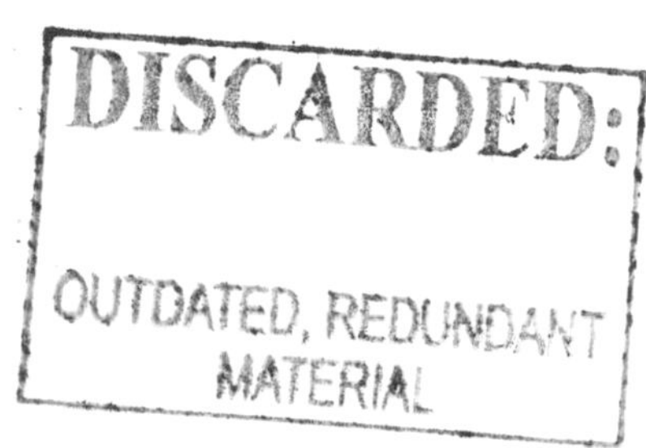

THE STATESMAN AND THE STORYTELLER

The Statesman and the Storyteller

John Hay, Mark Twain, and the Rise of American Imperialism

Mark Zwonitzer

Algonquin Books of Chapel Hill 2016

Published by
Algonquin Books of Chapel Hill
Post Office Box 2225
Chapel Hill, North Carolina 27515-2225

a division of
Workman Publishing
225 Varick Street
New York, New York 10014

Printed in the United States of America.
Published simultaneously in Canada
by Thomas Allen & Son Limited.

Photo credits: pages 9, 30: Mark Twain Project, Bancroft Library, University of California, Berkeley; pages 41, 91, 139, 199, 244, 325, 370, 383, 489: Library of Congress, Prints and Photographs Division.

The dollar amounts in this book are not rendered in current dollars. These sorts of calculations evade precision, but if the 2016 reader multiplies any dollar figures quoted by twenty-five or thirty he or she will have a fair and useful approximation of current value. —M. Z.

Library of Congress Cataloging-in-Publication Data
Names: Zwonitzer, Mark, author.
Title: The statesman and the storyteller : John Hay, Mark Twain, and the rise of American imperialism / by Mark Zwonitzer.
Description: First edition. | Chapel Hill, North Carolina : Algonquin Books of Chapel Hill, 2016. | Includes bibliographical references and index.
Identifiers: LCCN 2015034311 | ISBN 9781565129894
Subjects: LCSH: Hay, John, 1838–1905. | Twain, Mark, 1835–1910. | United States—Foreign relations—1897–1901. | United States—Foreign relations—1901–1909. | United States—Territorial expansion.
Classification: LCC E664.H41 Z96 2016 | DDC 327.73009/034—dc23
LC record available at http://lccn.loc.gov/2015034311

10 9 8 7 6 5 4 3 2 1
First Edition

For Gerri,

Now and Always.

CONTENTS

PROLOGUE

I SET OUT to write a simple and circumscribed book—the story of the final ten years in the life of one man, John Hay. Hay was the United States of America's ambassador in London in 1897 and 1898, at a time when that city was the seat of the most impressive empire the world had ever known, and then US secretary of state from 1898 until his death in 1905. He was appointed to his position in the cabinet by President William McKinley and stayed on at the command of his friend Theodore Roosevelt after McKinley's assassination. (Hay had first known of Roosevelt when he was a five-year-old called Teedie.) These public offices landed John Hay in the center of action at a pivot point of American history, a rampaging epoch that introduced habits of conduct our national leaders employ to this day.

The United States of America fought its first full-scale overseas war in those years and took its first steps toward displacing Great Britain as the most potent military and commercial power in the world. The United States took possession or control of Hawaii, Cuba, Puerto Rico, Guam, a piece of the Samoan Islands, the Philippines, and a good bit of Panama. The national reach spread east, west, and south; it would have spread north into Canada, too, if Theodore Roosevelt had had his way. The justifications for this explosive expansion of national aim and activity, much of which could be fairly judged by disinterested observers as extraconstitutional ("Oh, Mr. President," the US attorney general reportedly said after Roosevelt secured ownership and control of the Panama Canal Zone, "do not let so great an achievement suffer from any taint of legality!"), were explicitly and loudly articulated by its projectors: the spread of democracy and Western civilization, the opening of new markets for American business, the national defense, the supremacy of the white man, and even God's will. There was also much talk of abstractions such as patriotism, honor, and duty.

John Hay was not one to expound these things in public or to thump his own chest, but he was a force in shaping decisions and outcomes. He was also a thoughtful observer throughout, having arrived at the State Department with a long and personal perspective on national events. Hay's career in public service began in 1861, when he was just twenty-two years old, as one of Abraham Lincoln's two private secretaries in the White House. The beardless youth was shy to boast of his place. When a college friend congratulated him on his position, John Hay joked it away. "Yes," he answered, "I'm Keeper of the President's Conscience." But he was at Lincoln's side through the worst of the Civil War, when the country was in very real peril of disintegration and the sacrifice of hundreds of thousands of its slaughtered citizens appeared to be too little to save it. Hay had seen and felt the awful burdens the presidency could place on a single mortal man, and he wasn't one to forget. He also knew to keep a record.

Like his Civil War diaries, John Hay's letters, diaries, and official correspondence from 1895 to 1905 are clear eyed, frank, amusing, and intimate. They also reveal a rich supporting cast: Presidents McKinley and Roosevelt; Senator Henry Cabot Lodge; a forgotten media mogul and political gadfly named Whitelaw Reid; Lord Salisbury, who stood at the head of Her Majesty's vast empire; Her Majesty herself, Victoria, queen of the United Kingdom of Great Britain and Ireland and empress of India; her son Bertie, the Prince of Wales; and her Prussian grandson, the dangerous loon Kaiser Wilhelm II of Germany.

There are also Hay's closest friends, Henry Adams and Clarence King. Adams was, at the approach of the twentieth century, a nasty, crabbed little man who wielded a wicked pen, and King a renowned scientist whose hidden life hints at a future beyond John Hay's imagination. Then, too, there is Alvey Adee, a wee, near-deaf colleague of Hay's who anchored the State Department for more than a generation, and also Hay's own son, Del, then making his own first marks in public service. The Countess Marguerite Cassini, quasi-legitimate daughter of the Russian ambassador (her grandson Oleg would dress Jacqueline Kennedy, the First Lady) makes an appearance. So, too, do far-flung characters like the harried naval hero George Dewey and the Filipino freedom fighters Emilio Aguinaldo and Felipe Agoncillo.

But as I went deeper into Hay's public and private correspondence, and then into other contemporaneous accounts of the times, one of these side characters kept catching my eye, as if waving madly from the wings. *Pick me!* He just kept popping up, wheedling, cajoling, auditioning for a starring role. Samuel Langhorne Clemens is a hard man to deny. It wasn't long before he was a second leading man.

Once Clemens had forced his way to the front, I began describing the book to people who asked as the story of a friendship. But that was just shorthand and, withal, slightly inaccurate. Clemens's connection to John Hay in this time period was not one of great intimacy and was even a tad distant when compared with Hay's relationship to McKinley and Roosevelt. But it was more telling than any of Hay's other friendships. The two men had grown up in the same era, fifty miles apart, in remote and near-barbaric little towns perched above the

Mississippi River. They came of age out in the wild, in the same rural antebellum stew of race and class and want. They saw and heard the same steamboats and river pilots and roustabouts rolling in and out of their towns, sometimes a dozen different paddlewheelers in a day, filled beyond capacity with people bound for a wide world of possibilities the two boys could only dream of.

This shared history was among the commonalities that drew them to each other when they first met in the late 1860s, after Hay had become famous as Lincoln's private secretary, and as Clemens was just making a name for himself (or more precisely for his literary alter ego, "Mark Twain") with his comic lectures about the Hawaiian Islands and his first stories. Each had been an early supporter of the other's literary efforts. Sam Clemens credited Hay's *Pike County Ballads* as the first piece of American literature to capture the vernacular of their boyhood stomping grounds. "I cannot forbear telling you how much I have been encouraged and gratified by your generous commendation of my verses," Hay wrote to Clemens at the time. "I have sometimes thought that the public appreciation was a compound of ignorance and surprise—but when you, who know all about the Western life and character, look at one of my little pictures and say it is true, it is comfortable beyond measure." Hay returned the favor by booming Clemens's first travel essays and his first novels. Clemens invited Hay to partner with him in the ownership of a newspaper in 1871 and then to travel together down their old river on a research trip in preparation for a series of magazine articles about the Mississippi. Hay begged off on both adventures, but he wrote Clemens as soon as the first installment of *Old Times on the Mississippi* appeared in the *Atlantic Monthly*. "It is perfect—no more nor less. I don't see how you do it." The two men were already drifting apart by then, especially after they became fathers. They kept up with each other mostly through mutual friends until the late 1890s, when personal tragedies and public affairs drew them back toward each other.

The two remained, temperamentally, very different sorts of men. There was nothing about John Hay that marked him as a child of the coarse region of his youth; he was akin to the smooth-running eastern side-wheeler steamboats, which featured two paddles mounted on opposite sides of a single shaft. This was a boat engineered for straight-ahead journeys on deep and placid water. Clemens, though, remained like the churning western side-wheeler that ran the Mississippi River north and south of St. Louis, Missouri. These boats "geared their wheels on separate shafts," one of Sam Clemens's boyhood acquaintances would explain, "so that one wheel could go forward while the other was backing, imparting great mobility and adaptation to sudden turns." Clemens had a way of making sudden turns and of kicking up a commotion when he did, especially when there was an audience at hand.

So it was natural that John Hay would accept the US move toward global empire as his nation's destiny and its due—a course beyond his power to alter. Whatever doubts he may have had, and he did not have many, he was not going to raise them in public. Clemens just kept circling the question, churning, churning, churning. The two men ended up on opposite sides of the most compelling issues of their day. And they were not small issues.

But John Hay and Sam Clemens, whatever their differences in personality and outlook, remained tied till the end of their lives by unbreakable threads of affection and common experience. What joined them was a gut understanding of just how hard the other was running from truly desolate beginnings, and an admiration for how far the other man had traveled. John Hay was one of the longest-serving and most accomplished secretaries of state in history; Sam Clemens's books—*Innocents Abroad*, *The Adventures of Tom Sawyer*, *Adventures of Huckleberry Finn (Tom Sawyer's Comrade)*, *A Connecticut Yankee in King Arthur's Court, Personal Recollections of Joan of Arc*, to name a few—were among the best-known and most circulated books in the world. He had made "Mark Twain" a household name on multiple continents.

THE STORY OF Clemens and Hay's relationship (like the story of American expansion) was marked by missed opportunities. The final miss was the St. Louis World's Fair in 1904, on the banks of the Mississippi, just downriver from their respective hometowns. The formal and official name of this gathering was the Louisiana Purchase Exposition, and it commemorated the hundredth anniversary (a year behind schedule) of the most spectacular real estate deal in the history of North America. Fair organizers expected Sam Clemens and John Hay to attend, standing as they did as the most celebrated of the area's native sons.

Clemens's fellow Missourians, in particular the merchants in his hometown of Hannibal, were desperate for the author to make an appearance, not least because they knew he was a big draw—money in the bank. They enticed him to the great global convocation by proposing the organization of a Mark Twain Association to promote American literature and by offering to set aside an entire day of the fair in his honor. Clemens was in New York at the time of this offer and headed in the opposite direction—to a villa in a little town founded by the ancient Etruscans in the hills above Florence, Italy, in hopes of reviving his ailing wife. "I value the impulse which moves you to tender these honors," he wrote in scotching both the visit and the proposed Mark Twain Association, ". . . but I should stand in a sort of terror of the honors themselves. So long as we remain alive we are not safe from doing things which, however righteously and honorably intended, can wreck our repute and extinguish our friendships. I hope that no society will be named for me while I am still alive, for I might at some time or other do something which would cause its members to regret having done me that honor. After I shall have joined the dead I shall follow the customs of those people and be guilty of no conduct that can wound any friend."

The Missourians had to settle for a few consolation prizes: the planned construction of the Mark Twain Hotel, with eighty-seven feet and four inches of frontage on South Main Street in Hannibal, and a recent portrait of Clemens painted by an Italian artist named Gelli. "You will find it excellent," Clemens wrote to the governor of Missouri. "Good judges here say it is better than the original. They say it has all the merits of the original and keeps still, besides."

John Hay did make the trip to St. Louis, traveling in the company of Henry Adams. "History told little about these millions of Germans and Slavs, or whatever their race-names, who had overflowed these regions," Adams would write of the overland trip through the Ohio Valley, across Illinois, and into St. Louis. "John Hay was as strange to the Mississippi River as though he had not been bred on its shores. . . . One saw here a third-rate town of a half-a-million people without history, education, unity or art, and with little capital—without even an element of natural interest except the river which it studiously ignored."

Hay did not dawdle at the fair; he never even took the time to investigate its largest and most popular exhibit, the forty-seven-acre Philippine Reservation, which featured more than a thousand shanghaied natives from one of the new US possessions. The Filipinos served as props in a living diorama depicting the American effort to gentle the natives (benevolently) out of darkness and into the light of modern civilization. But Hay did perform his appointed duty, which was a speech. "The valley of the mighty river which rolls by the wharves of St. Louis can never be considered by me otherwise than as my home," he said wistfully, if not altogether honestly. "The great river was the scene of my early dreams . . . We built snow forts and called them the Alamo; we sang rude songs of the cane-brake and the cornfield; and the happiest days of the year to us who dwelt on the northern bluffs of the river were those that brought us, in the loud puffing and whistling steamers of olden time, to the Mecca of our rural fancies, the bright and busy metropolis of St. Louis."

Then he got down to the business at hand, which was the celebration of President Thomas Jefferson's (also extraconstitutional) land purchase, which doubled the territory of the United States with the stroke of his quill pen. "Jefferson gained an immortal fame by preferring an immense benefit to his country to consistency in a narrow construction of the written law," Hay told his audience, in words no less applicable in their own new century. "No man, no party, can fight with any chance of final success against a cosmic tendency; no cleverness, no popularity, avails against the spirit of the age."

John Hay had learned this lesson early and accepted it as an article of faith. He was not a man to fight a "cosmic tendency," and this served him well. Sam Clemens was less sure of this lesson. He learned it the hard way and, as you will see in the story that follows, kept unlearning it.

THE STATESMAN AND THE STORYTELLER

CHAPTER ONE

Making a Way in the World

As the *Warrimoo* steamed into open sea on August 23, 1895, churning out toward the setting sun, a lone man in a dark suit leaned over the deck rail, pulling hard on his cheap cigar, feeling every lurch and spasm of the wounded ship in his own body. The old man's lively gray eyes, hooded by a wild and windblown thatch of gray hair, scanned the flock of birds off the port side of the ship. He noted the natural ease of those brown seabirds—a kind of albatross, he figured them—riding the soft, forgiving currents of Pacific air. He had been watching them for hours, mesmerized by the improbability of their flight, tracking the lazy beat of their wing tips as they hovered just beyond reach of the waves, negotiating every rise and depression, every swell and crash, without thought or worry, *untouched* by what roiled beneath them. Meanwhile the tiniest pitch or yaw of the boat reverberated up through the marine-varnished planking and into his person. He had never found it easy to get the hang of a new ship, and in the few hours since the *Warrimoo* had sailed from the port at Vancouver Island, bound for Sydney by way of Honolulu, he had felt most every roll, felt it as sure as he felt the hot pinch at his swollen ankle, and the scratch of cheap serge against the gaping wound in his thigh, and the searing in his lungs that shortened every breath he took. Focusing his attention on the flight of those birds was his best hope for distraction, but his own discomfort bade his attention, and so, too, did the memory of the previous night's picture show.

His mind struck him as a machine that worked independently of his will; it had long ago adopted the habit of performing its most vigorous manufacturing while he slept. For as long as Samuel Langhorne Clemens could remember, his dream head had produced hyperreal running frames of scenery and narrative, rich in color, fine grained, and capable of physical effect both sharp and lingering. No waking effort had ever matched his sleep eye's conjuring. He had, for instance, resigned himself to the enervating fact that during his many long separations from his wife he had never been able to consciously bring to mind the particulars of her face. His dream machine, however, had perfected the art of reproducing Livy in fluid, lifelike motion, and the next morning he had always felt as if she had truly been there, with him.

But the thought of last night's moving images offered no comfort, his subconscious projector having spooled out one of its recurrent nightmarish set pieces in which he found himself alone on a stage, in front of an eager and expectant audience who meant to be *entertained* by "Mark Twain." He had stood there, as he always did in this dream, paralyzed, unprepared, without a notion of *where to begin*, clothed in nothing but his night garments—and not one of the long, flowing nightshirts that his servant girl Katy Leary had been making for him for the past fifteen years (the ones with the splendid red piping down the front), but a ragged, short shirt of older vintage, from his days of penury, the kind that exposed altogether too much. Thinking of that nightmare made him shiver.

A goddamned torment was what it was, this overactive subbrain of his, because it had a penchant for—no, a *delight* in—poking at him until it had riled his deepest insecurities. Sam Clemens was just three months shy of his sixtieth birthday, at an age where a respectable man would have put behind him the hard labor of life and packed the larder for generations to come, would have lifted his wife, his children, his unknown grandchildren, beyond the reach of financial worry. And here he was, a sick old man with a trunk full of fraying suits and scuffed brogans, more than a *hundred thousand* dollars in debt (to people who had trusted him), and he could think of no way to raise the funds to pay them back but to circle the entire godless globe—along the path of greatest circumference, no less—in search of folks who would part with a little money if he promised to amuse them.

He had worked up a talk that answered his side of the bargain. He was advertising it as the "Morals Lecture," and a little more than a month out and twenty-four performances into "Mark Twain's world tour," he was still sanding the roughest patches and inviting his listeners in on the process. "I would start with two or three rules of moral principles which I want to impress upon those people," he had told his earliest groups of auditors. "I will just make the lecture gradual, by and by. The illustrations are the most important, so that when the lecture is by and by written and completed, it will just be a waveless ocean with this archipelago of smiling green islands of illustrations in the midst of it." But he knew those "smiling green islands" for what they really were: a collection of hoary tales—"My First Theft," "Tom Sawyer's Crusade," "The Jumping Frog"—that played to every paying customer's expectation of what "Mark Twain" ought to sound like. All across the western United States and into Canada, Clemens's traveling entourage—Livy, his tour manager, and his daughter Clara—had pronounced the audiences well satisfied. "As to satisfying myself," Clemens had written his closest confidant, Henry Rogers, "that is quite another matter."

After almost thirty years plying his singular stagecraft, Clemens could handle most any crowd, could discern in a flash the subtle shadings of climate and mood. A full house was the easiest, once he got it started, laughter being contagious. But Clemens had also, and of necessity, mastered the art of playing to a small and spotty audience; he knew how to keep clear of the jagged shoals that lurked on the dark periphery of that sort of crowd, for if a talker got flummoxed or fumbled away his best material, he was sure to run himself out of the swift channel of sympathy and into snags of contempt. "And contempt," he had told a group of newspapermen not long before he boarded the *Warrimoo*, "is fatal."

As he stood silent and alone on deck that evening, Clemens knew well enough that the simple certainty that people would gather to his call forcing upon him the duty to perform for the scores (or maybe even hundreds!) of separate crowds that awaited him in the coming year could not fully account for his dark dread or the slow-sinking feeling in his empty stomach. (He rarely had an appetite for anything but cigars these days.) What gnawed at him was his awareness that he needed those audiences much more desperately than they needed him.

Livy Clemens didn't fully appreciate her husband's conundrum, but their daughter Clara, an aspiring performer herself—she got it. Clara had made a long study of her father on the stage and off. She was the only person in the family who could do a dead-on impersonation of his dinner talk: the slow drawl, the cavernous pauses, the incorporation of any prop available. "Papa always seems to be having a quarrel with his piece of bread," she explained. Clara was not possessed of expert timing, but she had inherited some of her father's wit, and all of his intense powers of observation. At twenty-one, she was the only one of the Clemens daughters with their father's hard-eyed view of the world.

Clara did not allow romance to cloud her vision, and consequently she didn't miss much. She had endured a thousand innings of her father's private rages against the lecture business, could recite every blasphemous word of them by heart. But after keeping a particularly close vigil on him in the previous month, Clara had come to understand the allure of the stage and why he *could not* give it up, why he insisted, against all advice, on rising from his sickbed to make the next date. She had come to understand her father's need to *connect* with his audience, to tap its energy. When it happened, she would always remember, "his cheeks and eyes glowed with color that resembled tinted sparks."

SAM CLEMENS UNDERSTOOD everything about himself that Clara did—and then some. He was nothing if not self-aware, mainly because he had built his life and his fame by depending entirely and exclusively on that self. He was self-made, self-propelled, self-promoted. He had never sought and never known the luxury of patronage; the entirety of his inheritance was between his own ears. The Civil War, back in '61, had cost him the only steady employment he had ever had up to that point, and the certainty of a life career with it. After fleeing west to avoid the fight, he had failed as an aide in Nevada's territorial legislature, as a miner, as a newspaper reporter who kept strictly to facts, and as a stockjobber. His ambition to preach the Gospel had been tempered by his tendency toward profanity and drunkenness—"could not supply myself with the necessary stock in trade—*i.e.* religion." The best he had going for him was his natural ability "to excite the laughter of God's poor creatures," he explained to his brother Orion. "It is nothing to be proud of, but it is my strongest suit." And once Sam Clemens had decided his course—he would talk and write his way out of poverty!—he had fought and scratched for everything he could get.

When Bret Harte got the jump on Clemens as *the* coming humorist from the West, Clemens stalked him with his nom de plume "Mark Twain" in tow, a meager dusting of celebrity that attended the nationwide publication of his "Jumping Frog" story, and blood in his eye. "I mean to go up ahead again & *stay* there," he told Orion five years into the back-and-forth scrap with Harte. That this particular contest was pretty far down on the undercard of American literary bouts did not diminish Clemens's ardor. "I will 'top' Bret Harte again or bust."

And hadn't he put Harte in the dust? Part of the reason, he knew, was native ability; but part was simple endurance and drive—the privilege of being able to sit all day at his writing desk and *outwit* the oily, insincere, heartless reprobate. But that wasn't the whole story of his thrashing of Bret Harte. Clemens had intuited early in his career that superior product and superior character would not be enough to secure the purse in postwar America. He had sold himself, and hard.

From the moment he landed on the East Coast in the late 1860s, Clemens had assiduously cultivated good feelings (and good press!) for "Mark Twain." It had been his joy as well as his mission to make fast friends and spread his own special brand of cheer among New York's young newspapermen, who gathered almost every evening in a loosely formed society of, as one of the young literati called it, "high aspirations and peregrinations." These were men on the move, and at a pace. The group picked up a new train of aspiring or visiting artistes as it made its way through New York nightlife. Harte fell in with them the minute he arrived in town, of course, as did the poet Edmund Clarence Stedman, and William Dean Howells, who was annoyingly quick to exhibit the Bostonian priggishness he had picked up in his adopted hometown, and Clarence King, who was fashioning his western experiences on the federally sponsored geological surveys into grand scientific theory and literary gems. America's best Shakespearean actor, Edwin Booth, stumped along at the rear of the procession some nights, though he generally took a pass on following the younger men in leapfrogging the ash cans that lined the sidewalks.

The club was, withal, unflinchingly democratic. The only necessity for membership was some sort of genius or the possibility of its later flowering. A man could rise as high as his talents took him. John Hay, a westerner who had entered adulthood, like Sam Clemens, with Mississippi mud caked on his trousers and had already made his first fame as one of two private secretaries to President Abraham Lincoln, was remembered as the "high priest of the revels." But among the nominal leaders of the gang was Whitelaw Reid, a tall, stiff-backed Ohioan with a forehead like a billboard and ambition to match. Reid was a newspaperman of a new stripe, which is to say high toned and apparently, if not actually, scholarly. But what put him at the front was the open secret—Whitelaw was not shy to tell it—that the imperious old Horace Greeley was grooming him for ascension to the editorship of the silken mouthpiece of the National Republican Party, the unquestioned choice of dailies among the nation's men of means, the *New York Tribune*. Hay, who worked under Reid as an editorial writer and assistant editor in those days, had a habit of poking fun at Greeley (behind his back) and his "Great Moral Organ." The GMO, Hay called the *Tribune*.

Reid, on his way up, was willing to favor his friends, so when the first full-length "Mark Twain" book was ready for sale, its author was not shy to push for a little publicity in the venerated newspaper. "To-day my new book [*Innocents Abroad*] will be sent to the *Tribune*," he alerted Whitelaw, "—& this is to ask you if you won't get your reviewer to praise the bad passages & feeble places in it for me. They are the only ones I am worrying about, you know—the meritorious parts can get along themselves, of course." And Reid did help. "The greater part of his book is pure fun," the *Tribune* offered in its notice, "and . . . the freshness is wonderfully well sustained."

Whatever *Innocents'* merits, and they were not small as far as Clemens was concerned, it was the book's stunning sales—wasn't it running second to the Bible for a time?—that provided "Mark Twain" entrée to the places where an ambitious young man had to be. Even that crusty old bastard Greeley had to invite Sam Clemens to his sixty-first birthday celebration in 1872, which dropped the new author into a scrum of the nation's most accomplished attention seekers—a decidedly *upscale* scrum. Senators, diplomats, judges, publishers, and other distinguished guests had arrived at the host's New York City brownstone at such a steady clip that chill winter evening that the doorman froze in an attitude of utter despair and simply gave up his attempt to make formal announcement of the various personages.

Almost a quarter century later, Clemens could still recall his own entrance, an hour late, when he swept into the crowded house with a contingent from New England and spotted across the room that blatherskite Bret Harte holding forth.

By the time Clemens got shed of his hat and coat, he was way behind. John Hay was already working the room, luring new admirers among the swells. Here was a man to be reckoned with in Clemens's judgment—the pride of Warsaw (né Spunky Point), Illinois, a poet who had sounded the vernacular of the boatmen and pioneers of the Mississippi Valley, and a multilingual raconteur whose tales of recent diplomatic service at the exalted courts of Europe were deliciously racy: about the empress of a certain Continental power, he would confide, "She has a wonderful power over senile envoys. She kept [American minister] Dix and keeps [his successor] Washburne in chronic priapism."

As early as 1870, Hay could provide a bracing commentary on the tilt of the table of European politics. The Spanish were shredding what honor remained to them, offering to sell island possessions like Cuba at a discount and choking down insults with nary a whimper. "They retain the speech of Don Quixote, but the heart and stomach are Sancho's." The Prussians stood ready to whet their martial blade fighting Spain's battles. The German kaiser was bewildered by the insolent march toward democracy of his peasantry. "France still lies in her comatose slumber," Hay would say, "—but she talks in her sleep and murmurs the 'Marseillaise.'"

Hay's finest parlor talk had that rarest of virtues: it was *first hand.* He had seen behind the gilt-threaded tapestries into the wormy rot of Europe's despotic monarchs. Napoleon III, emperor of the French, "moves with a queer, side-long gait, like a crab," Hay would recall when telling of his own presentation at the court of Versailles. The story would become a long, detailed remembrance of Versailles's outer salons, lined by footmen of "portentous calf development," and of the monarch-bedazzled sycophants arrayed about the throne in all their uniform and colorful inner-sanctum resplendence. Hay would lead his listeners toward a slowly building climax, when the emperor finally turned his dull gaze toward him, a poorly dressed factotum in the lowly American legation, the royal mouth a-twitch beneath his mustache: "You can imagine it a sort of wooden clock preparing to strike."

"But you are very young to be Col-o-nel." Hay would slur the words through puffed cheeks, in imitation of the emperor. "Did you make the war in America?" And thus the tale ended. Even when recounting the story, Hay never insisted on taking the last word for himself.

John Hay was three years younger than Clemens, and the older man—he was thirty-six already that night at Greeley's—envied the younger's wide experience and his enormous and unmistakable social gifts, all of which foretold a big future. And yet Clemens did not feel threatened by Hay. He was "a picture to look at," Clemens would say of him, "for beauty of feature, perfection of form and grace of carriage and movement. He had a charm about him of a sort quite unusual to my western ignorance and inexperience—a charm of manner, intonation, apparently native and unstudied elocution, and all that—the groundwork of it native, the ease of it, the polish of it, the winning naturalness of it, acquired in Europe . . . He was joyous and cordial, a most pleasant comrade."

Hay's appeal was almost animal. He had returned from his diplomatic postings with a downy elegance and a natural insouciance that made people want to reach out and *pet* him. Unlike Sam Clemens, John Hay never appeared to be selling. Nobody ever heard John Hay fashion himself the hero of his European sojourns; he would show up unannounced in his own stories, just another in a platoon of soldiers of mirth. Hay was always content to be the casual and caustic observer; and in social gatherings he had a way of holding himself apart, just beyond the possibility of true intimacy, but near enough that *everybody* felt—and remembered—the magnetic draw of his person.

Still and all, and in spite of his late start, Clemens had held his own that night at Greeley's party, or so the other guests remembered. "Bret Harte, Mark Twain, and Colonel John Hay ('Little Breeches') formed a trinity of wit such as has rarely been found under one roof," wrote one of the evening's lesser celebrants. "The three humorists were all looked upon as lions of the occasion, and each at once became the bright particular star of a group of admiring and attentive listeners." Even Greeley, who was on his way to securing the Republican nomination for president that year, had mentioned the triumvirate of young westerners in his letter of appreciation to the evening's host. "'To meet Bret Harte, John Hay and Mark Twain under the same roof with Samuel Bowles, Murat Halstead and Joseph R. Hawley, should be reckoned an event in almost any one's life."

About a year after that birthday party, and with understandable confidence, Clemens shipped to Reid and Greeley's *Tribune* a personal letter announcing the coming publication of his first novel, a political comedy written with his friend and neighbor Charles Dudley Warner (title as yet undecided), and suggesting some felicitous prose for the notice.

Reid forwarded the note to Hay, with instructions for a "rollicking bit of minion," adding "It shld be *must* for Saturday." And Hay had delivered: "[The novel] is known to contain all the profound philosophy, the sound learning, and geological truth which are found in 'Innocents Abroad' and 'Roughing It,'" he wrote for the *Tribune*. "It is no holiday work . . . and we are authorized to announce that the paper on which it is written cost eleven dollars." (The last bit was straight from Clemens's letter.)

But the small-type notice—*minion*, on a low-circulation Saturday—rankled Clemens. "A stickful of pleasantry down in a corner," he called it. The next day he fired off a note to Reid.

> You give us a notice which carries the impression to the minds of other editors that we are people of small consequence in the literary world, & indeed only triflers; . . . Now I hold that a novel from us is a literary *event*, (though it may sound pretty egotistical). . . . I am not a man of trifling literary consequence. . . . "Roughing It" had 43,000 subscribers already booked, the day it issued from the press. . . . "Innocents Abroad" . . . sells 1000 a month right along. . . . These things mean all this: that I have a good reliable audience in this country—& it is the biggest one in America, too, if I do say it myself. So a novel from me alone would be a good deal in the nature of a literary event, & the *Tribune*, to be just, should have made it so appear, I think.

Clemens went on to remind Reid of the good turns he had done the *Tribune* of late, how he had been loyal even when the *New York Herald* had come knocking at his door, ready to pay top dollar for his literary services. "Now confound you when I want you to do something for me, you shove my novel at the world as if neither it nor its father amounted to much! This isn't fair—I swear it is not fair. . . . Now just see if you can't do us a real outspoken good turn that will leave a strong wholesome impression on the public mind—& then command our services, if they can be of use to you. Title of novel is, 'The Gilded Age.'"

Clemens, in his dudgeon, had neglected his customary practice of swaddling his hard-edged ambition in humor, and Whitelaw Reid had a nose for naked ambition. It had dawned on Whitelaw as he read and reread this letter: the artless, grasping presumption of its author was something bordering on offensive. Sam Clemens, it was clear to Reid now, expected the *Tribune*—the stalwart of integrity, of Republican integrity—to toss editorial independence out the door . . . *for friendship.*

And, by the by, was that mention of the *Herald* a threat?

When Reid suggested to Clemens that he had poured more bile into his last letter than was properly manly, Clemens did not back down.

"All right! You go ahead and give us that other notice," he insisted two days later. "I want the *Tribune* to say it *right* and say it powerful—& then I will answer for the consequences. The consequences will be that all the other papers will *follow suit*, which you know as well as I do."

Sam Clemens, with his wife, Livy (in black, seated at left) and his daughter Clara (in black, seated at right) on the Warrimoo, *August 1895*

Reid did make good. His paper *was* breaking news by announcing the novel's title: "It is an unusual and a courageous enterprise for two gentlemen who have already won honorable distinction in other walks of literature, to venture upon untrodden paths with a work so ambitious and so important as this is likely to be," the *Tribune* offered, and with a placement Clemens felt more worthy of his stature.

By then, however, Reid was making it known around town that the *Tribune* was not of the opinion that any new book by "Mark Twain" was a literary event of great import, no matter the author's immodest assertions. "There is a nice correspondence on a part of the subject which would make pleasant reading; and if Twain gives us trouble, I'm very much tempted to make him a more ridiculous object than he has ever made anybody else." Ten years later, Reid was still reminding his subordinates that they had to be on guard against Clemens, editorially speaking, in "a paper which has good reason to think little of his delicacy & highly of his greed."

BY THE TIME Sam Clemens stood on the deck of the *Warrimoo* that August evening in 1895, he had long since written off Whitelaw Reid. What the hell did Whitelaw know about making his own way in the world? Reid had made a career playing the cheapest sort of political game, had hidden for years behind Greeley's skirts and then behind the institutional prerogatives of the upright and nation-dominating Republican Party. He had seen Reid at work, sucking up to presidents, senators, and moneymen, begging ambassadorships or places in the cabinet, sniffing around the White House invitation list whenever European royalty got in the vicinity. And as far as delicacy and greed were concerned, Clemens was pretty sure Reid hadn't been awarded the vice presidential nomination on the Republican ticket in 1892 because of his surfeit of delicacy and his freedom from personal greed. Twenty years since the feud had erupted, and Clemens still despised Reid . . . *the low-down yellow cur* . . . *the missing link* . . . *the eunuch* . . . *the goddamned—son of a bitch*!

Sam Clemens would never apologize to anyone for being the kind of man he had to be, or for what he had done to make a name for himself. It was not by humor alone, or even by the sympathy evident in his work for the lowliest of his fellow beings—a kind of human sympathy beyond Whitelaw Reid—but by furious and jagged-edged effort that Sam Clemens had raised himself from the privations of a small-town Missouri-pioneer boyhood to his position as the most famous living writer on the planet, at least the English-speaking swath of it (Tolstoy, the Russian, was enjoying mighty fine sales just then). Everywhere he went, people quoted him passages of *Innocents Abroad* and *Tom Sawyer* and *Huckleberry Finn*. His work might never be regarded with the reverence accorded the gleaming society jewels of stories wrought by Henry James, but he could live with that. "Yes, high and fine literature is wine, and mine is only water," Clemens liked to say, "but everybody likes water."

And he knew there was no shortage of esteem for him in high places. At a dinner in *his* honor in London just the previous spring, Clemens had been told he must, on his upcoming tour, look up the admiral in charge of England's fleet in the China Sea: the man slept with Mark Twain books under his pillow. ("P'raps it is the only way he *can* sleep," Clemens suggested.) President and Mrs. Cleveland had entertained him, unbidden, at the Executive Mansion. The emperor of Germany had professed affection for *Old Times on the Mississippi* and recounted—in English—his favorite section from *A Tramp Abroad.* Even the Prince of Wales had invited Clemens to dinner.

They had all wanted to know him; "Mark Twain" had met more European potentates than had any other private citizen, and invariably at the sovereign's invitation. American ambassadors might get five minutes of perfunctory diplodrivel at court, but when they pleaded for a private conference, they went begging. The ambassador in Berlin had been tremendously annoyed when he found out Sam Clemens was to have a *dinner* with Kaiser Wilhelm; he would have been furious to know that the German empress had also sent a card asking Clemens to join them *en famille* at the imperial breakfast table. "The way things are going," Clemens's youngest daughter, Jean, had remarked when the summons to dinner arrived from Kaiser Wilhelm, "there won't be anybody left for you to get acquainted with but God."

Just now, as Sam Clemens neared sixty, out on the open seas with no land in sight, standing aboard a rattletrap, roach-infested steamship that required government subsidy just to keep it afloat, the accumulated fame resulting from his thirty years' exertion didn't do him a hell of a lot of good. Fame was fine as far as it went, but he would have preferred a fortune. He was in fact, in midsummer 1895, the world's most famous bankrupt. Everybody knew—it was in *all* the newspapers!—that he had been forced to rent out his home in Hartford, the only one his family had ever owned, just to keep the taxes paid.

Losing that house, even for a short time, had cut Livy Clemens deep, and the thought of having wounded her so grievously pained Sam. Worse still, his promises to his wife that the rental arrangement was only temporary, that he would get them back to their home, where the family could be whole again and happy, rang false in his own ears.

His wife had never been a strong woman, and the previous three years had diminished her. She had lived every one of those days poised in anticipation of the imminent and total collapse of their publishing business, Charles L. Webster and Company. She had winced, in something akin to physical pain, when he boasted of striking a deal to pay the Webster creditors at fifty cents on the dollar; he sounded to her like some kind of chiseler. "You know my darling," she had reminded him gently, "*now* is the time for you to add to or mar the good name that you have made. Do not for one moment let your sense of our need of money get advantage of your sense of justice & generosity."

She had also looked on, bewildered, as he continued in the face of all good sense to throw tens of thousands of dollars a month into the production and perfection of a new printing press in the vain hope that its success would redeem *all* their debts and rescue them from the public embarrassment of the Webster failure. "I have a perfect horror and heartsickness over it," Livy had written to her sister. "I cannot get away from the feeling that business failure means disgrace. . . . If you were to see me you would see that I have grown old very fast during this last year. I have wrinkled."

Livy had remained a vision of light and good cheer in her husband's presence and had quietly constructed a few thin walls of defense against the coming disaster; she had economized mightily in the running of the household and sworn off trips to her New York dressmaker, Madame Fogarty. And when the new and inevitable thunderclap sounded—the printing press investment was lost, leaving the Clemenses deeper in debt, with no clear way out, since no sane bank would extend them more credit—Mrs. Clemens started peeling off other expenses. "Acres of figures," she made in her notebook, slashing their monthly budget by two-thirds. Without the horses and coachmen, and their daughter Susy's voice lessons, and Clara's piano lessons . . . and if they entertained in a less active and expansive fashion, and if she gave up her *private* maid, Livy was certain they could live on a thousand dollars a month.

Sam Clemens had no reason to doubt his wife's calculations, but he could not stand to think of her bent over those sorry, meager dollar numbers, pencil in hand. And it broke his heart when, on their silver wedding anniversary, not long after the final crash, he had made her a small gift of a single five-franc coin, and she smiled bravely and told him she was going to have it framed. His failure had made them small, made them *triflers.* And they were not triflers, not by his lights.

That's when Clemens had determined to do something to save them, and it had to appear—no, it had to *be*—heroic. That's when he had dreamed up this latest adventure: "take a breath & stand by for a surge," a round-the-world lecture tour. The tour receipts would allow Clemens to pay their creditors back dollar for dollar, he promised Livy. Their public dignity would be preserved. He would not allow their final chapter to be a story of his disgrace.

His creditors had mostly taken pity on him. They had almost all agreed to accept the fifty-cents-on-the-dollar settlement up front and to allow him the space he needed to work off the other half of the debt on his own schedule.

Clemens was beginning to understand by August of 1895 that the doing of this heroic deed would require plenty of time, even by his most optimistic estimates. The way he figured the numbers, if he kept at the lecturing full-time, and lived on the cheap along the way, and got good sales from his memoir of the trip, which he planned to snatch time to write aboard ships or trains and to finish soon after the tour had ended, it would still take him four years to pay off his creditors. But there was no turning back now, not since he had more or less made a point of telling the newspapermen, and thus the world, what he was up to. He would clear these gargantuan debts *and* protect his good name, or die trying. Just watch him!

So here he was, at fifty-nine, thrown back to the scratch line, back thirty years, to his first fevered attempts to win what money attention could bring. The memory of the handbills plastered across San Francisco in 1866, advertising his first lecture—"The Sandwich Islands"—could still make him blush.

A SPLENDID ORCHESTRA

Is in town, but has not been engaged.

ALSO,

A DEN OF FEROCIOUS WILD BEASTS

Will be on Exhibition in the next Block.

MAGNIFICENT FIREWORKS
Were in contemplation for this occasion, but the
idea has been abandoned.
A GRAND TORCHLIGHT PROCESSION
May be expected; in fact, the public are privileged
to expect whatever they please. . . .

Doors open at 7 o'clock. The Trouble to begin at 8 o'clock.

Thank God he no longer needed the brute thump of that desperate drumming. After thirty years in the public gaze, a decorous poster announcing MARK TWAIN'S TOUR AROUND THE WORLD filled the bill. And yet, Clemens knew, this latest lusty pursuit of crowd love was not altogether attractive in a man his age, even a public one. He also knew well enough the downside of the curve of his desire: once a night's electric high had worn off and left him hollowed out, he would start to feel a bit, well, tawdry. What kind of man, he had to wonder, got such joy from a passing stranger who thanked him—earnestly, profusely, reverently—for saying so many nice things *about cats*? What kind of man hauled himself and half his family around the world, prospecting for the affection of people entirely unknown to him? But the more pressing questions at the end of August 1895 were these: Was there enough Twain love out there in the world to sustain him through what was shaping up to be the most demanding year of his always demanding life? Would there be anything left of him when it was all over?

He took a long drag from his cigar. The sun dropped away in front of him. The breeze still warmed his face. And he was happy for the peace and quiet of the ship. They would be at least three weeks at sea on their way to Sydney. Maybe he would get a little rest. Maybe he would feel stronger by the time they hit land again.

He kept his eyes trained on that flock of birds alongside the *Warrimoo.* The divot in his leg felt smaller, didn't it, but it still hurt, and he thought he could feel another of the hideous boils about to rise. He took another drag from his cigar; it made his chest hurt.

Daaaaaam*nation*!

THE FAMILIAR DULL ache settled on John Hay as he sat evenings on his porch, gazing down the long, graceful slope of his thousand-acre estate, out over Lake Sunapee—moonlit and rippled by the cool breezes of a New Hampshire August—to the silvery rise of mountain. He had emptied his inkwell into a dozen plaintive letters of late, describing for his dearest friends the "languid, vegetable life" at his summer retreat, the Fells, "the Place-Where-Nothing-Happens," begging for their company. Henry Adams was a lost cause; he was at present chaperoning Senator and Mrs. Henry Cabot Lodge around England and would soon be bound for the Continent for a tour through the dusty Gothic wonders of Normandy. Clarence King had started making promises of a visit months ago—this private summer colony in the far-off New Hamsphire hills had been his idea in the first place—but King had gone silent, again, and could be anywhere between Madison Square and the Sierra Nevada. Their wayward friend had, as Hay wrote Adams, "evaded into space."

The time for visits was already running short. The family would be breaking up soon. Hay's older son, Del, was headed back to Yale in a few weeks; his daughter Alice back to her finishing school, "her jail on the Hudson," she called it; his youngest, Clarence, was going to Cleveland with Mrs. Hay; the oldest, Helen, now twenty, would probably return to their home in Washington to continue work on her first volume of poetry. Hay assumed he would end up in Washington, too, once Congress was back in session, though he wasn't certain what purpose he was to serve there. Until then, it would be more plodding sameness: hiking the worn, mossy circuit of his woodland trails, fishing trout from Sunapee, watching his wife worry her rose-and-hydrangea garden, and reading as much as his failing eyesight allowed. There were new translations of Balzac and Daudet that summer, though he had always preferred the original French; Henry Morton Stanley was just out with a new adventure book; and Henry James—his sad, beautiful friend Henry—had published a new collection of stories.

The life "suits elderly folks like Mrs. Hay and me very well," Hay wrote to his old friend Whitelaw Reid.

> My children are getting old enough to kick at the solitude, but they are more or less contented by relays of their friends. I listen to their clamor, and reflect that, after all, the world is still young. But I am sure that you and I were never so young as the boys of to-day. The riddle of the painful world suggested itself to us earlier and more imperatively. The fellows who came of age in the Lincoln year were forced to look at life in wider aspects than the Sophomores of to-day. I feel as though I should not look at anything much longer. . . . That is another reason for wanting to see you before the curtain drops.

John Hay was about to turn fifty-seven, older than Abraham Lincoln had been on that awful night in April of 1865. "The Ancient" had been dead more than thirty years now. Del was almost the same age Hay had been when he took up his post in Lincoln's White House. These sorts of statistics increased Hay's already keen sensitivity to the signs of his own decrepitude, even if none were apparent to the wider world.

He still *looked* trim and hearty; he even detected some added tone to his muscles after a summer's worth of outdoor activity. He never gained much weight, unlike Mrs. Hay, who enjoyed, as he said privately, a "good whack at the vittles." Fellow Americans who knew Hay only from Alexander Gardner's old wartime photographs of him standing next to the giant Lincoln were always surprised to find that Hay was of average stature. He was well short of the five feet eight he sometimes claimed, but not laughably so. When he had occasion to look in the mirror, Hay noted his high forehead, the subtle upturn of his nose, his pleasingly oval-shaped face, now sun burnished beyond its normal ruddiness; his eyes still flashed hints of youthful pride. And his mouth still pulled down a touch at the corners, suggesting a lurking melancholy. But there were no new worry lines on his face, and even at close inspection, he could find but a few new gray hairs on his pate or in his clipped and tidy Vandyke. And yet it was hard for him to recall the last time he had enjoyed a long string of days of simple, mindless physical well-being.

His health, as he remembered it, had started to falter around the time his son Del was born. John Hay wasn't even forty when he had begun hauling himself to general practitioners, oculists, and heart specialists on two different continents. How many times had he described the intricate web of his ailments, pulling apart the threads that made up the symptoms of his nagging physical malaise? Dizziness, rapid pulse, fogged vision, headaches, a sour stomach, insomnia, regular troughs of despair. The doctors had always listened attentively and earnestly, without betraying the least suspicion of their patient's possible hypochondria. John Hay, after all, was a man who would meet their bills, and promptly. But the diagnoses had always been vague. The eminent Philadelphia physician Silas Weir Mitchell had assured him it was nothing *organic*. And the brightest light in the firmament of Parisian neurology concurred: Hay was in the best of company, the French physician had said, suffering from the catchall affliction of the age, brought on by an unfortunate overexposure to modern civilization—weak nerves. That verdict, praise be to heaven, had been rendered in the doctor's native tongue, and the Gallic gravity of the phrase as it rolled off his tongue—*neurasthénie céphalique*—had made it seem sufficiently insidious and almost concrete. Like the bills that followed the visits, the courses of treatment prescribed, whether delivered in Philadelphia, New York, London, Paris, or Bad Nauheim, never varied much in final sum: *Get some rest! Get some exercise! Cold douches! Warm baths! Buck up!*

When John Hay had been in the earliest stages of his celebrity, a young bachelor whose worldly assets were a thousand acres of undeveloped land in the wilds of western Illinois and a small stake in a failing Florida orange grove, a young female admirer had asked his idea of happiness. "A bad character," he answered, with the mordant wit for which he was already renowned in the nation's capital, "and a good digestion."

He had to admit now, all these years later, that though he had been blessed with neither of those particulars, he had known happiness far beyond his due. "I really believe that in all history I never read of a man who has had so much and such varied success as I have had, with so little ability and so little power of sustained industry," he told friends. "It is not a thing to be proud of, but is something to be grateful for."

For nearly sixty years, John Hay had been floating gently down the stream of life, propelled almost entirely, as far as he could discern, by outside forces. He could call his life's successes destiny or fate, but that presupposed a higher being shaping the world, and Hay was free of that particular superstition. He could call them blind luck, but that wouldn't do them justice either. There had been no shortage of effort expended, but so little of it had been *his*. Ever since his boyhood in the tiny frontier town of Warsaw, Illinois, on the banks of the Mississippi, all he had had to do was be himself, *show* himself, and other people snapped to. They saw bigger things in John Hay than he saw in himself. His elders were awed by the effortlessness with which he sailed through his school lessons, his facility for languages, his natural ease in social intercourse. While siblings, classmates, and coworkers were left to fend for themselves, dozens of benefactors had taken pains to shove John Hay forward.

By 1895, Hay had won thoroughgoing respect among his nation's governing class, a colonelcy in the wartime army, a reputation as an astute collector of fine art, literary acclaim, and close confidential friendships among the leaders of the world's preeminent power, the British Empire. He had acquired a cosmopolitan familiarity with every world capital that truly *mattered*, and a place on the board of directors of Western Union alongside the business titans J. Pierpont Morgan and William Waldorf Astor. And he had wealth beyond his earliest imaginings, having gained his fortune in the way recently popularized by the sumptuously titled but cash-poor aristocracy of western Europe: he had married it. His bride, Clara Stone, was the beloved daughter of a former engineer and bridge builder who had managed to get controlling interests in railroads, rolling mills, coal and iron producers, and banks. The stout Ohio industrialist Amasa Stone presented John Hay with a wedding gift of $10,000 worth of railroad bonds and then lured his son-in-law to Cleveland, where Hay could work in the family business.

Less than ten years later, shamed by the deadly collapse of one of his railroad bridges, the fastidious old man stepped half-clothed into his bathtub and shot himself in the heart with a silver-plated Smith & Wesson pistol. As inheritors of half of Stone's fortune, Mr. and Mrs. Hay had overnight become, as Mrs. Henry Adams referred to them with a deep but mostly hidden reserve of New England envy, "tri-millionaires." The Hays owned, clear of liens and mortgages, the estate on Lake Sunapee, the mansion in Cleveland, and a bigger one in Washington, DC, which held Hay's most valued private treasures: the signed copy of the 1865 inaugural address (his last gift from President Lincoln, given just three days before the assassination), a public library's worth of smooth morocco-bound books, Sassoferrato's oil painting *Madonna and Child*, and a recently purchased Botticelli.

Hay and his old Lincoln White House coworker John Nicolay had recently won praise and thanks as the authors of *Abraham Lincoln: A History.* The two men had labored for nearly a decade on their epic and seminal ten-volume story of the president they had served so closely and known so intimately. The study had done much to secure Lincoln's reputation in history. Nicolay had been enticed by the money publication promised. But Hay had stuck with the difficult project mainly out of a sense of obligation to the country and his admiration for Abraham Lincoln and what he had accomplished in his brief presidency. Money, for Hay at least, was beside the point.

By 1895, Hay had accepted the central and defining condition of his life: he did not need to work for pay. This indisputable fact did not give him much comfort, because he feared boredom above all and sometimes fretted that his own death would be caused by chronic ennui. So he did his level best to keep active and engaged in the world.

Even at the distant remove of his mountain retreat, a steady current of news and gossip carried right to John Hay's doorstep. He read only one newspaper that summer, the Great Moral Organ, of course, but between that and his daily mail, he kept tethered to the still-spinning globe. He saw in the previous Saturday's *Tribune* that "Mark Twain" had got himself into a spectacular financial jam, which hardly qualified as an earth-shattering surprise. For as long as Hay had known him—almost thirty years now—Sam Clemens had exhibited a genius for inventing trouble where none could be bought, along with a proclivity to draw innocents into the fray. Hay still had, locked away somewhere from Mrs. Hay, an unpublished story Clemens had written, on the sly, for a few special friends—a tart rendering of dinner conversation among Elizabethan luminaries. The early seventeenth-century dialect was spot-on, and the dialogue put Rabelais in the shade: flatulence, masturbation, fornication, the intricacies of the female nether parts, and a spirited argument over the proper spelling of a certain subset of the male genitalia: "Ye contention running high betwixt ye learned Bacon and ye ingenious Jonson, until at last ye old Lady Margery, wearying of it all, saith, *Gentles, what matter it how ye shall spell the word? I warrant ye when ye use your bollocks ye shall not think of it; and my Lady Granby, be ye content; let the spelling be, ye shall enjoy the beating of them on your buttocks just the same, I trow."*

Hay's temptation to share the fun with other worthies had got the better of his official dignity—he was at the time the assistant secretary of state—and he conspired with a friend (in Cleveland, away from the seat of federal government) to facilitate a discreet circulation, without the author's prior approval. "The proposition which you make to pull a few proofs of the master piece is highly attractive, and of course highly immoral," Hay had written from his office at the State Department. "I cannot properly consent to it, and I am afraid the great man would think I was taking an unfair advantage of his confidence. Please send back the document as soon as you can, and if, in spite of my prohibition, you take these proofs, save me one."

Hay had admitted long ago the wisdom of his wife's insistence that he keep his distance from Clemens; Clara Stone Hay had an unerring radar for the sort of coarseness and vulgarity that Clemens cheerfully exuded, and she had the sublime Christian will to meet it without fear. She held him in contempt, and she showed it. The last time Mrs. Hay had laid eyes on Sam Clemens, beguiling her husband to violate the Sabbath *in her own parlor*, Mrs. Hay's muscular Methodist presence had caused the celebrated writer to go absolutely, uncharacteristically, impossibly silent. Mr. Hay followed suit. That was more than twenty-five years ago, and John Hay had made sure the three were never in the same room again.

News of Clemens was small beer for the *Tribune*, a paragraph here and there on the inside pages, but the paper was full of the doings of another friend of Hay's—the new president of the New York Board of Police Commissioners, Theodore Roosevelt. Even from afar, Theodore could be counted on to amuse, and Hay had sat rapt one morning at the Fells, reading the commissioner's latest interview. Summer in the city presented a wide-open field of opportunity for publicity, so the commissioner was in his glory, having made a show of foregoing his annual extended retreat to his home in Oyster Bay in order to redouble his public fight against crime and vice in Lower Manhattan. Roosevelt in full cry! Teddy talk had filled an entire column of the *Tribune* with the latest chapter of his ongoing crusade against that scourge of the modern metropolis: Saloons! Open on Sunday! Commissioner Roosevelt recounted for publication, in exhaustive detail, his most recent personal inspection of the Bowery's watering holes.

Theodore's campaign against the Sunday liquor sales had been bully, if he did say so himself, and he did say so, in every way he could conceive. "Last Sunday, let it be said what may, was dryer than any that have preceded since we began the effort to enforce the law."

At one point in the filibuster, the *Tribune*'s man conveyed, Commissioner Roosevelt had leaned back in his chair with an air of self-satisfaction, which was, as Hay knew from long observation, simply Theodore in repose. "I think that all the present Board of Police Commissioners feel alike; we like to smite the ungodly hip and thigh; we are believers in 'the sword of the Lord and of Gideon,' and we think that events here have shown the truth of the saying that 'Thrice armed is he who hath his quarrel just.' " Theodore Roosevelt bore watching.

There was news of real consequence that August, too, but Hay had a way of filtering larger stories through the narrow lens of personal acquaintance. The coalition of Conservatives and Liberal Unionists had routed the ruling Liberal Party in Britain, and Lord Salisbury had been restored to the prime minister's seat, much to the pleasure of Queen Victoria. "No doubt many causes combined," an old Liberal, Sir Robert Cunliffe, confided to Hay in a private letter, "but probably the most damaging effect . . . was a general want of confidence in men who seemed to have no very settled convictions, but a strong wish to win votes. People like their leaders to lead & that the late ministry did not seem able to do."

Salisbury's government appeared to be projecting the desired strength, especially its colonial secretary, Joe Chamberlain (another friend of Hay's), who was making speeches in Parliament about a new muscularity in his office. Great Britain's global holdings were untapped assets, and Pushful Joe, as the newsmen were now styling him, meant to make the underdeveloped colonies into viable modern markets for British exports.

But that was all talk, according to Henry Adams's latest dispatches from England. The British economy was reeling. Harvests were down, cotton and coal oversupplied. Nervous bankers were hoarding their pots of gold. The landed gentry were starting to sweat. "Neither party knows what to do," Adams had written Hay from the Scottish estate of their friend Sir John Clark, who had been forced to rent out his big house for the upcoming shooting season.

The British Foreign Office, meanwhile, was after the American State Department to help them excise a pound of flesh from China, as payback for the massacre of eleven Christian missionaries in Ku-cheng. "The outrage," the *Times* of London insisted, "must not be passed over as a trifle!" Alvey Adee, America's acting secretary of state (and another of Hay's old friends), was counseling calm, according to *Tribune* reports, at least until he had better information from Colonel Denby, minister to China.

Hay could imagine the scene outside the desk he had once inhabited at the

State, War, and Navy Building, where reporters would be waving recent press accounts in Adee's face: *Is there an American warship at Ku-cheng? Are the commissioners who were sent to investigate the massacre being menaced by the Chinese marauders? Why haven't you got word from Minister Denby?* Poor Alvey.

The China problem was just one in a dozen problems facing Adee that summer. The overworked assistant secretary would be tasked with keeping an especially close eye on Cuba, Hay knew, because Spain was getting jittery about the growing insurrection there. Hay was hearing from his own sources in Santiago de Cuba that the insurgents were "knocking" the Spanish army "like old boots" and that yellow fever was thinning the Spanish ranks. But thirty years of fighting off homegrown revolutionaries on that island, and the imperative of holding on to one of the few American colonies left in its shrinking empire, had hardened into a matter of stubborn Iberian pride. The Spanish government was making a show of defending what little remained of its honor, and it was hard to tell exactly how high a price they would pay to retain their battered dignity.

The most recent counterinsurgency had already cost Spain $20 million that they could ill afford, and the bill was growing every day. But the Spanish, from all appearances, were going all in. The new government of Antonio Cánovas del Castillo had reportedly dispatched to Cuba a fleet of seven cruisers, seven torpedo boats, and twenty-five gunboats small enough to negotiate the inland waterways of the island. Troop transports had just pulled out of Barcelona, Santander, La Coruña, and Cádiz with eight thousand reinforcement soldiers and boatloads of arms and ammunition.

What most interested John Hay in those last days of August, though, was Republican politics. Hay had stayed mostly on the sidelines of party politics, but he found himself increasingly pulled into the coming election cycle. The 1896 party convention was still nearly a year away, but the race for the presidential nomination was already gathering steam. The last Republican to hold the White House, Benjamin Harrison, was playing coy about running again, but that was because he didn't have a chance . . . which was all to the good for Hay, who had been passed over for an ambassadorship in the last Harrison administration. A "fine appointment," Harrison had said at the time, "but there isn't any politics in it!"

The Republican's recent Speaker of the House, Thomas Brackett Reed, was the acknowledged front-runner—Hay's friends Senator Henry Cabot Lodge and Theodore Roosevelt were carrying the Reed banner—but Hay was hearing from the Republican pooh-bahs in Ohio that the Speaker was too fastidious to get down in the mud and grovel and that Governor William McKinley was quietly gaining strength. McKinley's campaign manager was keeping Hay up on the latest developments. He had told Hay to hold tight, he didn't need money from him just yet, but maybe Hay could talk to his friends in New York and

Pennsylvania to find out where the state party bosses were leaning, and maybe he could make some personal appeals to his editor friends on McKinley's behalf.

Hay knew better than to spend energy pushing his old paper, the *Tribune,* to heed the early signs and get out front for McKinley. Whitelaw Reid, still running the GMO after all these years, would be, well, politic. Whitelaw would be seeking a place in the next cabinet no matter who was president, so he had to be careful not to make an enemy of *anybody* who had the slimmest chance of winning the nomination. But the *Tribune* was doing its Republican duty by kicking the stuffing out of the sitting president, Grover Cleveland. Just look at the economic destruction that feckless Democrat had wrought, the *Tribune* harrumphed almost daily. Who else could one possibly blame? The stock market had crashed two months into Cleveland's watch, and hundreds of banks had failed in the aftermath. More than fifteen thousand businesses had gone bust. The country's biggest railroads had declared bankruptcy. The Treasury's gold reserves continued to shrink, and the wealth of the nation with them. Farmers were taking bigger losses every year. Nearly a million American men were out of work.

The unwashed and now unhappy masses had their torches and pitchforks out, aimed at "capitalists." And Cleveland and his supporters had appeased the rabble by pushing through the first federal income tax since Lincoln's emergency war measure. The Democrat-controlled Congress wanted wealthy Americans to pay *two cents* on the dollar for any personal income over $4,000. Cleveland signed their bill, which was, by the *Tribune*'s lights, a blatant attempt at redistribution of wealth, confiscation of private property, and persecution of the rich. Here was the coming of the dangerous democracy that true Republicans always feared, the jealous, tyrannical majority bent on punishing a man for making money. This was *communistic*! The Supreme Court, fearful that the present "assault upon capital" would be the first shot in a ruinous class war, had negated the income tax law as unconstitutional, but the 5–4 vote had been far too close for Republican comfort. And Cleveland, the *Tribune* asserted that summer, offered no road to economic recovery except to prattle on about that fool's panacea, free trade. He had lowered tariffs just when the nation's faltering businessmen most needed protection from cheap foreign imports. There was something, well, *un-American* about Grover Cleveland, according to the *Tribune.* The best news of the summer, as Whitelaw's editorialists saw it: the president was on vacation. "There is at least a chance that in his absence some other official might show a little American spirit."

The *Tribune* was a tad strident for Hay's taste, but he had no qualms with the substance of its argument. The next president, no matter who it was, would inherit a nest of nasty complications. And the American economy might end up being the least of the worries. The Old World empires were shaky; the long-settled European balance of power was teetering. Spain was collapsing in on itself. The French were too weak to build a simple forty-eight-mile canal across Panama. The early death of Alexander III had thrust onto the Russian throne a scared twenty-six-year-old colt, "afflicted with the misfortune of being very weak on every point," the British ambassador in St. Petersburg noted, "except his own autocracy."

The British Empire was still supreme, but it was stretched thin. From the moment they took office that summer, Prime Minister Salisbury and Joe Chamberlain were fighting a rearguard action against what they regarded as their namby-pamby countrymen who wanted to "close the capital accounts on empire," forgetful perhaps that their island nation had been kept afloat in no small part by an enormously profitable opium trade in China and the gold and diamonds being dug out of Britain's far-flung colonies. The young German kaiser, meanwhile, sniffed blood in the international waters; the kaiser was making noise about building a navy to match Britain's and already had a small fleet skulking around the Pacific like a predator shark.

John Hay had been warning about a mindless European buildup of "enormous armaments" since he had been on post at his first legation abroad in the mid-1860s, and now, just when this race toward inevitable calamity was accelerating, loud voices in America, Senator Lodge and Commissioner Roosevelt right out front, were pushing President Cleveland to make bold and join the fight for the world's best commercial spoils. Lodge was calling for the United States to grab Cuba and Puerto Rico in the Caribbean, and Hawaii in the Pacific (maybe Guam and Samoa would be nice to have, too), and then to cut its own canal through Nicaragua to join the two oceans and open the path to the enormous markets in Asia.

Political cataclysm—that's what Hay's friend Clarence King would have forecast. King was no political theorist, but he was a man with his eye on distant horizons. King was one of America's renowned researchers in the natural sciences and was always ahead of the times. While the rest of his generation had been enthralled by Darwin's new scientific theory of natural selection and by its extrapolators' promises of the long, steady march toward higher civilization, King spent his early career putting Darwin's world-altering idea to the test in the American West. For nearly a decade, he had searched for answers buried in the tectonic plates of mountains and canyons in and around the Sierra, and he emerged with a jagged corollary that elaborated Darwin's elegant theory. King had found a definite pattern woven into the rocks: eons of geological stasis, punctuated by extreme and instantaneous upheaval. The force of nature had never been a constant, steady push, he argued, but a dormant giant given to violent, unforgiving, shape-shifting explosions. Change, King had divined, often happened all at once, spurred by the need to adapt quickly to extraordinary events—or be crushed by them.

Hay trusted King's work in the natural sciences, and wasn't it possible that what applied to nature must apply to man and his institutions? The world and politics were about to crack open, Hay could feel it, and something new would surely emerge. Was the final meaning of Lincoln's rescue of the American republic about to reveal itself? Had the time finally come for republican virtue to shove aside the decrepit body of Old World monarchy? There were days that summer when Hay felt the faintest intimations of a physical force gathering in him, something like vitality, or energy, something strong enough to meet the coming challenges. Hadn't he spent a lifetime in preparation? Wouldn't it be shirking his duty to stay on the sidelines?

The problem was, he wasn't quite sure how to make his way into the game. Maybe the field belonged to younger men like Roosevelt and Lodge. Maybe that was what accounted for that dull ache of longing in his stomach. He was lonesome in all ways as summer waned in New Hampshire: lonesome for his friends, lonesome for his many departed political comrades in arms, lonesome for his youth, lonesome for his own idea of himself. Would he ever be the man so many people expected him to be? Would he meet this new moment in time? Or had his best chances already passed him by?

This was a familiar sensation, not so different from its advent, acute and demoralizing, back when he was a fresh twenty-year-old graduate of one of the nation's few settled seats of higher learning. His uncle Milton had paid his way to Brown University, in Providence, Rhode Island, where Hay had got the idea that he had ahead of him a career of fashioning elegant and earthmoving poetry. Maybe he would stay in Providence, he thought, or go to Boston or New York. But after four years enfolded in the dark leather softness of Brown, cradled in the equipoise of its refined beauty and marbled solidity, John Hay had had no choice but to return to his frontier Illinois home, where he felt like an alien being. There was no young person like him in Springfield, let alone tiny Warsaw. He was, he was certain at the time, meant to be a man of large and artistic purpose—and his family was trying to make a country lawyer of him.

Hay could still remember the relentless grind of that cold prairie winter spent reading law at his uncle Milton's office in the clapboard capital of Springfield. He had plowed diligently through Hume, but a creeping sadness—were the best pieces of him being milled away?—had rendered him incapable of mounting a sustained attack on Blackstone's legal texts. "I still can console myself with a dream of possibilities that were once mine, and soothe my soul with the shadowy Might-have-been," he wrote to a friend back east. "I find only a dreary waste of heartless materialism [out west], where great and heroic qualities may indeed bully their way up into the glare, but the flowers of existence inevitably droop and wither. So in time shall I change. I shall turn from 'the rose and the rainbow' to corner-lots and tax-titles."

He still shuddered at the narrowness of his unlikely escape from that bleak future and recalled how pathetically he had held to the hope of a berth in the Illinois State auditor's office, with its promise of free access to the libraries at the statehouse. He still remembered how he had clung to the solace of the small triumph of his first public lecture, "History of the Jesuits." He had clipped and passed around the local paper's review of his talk. Amazingly, almost forty years later, its sentiments still applied: Mr. Hay, read the notice, "has the talents, and if he does not make his mark in the world as a bright and shining light, the fault is with himself."

CHAPTER TWO

A Bad-Luck Habit

The game played to his strengths; it required cunning, concentration, and nerve. And its prevailing formulas suited Sam Clemens: every man for himself, ample opportunity to overcome a bad deal by working off the weakest cards on your neighbors, and the ability to dig yourself out of a big deficit by one spectacularly played hand. Taking a trick full of scoring cards—every heart in the deck counted a point against you, and the dread Black Lady, the queen of spades, thirteen points—was to be avoided. When the points started to pile up against a player, he could always go for broke—*shoot the moon.* Take *all* the hearts and the Black Lady and you could shove twenty-six points on everybody else in the game. A player who managed to take every trick in a hand, to *shoot the sun*, could tally fifty-two points on every other player's ledger and put himself halfway to victory. But no matter how skilled a person was at counting cards, or how crafty at making the big go-for-broke play, winning usually required a fair portion of luck, which added tension and interest to the Clemens family hearts game the first week out on the *Warrimoo*.

There weren't many ways to pass the time aboard ship. Livy read, or wrote letters to the daughters they had left behind in Elmira, Susy and Jean. Clara did the same, or played shovelboard on deck with the other passengers, or flicked the lights on and off in her stateroom to see if she could get a hard count on the number of bugs she had heard in the night. "Their familiarity," she complained in a letter home to her cousin, "went beyond all bounds." But the pleasantest pastime was card playing, and the hearts games kept the family engaged for hours at a stretch. Once in a while it was just the three of them, but most days, Sam, Livy, and Clara rounded out a foursome with one of the ship's officers or even Captain Arundel, which meant the women had to keep a close watch on the proceedings, or, more specifically, on the family patriarch. When Sam Clemens had a couple of consecutive hands of rotten luck, and his point total started to run up, and he sat staring at the center of the table in boiling silence, the women knew an explosion was imminent.

The tiniest tremor of ill fortune set Clemens's teeth on edge just then, because it added evidentiary heft to his suspicion that he had suddenly acquired a bad-luck habit. This was a hard new future to reckon and a complete reversal of his lifetime horoscope. Sam Clemens had always believed he was born under a lucky sign, could tally dozens of scrapes he'd got free of, some surely fatal, through no particular skill of his own, but by the pure-gold luck he accepted as his personal privilege and his inheritance from on high. That's why he had been so damned sure the typesetting machine would make him as rich as Croesus, or at least Carnegie, right up to the moment it had helped to ruin him.

Clemens had been convinced that the Paige typesetter would perfect man in machine—would do all the labor of six hand compositors, only fifteen times faster and without error. The plan never lacked audacity. James Paige's patent application had totaled *176* sheets of intricate and filigreed mechanical drawings, including in sum each of the mechanical typesetter's *eighteen thousand* interlocking parts and pieces. The overawed clerks at the US patent office had taken to calling this application "the whale," perhaps because of its sheer size, and perhaps because it was, like Moby-Dick, both unattainable and dangerous to pursue.

Clemens had not been daunted by the oceanfuls of possible complications that attended the machine's effort to move its thousands of parts in perfect mechanical concert. And he had not been daunted when the elegant and delicate typesetter failed test run after test run, requiring another five-figure investment after each. He poured nearly $200,000 into it in all, and every new infusion of his cash, Clemens convinced himself, would be the one that allowed Paige to round the machine into its final, flawless form, so that every newspaper owner in the United States would clamber to have at least one! Never mind that Whitelaw Reid had already put the Mergenthaler Linotype to effective and efficient use at his *New York Tribune*, and other publishers were well satisfied that it would be hard to beat. Sam Clemens meant to beat it.

He would later claim that he kept pouring money into the project because he had been entirely swept up by the inventor's powers of persuasion, calling James Paige a "most great and genuine poet, whose sublime creations are written in steel." "He is the Shakespeare of mechanical invention," Clemens insisted. "He is a dreamer, a visionary. His imagination utterly runs away with him." But Sam Clemens knew in his heart that it hadn't been Paige's imagination that got him into trouble, but his own. Sometimes the sheer ecstasy of his private reverie had been impossible to keep to himself, and he would wonder aloud to the family servant, Katy Leary—and only half-jokingly—about the day he could buy up every newspaper in New York, and the railroads to boot. "He was always calculating all the millions that the typesetting machine was going to bring in," Katy would say. "They was just waiting for it to be perfect—to astonish the world. . . . Mr. Clemens never lost faith."

He had been so sure, every time he doubled down on that typesetter, that fortune's fickle hand would pull him through, because it always had. So in the great typesetter game, he shot for the moon, the sun, *and* the stars. But he had misplayed the game, badly. And it had landed him in the middle of the Pacific Ocean, shuffling cards on the *Warrimoo*, dead broke, his faith in himself sorely tested.

If it was the ship's captain across from him, making up the game's fourth, that was cause for further concern. Clemens had always been careful not to have truck with the unlucky, and Captain Arundel seemed to qualify as an untouchable. On his way to Vancouver three weeks earlier, where he was to pick up the Clemens family and other Sydney-bound passengers, the captain had run the *Warrimoo* onto the rocks within sight of the Canadian coastline. It was a nasty accident and would have been worse had the weather been stormy that night, but in the aftermath of the event, nobody questioned Captain Arundel's seamanship. Newspapermen noted the dense fog, the puniness of the warning horn near Carmanah Point, and the out-of-date maps the captain had been forced to reckon with. They noted the captain's slow, cautious approach to port, the assiduousness with which he sounded, repeatedly, the depths ahead; "200 fathoms, and no bottom," was the last reading, just moments before the *Warrimoo* heaved up, with a frightening metallic scream, onto the reef ledge.

She was hard and fast on those rocks for five hours, and by the time the high tide floated the ship enough to be worked off the reef, her underbelly was creased, gashed, buckled, and punctured. Her propeller blades had been violently warped. But Arundel, it was noted, had done all he could under the circumstances. The captain, said the *Victoria News*, "can scarcely be blamed in any way for the accident." Just bad luck was all.

While the *Warrimoo* was being patched up with the maritime equivalent of chewing gum and baling wire, reporters in Vancouver stopped in to ask "Mark Twain" what he thought of taking his appointed berth on the damaged vessel, and he had played nice with the feelings of Captain Arundel; he would gladly, he insisted, entrust his family's safe passage to the skipper's care. The celebrated humorist, the *Vancouver Daily News-Advertiser* reported, had been "looking for a ship of that kind—a ship with the rock habit, and one which never allows such mishaps to disconcert her, but always got off again." But that was just for show. Sam Clemens was not at all pleased to be forced onto this bad-luck bark. The time spent on stopgap repairs had put the *Warrimoo* nearly a week behind schedule when it finally pulled away from Vancouver, and there was no way to know if there would still be time enough for Clemens to make his advertised lecture during their brief layover in Honolulu.

He was always attuned to possible trouble on this ship, so that even an unhappy trend in the family card games felt like a sign of coming woe. Clara Clemens could see it prey on him. When a new hand was dealt, she would watch him as he regarded his cards, and if it was another bad deal for her father, she knew it right away by the onset of tremors just below his eye. Then the first pass would be made, and Clara would see the Clemens jaw set hard, her father burning with rage until, in a sudden and dramatic movement, he would slam his cards facedown on the table.

"By the humpin' jumpin' Jesus," he would yell, "who can play with a hand like that?" And Livy would fix her eyes on her husband in a silent but unmistakable plea for calm.

"*Look at those cards! Just look at 'em!*"

"Youth," Livy would purr, her pet name for her husband.

"*Products of the devil and his ancestors!*"

"Youuuuuth," Livy would purr again, with a little more edge.

Clara thought it was her mother's gentle cooing that calmed him, but Sam Clemens always caught the measured but resolute insistence in the cold blue steel of his wife's gaze.

"Youth . . ."

"But I can't stand the sight of such cards," he would mutter, by way of excuse, as he picked up his cards. "Only a saint on ice could keep cool."

And then he would punctuate his outburst with a sheepish little laugh, and quiet himself, and accept his new fate, and determine to play out the hand as best he could with the cards he'd been dealt.

BY THE SEVENTH day at sea, Sam Clemens was beginning to calm. He had not committed to paper a single word toward his round-the-world book, had made only a few jottings in his notebook, and had kept up a spotty correspondence with friends back home. Mainly he stuck to a daily routine of reading, playing hearts, smoking, and watching the sun paint the Pacific a fanciful range of blues. The trip had been uneventful, the weather serene and bright, and for a vessel so recently ruptured and bent, the *Warrimoo* had been surprisingly swift. And though Clemens was admitting to friends that he had already got "mighty tired plat-forming," he was beginning to feel the return of some of his normal energy. The closer the ship got to the Hawaiian Islands, he noticed, the stronger he felt.

The port city of Honolulu was the *Warrimoo*'s lone stop between Vancouver and Sydney, and the original plan was for a quick lecture there, while the ship was off-loading cargo, mail, and passengers and taking on the Sydney-bound traffic. A local promoter had engaged an outdoor dance pavilion at Independence Park in Honolulu and papered the city with broadsides announcing the "Mark Twain" lecture program, which would also include traditional musical airs from the Kawaihan Quintette Club. The *Evening Bulletin* had already run a long sketch of "Mark Twain," including a full reprint of his *Encyclopaedia Britannica* entry, a signature Twainian bon mot ("There is nothing that disagrees with me so much as working between meals"), and a nod to the jaunty irreverence and sharp satire the performer was bound to display. Word of the author's imminent arrival had radiated out through the city's thirteen hundred new telephones. More than five hundred tickets to the "Mark Twain" lecture had been sold in advance, and the city fathers had agreed to scramble extra tramcars to haul the multitudes up and down King and Beretania Streets for the Saturday night performance. Even after the *Warrimoo* failed to steam in on schedule, on August 24, with no word yet as to why, people held on to their tickets in hopes that the funnyman would appear. Better late than never.

ON THE EVENING of August 30, Sam Clemens was on deck, scanning the horizon, when he finally caught sight of the murky shape of Oahu emerging in the distance and presently recognized the outline of Diamond Head, that majestic, 760-foot-high promontory that rose up 300,000 years earlier, give or take, in a series of violent, spasmodic eruptions. A certain affinity existed, in terms of personality, between himself and the old volcano; it was like seeing a dear and long-lost friend. "Not any other thing in the world," he would write of that moment, "could have stirred me as the sight of that great rock did."

Once Oahu was in view, Clemens knew, it would be only a few hours to the Honolulu roadstead; he was so near he could almost smell the jasmine. With every passing minute, he grew increasingly anxious to step again into the circle of that ancient Hawaiian magic. "The peacefullest, restfullest, sunniest, balmiest, dreamiest haven of refuge for a worn and weary spirit the surface of the earth can offer," he called these islands, with hard evidence to back it up. He had been there once before, in 1866, arriving as a penniless and bitterly depressed thirty-year-old newspaperman on assignment for the *Sacramento Union* and returning—after six months of occasional spurts of industry, followed by the first prolonged stretches of indolence he had known since his preadolescent larks in Hannibal, Missouri—with the goods to remake himself. It would not be an exaggeration to say that Hawaii was the pivot on which his life turned, and toward the good, or at least toward the lucrative.

Sam Clemens with his nephew Samuel Moffet.
Clara and Livy in the background.

His lectures on the exotic Sandwich Islands had brought him, for the first time in his career, a celebrity he could bank on. That was the miracle of the islands: Hawaii replenished, restored, revivified. For the rest of his days, glancing associations with those islands moved Clemens to uncharacteristic and unexpected flights of public sentimentality. "No other land could so longingly and so beseechingly haunt me, sleeping and waking, through half a lifetime, as that one has done," he would say.

THE *WARRIMOO* DID not sail into Honolulu that August night in 1895 but anchored a mile offshore, and its passengers stood on board in the warm dark, rocked by a gentle tide, waiting for a pilot boat to take them ashore. The scheduled layover had already been squeezed. Captain Arundel had in mind to make up some of the time lost to the accident, and planned to pull anchor by eleven the next morning—too fast to accommodate a "Mark Twain" lecture show. Still, it meant something to Clemens to be able to put his feet in the Hawaiian sand, gaze up Nuuanu Valley to the mountains beyond, hear the delicious rustle of palms, feel the balm of warm, wet air, and *smell*, if even for a moment, the redolent floral aroma that rode the island breeze. By the time a boat finally drew up alongside the *Warrimoo*, Sam Clemens was damned impatient to be on Oahu.

"We cannot board you," came a voice from the smaller vessel. "There is sickness on the island. We want to speak to the captain."

"What kind of sickness?"

"I'm sorry. We must speak to the captain first."

The news delivered to the captain was grim: Asiatic cholera was abroad in Honolulu, and the incidence of infection seemed to be accelerating. Twenty cases had been reported over the previous week, and fifteen people were already dead; today's daily bulletin had eight confirmed new cases and at least two deaths. The local board of health was working night and day to prevent a full-blown epidemic of the deadly intestinal ailment. The board had ordered the city scoured with chloride of lime and carbolic acid, set political prisoners from the Oahu jail to the task of sanitizing a suspect fish market, quarantined and burned the homes of the already infected, warned citizens away from Chinese restaurants, and—being a board possessed of the most up-to-date principles of Western medicine—offered such inane advice as affixing copper disks on the skin over the abdomen and remaining calm. "It is a positive fact," one board member wrote, "that fear has killed as many people as the most virulent epidemic."

The board had also placed strict limits on traffic into and out of the port; no people, cargo, or mail were allowed to leave Honolulu, for fear of spreading the disease in a manner that would invite the wrath of its Pacific neighbors, most specifically the United States of America. The government of the new Republic of Hawaii did not want to antagonize the United States. Captain Arundel had broken the hard news to the Clemens family: any passenger who disembarked at the port would be forced to stay on Oahu until the health emergency passed, and that could take weeks, even months, which meant the Clemenses would not set foot on the island. The next day's newspaper headline would sum it up neatly: THE UNLUCKY WARRIMOO.

At one thirty in the morning, the lighters began off-loading the *Warrimoo*'s hundreds of tons of Honolulu-bound cargo, while passengers stood around the deck and tried to make sense of the little information they had been given. The staterooms were too hot for Livy and Clara that night, so they remained on deck, offering a friendly ear to people who were being forced to decide whether to disembark and be trapped in Honolulu or continue on to Sydney. Sam Clemens, meanwhile, kept to himself; he could not take his eyes off the island city, lit up like Chicago. The dark hulk of the mountains in the distance was just as he remembered it, but the shimmering electric brilliance of the foreground was something new. Things had changed in thirty years.

WHEN SAM CLEMENS had first arrived in 1866—the British appellation of the Sandwich Islands was still common then—Honolulu was a sleepy port town of sea captains, seedy merchants, missionaries and their offspring, and Native Hawaiians or *kanakas*. The profits to be had from whaling were shrinking fast in those days, but what ships still worked the Pacific stopped in Honolulu to resupply and could sometimes be found in bulk, bouncing next to one another in the harbor, or "bulling," as the old salts called it. A few blocks up from Honolulu's main wharf was the seat of central government for the eight nearby islands, unified under the banner of Hawaii in the 1790s by the physically imposing and politically ambitious Kamehameha I, who made haste to invite commerce. And with foreign trade came foreigners.

A smattering of Germans, Dutch, Swedes, and Portuguese had worked themselves into banking, shopkeeping, and cottage industries. But the rising powers when Clemens first alighted were the descendants of the earliest Euro-American missionaries. They had been driving Hawaii toward "civilization" for a few generations by then, first steering the natives toward Christianity and then steering their government from feudal kingdom toward constitutional monarchy and republicanism.

A son or daughter of the Kamehameha line still ruled Hawaii in 1866, with the assistance of handpicked ministers (many were white) and titled native aristocracy. Though the kingdom held most of the land in trust for the nation, the sons of the earliest white settlers and missionaries had introduced to the Hawaiian ruling classes the benefits—in terms of revenue—of private property and then bought themselves huge tracts for planting sugar and raising cattle. Powerful landowning families, white ministers, and royal advisers then persuaded Kamehameha V to narrow the franchise to the "intelligent classes" by tying voting rights to ownership of property, which meant that the only *kanaka* voters were those few capable of wriggling free of a "civilizing" tool new to the islands—foreclosures by private banks.

The groups jockeying for dominion in the commercial arena in 1866 were the two that made up the bulk of the white, or *haole*, population. "English and Americans were well to the fore," wrote an observer at the time. "Socially and politically each was arrayed against the other; the Americans quiet, but confident, the English watchful but aggressive." As a young journalist and observer, Clemens had done what he could to put his finger on the scale for his fellow countrymen, booming their can-do energy and enterprise. "Whatever of commercial and agricultural greatness the country can boast of," Clemens claimed in his early letters home to the *Sacramento Union*, "it owes to them [Americans]."

Clemens trumpeted the bounty of the Sandwich Islands to his California audience with the enthusiasm of a chamber of commerce mouthpiece. Hawaii had natural resources to be *worked*, he reported. He totted up the remarkable yield of the land itself: an acre of island soil—unmanured!—produced a sugar crop five times the world average; in five years, the annual sugar output on the islands had grown tenfold, to twenty-seven *million* pounds. Ten separate plantations produced more than a million pounds a year. And here's how you could tell American-style ingenuity and capitalism were galloping in tandem through the kingdom: consolidation. The top five plantations accounted for nearly 40 percent of production and—owing to industrial efficiency, economies of scale, and cheap Asian laborers who resembled indentured servants—more than half the profits. One American-owned plantation on Maui was so comely, Clemens admitted, he wanted to marry it.

But Clemens had offered up all that overheated journo-chatter back when his country was the underdog, and precisely because it was the underdog. By 1895, however, American interests had triumphed in the islands. Trade with the United States accounted for four-fifths of Hawaii's foreign commerce. US gold coin was the only legal tender for denominations over ten dollars, the electric lights and the tramcars were American made. *Haole* sugar planters owned more than three-quarters of the private property in the islands in the 1890s and had risen from merely rich to filthy rich, largely by securing the rare privilege of selling their colossal annual crop tariff-free in the United States. The planters gained and held this rare trade concession by convincing the Hawaiian sovereign to forswear alliance with any other nation on the planet and to cede to the United States exclusive rights to build a naval station at Oahu's Pearl Harbor. They were hard at work trying to make the United States Congress see the wisdom of making the Hawaiian Islands America's first possession in the Pacific.

The decided underdogs, by 1895, were the Native Hawaiians. Most worked as wage laborers or languished in Honolulu's impoverished urban-tropical ghetto of Iwilei. Chinese and Japanese immigrants shipped in as cheap plantation labor accounted for almost half the population of the Hawaiian Islands, though as in the United States, Asians were denied the right to vote, or to own property, or to enjoy any other benefit of citizenship. The native nobility, meanwhile, was in a death struggle with the *haole* money crowd for control of its homeland.

The elected sovereign of Hawaii, Queen Liliuokalani, was under house arrest in August of 1895, having been forcibly removed from the throne two years earlier by the Citizen's Committee of Public Safety (also known as the Annexation Club), a secret society of American businessmen who had grown increasingly annoyed by the new queen's professed desire to disperse the nearly monopolistic commercial and political power a few dozen *haole* families had enjoyed for a generation or more. Liliuokalani, they feared, meant to promulgate a new constitution that restored franchise to all her native people.

The citizen's committee coup against this incipient island democracy was long nurtured and executed with both alacrity and a lively appreciation for what later American conspirators would call "shock and awe." The Annexation Club had funded and weaponized a sizable cadre of soldiers but held its powder until January 16, 1893, a day when the USS *Boston*, a well-armed, steel-hulled American cruiser on a nine-month tour of the Pacific, happened to be in port in Honolulu. The plotters picked that day to sound a panicked alarm on the doorstep of the US Consulate. "The public safety is menaced and lives and property are in peril," the committee pleaded in their official correspondence, which was carefully composed as evidence for the historical record. "We are unable to protect ourselves without aid." The US minister in Honolulu, who was among the planners of the *haole* plot against the queen, requested of the commander of the *Boston* an immediate landing of marines and sailors, "for the protection of the United States Legation, and the United States Consulate, and to secure the safety of American life and property."

Hawaiian officials watched from the second floor of their government building as the 3,189-ton US warship wheeled around its big guns and took direct aim at their sovereign kingdom. A few hours later, two battalions of the US Marines double-timed through downtown Honolulu with their rifles shouldered, rolling two small artillery pieces unimpeded down the quiet streets, and set up shop near the queen's royal residence and the legislative building, exhibiting a boldness that shocked the representative of the most accomplished native-subduing nation on the face of the earth. "If the troops were landed solely for the protection of American property," said the British minister in Honolulu, "the placing of them so far away from . . . the property of Americans and so very close to the property of the Hawaiian Government was remarkable and suggestive."

The next evening, fearing a senseless and bloody fight, the queen took temporary leave of her throne and handed the reins of government to the attorney Sanford B. Dole and the other *haoles* of the Citizen's Committee of Public

Safety. "I yield to the superior power of the United States of America," she wrote, "whose Minister Plenipotentiary, his excellency John L. Stevens, has caused the United States troops to be landed at Honolulu and declared that he would support the Provisional government." This event, the queen knew, was something new in history, which is to say the first US-backed overthrow of a sovereign government; and she was convinced the news would not play well in the States. The queen expected subsequent moves by the American government to strictly conform to international law in general and the treaties between the United States of America and the Kingdom of Hawaii in specific. The US minister in Honolulu was sending another message: "The Hawaiian pear is now fully ripe," he alerted the secretary of state soon after the queen's overthrow, "and this is the golden hour for the United States to pluck it."

The two years that followed had been a tug-of-war that left the islands in political limbo, albeit a relatively peaceful one. The queen and her counsel argued the case that her American-made ouster was a blatant violation of international law and of US law, and she called for her immediate and unconditional restoration to the throne, while President Dole begged the US Congress to put his new republic under its protection, began cutting up the suspended kingdom's publicly held lands for a private fire sale, and sought expert legal advice in quieting the natives, who were, in his ugly and unfounded claim, "comparatively ignorant of the principles of government [and a] menace to good government."

"If I understand your situation, it is as follows," an esteemed professor at New York City's Columbia School of Law wrote in answer to President Dole. "You have a population of nearly 100,000 persons, of whom about 5,000 are Teutons, i.e., Americans, English, Germans and Scandinavians, about 9,000 are Portuguese, about 30,000 are Chinese and Japanese, about 8,000 are native born of foreign parents, and the rest are natives. With this situation, I understand your problem to be the construction of a constitution which will place the government in the hands of the Teutons, and preserve it there." An ivy-covered law school was already the best place in America to go in search of legal niceties to paper over criminal activity.

President Grover Cleveland, inaugurated two months *after* the overthrow, had denounced the US role in the revolution as a "lawless occupation of Honolulu under false pretexts." He had also refused to resubmit the already failed treaty of annexation. The House of Representatives had censured the American minister in Honolulu for his unbecoming actions against Hawaiian sovereignty—actions that betrayed an uncommon lack of good sense, good manners, and good diplomacy; the Senate remained boisterously and violently split on the question of annexation.

Well, one good thing would come of this cholera quarantine, Clemens figured:

he wouldn't have Honolulu's newspapermen begging him to weigh in on the current to-do. Even the most nimble social commentator entered that thicket of briars at his own peril, and Clemens's settled policy was to avoid taking sides on the divisive political questions of the day; in his long observation, the opinions of a private citizen, no matter how famous, could have little or no effect on public matters. And tweaking the noses of folks on the other side of an issue could have unfortunate commercial consequences. Sam Clemens's financial success was built on "Mark Twain's" being *liked*. Precious few causes merited championing if it meant alienating the affections of a potential book buyer.

AUGUST 31, 1895, a Saturday, dawned hot and still. The staterooms of the *Warrimoo* were nearly uninhabitable, and the psychic forecast for the captive passengers called for general mind warp, with a chance of scattered crack-up. Clemens spent most of that Saturday under the shade of the ship's awning, a lit cigar in hand, mesmerized by the distant waves sweeping continually to shore, "with no crash, no sound that we could hear." He sat alone, happy to be dressed in his new suit of snow-white ducks (as was the custom when a ship entered the tropics), and thumbed through the local newspapers.

The big political questions of the day had been pushed aside by a slate of advertisements for Dr. Hall's twenty-five-cent cholera-remedy medicine and an assortment of household disinfectants—"Cleanliness IS NEXT TO Godliness"—and by the latest bulletins from the board of health: ten new cholera cases as of that morning, and six more dead. The increasingly cautious board had shuttered schools in Honolulu until further notice, shortened the hours of operation for saloons, and—more shocking for this ultrapious little city—forbidden church services or Sunday schools the next day.

At one point that afternoon, Clemens opened his notebook and scrawled out a few random thoughts. He might not have the energy and inspiration to begin the travel book in earnest, but he meant to record as he went, and not just the visual images of the trip but the *felt* impressions: "Oahu—Just as silky and velvety and lovely as ever. If I might I would go ashore and never leave. The mountains right and left clothed in rich splendors of melting color, fused together. Some of the near cliffs veiled in slanting mists—beautiful luminous blue water; inshore brilliant green water. Two sharks playing around, laying for a Christian." The shark gods, Clemens recalled, were guardians of the native people.

This was Hawaii in a coconut shell, for Clemens, the yin and yang of it—the radiant beauty of the natural world serving as an arena for the sharp, nasty play of man and beast. As a young man, Clemens had been as fascinated by Hawaii's clash of cultures as he had been by its blessed pulchritude. In fact, it was the tragicomic spectacle of the earnest Christian assault on the ancient customs of the natives that provided Clemens with material enough to establish himself as something more than a one-horse humorist of the American West.

In the essays and public lectures that grew out of his six months in the islands, he had called it as he had seen it. He did not, in his telling, smooth the edges of the Native Hawaiians' most barbarous and backward customs: the tradition of executing a commoner who stood upright in the presence of the king, or the practice of mourning royalty by plucking out one's own tooth or *eyeball*. And he did not avert his gaze from their bold sexuality. He had noted, with a nod of respectful awe, an unmarried princess who kept a man harem nearing three dozen, and "it had been her pride and boast that she kept the whole of them busy, and that several times it had happened that more than one of them had been able to charge overtime."

"Mark Twain" had been willing to credit the early American missionaries with clothing, educating, and generally uplifting the native population, but he wasn't blind to the ways they were redistributing the material blessings of the islands; the missionaries and especially their descendants had profited, and handsomely, by their works. (The missionaries came to do good, went the old saw in Hawaii, and they did well.) And Clemens had chuckled more than once at the various Episcopalians and Catholics and Presbyterians and Methodists and Mormons whose patience frayed and spirits wearied in the continuing efforts to inhibit the native generosity in matters pecuniary and sexual: "The example of white selfishness does not affect their native unselfishness any more than the example of white virtue does their native licentiousness."

The longer Sam Clemens had stayed in Hawaii, the more his sympathies tended toward the ancient inhabitants of the islands. A boyhood of enforced churchgoing had made him sensitive to what was lost in the icy drizzle of Christian piety, and he lamented the missionary success in making the Hawaiians "permanently miserable by telling them how beautiful and how blissful a place heaven is, and how nearly impossible it was to get there; and showed the poor native how dreary a place of perdition is and what unnecessarily liberal facilities there are for going to it; showed him how, in his ignorance he had gone and fooled away all his kinfolks to no purpose; showed him what rapture it was to work all day for fifty cents to buy food for the next day with, as compared with fishing for pastime and lolling in the shade through eternal Summer, and eating of the bounty that nobody labored to provide but Nature." While Clemens was no apologist for the sitting sovereign of his early visit, he did appreciate the horse sense exhibited by Kamehameha V when it came to questions of doctrine and devotion. "The foreigners like their religion—let them enjoy it, and freely," the king had said. "But the religion of my fathers is good enough for me."

Apart from the questions of money and religion, Clemens made a point of revealing the unintended but near-genocidal damage done to natives by Europeans and Americans, whose imports included small pox, influenza, measles, whooping cough, venereal disease, and assorted other maladies that marched relentlessly through the immunologically defenseless Hawaiian people. "The [Hawaiian] population was about 400,000," Clemens had told his first audiences in 1866, "but the white man came and brought various complicated diseases, and education and civilization, and all sorts of calamities, and consequently the population began to drop off with commendable activity. . . . [It was] proposed to send a few more missionaries and finish them."

THIRTY YEARS LATER the Native Hawaiian population was down around thirty thousand and still dwindling. The Honolulu epidemic that Clemens sailed into in August of 1895 turned out to be a tragic epidemiological repeat of a century of island history. Among the eighty-eight known cholera cases, according to statistics compiled for public health officials in the United States, there were four Americans, two Portuguese, one Chinese, one Japanese, four part-Hawaiians, and *seventy-six* Native Hawaiians. Native Hawaiians accounted for all but a handful of the sixty-three dead. The local board of health, with the assistance of the US consul general, constructed a pat little narrative of the cause and spread of Asiatic cholera in the capital city of the Republic of Hawaii. "There is no question," read the official US report on the epidemic, "that the *Belgic* brought cholera here through her Chinese steerage passengers. . . . The harbor became infected and formed a good culture medium for cholera germs, due to its sluggishness, alkalinity, and the organic matter contained therein. By eating raw crabs, which had been feeding on the infected material in the harbor, the first native woman became infected, and from a feast held in her house it spread to various parts of the city."

The fact that tons of raw sewage from the city of Honolulu emptied from the Nuuanu River into the open harbor, near the neighborhoods where the shanty Hawaiians had been ghettoized, was given less prominent play in the official document. The report did cite the "indefatigable efforts" of the US consul and local health officials in stamping out the epidemic before it could get abroad to other port cities in the Pacific—and this in spite of the stubbornness of the Native Hawaiians, who hindered the best medical efforts "by secreting the cases that were taken sick and not reporting the same," according to the report. "They were ill advised," it continued, "thinking that the foreigners were trying to kill them off."

As to where in the world the natives got *that* idea, the official US report offered no theory.

CAPTAIN ARUNDEL EXTENDED the *Warrimoo*'s stay off the coast of Oahu as long as he could; ticketed passengers in Honolulu, bound for Australia, had written the captain pleading with him to take them aboard in spite of the cholera scare, and he agreed to delay departure through the weekend in case the board of health lifted its quarantine. But he made it plain that the *Warrimoo* would pull anchor first thing Monday, at the stroke of midnight. The Sunday sunset, Sam Clemens knew in his heart, would be the last glimpse he would ever have of this paradise, and so he sat on deck that evening watching the far-off mountains produce the show's vivid prelude, noting the "dainty browns and greens, blues and purples and blacks, and the rounded velvety backs of certain of [the mountains] made one want to stroke them, as one would the sleek back of a cat." The scene softened into a diffuse haze of pink, followed by a final explosion—"the cloud-rack was flooded with fiery splendors, and these were copied on the surface of the sea, and it made one drunk with delight to look upon it"—just before the far mountains fell gently away into the darkness of the heavens. A few hours later, Clemens felt the rumble of the ship's engines firing up, and sometime after midnight the unlucky *Warrimoo* carried its passengers away from the bright lights of Honolulu.

Clemens kept a watch as the ship skirted Oahu in the darkness and headed for open seas. His Hawaii dream had come to an end. He didn't much feel restored.

CHAPTER THREE

With Friends Like These

John Hay sat in the dull stillness of the fussily upholstered, wood-paneled Pullman car of the Congressional Limited Express as it crossed the Potomac, ducked into the tunnel just south of the Marine Barracks, emerged again within sight of the Smithsonian Castle, and finally eased into the railroad yards at Sixth and B Northwest. He was home again, or as *home* as he would be anywhere.

The news of Hay's return to Washington in the last week of November 1895 rated a mere squib on page 5 of the *Evening Times*. "Mr. and Mrs. John Hay and family," read the notice in its entirety, "have returned to the city after an absence of several months and are established in their handsome home on Sixteenth street northwest." Hay would not argue the length or the placement of that notice. It was about what his arrival in the nation's capital warranted, as far as he could tell. His time of splendid public personage had surely passed. His life, he had recently confided to a friend, "drags on with a broken wing."

He had spent most of the autumn lamenting his indolence ("I have done nothing for McKinley or Heaven") or making quick trips from his New Hampshire estate into New York to tend to his corporate directorship or to his wife's prodigious shopping requirements. When cornered by a newspaperman at his Madison Square hotel that October, Hay had pled absolute ignorance of the day's political doings, explaining that what minimal concentration he could muster was wholly trained on his upcoming hunting trip to Sandusky. But then, once settled into his duck blind on the banks of Lake Erie, alongside the esteemed barons of industry who made up the exclusive membership of Winous Point Shooting Club, he wasn't sure what the hell he was doing there. "This last fortnight has been the longest of my life," he wrote to Henry Adams from Lake Erie.

The new session of Congress, at the very least, promised some excitement. Capitol Hill was already abuzz with war talk when Hay arrived in Washington. Senator Henry Cabot Lodge had pronounced himself "on pins and needles."

Senator Henry Cabot Lodge

"I am worried and angry beyond words at what I see," he wrote. "England is simply playing the Administration for what she can get."

Henry Cabot Lodge—his intimates called him Cabot—was a wonder to his friend John Hay. The first-term senator was a puckish, auburn-haired child of Boston privilege twelve years Hay's junior; the two men shared an appreciation of fine literature and an abiding concern for the welfare of the Republic. But Cabot, it had to be admitted by even his closest friends, had the temperament of a wet ferret. He was a darter, a worrier, a doer who would not be still. His electric, restless energy (along with impatience to *get something done*) stood out in the staid and musty halls of the United States Senate.

Hay had tried his best to put Cabot at ease over the years; he was always sensitive to the younger man's vanity. Like the rest of their insular social set, Hay was careful not to laugh too loudly—or to read too much into it—when Nannie Lodge called her husband by his pet name, Pinky. On the occasion of Cabot's fortieth birthday, Hay had presented him with a Rubens sketch he had bought at an estate sale at Christie's. "Mrs. Hay tells me you liked it when she showed it to you," he wrote in his accompanying note. "I congratulate you upon everything—your position, your talents, your time of life. You have a right to adopt the motto Charles V. assumed in his young manhood, '*Plus ultra*.'"

Cabot's friends found him much easier to stomach when he was away from his official duties—"I don't need to murder Cabot here half so often as I do at Washington," Henry Adams wrote of his friend while on a trip to Europe—but when he was at his politics, Henry Cabot Lodge's charms were greatly diminished. "Rather enjoys kicking his enemies," Hay would say of him. And when Congress convened in the first week of December 1895, Hay knew, Cabot would be ready to kick. After a full year's worth of nearly athletic agitating—in the well of the United States Senate, on the stump in Massachusetts, in the pages of the nation's leading periodicals, in the high government offices of Madrid, and even in the shadows of the British Parliament itself—Senator Henry Cabot Lodge set the table for some real drama. He had picked a fight (on behalf of the rest of his countrymen) with the richest and most powerful empire on the planet, and it looked as if he just might get it.

THE WHOLE THING had kind of snowballed on Cabot in the previous year. He had started his Senate career doing what any blooded Republican would do: flailing away at the Democratic president, Grover Cleveland. His shrill assaults on the Cleveland administration's modest proposals for a little more government purchase of silver or a little less tariff didn't get much traction. Cabot had, however, managed to get a bit of political purchase by attacking President Cleveland's foreign policy, which was, by Cabot's reckoning, "immoral" and "un-American," especially in regard to Hawaii. He had been apoplectic when the new Cleveland administration refused to press for annexation. And when it appeared the president was maneuvering to help put what Cabot called "the savage" queen back on her throne, the senator from Massachusetts began to spray invective—on the president, on the president's State Department, on the president's defenders in the Democratic Party, who, Cabot suggested, were too daft to understand the strategic and commercial necessity of taking control of those islands.

This far-flung venom eventually lighted on Her Majesty's government in Great Britain. In a speech on the Senate floor in January of 1895, Cabot accused the British of fomenting an uprising against President Dole and his new Republic of Hawaii; of arming Queen Liliuokalani's supporters with guns and ammunition shipped from Vancouver, *British* Columbia, and of promising them that if they could seize and hold the palace in Honolulu for just three hours, the British Empire would recognize them once again as the only legitimate government in the Hawaiian Islands. "It is perfectly clear that Great Britain is seeking, with wise aggressiveness which characterizes her foreign policy, to establish British commercial supremacy in those islands," Cabot charged. "I am the last to find fault with [Great Britain]. I believe she is wise in doing so. My criticism is that we do not exhibit the same spirit, the true spirit of our race, in protecting American interests and advancing them everywhere and at all times."

Cabot followed that speech with an article for the *Forum* titled "Our Blundering Foreign Policy," in which he accused President Cleveland of having "labored to overthrow American interests and American control of Hawaii." This was no time to bow down to the English, Senator Lodge maintained. It was, rather, time for the great people of the United States to push its Manifest Destiny out onto the open seas. By the time the article was done, the senator had sketched an ambitious campaign of conquest: he had called for an American-built and -controlled commercial shortcut through Nicaragua to unite the Atlantic and the Pacific and to provide the surest pathway to the commercial honeypots of Asia; for US dominion over Hawaii and Samoa in the Pacific, and over Cuba and Puerto Rico in the Caribbean; and for US sovereignty over pretty much every bit of land, every mineral of value, and every earthly inhabitant from the Rio Grande to the Arctic Ocean. "The great nations are rapidly absorbing for their future expansion and their present defense all the waste places of the earth," Cabot concluded. "It is a movement which makes for civilization and the advancement of the race. As one of the great nations of the world, the United States must not fall out of the line of march."

On March 2, 1895, at two o'clock in the morning, as the clock was running out on the fifty-third Congress, Cabot had taken the Senate floor to make the point that Cleveland and the rest of the Democrats would be derelict if they did not make haste to equip the United States with a proper fleet of steel-hulled battleships, torpedo boats, and necessary naval outposts in the Pacific. The senator had even prepared a visual aid for his speech: a map of the world and its oceans, with bloodred Maltese crosses to mark the British naval stations. "Now, every one can see here at the Falkland Islands is a British naval station," he said, pointing to his map. "Here is another at Vancouver. Here is another at the Fiji Islands. In that great triangle marked by these three points Great Britain does not hold a naval station. There in the center of that triangle, in the heart of the Pacific, where I am now pointing, lie the Sandwich Islands. They are the key to the Pacific. If we are ever to build the Nicaraguan Canal, it would be folly to enter upon it if we were not prepared to take possession of those islands."

By the time a fellow senator got around to asking how exactly US warships would check British aggression in Hawaii, Cabot had got himself worked into a frenzy. "All the great routes from San Francisco and from Vancouver, all the great routes to the East, to and from the Nicaraguan Canal, pass those Islands," he asserted. "In the hands of this country they would rapidly increase in population, and they would be a source of wealth and strength. . . . As I have said once before, in speaking on this subject, we hold the citadel of our greatness here on this continent within the borders of the United States, but we should not neglect the necessary outworks."

And here he went back to his map, tracing the short distance from the British naval station in Bermuda to the East Coast cities of Charleston, Washington, New York, Boston.

> I have no idea that England desires to go to war with this country. I do not think she does; but we may as well look facts in the face. This country is the rival and competitor of England for the trade and commerce of the world. . . . [England] has always opposed, thwarted, and sought to injure us. She desires to keep her control of the great pathways of commerce. She desires to put us in a position where we cannot fight, if we wish, except at a great disadvantage. I have said that I do not fear a war. I do not think we have any reason to. England is quite as well aware as we are that, though she might bombard a few of our coast cities, her great territory of Canada in the event of a war would pass from her never to return.

"When I sat down," Cabot later boasted to his mother, "everybody crowded around to shake my hand, something quite common in the House but which hardly ever happens in the Senate."

"A notable little speech," the newspapers called it, which was somewhat deflating. The map and the Maltese crosses were nice and all, but the whole enterprise seemed a tad fanciful. Was Senator Lodge calling for an invasion of *Canada*?

The president certainly hadn't paid Cabot much mind. Grover Cleveland would not be spurred into action on Hawaii, or Samoa, or Cuba, or a Nicaraguan canal, or extra battleships, or anything else Senator Lodge screamed for. The president had little interest in inviting a row with the British, and none in provoking one. So Cabot continued on like a frustrated picador wielding one dull blade after another, looking for one that might pierce the president's thick hide and induce him to make some sort of menacing feint in England's direction.

Cabot kept thrusting at Cleveland, and with a new weapon, even after the Congress slid into a long recess. In the June 1895 issue of the *North American Review*, Senator Lodge drew up a new bill of particulars against the British—cribbed in the main from a pamphlet by a former American diplomat hired by the government of Venezuela to solicit support in the United States in their recent dispute with Great Britain. Cabot's article was succinctly titled "England, Venezuela, and the Monroe Doctrine." The British government's recent activities in the Venezuelan goldfields, Cabot insisted, had besmirched the dignity and honor of the United States of America, by wantonly violating the seventy-three-year-old Monroe Doctrine, which, in Cabot's expansive interpretation, had "announced it to be the settled policy of the United States to regard any attempt on the part of any European power to conquer an American state, to seize territory other than that which they then held, or to make any new establishment in either North or South America, as an act of hostility toward the United States, and one not to be permitted."

Her Majesty's government had been surreptitiously extending the borders of British Guiana into sovereign Venezuelan territory for fifty years, Cabot wrote, and doing so in spite of Venezuela's official protests. One British prime minister after another had refused pleas to submit the boundary dispute to international arbitration. "All that England has done has been a direct violation of the Monroe doctrine, and she has increased and quickened her aggressions in proportion as the United States have appeared indifferent. The time has come for decisive action."

Cabot's own decisive action had been to take an extended pleasure jaunt to Europe that summer, beginning in London, where, according to Associated Press reports, he and Mrs. Lodge lived "in comfortable style here just off Piccadilly, and within easy reach of some of the great clubs." For a full month, the senator was fed and feted and entertained by the leading lights of Lord Salisbury's new government.

John Hay had followed the progress of Senator and Mrs. Lodge with the help of detailed letters from their traveling companion that summer and fall, Henry Adams. Cabot "has been prancing about with Dukes and Premiers all over the place," a bemused and slightly bewildered Henry Adams reported. "He that kicks the Britisher gets his reward. Cabot is treated with the utmost civility."

According to Cabot's own letters home to his closest friend and political confidant, Theodore Roosevelt, the senator found the company in and around Whitehall lively and pleasant and altogether agreeable. So uncharacteristically relaxed was Cabot that even when the empire's new colonial secretary, Joseph Chamberlain, all but patted the senator on his red head and told him how fortunate he was to be a statesman in a country "untroubled by a foreign policy," Lodge kept his cool and suggested politely that within the Americas, the United States had "a very definite one."

Cabot did express some frustration to Theodore that the New York–based correspondent of the *Times* of London was not conveying to his British readers the actual gravity of the Venezuela situation. "He keeps saying that there is no general interest in the Monroe doctrine, that only a few jingos talk about Venezuela, that there is no real objection among our people to England's going there," he wrote to New York City police commissioner Roosevelt. Then he suggested that Theodore apprehend the reporter and set him straight. "He ought to discourage British aggressiveness which our people dislike." But aside from the time spent reading the *Times*'s misbegotten dispatches, Cabot told Theodore, his London sojourn "has been a delightful month and well worth while."

THE SUMMER PROVED anything but delightful for the American ambassador in England, Thomas Francis Bayard, thanks at least in some small measure to Senator Lodge. In the first week of August, just as Cabot was preparing to leave London and skip over to the Continent, a diplomatic pouch landed on Ambassador Bayard's desk with a thud; it contained—to his surprise and regret—a forty-page, ten-thousand-word indictment of Britain's ongoing bad faith in Venezuela, signed by United States secretary of state Richard Olney but authored in the main by John Hay's old friend and colleague Assistant Secretary of State Alvey Adee. The document was shot through with the punctiliousness, the thoroughness, the combativeness, and the attention to fine detail for which Adee was known. The assistant secretary had also shipped to Bayard by separate mail an extra citation for the most remarkable charge in the original dispatch: that in two years alone, England had added thirty-three thousand square miles to the size of its colony of British Guiana by unilaterally redrawing the boundary line deeper into Venezuela, thus gaining a sizable portion of the goldfields and control of the mouth of the Orinoco River, the Mississippi of South America, pathway to all the gold and all the commercial markets of the interior.

President Cleveland, it seemed, had grown weary of turning the other cheek or of being poked and prodded by the likes of Senator Lodge. And through his new secretary of state, the president had handed Bayard the unenviable job of delivering the message, in accordance with proper diplomatic etiquette, in person, to the British prime minister. "You are instructed, therefore, to present the foregoing views to Lord Salisbury by reading to him this communication (leaving with him a copy should he so desire), and to reinforce them by such pertinent considerations as will doubtless occur to you." As Bayard looked over the "foregoing views" contained in the message, he grew less and less keen to make the trip to the prime minister's office: "Venezuela for a quarter of a century has asked and striven for arbitration," the dispatch read.

> Great Britain, however, has always and continuously refused to arbitrate, except upon the condition of renunciation of a large part of the Venezuela claim and of a concession to herself of a large share of the territory in controversy . . . by offering to act as arbitrator, by expressing its grave concern whenever new alleged instances of British aggression upon Venezuelan

> territory have been brought to its notice, the Government of the United States has made it clear to Great Britain and to the world that the controversy is one in which both its honor and its interests are involved and the continuance of which it can not regard with indifference.

The paper then ran through the history and meaning of the keep-your-European-paws-off-America-where-you're-not-grandfathered-in Monroe Doctrine, which Adee pointed out "was unquestionably due to the inspiration of Great Britain, who at once gave to it an open and unqualified adhesion which has never been withdrawn." It called any political union between a European and an American state unnatural; belittled the spectacularly idiotic arms race England was running against other European powers; and made a slightly beside-the-point point that England's imperial monarchy—constitutional though it might be—was by comparison a form of government inferior to the American republic. It also called out England for its peremptory treatment of Venezuela: "Upon what principle—except her feebleness as a nation—is she to be denied the right of having the claim heard and passed upon by an impartial tribunal?" Adee's treatise laid on extravagant claims that might have made even Cabot blush.

> To-day the United States is practically sovereign on this continent, and its fiat is law upon the subjects to which it confines its interposition. Why? It is not because of the pure friendship or good will felt for it. It is not simply by reason of its high character as a civilized state, nor because wisdom and justice and equity are the invariable characteristics of the dealings of the United States. It is because, in addition to all other grounds, its infinite resources combined with its isolated position render it master of the situation and practically invulnerable as against all other powers.

For now, wrote Olney and Adee, the United States would content itself with its own investigation into the boundary question to see what action against England, if any, the Cleveland administration would be justified in taking. The message Bayard delivered to Lord Salisbury concluded with the president's suggestion (or was it a demand?) that any future unpleasantness would be avoided if England agreed to submit its case to an impartial arbitration of *all* the territory in dispute. Grover Cleveland needed an answer by December 2, 1895, when the new US Congress was scheduled to convene.

The prime minister had plenty of more pressing problems in his vast empire and would only promise Bayard that the American demand would be given careful consideration by the law offices of the Crown. So while the British government dawdled, the American ambassador fielded a series of increasingly nervous dispatches from his boss, the anxious secretary of state—he wanted an answer!—and a series of increasingly insistent press inquiries. News of the secret dispatch got around, and Bayard was forced to squelch sensational and false reports in the anti-Anglo US press that Lord Salisbury had gravely insulted the United States by rudely interrupting Bayard's initial presentation midstream and waving him away.

The difficulties surrounding the Olney-Adee missive forced Bayard to decline a bevy of grouse-shooting invitations from the British gentry, and he held out but faint hope that he would get to the Highlands for the opening of partridge season. Cabot, meanwhile, with his work in London now being done for him, pranced about the Continent. He spent time in Paris, took in the Gothic architectural wonders of Normandy, and then headed south for a quick trip through Spain, which he regarded as much more than mere sightseeing.

To get possession of Cuba and Puerto Rico, which Cabot dearly wanted, the United States would have to wrangle with the Spanish, and the senator wanted to take their measure. He judged (with some real glee) the Spanish prime minister, Antonio Cánovas del Castillo, quite nervous at the prospect of American intervention in Cuba; the rest of Spain he found wanting. "You never saw such desolate dreary plains and here and there a dying town," he reported to the Roosevelts. "The people . . . seem sullen and indifferent. . . . They are beaten, broken and out of the race and are proud and know it. They depress and repel me like their landscape." All in all, Senator Lodge's trip to Spain had confirmed what he had also felt in England: "Oh, how I am glad to be an American! How much better—and then we are so much more interesting and amusing as people."

By the time the Lodges had doubled back to Paris, news of the Venezuela ultimatum had reached the Continent. Lord Salisbury remained intent on ignoring it, and Chamberlain had upped the ante by demanding of the Venezuelan government a cash indemnity for recent crimes against British subjects in the disputed territory. Henry Adams was clucking in private that Secretary of State Olney had stolen Cabot's thunder, when the Massachusetts senator let loose another roar in the form of a letter cabled across the English Channel, warning that if Lord Salisbury didn't relent on arbitration, the likely result would be war.

Cabot even got a little unexpected backup when Senator William Chandler of New Hampshire announced—with what appeared to be some delight—the certainty of a war with England. On his way home in the middle of November, Cabot stopped off in London long enough to give an interview to the *Daily Chronicle* so that he might educate the Brits on both the meaning of the Monroe Doctrine and the American people's determination to uphold it at all costs.

LEAVING ASIDE THE Monroe Doctrine, Americans and Englishmen were anything but indifferent to one another by the tail end of 1895; in fact, by the time the new Congress convened in the first week of December, Uncle Sam and John Bull appeared to be spoiling for a fight. Of course, as John Hay knew well, politics alone was not sufficient to inspire the level of bitter acrimony echoing back and forth between what he had thought of as "kindred nations." Neither of the two publics was quite clear on the actual import of boundary lines in some South American country, or about just how urgently exercised they should get over a statement of international principle laid down by a US president who had been in his grave more than sixty years. What had got the average run of citizenry riled up had less to do with mapmaking and international law than with two more compelling fields of battle: sport and romance.

The worst of the recent hard feelings between the United States and Great Britain had started with a yacht race, after the Earl of Dunraven, a leading member of the Royal Yacht Squadron, had manned up to challenge the New York Yacht Club for the America's Cup. After sailing his *Valkyrie III* across the Atlantic at the end of August 1895, Lord Dunraven was met with the near-universal applause and good wishes that generally attend a sportsman who has the courage to test his mettle against foreigners in foreign waters. American yachtsmen observing the boat as it was being prepped for the races in dry dock were unembarrassed to voice admiration for the *Valkyrie*'s sleek lines and formidable spars. "She is a smoother and fairer boat than I had any idea of," said one. The consensus was that the yacht co-owned by William K. Vanderbilt was in for a real contest: "People are saying," reported the *New York Tribune*, "'There is a boat that is likely to carry the cup back if the *Defender* is not trained to the hour, as it were, when she meets her.'"

Theodore Roosevelt couldn't resist this sort of mano a mano, and on September 7 he took a break from saloon busting, commandeered an official New York City police patrol boat, and took his wife and a few friends to watch the first of the three yacht races in New York Bay. Commissioner Teddy had been nervous and uncharacteristically unsure of the American chances until the contest got under way. "In a very low wind and in smooth waters the two boats were nearly equal," he wrote after the first race, "but when there was a sea on the *Defender* was the better boat; and as soon as the wind rose her superiority became very marked."

The *Defender* won that first race going away, and Lord Dunraven wasted no time in suggesting to the host New York Yacht Club's America's Cup committee (in private, of course) that the captain and crew of the *Defender*—which appeared, to Dunraven's eye anyway, four inches deeper in the water on the day of the race than it had been when measured the day before—had probably cheated by adding ballast in the overnight hours before the first race. The committee wisely kept Dunraven's impolitic charge under wraps; they were not going to let the visiting earl embarrass himself in such a frightfully unsportsmanlike fashion.

Dunraven's dander was apparently still well up three days later when the tugs hauled the two racing boats out into the bay for their second run. As the boats approached the start line that morning, Dunraven's yacht swung so near the *Defender* that the *Valkyrie*'s mainsail boom crashed into and splintered the American boat's topmast. Emergency repairs on the *Defender* were hasty and ineffectual. The crippled vessel was forced to sail the entire race without use of its headsail, and still she came within forty-seven seconds of overtaking the *Valkyrie*. Dunraven was shaken by the *Defender*'s game performance and loathe to offer even an oblique apology about the injury to Mr. Vanderbilt's boat. He *was*, however, quick to offer public alibis on two separate counts: claimed he had been forced in on the *Defender* at the start line by all the excursion steamers and tugboats and police patrol boats that crowded the waters for a close view of the race; and besides, he assured a sympathetic correspondent, he would have won by five or six minutes had the excursion boats not interfered. "To-day on the reach home eight or nine steamboats were to the windward of me," he wrote to the Cup committee in a new complaint, "and, what was worse, a block of steamboats were steaming level with me and close under my lee. I sailed nearly the whole distance in tumbling, broken water, in the heavy swash of these steamboats."

While race officials mulled the question of whether to disqualify the *Valkyrie* for the foul against the *Defender* and award the second race to the Americans, Dunraven began to hint at abandoning the waters altogether. To continue to race among all these excursion boats, he suggested to race officials rather too theatrically, would be to risk the lives of his men and his ship. But again, none of this went public, and on the day of the third and deciding race, the weather advantage was to Dunraven: the breeze was gentle, the water glassy and rolling. Word was out, well before ten o'clock that morning, that the *Valkyrie* and the *Defender* had both left anchorage and were making their way to the start point. New York Bay was thronged with fifty thousand excited onlookers, but the scratch line was kept clear for half a mile in all directions. At just after ten o'clock, the two boats could be seen near the start line. The *Defender* made ready for the deciding race, while *Valkyrie* sat in motionless calm.

More than an hour elapsed after the first sighting and still there was no real activity on Dunraven's boat. Even after the course signals were set and the preparatory gun was fired, *Valkyrie*'s crew made no visible preparations. Finally, at 11:20, the starting gun fired, and twenty seconds later the *Defender* crossed the start line and made for open water. Nearly two minutes later, the *Valkyrie* crossed, too, making it an official race, but as one newspaperman wrote, "As soon as she crossed she luffed right around the old red Lightship, describing a semicircle, and pointed her bow toward Sandy Hook. Lord Dunraven's private signal was hauled down from the main truck and the New-York Yacht Club was hoisted."

The Earl of Dunraven, it was now obvious to everyone in attendance, was refusing to compete. There would be no deciding race. The *Defender* would win in a walkover. Reaction to Dunraven's retirement was fast and furious. Tugs and steamers let loose with whistles of derision; some boats pulled near enough to the *Valkyrie* that her crewmen could hear the taunts and jeers from normally genteel excursionists. When a boatload of reporters approached the British sloop, they were told to shove. Dunraven hadn't been impeded, they wanted to know, had he? "Oh, yes, it was clear enough at the start," said a crewmember speaking for His Lordship, "but how about the finish? You must look further than your nose, you know."

Dunraven threw more fat on the fire by refusing to concede anything but the ineptitude of the Cup committee. "The two yachts have not been fairly tried," he insisted. Dunraven had had defenders among the Americans after the second race, but not after his infuriating retirement. "He saw he was beaten," Theodore Roosevelt wrote to friends. "He sulked, and showed the white feather." Another disappointed race watcher made a more sweeping indictment: "The action of the *Valkyrie* gave expression to a deliberate and gratuitous insult to the American people."

The British press, unsurprisingly, rushed patriotically to Dunraven's defense, deeming as "amply justified" his withdrawal from the America's Cup, which one paper called a "rather ghastly farce." A few of Queen Victoria's Canadian subjects piled on, too, asserting that among their neighbours to the south "the spirit of honorable sport is wholly absent . . . if [the *Defender* syndicate] claim yesterday's race and the American public do not sharply repudiate the whole business, the friendship between the two countries will be severely strained, and the cause of an Anglo-American alliance for the preservation of peace will be set back a hundred years."

The Earl of Dunraven started home for England the day after his forfeit, but London correspondents for Anglophobe papers like the *New York World* kept stirring the pot. "The vast majority of opinions at clubs and places of public resort [in England] are brutally denunciatory of our committee, of the *Defender* syndicate, and the American public," the *World* correspondent wrote, citing an American who had been in residence in London for thirty-five years, who was certain that fear and envy of America's growing commercial and industrial power—

the United States had overtaken the empire in annual steel production—was the actual root of Anglo anger. "So bitter and unreasoning is the almost universal sentiment, that the present good feeling of England toward America would seem to be only on the surface and that underlying it there is real hatred of us."

Ill will between the two countries was still running high when, on September 20, just a week after Dunraven skipped town, potential good tidings about Anglo-American relations hit the New York papers. Alva Vanderbilt (lately divorced from the *Defender*'s co-owner William K.) announced the engagement of their daughter, Consuelo, to Charles Richard John Spencer-Churchill, the 9th Duke of Marlborough. This was, for Mrs. Vanderbilt, a triumph. She had coveted a title for her daughter, and now the eighteen-year-old Consuelo was to be welcomed into British society as a full-on duchess. Lord Dunraven's indelicate behavior faded to the inside pages as newspapers filled their columns with details of Consuelo's exquisite wedding trousseau and of the engagement ring the duke presented to her, containing a ruby once owned by an Indian maharaja. But it didn't take long for the financial angle of the engagement story to take hold, partly because within weeks of the engagement announcement, the duke's legal counsel, R. Harding Milward, arrived in New York to negotiate the marriage treaty. Miss Vanderbilt's twelve-year-old brother more or less summed up public opinion on the matter when he chided his sister, "He's only marrying you for your money."

American reporters began to uncover the sad state of the duke's family finances, and a whiff of the mercenary attached itself to Marlborough's motives. Merging with the Vanderbilt fortune, it was clear, would give the duke his best chance to fulfill his single purpose in life: to rescue his family's vast and collapsing estate. The Spencer-Churchill family was like most of the land-rich, cash-poor British aristocracy. It had been about four steps back in the ducal lineage since the Marlboroughs had been able to afford the upkeep on the seat of their estate, Blenheim Palace. They had been living off principle for a few generations too many. The family had already sold off its library as well as its collections of old European masters and Chinese porcelain; they had even accepted within their ancient palace the footfalls of any tourist willing to part with a shilling. The 9th duke's father had formed a second marriage with a plain-looking, mustachioed American widow whose dead husband's middling fortune bought the palace the sort of modern conveniences (like electric lighting) that were already common in the nicer neighborhoods of most American cities.

Speculation as to the amount of the Vanderbilt fortune to be traded for the title traveled far and wide in the days after the engagement announcement and even caught up with Sam Clemens, then traveling to his next speaking date on a dusty train in Australia. Expecting to get a comedic rise out of "Mark Twain," a newspaperman from Melbourne handed him a report that put the price of Miss Vanderbilt's title at $10 million. "It seems that American heiresses are showing a disposition to go after young English aristocrats," the reporter goaded.

Clemens was uncharacteristically terse: "No," he answered. "It is the English aristocrats who run after American heiresses."

"Ah, that is your American way of putting it."

"Well, and the other is your English way of putting it."

Reliable reports of the dollar amount quickly receded back to $5 million, which seemed a bit more appropriate—it was not as if the Vanderbilts were trying to make their daughter a princess. But the new figure did not reduce American skepticism regarding the young Briton. He put one in mind of the empire's Colonial Office—always sniffing around somebody else's precious metals. What was more pathetic, the duke simply didn't have personal charm enough to endear himself to his prospective bride's countrymen. The American grandees in Newport were taken aback that the young man was such a poor model of British manhood. "A pale-faced, frail-looking lad," was how the *Newport Mercury* described him on first sight, "with a voice of that affected drawl peculiar to the English, and as soft as a debutante."

For the next six excruciating weeks, American newspapers followed the duke's less-than-epic career through his fiancée's homeland with a delight bordering on sinister. On a trip to Kentucky to inspect thoroughbred racehorses, it was reported, the diminutive duke was thrown out of a theater for harassing an uninterested chorus girl named Sophie Erbs. "The little lady," a local reporter noted, "sent word that she did not care to sup with his 'dukelets,' that 'a good American mister was good enough for her.'"

Marlborough then ditched a private meeting with President Cleveland arranged by the British ambassador, skipped his own wedding rehearsal (all that's good enough for the women, he reportedly said), and was entirely unable to think of anything nice to say about his host country at a dinner in his honor. "He said that, having been so short a time in the country, it would be fair neither to himself nor to the United States to express an opinion," reported the *New York Sun*. What good Marlborough's best man had done at that dinner by reciting the many qualities he *believed* the duke had come to appreciate about America was undone by Milward, his legal counsel, who told the gathering that "by [the duke's] allying himself with one of your great families that family and Americans have received honor."

Hard as it was for Americans to grasp, the duke was not going out of his way to insult them; it came quite naturally to him. When a friendly reporter sent to write a damage-control story told Marlborough that famous American men were usually happy to be interviewed, the duke scrunched his pale little face. "No, really?" he said. "They can't be such flats."

Then came the Custom House debacle. Wedding gifts from England had piled high in the bonded warehouse in New York in the weeks before the ceremony, and when the duke and his entourage went to retrieve them, it was determined that these luxury items were dutiable to the tune of thousands of dollars. The duke found the bill rather in bad taste and asked that the gifts instead be shipped back to his palace in Oxfordshire, where they could be unwrapped free of charge.

In the aftermath of this story, Miss Vanderbilt received a host of marriage proposals from strapping young Americans who wished to save her from the cruel fate that awaited her at Blenheim. A few threatened violence against the duke; others threatened the elder Vanderbilts themselves for allowing the flower of American womanhood—and her personal millions—to be shanghaied to a foreign country.

Alva Vanderbilt parried by dispatching press agents to fill the journalistic maw with details of the upcoming wedding, including the guest list and seating chart for the reception to follow at Mrs. Vanderbilt's Fifth Avenue mansion. Alva's clever factotums even managed to make a mathematical case for romance, planting the story that the duke had chosen Consuelo over the heiress to an English ale-brewing fortune who was in sole possession of $20 million. "That the Duke should prefer to wed with $15,000,000 less in sight is said to be evidence that his alliance with Miss Vanderbilt is a true love-match," one American newspaper syndicate reported.

The coverage of the splendid public spectacle of the wedding itself, held on November 6, showed the duke and his countrymen in a softer and more appealing light. At the breakfast reception afterward, it was reported, the duke presented his bride with a girdle of gold set with diamonds—or at least told her about this girdle, which awaited her at Blenheim. British ambassador Julian Pauncefote read cablegrams of congratulations from the Prince of Wales and Queen Victoria herself. "As a social happening," gushed the *New York Tribune*, "it was of unsurpassed splendor and magnificence." There was also some satisfaction in Democratic circles when it got around that the Vanderbilts had settled on the duke the income *only* from $2.5 million worth of shares in Beech Creek Railroad, payable at 4 percent per annum. The new duchess judiciously withheld from the public the details of the after-ceremony carriage ride from St. Thomas Church to the reception at her mother's new mansion. Her new husband wished Consuelo to know that he had given up the woman he had truly loved and married Miss Vanderbilt out of "a sense of duty to his family and to his traditions." He also informed her that it would be a cold day in hell before he returned to America, for he truly hated "anything that was not British."

Three days after the wedding, for no reason anybody on either side of the Atlantic could discern, Lord Dunraven—recently elected to the vice presidency of the Royal Yacht Squadron in England—emerged from two months of relative silence by revealing to the public for the first time his real reason for abandoning the Cup challenge: the American team had cheated in the most dastardly fashion by secretly adding ballast before the first race. The managing director of the *Defender* shot back that Dunraven was a "liar and a blackguard." The New York Yacht Club promised a "most searching and complete investigation" and requested Dunraven's presence in New York to provide any actual evidence he might have to support his scandalous accusation. The club convened a jury that included America's only internationally celebrated naval officer, Captain Alfred Thayer Mahan.

Dunraven announced he would be sailing for New York at "the earliest possible moment," and other members of the Royal Yacht Squadron cringed at what the hothead might set off.

SO THAT'S WHERE relations stood between the two countries when the Hays and the Cabot Lodges and Henry Adams and all of America's elected representatives descended once again on Washington for the opening session of the Fifty-Fourth Congress in December of 1895. Hay had not got the game of politics entirely out of his blood, but he considered himself nothing more than an interested observer. The national questions of the moment, like war and peace, he had long ago left to younger men. The best he could do was commiserate with his friend the British ambassador Julian Pauncefote, who was getting beat about the head by the American press for suggesting that Great Britain was as likely to arbitrate possession of territory she had claimed in Venezuela as she was to arbitrate possession of Essex and Sussex Counties on English soil itself. Poor Pauncefote was also much worn down by a month of largely unsuccessful attempts to smooth the Duke of Marlborough's path through Washington and New York.

Hay spent most of the hours of falling light in those December days with Adams, who remained as he had been since his wife's suicide ten years earlier—affectless and uninterested. "So we are going to war. It sounds droll, to you and me," Adams wrote to one English friend. "Luckily war makes no difference in social relations, except to lend them a shade of deeper interest. It only breaks postal conveniences. You'll not hear from me so regularly, but you will read my fewer letters with a good deal more interest."

Adams's lack of concern was at least sincere, as far as Hay could tell, while Cabot and Theodore Roosevelt betrayed more than a hint of playacting in their loud insistence on defending the Monroe Doctrine as if something akin to the virtue of American womanhood was at stake. The martial step they showed was too obviously studied, the passion behind it too plastic, Hay believed, for their war hawking to get any real public support.

Things might have been smoother, Hay noted, had the British prime minister shown the minimum courtesy of providing his reply to Olney and Adee's Venezuela paper, as Grover Cleveland had requested, in time for the president to relay this answer in his annual message at the beginning of this new Congress. Lord Salisbury, however, was tardy by a week, which most American lawmakers regarded as an intentional and insulting slap. Congressional anger and impatience was marginally tempered by Cleveland's decision to order the USS *Texas* out from its berth on Staten Island for a little shakedown run, to blow out the cobwebs, just in case. But members of the House and the Senate were beside themselves to learn that Cleveland had refused to sit at his desk awaiting the steamship that carried Salisbury's reply and had actually *left town*. So on the fourth day of the new Congress, when Ambassador Pauncefote finally trotted up the steps of the State, War, and Navy Building with the blue envelope containing Salisbury's answer, Grover Cleveland was on a duck-hunting trip off the coast of North Carolina. The president meant to project a magisterial calm and had announced no set time for his return, so the substance of Salisbury's message would remain under wraps indefinitely.

The Republicans in both houses of Congress were howling for action by the time Cleveland arrived in Washington a week later. And neither was the president well pleased with what he found awaiting him. Ambassador Pauncefote had delivered two separate communications to the State Department: one was a disquisition from Lord Salisbury on the ways in which the Monroe Doctrine did *not* pertain to the question of boundaries in Venezuela, and the other a point-by-point correction of the American understanding of the boundary dispute itself.

What really galled Cleveland was exhibit A. Like the Duke of Marlborough, Lord Salisbury had not gone out of his way to insult the Americans; it came to him quite naturally. The British prime minister's first salvo not only asserted that the American secretary of state had mischaracterized the import and meaning of the Monroe Doctrine, but also suggested that these 1823 "political maxims" had been written largely at the insistence of Great Britain in an effort to check the Catholic monarchies of Europe, that in Olney's hands the doctrine had been expanded beyond parameters of credulity, and that "the dangers against which President Monroe thought it right to guard were not as imaginary as they would seem at present day." *Imaginary*? Cleveland was "mad clean through." He and Olney spent a long weekend writing a terse report and announced to Congress that the president would like to append to his annual message of two weeks earlier a special message about Venezuela. He would be sending it over to Capitol Hill on Tuesday.

Anxious spectators swarmed the galleries of the House and the Senate on Tuesday, December 17, to hear their president's answer read aloud. Cleveland made one simple request of Congress: the funding of an American commission to determine the Venezuela boundary so that the United States could be certain of its case. But he was also making crystal clear, to Americans and Britons alike, that the United States of America was prepared to go to war if the investigators concluded that Her Majesty's government was flouting the Monroe Doctrine. The doctrine, according to Cleveland, "was intended to apply to every stage of our national life and can not become obsolete while our Republic endures."

At the moment the clerk finished reading the presidential declaration that "nothing remains but to accept the situation, to recognize its plain requirements, and deal with it accordingly," three hundred members of the House broke into applause. The audience in the gallery joined in. Even in the Senate, a traditionally dignified chamber of old men with ear trumpets, the president's message was roundly and loudly applauded. Lord Salisbury could not possibly misapprehend Cleveland's warning, the outgoing chairman of the Senate Foreign Relations Committee whispered to nearby colleagues. His fellow Alabaman was more direct: "There will be war unless England backs down."

The next-day lead in the *San Francisco Call* treated the presidential message as an announcement of a new power entering onto the world's stage—an announcement that had necessarily created a "profound sensation" in capitals around the globe. Cleveland's message, according to the *Call*, was "the most startling and important occurrence in American history since the close of the War of the Rebellion."

The much-stimulated House passed the president's requested appropriation for the Venezuela boundary study inside twenty-four hours. A congressman who suggested on the floor that legislation of this significance might be handled in a more decorous and deliberate manner was shouted down by cries of "Ready! Ready!" In the Senate, Cabot implored men on both sides of the aisle to stand with the president, while patting himself on the back. "As a matter of course I heartily approve of [the message's] spirit, its conclusions and the general position taken, for I took the same grounds myself last June . . . before public attention had been drawn to the matter at all." Commissioner Roosevelt concurred! "This is a most remarkable vindication of your attitude last Spring," he wrote to Cabot. "I do hope there will not be any back down among our people. Let the fight come if it must; I don't care whether our sea coast cities are bombarded or not; we would take Canada."

INITIAL REACTION IN Britain did not suggest a similar level of arousal. The members of the London Stock Exchange cabled a humorous message to the New York Chamber of Commerce expressing their desire that, in the case of actual armed conflict, the Americans keep their excursion steamers from interfering with the progress of British warships. (The chamber cabled back, wondering whether the British warships would be more capable than their yachts.) The rest of the public and the press and the parliamentarians in England exercised the kind of patronizing restraint for which the British were known; nastiness only seeped out at the edges. "Can those be serious words addressed to us by the descendants of the little ship load of English folks who sailed in the Mayflower?" asked the *Daily Chronicle*. The Americans had "always shown themselves a sentimental, excitable nation," the *Times* of London reminded their readers. "They have the haziest idea of what the Monroe doctrine really is, but nevertheless they are quite willing to enter upon a holy war to defend it. We must reckon on this feeling and be prepared for the wildest aberrations it may cause. . . . Indeed, it rather increases our sense of the peril to which immense international interests are subjected by combined sentiment and ignorance."

Discussions around the empire's Colonial Office were not so mirthful. Colonial Secretary Joseph Chamberlain privately called Cleveland's December 17 message "the greatest crime of the century"; called Cleveland himself a "coarse-grained man, with, I think, a good deal of the bully in his composition"; belittled the American Senate as a dingy collection of country lawyers and self-dealing ward heelers elevated above their abilities, and let it be known among his staff that the British Empire "can no more arbitrate about this than we can about the Isle of Wight."

Salisbury's government made available to its public all the correspondence concerning Venezuela, and the more closely the British press read it, the more exercised the newspapers became: "The concessions that this country is imperiously summoned to make are such as no self-respecting nation, and, least of all one ruling an empire that has roots in every quarter of the globe, could possibly submit to. . . . If it comes to [war]—well, we won't imitate Cleveland's bluster; but Englishmen would not expect to get whipped."

American papers reprinted all these pronouncements and more—and, John

Hay noted, with increasing truculence. This Venezuela business was no longer looking like one of Cabot's painted hobbyhorses. The national temper was something Hay had not seen for years: Americans were atremble at the prospect of a call to arms. "On the streets the message was discussed and old veterans of the late war talked exultantly of what they were prepared again to undertake at the call of their country," reported a wire service correspondent in Washington. "In the great hall of the pension building the employees gathered and sang with great gusto the 'Star Spangled Banner' and 'My Country, 'Tis of Thee.' " American citizens who stood athwart this accelerating martial juggernaut did so at their peril. Speakers at a peace meeting at New York's Cooper Union were shouted down. *Three cheers for Cleveland! Hurrah for patriotism! Rats! War on England! War on Spain!*

Serious and generally sober legislators introduced bills to fund the construction of six new steel-armored battleships and twenty-five torpedo boats and to repeal the lifetime ban on Confederate veterans holding commissions in the United States military; US Army enlistment quickly hit the statutory ceiling of twenty-five thousand; news leaked out that the Navy Department had laid on an extra shift to keep its munitions factory humming through the night, and the powder works in California was also operating around the clock to fulfill the biggest contract in its history.

Newspapermen trotted out old battle dogs for fresh barking. "War is a very serious matter and a very great calamity, but cowardice and dishonor in a great nation is far worse," Rear Admiral George E. Belknap explained to an inquiring reporter from the safety of his study on Beacon Street in Boston. "Great Britain must be made to understand that she must respect the rights, the dignity, and the power of this people and government." Retired major general Lew Wallace, who, as the author of *Ben-Hur*, was clearly fond of epic struggle, said, "It would go hard with us at first, but we would not be idle. . . . At the end, as I see it, we would own everything on this side of the globe from the Gulf of Mexico to the North Pole."

William K. Vanderbilt, co-owner of the *Defender* and father to poor Consuelo—a man who had held his powder through the America's Cup and the public negotiation of the marriage treaty with the Duke of Marlborough—finally let loose. He was traveling in Belgium in the final days of 1895 and gave an interview to *Le Soir* that was reprinted in London and New York. He let it be known that Americans did not intend to yield an inch more to the British Empire in Venezuela or anywhere else. He had just received a private telegram, he said, that suggested that all the Central and South American republics were about to make an alliance to stand by the United States in a war against England.

And he warned the British antagonists that they might take special heed of the self-steering torpedoes Thomas Edison had invented. "Referring to England's navy," *Le Soir* reported, "Mr. Vanderbilt exposed the palm of his hand and said: 'In a month from the declaration of war the entire ocean will be as clean as this of British ships.'"

CHAPTER FOUR

Right and Kind towards the Others

Just Sam Clemens's luck, of course, that his countrymen would choose this particular moment to pick a fight with the British Empire. Wasn't this rich? His prospects for getting free of debt rested almost entirely on the warm feelings for "Mark Twain" that were shared, he was pretty sure, by the millions of British subjects strewn around the world. This scheme of his to barnstorm the globe—the English-speaking part of it anyway—and shake the change out of British pockets had looked like a no-brainer when he had set off. His friend Henry Morton Stanley, the famous English explorer, had done a brief lecture tour of the British colonies in Australia, New Zealand, and Tasmania, and he had assured Clemens there was still plenty of cash to be had by traveling fast and flapping one's lips faster. The people in those distant lands were starved for entertainment.

Temperamentally competitive, given to overreaching, and fascinated by figures, Clemens had ciphered the potentialities of this enterprise as only he could. The little island nation of England had, as its far-flung citizens liked to say, painted the world British. Her Majesty's government, as Clemens figured the numbers, ruled more than 40 percent of the habitable portion of the planet in 1895 and somewhere in the neighborhood of four hundred million human beings, a third of whom spoke English, and a reasonable percentage of whom knew of "Mark Twain." Factoring in what his London-based publisher told him about his sales in England and India, and his own guess at the number of pirated versions of his American titles, Clemens thought there were well over half a million of his books at large in Great Britain and its colonies, protectorates, and dominions—and maybe more. "The number of those who have read Mark Twain," one friendly British literary critic offered, "must be numbered by the million." And they also numbered, Sam Clemens believed, a good portion of the highfalutin in British society.

When Stanley had thrown a dinner party in Clemens's honor the previous spring, Clemens described for a friend in America the lavish and congenial scene at his friend's mansion, right down the street from the prime minister's residence in London.

> He had an extraordinary assemblage of brains & fame there to meet me—thirty or forty (both sexes) at dinner, & more than a hundred came in after dinner.... There were cabinet members, ambassadors, admirals, generals, canons, Oxford professors, novelists, playwrights, poets, & a number of people equipped with rank *and* brains.... One was the wife of His Excellency Admiral Bridge, Commander-in-Chief of the Australian Station, & she said her husband was able to throw wide all doors to me in that part of the world & would be glad to do it; & would yacht me & my party around, & excursion us in his flag-ship & make us have a great time; & she said she would write him we were coming, & we would find him ready.

So it had seemed fairly elementary when he set out: all Sam Clemens had to do was follow the march of the British Empire around what he called the "fat rotundity of the globe." The empire was good for about $25 *billion* worth of commerce a year. Surely he could siphon enough from that mighty river to satisfy his creditors. The itinerary as planned took him through Australia, New Zealand, Tasmania, Ceylon, India, and South Africa. Once he had circled the earth, Sam Clemens planned to settle in the English countryside to write his travel book about the adventure. It would be cheaper to live there than in America, and he wouldn't have to answer as many questions about being a bankrupt. But as his colonial hosts would say, *Best-laid plans and all that . . . rather . . . yes, mmm-hmmm . . . oh, bugger.*

THE TRIP HAD been anything but smooth, even before the president of the United States had all but declared war on Clemens's hosts. When the *Warrimoo* carried America's most celebrated and best-known author into Sydney in the middle of September 1895, the Australians seemed at first somewhat underwhelmed by his actual presence. Sam Clemens wore a rumpled dull-black suit and a pair of tan shoes in desperate want of a good polishing. His gray-streaked hair jutted out at odd angles from beneath a worn silk hat. His voice was surprisingly nasal, even for an American. He seemed well past middle age, sniffed one newspaperman who was there to meet him at the docks. "He is spare and undersized, and there is nothing about him to fill the eye," another wrote. "Physically he is disappointing." And the truth was, by the time he got off the bad-luck boat, Sam Clemens was kind of a mess, suffering both from the generalized mental anguish attendant to living under a mountain of debt and from a quite specific egg-size growth that had boiled up "half way between my left knee & ancle, right astride a big tendon."

The first of these carbuncles had actually arisen in the middle of his thigh while he was still in America, and the incessant and sometimes sharp pain made it nearly impossible to prepare the three separate lectures he felt he needed to meet the demands of the tour. "I have found it exceedingly difficult to memorize readings & curse a carbuncle all at the same time," he had reported to a friend, "& I have done only one division of the job really well." That growth plagued him for more than two months, and he just barely got rid of it in time to set out gingerly and underprepared on his round-the-world lecture campaign. This second carbuncle had bubbled up on him as the *Warrimoo* steamed from Honolulu to Sydney, and it would not be the last.

Every few weeks for the next six after his landing in Sydney, a new pustule formed. Doctors in Australia and New Zealand dutifully lanced and drained the boils as they made their individual debuts, and administered opium hypodermics that gave him temporary relief from the worst of the pain. But just as one carbuncle seemed to be healing, another came—one of the last, in the tender fold of his armpit. He braved as many of his scheduled lecture dates as he could, but he was increasingly agitated by all the dates he had to cancel and all the money he left on the table in Sydney and Melbourne. He spent an entire frustrating week confined to a sickbed in the latter city.

The occasional packets of receipts he was able to send to his friend and financial consultant, Henry Rogers, to pool for the eventual satisfaction of his creditors contained dribs and drabs of money, fractions of what he had counted on. Clemens fretted aloud about the meager take and about not yet being in command of three solid platform lectures: a hellfire embarrassment was what it was, to do the same three talks three nights in a row in the same city. His tour manager was a bit shaken at the number of times Clemens was unable to recall specific episodes from his own novels.

The author did his best to avoid turning the trip into a sympathy tour. He kept his physical maladies out of public view unless forced to explain a canceled date: "[The carbuncle] sits on my leg like the nation," he confessed to a reporter from the *South Australian Register*. "It keeps quiet awhile, but at times it gathers itself together and gives an almighty hard twist. It's pretty vigorous." And sometimes he would have to send last-minute regrets for private dinners he had already agreed to attend. "Dear Miss Buckley," he wrote in apology, to one of a number of disappointed hostesses. "I have spent the last few days in bed trying to check a very persistent carbuncle—with no success— & I find I must continue that discipline. The society of carbuncles is full of interest, but to get the fullest enjoyment out of it, one must seclude himself from other society & give all his devotion to *that*."

The most disheartening of the entire disheartening carbuncular menagerie put him flat on his back on the occasion of his sixtieth birthday. He spent that day in bed in a seaside resort in Napier, New Zealand, dueling with a Ballarat fly—worse than a hundred mosquitoes, he complained—and lamenting the box office take he had lost when the doctor forced him to scratch the previous night's lecture. Livy did what she could to soothe her husband, though she, too, was rattled by the minimal cash proceeds to date. "I wonder if we shall ever get all our debts all paid and live once more in our own house," she wrote home to her sister. "To-day it seems to me as if we never should." But Livy kept her worries hidden from Sam and bent herself to nursing her husband through his ailments, making sure the gouges the carbuncles left behind were full of salve and freshly dressed.

He meant to give his audiences what they wanted, and he knew what it was. He drummed the British Empire for all it was worth . . . and a damned sight more than it was worth. He told all the queen's loving subjects and all the patriots of New South Wales and Queensland and Tasmania and New Zealand just what they wanted to hear about their dear mother country: "There is only one London. It is unique. . . . The wealth and intellect of the world is centralized there. It is wonderful, and what cannot be said of the nation which has evolved such a city!" And he parried reporters' *many* invitations to tweak the world's greatest living empire; he was a political babe in the woods, he insisted, especially where international relations were involved.

He praised the loving and open reception that characterized audiences in England, Australia, and New Zealand. As good as Americans? No, better! He patted Australasians on the back for their spectacular landscapes, their nowhere-else-on-earth collection of wild beasts, their rousing horse races, their modern systems of transportation, their ripening literary talents, and especially their splendid advancement in the field of journalism. The longer Sam Clemens was there, the more the locals grew to like him. "He has soulful eyes," one reporter wrote fawningly, describing a railroad trip with Australia's new favorite American. "They beam on you when he refers to the welcome he has been accorded in Sydney—and when, after a long gaze through the carriage windows upon the speeding landscape, he turns, and, a little above a whisper, says, 'I am learning to love your Australia.' "

He did signal to the Aussie reporter, however obliquely, that things were not always what they seemed—a lesson he had learned as a riverboat pilot on the Mississippi, where treachery lurked just beneath placid and pacific surfaces. "It is true indeed," he told him, still peering out the window of that train, "that very often the greatest beauty indicates the gravest danger."

He heaped praise on the Kiwis, too, when he got to their land. "New Zealanders are all enthusiasts—and rightly so—as to their country, which they contend is the finest in the world. From the glimpses I have had I am inclined to believe them," he boldly told a newspaper in Christchurch. They loved him there, too. Viceroys had him to concerts in their private boxes, and the hoi polloi dragged him into pubs to toast his health. Whenever he left a town, dozens of well-wishers would show up at the railroad tracks or the docks to see him off; whenever he passed through some sunbaked inland outpost, people would show up at the station just to catch a glimpse of "Mark Twain." Colonists delivered flowers for his wife and daughter, offered gifts of ancient Maori art, books by local authors, petrified insects, a platypus. "Mr. Clemens does not allow his Ornithorhynchus dear to leave his arms while we are moving from boat to train and train to boat," Livy wrote to the donor of the platypus, by way of thanks. "He says it is his most treasured possession."

The auditoriums and concert halls he played were packed and primed for fun. One night a young man sitting next to Livy got to laughing so hard in the early innings of the lecture that he was forced to start pounding and rubbing at his sides, as if trying to quiet some excruciating pain. "Well, if it is all as funny as this," he told Livy, "I shall die." People would trail Clemens back to his hotel after a show to buy him a drink and watch him smoke cigars and would listen to him talk some more about what a wonderful time he was having among the finest folk in all the world.

The effort of this charm campaign wasn't so much thinking up nice things to say. Saying something nice had always come easy to Sam Clemens, especially after some particularly good audience had given him the juice. Suppression of the less flattering actualities he had observed in these British colonies was the hard part. He liked to call things as he saw them, but what good would it do to kick the outback dust in people's faces when they were being so hospitable? He kept to himself his criticism of the steamships he traveled on ("that floating pigsty"; "smelt like a kennel"). He certainly wasn't going to dwell on the colonists' unfortunate and near-genocidal treatment of the aboriginal people of Australasia. Nor would he be goaded into an ill-conceived outburst over the Duke of Marlborough–Consuelo Vanderbilt engagement to-do. He knew better—why give some colonial homer a reason not to buy a ticket to his show?

Sam Clemens had long ago discovered the value of doing his venting *in private*. When the day's newspaper interviews were done, and the evening's post-lecture toasts ended, and he had done all the hand shaking and backslapping and small talking required of him, Clemens would sit down with his notebooks and fill them with jottings meant for his eyes only, at least while he was on terra firma Britannia: "They are innocently & provincially vain of everything colonial

& want it admired. The interviewer is pathetically persistent in trying to worm out of you your 'impressions' of NZ and her people & audiences & which city did I like best, there, & which audience; & are the audiences there as quick and bright as Austra.; & which do I think the most remarkable city, Syd or Melb; & which newspapers do I consider the best; but don't I think them *all* remarkable—& a dozen other questions of the same guilelessly idiotic sort, which only another idiot would answer."

The old British convict system—these islands had been home to viciously inhumane prisons—was "invented in hell & carried out by Christian devils," he noted to himself. "The *spirit* of the old brutalities remains in England, where they still punish poaching heavier than brutal wife-beating."

About that inimitable landscape: "The truth is that the native Australian is as vain of his unpretty country as if it were the final masterpiece of God, achieved by Him from designs by that Australian," he recorded. "He is as sensitive about her as men are of sacred things—can't bear to have critical things said about her."

"It is the strangest thing that the world is not full of books that scoff at the pitiful world, and the useless universe and violent, contemptible human race—books that laugh at the whole paltry scheme and deride it," he recorded in his notebook one day in New Zealand when his rancor apparently skipped the rails of the British Empire and lit on humanity in general. "Curious, for millions of men die every year with those feelings in their hearts. Why don't *I* write such a book? Because I have a family. There is no other reason."

LIVY AND CLARA were powerfully attuned to the danger inherent in the darkening moods of Clemens père; they knew how important it was that nothing impolitic seep out of him in public. So they were careful not to add weight to the burden he carried. Sam Clemens never heard Livy complain about how much she missed her maid Katy Leary, who had come to the Clemens family from Livy's hometown and served them for fifteen years. Katy was back in Elmira, New York, with Livy's sister, mothering the two daughters Livy had grudgingly left behind, and Livy was making do with a hired German girl, who was perfectly capable, but still a stranger. "I always want her to get away as soon as possible," Livy confided in a letter to her oldest daughter. "Katy never makes me nervous personally and this girl does so that I often find it difficult to be pleasant with her."

Clara, meantime, was chafing at the duties thrust upon her, and slightly jealous that her older sister, Susy, and her younger sister, Jean, were back in America, living a life of their choosing. She resented it sometimes, being the only daughter her father could depend on, and wondered on occasion if her chance at a future of her own making would be extinguished by her father's smothering demands. But Clara wouldn't bring that up with him, not now. As for the letters she and her mother were getting from Susy, the Clemens women decided the less Sam knew the better.

Susy Clemens had put her foot down about this round-the-world trip. She was twenty-three years old now, ready to get on with her own life, and she simply refused to go. Susy hated ocean travel, especially aboard steamships, where she was likely to lie awake nights imagining the coal-fired engines sparking a conflagration beneath her, imagining the vessel and its passengers becoming cinder and ash in the vastness of the open sea. She was nervous and frail by nature and had trouble sleeping in the best of conditions. So the oldest Clemens daughter had told her father she was going to spend the year of the lecture tour on her aunt's farm in upstate New York, drinking milk, eating healthy food, and building up her lungs. Her voice teacher from Paris had recently convinced Susy she had a future onstage if she could gather some physical strength. Besides, Susy knew she was no good for the role her father had suggested for her when he told her about the trip; the job was to keep Livy free from work and worry. Susy would be expected to act as nurse and companion to her mother and as secretary to her irascible, sometimes impossible father. She had practically crumbled at the *idea* of that responsibility—better to let Clara take the reins. Susy was convinced she was making the right decision at the time, but she quickly came to regret it.

As Sam, Livy, and Clara traveled west and the distances between them and Susy widened, the stay at home started to beat up on herself. Why did she have to be the outlier in this adventurous family? Why was she so prone to this unspeakable *cowardice*? Why had she forsaken her own mother? Why did she have to feel so alone? "I am often deeply cast down with the thought of how I have failed to be what I should have been to you all," she wrote to her sister at the beginning of August, when the traveling party was still in the United States. "This realization takes possession of me and horrifies me often in the middle of the night," she had written at the beginning of August. "But perhaps I shall have a chance to try again. In any case, you *know* I love you all and *could not* have *wanted* more to be a 'nice child.' The only difficulty is that our duty doesn't end with wanting."

And a month later: "I am tired *tired* of all my *sins*, and all myself! This hitch, this discord, this restlessness making every undertaking impossible, and spoiling and frittering away my life."

And three days after that, as the Clemenses neared Sydney: "*If* I ever can be with you again, I shall stick like a burr indeed! . . . We *do* belong together. . . .

How, how, why, *why* did I ever let you go? . . . It is a mistake to separate from the people we love and whom we belong to. I do not really love anybody but you dear three, and of course nobody loves me."

Clara sent back letters to buck Susy up and to reassure her about their mother's always shaky health. "She has borne this hard travelling so *excellently* that I am not afraid of the future," Clara reported. "Don't worry at all about us for Providence will see us safely through our journeys I am sure, and I shall look out for Mamma and see that she does not get overtired. This year will be quickly gone I hope."

Livy offered Susy happy depictions of the Clemens family's progress—"it is constant unceasing adulation of Papa"—and tried to tend Susy's cries for emotional support.

> You dear sweet darling little child in your self reproachings you seem to entirely forget that we had many, many, many happy beautiful hours together, beautiful hours that I remember with such infinite pleasure. Do you remember oftener times that I was impatient and disagreeable to you, or the times that we were happy together? I am sure you do not think very often of the fact that I often spoke in a way that a mother ought not to speak—I am sure you do not hold those things in your heart; neither do I, I think *much much* oftener of your lovable, dear, sweet ways than I think of the times when you were not absolutely perfect. . . . So my darling child do not repine for the things that you did that were wrong. I feel that when we come together again we shall feel alike that we never shall want to be separated.

LIVY THOUGHT HER husband was gaining, in spite of the blistering heat; he was even starting to talk with excitement about the upcoming jaunts through Ceylon and India and South Africa. As the 1895 Christmas holiday approached, before the United States' near declaration of war on Great Britain anyway, Clemens was beginning to feel somewhat more hopeful about the prospects of this lecture trip. He had gone nearly three weeks without threat of another boil. He had mastered and memorized his three lectures and could mix and match stories as he pleased on the platform. On December 17, Clemens boomeranged back from New Zealand to Sydney. He had at least a week, maybe two, before he had to set sail for India, which meant he had some time to make up for the dates and dollars he had lost to the carbuncles.

He felt well enough to agree to two lectures in Sydney and two in Melbourne—billed as last-chance finales all. He didn't even appear to mind the ham-handed advertisements in the *Sydney Morning Herald*.

MARK TWAIN'S LAST NIGHT
Prior to Sailing for India on Monday by the Oceana
SCHOOL OF ARTS,
TO-NIGHT

POSITIVELY LAST APPEARANCE
OF

MARK TWAIN
MARK TWAIN
MARK TWAIN

THE ONLY
THE ONLY
THE ONLY,

being the
COUNTRY VISITOR'S ONLY OPPORTUNITY
of hearing
THE FUNNIEST MAN OF THE AGE
THE FUNNIEST MAN OF THE AGE

HOLIDAY PRICES

Clemens's habit was to read all the newspapers he could get hold of, every day, wherever he was, and what there was to read in the first few days after his return to Sydney made him edgy in spite of himself. The front pages shouted about President Cleveland's ungentlemanly warning to Lord Salisbury as to Venezuela and about the suspected whereabouts of a fleet of US warships.

Clemens had hoped for a couple of quiet days to prepare his last few lectures in Australia—he had promised to unveil "Mark Twain's Australian Poem," including a rhyme for *ornithorhynchus*, and he needed to be working on that—but the sound and fury of the "war scare" was impossible to ignore. Clemens never cared much about boundaries and borders. He thought of himself as a citizen of the world; leaving off France, there was no nation or people for whom he did not feel a genuine human sympathy. He had already seen the waste of one war and its aftermath, and it had made him exceedingly wary of patriotism in its boldest coloration. But Sam Clemens was an American, after all, and a proud one at that, and some of these Aussie newspapers were, well, provoking.

The *Sydney Morning Herald* reported that President Cleveland's slap at the empire was an inevitable outgrowth of America's penchant toward "jingo mania." The Tasmanian Press Association syndicate gleefully quoted French journals on "American arrogance." As to the Monroe Doctrine and the question of just who held sway in the New World, the *South Australian Register* suggested that President Cleveland and the Congress might want to take a moment to recall that Britain governed more territory in the Americas than did the United States. "The Monroe Doctrine when directed against England is in itself sufficiently absurd," the *Register* opined. "The Venezuelan application of the principle is, however, beyond measure preposterous."

There were bald (and of course knowing) assertions that President Cleveland's "discharge of theatrical thunder" was a cynical political ploy to whip up support for his candidacy in next year's election. Second- and third-day stories suggested that Cleveland was already growing fearful of what he had unleashed. Less generously, and without any particular evidence to back it up, the *Mercury* of Hobart, Tasmania, printed this stark statement: "Cleveland is at present moment the most notoriously unpopular man in the world among thinking people." These were not easy things for Sam Clemens to let pass. He counted the president as a personal friend and as one of the few American leaders whose integrity transcended cheap party politics.

Clemens felt honor-bound to stand up for a man like Cleveland and for his own country and no doubt would have if, like William K. Vanderbilt, he could have afforded to. He might not have held his tongue, for instance, when an English lady, dripping condescension, said to Livy, "Your American threats of war we merely smile at."

Clemens still had plenty of good feelings for England, even in this maelstrom, but when crossed, by *anyone*, his first instinct had always been to hit back with force. Livy still remembered her husband's answer some years back to the British publisher who wanted to make revisions in one of his books in an effort to make it somewhat less offensive to the English reader. There were to be *no* changes, he insisted: "This is important, for the reason that the book was not written for America; it was written for England. So many Englishmen have done their sincerest best to teach us something for our betterment that it seems to me high time that some of us should substantially recognize the good intent by trying to pry up the English nation to a little higher level of manhood in return." And that had been written when he was in a good mood.

THE FIRST OF the two farewell lectures in Sydney, on Friday night, December 20, shaped up as trouble. War talk was at its hottest, and Clemens was at the tail end of a fourteen-hour round-trip rail journey to make a quick hit at a lecture hall up north, in a two-farthing town that had produced only a portion of the large house it had guaranteed. He had been late getting back to Sydney that Friday, had to change into his performing clothes in the horse-drawn cab on the ride from the railroad station to the School of Arts, and arrived onstage a bit tardy and more than a bit weary. The Clemens women might have worried; this was the sort of day that set him on a hair trigger. The initial reception in the auditorium, as described by observers on hand, was merely "cordial."

He pulled it off, though, to judge from the next day's *Sydney Morning Herald*, which took a pause from its America bashing to make approving notice of "Mark Twain at Home." The *Herald* reporter recounted the author's heroic efforts to make it to the stage in the vicinity of curtain time and the ease with which he tickled his listeners out of their apparent irritation at being made to wait. "What may happen when a woman has the dread of lightning in her composition was told with great drollery, and the end, if not the moral, of the story was that a respectable married man may be discovered by his friends, at a late hour of the night, standing on the verandah and dressed in pyjamas, a military helmet, with spurs on his heels, and grasping a military sabre," the *Herald* explained. "Throughout his lecture the audience was in a simmer of laughter."

The finale that night turned out to be the triumph, though Clemens began it by sorrowfully announcing he was scrapping the promised premiere of his new Australian poem featuring its ornithorhynchus. "Advancing to the edge of the platform and speaking with great earnestness," the *Herald* reported,

> "Mr. Clemens said that, in bidding his audience good night, he wished to express his belief, as well as his earnest hope, that the "little war cloud" which had been lowering over England and America during the last few days would be quickly blown away under the influence of cooler and calmer counsels. (Loud cheers). He trusted sincerely that the fruitful peace which had reigned between the two nations for 80 years would not be broken—(cheers)—and that the two great peoples would resume their march shoulder to shoulder, as before, in the van of the world's civilization. (Prolonged cheering.)

That little paragraph of peaceful tidings from the colonies' favorite American was picked up in Adelaide and Bathurst and Brisbane and Broken Hill and Melbourne. Clemens repeated the windup almost word for word the next night in Sydney, adding for effect that all this war babble was "unpleasant, unprofitable and unbrotherly." It was clear to him by then, however, that his tour was not going to steer clear of the line of fire in this international dustup. The potshots had already started. A magazine in Sydney quoted a disappointed attendee who had traveled from northern Queensland to hear the Friday night talk: "I've come 3000 miles to hear [Mark Twain]," he complained, "and, blow me, if the heat hasn't taken all the gas out of him."

"He is lacking in variety," said the *Clarence and Richmond Examiner.* The *Examiner* also used Clemens's peace offering to pivot into another brisk verbal crack across the American bow. "By their insane howlings about the British claims regarding Venezuela," the paper concluded, "the Americans have earned the contempt of all the continental nations, and the sooner they come to their senses the better it will be for their reputation."

THE MARTIAL STARCH did seem to be softening a bit in the States; not that Americans were much concerned that this war scare was unpleasant and unbrotherly. But the whole deal was starting to look alarmingly unprofitable. Grover Cleveland had started the fight with England, with Henry Cabot Lodge and a few others jabbing him forward, but it was the American money crowd who were getting their noses bloodied. The banks and stockjobbers in London started selling off American assets and securities as soon as Cleveland's hostile message became known among the financiers in the City of London, and they prodded investors to get out of the American market in a hurry, before the bottom fell out. At the open of the business day on the Friday morning after the Cleveland message went public, news came that investors were dumping American stocks in London, which started a spasm of panic selling on the New York Stock Exchange. Volume was pumped up by Wall Street speculators who had schemed the Venezuela war scare as a way to make a quick buck selling short: nearly a quarter-million shares were unloaded in the first hour.

Prices began falling across the board, and fast; the sinking values churned up rumors that the great London banking house of Rothschild was going to sell notes and pull $25 million worth of American gold out of the already depleted US Treasury. Ships were already loading up with gold for the trip across the Atlantic. Suddenly undercapitalized banks in the States started to call in loans; at least three suspended operations. More robust US banks were obliged to flood the market with cheap paper to keep the overseas speculators from pushing money rates through the roof and making the day an all-around rout. By the end of the session that Friday afternoon, December 20, 1895, shareholders in the American stock market were down hundreds of millions. The markets gave away only a bit more ground in the abbreviated session the next morning, which was a pathetic cause for cheer. Everybody agreed that the pair of private banks that went under that day was of little account. But railroad paper was still heading downhill, without brakes. Monday's open might be a bloodbath.

Chauncey Depew, the big mutton-chopped blowhard who ran the New York Central Railroad for the Vanderbilts and other investors, was apoplectic at what he thought was Cleveland's ill-considered blunder concerning Venezuela. This transatlantic run on American financial markets made the Duke of Marlborough's raid on the domestic house of Vanderbilt look like penny-store shoplifting, and for what? Some malaria-soaked piece of real estate in Latin America? "The 'war' has already cost the country $1,000,000,000 in depreciated values, and it has been going on for only three days," Depew told reporters. "I met a man yesterday who owns most of the swamp in Venezuela which is in dispute and he said he would sell it to me for $25,000."

Chauncey, as was his wont, was exaggerating for effect. But he was not overplaying the level of panic, especially among the directors of those big American banks who would have to cool their heels until Monday to see how the markets broke. "I dined on Saturday night with a lot of financiers," Depew explained in a letter to Whitelaw Reid,

> among them [J. Pierpont] Morgan, Lanier and Sturgis, President of the Stock Exchange, and they all believed on Monday that the frightened English investor and European holders of our securities would be tumbling them across the Atlantic at a rate which would take out all the gold from the Treasury to pay for them; that they would find no market here capable of buying them, and so they would sell for nothing; that they would cramp the banks; that the loans would all be called in and no new ones made; that everybody owing money would fail in business, and that we were on the eve of a financial cataclysm the like of which had never been witnessed.

President Cleveland had already made a late-night plea to Congress to take quick action to protect the diminishing gold reserves; he wanted the legislators to stay in session and do something to reassure American citizens and investors around the world of the strength of the nation's finances. This request was received in "a manner that might be termed frigid," particularly among legislators whose constituencies believed Cleveland was the tool of oily Wall Street brokers. Congress adjourned as scheduled.

American bankers were cheered by gossip that the flustered president was begging the financial sun kings, J. Pierpont Morgan and August Belmont Jr., Rothschild's American agent, to come to Washington that Sunday to discuss how they might pull the US Treasury chestnuts out of the fire, which the men had already done once that year. Nobody would confirm that any such emergency measures were imminent, and neither Morgan nor Belmont, the papers reported, cared "to make any public utterances just at the moment."

A Wall Street crowd gathered at the Windsor Hotel in Manhattan, as it did every Sunday, to chew over possibilities and predictions for the next day's open at the stock exchange and to receive useful commercial intelligence from their acquaintances and allies at the center of financial power, in London. What they got was nothing. "This in itself was regarded as one of the singular incidents of the situation," the *New York Sun* reported. "In all previous flurries in Wall street in which the London Stock Exchange has had a sympathetic interest, the big men . . . have received private cables from their friends in London giving points on the prospects for the immediate future. Yesterday the bankers and brokers were left entirely in the dark."

Commercial titans at the Windsor, at the Racquet Club and the Metropolitan Club and the Union Club in New York, and at private enclaves around the country were understandably shaky that Sunday. They were terrified at the prospect of being swept back into the miserable hole they had recently crawled out of. The last market crash, two years earlier, had ushered in the most frightening and costly depression in the country's history. In the summer and fall of 1893, one wave of panic after another had eaten away chunks of the beautiful new sand castles of the US economy. More than five hundred banks failed, and fifteen thousand businesses. Hundreds of thousands of men and women lost jobs, leaving them without even a meager income. Armies of unemployed and angry men had roamed the streets in Chicago and Cleveland and Pittsburgh.

The Boston Brahmins Henry Cabot Lodge represented had felt the pinch deeply as well. Bankers on State Street, manufacturers, commodities brokers, even trust-fund artists and scientists and historians who were heavily invested in the market, felt pushed to the precipice of disaster. "Everyone is in a blue fit of terror, and each individual thinks himself more ruined than his neighbor," Henry Adams had written in the middle of the panic, while watching friends and family collapse around him. "Men of sixty wear out fast under steady anxiety."

Adams and much of his class were starting to emerge from the depression at the end of 1895 atop nest eggs still sufficient to provide a life free from actual toil, jobs were just starting to come back for the people who had to work for a living, and the threat of a violent proletarian explosion had eased, but a generalized fury at having been shoved through the wringer had been loosed in the land. Adams—like many in the country, of every class—was meaner for the experience and stalking scapegoats. "In a society of Jews and brokers, a world made up of maniacs wild for gold, I have no place," he wrote. "I am myself more than ever at odds with my time. I detest it, and everything that belongs to it, and live only in the wish to see the end of it, with all its infernal Jewry."

That pungent anger still hung in the air like just-fired gunpowder as the Venezuela-fueled financial panic appeared to be gaining momentum over that long weekend in December of 1895, especially among Cabot's constituency. Boston had made its money as a port of international shipping and trade. Lodge's own family fortunes, for instance, rested largely on the opium markets in China. Manufacturing margins throughout Massachusetts depended on overseas markets; the last thing the banking and producer crowd needed right now was their own government roiling the sea lanes and the financial markets with this defend-the-Monroe-Doctrine-at-any-cost stunt. They were not at all sanguine when a few senators used the threat of armed conflict as an excuse to revisit the income tax on the wealthiest Americans. They didn't need to be reminded that patriotism was, after all, dear. The mere *talk* of war was about to tank the market and ravage corporate and private bank accounts.

Senator Lodge's office filled with telegrams and letters imploring him, as he whined to his mother, to "eat my words and swallow my convictions." The senator was still receiving such missives from Boston months later. "You were sent to Washington to represent one of the largest business states in the country," he was reminded by a cotton and woolen broker who depended on international (i.e., British) markets. "The business interests of the state require peace and quiet, not war."

There were calculations beyond profit and loss that gave pause to the more general run of informed Americans. For all the newspaper ink expended on the moxie of the country's fighting force, there wasn't much in the way of actual military resources to back the claim. The United States had a standing army of 25,000 men in 1895, though the War Department knew the actual number was probably far less: one in seven soldiers had deserted from the US Army, on average, every year for the previous twenty-five. The Belgian army was double the size of the American's, and the kaiser's army twenty-five times larger. The English, by way of more signal comparison at the particular moment, had a ground force of more than 150,000. The disparity in naval forces was even more embarrassing.

At present, the US Navy could count something less than three dozen vessels fit to be put to use on open seas, and only two of them battleships; this was as against forty-four battleships and nearly three hundred vessels for the British. The British fleet in the Pacific could very easily penetrate to within firing range of the West Coast of the United States.

Then, too, early efforts to "extemporize" US naval power did not seem promising. Three new first-class battleships were still some months away from completion. The iron-hulled coastal monitor *Monadnock* was to come on line at any time, the country was assured, but this assertion seemed dubious given that the ship's builders had, at that late date, been at the job for twenty years. The secretary of the navy was eyeing old wooden flagships on Rotten Row. "The *Swatara* is not of much account," was the report, "but the *Pensacola* could in three or four months' time be placed in commission and would then be practically as good as when she came in port a few years ago and was put out of commission." One of the finer cruisers in the Asiatic Squadron, the *Charleston*, was sitting in the far-off port city of Nagasaki, Japan; the ship had two broken pistons and was unable to move under its own power. When the USS *Texas*—billed as the fastest battleship in the world—arrived in Staten Island for its little shakedown jaunt, an anchor fell off and dropped to the bottom of the bay. Ten days later, on a four-hour run into the Atlantic, its bearings overheated, its drainage system faltered, the engine room flooded with water and oil, and the trial had to be abandoned.

Theodore Roosevelt, who was a recognized authority on naval history, didn't give a damn about all that. The weaklings who doubted America's ability to make a good fight were driving him near crazy, which was, admittedly, a short drive. Roosevelt was a man who, when agitated, was known to shoot a neighbor's dog for barking at him. But what, or who, could he shoot now? The do-nothing legislators who had allowed the United States Navy to sink into such a sorry state? The weak-kneed whiners in the financial class? The cosseted Harvard crowd and office-bound newspaper editors who thought peace was something you could win by *talking*? All they knew to do, Roosevelt carped, was to flinch and show the white feather. "The moneyed and semi-cultivated classes, especially of the Northeast, are doing their best to bring this country down to the Chinese level," he complained, again to Cabot. "If we ever come to nothing as a nation it will be because the teachings of . . . the futile sentimentalists of the international arbitration type, [bears] its legitimate fruit in producing a flabby, timid type of character, which eats away the great fighting features of our race."

The Roosevelt family, as well as friends like John Hay and Henry Cabot Lodge had come to understand that this war thing was personal to Theodore. Roosevelt had been trying to find a real man-size battle to throw himself into for nearly as long as Hay had known him. Theodore's own wife had taken to calling him "the Chilean Volunteer" a few years earlier, when he was agitating for military action over the minor incident involving a few jailed American sailors in Valparaíso, Chile. "Do you remember," Mrs. Roosevelt was still joking with their friend the young British diplomat Cecil Spring Rice, "how we used to . . . tease him about his dream of leading the cavalry charge?"

Edith Roosevelt knew her husband better than most. She nursed him through the asthma attacks that had plagued him since childhood and through his uncomfortable bouts of nervous diarrhea; she swept up after Theodore when he made financial missteps most grown men knew to avoid, and she listened to him complain that he had been too "nearsighted" to play that most manly of sports at Harvard, football. Out of earshot of all but their closest friends and family, Edith called her husband "her sensitive plant." When Roosevelt complained that his wife treated him like "a frail invalid needing constant attention," his friend Cabot sided with Edith: "Pray take care of yourself and be reasonable."

Yet—and perhaps one could chalk this up to overcompensation—no foe daunted Theodore Roosevelt, at least to hear Theodore Roosevelt tell it. And now that President Cleveland (or more probably Secretary of State Olney, as Roosevelt decided, who was "far more of a man than the President") had finally taken the country right up to the battle line with the world's most formidable military power, Teddy was in a swivet. "If there is a muss I shall try to have a hand in it myself!" he wrote to his sister's new husband, a naval officer attached to the American embassy in London. "They'll have to employ a lot of men just as green as I am even for the conquest of Canada; our regular army isn't big enough."

Soon after Cleveland issued his ultimatum to Lord Salisbury, Roosevelt piped up to make the public case for facing down the mighty British Empire; he lashed out at anybody who had the temerity to recommend caution where the self-respect of the United States was involved, which he seemed to believe was located somewhere along the border of Venezuela and British Guiana. The peace crowd, as Roosevelt churlishly styled them, was unpatriotic and cowardly, made up of "prized idiots" or—drawing on his interest in the natural sciences—hermaphrodites. These peacemongers were, as he later wrote, "people who are soft physically and morally, or who have a twist in them that makes them acidly cantankerous and unpleasant as long as they can be so with safety to their bodies." He was particularly proud, he explained to Cabot, of "a pet sentence in which I state that [one editor] combines the imagination of a green grocer with the heart of a Bengalee baboo."

One of Theodore's chief targets, the editor of the *New York Evening Post*, was already flagging in the effort to hold back the force of the militant tide. "The situation to me seems this," he wrote. "An immense democracy, mostly ignorant, and completely secluded from foreign influences, and without any knowledge of other states of society, with great contempt for history and experience, finds itself in possession of enormous power and is eager to use it in brutal fashion against any one . . . and is therefore constantly on the brink of some frightful catastrophe."

Theodore just kept coming. "As for the Editors of the *Evening Post* and *World* it would give me great pleasure to have them put in prison the minute hostilities began," Roosevelt told Cabot, once again neglecting to factor in the limited authority of his New York City police commissionership. "Personally I rather hope the fight will come soon. The clamor of the peace faction has convinced me that this country needs a war."

Roosevelt's rage was no great surprise to John Hay, and more to the point, Theodore was in no position to do any real harm, but Hay was troubled that the war talk among the general population and the popular press had not much subsided after a week. "Frankly I lose my Latin in this confusion," Hay wrote to Whitelaw Reid on Christmas Eve of 1895. "When I see Cleveland, who could not be tricked into any assertion of Americanism a while ago, now roaring defiance at the Universe, amid the plaudits of Lodge and Chandler . . . I can only rub my eyes and ask 'where am I at?' . . . The situation looks very mixed. Neither side wants to fight, but more than one war has begun in spite of the real wishes of both sides."

THE DAY AFTER Christmas, on the day of the first of two "Mark Twain" finales in Melbourne, a reporter from that city's *Herald* appeared at the door of Clemens's local host. "I have come to ask you," he told the author, "if you can tell our readers anything about this trouble between Great Britain and the United States." The prospect of war was clearly not fading away, and Clemens did not care to make light of the situation or speak to it at all. He insisted to the reporter that he was no expert. "In politics," he demurred, "I am all dense ignorance." And as he did not have at his fingertips the actual correspondence between the two governments, he insisted he could draw no definite conclusions on the merits of either side's argument. The *Herald* reporter pressed, and Clemens danced a graceful and sprightly Missouri reel right down the middle of the road.

"It has been suggested that the opposition to the President arises from a knowledge that the United States are unprepared, especially in the navy, and not from any aversion to war itself," the reporter started in.

"Nations do not consider these things at first," Clemens reminded him. "They act first and think afterwards." And more important, he explained, the stated reasons for the recent American outburst over Venezuela should not be summarily dismissed. President Cleveland was not simply grasping for votes, Clemens explained. Cleveland "would never so degrade his high office," he said. "Whether he be mistaken or not, I am sure he believes that he is doing what is right for the honor of the nation, and just what Lord Salisbury would do were they in reversed positions." Clemens wanted the *Herald* man to understand that the principle Cleveland had staked out was an important one to Americans.

"I presume you refer to the Monroe doctrine. Is it not possible that Mr. Cleveland has taken an extreme view of that doctrine?" the reporter asked.

"Yes; any one may take an extreme view of any subject," Clemens countered. "To Americans, who like myself, are not politicians, the Monroe doctrine has some vague meaning, but we do not know exactly what it is. We have a general idea that [if] anything attacks the Monroe doctrine it attacks something that is good for the nation, and must therefore, be resisted, but our ideas are vague."

Clemens then offered his assessment that nobody in the United States government was insisting on dictating the terms of anything, to anybody, until they knew facts. "Suppose that you and another man—Mr. Venezuela, say—are in this room, and have a dispute as to how much of it belongs to each of you," he explained, speaking as always, for effect, in his deliberate, nasal drawl. "Venezuela says the line ought to be here and you say it ought to be there. I am also in the room, but not directly interested. I say I think Venezuela is right, and I appoint a commission to survey and determine the line. It may be that you are right and then I must withdraw. That appears to be what the United States Government has proposed."

"Then you do not think the people of the United States wish to go to war?"

"They do not wish to go to war with any nation, and if war is to be avoided with other Powers, it is to be supremely avoided with England. There is a strong feeling of sympathy, civilization, and kinship between the two peoples, and each country should nurse that feeling. It wants nursing. . . . But if the honor of [the United States] or its integrity be attacked it will not shirk it, and the honor of the nation is, I am sure, safe in the keeping of Mr. Cleveland."

And so Sam Clemens shimmied through that interview unharmed. He had succeeded at protecting his own financial imperative: he had offended no one. He had to be pleased by the *Herald*'s windup paragraph, which concluded that Clemens was as patriotic as the next American, without being a "Whip-All-Creation" crackpot so common in the news those days. Clemens's final two stage appearances in Melbourne proved pleasant, brotherly, and profitable.

THIS WAS THE curse of being Cabot, as Cabot saw it: he was terribly misunderstood. Boston's Beacon Hill and Back Bay crowd "seemed to think we had gone crazy here," the senator wrote to his mother from Washington, "& were running the country into war just for fun." The commercial crowd in Boston was simply unable to take the long view on the Venezuela business, he complained. They kept their eyeshades down and worried over tomorrow's balance sheets, while he, the statesman, was trying to crack open the world—*for them.* By his own lights, Cabot was about to rescue the American economy from the demoralizing vicissitudes of its traditional boom-bust cycles. What was punishing the economy of the United States was its inability to restrain its energetic production; US manufacturers needed opportunities to expend their surplus vitality. The obvious fix was to open and secure new markets all over the globe. And, as Cabot would say, Americans had to be white men about it; they had to be willing to *compete* for those markets.

The Venezuela boundary dispute was just the first step in Senator Lodge's large scheme, a chance to chisel the Monroe Doctrine into the canon of international law. If the British acquiesced, he believed, the rest of Europe would fall in line. But he knew the British Foreign Office wasn't going to stand by and watch it happen; the United States government had to shove neo-Monroeism down its craw. The whole idea of "international law" was make-believe anyway: a maxim dear to a single country was honored by the rest of the world only when that country proved itself willing and able to enforce it. Standing firm on Venezuela would prove the point, Cabot believed: America for Americans. Then we could kick the British out of Central America, take control of a new canal linking the Atlantic and Pacific, annex Hawaii, and have a straight shot to the Orient. US manufacturers would own trade in Latin America, in the South Pacific, in China!

Cabot had already publicly warned the British government that Americans would stand as one and would not be cowed by England's dishonorable efforts to get their way by forcing a financial catastrophe. His next job, as he explained it to his mother, was to calm the nerves of the bankers on State Street and Wall Street, to gentle them into line.

Christmastime found him holed up in his library at his Massachusetts Avenue mansion, poring over maps and documents pertaining to the disputed Venezuela territory and tearing through newspaper clippings in preparation for yet another speech on the purport and the dignity of the Monroe Doctrine.

The tables, the chairs, the floor of Cabot's library, were always strewn with papers and books as he worked on a speech. He would write it out longhand, show it to Mrs. Lodge for emendation, and then take it back to the library to practice his delivery. "This action on the part of the President and of Congress has led to a great deal of discussion and much wild talk. Those persons in this country who, for one reason or another, believe that we should never do anything which can clash with English interests have filled the air with their cries and lamentations. It is true that they are more vocal than numerous, but they are very vocal indeed." Cabot, his hands clasped behind his back, would pace back and forth across the Oriental rugs of the library, memorizing what he could, familiarizing himself with the feeling of the words forming in his mouth. "This outcry, however, coupled with London's attempt to frighten Congress by producing a stock panic, has tended to confuse the issue and to mislead many persons."

The full Senate did not go back in session until a few days before New Year's, and by then the situation had cooled considerably. The threat of financial panic had passed; the US markets were on the upswing. As it turned out, the American economy was where a lot of international money wanted to be. Half of Europe had been happy to jump in and buy American stocks and securities Englishmen had dumped; the other half had been happy to stand on the sidelines and cackle at British losses. Baron Rothschild had reversed himself and started buying up "heavy parcels of American stocks" to help bolster the US market, he said. That seemed brotherly.

Lord Salisbury had retreated to celebrate the holidays with family and friends at his residence outside London, "the atmosphere motionless and not a trace of the recent supposed excitement," the *Washington Evening Times* correspondent cabled from London. When news came to the prime minister that Congress had officially sanctioned the US boundary commission and study, Salisbury let the news pass without comment. Having recently been elected a member of Parliament, Henry Morton Stanley was now on record saying that a third war between the United States and Great Britain would be "the biggest blunder of the age." Even Joe Chamberlain was starting to preach conciliation in the Colonial Office.

It might have been a good time for Cabot to hold his fire as well, but this was not his way. He had worked too hard, for too long, to keep quiet now, and besides, Roosevelt was riding him pretty hard. "I most earnestly hope that our people won't weaken in any way on the Venezuela matter. The antics of the bankers, brokers and anglomaniacs generally are humiliating to a degree; but the bulk of the American people will I think surely stand behind the man who boldly and without flinching takes the American view."

For more than two hours on the Senate floor, Cabot made yet another unneeded and unwanted and somewhat dated recap of the state of affairs. He careered through such already trod Venezuelan boundary minutiae as Columbus's discovery of the Orinoco in 1498, the Treaty of Münster in 1648; the Dutch aggressions across the Essequibo; the long-moribund Holy Roman Alliance; the Canning protest of 1823; and Britain's amateur mapmaker of 1840 (hadn't Mr. Schomburgk been in the tobacco business?), before finally tacking around to the immediate issue of recent British aggression. "If England can seize territory under a claim which has grown larger with each succeeding year, there is nothing to prevent her taking indefinite regions in South America," Cabot told his colleagues and the press and public that filled the gallery.

> If England can do it, and is allowed to do it, by the United States, every other European power can do the same, and they will not be slow to follow England's example. We have seen them parcel out Africa, and if we do not interpose now in this case the fate of large portions of South America will be the same. . . . We have permitted this English advance upon Venezuelan territory to go unchecked for years. . . . [Americans] are resolved that there shall be an end to these encroachments. They are resolved that the United States shall not sink in the scale of nations; that it shall not be menaced even by that nation to whom we are united by the bonds of blood and speech; but that it shall fulfill abroad, as at home, the great destiny to which it has been called.

Oh, and in case anybody had forgotten, "the necessity of our controlling the Hawaiian Islands," Lodge reminded his auditors, "becomes more pressing with each succeeding day."

HANG LODGE. LET him suck on his sour pickle of international doctrine. Sam Clemens was having some fun, like a gray-haired Tom Sawyer in enemy territory, with an Injun laying for him behind every scrubby bush in South Australia. He was enjoying the adventure of his one-man make-it-up-as-you-go diplomacy in the wilds of a frontier. "Mr. Clemens is naturally perfectly happy, entirely in his element," Livy had just written home to her sister, regarding the recent want of comfortable accommodations. "He was born for just this kind of luxury, I think. This morning we had Johnny cake and buckwheat cake for breakfast."

But Livy was even happier after the three Clemenses took up residence on the steamer *Oceana*, in a commodious stateroom overflowing with fresh-cut flowers from well-wishers in Sydney, to begin their long sea voyage to India. In the last few days of December they were skirting the lower coast of Australia, stopping for a day or two in various ports to load freight and passengers. And when Clemens got an invitation to step off the boat for a few hours to be the guest of honor at an annual South Australian celebration, he allowed as how he would be pleased to attend.

They were commemorating the biggest day in their history in South Australia, "this 'ere bein' the anniversary of the colony," as one boardwalk barker put it. The day had dawned bright and fair in Glenelg; the sun sparked in a crystal blue sky. Cooling breezes kept the temperatures hovering at pleasant all afternoon, while thirty thousand South Australians thronged the ocean-side resort town's esplanades and beaches. The mood was cheery all around.

At noon, the HMAS *Protector*, anchored in the bay and festooned from stem to stern with red, white, and blue bunting, fired off a volley of salute. Then the queen's new man in the colony, His Excellency Sir Thomas Fowell Buxton, KCMG, governor of South Australia, rode into Glenelg's town hall to preside over the formalities of the occasion. Everybody was pleased to see the American consular agent Mr. Murphy arrive for the banqueting. They had thought Murphy might be afraid to venture into the gathering, given the current state of affairs between the two nations, but as the province's commissioner of public works noted, "he was under the guardianship of 'Mark Twain.'"

His hosts settled Sam Clemens into a seat of honor at the head table, where he hurrahed for two straight hours while Their Excellencies from England toasted the handful of original pioneers in attendance. He hurrahed some more while the colonists proclaimed their continuing loyalty and devotion to the queen and her empire.

There were a half-dozen little speechlets, and at last, after a cheery and heartfelt introduction and a toast—with musical accompaniment—to "Mark Twain," Clemens was invited to "speak a piece" for the visitors in attendance. He got right to what he knew people wanted to hear. No sane man should so much as contemplate a war between England and America, he insisted. They were brothers in blood and bone. He echoed his old friend Henry Morton Stanley: a pitched battle between the two great powers would set back the progress of humankind for generations at least; ill effects might be felt for five hundred years. Then he laid it on thicker than ever. Tom Sawyer would have blushed, but what the hell? He wouldn't be back here again, he knew, and his sentimental streak had increased with his age. "It seems that in appointing me to respond for the visitors there is a sort of incongruity. It seems impossible for me to stand here in so chilly an attitude as that of a visitor. I have been among you in Australia for three and a half months, and from the beginning to the finish I seemed to be regarded rather as a member of the family."

FOUR DAYS LATER, as the sun dropped toward the horizon ahead of them, the *Oceana* got up anchor in the shallow roadstead, and the old riverboat hand in Clemens stood on deck and took note of the scene on the bridge, where the "small pilot in elaborately gold-laced uniform, stood by our giant uniformed Captain on the bridge and began a fine piece of seamanship. Our stern pointed straight at the head of the narrow buoyed channel; we set a jib to help and turned around in our tracks in spite of the strong wind." The ship churned up a storm of mud but skirted the bottom, and Sam and Livy and Clara were loosed from the tiniest continent, out on the open seas again, headed for India, and feeling much better about future prospects.

There were plenty of other passengers, but there was no emergency diplomacy to be conducted, no expectant audience to be satisfied, no reporters to be inveigled. Sam Clemens didn't even feel the need to curse the trifling box office haul from his four months in Australia and New Zealand. The burden of debt didn't weigh so heavy when he was out on the water.

"The sea is a splendid Mediterranean blue today with a delicate but pronounced copper tint on the shady side of the waves," he wrote a few days later, in the middle of thousands of miles of Indian Ocean. He was content to leave his troubles on land and lazy along, like Huckleberry Finn and Jim on their raft, floating where the current took them, pipes lit, legs dangling in the water. "It's lovely to live on a raft," he had written in his finest novel, ten years earlier, from the memories of his youth. "We had the sky up there, all speckled with stars, and we used to lay on our backs and look up at them, and discuss about whether they was made or only just happened."

All these years later, water voyages still made him feel easier in the world and connected to his fellow travelers, whoever they might be, "for what you want, above all things, on a raft," according to his Huck, "is for everybody to be satisfied, and feel right and kind towards the others."

CHAPTER FIVE

Something More Than Nothingness

John Hay had never known an arrival in England to be so joyously free from complication. His previous eastbound Atlantic voyages had always ended in a body-battering tugboat ride from the steamship to the wharf in Liverpool, a struggle through the dank Custom House to secure baggage, a banging horse-drawn transit across the drab little city to the railroad station, and a search for a second set of porters who would load everybody into a crowded compartment to endure the five-hour train trip to London. But on this happy late-spring day in 1896, Hay found Liverpool's new landing stage a wonder. The White Star Line's luxurious and powerful ocean flyer, the RMS *Teutonic*, steamed right up to port, where Hay and his party walked down the ship's sturdy gangplank, swept up their baggage—thoughtfully sorted, waiting under *H*—and followed their porters a few short steps onto a platform of the new and sun-drenched Riverside Station and into a railroad car for the trip to London. As the train ran its smooth rails southward, Hay sat admiring the manicured English countryside, lit bright by a high sun, "the hedges," as Hay put it, "all white with May." The English had become downright welcoming to New York arrivals by the spring of 1896. The Venezuela dispute, praise be, had quieted down considerably, owing in the main to British concessions, which owed in the main to the empire's concurrent wrangle in South Africa.

Right around the time Colonial Secretary Joe Chamberlain was clubbing President Cleveland for his recklessness in challenging the Brits on Venezuela, he had also surreptitiously encouraged an attempt to overthrow the Boer Republic of Transvaal. The diamond and gold mines in the independent South African Republic were apparently too enticing to be left to somebody else. The conspirators had bungled and had been tossed into jail by the Boers. Chamberlain made it known that he had tried to stop the plot at the last minute (he suspected a failure was certain) and won plaudits for the quick and sharp public scolding he had laid on the revolutionaries: their actions, he asserted, were decidedly un-British.

Unfortunately, Chamberlain's attempt to calm things in South Africa had been slightly overshadowed by Kaiser Wilhelm II of Germany, who broke diplomatic protocol by taking sides. The German emperor shipped a letter of congratulations to the Boer president for slapping down the British-instigated raid, and this kaiserly pat on the back had rattled Her Majesty's government and Prime Minister Salisbury. The German missive in itself wasn't construed as a direct threat to the British Empire, but it was clearly a breach of international etiquette, an act of full-on disrespect to the queen herself, and, as such, another in a series of eruptions in an increasingly dangerous family feud.

The queen and the kaiser were more than just fellow sovereigns. Victoria was also Wilhelm II's maternal grandmother and seemed incapable of letting him forget it. She insisted on calling him by the Anglo name William instead of the Germanic Wilhelm, which he preferred. "She thinks very badly of him," Salisbury once complained, "and has more than once shown her resentment very plainly. [The kaiser] is intensely irritated at this treatment, being quite conscious of his position." Lord Salisbury had come to understand, even if the kaiser's grandmum refused to acknowledge it, that the German emperor required careful handling. The prime minister knew Wilhelm to be, according to the medical reports slipped to Lord Salisbury by a German doctor who had attended the kaiser, a dangerous loon. And unlike the American president, the kaiser had a respectable navy and a big army and didn't have to round up the support of any political body to start a shooting war. Absolute monarchy had its privileges.

As Henry Adams would tell Hay and anybody else who would listen, the kaiser "stepped in just in time." Adams was certain that "the sudden appearance of Germany as the grizzly terror . . . frightened England into America's arms."

Lord Salisbury had been backpedaling on Venezuela for months by the time Hay and Adams arrived on British soil. The prime minister had let go of the fiction that "British settlements"— that is, lands pirated from Venezuela in the past few decades—were, like the Isle of Wight, undisputed legal property of the empire and beyond the reach of arbitration. Salisbury had also agreed to comply in full with requests from the new US commission studying Venezuela's boundary history to turn over maps and documents and other scraps of the historical record that Britain possessed. He had even sent out his right-hand man and nephew to disclaim his recent broadside on America's pet precept of international intercourse. "I am certain that everyone, American or British, who is impartially considering the subject will be convinced that there never has been and there is not now the slightest intention on the part of England to violently attack the substance or sense of the Monroe Doctrine," Arthur Balfour, first lord of the Treasury and leader of the House of Commons, assured the members of that chamber, in a generous but questionable rewrite of Salisbury's insulting answer to Secretary of State Olney.

Perhaps most important, Lord Salisbury had declared a halt to diplomatic amateur hour. He had wisely relieved the excitable Chamberlain and that dullard of an American ambassador, Bayard, of the job of negotiating a reasonable solution and deputized Britain's ambassador in America, Sir Julian Pauncefote, to work out something with the State Department in Washington.

The leader of the Liberal opposition in the House of Commons was meanwhile nudging Her Majesty's government toward even greater shows of sympathy toward America and its wounded honor. "We have no desire whatever," Sir William Harcourt announced, "to assert any claim to any territory to which we are not clearly entitled."

If the sweetness and light of John Hay's Liverpool welcome was a reliable augury of the relations between the two countries, there was an intriguing future ahead, which might just add a touch of political interest to Hay's summer jaunt.

HAY HAD BEEN talked into this pleasure trip by his oldest daughter; he found it nearly impossible to say no to her. Helen Hay was, to her father's great delight, carrying the Hay family's literary hopes on her lovely, slender shoulders. Her first sonnets were already headed to press. So when his daughter had asked him to take her and a friend on a tour through Europe that summer, he had relented, and then he had roped "Uncle" Henry Adams into making the trip as assistant chaperone and all-around guide.

Hay wished his lone age-appropriate traveling companion had embarked on the journey in better fettle. From the moment they boarded the ship in New York, Henry Adams had cosseted himself in his luxurious stateroom "to avoid seeing the Jews," he suggested, only half-jokingly, and stayed there for the entire week reading books from the *Teutonic*'s well-stocked, oak-paneled library or writing letters to Lizzie Cameron, for whom he was already desperately homesick. "A quick voyage, without wind or rain or cold or complaint," was how he described the ocean passage to her. "I've exchanged not a word with man or beast."

Adams's mood was not much improved once they disembarked from the *Teutonic*. Even as the American Special train raced toward London through the pleasing scenery of the English countryside, Uncle Henry remained low in mind, which, as Hay knew from long years of experience, was nothing out of the ordinary. Part of what had Adams so downhearted lately was the unfolding realization that John Hay's destiny was about to depart from his own. Hay and Adams had been attached for most of their adulthood by a cord of intimate friendship and by the surprisingly strong bond of circumstance and *place*.

Their mutual friend the expatriate novelist Henry James theorized that Hay and Adams chose to live in the culturally, aesthetically, and monetarily backward national capital because "they are, vulgarly speaking, 'someone' here." But James guessed wrong. It was not to feel *more* potent that his two friends had planned and built adjoining houses in Washington, where they could gaze out their respective windows, across Lafayette Square, at the nation's Executive Mansion. Each man was tethered to that official residence, Adams by remote family history—two of his antecedents had been president of the United States—and Hay by remote personal history, having lived in that house for nearly four years while serving Abraham Lincoln. Adams had been quietly tortured by his inability to live up to the Adams family legacy, while Hay had been vexed for decades by his inability to rise again to some semblance of the usefulness he had felt while rooming in that mansion, in daily service to the most consequential president in American history. Nothing in his life had been the same since Abraham Lincoln's assassination. "It is odd to live in a small city like this," Hay had written to a friend, "and see the world at a distance, and be like a dead man, if dead men can read the newspapers."

For Hay, though, there appeared to be new possibilities ahead, because he was once again tied to a man who might be headed to the presidency—a man who just might drag Hay across Lafayette Square and back into the tides of national purpose.

John Hay and William McKinley did not know each other well, but McKinley's regard for Hay's personal and professional capabilities had grown enormously in the past few years. McKinley had come to appreciate Hay as a rarity in American political life: a man who gave aid and comfort without expectation of something in return and without advertising his place in the candidate's affections. When McKinley nearly torpedoed his own reputation and nearly derailed his nascent presidential hopes by losing about $100,000 in a tinware factory he had personally championed, Hay wrote fat checks to help pay off McKinley's creditors. He also helped to keep the real story (that McKinley had acted with some measure of venality) under wraps. As far as the public knew, the former congressman and then governor of Ohio had been an unsuspecting and unfortunate dupe of a dear friend who had tricked McKinley into signing banknotes while he was focusing on the affairs of the state. By the time people started paying attention to the race for the presidential nomination, that potentially explosive scandal had been defused, owing to the favor of Hay and a few others.

William McKinley, "the Major," did not cut a particularly compelling figure; the *New York Times* described his intellect as "fluid and flabby." But he was a decorated veteran of the Civil War, a seven-term congressman, and a popular governor from the strategically situated state of Ohio. His campaign manager, Mark Hanna, had trained in finance and industry; he was a hard-skull operator who did the dirty work of electioneering without regret or apology. McKinley was also the political figure most identified with the high tariff Congress had imposed on foreign goods in 1890, an act of commercial protection that proved tremendously lucrative for American bankers and manufacturers.

McKinley's only serious opponent among the Republicans, the political touts and handicappers figured, was the Speaker of the House, Thomas Brackett Reed. Reed was able, intelligent, and principled. "The country has not bred a nobler man," Sam Clemens said of him. The Speaker's electoral strength lay in heavily populated New England, and he had energetic support from young political friends like Henry Cabot Lodge and Theodore Roosevelt. But Reed proved a bit too scrupled for modern campaigning. He refused to accept cash offered by industrialists to buy delegates at the state conventions. "Why?!" one railroad baron complained. "The others have taken it." Reed's punctiliousness left the field of creative financing open to McKinley's manager, Mark Hanna, who exploited this advantage from one end of the country to the other.

Delegates had dropped out of the Reed column and into the McKinley column with surprising velocity at the beginning of 1896. "They were for me until the buying started," Reed said of the southern delegates who fled him. By early spring the only real obstacle to McKinley's nomination was a cabal of the party's big-state kingmakers led by Senator Matthew Quay, boss of Pennsylvania, and Thomas Platt, boss of New York. Here is where John Hay proved his special value. He was a discreet gatherer of backroom intelligence, and his private reportage was accompanied by his own wise analysis.

After thirty-five years of hanging around the fringes of politics, watching closely, and making no enemies, Hay had a lot of sources to tap. When the McKinley men started getting signals that Quay's support for Reed was going soft, Hay warned them that they shouldn't be too eager to press for Quay's endorsement; it would be folly to rely on any pledge or promise made by the Pennsylvania boss. He kept them advised as Boss Platt began to swing all the New York delegates behind the state's governor, Levi Morton. When Platt prodded Morton to start expending some of his own personal fortune to buy up delegates down south, Hanna heard the news from Hay. Hay also confirmed McKinley's instinct to refuse to bargain with the bosses. When Quay and Platt asked for places in the cabinet or for dominion over all the federal patronage in their states, McKinley put out a stiff arm.

Hay also alerted Hanna when McKinley's success in rolling up delegates in state conventions made Quay and Platt nervous enough to promote—in stealth—a series of "favorite son" candidacies in hopes of forcing a brokered convention, allowing them to pick a candidate friendlier to bossism in general and to them in particular. When newspapers floated the rumors that Platt and Quay were going to boom former president Benjamin Harrison as their anti-McKinley candidate on the floor of the convention, Hay could ease Hanna's busy mind. "I do not see how anyone can make a successful administration," Harrison had confided to Hay's friend Whitelaw Reid, "and I do not feel that I could stand the worry of another term."

The early McKinley campaign was as close to politics as Hay had been for years, and he actually had some fun. Hay and Reid had had a fine cackle over the spectacular contortions performed by Chauncey Depew, who wanted a senatorship from New York badly enough that he was willing to suck up to Platt by publicly pledging himself to the boss's chosen candidate, but also wanted a cabinet post badly enough that he was telling Hay on the sly that his personal loyalties were with McKinley, and of course he would like McKinley to be apprised of this. "You remember Chauncey Depew's uproarious mirth [last fall] over the comic aspect of McKinley's candidacy," Hay wrote to Reid, "and now, no lover under a waning moon ever protested more unstinted devotion."

BY THE TIME Hay landed in England with his daughter and friends, the Republican National Convention was just a few weeks away and McKinley's nomination was a certainty. Pennsylvania's Quay had resigned himself to the hard facts of the case and quieted down, but Platt was still making mischief. He had started the rumor mill grinding about McKinley's dangerous game: The Ohioan, Platt and his boyos whispered around, was wavering on the sound-money, gold-only backing of US bonds and notes, which kept American financial markets afloat and humming. McKinley was flirting with . . . *bimetallism*! And perhaps even more worrisome . . . *free silver*!

The New York correspondent of the *Times* of London, George Smalley—supposed to be a friend of Hay's—had reported Platt's sub-rosa assertion that there was reason to believe that McKinley would cave to pressure from the western states and stand for unlimited coinage of silver, so that by the time Hay and Adams and the girls took up residence at Brown's Hotel in London, dread of McKinley's possible financial apostasy was afoot from one end of Piccadilly to the other, at the palace, at the government offices in Whitehall, and at powerful financial institutions in the City of London. The leaders of Her Majesty's royal government already had a jaundiced view of Hay's man. The McKinley

Whitelaw Reid, circa 1880

Tariff had been bad business for manufacturers throughout England, even after the Democrats watered it down. The British had held tight to their free-trade doctrines in the six years since and had watched American goods flood into the United Kingdom and the empire's colonies in Latin America.

The prospect of America's next president's being its most vigorous protectionist was bad enough, but word that McKinley might also support the monetization of silver sent cold shivers down the bespoke suit jackets of Lombard Street's international banking set. Would the Americans really try to pay off their notes and securities in devalued silver? "The English public distrusts [McKinley]," the *New York Times*'s London correspondent reported. "His record on the silver question needs to be looked up."

This silver balloon did give Hay a chance to do another good turn for the Major, which the soon-to-be nominee no doubt read about in Whitelaw Reid's *New York Tribune*. (The Great Moral Organ had been doing the most comprehensive delegate canvassing for months, and McKinley kept up.) "The first emphatic word for McKinley which has been spoken in any English journal appears in to-day's *Times* [of London] over the signature of John Hay," the *Tribune* reported as the convention neared. "A trenchant, plainspoken word it is, too, and one that commands the attention from sheer weight of utterance. . . .

While admitting that protection would be the main issue this year in American politics, he contradicted the assertions that the West wants free silver and that Governor McKinley will stand for that policy. . . . This letter has an authoritative tone which ought to arrest public attention in England and to involve a suspension of current criticism of McKinleyism as the cause of free silver and reckless and dishonest finance."

Hay had insisted in his letter to the *Times* that McKinley was a man of "extraordinary ability, integrity and force of character" and told the English public to expect "an administration in a high degree wise, pure, politic and magnanimous." In other words, Hay was swearing on his honor: McKinley could be trusted.

He knew he hadn't changed many minds in the British Isles, but Hay wrote home to his wife that the *Times* letter seemed to be the most read article he had ever written. He was kind of enjoying his public attachment to a potential president, though he did not intend to let himself appear overly eager. "The *Chronicle* was after me for several days for an interview," he told Clara. "I fought it off till the last day and then concluded I might as well say a good word for McKinley."

THEY WERE IN London a short week, time for a few social calls, a little shopping, a morning at Guildhall to see a collection of watercolors on loan, a morning at the Royal Academy to see the new Sargent portrait of the Right Honorable Joe Chamberlain and to take in Edwin Austin Abbey's painting *Richard, Duke of Gloucester, and the Lady Anne*. Hay could spend days looking at great pictures, or buying them, and he was especially enthralled by the power of Abbey's composition and his bold use of red and black. Abbey was a friend, so Hay decided to put a few bids in on the new work.

On their next-to-last day in England, the foursome made a quick trip to Oxford, from which Hay and Adams returned with very different memories. "The day was beautiful and we spent it pleasantly enough wandering about the different buildings and gardens," Hay wrote. Said Adams: "Hot as blazes and burned to a crisp, and [we] languished in the meadows and gardens."

The tiny grace note for Adams was his growing fondness for his new charge, Elizabeth Warder, who refused to betray the tinge of melancholy she felt when left out of some of John and Helen's choice engagements in London society. Adams found it endearing; he had even stopped referring to her as Cleopatra Jr. "She shows on closer acquaintance, the reason why the boys like her," Adams observed of Miss Warder. "She is amiable and intelligent, and has a rather keen sense for what is good. I am struck with it in her appreciation of art, which does not always agree with mine, but is very natural and refined."

Adams was most pleased for Elizabeth when she was included in the final-evening-in-London dinner at the home of the English aristocracy's favorite Americans, Henry and Daisy White. Adams chose not to attend; he didn't trust his ability to avoid offending somebody. He may also have been a bit on edge on account of Miss Warder. She may have debuted beautifully in Washington, but this was upper-class London, and her refined and assured taste notwithstanding, she was still a young American woman whose father had only recently secured the family fortune by the manufacture of Champion brand farm machinery and implements.

This dinner at the Whites was no trifling affair. Henry and Daisy White were Americans by birth, but they had climbed well up the slippery ladder of London society. The Whites lived at Grosvenor Crescent, just a few convenient steps from Buckingham Palace and its gardens, which delighted their personal friend, Queen Victoria. Harry, as he was known, had worked until recently as first secretary of the American legation in London, but he was much more than that meager job title implied. He was a European by education and upbringing, erudite, full of wit, impressive at a fox hunt, and an easy companion to marquesses and earls and counts. "He is good nature itself," Cecil Spring Rice wrote of him, "and agrees with everyone in turn without irritating them as much as one would expect from the habit." He and his wife were charter members of the self-styled Souls, a literary-minded town-and-country social club that rivaled the Prince of Wales's horsey Marlborough set for celebrity and sway. Daisy White was old-money New York, without need of showing it, and she mingled without the least tremor of discomfort among the titled and landed British aristocracy. She knew how to treat a duke, and she knew how to treat a commoner, and she knew they were not to be treated the same.

For John Hay, the Whites had planned a lavish evening. "Dazzling," Hay said of the company: four lords, a knight, and the favorite sister of a recent Prime Minister. The dinner was not merely social. White had been relieved of his first secretaryship at the US Embassy three years earlier, when the new Democratic administration of Grover Cleveland took office and the president wanted White's job as a plum to hand out to one of his party men. Despite vocal outrage by eminences on both sides of the Atlantic, Cleveland had refused to restore White. In the governmental divorce, President Cleveland and newly appointed ambassador Thomas F. Bayard got the embassy offices in London, along with the desks, the stationery, and so forth, while White alone retained good relations with all the informed and important men in the British government. In fact, Cleveland's own secretary of state had, by the middle of 1896, given up on Ambassador Bayard and had confidentially asked Harry White to articulate to the powers in London the American position on Venezuela and to gather

British views on the same. Lord Salisbury had recently summoned White to his private residence for a day of conversation on the matter.

So the Whites' table that night was, as always, a fresh and fragrant admixture of aristocracy, artistes, and raw political power. Sir William Harcourt, the leader of the Liberal opposition in the House of Commons, was among the guests that evening, as was the Right Honorable Joseph Chamberlain, secretary of state for the Colonial Office. Another of Salisbury's deputies, the undersecretary of the Foreign Office, George Curzon, was in attendance, too.

Hay had been a social friend of Chamberlain's and Curzon's for years, and he knew both men to be conflicted in the extreme about America and Americans. Chamberlain, born a commoner himself, often complained that the United States lacked civility and culture; he had pronounced New York ghastly, the ugliest city he had ever seen—"no flowers, no good statues, no monuments of any kind." That city's elite, he wrote, "have learned to create wealth but have not yet reached a stage where they know how to spend or enjoy it." Curzon was rather less dismissive of America's moneyed class—the Whites, his fellow Souls, were dear—but he assessed middle-class Americans as "the least attractive species of the human genus," worse even than the Germans.

Hay didn't disagree entirely with these harsh judgments, but he did forgive America its philistinism; it was a young country on the make, after all, and it takes time to develop the proper soil for husbanding aesthetics. Besides, Hay could also remind both Chamberlain and Curzon, they had both chosen to marry American women—very wealthy American women.

What Hay would remember most about the dinner at the Whites' that night was the striking vision of one of the young American women in his care. "Elizabeth [Warder] was placed between Joseph Chamberlain and Sir Wm. Harcourt, and had a very merry time," Hay wrote to his wife, Clara, a few nights after the event. "Old Sir William flirted with her in his most elephantine manner and occasionally he and Chamberlain would fight across her, on politics, in a very savage though courteous manner. It was a chance that a girl of her age rarely gets to see the greatest politicians of the time, in their hours of ease."

The real fun began for Hay, he reported to Clara, when the men retired to the smoking room after dinner. "I sat between Lord Curzon and Chamberlain and had some very interesting conversation with each of them. My talk with Chamberlain was especially important." The colonial secretary wanted to talk Venezuela.

Joseph Chamberlain was as smooth and silken as John Hay; he was just about Hay's age, fastidiously turned out, as always, with his short hair swept back off his forehead, a fresh orchid on his dark lapel, his dainty monocle at the ready, his nose pointed up a smidgen. He was a delicately formed man, with the pale mien of a dedicated indoorsman. "Seems like the model of a head clerk at a West End draper's," a colleague in the House of Commons once said of him. Chamberlain's appearance, however, belied the steel in his spine. The colonial secretary was used to getting his way in the world and apt to combust when challenged. He had described himself to his young American bride as "obstinate & self-willed—very proud & arbitrary—very impatient of contradiction & masterful in temper." And this while he was still wooing her, for he may have counted these among his admirable traits.

Chamberlain was a staunch protector of British power, and he had been prodded into more and more forceful advocacy of the empire by the recent hostility from what he called "jealous competitors" like Germany and America. Great Britain might stand alone these days, but it stood proud as far as Chamberlain was concerned. American politicians could call the British actions in Venezuela a "land grab" if they chose, but the colonial secretary saw no reason to apologize or to back down.

In fact, since President Cleveland's challenge on the border question, Chamberlain had been busy staking a greater claim to the disputed territory in Venezuela, throwing resources from the Colonial Office into the development of new gold mines there, building good, safe roads to those pots of precious metal, and arming soldiers in British Guiana with deadly Maxim machine guns. He was willing to take some chances, but he wanted to gauge just how far he might go before running afoul of America and its new adhesion to the Monroe Doctrine.

In the smoking room that evening, Chamberlain assured Hay that Her Majesty's government was seeking a fast and fair agreement. The holdup was all on the Venezuelan side, which refused to come to the negotiating table without the benefit of US muscle. Hay knew better; Salisbury's government was stalling because they hoped a new American president might be more willing to accept the "British settlements" argument. Hay had also heard around town that Chamberlain did not have much backing for his hardball play, and he told Chamberlain point-blank that Lord Salisbury's government might as well settle the Venezuela question right away, because McKinley was going to be the next president, and the Major would give no quarter. Chamberlain shouldn't be fooled by all this newspaper talk about McKinley's being amiable and irresolute. With McKinley as president, America would be standing firm on Venezuela and on the rest of the Americas.

ENGLISH ACQUAINTANCES DIDN'T understand why Hay and Adams were leaving the tiny isle so soon; they had invitations to Lord Acton's and to the Gaskells' at Wenlock Abbey and to Sir John and Lady Clark's at Tillypronie.

One London matron cocked her head reproachfully and looked at Hay and Adams "as if to insinuate that we two dissolute old boys were in a hurry to get to Paris," which, when Hay thought of it, was kind of funny. Pleasure of the flesh, Hay knew full well, was not Adams's cup of tea. And this was just as well. The prospect of wallowing in Gallic depravity held little interest for John Hay, and he was in no hurry to be anywhere special just then. Hay had resources to buy an expansive and comfortable round of European sightseeing, and he was hopeful of arousing the innocent excitements of original discovery—seven weeks to play in Europe, with no hard-and-fast itinerary, as when he and Henry Adams had been young.

John Hay had first arrived in Europe at age twenty-six, a few months after Lincoln's assassination, and had spent nearly four years adrift on the Continent as an underemployed, threadbare aesthete-in-training. Even on the paltry earnings of a secretary of the legation in Paris and Vienna and Madrid, he fed well. He brushed up on his German and became fluent in French. He cadged an opera box from a minister in Vienna, prowled museums and galleries and cathedrals in France, Austria, Spain, Holland, Italy, Turkey; the theater amused him, the opera inspired, even a ballet could occasionally hold him rapt. But what really moved the poet aspirant had been paintings.

Hay found himself drawn in by the primal authority of the old masters. He didn't see divine inspiration at work, but the ultimate expression of human genius: the guiding hand of the best of men.

This trip with his daughter in the summer of 1896 would probably be the last best chance John Hay had to share with her the ancient enameled figures at St. Mark's in Venice, Rembrandt's finest scenes, France's most exquisite private residences, the history of the Valois kings, the manuscripts of Leonardo da Vinci and Dante and the Medici family at the Ambrosian Library in Milan, the glorious public statuary of Bologna. Hay's oldest son, Del, and a couple of his Yale classmates were going to join the party in a few weeks, too. This would probably also be the last best hope to light a little spark of intellect and culture in Adelbert Stone Hay. There was no gentle way to put it: Del was thick, like a side of beef with eyes. He was big boned, incurious, and slow witted by Hay's standards. A generous patron of the fine arts of football and rowing, Del wouldn't have known a Tintoretto from a Rubens from a Turner. So this was important, this trip, and Hay had the resources to buy for his children and their friends a key to the world's treasures; his caravan could go where its fancy took it. They would recline at the most luxurious hotels in any city they chose, and they would keep on hand a hired girl to save them the proletarian bother of wrestling baggage from conveyance to hotel to conveyance to hotel.

Helen and Elizabeth had been sketching and resketching plans since they set out from New York: Amsterdam and Venice and Milan and Ravenna and Rimini for certain; Hay wanted to show them Florence, Nuremburg, Munich, Vienna, of course, and as much of France as they could get. Adams threatened to drag the troop to a few esoteric and remote Byzantine wonders. Little was set in stone; they were still remapping their cultural safari after they crossed the channel from London and settled in Paris.

The foursome was content to keep that city as its base for three or four weeks at least, wander the Louvre, stop by this season's exhibitions at a few noteworthy salons, and make quick trips up into Belgium and Holland or down into the Loire Valley. "We fill the days with different kinds of idleness," Hay wrote to Clara from his suite of rooms at the Hotel Westminster. And to another correspondent back home, he admitted, "We drift at the will of the wind."

JOHN HAY DID not appear to Henry Adams, in that second week of June, to be entirely at ease in this amiable drift. The Republican convention was just a week away now, and Hay was anxious for news of McKinley; he spent a lot of time scanning the papers for the daily updates on the American political scene. One of the first mornings in Paris, Hay and Adams both caught sight of a brief item describing Whitelaw Reid's not-so-brief private audience with Major McKinley. Whitelaw had made a detour to McKinley's home in Canton, Ohio, on his return to New York from a long stay in Arizona. If Hay knew his friend, Whitelaw was in Canton trolling for high office in a new administration. By then, McKinley was a lock for the party's presidential nomination, and no doubt Whitelaw wanted to remind the Major what he had risked to stand up for him against Boss Platt in New York, and to thank McKinley for thanking him for the *Tribune*'s enthusiastic (if fairly recent) support. McKinley, Hay would understand, was in no position to ignore the call.

Hay took a moment to dash off a quick note to Reid that same morning, congratulating him on his health and on securing three hours of private time with the Major. In his heart of hearts, Hay coveted a position in McKinley's administration, too, but he was a very different man from Whitelaw Reid; it was not John Hay's way to show need or to act on desire. So having the English Channel, the Atlantic Ocean, and a couple of Great Lakes between him and the gory scenes of sycophancy he imagined at McKinley's home in Canton, Ohio, was fine with him. He had no desire to be in the vicinity of Camp McKinley.

Hay knew from many years of close observation how a cadre of fresh new supporters would be attempting to endear themselves to the nominee-to-be, mostly so that they would have a place at the trough when a new president started slopping jobs. The Major would have to play it safe in the early innings of the spoils game, of course, especially in what was sure to be a close-run election against the Democrats, but Hay trusted McKinley to play them well. Like the most successful American pols, McKinley knew how to wear the mask. "It is a genuine Italian ecclesiastical face of the fifteenth century," Hay said of McKinley. Nobody who made the pilgrimage to Canton would leave the McKinley residence with any actual commitment, but every man would bound off the McKinley front porch knowing the Major was *for him*.

Whitelaw Reid, for instance, left Canton believing his counsel was enormously valued and always welcome. McKinley handed Whitelaw a memorandum concerning the prospective "sound money" plank in the Republican Party platform and invited his comments on how to handle the question of the gold standard. Reid's responses to the question over the next few weeks were voluminous, though not altogether consistent, except as a barometer of Reid's own protean nature.

Reid had warned McKinley at their meeting in Canton that coming out explicitly for the gold standard would cost them electoral votes in the West. So the Major must have been surprised to receive Reid's anxious note from New York a week later. Reid was still wary of actually using the word *gold*, but he was now certain that the Republican Party's firm insistence on sound money was an electoral imperative as well as a sacred obligation. "There seems no doubt that the most conservative bankers are extremely apprehensive that any hesitation on our part to take the squarest sound money ground would bring on a great and probably sudden depression in values."

Hay would learn later from his friends on the McKinley squad how Cabot had worried the "sound money" bone, too. The Massachusetts senator was a key manager for McKinley's vanquished rival and was scheduled to make the pointless nominating speech for Speaker Reed on the floor, but he showed up in the office of McKinley's campaign manager, Mark Hanna, the evening before the convention opened, leading with his inimitable sense of tact. "Mr. Hanna," he said, without hesitating to be announced, "I insist on a positive declaration for a gold-standard plank in the platform."

"Who the hell are you?" Hanna asked.

"Senator Henry Cabot Lodge, of Massachusetts."

"Well, Senator Henry Cabot Lodge, of Massachusetts, you can go plumb to hell. You have nothing to say about it."

Cabot spluttered at the red-faced Hanna that he would take his fight for gold to the convention floor. Hanna was unmoved by this threat. "I don't care a damn where you make your fight," replied Hanna.

Things did cool down after Cabot stormed away, and Hanna sent an emissary to Cabot's hotel to show the senator the plank. Written weeks earlier, it was firmly for the gold standard, unless and until the European powers agreed on bimetallism and set a consistent and hard ratio between gold and silver.

It didn't matter much in the end anyway, according to the newspaper reports Hay read in Paris. The revolt of the silver backers from west of the Mississippi didn't happen. Only a handful of delegates bolted. The "sound money" gold plank had plenty of hedge in it—"we'll willingly follow Europe into bimetallism" left a lot of wiggle room—and it won the support of eight of every nine delegates. McKinley took the Republican presidential nomination on the first ballot, with delegates to spare. The McKinley team didn't even bother to correct the record when Henry Cabot Lodge took credit for the convention's gold plank. McKinley was going to need the senator's help in Massachusetts in the general election that fall.

NEWS OF MCKINLEY'S nomination greatly cheered John Hay, as did the gently stirring and pleasant June winds on which his entourage drifted through Europe; it was wet and gray for only the first few days in Paris. After that, the skies brightened without bringing heat or humidity. Hay and Adams managed to steer the group clear of social engagements in Paris, so the party of four remained a tidy little world unto itself . . . but it was not dull. The contrast between Adams and Elizabeth Warder made for interesting squalls of light and shade. Elizabeth had an electric energy and, as Hay described it, "the happy gift of spontaneous enthusiasm." At the theater one night, she and Helen got themselves worked into such a fit, laughing at all the dewy Parisians weeping and blowing their noses at a broad and artless melodrama, that Hay feared "the police would put us out." Elizabeth next fell under the spell of the pythons at the zoological gardens in Antwerp. They couldn't drag her away that afternoon, and when the four tourists passed another zoo in Amsterdam a few days later, she grabbed a surprised Adams by the arm, announced she must see her dear new friends at once, and led him off to the snake cages.

Adams followed Elizabeth in spite of himself, taken up by the lift of the young woman's momentary fancy. Most of the time, though, Henry managed to keep Miss Warder and the rest of the world at a safe distance, by offering little more of his phlegmatic self than amusing and caustic grousing. The season's salons, said Adams, were "what they always are, a chaos of shrieking artists, each one trying to carry some trick to an excess which will advertise him"; the theaters were full of ugly middle-aged women who "seem to enjoy most the crudest indecencies"; the city's celebrated chanteuse struck him as a raunchy and *utterly* inane exhibitionist. He did relish taking his companions to the skeleton beer shop for a drink one evening. The waitstaff dressed as undertakers, and human skulls and bones hung over the dim-lit coffin-tables. They celebrated death and decay with sincere feeling at the Cabaret du Néant ("Cabaret of Nothingness"), and Adams claimed to be right at home amid the ghoulish display. "We . . . did the microbes de la mort, etc.," he wrote to a friend, "which seemed to me rather the most suitable show in Paris." He found little else as charming as nothingness.

The group was small enough that the magnetic tension between the polar opposites of Elizabeth and Henry was always present, and Hay knew where he tended. He could not agree with his old friend about the charms of nothingness, or the "too too utter" pointlessness of the modern age, or the inevitability of the coming collapse of human institutions; Hay would not agree with Adams's fatalistic insistence that it *did not matter* whether it was McKinley or Cleveland on the American throne a year from now. Hay found himself drawn toward the youthful *enthusiasms* of Elizabeth and his daughter Helen. John Hay still wanted to be among the living, with something at stake. He braved a series of footsore marches through Paris and its outskirts and then around Belgium and Holland, pleased to find his own robust appetite for happy experience still intact. After a long day of sightseeing in Amsterdam, he arose early to write to his wife: "Our legs are broken and our eyes are like boiled gooseberries with the work of going through the Museums. . . . The treasures of art this city contains are simply amazing." He was bowled over anew at revisiting *The Night Watch*, one of his favorite Rembrandts, as powerful to him as when he had first seen it. His newfound avidity even got the better of him one day at the château in Loches, when he followed Del in a dangerous and forbidden sprint up into one of the towers. (They had missed the warning signs.)

Hay's regret at the beginning of this trip was that he didn't have more time with his son, who arrived in Paris with his two traveling companions when the rest of the group was more than a month into the tour. Del's earlier European trips had never taken him much beyond Paris, and Hay was looking forward to showing his son Florence and Venice and Munich and Vienna, his tramping grounds when he was not much older than his son was now. But the boy had his own agenda; he was only on hand for a few days in France before he and Reynolds Hitt peeled off to go see the team from Yale row at Henley. He promised to return to the group in Florence, or Bologna, or somewhere in Italy.

Del and Reynolds left behind the third of their group, Eugene Hale, who was busy mooning over Elizabeth Warder and couldn't tear himself away, Hay noted. So when Hay and Adams loaded their charges onto a train for the ride from Paris into northern Italy, the party was five. Six if you counted the maid, Charley, who couldn't stop shaking her head at two young women who would give up the comforts of the Hôtel Westminster in Paris for the wilds of northern Italy. Hay was getting a real kick out of Eugene by then. Young Hale had taken up the role of eager museum acolyte in place of Del. Hay watched the boy take the time to really *see* the paintings, to ask questions; Eugene made mental notes of the artist, the school, the dates. Maybe it was all just to impress Miss Warder, but Hay encouraged Eugene nonetheless, and he enjoyed watching the young man on trains and in hotels, working diligently at the sewing patterns Elizabeth had bought for him in Paris. "You never saw anything so funny as Eugene Hale with his embroidery," Hay wrote to Clara. He "has worked like a Turk over his, making full as much progress as Elizabeth." Hay added, "You ought to have a piece on hand to occupy him when he comes to the Fells."

When the caravan rode the train through the Alps toward Italy, Hay found himself awestruck and somewhat churlish that nobody else paid much mind to the view out the train window. "I don't know what to make of the youth of the present day," Hay mused when they arrived in Milan. "While we were passing through some of the loveliest scenery of the world, Eugene and Elizabeth played cribbage, and Helen kept her nose between the leaves of a novel." Probably a good thing Del hadn't been along for the ride. He was likely to have spent it in the bar, drinking beer with Uncle Henry.

THERE WERE MOMENTS of tour bliss in Italy, and Hay was surprised at his capacity for new thrills. "I used to care nothing in particular for Giovanni Bellini," he mused. "Now his pictures charm and attract me more than anything in Venice." But Hay's mood was increasingly ragged as the trip wore on. He was frustrated that Italy was so backward. Why did the *valet de place* at his favorite hotel in Verona smell "of garlic in a style that drove me frantic"? Why was it impossible to find out which candidate the Democrats had nominated to run against McKinley? Were the timetables for Italian trains merely for decoration? The trains themselves were often slow, hot, and packed, and Hay and Adams noted that they had gone weeks without running into anyone they knew. For Adams it was another sign of the decay of society. "Decent people have stopped travelling," he told Hay, and Hay could not argue. "Formerly everyone you met in a first-class carriage was a person of some distinction. Now they are not even clean," he wrote to Clara one morning. "Where they get their money is a dark mystery."

By mid-July, the girls' need of excitement and adventure was taking its toll on the older men. Hay had started calling Elizabeth "the cyclone," and not always fondly. Adams was weary of being "whacked . . . around Europe," and his private letters were becoming less generous toward the females of the party.

The return of Del and Reynolds Hitt grew the procession's youthful number back to five, and not happily. Del's presence was especially hard on his father. Hay had been disappointed to have his son miss so much of the trip on account of sporting events, but he knew better than to press. Del was still, as Adams noted, a spoiled little boy and unwilling to be dragged where he didn't want to go. Hay reported glumly to his wife about their son's dilatory influence on the traveling party: "Eugene seemed to be enjoying the pictures while with us. . . . But as soon as Del arrived and began his ignorant buffoonery about them, calling them old daubs, etc., Eugene gave way and said he did not like them much himself." Del did allow as how he had actually *liked* Venice. "High praise from Sir Hubert," his father sniffed.

By the time he hustled his flock through Munich—they had to take a pass on Vienna—dropped Henry Adams in Paris, and then hopped back across the channel to London, Hay was a knackered soul. A peaceful Sunday worship at Westminster Abbey set him on edge: "An unbroken stream of Americans kept crowding in till the seats were occupied, and then they packed the aisles," Hay whined. "Where they came from I have no idea. No race so restless ever appeared on the face of the earth." The good and refreshing news for Hay was that the Democrats had apparently lost their good sense and selected as their presidential candidate a thirty-six-year-old Populist sympathizer from Nebraska named William Jennings Bryan. The ex-congressman had shot to the nomination with a dramatic convention speech condemning the idle rich and banking interests for putting their narrow welfare above their less fortunate fellow countrymen. Bryan argued that their insistence on the gold standard had been punishing to the simple country lawyer and doctor, the Main Street merchant, the miner, the laborer, the farmer: "We beg no longer; we entreat no more; we petition no more. We defy them," Bryan preached. "Having behind us the producing masses of this nation and the world, supported by the commercial interests, the laboring interests, and the toilers everywhere, we will answer their demand for a gold standard by saying to them: You shall not press down upon the brow of labor this crown of thorns; you shall not crucify mankind upon a cross of gold."

The more Hay read about Bryan, the more he thought him a crank. Hay was rich and idle himself, but he wasn't going around sticking thorns in anybody's skull. He took to calling Senator Bryan "the Baby Demosthenes," "the Boy Orator," "this blatant wild ass of the Prairie." If "the men who have money refuse to do anything in their own defense," Hay would say of Bryan, "they will deserve to be robbed to the enamel of their teeth." But as he reminded Adams, "In politics the appeal to the lower motives is generally for the moment successful."

Adams was telling friends that he preferred what he saw as Bryan's destructive lunacy to "the crushing intellectual imbecility of McKinley and his Ohio-Pennsylvania following." He didn't think McKinley was up to the job, and he didn't think Bryan could destroy anything worth saving. What did it matter who won the next presidential election? Nobody could save the patient. "The whole carcass is rotten with worms—socialist worms, anarchist worms, Jew worms, clerical worms—God alone knows his own microbes," he wrote to Hay from Paris. "The very brain and heart are alive with morbid bacteria. The very source of life is tainted. Nothing like it was ever seen in history."

Hay could tell already that this campaign was going to be livelier than any in recent memory, and some fun, too: he would be needling Adams all the way to November and beyond. "Once more, let me tell you, young man, now in the morning of your life," he wrote to Adams about the upcoming campaign, "there is nothing unimportant." And yet John Hay did not choose to let Adams in on his private meetings in London with Sir William Harcourt and Arthur Balfour. Balfour, the prime minister's closest political ally, had summoned Hay. Everybody, it would appear, wanted to talk with him about McKinley's position on Venezuela.

Hay was fairly puffed up about the whole episode, and pleased with how very *diplomatically* he had handled it. He had been forthright and direct with his British friends, and instead of making light of it to Adams, he had dutifully reported the talks to Secretary of State Olney. "In neither case did I seek the interview and in neither case, I hope I need not say, did I assume any representative character, or any means of information not open to everybody," Hay wrote to Olney. "From what I have been able to gather in conversation I infer that most of the leading men are convinced that Lord Salisbury's tone a year ago was a mistake, and that our attitude is on the whole reasonable. Everybody wants the matter settled if it can be done without damage to the pride and prestige of England."

On July 31, 1896, having posted the letter to Olney and dropped Elizabeth Warder with her parents in London, Hay and his daughter Helen passed again through Liverpool's Riverside Station and settled into their separate staterooms on the *Teutonic* for their trip home. This was one of the fastest ships on the Atlantic, propelled by triple-expansion engines and the newest in forced-air technology, and could run more than five hundred miles in a single day, which was all to the good. Hay was anxious to get back to New York, where Mark Hanna and a few others in the McKinley brain trust awaited his arrival. The ship made one brief stop at port in Ireland to pick up passengers and mail. There was a letter waiting there for him, from Adams, who was still in Paris recuperating from the summer's taxing excursion. "Dear Pilgrim, My last benediction dear! Dear!! What a good time you're going to have! . . . Now is your time, if you want a career in politics. You will undoubtedly get chawed up, but you will have the fun. . . . May you ride the whirlwind. I know you can't direct it. At least we have had an awfully pleasant vacation."

CHAPTER SIX

Still at Sea

The day John Hay shipped out of Liverpool, Sam Clemens approached the far shore of England, 250 miles away. Clemens wasn't paying much mind to the gold standard or diplomatic relations with Great Britain or the upcoming presidential election back home. He was simply looking forward to landing at the Southampton pier and to completing his circumnavigation of the planet. Livy, meanwhile, was pining to get off the ship so that she could get their threesome settled into a house in the hush of the English countryside and send the signal for Susy and Jean and Katy Leary to book their passage from New York. Just two more weeks at most, Livy reckoned, and her household would be whole again. Finally, for the first time in more than a year, she would have all her daughters back under her watchful care.

Reports from back home in the previous few months had only made Livy more anxious. Jean had suffered a seizure so harrowing that Aunt Sue had called in a specialist. The doctor diagnosed epilepsy, for which little could be done. He counseled Sue to be on the lookout for more attacks, which, "though disagreeable to see," he said, were neither harmful nor dangerous. "Keep her quiet, loosen her dress, put a spoon between her teeth, and cool cloths to her head," was his advice. Susy's situation was no more comforting. She had run away from her aunt's house in Elmira and was staying with friends in Hartford, spending her time alone at the Clemens's now unrented house or with the gaggle of "mental scientists" down the street. Their "mind cure," according to Susy's reports, had proved a great help in combating her physical maladies, her dark moods, and her social ineptitude. But Livy had been disquieted by the growing intervals between letters from Susy and by the chords of false and forced optimism in the notes she did write. Susy and Jean were in need of their mother, and Livy meant to give them what they needed. Her husband, meanwhile, was going to require some fortifying as well.

The final legs of the lecture tour—a six-month run through India and South

Africa—had taken the last of the luster off the honorable debt-clearing crusade Sam Clemens had envisioned when he started out. The carbuncles had finally abated, but Clemens arrived in Bombay in January of 1896 with a cold that had settled deep in his lungs, and he fought it for the entire passage through India. The doctors were little help; he did manage to starve it out one day, he believed, by limiting his diet to liquids and cigar smoke, but his lungs never really cleared. "I barked at audiences all about India for six weeks," he later wrote. "Then the cough expired by statute of limitation."

India's heat was debilitating and maybe even dangerous to the weakened lecturer. He had been so frightened by tingling and numbness in his left arm one morning that he sent for a doctor. The doctor ordered him to bed for ten days, all engagements canceled, at which point Clemens sagged into a depression and pulled Livy in with him. Factoring in all the canceled lecture dates and the travel expenses and the doctor's bills, Livy explained in a letter to her sister, Sue, the best they could hope to net from more than two months in India was maybe $1,000. "You know I have pretty good courage, but sometimes it comes over me like an overwhelming wave, that it is to be bitterness and disappointment to the end. . . . Still, most of the time I keep up my courage. Mr. Clemens has not as much as I wish he had."

South Africa had been easier in some ways. Clemens recovered some of his strength on the seventeen-day crossing to Durban, and though the country lacked the beauty and exoticism of India, he did find political issues worthy of investigation. Everybody in South Africa—Boers, Uitlanders, British mining engineers, and German businessmen—was talking about the recent failed attempt by a militia led by a Scotsman named Jameson to overthrow the sitting government of the Transvaal Republic, led by Boer president Paul Kruger. Joseph Chamberlain's disavowal of the Jameson Raid notwithstanding, the English financier and head of the British South Africa Company, Sir Cecil Rhodes, had been fingered as the mastermind of the armed attack on the government of the old Dutch-descended settlers (and their commercial sponsors in Berlin).

Clemens had taken the long view of the incident at first, assessing the Jameson Raid as another episode in a long history of "land robbery" and "claim jumping" by the Imperial Powers. "Africa has been as coolly divided up and portioned out among the gang as if they had bought it and paid for it. And now straightaway they are beginning the old game again—to steal each other's grabbings."

After a month of drilling down on the particulars of the misbegotten adventure in the Transvaal, he still found it difficult to untangle the politics and the morality of the situation or to take sides. He bent his efforts instead to a statistics-based assessment of the military tactics employed by Jameson's raiders. Their mistake, Clemens noted, was in ignoring the precedents of history.

The British and the Boers had wrangled over this territory once before, in a three-month-long war fifteen years earlier. The casualty count for the four battles comprising that war was seven hundred British soldiers lost, as against four Boers. The British mistake in planning the later excursion, Clemens would say, was in failing to use those counts as a guide: Against 8,000 Boers, Jameson would need 240,000 men to even up the odds. He had on hand 530. Clemens also questioned Jameson's judgment in breaking out the new five-hundred-round-per-minute Maxim machine guns against the cagey Boers, who were dead shots and liked to hide behind rocks. "He worked the Maxims so hard upon the rocks that five of them became disabled—five of the Maxims, not the rocks. It is believed that upwards of 100,000 rounds of ammunition of the various kinds were fired during the 21 hours that the battles lasted. *One man killed*. He must have been much mutilated."

The downside of South Africa had been the separations from his wife and daughter; Clemens had grown worried about Livy's state of mind, so he did his final six-week sweep alone except for his lecture agent, Mr. Smythe, while Livy and Clara stayed behind to rest at a seaside hotel in Durban. Livy sent her husband off with strict orders to write to her every day and to cable her at the first sign of sickness. She instructed Mr. Smythe to make sure her husband ate well and got sufficient rest.

Sam's long missives to Livy had been cheery at first, wishing she and Clara could be on hand with him to "join culture & beauty to talent & make the fambly show up fine." But just ten days out, his letters took a turn. "I am driven—driven—driven—& without you to save me from blunders I make them all the time."

"Con*sound* it! it was such a *cussed* mistake that I left you two behind," he wrote to Clara a day later. "Good bye, Ash Cat. I love you very dearly; & as for Mamma, nothing can describe it."

"Pretty soon we will be together, again, & then we'll stay together Sweetheart," he wrote to Livy after nearly a month on his own. "I am homesick for you all the time."

The receipts remained a disappointment, and he was horrified to learn that the promised serialization of his Joan of Arc novel appeared to be on hold. "I find myself well scared," he wrote to a friend back in New York. "I don't think it is of any use for me to struggle against my ill luck any longer. If I had the family in a comfortable poor-house I would kill myself."

By the time he made his way back to Livy and Clara and got them all settled on the RMS *Norman* for the trip north into English summer, Sam Clemens had a lot of reasons to kick himself. He had worn himself ragged on the lecture circuit for a full year, and for what? He had raised maybe a quarter of the money he had hoped to earn on the platform, and he hadn't even started to write the travel book he had intended to nearly finish while on the trip. His great hopes for *Personal Recollections of Joan of Arc* had been badly shaken. Prospects for big sales appeared dim. He was too embarrassed to return to the States until his financial affairs were in better shape, and he couldn't afford the expense of living in America anyway.

The only good news: the worst was about to be over.

When they floated into Southampton on July 31, 1896, Clemens was at last within reach of being able to reunite his entire family. Susy, Jean, and Katy Leary were set to sail from New York in five days, which meant they would be together again, all of them, in less than two weeks. Sam Clemens had half a mind to send for their old butler, George Griffin. They would rent a nice big house in the English countryside—cheap. Livy was already talking about what kind of house they might find, and where. The Isle of Wight would be nice, or maybe somewhere closer to London so that Clara could be within reach of a good piano instructor.

Clemens meant to get right to work and have his round-the-world travel book completed by the first of November, and he suspected the reporting he had done on the Jameson adventure in South Africa might just give him material enough for a second book. His new best friend, Henry Rogers—the man who was running Standard Oil just then—was renegotiating a new publishing contract, playing a robber baron's game of pitting Clemens's longtime publisher, Frank Bliss, against the new suitor, Harper & Brothers, which was already publishing his Joan of Arc book. Rogers was aiming to line up all the copyrights for "Mark Twain" under one flag, get the older books back into circulation again, and make sure the profits would go to Livy and the girls. Rogers was also working up better terms for any future books. Sometimes it overwhelmed Clemens to think of all Rogers's effort on his behalf; a man he had known only a few years was doing all this out of friendship, pure and simple. Maybe things were looking up for the Clemens clan after all. He might yet be strong enough for a lucrative season of lecturing in London.

The minute they got off the boat and hit land, Livy went down in a heap: she had sprained her ankle.

CLARA WAS DEPUTIZED to run around the countryside south of London looking for a rentable house, so Livy was in the hotel room when the cable arrived that day, August 5. Susy, Jean, and Katy were delayed a week, it said. No reason was given. They would be aboard the *St. Louis* instead, a week behind schedule.

This unwanted news did allow Clara more time to find a house, but the best she could do was a temporary rental in Guildford, an hour from London by rail. She knew her father would like the sun-splashed morning room and, especially, the billiard table of Highfield House. Livy was not well pleased, though it did give her five weeks' leeway to find a long-term residence suitable for the winter, and the reasonable rental price of Highfield included a housekeeper and maids. At least Livy would have a proper place to welcome her daughters when they did arrive.

The mood at Highfield headed toward jolly as Susy and Jean's new travel day approached, as evidenced by Clara's letter to "Mark Twain's" London publisher, Andrew Chatto, who was to be their first visitor to Guildford. "My Father has asked me to write his notes for him this morning as he is unable to use his right hand owing to a cut in the left, his leg was also injured trying to walk to the village the other day, & his hair is falling out fast," Clara wrote. "These he considers causes enough to be shoving all his affairs onto the shoulders of an other. He wants you to know that we shall be very glad indeed to see you on Monday & we hope that you may have as pleasant a day for travelling as it is today." Sam Clemens even joined the women in the renewed house scouting and showed remarkable patience.

The air around the Guildford rental began to get a bit electric, however, on the day the *St. Louis* left New York for Southampton: no cable arrived announcing the Clemens girls departure. A cable from Livy's sister came two days later, explaining that Susy was not well and it wasn't clear when she would be sufficiently recovered to travel. That settled it for Livy. She started preparing herself for another leg of her yearlong journey. There was a steamship leaving Southampton for New York the next day, and Livy was going to be on it. If her stricken daughter was unable to come to her, she would go to her daughter. They had been apart long enough. There would be *no more delays*. Clemens was not the man to calm his wife when she was in a state; he was pulled without much effort into the addling web of family anxiety.

He hurried off to the post office at Livy's insistence to send a cable instructing Katy to get Susy back to Elmira—Livy didn't trust her to the care of the "mind cure" crowd around Hartford—and to cable news of Susy's condition right away. The response did not bring much comfort: "Wait for cablegram in the morning." Clemens sent a renewed demand for immediate and specific news of Susy, then prowled the grounds of the Guildford post office the rest of the afternoon and evening, checking in with beleaguered clerks about cables addressed "Clemens, Guildford." He was still pacing around in the dark after eleven o'clock that night, but when the doors finally closed for good at midnight, there was nothing left for him but to trudge home to Livy empty handed.

Livy had spent the day in a round of frantic packing and had worried herself to exhaustion. The ship was to leave Southampton for New York at noon the next day, and Livy was going to be on it unless positive good news awaited them the next morning, she informed him. Her husband could not dissuade her.

THE CABLE THEY found in Southampton the next morning was terse, and its message mixed: recovery would be long but certain. Sam Clemens was relieved—*certain recovery*, it promised—but Livy was not convinced. She and Clara were getting on the boat! Clemens said he would stay and await more definite news and sail in three days if needed. He got the baggage loaded onto the SS *Paris* and nodded good-bye to his wife; a show of physical affection in public, even in duress, was beyond him.

As soon as Sam left the ship, Livy realized there were things her husband had to know, things she hadn't told him, so she sat down and wrote out a list: a few bills had to be paid, their tableware was arriving any day from Hartford, and the housekeeper in Guildford, Emily, had asked for the day off on the twenty-sixth. "Youth, please, you must remember these things." She managed to get the letter of instructions off just before the ship sailed.

CLEMENS WAS LUCKY to have the company of Mr. Smythe to take his mind off the gnawing discomfort occasioned by this new and unexpected scattering of his family. The two men walked into town to have lunch that afternoon and to do a few errands, but Clemens was so distracted he forgot to send the cable to America warning of Livy's arrival the following Saturday. He and Smythe had to make a return trip to the village post office late that afternoon to get that done. After dinner that night, Clemens forced Smythe to stay up late playing billiards and meanwhile persuaded him to bed down in Guildford for a few days. Sam Clemens could not stand to be without company even in the best of times, and a houseful of maids didn't count.

Clemens thought he could entice Smythe into a long visit by making a gift of the pajamas someone had given him in India. The pajamas were not a big draw, but Smythe knew a man in need when he saw one, and he made arrangements for a quick trip to London the next day to pick up enough clothes and shaving gear for an extended stay. It would be weeks, at best, before Mrs. Clemens returned.

After the two finally retired from their billiards game that first evening, Clemens went to his bedroom and had a fitful sleep. The night was too cold for comfort, even after he got up and shut the windows, and when he arose a second time to look for extra blankets, the best he could find was Livy's dress cloak, which she left hanging in the bathroom. The thought of Livy at sea without her cloak or her gray shawl (he had found that, too) filled him with remorse. For the rest of the long night, his godforsaken overactive conscience clawed at him. When he hauled his haggard self out of bed the next morning, he was pining for Livy and upset with himself for allowing this new separation. He wrote her a long and remorseful letter that morning. He promised to do all the chores she had laid out for him. He promised to look after the bills. He promised to remember Emily's day out on the twenty-sixth.

SMYTHE MADE IT back later that day, and the pair fell into a round of smoking, long walks, short meals, smoking, reading, smoking, letter writing, smoking, and hours upon hours of evening billiards. A few days into their bachelor visit, a package arrived from Clemens's London publisher, Chatto & Windus, with five books and a sheaf of reviews of *Joan of Arc*. Some of the reviews were pretty good, certainly better than the notice in that skinflint Whitelaw Reid's *New York Tribune*, whose critic had indicted him for lacking "a streak of poetic genius."

The *Daily Chronicle* of London was his favorite of the new bunch, the one Susy Clemens would most appreciate. Susy had been his spur in the writing of *Joan of Arc* and a good bit of its inspiration. His oldest daughter had a rare and fleeting kind of courage. She was the only one in his family brave enough to reproach him for not wringing the most out of his prodigious native talents, for playing it safe by settling for "Mark Twain" the jester. "How I hate that name!" Susy had once told a friend. "My father should not be satisfied with it! . . . He should show himself the great writer that he is, not merely a funny man. Funny! That's all people see in him—a maker of funny speeches."

He had started in on the story of Joan of Arc, the brave and selfless seventeen-year-old heroine and martyr, with Susy as a guide, and when he had finished a day's work on the manuscript and read it aloud to the family, it was Susy's reaction he watched for, and it was her flinty sense of selflessness and public virtue he played to. He suspected that Joan's momentous change from "playful girl" to unquestioned leader of a vast army would appeal to his shaky oldest daughter.

Susy became *Joan*'s great champion, and while his oldest remained the person in the family most likely to be rattled by her father's sudden outbursts of rage, Clemens could tell the new novel had raised him up in her eyes. "The character of Joan is pure and perfect," Susy reported to Clara. "Many of Joan's words and sayings are historically correct and Papa cries when he reads them. In fact he almost always fills up when reading any speech of hers."

Well, Susy would love the *Daily Chronicle* review. "A work destined to be remembered for its humour least of all," the notice read, and it concluded by seconding another recent review: "The creator of *Tom Sawyer* is something far more than a mere man of letters, even a great one; he is something far more than a humourist, even a thoroughly genial and whole-souled one—he is a great writer. Like Balzac himself, he can afford to let the critics have their say about his style, in the consciousness that he has understood and expressed the workings of the human heart." Sam Clemens went straight to his desk to write a letter with news of the good reviews. That would cheer the entire family, especially Susy.

After he had sent off that missive, he remembered to write a quick note of thanks to Andrew Chatto. "I am cumulatively obliged to you. The Chronicle notice is very, very fine. If ever I lecture again—but I hope I shan't—I shall be glad to be interviewed for the Chronicle, & you & I must not forget that."

That letter was still on his desk, unsealed, and Clemens was mindlessly puttering around the dining room in Guildford—*will there be room for the tableware when it arrives?*—when a maid put the just-arrived cablegram in his hand. As he reached out for it, he would later tell his brother, he had "supposed it was going to be something pleasant."

HE DID NOT share the contents of the cable with the maids or even with Smythe. When he had sufficiently gathered his wits, he sat down at a table, numb, to add a postscript to the letter to Chatto. "Will you hand the enclosed half-sheet to the Chronicle . . ." No, he thought, and crossed out "the Chronicle." "Will you hand the enclosed half-sheet to any newspaper you please—no *copy* it & give them the copy, so that they will not know it came from me. I have many personal friends in England & they should know of my disaster. Susan Olivia Clemens, aged 24, eldest daughter of S. L. Clemens (Mark Twain), died on Tuesday of this week in the home she was reared in, in the city of Hartford, Connecticut. The illness was brief, the disease brain fever. News of the illness, with the intimation that it was not serious, was received by cable on Friday last, & Mrs. Clemens & her second daughter sailed from Southampton the next day, hoping & expecting to be able to bring the patient to England for some months' stay. They are still at sea."

HE LOCKED HIMSELF away in the morning room after that and fingered through the few letters he had received in the four days since he had seen Livy off on the steamship voyage. Jean had written, and Livy's brother, Charley, and her sister, Sue Crane. The news was dated; the letters had all been written a week to ten days earlier. All he could gather was that Susy had been taken to the Clemenses' house in Hartford to fight off the brain fever or meningitis or whatever it was. He was a little comforted to know that his oldest daughter had been at their home in Hartford when the end came, but the image that kept pushing itself into his mind was Susy, *at this moment*, in her coffin. They would take her to Elmira for burial, he knew, so she would soon be laid out at her aunt Sue's house, where the Clemens family had spent most of the summers of Susy's growing up. He hoped they would put her in the library, *for there she & Clara & I mostly played when we were children together and happy* . . .

This final forced separation he apprehended as his punishment, and as he turned it over in his mind, he was convinced his sentence was well earned. He was to blame for Susy's death after all. This disaster was the culminating blow, the destined outcome, of the myriad ways great and small in which he had failed his wife and daughters: the Webster bankruptcy, the hundreds of thousands of dollars thrown away on that wild printing contraption, the stubborn insistence on making a public display of saving himself and his precious reputation on the round-the-world tour, with or without Susy and Jean. *I have brought misfortune and sorrow on this family.*

It drizzled all day in Guildford, and the raw, damp gray of ache thrummed in on his lonesome vigil. There were shy knocks at his door throughout the morning and into the afternoon; the maids wondered, every few hours, if there was anything Mr. Clemens needed. When Smythe came to collect him for the daily trip into the village for lunch Clemens did his best to decline without raising suspicion, but he was pretty sure he had failed. Not long after Smythe left for lunch, the housekeeper forced herself into the morning room and, without speaking a word, placed a decanter of port wine and a plate of biscuits at Clemens's elbow, then backed out in silence. *The maids seem to suspect something is the matter.*

He could not stop thinking of Livy. The ship carrying his wife, the *Paris*, would not arrive in New York for another three days. Livy had three days of blissful ignorance before the ax fell on her. He would send a cable to Mr. Rogers tomorrow, asking him to have a mutual friend, a doctor of medicine, board the *Paris* in quarantine and break the awful news to Livy. If his wife made it to the dock unaware, Clemens feared, a big, tearful welcoming party would be too shocking for her fragile heart; she would come near to dying herself. And he meant to provide his wife with what solace his own distant words could bring; he could do that much. Livy would cling for life and sanity to her Christian faith, to her cherished certainty that she and Susy would be together again in some heavenly afterlife. He had tried, in spite of himself, to be her partner in this strange conviction. "Let us believe in it!" he had written to her the year before. "I will believe in it with you. It had been the belief of the wise and thoughtful of many countries for three thousand years; let us accept their verdict; we cannot frame one that is more reasonable or probable. I will try never to doubt it again." He could not now allow Livy to doubt his sincerity in that.

So Sam Clemens sat down and wrote his wife that he, too, blasphemous old apostate that he was, *knew* that Susy was in a better place. "I would not bring her back—no, not for the riches of a thousand worlds. She has found the richest gift that this world can offer; I would not rob her of it." Then he assured Livy of her own innocence in the horrible long-unfolding episode of Susy's demise; their daughter's death might have been an inside job, but Livy had had no role in it. "How you wrought for her!" Clemens reminded his wife. "How you gave yourself to her, night & day, at cost of strength & sleep; how faithful you were to her; you did all for her that a mother could do for a child, you were all to her that a mother could be; let it assuage your grief to know that you have nothing to reproach yourself with."

The rest of the afternoon he spent reading and rereading the recent letters from Hartford, and when he had wrung from them all he could, he began searching his belongings for any letters he had received from Susy in the separation of the past year. He couldn't remember any offhand, and his despair grew as he rifled his papers for some tender word from the daughter he would never again see. *No letter from Susy—oh, not so much as a line.* At six o'clock that evening he sat down and wrote a postscript to his letter to Livy. "Sue says that in our house after they took her there she was up & dressed and writing all the time—poor troubled head!" he wrote. "I hope they kept every scrap; for they must often have suspected that these were the last things that would flow from that subtle brain. I know that if they are there you will find them. I wish she had written something to me—but I did not deserve it."

HE SENT THE cablegram to Mr. Rogers the next day, posted his letter to Livy, and then reentered the puny society of Highfield House. He took his walks and his meals with Smythe (they even started house hunting again) and in the afternoon and after dinner he spent his time stalking the edges of the billiard table, stick in hand, measuring the angle of the next shot, concentrating his mind on the complicated scoring, reminding Smythe of their shared disdain for fluking—anything to keep his mind sufficiently occupied to block out the sharp stabs of grief and resentment. "Hour by hour my sense of the calamity that has overtaken us closes down heavier & heavier upon me," he wrote in a second letter to Livy, "& now for 48 hours there is a form of words that runs in my head with ceaseless iteration—without stop or pause—'I shall never see her again, I shall never see her again.' *You* will see the sacred face once more—I am so thankful for that."

TWO DAYS AFTER the *Paris*'s scheduled arrival in New York, there was a cablegram from Livy. She asked after his health, and he took her meaning: she had survived the first shock, and this knowledge was the first relief he had had in six days. He lashed himself to routine after that: a bath at nine, breakfast, a short look at the newspapers, and then a two- or three-hour walk through the last summer blooms of the English countryside, luncheon, billiards, rereading the old letters from Hartford, dinner. "After dinner, billiards till 1 a.m., or a trifle earlier if Smythe finds he is no longer able to stand up," Clemens explained in a note to Livy. "I get so tired that in bed if I drive poor Susy out of my mind I go to sleep at once. I do not wake until I am called."

TEN DAYS AFTER Susy's death, he had not yet heard from the world outside his Guildford cottage. The death notice in the London papers had not fetched a single note of condolence. Neither had letters arrived from *any* of his friends in America. The one card of sympathy that had been delivered was from his new publisher, Harper & Brothers. Every day he watched for the postman, and every day he came up empty handed. Clemens knew nothing of Susy's funeral, of the state of Livy's health, of when the remains of his family might return. He still did not know exactly how Susy had been carried off.

"Forasmuch as you had sailed, did those friends think none was left behind who would care to know the pathetic details of those last days?" he wailed in a letter to Livy. "I get a cablegram: . . . 'Susy could not stand brain congestion and meningitis and was peacefully released to-day'—& I sit here & try to believe that there are any human beings in the world, friends or foes, civilized or savage, who would close their lips *there*, & leave me these many, many, many days eating my heart out with longings for the tidings that never come. . . . I think that Jean could have remembered me. Or Katy, or Twichell, or somebody."

Eleven days after, and still no letter. Was it him? Had his selfishness been found out by the others? Had it repulsed his friends, his family? Did they indict him for abandoning his wife and daughters in their time of need? Were his feelings, his hurts, not worthy of consideration? And what about Susy? He still could not find a scrap of a letter she had written to him during the latest separation. Had the merest scintilla of a memory of him been a part of her final days? He started to beat up on himself.

> My remorse does not deceive me. I know that if she were back I should soon be as neglectful of her as I was before—it is our way. We think we would do better, because of our lesson. But it is a fallacy. Our natures would go back to what they had always been, & our conduct would obey their commands. My selfishness & indolence would resume their power & I should be no better father to her, no more obliging friend and encourager & helper than I was before. If I could call up a single instance where I laid aside my own projects & desires & put myself to real inconvenience to procure a pleasure for her I would forget all things else to remember that.

Next day, day twelve after Susy, was bleak and gray, Sunday-like, he called it, and the postman brought no relief to the door of Highfield House, Guildford. "Not a line yet, not a single line. It seems as if I cannot bear it. . . . It is an odious world, an horrible world—it is Hell; the true one, not the lying invention of the superstitious; & we have come to it from elsewhere to expiate our sins. And now what can we do? Where can we go & hide ourselves till we earn release? For what have we further to do in this world?"

A few days later, the postman delivered to Clemens a second pathetic letter of sympathy. "No," he answered the friend in New Jersey, "there is nothing you can do for me, I am hurt past help."

HE MET THE return ship at the docks in Southampton, eager to reunite with all he had left in the world: Livy, Clara, Jean, and Katy Leary. Livy was more drawn than usual and dressed in mourning black, which set off her frightfully pale complexion. She had not seen the sun for a week, having spent the entire voyage hiding in the cabins Henry Rogers had secured for the Clemens party so that they could avoid the pitying gazes of fellow passengers. Rogers had also put in Livy's hands a package of letters that told the story of the long (and now completed) negotiations he had made on behalf of the "Mark Twain" publishing interests. While not busy overseeing Standard Oil, Rogers had all but secured ownership of the copyrights of "Mark Twain's" earlier books in Livy's name, and he was close to working out favorable terms with Harper & Brothers for the trade editions of new books and with Bliss for the subscription editions. Clemens almost wept as he read those letters. *Somebody* was thinking of him. *Somebody* was protecting his battered family.

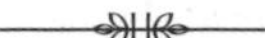

CLEMENS HAD NO desire to linger at the scene of his despond. He also thought a big city would be easier on them all. The day after the Clemens women disembarked in Southampton, they packed up the house in Guildford and went to London, "not to live in public there," he told a friend, "but to hide from men for a time, & let the wounds heal." We "shall get a house there & shut ourselves up in it & bar the doors & pull down the blinds & take up the burden of life again, with one helper the fewer to put heart into my work as it goes along. I shall write the book of the voyage—I shall bury myself in it."

CHAPTER SEVEN

Accepting the Inevitable, or Not

John Hay was something near giddy as the presidential campaign heated up in the fall of 1896; his friend McKinley seemed a good bet to win the nation's highest office and the vast spoils that came with it, which meant Hay stood a fair chance of becoming the new ambassador to the Court of St. James's. If things went well, he would be in London to take up the post before the next spring. He had certainly won the right to McKinley's sincere consideration, having applied himself to the Major's campaign with powerful efficiency and an equanimity rarely seen in politics. Hay had been an early and loyal supporter, which the Major was not likely to forget. Late-coming McKinley supporters like Henry Cabot Lodge and Theodore Roosevelt had been at pains to exhibit their allegiance to the Republican standard-bearer. The dynamic duo—leaders of the Reed faction at the convention—journeyed through New England and western New York that fall of 1896, braying on the stump for McKinley, and then swung into the nominee's hometown, where the candidate himself was sitting tight through the campaign.

The day Cabot and Theodore showed up in Canton, Ohio, the sun was just starting to peek out from behind dense clouds, clearing the skies after a dull week of rainstorms. The pair trudged through the soft, muddy grass toward McKinley's front porch, stopping to assure newsmen that the Major was a sure thing in Massachusetts and New York and, Theodore added with no logic to back it, that the Republican chieftain enjoyed such a tidal wave of support in the East that it was sure to roll over itself into the western states.

The two former Reed backers then went inside the McKinley home and assured the Major they were doing all in their power to aid his election. In a scene later recounted to Hay by amused McKinley aides, Cabot and Theodore prostrated themselves in pledging absolute and unwavering fealty. Theodore was clearly angling for a job in the McKinley government, and he knew there would be a lot of applicants from his home state of New York—Whitelaw Reid,

Secretary of State John Hay

Chauncey Depew, Levi Morton, maybe Boss Platt himself. And Cabot, well, Cabot *always* wanted to be heard. They "have been to Canton to offer their heads to the axe," Hay reported to Henry Adams of Cabot and Theodore, "and their tummies to the harikari knife."

Those two tummies were upside down in the early days of that general election campaign; Lodge and Roosevelt were doubtful of their own political instincts, which meant that in spite of their confident public pronouncements, they were terrified that William McKinley was headed for defeat. This made the two men, Hay noted, like much of the moneyed class in those days. "The election scare which I have observed with more or less detachment for twenty years has set in with unusual vigor," Hay wrote to Adams. "Most of my friends think Bryan will be elected and we shall all be hanged to the lampions of Euclid Avenue." Cabot and Theodore were already prone to bouts of nervous diarrhea (the Roosevelts insisted on calling it "cholera morbus"), and this imagined electoral disaster roiled their overwrought bowels. "The hatred of the East among many Westerners, and the crude ignorance of even elementary finance among such a multitude of well meaning, but puzzle-headed, voters, give cause for serious alarm throughout this campaign," Roosevelt told Cabot. If the worst came to pass and William Jennings Bryan won election, they agreed, America's republican form of government had a life expectancy of no more than fifty years. Poor Cabot worried fifteen pounds off his already slender frame, while Nannie

Lodge wrote to friends about what an impressive figure the brash and youthful Bryan cut. Roosevelt, meanwhile, was one of the hundreds of Republican proxies Mark Hanna funded to chase all over the country in hopes of counteracting the excitement of Bryan's unprecedented whistle-stop tour. Theodore's speaking voice constricted to a shrill metallic screech as Election Day neared. "Mr. Bryan and his adherents have appealed to the basest set in the land, the farmers," he reportedly told one audience before tying the Democratic presidential candidate to the controversial Illinois governor who had pardoned rioters in Chicago. The convention that renominated the Illinois man, Roosevelt exclaimed, according to newspaper accounts, was thick with "murderers, horse thiefs, burglars, libertines, crooks of all kinds, men who had been convicted of crimes ranging from pocket picking to arson and from mayhem to rape."

Hay remained calm and spent much of his time twitting Henry Adams, who remained a Bryan man. "The Majah is a cinch," Hay wrote to his friend, "and don't you forget it." Hay made only one campaign "speech"—which was not actually a speech but a written pamphlet distributed to a thousand students at Cleveland's Western Reserve University, where his father-in-law's generous donation a generation earlier had made Hay a trustee. Hay was playing mostly to an audience of one—William McKinley.

The portions of Hay's address celebrating the Major and Republicanism were certainly a cut above the rank verbal spillings of most of McKinley surrogates; the best of it tended toward poetry: "The tariff law which bore Mr. McKinley's name had gone into effect and had resulted in a great wave of prosperity, which, like a Nile inundation, had fertilized every field of commerce and industry throughout the land. Never in our history were days' works so plentiful or so well rewarded. The humming of thousands of looms, the ringing of the hammer on the anvil, the murmur of trade in thousands of marts, the peaceful sounds of tillage from myriads of farms, all testified in one great chorus to the wisdom and justice with which the country was governed."

McKinley himself, in Hay's description, was the exemplar of American manhood and civic virtue, "without malice or meanness of any kind: a man whose heart is as liberal as his mind, of high intelligence and ardent patriotism; to whom every American is a brother; who knows no such thing as classes in our Republic; who does not know what it means to look on an other as his superior or his inferior, a man of the people to the marrow of his bones."

John Hay did lend a certain whiff of class to the political season. As Sam Clemens had written to a friend of theirs, Hay's presence in politics "is like a vase of attar of roses in a glue-factory—it can't extinguish the stink, but it modifies it." But when Hay turned his talk to William Jennings Bryan, he made no effort at perfumery. He skinned Bryan and tossed his carcass on the smelly heap, calling him out as "an ignoramus" offered up by a "bedlamite" convention in Chicago. "Civilization itself is attacked," Hay wrote. The Boy Orator of the "muddy and wide-mouthed Platte . . . tears his vocal cords" to "roar out his voluble ignorance in public," Hay claimed. "Not one appeal to pure and lofty motives do we hear in all the endless wash of his oratory. Envy, hatred, greed, sectional distrust, the fury of the tramp against the citizen, of the shiftless against the thrifty, are the only strings he plays upon."

Who was William Jennings Bryan, Hay suggested, to share the political stage with the Republican nominee? Major McKinley's "speeches are an arsenal of facts; his arguments have the force and weight that come from full knowledge and perfect conviction," Hay concluded. "He has the calm temper, the liberal view of the statesman. He is as free from malice or sectionalism as the best of the simple great ones of our past. His every utterance is distinguished by that lofty courtesy to his opponents which is the infallible sign of the men born to high destinies."

McKinley, in fact, was doing a masterly job of hiding this remarkable self. The Major's most compelling campaign promise was "a full dinner pail" for all, but he was leaving it to others to make his case. McKinley was content to sit home in Canton and receive trainloads of visiting civic groups: the McKinley and Hobart Sound Money Club of Sewickley, Pennsylvania; an aging party of former Union generals; a host of ex-Confederate soldiers; miners and mechanics from the Lehigh Valley; women's clubs from neighboring midwestern states; the McKinley Club of Mingo Junction; and on and on, day after day. The Major would step out onto his rain-softened lawn and accept gifts from the delegations—a whale's tooth from New Bedford, coal from the anthracite regions, fresh-cut chrysanthemums for Mrs. McKinley—and then offer up some milquetoast cant. He was careful not to tread, even lightly, on the specific planks that made up his party's platform. Why take the chance of offending some independent-minded voting man? The Major would give his audiences to understand that he was for all the things they were for: national honor, the preservation of free institutions, confidence in business and lower interest rates, motherhood, truth and virtue, patriotism, a free and independent citizenry, good government, good morals, clean politics, and wise legislation. Who could argue?

Hundreds and thousands of words spent every day, and McKinley said nothing. He was happy to leave the stimulation of the Republican nerves to Bryan, whose daily orations were doing the trick. The Democrat's nominee was proposing that the federal government take over the management of currency and the money supply, insure bank deposits, tax *income*, permit laborers to form unions, and defy the world economic powers by coining silver at a ratio of sixteen to one as against gold, when everybody knew that the proper ratio was thirty-two to one. He wanted to promote free trade, which meant further reducing (if not outright killing) the protective tariffs that stood, as the banking and manufacturing crowd told it, as their bulwark against certain economic ruin. He wanted to find a way to put a floor under falling crop prices and get farmers out from under 20 percent mortgages. Bryan volubly—and at least twice a day—repudiated the Republican Party's insistence that if the government protected and propped up the well-to-do, their prosperity would, as a matter of natural law, leak through to the lower classes. "The Democratic idea," Bryan liked to say, "has been that if you legislate to make the masses prosperous, their prosperity will find its way up through every class which rests upon it."

All this wild-hare Paris Commune–like talk from a serious presidential candidate was the Republican nominee's best advertising. Conservative leaders called Bryan's economic program an "anarchist" agenda "made in hell." This was communism on the march! When McKinley's campaign manager, Mark Hanna, trolled through the banking and business corridors in New York and Boston, money poured in. Hanna's boyhood pal John D. Rockefeller dumped $250,000 in the McKinley war chest, almost as much as Bryan would raise in total. It would be more than a century before another candidate raised and spent so much cash on a national election. And even while McKinley stayed indoors, the public square of Canton would fill up with excited well-wishers rallying to his studied and unoffending nothingness or, rather, *against* Bryan's frightening somethingness. They sang "Yankee Doodle" and "The Star-Spangled Banner," then "Dixie" and "Maryland, My Maryland." According to wire reports, the old Confederate ditties were sung "as lustily and as patriotically as were 'John Brown's Body' and 'Marching Thro' Georgia.'"

SAM CLEMENS WAS keeping only half an eye on the American presidential campaign that fall. "If they elect Bryan & a silver Congress," he wrote to Henry Rogers, "send me our balance & I will wait & buy silver & settle some of those debts on an economical basis." But he could not work up much real interest in the distant political battle. He was too busy trying to keep his family from collapse. Clemens had only just got his wife and daughters situated in London that fall, after nearly a month of hunting, in a nice big four-story house with rented maids and a handyman included, in an affordable area of Chelsea. He had also taken over the household management and had drawn up a detailed and comprehensive weekly budget that included rent, household wages, postage, food, coal, gas and electric, washing, clothing, newspapers, music lessons for the girls, cabs and buses, whiskey, beer, claret, cigars, and also physicians for his ailing wife. Mrs. Clemens could not stop beating up on herself about Susy's death: "We left her. She was not a child that we should have ever left. . . . I can never forgive myself that desertion."

Livy was suffering from dyspepsia, insomnia, a lack of appetite, and low spirits. She insisted on staying indoors day and night, so it was Sam who took their daughters for long walks in the nearby parks, where Clara spied hazy kindred spirits in the London fog. "A stray cat, a stray leaf, a stray—Oh," she wrote, "everything looked adrift and unattended."

Sam Clemens's fury was never far from the surface that fall, and he tried to give it sufficient vent in the outside world to spare his wife the worst of it. He fought a pitched battle with the Chelsea post officers, who would not quit sending the previous tenant's mail to their house, and with the Chelsea water utility, which insisted that Clemens was responsible for the previous tenant's water bill. "They decline to know anybody in the matter but the *house*. It saves (them) trouble." He angrily accused the local lending library of giving out his address. That was *private*. No one was to know where he was.

He railed to Henry Rogers about the hapless law firm he was paying to recover royalties owed him for theatrical uses of his work. "If Colby's senior, Russell, were dead, Colby would be the head idiot of this century; & I wish Russell would die & give him the chance." He sent bitter notes to the agent who had been in charge of renting their house in Hartford. Last year's tenants, Katy Leary had told him, "crippled & battered & destroyed" crockery, kitchen utensils, and glassware. "It will cost them considerable to repair that damage," Clemens insisted to his agent, "but they shall pay to the last farthing."

There were days, however, when he was unable to work off his anger in extracurricular activities. Clara could tell when he was at full boil, and all she could do was shake her head and dread the unfolding scene when her father, his dark mood rising, made Livy sit through one of his long, grim sermons about the various foul and filthy properties of the *entire goddamned human race*. Clara understood that her father was a weakened vessel—knew he lacked the strength to keep his ferocious anger from leaking out—but that didn't make it any easier to watch. "Do you remember, Livy, the hellish struggle it was to settle on making that lecture trip around the world?" he would say, pacing the floor of their drawing room, his voice rising. "But once the idea of that infernal trip struck us we couldn't shake it. Oh, no! for it was packed with sense of honor—honor—honor—no rest, comfort, joy—but plenty of honor, plenty of ethical glory. And as a reward for our self-castigation and faithfulness to ideals of nobility we were robbed of our greatest treasure, our lovely Susy in the midst of her blooming talents and personal graces. You want me to believe it is a judicious, a charitable God that runs this world. Why, I could run it better myself."

He would realize his error even before his splenetic tirade was complete and would look in shame at his poor, pale, diminished wife. (Why did he think of no one but himself? Why was he attacking Livy's God and comfort?) And then he would apologize as best he could. "Don't mind anything I say, Livy. Whatever happens, you know I love you."

Clara was watching her father closely again in those days; she noted how "under stress of thought or feeling" his gray eyes paled to a milky aqua green. In his grief, she also noticed, he was no longer dedicated to maintaining his practiced public drawl; there were days when it disappeared altogether, as if he was actually losing some vital part of himself. So no one was more pleased than Clara when her father finally, in the last week of October of 1896, emerged from his study with the opening of his travel book: "The starting point of this lecturing-trip around the world was Paris, where we had been living a year or two. We sailed for America, and there made certain preparations. This took but little time. Two members of my family elected to go with me. Also a carbuncle. The dictionary says a carbuncle is a kind of jewel. Humor is out of place in a dictionary."

JOHN HAY HAD no desire to be one of the obsequious "millions who trampled on McKinley's lawn," as he put it. But in late October, exactly two weeks before the vote, he accepted the Major's long-standing invitation and traveled to Canton, where he did what only a handful of living men could: right there on the candidate's front porch, John Hay summoned the political Holy Ghost of the United States of America and gave McKinley his benediction. Hay hadn't seen a national contest of such import and interest since he had been at the side of his old boss, Abraham Lincoln, he told the assembled reporters. "Major McKinley has made a remarkable campaign from his front porch," he said. "When Mr. Lincoln was a candidate he received at his home a large number of visitors, but they were by no means as numerous as those who come to see Major McKinley, and Mr. Lincoln made no speeches. Many persons regard it unsafe for a Presidential candidate to discuss public questions, but Major McKinley has not uttered a wrong word or made a mistake of any sort whatsoever."

A week later, John Hay was confident enough in the wisdom of the American electorate to keep his annual appointment at the Winous Point duck blind, and there was an entirely new aspect to the proceedings that fall. His sights were no longer empty. "Light of Mine Optics," he wrote to Adams, "I send you by express a duck or two in a basket. If they arrive in good condition, accept them with my love. If otherwise, blame . . . the President of the Express Company, and I fear, no true friend of us McKinley men. The Bryan men still claim they have us where the capillary integument is brief [i.e., the testicles], but Hanna gives them the hoarse hoot. Me too!"

A week later, McKinley slid safely into home. Hay's man whipped Bryan where the votes were: New York, New England, Pennsylvania, most of the Midwest. He won a squeaker in California. So John Hay had a friend headed to the White House—a friend who favored him.

IT PAINED HAY to watch the postelection proceedings. President-elect McKinley, like every president-elect Hay had observed, was in a Lilliputian bind—tied fast by a thousand small concerns. There were only so many cabinet positions and assistant secretaryships and plum diplomatic posts to be handed out and a lot of supporters to be satisfied. The toughest nut was New York State. McKinley had debts there, big ones. Of the record millions Hanna had raised and spent for McKinley in the campaign, nearly 90 percent of it had come from Wall Street banks, commercial houses, and business barons like Rockefeller and Morgan. The railroad interests would want Chauncey Depew to have a big job (he had been an energetic stump speaker for McKinley); then, too, Boss Platt needed stroking. McKinley worried that if he failed to hand Platt some prize for his New York regulars, the boss would be an active blockader for the next four years. And then there was Platt's sworn enemy in the state, Whitelaw Reid, whose Great Moral Organ, the *New York Tribune*, had helped neutralize Platt's play against McKinley in the nominating process. McKinley needed to keep Reid happy because his *Tribune* would be key to building support for McKinley's signature pieces of legislation—if he ever came up with any.

Hay suspected his friend Reid would be, as usual, the most extreme case of the unfortunate and unattractive seasonal disorder that hit public men post-election. Whenever a new Republican administration came into power, and jobs were to be distributed, Whitelaw was first in line—and hungry.

Whitelaw did not surprise; he was like a moose in rut. Three weeks after the vote, he made the pilgrimage to McKinley's Canton home, where he cut in on a party including Mr. and Mrs. Mark Hanna and cost McKinley and his wife a precious hour with dear and old friends. Reid was unaware of this social faux pas, anxious as he was to explain to the Major the proper way for a president to people his administration. McKinley had little choice but to endure this long, private conference, nod politely, and assure Reid that he wanted to hear from him often, with whatever suggestions he had.

So ten days later, just in case McKinley hadn't got the message orally,

Whitelaw shipped him a long letter with instructions on how to handle Boss Platt and the New York regulars. The message was simple: McKinley needed to smite Boss Platt across the chops, and the best way to do that was to make a place in the cabinet for Platt's biggest rival—Whitelaw Reid. Reid followed up with a letter to John Hay, because Whitelaw was counting on Hay to carry the Reid banner in the battle for the cabinet. The McKinley crowd "will make a mistake if they imagine that friendly independence can be attained in [New York] by beginning with conciliation," Whitelaw reminded Hay. "Conciliation at the outset will confirm [the Boss Platt] people in their estimate of the nerve and staying qualities of the man they have to deal with; and nothing thereafter but absolute surrender on every point will satisfy them."

John Hay felt bound by long years of friendship to make the pitch for Reid, but McKinley showed no interest in putting Whitelaw in his cabinet. He made little headway with the Major. The president-elect asked Hay, instead, to take on the difficult task of making Whitelaw understand that McKinley's hands were tied, that he needed to make a friend of Platt. There would be no cabinet job for Reid. Whitelaw grudgingly gave up on becoming McKinley's secretary of state or his secretary of the navy. He decided after a tortured application of his typical solipsistic calculus that he would be willing to *settle* for the role of United States ambassador to England.

CLEMENS HAD RECEIVED the news of the McKinley victory with quiet despair—an acceptance of the inevitable. "Does the human being reason?" he recorded in his private notebook as the campaign wound down.

> No; he thinks, muses. . . . Thinks *about* a thing; rehearses its statistics & its parts & applies to them what other people on his side of the question have said about them, but he does not compare the parts himself, & is not capable of doing it.
>
> That is, in the two things which are the peculiar domain of the heart, not the mind—politics & religion. He doesn't want to know the other side—he wants arguments & statistics for his own side & nothing more.
>
> Take the Silver question, for instance.
>
> And the slavery question.
>
> To remove slavery would destroy prosperity—it didn't do it.
>
> To take the 13 colonies from under the shelter of Eng. would destroy them. It did not do it.
>
> To make France a Republic would destroy her. It didn't do it.
>
> Half of our people are for silver—are all the fools on that side?

And there he closed the book on McKinley's election. No reporter sought him out for an opinion, and he made no effort to offer one. What did it matter to Sam Clemens who sat in the White House anyway?

He was working like a ditchdigger on the travelogue by then, and more or less in seclusion. Clemens took no physical exercise and declined all social invitations. He went to his desk seven days a week and was still there well after dark, bent over his manuscript, pen in hand, taking long, heavy pulls from his cigars at regular and thin intervals. "The constitution which tolerates this abuse," Mr. Smythe would say, "is the puzzle of physicians." Sam Clemens was a mystery to himself, too. At the end of the long workday he would write letters to friends just to try to make sense of his strange machine self: "It will puzzle me to know what it is in me that writes and has comedy fancies and finds pleasure in phrasing them. It is the law of our nature, of course, or it wouldn't happen. . . . I work all the days, and trouble vanishes away when I use that magic. . . . I myself can keep cheerful—much more so than the others."

The mental demands of the book crowded out the nagging scene of Susy's death ("My brain is worn to rags rehearsing it," he had written), and grinding out work for pay served his desperate need to believe himself, still, a proper father to his remaining daughters. He was going to spend whatever time he had left in this life, he told friends, scraping out of his brainpan every last book he had in him. He had privately given up on his honor vow to satisfy to the last penny his creditors back in America, but he was going to make sure Clara and Jean Clemens would not want for anything in their lives. His attitude hardened into animal fierceness that autumn. He shipped Clara out to find the best piano teacher in the city, cost be damned. He bought the girls fancy new bicycles and paid for lessons. He chaperoned them around the city when he could, and he lashed out at anyone who showed "Mark Twain's" daughters the tiniest indignity—especially when that person reminded the girls of their reduced circumstances. His old acquaintance Bram Stoker, who was managing Henry Irving's Lyceum Theatre, got a snootful of Clemens's temper one evening in early November, after Clara and Jean returned home from a ticket-buying excursion bruised in spirit and ego. "The large blonde man with spectacles who was selling seats in your box office this afternoon at half past 4 or 5 grossly insulted my two daughters by his brutal & surly behavior," Clemens wrote to Stoker, apologizing for the angry tone of the letter, but reminding him it was that "mangy cur" of a box office man who had provoked it. "Apparently their offence lay in wishing to buy cheap tickets—4-shilling ones. Perhaps he can imitate a gentleman's gentleman when people apply for boxes. But in any case he is a hog; he was born a hog & will die one."

Livy was a harder case; Clemens wasn't sure how to protect his wife. He would emerge from his study in the evenings to find her in the parlor, staring blankly at the walls—and the ache he had kept lidded all day would be at him again. "She does not see people, and cannot; books have lost their interest for her. She sits solitary; and all the day, and all the days, wonders how it all happened, and why." Beyond the self-imposed prison of her rented home, Livy knew and cared for nothing. News of the wider world simply passed by her; the presidential canvass in the United States had barely registered in Livy's consciousness. Clemens wrote to their closest friend in Hartford, the Reverend Joe Twichell, who had presided over their wedding and Susy's funeral, and begged the man of God for words of solace for his wife: "Livy stands so in need of help; and none among us all could help her like you." He was also trying to get Livy a copy of one of Susy's favorite poems, "In Memoriam," by Tennyson. He knew this gesture would not suffice, but it was something.

On Livy's birthday, November 27, Clemens sent his wife a hapless little note: "We still have the others, & that is much; & also we have each other, my darling, & this is riches. . . . With worlds of love, Saml."

His birthday, three days later, was not celebrated within the home or without. Thanksgiving passed unmarked by the Clemens household. Christmas morning, Sam sat down at his desk and confided to his notebook: "Because of the smoothness and excellence of the paving, London is the least noisy city; but the silence of today! Oh, it is the silence of the tomb. The family have been to breakfast. We three sat and talked as usual, but the name of the day was not mentioned. It was in our minds, but we said nothing."

HAY'S INITIAL INSTINCT was to accept the inevitable and step aside. If giving Whitelaw the ambassadorship in London helped McKinley, Hay would of course be willing to back away gracefully. But he was not without political instinct, and he was not without personal pride, and as he worked it around in his head, Hay determined that he might actually be doing the Major a favor by taking over the embassy in London. He found himself making a nearly unprecedented entreaty on his own behalf. "I do not think it is altogether selfishness and vanity which has brought me to think that perhaps you might do worse than select me," he wrote to McKinley.

1. My appointment would please a good many people & so far as I know would offend nobody. Any appointment from New York would rouse bitterness in some quarter. If Reid can't get it, he would rather have me go, than any one else.
2. I should not hold the office very long. It would be at your disposal in some critical time when it might serve a useful purpose.

3. As I have no claim on the place, and as it is really above my merits and deservings, I think I would be more grateful than any one else would be, and would do as much to show my gratitude.

He then apologized for any difficulty or discomfort his plea might visit on McKinley. "But I cannot help feeling that perhaps you can do this with some relief or advantage to yourself," he concluded. "If this is not so, do not give the matter a moment's thought. Perhaps the best way to dispose of this letter will be to send it back to me in the inclosed envelope. I do not want it to be filed. You need not answer it. I will understand your silence. There will be no embarrassment between us."

McKinley had plenty of other personnel problems to solve before he decided on the coveted ambassadorship, but he did hit on an idea to save face for Reid. He asked Hay to work on a public statement that president-elect William McKinley's great desire was to give Whitelaw an office, but that he could not in good conscience risk the editor's fragile health by tying him to a difficult public job right now.

Reid, however, did not appear willing to relent. He agitated again and again for the English embassy, until Hay's patience finally gave out. The way the politics shaped up, it looked as if Hay was going to be left out, too, and Reid had offered not a word of support or comfort. "It is the only chance I have ever had, or ever shall have for an important place," he wrote to Reid, "while you have had the highest honors three administrations and a national convention could give."

Whitelaw, adhering to character, offered no response, and when he finally began to accept the plain fact that he would not have his plum, his demands became churlish. Whitelaw asked that McKinley *offer* the ambassadorship so that he could make a public show of turning it down. And he also wanted a personal letter from the president expressing regret that Whitelaw's ill health would not permit him to serve. Hay drafted both instruments for McKinley to look over. "In all this, I am only thinking of you," he wrote to the Major. "I have ceased thinking about Reid; he thinks enough about himself for two."

McKinley was wary of sending anything in writing offering Reid the ambassadorship; he thought Whitelaw might double-cross him and accept the post. McKinley chose the safer option instead, the health canard, and Reid made sure the contents of the president-elect's letter got wide play in the newspapers.

Shortly thereafter, McKinley surprised John Hay with instructions to start making arrangements to move his household to London, and before the appointment became official, the *Times* of London broke the story that Hay was McKinley's pick to be the ambassador to the Court of St. James's. Just before inauguration day, March 4, 1897, a letter arrived at Hay's doorstep from England. News of the appointment, one of Hay's expatriate friends wrote, agitates me too deeply to permit any mere routine of make-believe romance in the presence of such a romantic reality. You make the plot of existence thicken more delightfully—even across the hiatus of the Atlantic—than anything I can manage on paper this morning, at least until I have embraced you. I long for the hour when I shall come as near as I dare to laying hands with that intent on your inviolable ambassadorial person. You change the whole prospect—you light it up in a manner more festive than any sight I supposed still reserved for these aged eyes. I can't decently take up your time, and this is only one of the million handshakes. But it goes all round your house—goes straight on to the Ambassadress. . . . My dear Hay, rejoicingly, restlessly, impatiently, devotedly, Henry James.

Another letter had arrived from the son of Hay's diplomatic mentor John Bigelow, who had been one of Lincoln's most trusted foreign ministers. "My dear Colonel Hay—Blessed be God and the President that you are to come here as Ambassador—my friends here are all asking about you & I am puffed up with the glory of having known you 'from a Babby,'" Poultney Bigelow wrote. "You have thousands of friends here but none warmer than me & I congratulate my country if it is true that you are really to be here as Ambassador. At any rate I claim the pleasure of proposing you here as honorary member [of the Reform Club]—Mark Twain was the last one put up here—by me—he has also become a fellow citizen of Chelsea."

CHAPTER EIGHT

Easing Burdens

Poultney Bigelow was one of the few people Sam Clemens was willing to allow across the threshold of his temporary residence in the first months of 1897. A newspaperman who weaseled himself uninvited into 23 Tedworth Square noted the eerie silence in the darkened house, the muffled murmur of the servants, the "prevailing sadness in the atmosphere." "Mark Twain," he quickly apprehended, was in no mood to humor reporters, or anybody else. Clemens was guarding this family sanctuary in Chelsea with ferocity characteristic of the wounded and wary. "*Don't tell any one my address.* . . . We keep in hiding," he wrote to Poultney, on first invitation. "I do not go out and my wife and daughters never see anybody—they cannot bear it yet; but I shall be glad, and more than glad to see *you*; and the sooner you come the gladder I shall be."

Clemens had put his new home through its shakedown cruise by then, having discovered and remedied the most obvious flaws of the big four-story house: broken chimney pots that caused the drawing room to fill with smoke when the first fires were lit, the continued arrival of the previous tenant's mail; the overabundance of artificial light in the basement, hallways, and dining room; and far too little illumination in the main bathroom, bedrooms, and drawing room. "Properly constructed people like a subdued light," Clemens explained to his landlord, "but I love a glare." He had also fallen into accepted British customs where the household staff was concerned, making sure to provide for their "leavings"—beer on tap in the kitchen for all and a weekly stipend of whiskey for those who bargained for it.

The street life suited Sam Clemens when he did venture out. A roster of artists and writers had lived in this area of Chelsea for some time, so the neighborhood was accustomed to a low simmer of celebrity and generally quiet. The only truly notorious neighbor had long ago been removed to one of Her Majesty's prisons, so curiosity seekers were rarely in evidence any more at his house on Tite Street. "He was a very bad man, Oscar Wilde was," Katy Leary concluded after hearing the back-porch gossip among the serving staff, "so bad you couldn't talk about what he done."

Katy recoiled at the smoke and fog of London, pronounced the city the dirtiest she had ever seen, and couldn't quite get the hang of the calcified class system that prevailed within the rented servant staff at the Clemens home. The head housekeeper would not deign to speak to a scullery maid; the cook held sovereign sway over her kitchen; the butler high-hatted everybody. This was all new to a woman who had been raised in service to Sam Clemens and his family. "I never could be on my dignity," Katy would say. "Upper housemaid, under housemaid; upper chambermaid, under chambermaid; upper and under everything. It made me laugh, for I didn't take my position very lofty, you know."

Katy was on her guard in this alien land, which made her especially aware that she was the only one of the staff with intimate knowledge of the family they served, and especially vigilant in the care and feeding of her charges that winter. She made sure to spend a little extra time combing out Mrs. Clemens's hair each morning and night, because those familiar old routines seemed a comfort to Livy and because Katy was one of the few people to whom the grieving mother could talk freely about Susy. Katy made herself available to do the squiring when the Clemens girls wanted to step out of the house during the day and Mr. Clemens was hard at work. And she kept an eye on Mr. Clemens, too. His moods were still the weather of the house, and he had his calm days and his stormy ones, but he was absentminded about his health every day that winter. Sometimes when he had gone days, even weeks, working straight through every hour of dull light without a bite to eat, Katy would entice him into taking a little nourishment by mixing up a batch of johnnycakes.

When the cook took her night off and Sunday supper preparations fell to Katy, she made sure the family got all their old favorites, as in the good-time Hartford days. "I could make creamed potatoes perfectly luscious," Katy was proud to say, and she knew that on Sundays she didn't have to hear the regular cook and her staff complain about this American extravagance: "Who ever heard of such a thing—creaming potatoes!"

All in all, and in no small part because of Katy's ministrations, Sam Clemens professed himself and his family comfortably situated in the quiet of Chelsea, but domestic tranquillity and familiar routine hardly sufficed for a man with his animal need of company. He was lonely for familiar *people* that winter, and Poultney Bigelow's presence in London was a lifeline. Poultney was a generation younger, and the two men shared a relatively short history, but it was a happy one. Their acquaintance had started just six or seven years earlier with Poultney as a literary idol worshipper, but Clemens quickly grew fond of the younger man—and was soon enough treating him as an equal. Poultney came from a distinguished family; his father was a renowned diplomat and publisher. Both men valued travel, fine prose, and a well-wrought joke.

The friends had met often at the Players, a social club, when Clemens was in New York trying to stave off his imminent bankruptcy, and when Clemens's financial bust-up became public, Poultney had shipped him a $1,000 check, a sum he could not truly afford. Sam Clemens, abashed, sent it back, but he never forgot it. And neither did Mrs. Clemens. She didn't take part in Poultney's visits to Tedworth Square that winter, but she didn't discourage them. The visits from Poultney were among Sam Clemens's few hours of relief in the long, gray, coal-smudged London winter.

SAM CLEMENS HAD started 1897 with big plans, committing himself to work as he had the previous two months—every day of the week, thirty-one in a month. "I shall get 31 into February," he wrote to Henry Rogers four days into 1897. "It will crowd me, but I shall do it." This resolution, though, proved a hard one to keep, largely because he was not yet ready to let go of Susy and found himself unwilling to allow his work on the new book to entirely eclipse his memory of her. He found himself spending long work hours that January reading the letters and papers left behind by his daughter or bent over his own notebooks, scrawling out a stream of consciousness, reconjuring all he could about her, as if to make sure she was not all *gone*—as if the essence of Susy, even without its vessel, could still be felt.

He started musing one day about how Susy had tried to reform their Hartford butler, George Griffin. George had played along with Susy's girlish attempts to convince him to renounce once and for all his immoral practice of gambling, but he was too able and too successful a betting man to let go this steady stream of income. George rarely lost, whether at the horse track or the boxing arena, because he did his homework and worked from the head. Clemens had been with George in New York one day when he was asked why he had bet on a white fighter against a black one: "Was it quite patriotic to bet against your own color?"

"Betting is business, sir, patriotism is sentiment," George explained. "They don't belong together. In politics I'm colored; in a bet I put up on *the best man*. I ain't particular about his paint."

Sam Clemens loved George Griffin as Susy had. He was with the family, day and night, for sixteen years. Like Katy Leary, and their old coachman Patrick McAleer and his wife, George was *family*. Clemens missed his friend George, and he knew the feeling was mutual. "Don't think I have lost sight of the old family," George had written to Clara one recent Christmas, "for that cannot be."

The weight of the money problems made it difficult to focus on the new book also, because Clemens's burden was feeling heavier than ever; Henry Rogers had just informed him that liquidation of the Webster company assets would not settle as much as they had hoped. Sales of *Personal Recollections of Joan of Arc* were too slow to offer much relief. And now Bliss, his longtime publisher, who had agreed to pay $10,000 on delivery of the new manuscript, was caviling about signing the contract. "He is the most *indefinite* man that ever was," Clemens complained to Rogers. "He is intangible. He is a gas, & nothing but a pressure of 250,000 atmospheres can solidify him."

And then again: what the hell was $10,000 against the money he owed? Clemens could reckon no conventional means for working off his debt, which left him momentarily despondent, until . . . he hit on a new scheme. He would do one final and spectacular lecture burst in America, just a few nights in a few target-rich cities, with $1,000 seats sold by private subscription to his friends of means. He did not dare tell Livy until he had it worked out, but he began expending precious time and energy on the planning. He would dump Major James B. Pond, he decided, and give over the organization of this world-record box office event to old Frank Fuller, who had promoted his very first lecture thirty years earlier, and he penciled in a list of dear old friends who might subscribe (Andrew Carnegie, Adolph Sutro, Grover Cleveland, John Hay) and rich acquaintances who might be publicly shamed into purchasing seats (Vanderbilt, Rockefeller, even the loathsome Whitelaw Reid).

None of them would be surprised when the ask came, he figured, because "Mark Twain's" embarrassing predicament was back in the news that January. His uncharacteristic refusal to show himself in public inspired rumors of abject poverty and failing health, some of which began appearing in print. "It is probable that the end has come," read a newspaper story that spread across both sides of the Atlantic in the middle of January. "Mark Twain is 62 years old and handicapped by the fact that his best efforts have not been his latest. There has been a steady decline in his humor since it became a treadmill grind. The sooner the end comes the fewer will be the excuses when the record of his reputation shall be written as a matter of literary history. He seems to realize this. . . . The struggle is really one of most tearful contemplation, with every indication that the poor man will not be able to realize his last faint hope."

Clemens did not see any good reason to challenge these fictions in public. "This would enrage & disgust me if it came from a dog, or a cow, or an elephant or any other of the higher animals, but it comes from a man, & much allowance must be made for Man," he recorded in his notebook. There was one particular newspaper hack, however, who did demand attention—his next-door neighbor, a reporter for the *Times* of London named J. Woulfe Flanagan, who issued a formal written complaint about the "intolerable nuisance" of Clara's piano practice. Flanagan explained that he worked late hours for his venerable paper and needed to catch up on his sleep in the mornings. Piano noise made it impossible.

Clemens was bound to make an answer, but first he had to calm down, lest he send the "rude, uncourteous, goddamned son of a bitch" a letter he might regret. It took some effort—and no little time—to achieve a suitably diplomatic tone, but he did: "If my daughter used the piano for amusement, it would be simple: she would accommodate her hours to yours, & find it a pleasure, not a hardship. But she merely practises her lessons," he finally wrote. "I & my family are most sincerely sorry that things are as they are; but as I have said, we do not know which way to turn nor what to do, to make them easier for all concerned—easier for you, & for ourselves. Can you suggest anything? I shall be glad to examine it; & if possible, fall in with it." This calmed Flanagan temporarily, but not Clemens, who kept mulling devious little strategies for punishing the idiot next door.

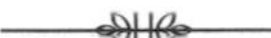

HE PUSHED ON with his book as best he could for the next month, temporarily cheered by a dinner invitation from the lord mayor of London (though Livy asked him to send regrets) or, on one of his occasional strolls down King's Road, by the sudden, unexpected appearance of glinting February sunshine, only to be taunted by new reports in the press: he was "lost in a great city, struggling with other millions against the adversities of life," it was said. "The days are dark and dreary for Mark Twain." The reports were consistently in error about his living conditions, but they weren't entirely inaccurate, and this fact fed Clemens's rattling unease in the intervals when his lumbago kept him from his desk, or when a new complaint from J. Woulfe had to be answered, or when he simply broke down for days at a time, unable to pick up a pen, or when he got the news that Bliss still refused to sign off on their latest publishing deal. "I am grown so nervous about the contracts that such sleep as I get doesn't do much good, & so my work drags body & lacks life," he confessed to Henry Rogers. "I am ashamed to seem so nervous & scared, but by gracious it's just the way I feel."

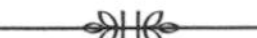

HE DID START to get out for an occasional meal with Henry Morton Stanley or Bram Stoker near winter's end, and he even managed to gather up a few new friends, like the literary-minded medical man who was helping him find the Tennyson volume he wanted for Livy. "You speak a language which I understand," he wrote in an invitation to the doctor, J. Y. W. MacAlister. "Could you come and smoke some manilas; I would, of course, say dine, but my family are hermits & cannot see any one, but I would have a fire in my study, & if you came at any time after your dinner that might be most convenient for you you would find me & a welcome."

On the evenings Clemens had the luxury of time and some leftover energy after the day's writing session and the family dinner, he would answer letters. In spite of the news of his miseries, and perhaps because of it, there was no end to the correspondence from friends, or people he had met in passing in his world travels, or just plain fans. Only a handful of people had the London address, but letters found their way to him through his British publisher, and he even received a few addressed simply "Mark Twain, Somewhere in the World." He left the bulk of the day-to-day correspondence to Clara and Livy, but he made a point of answering a few close friends, like Rogers and Twichell and Howells, to assure them that he was making progress; whatever they might read in the newspapers, he wanted them to know he had not lost hope. He reported that Jean was surprisingly healthy and Clara better every day. "They have youth," he wrote to Howells, "the only thing that was worth giving to the race." As for himself, he was confident of regaining some measure of his good cheer, no matter how hollowed out he felt most days: "This mood will pass, some day—there is history for it. But it cannot pass until my wife comes up out of the submergence. She was always so quick to recover herself, but now there is no rebound."

THE CLEMENSES MADE no occasion of their twenty-seventh wedding anniversary that February—Livy didn't want it. But in March, Sam thought he began to see some light behind his wife's eyes. She agreed to have Poultney Bigelow and his wife to 23 Tedworth for supper one evening and was delighted that they so enjoyed the potato dish she served. "Why, you've surely got some one from *America* in your kitchen," Mrs. Bigelow said, "because there's no cook in England that could cream potatoes!" And Livy appeared truly pleased when an unknown Clemens cousin who was living in London surfaced. Dr. James R. Clemens, native of St. Louis and resident surgeon at St. Thomas's Hospital in London, had read the accounts of "Mark Twain's" pathetic decline—one report claimed his wife and remaining daughters had abandoned him to die alone in a dank London garret—and had written with an offer of financial assistance. Clemens shooed away that offer. "The report of my poverty was an exaggeration," he told James Clemens. But he invited the young doctor and his wife to dinner. Family was family, after all, and pretty soon Livy was regularly summoning "Dr. Jim" and his wife and his autoharp for dinners and music recitals with Clara.

And then, in early April, Clemens announced to his wife that he had written through to the end of his book, which was an invitation to his wife to once again take up her life's work—which had been, for the previous twenty-seven years, saving Sam Clemens from himself.

The couple fell comfortably back into their pattern of in-house editing. No "Mark Twain" manuscript left the Clemens home, ever, without Livy's signing off on every word and phrasing, and they found themselves fighting and cooing and teasing over the new manuscript. Each took up the long-assigned roles: Livy was the sober adult, and Sam the rebellious and shamefaced "Youth."

"Page 1020 I think some other word would be better than 'stench.' You have used it pretty often."

"But can't I get it in anywhere? You've knocked it out every time. Out it goes again. And yet 'stench' is a noble, good word."

"Page 1038. I hate to have your father pictured lashing a slave boy."

"It's out, and my father is whitewashed."

The renewal of this familiar back-and-forth nudged Livy back toward life, but it did not fill the gaping canyon of her grief. "I am a changed woman," Livy wrote to old friends from Hartford. "Life is so dull, the poetry seems gone out of it. I have always had much courage even when things seemed hard but now I have none. I long to be with Susy."

JOHN HAY WAS once again pleasantly surprised by the ease of the crossing. The Atlantic Ocean was a path of divine liquid gentleness all the way to England. His private dinner table on the *St. Paul* was full every night of the weeklong voyage. Neither his wife nor his daughter Helen had to miss a meal on account of seasickness, which counted as a Hay family record. Henry Adams, so blue at the news of his friend's appointment as ambassador to the Court of St. James's that Hay invited him to make the trip over, was dressed for dinner and almost cheerful every night. Hay's personal assistant, Spencer Eddy, and Chandler Hale, who was on his way to take up his post as secretary of the US legation at Rome, added to the proceedings the jangly first-job excitement of youth. The newly appointed naval attaché to the American embassy in London was along for the ride, too, and stood anxious to impart "quaint seafaring wisdom" to his new boss.

John Hay was careful not to show it, and certainly wouldn't talk about it, but the month since McKinley sent his nomination for the ambassadorship to the Senate had been among the most satisfying of his life. There had been virtually no opposition to Hay's appointment. Newspapers in all parts of the country praised the wisdom of his selection. Elected officials showed overwhelming approval. Felicitations from around the country poured into his house at Lafayette

Square, many from old friends from the Lincoln administration. The most treasured message was from John Bigelow, the father of Poultney. The older Bigelow had schooled Hay in diplomacy thirty years earlier, but he himself had never won the post he coveted, the embassy in London, in large part because Mrs. Bigelow was thought to be a bit unhinged and possibly even violent—a decided liability for a diplomat's wife.

Bigelow was thrilled for his old charge. "Your selection for the London Embassy in these portentous times is even more an occasion for congratulating the Country than you," he had written the day after the news became public. "I do not think the President could have found either inside or outside of his party a person better equipped for the discharge of the critical duties that will devolve upon you."

John Hay was not without genuine doubts about his ability to keep up with the frantic demands of this new job, but he was also resigned, no, *determined*, to perform at the required pace for as long as he was able. For the first time in nearly twenty years, he was beginning to feel that he could be useful. His duty would be to take what load he could from the shoulders of the new president.

The Major, it was plain to see, was no longer as comfortable as he had been in his parlor in Canton; four weeks in, he was already flagging under the demands of his new office. Hay had remained at home in Washington for a month after the inauguration, and it pained him to see the Major so continuously knackered. Every day at the 10:00 a.m. rope drop—*Go early and avoid the rush!* was the mantra on Capitol Hill—the Executive Mansion filled with the querulous and obstinate importuners the free nation produced at every change of administration. Senators and representatives and state party officials and campaign donors lined up at McKinley's door in droves, most of them "repeaters"; some came twice a day, every day. A handful showed up three times in a single day. They were there to promote able men and women in their districts and states for all the jobs McKinley held in his executive pocket: governor of the Arizona Territory; US marshal in the Southern District of New York; assistant secretary of the interior, of war, of the navy; district judge in California, Wisconsin, Indiana; minister to Denmark; consul in Antwerp, Bogotá, Calcutta, or Kingston, Jamaica; auditor at Treasury; postmistress in some rural outpost in Tennessee. Occasionally a couple of university professors would slip through and rattle McKinley's cage about sending a torpedo boat or two to Crete, where the Turks and the Greeks appeared ready to make a war. "As things now are," reported one newspaperman, "the President finds no time for business of State until the shades of night hover over the mansion, and even then he is repeatedly interrupted by Senators and Representatives who claim the right to make evening appointments."

Senator Henry Cabot Lodge's visits alone would be enough to drive McKinley around the bend. Cabot had been agitating McKinley since before his election to seize Hawaii once and for all and put some coaling stations in the Pacific, and to get going on the interoceanic canal through Nicaragua, and to run the Spanish out of Cuba—by force if necessary. The senator was still advocating for a fleet of US battleships sufficient to patrol the Atlantic and the Pacific Oceans. But most of all, he wanted his friend Theodore Roosevelt to be made assistant secretary of the navy to vanguard this bold new Americanism on the high seas.

On top of the continuing onslaught of *official* prerogative, President McKinley had to contend with the great unwashed. Three days a week—at set and advertised times—Hay could look out his window across Lafayette Square and see thousands of private citizens arriving at 1600 Pennsylvania Avenue simply to be received by their president, which meant McKinley might have to shake thousands of hands. The president, somebody noted at the reception a few days after Hay left Washington for his journey to London, "was not as active and sprightly as on previous occasions."

McKinley was being crushed, Hay understood. He had seen it up close, with Lincoln, who wore himself to a nub trying to satisfy the unsatisfiable wants and needs of the public. And Hay suspected the Major didn't have the wily sense of self-preservation the Tycoon had had. Hay had seen Lincoln deal with office seekers in every way conceivable. Once, when a slight acquaintance came to the Executive Mansion and started to tell Lincoln how he had done more than anybody in Illinois to get him elected president, Lincoln escorted him to the door, with his arm around the man's shoulder, and agreed. "Well, I'll forgive you for it," he said, and he sent the man away empty handed. Sometimes Lincoln's natural good humor failed him, as when he scolded a private soldier who was asking the president of the United States to intervene in a personal row with his commanding officer. "Go away!" the president finally yelled. "I cannot attend to all these details. I could as easily bail out the Potomac with a spoon." Hay had also witnessed Lincoln grab a particularly insolent "repeater" by his coat collar and physically throw the man, ass over teacups, out his office door. Unfortunately for McKinley, hog-tossing somebody into the anteroom did not seem a viable option.

McKinley was a man in need of support, and by the time Hay sailed for England in the middle of April 1897, the new ambassador meant to ease one burden: he would do whatever it took to diminish the ill will between the United States and the British Empire. It would take some doing. The only give on the British side had been a willingness to settle the Venezuela dispute. Prime Minister Salisbury was dragging his feet on nearly every other issue at hand: an international conference to sort out the issue of bimetallism; a boundary dispute with Canada; a fight about the near extermination of the fur seal population in the American territory of Alaska.

The new president might also find himself in a position to ask British favor on the thorny issues the United States faced in Hawaii and Cuba. McKinley, who had no previous experience in foreign affairs, was counting on his new ambassador to take these problems in hand. This was John Hay's charge as he steamed toward Britain—to remove from McKinley's plate the worry of rebuilding reasonable and mutually beneficial relations with England.

THE *ST. PAUL* would have made Southampton in record time, but near the end of the voyage the steamship made a sharp right turn and detoured 180 miles off course to avoid icebergs—a prudent move, but an annoyance. Hay was anxious to get to London to see how his household and embassy were shaping up. He had reason to be optimistic; for one thing, he was going to have Harry White as first secretary there. President McKinley had wanted White to go to Madrid as minister to Spain, to see if he could help settle the Cuba matter peacefully. But Hay, with *very* strong assistance from Mrs. White, had managed to persuade White to remain in England. The young diplomat was already in London seeing to business. Hay knew he could leave all details domestic and diplomatic to a man of White's impeccable social graces and wide and deep knowledge of the ways of both London and the US State Department.

Ambassadors in service to the United States were expected to pay out of their own salary (or their personal fortunes) the expense of suitable living arrangements abroad, so White had helped Hay find a regal and commodious mansion not far from his own home and within walking distance of the court and the British Foreign Office. He and White had also discussed the advisability of leasing an enormous sixteenth-century country estate for entertaining outside the city. Hay was also counting on White to be on the lookout for the arrival of the Hay family silver, and the carriages and five horses, and to see to the proper markings for an ambassador's accoutrement. "I went to Harris & Alison's & could get nothing from them in regard to a monogram on the harness other than the one I sent you," Hay had written to White as he prepared to leave Washington, "—so I am afraid I must leave that matter to your taste and judgment, along with so much else. Anything you and the livery man get up will be quite satisfactory."

He could also trust in White to dissuade (in the least objectionable manner, it went without saying) the scores of friends and admirers who wanted Hay for receptions and dinners and speechifying. Londoners had grown accustomed to an American ambassador's being a figure of pronounced public plumage. Hay's predecessor at the embassy was still, as Hay approached England, running the final laps of his personal charm marathon. There was no audience from which Thomas Bayard shrank, and after four years of constant banqueting, the ambassador's addiction to making bombastic hour-long orations extolling Great Britain had begun to rankle. England was sick of Bayard, and about half the United States Congress wanted him censured.

John Hay was going to run a different kind of shop: he would stick to business. His evening entertainment would be confined to small, private dinners with men of import and influence over British policy, officials like his friends Balfour and Chamberlain and Curzon. His public events, he promised himself, would be few and far between.

AS THE *ST. PAUL* entered Southampton waters, it had already become clear that Hay's simplest plans would not be so easily realized. "I quake a little in the knees and pale a little about the gills as I am informed the Mayor and Corporation of Southampton are to meet us at the dock and make me an address of welcome and flapdoodle," he jotted in a quick note to his brother-in-law. "I heard a horrible rumour on leaving New York that they were planning a banquet and public reception. If that should turn out to be so, there will be no London for me till after midnight. I wired Mr. White to stop it if possible, and hope he will have done so."

When the steamship finally pulled within sight of the docks in Southampton a few hours later, near noon on that bright spring day, the scene that unfolded below Hay was much worse than he had feared. A sizable and expectant crowd milled at the pier; he could see a special VIP section filled with the local elect in official robes. From the deck above, Hay smiled gamely, returned the waves of welcome, and bid his wife and daughter to do the same. When the great ship docked, the mayor and the corporate officers of Southampton, along with the American dignitaries on hand, marched in official procession up the gangway and into the ship's saloon, where they cornered Hay and his family. The only people Hay recognized in the party were Harry White and Henry James.

The US consul in Southampton made the formal introductions, and the mayor spoke the first welcome. "Allow me to offer you, in behalf of my fellow-townsmen and countrymen, a hearty and cordial welcome to these shores," he began. He followed this with a short sermon about Hay's eminence and his fitness for his new job. "Your diplomatic career is well-known to us, and the personality you exerted at the various posts you have occupied assures us that we shall find in you a man who will cement closer than ever the affectionate regard of the two countries."

Hay could see Henry Adams out of the corner of his eye, "gloating over my sufferings," as he would later explain to a friend of theirs. Meanwhile, the mayor droned on. "If anything was needed to assure us of your country's affection of our beloved Queen your own words, written when you had no thought of occupying your present position, would suffice." And then he quoted from a poem Hay had published a few years earlier:

Once more hail, England! Happy is the day
When from wide wandering I hither fare,
Touch thy wave-warded shore and breathe thine air,
And see, again, thy hedges white with May.

The president of the local chamber of commerce had to say a few words also, and there were gifts to present to the incoming ambassador, before Hay was invited to make a reply. He kept it short. "I come to work for the welfare of my country," he assured the crowd, "and it is my profound conviction that this can best be served by promoting a cordial feeling between countries." His brevity seemed to disappoint.

When it was all over, Henry James, who had stood off to the side, aghast at it all, got a private moment with Hay. "What impression does it make on your mind," the novelist asked, "to have these insects creeping about and saying things to you?"

Hay and his traveling party escaped the banqueting in Southampton, through White's good offices, so the party was able to get on a fast train and head straight for London and the new home at 5 Carlton House Terrace. As Hay's train sped north, newspapers were already beginning to praise the new ambassador's "dignified reticence, compared to the volubility of his predecessor" and to remark on the import of Hay's arrival. "There would be no use in denying," opined London's *Daily News*, "that Mr. Hay comes at a rather critical moment."

CHAPTER NINE

Bluff, Brutal, Blunt

John Hay did not slide into his new life without a hitch or two, owing mainly to the high standard he had set for himself. As representative of the world's greatest republic in the most important international court on the globe, Colonel Hay meant to present well. The many moving parts of the household, as a consequence, were not yet in place when John Hay and his traveling party turned onto the marble-lined path of London's Lower Regent Street on the afternoon of April 21, 1897, rolled down through the gardens of Waterloo Place, and caught first sight of the sun-flashed stucco of his regal new home at Carlton House Terrace.

The Hay silver and some of the ambassador's favorite household relics were already inside the rented mansion. He couldn't be sure whether his two carriages or his five horses had been freed from consignment at the stable on King's Road, or whether the animals would recover sufficiently from the buffetings of the Atlantic crossing to shoulder their load anytime soon. The equipage plan was a blind gamble. John Hay was the first American ambassador in London to attempt the importation of his own American-made carriages and his own American-bred horses.

Once inside, in the sweet spring light of their four-story terrace residence, puzzlement ensued. When Henry Adams arrived later that afternoon, having checked into a hotel just on the other side of Piccadilly, he found John, Clara, and Helen "sitting solemnly in the midst of the grandeur, having lost all the keys of the trunks." Adams did not find his friend more anxious than usual about the key issue. The situation was hardly beyond remedy, and the regal bearing of the house clearly took the sting out of any niggling inconvenience. The eleven-person servant staff was already on hand, ready to keep 5 Carlton House Terrace in trim for entertaining—the coal-fired furnace burning, the pantries stocked, the kitchen humming. The house afforded Hay and his wife separate bedrooms and Helen had a suite of rooms, including her own private parlor.

The family was not unaccustomed to this style of living. Hay's solid manse on

Lafayette Square in Washington was regal by American standards, but *location* meant his temporary London residence was of an altogether higher order. A view of Lafayette Square and a piece of the White House was fine, but here on Carlton House Terrace, Hay could peer out through the Corinthian columns rising two stories above St. James's Park, or walk out onto his balcony and survey the Mall, the sun-dappled lake in the park, the Birdcage Walk, the houses of Parliament, the Horse Guards Parade, and Westminster Abbey. He could even catch a glimpse of the gardens at Marlborough House, the city residence of the Prince and Princess of Wales. John Hay stood with the elite, in the radiant warmth of the greatest empire the world had ever known. The new ambassador, one newspaper noted, had taken up residence in the most expensive private residential block on earth.

The terrace was also, Hay knew, something of a touchy spot for the crumbliest of the British upper crust and their ardent down-class supporters. In the score of attached houses that constituted Carlton House Terrace there still resided a preponderance of homegrown aristocracy—marquesses and earls and duchesses—along with a sprinkling of old-line merchant bankers, decorated soldiers, dedicated sportsmen, and even the home secretary, Brits all. In recent years, however, there had been a notable influx of American arrivistes. Here, as at other fashionable addresses in the imperial city, money was beginning to tell. The lease on 5 Carlton House Terrace was available to Hay chiefly because he could comfortably afford the $2,000 monthly rent, while the most recent lessee, Her Majesty's undersecretary for foreign affairs, the Right Honorable George Curzon, could not, even with his recent financial windfall from his marriage to the belle of Washington, DC, Mary Leiter. Her American millionaire father had settled on his daughter as a wedding gift enough fixed-income railroad stock to throw off the lordly sum of $33,000 a year.

Curzon had had big eyes when he returned to London with his twenty-five-year-old bride and her ample dowry, but the tariff on the terrace town house proved dear, and considering the upkeep on the country estate in Reigate and on the little castles he rented for grouse-shooting season in Scotland, Curzon quickly felt the need to economize. So after just a few months on the terrace, he leased a smaller and cheaper home around the corner at the regal but less costly Carlton Gardens. His wife, however, was little comforted by this short move.

The Hays had sympathy for Mary Leiter Curzon, whom they had known as the most radiant and exotic young swan in Washington's society pond. By April of 1897, the month of her second wedding anniversary, Mary was just another restless political wife—lonely, bored, and addled by a staff of servants she found insolent and inept. She spent nearly all her evenings at home, pining for the London social whirl she had dreamed of inhabiting by right of marriage, while her husband toiled away for the prime minister, Lord Salisbury, and the glory of the British Empire—"the greatest instrument for good that the world has seen," Curzon had written. "In the Empire we have found not merely the key to glory and wealth, but the call to duty, and the means of service to mankind."

Mary did not share the Right Honorable George Curzon's ardor for her adopted country's duty to all mankind—"He sits and sits at those Foreign Office boxes until I could scream," she wrote—but she was determined to be a dutiful wife. She had been a vigorous campaigner in his last election (which had been funded almost entirely by her father) and exhibited sincere pleasure when her thirty-eight-year-old husband became the youngest man in generations to be invited to sit on Her Majesty's Most Honourable Privy Council. Mary was determined to make no domestic or social demands that might impede his political rise.

Curzon, as an instrument of Her Majesty's government, embodied what Henry Adams had long ago apprehended as the three Bs of British assertiveness: he was "bluff, brutal, blunt." Hay was nonetheless fond of Curzon and suspected that the young man could be a useful friend, professionally speaking, or at least a useful barometer with which to read the likelihood of a thaw in Anglo-American relations. A favorite of Lord Salisbury's, Curzon had always appeared to be sympathetic toward the right sort of Americans, if not America itself.

Carlton House Terrace already housed a sprinkling of noteworthy American millionaires—transatlantic Midases, as they were styled in the British press. They were the type being lampooned nightly on the London stage, or in the occasional speech in Parliament, and generally spoken of, though rarely to their faces, as pork and peltry kings, or former washerwomen, renowned for their recent acquisition of money and little else. But these commoners were grudgingly abided; times were tough for the landed in Britain, after all, and the earls and dukes who needed income from their Carlton House Terrace real estate could not afford to be overly choosy. Hay's landlord, the Earl of Caledon, had drawn the line at renting to the minister from Mexico, but he could stomach just about any white man who could pay the freight.

Next door to Hay at number 6 was Mrs. John Mackay, the wife of the famous Bonanza King silver miner of Virginia City, Nevada, whose current riches were so diverse and far-flung that his private secretary could say with some measure of pride that his boss was unable to estimate his personal wealth within the nearest $20 million. "The Mackay residence has been thought to surpass every other London mansion in the elaborateness and artistic character of its ornamentation and the richness of its furnishings"—or so boasted the *Milwaukee Journal*.

Hay's other new neighbor, William Waldorf Astor, was preparing for a right brisk round of socializing down at the east end of the terrace, especially now that his dear friend the Prince of Wales was back in London to officially open the social season. To Willie Astor's delight, this was shaping up to be the most extravagant season in the long life of London, which was readying to host the Diamond Jubilee, a twin celebration of Queen Victoria's sixty years on the throne and of the dazzling empire she ruled. The jubilee promised to draw titled dignitaries and potentates from around the world.

The forty-nine-year-old Astor, heir to a $200 million fortune, had made himself a useful friend of the Prince of Wales largely because the prince was a man with expensive tastes and very definite ideas about how the heir to the British throne should be allowed to comport himself, namely, free from restraint.

Bertie, or Prince Baccarat, as he was sometimes known, was a genial sporting man, a yachtsman, a horse breeder, a gambler, a ladies' man, and an unrepentant spendthrift. His annual stipend from Her Majesty's government never sufficed. Even in the years when a chancellor of the Exchequer persuaded Parliament to increase its expenditure for the heir to the British throne, Bertie blew the budget; every year, without fail, the Prince of Wales fell deeper and deeper and deeper into debt, yet he continued to entertain his many friends, and his many girlfriends, in kingly style, cheerily building for his preferred mistress a sprawling Tudor mansion near the sea at Bournemouth. But the longer he waited for his mother to expire and cede the throne, the more his debt grew. And then along came Willie Astor, who seemed happy to use some of his own bottomless inheritance to pay the prince's bills, gratis.

How could Bertie not be charmed when the wayward American commissioned a portrait of His Royal Highness to hang in a place of pride in Astor's new country estate, Cliveden? Or gave his daughter, Princess Maud, a cobnut-size diamond as a wedding gift? When editorialists on both sides of the Atlantic flogged Willie Astor for using his fortune to wheedle his way into the highest tiers of British aristocracy, or Kaiser Wilhelm made known his displeasure that his royal cousin was on such intimate terms with a commoner, Bertie defended his friend Astor and drew him and his prodigious checkbook closer.

JOHN HAY HAD no interest in following Astor into London's jubilee-mad social whirl that spring, or to comport himself in a way that made him appear desirous of status or celebrity, but it was excruciatingly clear to him from the day he arrived in London that there was little a wealthy and prominent American could do to avoid attention, wanted or no. A London publisher had already issued an affordable little collection of Hay's poetry, with "Jim Bludso of the Prairie Belle" and "Little Breeches" leading the volume. Hay could stomach the reappearance of "Bludso," the story of an engineer who had sacrificed his life to save his steamboat passengers, but "Little Breeches" made him cringe. And once the British publisher had dredged them up out of his ancient past, the poems became immediate currency. Not only was a stalwart of the London stage already selling tickets to her recital of "Little Breeches," but the newspapers were having great sport in attaching the hayseed colloquialisms to the new head of the US Embassy. "[Mr. Hay] will always do well to remember that looking after the best interests of his country 'is a derned sight better business than loafin' round the throne.'"

Hay felt compelled after the first few weeks of the "Bludso" boom to make a statement, which was part excuse, part explanation, part plea to dispense with the entire business. He wanted it understood that he himself had never estimated these particular works very highly: "I sometimes wrote two ballads in one evening," he told a reporter he invited in for an interview. "The ballads were nearly all rough, hurriedly-written pieces, and it is a wonder how they have lived; but they are founded on fact, and I suppose they touch a chord in the popular heart."

Hay also had to endure in print the story intimating that the real secret of his success was Mrs. Hay, who had afforded her husband a "handsome dowry besides a quarter of a million sterling which came to him on her father's death." The Hays' Lafayette Square home was described as "her residence," while rumor had it that her friendship with the wife of President McKinley's right-hand man was the real reason John Hay had secured the coveted ambassadorship in London.

Hay did continue to get some good early press, especially for being less voluble than his predecessor, Bayard, and also for his apparent style. Newspapers commented approvingly on the liveries of his coachman and footmen, who showed handsomely in green jackets, scarlet waistcoats, and silver buttons, and also on the handsomeness of his imported horses and his finest carriage, which was becomingly sleek and modestly ornamented, obviously capable of grace *and* power. The new American ambassador seemed to belong at the seat of empire, as one of the "right-of-way people." At any crowded crossroads in Hyde Park, provided the queen's royal landau was not in sight, John Hay would be among the elect whose driver barreled him through traffic with, as one observer of the time described the scene, "the easy and not unkind authority which makes sons of Britain masters of strange races."

AMBASSADOR HAY SETTLED into a fairly straightforward routine. His daily trip to the official US Embassy on Victoria Street was a pleasant mile-long walk, much of it through St. James's Park, but once there, Hay rarely tarried at his office more than an hour or so. The embassy was an unprepossessing and unwelcoming little warren—generally described by disappointed visitors as "dark and dingy"—tucked into a building of inexpensive flats in a bustling block overtaken by the Army and Navy Cooperative Society, a discount department store drawing scads of bargain-conscious middle- and lower-middle-class shoppers. Then, too, the more time Hay spent at the Victoria Street office, the more likely he was to get wrangled into the most enervating of his routine duties: looking after moneyed Americans on holiday. They wanted, and wanted, and wanted some more: tickets to watch Parliament in action, an audience with the queen, reserved seats for the jubilee parade: "Wasn't there *any*thing available at St. Paul's Cathedral? We hear the Queen might get out of her carriage there, if her lumbago doesn't flare."

Hay chose to do the bulk of his work in the quiet expanse of his Carlton House Terrace residence. He would scan the day's newspapers and report back to the State Department anything of interest—augmented with inside information gleaned from his (and White's) circle of London friends. The papers carried plenty of wire news from back home, and Hay felt compelled to keep up with that. There were interesting little squibs about American politics his first week on the job, like a story about the growing rupture between the new McKinley administration and various prominent members of the Republican Party who had been locked out of jobs. "Among the chief of the malcontents," it was reported, "is Mr. Whitelaw Reid, formerly Ambassador to France, who is deeply chagrined that he was selected neither for a post in the Cabinet nor as Ambassador to England, although his friends worked hard for him." No doubt Reid's *Tribune* would start grinding away at McKinley's tariff bill, and his Hawaii policy, and his choice in foreign consuls, and whatever else might come up. An ocean away from Whitelaw's bilious output, it seemed to Hay, was just about the right distance.

Hay's shaky health improved once he was in harness. The demands of his ambassadorship were not great, but they afforded enough consequential business to keep him engaged. William McKinley's middle-of-the-road tack on the gold-and-silver question, for instance, landed the issue of bimetallism on Hay's desk also. The president was using Great Britain for political cover, continuing to say that it would be wisest, just in terms of economic stability and market confidence, to defer to the British preference on the question. The Brits, after all, remained the world's unquestioned commercial behemoth. The Royal Navy ruled the world's shipping lanes. "I do not say the French cannot come," one of Her Majesty's admirals had famously remarked, "I only say they cannot come by sea." Britain accounted for half the merchant vessels on the seas at any given moment and nearly three-quarters of the goods shuttling between Europe and Asia through the Suez Canal. The empire's gold reserves dwarfed the rest of the world's, and just kept growing. And because they dominated global commerce, the British also dominated world finance. The stock exchange in London was an international marketplace; more than half the listings were companies outside England. Prices and futures contracts on all the world's important commodities were set by the markets and exchanges in the City of London. And just as Greenwich mean time was the standard by which all clocks were set, so the British pound sterling was the stable currency against which all others were measured. America and Germany were nations of obvious industrial and financial ambition, but neither was a real threat as far as the British Foreign Office was concerned.

President McKinley had decided to ship a trio of prominent American politicians to Europe to see if they could work out a reasonable and internationally sanctioned ratio for valuing gold against silver so that the two metals could live in perfect harmony as a dual standard. This effort to effect an international agreement, McKinley reckoned, would serve to tamp down the Populist crowd's push for free silver in America. And if it didn't work out, well, that was fine, too; the president could always explain that he had done his best, but his hands were tied by a greater power. Hay did hasten to make a brief survey of British sentiment, conferencing with the most powerful banker in London and his acquaintance of nearly twenty years, Baron Rothschild; with Lord Salisbury's chancellor of the Exchequer; and with some liberal friends of Henry Adams's. But it would be months before the American commissioners arrived, so Hay could let that issue simmer quietly on the back of the stove.

Hay was faced with only one immediately pressing issue, which would give him his first practical lesson in dealing with the most powerful empire on earth: fur seals. The first Tuesday after his arrival, Ambassador Hay headed for the Foreign Office to see if he could untangle what had recently tightened into a perilous little knot: the question of the rapid diminishment of the valuable fur seal population in the US-owned Pribilof Islands, off Alaska. There was a long history at play here. When William Henry Seward, Hay's old friend and champion and President Lincoln's secretary of state, had bought Alaska from Russia back in 1867 (the nearby Pribilofs were included in the purchase price), there were somewhere between two million and five million seals in the Bering Sea. But in the thirty years since, sealing had become a big and consequential *industry*. A sealskin, it was discovered, made simply smashing fur-trimmed outerwear—it was warm and waterproof but also breathable. Manufacturers and department stores across Europe and America were at pains to satisfy the demand for sealskin coats and gloves and boots. The first time the writer

William Dean Howells laid eyes on him, Sam Clemens was wearing one of these fashionable overcoats, "with the fur out," Howells later remembered, "in the satisfaction of a caprice, or the love of strong effect which he was apt to indulge through life."

Feeding the maw of an international mass market had brought the seal population off the coast of Alaska near extinction; by the time Hay hit London, only about two hundred thousand fur seals remained. The overwhelming danger to the herds now was pelagic—or open-water—sealing. Canadians who did not have access to easy club-and-carry hunting on the American-owned islands had started outfitting boats back in the 1880s to pluck the seals out of the water on their long ocean swims. The Russians and the Japanese, who had sizable seal populations within their own territory, also began to follow the seals into open water, and American hunters joined in, too. The United States had tried to assert jurisdiction and to close the nearby waters to the hunt, but the single US revenue cutter on patrol was unable to keep watch on the entire Bering Sea. The Canadians, meanwhile, complained of harassment and general mercantile injustice. They were, they claimed, being reduced to poverty by the high-handed American restrictions. They didn't appreciate being treated as pirates or poachers. They felt betrayed and neglected by the British Colonial Office, which had not protected their simple right to make a living killing and selling fur seals.

An 1893 arbitration conference with representatives from the most interested parties (America and Britain, representing their dominion Canada) and three neutral countries (France, Italy, and Sweden and Norway) produced a multivolume door stopper of minutes titled *Fur Seal Arbitration: Proceedings of the Tribunal of Arbitration, Convened at Paris* . . . and a series of reform measures for ensuring "the proper protection and preservation of the fur seal resorting to Bering Sea," which really meant the proper protection and preservation of the sealing industry. Vessels were enjoined from hunting seals within sixty miles of the Pribilof Islands, hunting with firearms was prohibited, annual catch limits were set. These terms were to be in effect for five years, until 1898, when the conferees would meet again, with a new assessment of the seal population, and revise the provisions as needed. It had already become apparent, however, that the 1893 rules didn't much help.

The number of boats on these international "fishing" expeditions grew to sixty-seven in the 1896 season, with ugly results for all involved. The crews had worked harder than ever that season for *half* the usual catch and held out little hope for a profit. The damage to the seals was compounded by the outright waste of pelagic hunting: about two-thirds of the seals captured in the Bering Sea were mamas out on hundred-mile swims to gather food for their newborns. Nearly fifteen thousand orphaned pups had died of starvation in

1896, according to David Starr Jordan, the US government ichthyologist sent to study the problem. "Facts lead Dr. Jordan to the positive conclusion that pelagic sealing will ultimately result in the practical extinction of the herd," his study concluded.

The problem had been deemed so acute in the spring of 1897 that the US secretary of state had decided he could not wait for Hay's ship to arrive in England and had dispatched Harry White to the British Foreign Office with marching orders: "You are instructed to bring subject to immediate attention of British Government, communicate President's concern and urgent expectation that effective measures be at once adopted by the respective Governments." White had made it plain that President McKinley wanted all pelagic sealing suspended for the coming season and a new conference of the parties concerned to make a plan to preserve enough of the seal population to ensure a commercially viable industry. "It will not satisfy the President," was White's message, "to be informed that the British Government proposes to take up the subject at the close of next year's season, as contemplated in the Paris award. If destruction goes on meanwhile, there will be no occasion for conference, then. Action as indicated must be taken now if herd is to be saved." Time was of the essence, as the seal fishermen were preparing to ship out for the beginning of the 1897 season.

The Brits did not share this sense of urgency. For one thing, White was told, they were still waiting for their own man of science to weigh in with *his* count from the previous season. For another, the prime minister, Lord Salisbury, who ran all foreign affairs, was spending his Easter holiday in France. The Foreign Office factotum could only promise to send the message along to Lord Salisbury in France and told White that the United States might even hope for a prompt response. Lord Salisbury, who had a habit of sitting on American requests for months, made a surprisingly quick answer from his holiday retreat; his message was already en route to Washington, but the contents were not yet known when Hay took up his new post.

This was the situation the new American ambassador was facing on April 27, 1897, less than a week after he took up residence in London, as he walked, "at the earliest possible hour," into the holiday-thinned Foreign Office to push for an answer. Salisbury was still resting in France. Curzon was away from London. And Francis Hyde Villiers, who had been paying close attention to the seal issue, was also vacationing. So Hay was left to take his argument to the reedy, whiskered, and thick-spectacled permanent undersecretary, Sir Thomas Sanderson.

Hay repeated the president's earnest desire to call a halt to the sealing that season and to negotiate a new agreement in order to avert the extinction of the fur seal. Sanderson let it be known that Her Majesty's government had come to a different understanding of the question: the American suggestion of near extinction was overblown and unfounded. Hay countered that the British interpretation sounded suspect, as "the conclusion of [the British expert] Mr. Thompson did not seem in entire accordance with the facts on which they were based." When Sanderson held to the prime minister's line, Hay veered slightly from the official American argument. "I said the interests of England and the United States were identical in the matter," Hay reported back to his boss, Secretary of State John Sherman, "that the business of sealing would be lost to the Canadians by the extinction of the seals, [as would] the handling of the product in London."

A second British foreign officer told Hay, in all frankness, that if any British subjects were forced to forgo the hunt this season, they would have to be paid off. There was no chance, failing such a payment, that the British Colonial Office was going to tell the Canadian sealers they couldn't make their hunt. Hay didn't waste any more breath; he understood that these men, whatever their rank, were little more than Salisbury's tools. The prime minister kept his own counsel and set *all* policy.

So Hay requested a meeting with Lord Salisbury himself, at the prime minister's earliest convenience. He retreated back to his terrace and wrote home to the State Department that the chances of successfully stopping that season's hunt seemed small because the British Colonial Office was working hard to persuade the empire's "white dominion" in the Americas to sign a trade deal giving Britain special privileges. "There can be no doubt that the influence of the Dominion was never stronger in England than now," Hay explained to Washington. "Whatever might be the real merits of the case it would be difficult for the British Government to go counter, at such a time, to the wishes of the Government and people of Canada."

Hay did get quick word that his audience with the prime minister would take place on Salisbury's return from France, in just a few days, but knowing what he did about the leader of the British government, he still held out little hope for a fast and happy settlement. The sixty-seven-year-old marquess, Robert Arthur Talbot Gascoyne-Cecil, was a large, bearded, rumpled, brusque, and imposing statesman who had been prime minister for nearly nine of the previous twelve years. In addition to the prime minister's hat, Lord Salisbury wore a second official bonnet as chief of Her Majesty's Foreign Office. This vast portfolio might have harried another man; Lord Salisbury appeared unruffled. He conducted his business with chilly and efficient detachment. The 3rd Marquess of Salisbury did not waste time trying to make friends among men or nations. He saw himself as he saw his nation: self-sufficient and beyond need of alliance. The prime minister tended the vast empire as a landlord, without sentiment and without illusions of any great and noble national mission. He cared only to run a smooth and profitable operation.

"British policy is to drift lazily downstream, occasionally putting out a boat-hook to avoid collision," the prime minister once said. He was keeping his eye on what mattered: ruling Egypt and the Suez Canal, which allowed the empire to control and defend the jewel of its crown, India, and its passageway to the Far East; and maintaining the delicate balance of power in Europe. But he expended precious little time or energy trying to herd the great powers on the Continent in any particular direction. "The utmost we have is a slight negative influence by which we prevent them from flying at each other's throats," he once told Arthur Balfour. His preferred method, according to Curzon, was to throw bones to the big dogs like France and Russia and Germany—a little piece of Africa here, a little piece of Asia there.

Salisbury had only slight interest in the United States of America in 1897, and saw no need of any happy understanding with the former British possession; the United States was just another niggling headache, annoyingly loud but easy to push aside. The Venezuela affair had been a terrific bother, but it had also convinced Salisbury that the men who governed the United States were mostly talk. The Americans would continue to threaten Spain over Cuba, he told the queen, but it would stop there: "The United States will do all the mischief they can without going to war."

When Hay and Salisbury met at the Foreign Office on the afternoon of April 30, 1897 (his lordship rarely got to his office before three thirty), the well-rested prime minister simply stuck out his boat hook and gave Hay a firm little push. Lord Salisbury explained that he had been going over the report of the British scientist and had concluded, as he had written to the secretary of state, that "the President is mistaken in supposing that in the opinion of the British agent there is any immediate cause for alarm." Hay protested; Salisbury was unmoved. He refused to endorse the well-founded theory that pelagic sealing had destroyed nine-tenths of the seal population. The reason for the previous year's diminished seal catch, he declared rather *un*scientifically, was "stormy weather." The Canadians would be left free to hunt as they pleased this season, he peremptorily reiterated, and there would be no conference until the five-year agreement expired two seasons hence.

The meeting was perfectly cordial, and Salisbury's clarity and frankness were worthy of appreciation, but his manner confirmed Hay's long-held belief that English diplomacy was "overbearing and pigheaded." He well understood, as a frequent auditor of a London salon wrote at the time, "one of the Englishman's distinctive traits: he has battle-ships back of his opinions." While Hay was confident he could keep happy relations with his many British friends, it was already apparent that it would be difficult to achieve any official friendship with the British Empire. The imperial bosses were not interested in a relationship of equals, because as far as they were concerned they had no equals.

THERE WERE A few diplomatic formalities for Hay to see to in his first days in London, the most important being the official presentation of his credentials to Queen Victoria. He was kept waiting for nearly two weeks, but when the day of presentation finally arrived, Hay and his wife were scooped up from Carlton House Terrace, placed in the royal carriage, and conveyed to the queen's doorstep at Windsor Castle, where festivities began with a luncheon, at which Lord Salisbury was on hand to make the formal introduction.

Queen Victoria was enjoying a wave of popularity at home and across the empire in general in the early spring of 1897. The seventy-seven-year-old queen had recently hurdled over her grandfather, George III, to become the longest-reigning monarch in Britain's long history, and this record-breaking rule was judged fruitful to the nation, and at not too steep a price. The chancellor of the Exchequer had reported to Parliament the day before Hay's presentation that maintaining the queen in her deserved and desired lifestyle cost the British taxpayer less in 1897 than it had when she ascended to the throne in 1837. If one studied the numbers closely, they suggested that the interest alone from William Waldorf Astor's estate could float the queen in perpetuity, along with the entire royal family (spendthrift Bertie included) and entourage, and still allow for a steady increase in principal.

Queen Victoria hardly thought of herself as a dependent or a mere figurehead; she nodded without doubt when Lord Salisbury referred to her as the personage "from whom, legally, all power flows." And she had much on her business agenda the day of her formal recognition of John Hay. She was meeting with the prime minister and members of her Privy Council that day to discuss, among other things, the storm her increasingly difficult grandson, Emperor William of Germany (the kaiser), was stirring up between Greece and Turkey. In spite of Salisbury's efforts, the two countries *had* gone to war over the island of Crete, and the Turks—with secret assistance from Germany—had gained the upper hand. There were fears the sultan's army would be strong enough to take Athens, home to Victoria's granddaughter and William's *own* sister, Princess Sophie, who had married the crown prince of Greece. The queen was sending Willie little notes of advice on the matter, in cipher. And he was returning the favor with rude retorts, in the clear, for any telegraph operator to see, which had caused her to uninvite Kaiser Willie from her own jubilee, in spite of warnings from her Privy Council and others who tried to point out that her oldest grandson not only was extraordinarily sensitive to slights but also had at his disposal the world's most powerful standing army.

The presentation of diplomats was generally short and formal—the sovereign accepting the credentials, the ambassador offering a private message from his own seat of government. The queen hastily dispatched the new ministers from Portugal and China that day, but she lingered a bit with John Hay before offering the customary dismissal: her genial half smile and soft bow of the head. Unlike her current prime minister, Victoria had softened toward Americans; intemperate and treasonous though they had been toward her grandfather George III, she saw no margin in holding the grudge. She and Great Britain had had plenty of big innings in the 120 years since the American Revolution, and the queen had been given to understand she was a fairly popular figure in the former colonies. "[Americans] have always had a kind personal feeling for me," she told Henry White's wife, Daisy, "and I don't know why."

Victoria's graciousness toward Hay did not owe chiefly to any exalted standing of the nation he represented; good relations with America were about as important to Her Majesty as good relations with Portugal and much less crucial at that particular moment than good relations with China. But the queen had friends and acquaintances in common with the new American at court, and Hay was the rare commoner who put Victoria at ease. He was respectful and aware of protocol but not fawning: plainspoken, unperturbed in the presence of power, and well read. The queen was not particularly fond of sportsmen, like her son Bertie. She had tried to watch golf—"people walking about with sticks in the distance," she said, "and it looked very dull." She was, however, forgiving of literary men and poets like Hay. Tennyson "was like a person who had never been contradicted or disciplined," she said of the truculent and mostly unlikable poet, "but he had noble thoughts."

The new American ambassador, the queen would record in her diary that day, "is very gentlemanlike & pleasing."

John Hay had grown less acidic about royalty in general since his days in the rouged and powdered courts of France and Spain, and besides, Queen Victoria was a constitutional monarch, which made her country very nearly a real republic. But he still couldn't understand the hold the institution had on the general public. "What a curious thing it is," he wrote in the jubilee year, "that there has been no King in England since Elizabeth of special distinction; most of them far worse than mediocre . . . and yet the monarchical religion has grown day by day, till the Queen is worshiped as more than mortal." Hay did have to admit his delight when the queen insisted on hosting Clara for a separate private meeting that afternoon, and he was charmed when his wife came away with the assurance that a "dine-and-sleep invitation" would soon be proffered.

The now official American ambassador liked the aged queen in spite of himself. The Hays had seen her both at a distance and up close over the years, including at her Golden Jubilee in 1887, and the dough-faced sovereign appeared to them now, ten years later and within weeks of her seventy-eighth birthday, to have been much worn in that interval. There was a little less color in her once-florid cheeks; her eyesight was failing; her hearing iffy; she seemed stiff in the joints, in pain walking even a short distance; and she was thinner, even somehow smaller. She looked to Clara Hay like "a nice little old lady."

Here was the living embodiment of the world's most impressive empire, Victoria, queen of the United Kingdom and empress of India, and yet she appeared haggard and fragile. She was also sensitive to her current predicament. She had a self-awareness sharpened by a lifetime in the public eye, and with her Diamond Jubilee approaching, and the queen's own self set to be the focus of the most brilliant celebratory capstone of the nineteenth century, the century Britain had ruled, Victoria was more and more vexed by this problem of image, as she was more and more mindful that even a monarch was powerless against the sad sag of mortality.

She had begun to make requests that might be considered vain by the less charitably inclined: she had asked that a recent likeness, a statue unveiled a few years earlier, embody her at her best. "Make it like me when I was young," she had pleaded with her daughter Louise, who was also the sculptor. When Princess Louise protested that she was modeling from life and wasn't old enough to remember her mother when she was young, the queen insisted. "I shall be gone in a few years; then no one period of my past personal appearance will represent me any more truly than any other. Why not select for posterity the aspect of me which I liked the best, when I looked my best and was young and happy?"

Hay was happy to do his own small part for the queen's vanity, having been informed that she might appreciate a special American mission to help celebrate her anniversary and that, as the British ambassador to the United States expressed it, "if your Government should find it convenient to send a ship of war flying an admiral's flag to attend the festivities the visit will be very welcome." Hay endorsed the warship idea and the special mission, shortly after his presentation, as a show of friendship. "I am aware that it is not in the traditions nor in the habits of our country to compete with other powers in the matter of ceremony," he wrote to his boss at the State Department. "At the same time it might not be advisable to pass by without notice of an event of so much interest and significance, and one which so strongly engages the feelings of all people of the British empire."

Chapter Ten

The Town Begins to Grow Abominable

Sam Clemens had his head down in his book work when John Hay took up his post in London, but Clemens did follow the news of the ambassador's first meetings with Lord Salisbury and his audience with the queen. Clemens had been in the company of plenty of statesmen and celebrities, but he had never had a friend of such long standing ascend to this level—and certainly not one who had grown up as he had, with the Mississippi mud between his toes. Still, though this was the first time in their thirty-year friendship that John Hay and Sam Clemens were living in the same town, it was unlikely that the two men would cross paths. Clemens planned to stay in London only a few more months, and he and his family intended to remain exiles from society until then.

Clemens's desire to keep company with John Hay had a long history of coming to naught. Hay had politely declined Clemens's offer of a fifty-fifty partnership in a newspaper in Buffalo in the early 1870s because he had no capital to bring to the enterprise. Hay also took a pass when Clemens invited him along on a Mississippi River research excursion a few years later, explaining that his daughter had just been born. "She is well and hearty," Hay told Clemens. "So is her mother. Of the two the mother is the handsomer and makes less row." Then came that fateful day when Clara Hay had caught her husband yukking it up on the Sabbath with Clemens, *in her own parlor*; the two men had rarely been in the same room since. They had exchanged letters of fun and congratulations over the years. Clemens had sent Hay a note of applause on the publication of his *Pike County Ballads* and publicly championed Hay over Bret Harte as the man who introduced frontier vernacular to American literature. Hay could be dismissive of Clemens's books to friends like Henry James and Henry Adams, but he applauded Clemens for the "documentary" powers he brought to bear in writing *Adventures of Huckleberry Finn*: "I, who grew up in the midst of it, have almost forgotten it, except when I read of it in your writings—the only place, I think, where a faithful record of it survives," he had written to Clemens when the book was first published. "Huck Finns and Tom Sawyers were my admired and trusted friends—though I had to cultivate them as the early Christians did their religion—in out of the way places. I am glad to meet them again in your luminous pages."

Hay's fondness for Clemens never dimmed over the years, but he understood that this, too, was a relationship he had to cultivate in out-of-the-way places. Their politics differed, for starters. Hay was not loud about it, but he remained a Republican in the original party sense: a defender of government by educated and accomplished white men, a believer in the genius of capitalism and of the capitalists who made it big, a champion of shielding their profits from what he regarded as the insistent and unmanly grasp of foreign competition and labor unions. He was especially wary of a shift of money and power to the working class and immigrants. Clemens was on the other side. He was never a party man, but he was a small-d democrat and skeptical that anybody in power would long remain interested in the common good. Clemens wanted fairness across the social, political, and commercial structure, even if it meant shaking the foundations. He was shy to do the shaking himself, except behind the cover of one of his fictional characters. "And now here I was, in a country where a right to say how the country should be governed was restricted to six persons in each thousand of its population," was how his Connecticut Yankee in King Arthur's court called it. "Nine hundred and ninety-four of the members furnished all the money and did all the work, and the other six elected themselves a permanent board of direction and took all the dividends. It seemed to me that what the nine hundred and ninety-four dupes needed was a new deal."

Politics couldn't really separate the two men, but class could, especially after Hay married into his pots of money. The two men weren't going to travel in common circles or live in the same neighborhood, whatever the city. Renowned and well loved as he was, Sam Clemens was not going to be a guest at the terrace that spring or summer. Clara Hay was in town until early August, and she wouldn't stand for having Clemens in the house. Harry White would be her ally on that count, too. White had met Clemens on a long ocean voyage a few years before and found the author a blusterer—charmingly amusing but uncommonly profane. "He is a quaint, rough, and rather uncouth person in manner, very frank and open in expressing his opinions," Harry explained to his wife, who much preferred an author who respected the accepted social hierarchy, like Henry James. And it must be admitted that even people who loved Sam Clemens for his fellowship, his brilliance, his extraordinary sense of fun, and his facility for entertaining any audience still found him a challenge. He is "not at all refined," wrote the author Grace King, who had known him all through the Hartford years, "and ate like a corn-field darkey."

CLEMENS WAS UNLIKELY to be invited to Lady Ancaster's ball at Belgrave Square or to put on silks and buckles and velvet knee breeches to attend one of the drawing rooms at Buckingham Palace. His usual social circle did not run toward prime ministers and members of Parliament and British royalty. His relationship to the houses of Hanover and Saxe-Coburg-Gotha was mostly epistolary; his chief intercourse with the reigning family was an ongoing burlesque of a kerfuffle over taxes. The British government had been after Clemens for a decade to pay taxes on income earned from sales of his books in the British Isles and the colonies; unlike the American government, which could still run itself on revenues from protective tariffs, post office receipts, and a small cut on all sales of alcohol and tobacco, the British Empire needed a lot of ducat to fund a navy capable of controlling the traffic of five separate oceans and an army equipped with enough new weaponry—Maxim machine guns, exploding dumdum bullets, fast transport—to perform the "butcher and bolt" raids that terrorized into submission the most obstinate native population.

The Inland Revenue Office had first contacted Clemens in 1887 requesting that he pay a Parliament-sanctioned tax on foreign authors. He did not write a check right away but chose instead to make a plea for lenience to Queen Victoria in an open letter, explaining right up top that he had a passing acquaintance with her oldest son. He had "met the Prince of Wales once in the fall of 1873," he wrote, but it was not in any familiar way,

> but in a quite informal way, being casual, and was of course a surprise to us both. It was in Oxford street, just where you come out of Oxford into Regent Circus, and just as he turned up one side of the circle at the head of a procession, I went down the other side on the top of an omnibus. He will remember me on account of a gray coat with flap pockets that I wore, as I was the only person on the omnibus that had on that kind of a coat; I remember him of course as easy as I would a comet. He looked quite proud and satisfied, but that is not to be wondered at, he has a good situation.
>
> And once I called on your Majesty, but you were out.

Clemens then explained to the queen that he had received this thick document from Inland Revenue, which was a demand for payment, and he showed it to an eminent scholar who counseled that he was expected to make good not only on that year's tax but on three years' back taxes. But when Clemens looked again at the opening lines—"To MR. MARK TWAIN: IN PURSUANCE of the Acts of Parliament for granting to Her Majesty Duties and Profits"—he decided to take it up with Her Majesty directly.

> I saw that it was a private matter, a family matter, and that the proceeds went to yourself, not the Government. I would always rather treat with principals, and I am glad I noticed that clause. With a principal, one can always get at a fair and right understanding, whether it is about potatoes, or continents, or any of those things, or something entirely different; for the size or nature of the thing does not affect the fact; whereas, as a rule, a subordinate is more or less troublesome to satisfy. . . . Now then . . . this is not going to be an Irish question; it is going to be settled pleasantly and satisfactorily for all of us.

This little joke could have gone either way, but Clemens had got word that the queen had had a good laugh at the letter, and when he had run into Bertie a few years later, at a spa in Homburg, Germany, the prince insisted on an introduction. Chauncey Depew had been slightly embarrassed to introduce Clemens, who was wearing a well-worn and slightly soiled "tramping suit," but he did as Bertie asked. Joe Twichell, who was traveling with Clemens at the time, would never forget the scene: "The Prince took Mark Twain's arm and the two marched up and down, talking earnestly together, the Prince, solid, erect, and soldier-like, Clemens weaving along in his curious, swinging gait in a full tide of talk, and brandishing a sun-umbrella of the most scandalous description."

As Clemens later described it to Twichell, the prince's parting words were, "It is a pleasure, Mr. Clemens, to have met you—again."

"Why, have we met before?" Clemens asked.

"Oh yes, don't you remember that day on the Strand when you were on the top of a 'bus and I was heading a procession and you had on your new overcoat with flap-pockets?"

The Prince of Wales told Chauncey Depew he would have been pleased to invite Clemens to supper that evening, "if I thought he had with him any dinner clothes."

CLEMENS WASN'T LOOKING for any invitations in early 1897. He was all business. Frank Bliss had finally signed the new book contract, but not before insisting that his author include a section on South Africa and the Jameson Raid, which was still in the news. It was starting to look as if Joseph Chamberlain might be implicated in the violent plot to overthrow the Boer government. Clemens protested at first, because he was still hoping his reporting on the raid would provide him with enough material for a second book and thus a second stream of income from that god-awful trip. But he didn't have the legs to put up a real fight. So he went back to his desk, with his wife in harness now, too, to add another thirty thousand words.

They finalized the manuscript together, Sam and Livy, and Katy Leary could sense the change in the house, like the lifting of the fog. "When spring come, and the sun came out and everything was gay, and it was the 'Season,' then London was wonderful," she wrote. The full manuscript was almost ready to ship, and Clemens could feel the family fortunes swinging up. Harper & Brothers had started issuing and advertising the New and Uniform Library Edition of Mark Twain favorites, including *Life on the Mississippi*, *The Prince and the Pauper*, and *Huckleberry Finn* and new collections of essays and short stories. Bliss was ready to set sail for England to retrieve the new manuscript and fork over the $10,000. Clemens was feeling better than ever in the first week of May, when newspapers in America pronounced him dead.

It was true that he had been in and out of St. Thomas's Hospital across the river in Lambeth quite a bit recently. Maybe somebody slipped a reporter the news that there was a Clemens near death. Maybe somebody had seen Sam Clemens enter one day and not leave and, what with all the talk of his ill health recently, assumed the worst. There was actually no great mystery, had anybody bothered to ask. Clemens's newfound cousin, "Dr. Jim," had suffered a bad case of pneumonia, and Clemens had dutifully visited every day, just to keep his cousin's spirits up and to tell him—or forget to tell him—that Livy stood ready and able to serve, whatever he needed. Of course, nobody asked. Instead the London correspondent of the Associated Press cabled home to America the sensational news: "Mark Twain" was dead. Clemens didn't bother to make a statement. This was getting to be old hat. But refutations from Clemens's friends began to cross the Atlantic the same day. His publisher Frank Bliss, for one, was not going to pass up an opening for a little free publicity. He told his reporter friends that "Mark Twain" was alive and well, making the final edits on his new travel book, which might well be his masterpiece. Bliss also showed reporters a private letter he'd recently received from the author: "I wouldn't trade it for any book I have ever written," read Clemens's note, "& I am not an easy person to please."

Clemens still did not join in Bliss's little publicity boomlet, but the reports of his death, coupled with his emergence from the long winter's work on the book, made him eager to be back among the living. "Now I am ready for dissipation with a good conscience," Clemens wrote to his new friend MacAlister. "What night will you come down & smoke?"

Clemens was full of vinegar now, and he had enough free time again to be dangerous. He was, once again, determined to do something heroic for Livy. At times he even felt lionhearted enough to attempt to convince his wife, for her own good, that they should let go the crusade to pay off every creditor at par. No less a legal personage than a former United States attorney general had advised Clemens that he needn't pay dollar for dollar, which ought to carry *some* weight with Livy. "He told me to bust up Mrs. Clemens's desire to pay some of the small debts in full," Clemens reported to Rogers. "I said that was your view, too, & he said it was sound. I shall try to do the busting."

He was also dreaming up new ways to remarket his old stories. How about a special thousand-set deluxe edition of his collected works, which he would sell personally? The scene of his triumph was already playing in his head: "Mark Twain" shuffling through the marble halls of Capitol Hill, closing deals. "I would go to Washington & stay there 2 months & make the 700 Senators & Congressmen & each give me the name of a man at home who, to please his representative & keep on the good side of him, would take a set—heelers, barkeepers & other persons near & dear to Congressmen. I would load up every important jail & saloon in America." He wondered whether Rogers might be able to get Doubleday to issue the deluxe set. That was a publishing house of quality; Bliss could never handle it.

He hadn't given up on the special $1,000-a-seat lecture either, and that event was starting to come into focus, too, so he sat down and sketched it, *enthusiastically*, for his would-be promoter, Frank Fuller. "Lately the matter has come to me again," he wrote to his sensible and discreet old friend.

> This time, with this suggestion: that a dozen men, each with influence over a millionaire go each privately to his millionaire and get him to put up $1000, and sign his name to an invitation to me to come and do a 'benefit'-lecture in the lecture hall of the Waldorf hotel, and sell our seats privately at auction to the highest bidder. Now if *that* scheme could be worked—well, it appeals to my vanity. I *would* like to sail up like that, and go into history as the only lecturer that had ever made so immense a scoop on the platform in any country. . . . Is the scheme practicable?"

Clemens wanted his old friend Fuller to understand that he was aware of the possible humiliation of another public failure, but the lecture event seemed worth the risk. "Would it 'go'? and pull me suddenly out of debt?" he pleaded to Fuller. "If it would the income from my wife's inheritance would enable us to go home and live in a modest way in our own house [in Hartford]."

VEXATION PILED UP on Ambassador Hay's desk over the next weeks, in large part because the State Department in Washington was a listing ship with a dotty captain. McKinley's chosen secretary of state, seventy-three-year-old John Sherman, turned out to be suffering early-stage dementia. Alvey Adee was capable enough to keep the diplomatic trains running, and McKinley had persuaded a trusted friend and legal adviser, William R. Day, to take over daily operations as Sherman's chief deputy, but Day was not yet in Washington when Hay began his ambassadorship in London.

McKinley was basically acting as his own secretary of state and had been forced to hand over large swaths of diplomatic acreage to special envoys like General John W. Foster, who was put in charge of the Bering Sea fur seal problem. Foster was already preparing to sail from New York to try to push the British, the Russians, and the Japanese to work toward a new agreement on restrictions. The former secretary of state, it had to be admitted, knew the issue as well as any man in America; he had been the US representative to the Paris fur seal convention in 1893. But Foster was still stewing about what he believed were the unjust and feckless final terms of that conference. Prime Minister Salisbury's sharp rebuff of the president's request for a temporary moratorium on seal hunting had not improved Foster's mood.

The week before he boarded his boat for Europe, Foster wrote, under Sherman's official State Department signature, a provocative new set of instructions concerning the seal problem for Ambassador Hay to transmit to Lord Salisbury. The paper contained a long history of the fur seal problem from the American point of view, followed by a run of barbed imputations. The dispatch accused Lord Salisbury of cooking the seal data for political purposes and laid blame for the decimation of the seal population squarely on Great Britain, which, in refusing to check its subjects in Canada, had "failed to respect the real intent and spirit of the Tribunal or the obligations imposed by it," wrote Foster. "Upon Great Britain must therefore rest, in the public conscience of mankind, the responsibility for the embarrassment in the relations of the two nations which must result from such conduct." Hay's unhappy task was to deliver this pointed message to Lord Salisbury and his boat hook. While Foster set sail for England, Hay decided to pocket the instructions temporarily. "I have this week twice kicked at my orders," Hay confessed opaquely to Henry Adams, "a thing beyond reason and utterly unjustifiable. But I really must not talk about it."

LONDON, MEANTIME, WAS experiencing Diamond Jubilee fever, now that the queen was back in residence at Buckingham Palace to play drawing-room hostess and to take her afternoon rides, wearing her sporty dark spectacles, in her open landau. Londoners commented on Her Majesty's surprising endurance and on her willingness to extend her usually circumscribed orbit to neighborhoods she had never much frequented. "The streets & Park were immensely full & there was much cheering & waving of handkerchiefs," she recorded in her diary on May 10, 1897, five weeks before the jubilee observance was to commence. This was a woman who craved public affection. It had been "worth being shot at to see how much one is loved," she had said after an assassination attempt some years earlier.

As the queen began to show herself in London again, details of the weeklong jubilee fete, set for the end of June, were becoming clear to the public. The six-mile-long parade route had been finalized, and it was noted with pride that the queen would make display even to her subjects in the "humblest quarter" across the Thames. "Half of the route," it was reported, "lies through the abode of poverty." Her Majesty's government did, however, plan to employ a guard of twenty-five thousand soldiers to keep the dregs at a proper distance.

The jubilee was to be a celebration of the empire, and invitees from its distant colonies were already beginning to assemble. "Native officers" from India, including cavalry and lancers from Bengal, Madras, Bombay, and Hyderabad, were steaming toward England, as were uniformed representatives from Canada, Australia, and New Zealand. The New Zealand military outfits "are a smart, well-set-up lot," it was reported. "The average height of the company is 5 ft 10 in." Colonial Premiers were already en route from Britain's cherished "white dominions," that is, the places where they had pretty much exterminated the native populations—New South Wales, Queensland, Tasmania, South Australia, Western Australia, New Zealand, Cape of Good Hope, Natal, Newfoundland, and, with pride of place, Canada.

Jubilee commerce was already moving at a gallop. Smithies were striking commemorative coins and plates and medals. Charity subscriptions in the queen's honor were funding hospitals, infirmaries, convalescent homes, nursing brigades, parish churches, and agricultural benevolent societies. Hotels and landlords along the parade route had been advertising overseas for months. A reviewing stand with something near a million seats was being constructed and priced out. Blocks of prime viewing spots, flats and mansions with windows overlooking the procession, were being auctioned off to the highest bidders. The newspapers predicted a crowd of two million and fourfold inflation in the price of food in London. "The town begins to grow abominable," Hay complained to Adams. "Six miles of lumber deform the streets. The fellow-being *pullules* [multiplies]. How well you are out of it!"

Ambassador Hay was in it up to his neck; it fell to him to ensure and maintain the official dignity of the American presence among the gathering nations of the world. The United States was sending a warship, the *Brooklyn*, for the naval review at Portsmouth, but so were France, Germany, Austria, Spain,

Holland, Sweden, Russia, Portugal, Norway, the Netherlands, and Italy. Those countries had something the United States did not: royal persons to offer to the Victorian altar. The queen had forbidden the presence of any other national sovereign—mostly as a ruse to keep her petulant grandson Kaiser William close to calm. Not that William was anxious to celebrate "the old hag," as he called his grandmum, but he had remembered Victoria's Golden Jubilee ten years earlier, when he had begged the queen to let him represent Germany. She had brushed him aside in favor of his own father and had given the dying Frederick III the place of highest honor in that parade. Willie had seen the pictures of his father that day, astride his white steed, the glare of the sun on his bleached uniform, and he wanted that for himself. When Victoria refused to relent on the no-sitting-sovereign edict, Willie decided to send his brother Prince Henry of Prussia and a naval band from Kiel, but he kept whining right up to the end. "I feel like a charger chained in the stables who hears the bugle sounding, stomps and chomps at his bit, because he cannot follow his regiment," he wrote to the queen.

Near the end of May the papers had items every day about newly designated royal representatives: princes from Naples, Bavaria, Schleswig-Holstein, India, Persia; a princess from Saxony; dukes from France, Spain, Portugal; the Grand Duke Cyril of Russia. The heir presumptive of Austria, Archduke Franz Ferdinand, was emerging from a year-long illness with plans to don his uniform and represent his uncle, the emperor. The pope was sending a monsignor from the Vatican. Secretary of State Sherman, meanwhile, was still dithering. As far as Hay understood it, the envoys from the United States were to be the admiral commanding the *Brooklyn*, a general of the US Army, and two as-yet-unnamed "eminent civilians." Hay himself would act as official head of the special embassy.

Plenty of other distinguished Americans were already drawing up on the English shore and paying huge sums for good views of the queen's jubilee parade. Mr. and Mrs. Bradley Martin, whose excessively lavish society masquerade ball at the Waldorf Hotel that spring had made them infamous on at least four continents, were getting plenty of local press. Their $9,000 expenditure "to engage a couple of windows" overlooking the parade even managed to improve the normally low standing of that American punching bag of long standing. "Mr. [William Waldorf] Astor shines as quite a splendid example of good taste," offered the *Gloucester Citizen*, by way of comparison. "Good taste is not being shown very much by American millionaires in connection with this event."

The problem, from Hay's perspective, was that the flood of Americans into London—millionaires and elected officials or no—crowded his time with a torrent of entreaties for information and for special privilege. The American visitors all wanted tickets to Parliament, which was back in session again. "I go to bed aching with petty anxieties, and I get up unrefreshed to grapple again with futilities too trivial to think about much less talk," Hay wrote to Adams. The kicker came on May 22, 1897, a Saturday—a cable from Secretary Sherman, an instruction finally about the jubilee delegation.

The president, it seemed, had decided to use the jubilee mission to repair some domestic political damage. McKinley thought he could mollify the most embittered failed office seeker in the land. Hay would still lead the delegation, but there would be just one "eminent civilian," officially designated "the bearer of [the president's] message": *Whitelaw Reid*.

Hay was alert to the problem the moment he read the name. As with the ambassadorship itself, there wasn't room for both men. Queen Victoria would be recognizing and receiving only *one* emissary from each delegation; if Hay remained the head of the delegation, Reid would be left holding his bib and tucker, outside the Buckingham Palace drawing room, looking in. As Hay knew from long years of experience with Reid, this would not do. "Whitelaw would have gone clean daft," was how he put it.

Whitelaw Reid was the Kaiser Wilhelm of the editorial set: he was extraordinarily sensitive to slights and had the nation's most powerful newspaper at his disposal. The president could not afford to have Reid's *New York Tribune*, a Republican paper in the most populous state in the nation, on the warpath against him. The president needed strong backing on his proposed tariff, and on the Cuba problem, and on the annexation of Hawaii, and he wasn't getting much of what he needed from the *Tribune* just then. But Hay also knew from long years of experience that while Whitelaw was, as a mutual acquaintance once said, "quite likely to be amenable to the gentle influences of society, in his political relations."

So Hay sat down and wrote a personal wire to the president, with a message McKinley could not fail to miss. Whitelaw, Hay explained, "coming so far, with special commissions, would naturally feel aggrieved at being relegated so entirely to the background." Hay offered to step aside, stick to his duties at the Victoria Street embassy, and let Reid represent the United States as a *special* ambassador. McKinley wrestled with the question for a few days before conceding Hay's logic and announcing Whitelaw Reid's appointment as the US ambassador extraordinary on a special mission.

Reid got his brother-in-law appointed as a secretary to the mission, rented Lord Lonsdale's double mansion a few doors down from Hay on Carlton House Terrace, and put the boys at the *New York Tribune* to work. "The appointment of Mr. Whitelaw Reid as special envoy has led to fresh expressions of . . . satisfaction as is shown by the cordial references to it in many of the London and provincial journals," the paper said of its owner and captain. "The action of

President McKinley's Administration in honoring in an exceptional way the gracious sovereign who has always been a sincere friend of America will be heartily appreciated in England and tend to promote good feeling."

But it was Hay's astute and politic reading of the Reid matter that had caught McKinley's eye. The day after the announcement that brought Whitelaw so much joy, the president sat down at his desk and wrote Hay a personal letter. McKinley complimented the new ambassador on his reception in London, on his recent speeches—"models of good-taste in every respect"—and on his "conservative course" in accepting social invitations. He expressed confidence in Hay's wisdom and in his ability. "Let me assure you of my appreciation of your friendly cooperation in arranging for our representation at the Queen's Jubilee. Mr. Reid is of course delighted with his appointment and must recognize the courteous manner in which you paved the way for his appearance at this interesting function. My time for personal letter-writing is very limited now-a-days as you may readily imagine; and for this reason this letter is I believe the longest I have sent to any one, but I want you to write me often."

There was a separate note, scrawled on the bottom of the page: "How does situation in Cuba appear to you & what comments do you have?"

CHAPTER ELEVEN

Theodore Beats the Drums

John Hay recognized this as an unusual request for the president to make of an ambassador in London, this thing about Cuba. But the problem of that nearby Spanish colony was the most perilous issue McKinley faced at the beginning of his first term. The American polity—still aquiver with frustration at the *bellum interruptus* on the Venezuelan border—seemed anxious to take up the fight for Cuban independence. McKinley's own secretary of state, the usually irenic John Sherman, was already on the record for putting a stop to the reported Spanish atrocities against the native Cubans. "If this continues," Sherman had said while he was still in the Senate the year before, "no earthly power can prevent the people of the United States from going to that island, sweeping over it from end to end, and driving out these barbarians."

Henry Cabot Lodge was prodding for action, too, having assayed the geostrategic and mercantile implications of the situation. The island just ninety miles from Florida "lies athwart the line which leads to the Nicaraguan Canal," Cabot reminded his colleagues. "Free Cuba would mean a great market for the United States; it would mean an opportunity for American capital invited there by special exemptions; it would mean an opportunity for the development of that splendid island."

All through the first months of McKinley's presidency, the outgunned revolutionaries in Cuba kept up the battle against their Spanish tormentors, and bravely so, according to American newspapers. The war tom-toms in Washington were growing louder by May of 1897; McKinley wasn't sure how to do it, but he meant to muffle them. "If I can go out of office at the end of my term with the knowledge that I have done what lay in my power to avert this terrible calamity," McKinley had told his predecessor, Grover Cleveland, on assuming office, "I shall be the happiest man in the world."

John Hay, who had seen a new president crowded by a real war thirty-five years earlier, had thoroughgoing sympathy for McKinley. There was a hoary maxim in the capital, one Hay heard Abraham Lincoln and his secretary of state, William Henry Seward, joke about three decades earlier: God pity the elected official who voices opposition in an American run-up to military action. "I opposed one war and that was enough for me," Lincoln remembered an old Whig advising him during the Mexican-American War. "I am now perpetually in favor of war, pestilence and famine." When Americans are bent on making war, one peace-minded congressman commented ruefully, a man has a better chance of standing on the prairie and stopping a cyclone.

Hay was reminded of this on May 20, 1897, the same week President McKinley decided to ship Whitelaw Reid to London, as the Senate debated its most muscular resolution to date in support of Cuban independence—one with hardware behind it. "Let us now dispatch the mightiest battle-ships in the United States to the harbor of Havana," one senator had offered on the floor. McKinley dispatched a messenger across town to the Senate during the debate on the resolution. While the president was in sympathy with the revolutionaries, he found it preferable to secure some measure of Cuban independence through a more peaceful means than the threat of—or the use of—battleships.

This battleship talk was almost too good to be true as far as the new assistant secretary of the navy was concerned. Theodore Roosevelt was *dee*-lighted. He had been fretting about McKinley's obvious reluctance to challenge Spain over Cuba since before the man was elected. McKinley was "not a strong man," Roosevelt had confided to a political friend. "I should feel rather uneasy about him in a serious crisis." But with war talk in the Washington air, thicker than ever before in his adulthood, Theodore could hardly believe his good fortune. This was better than Chile and Venezuela rolled up together. Not that he was a great supporter of the Cubans, who were, after all, not white men. "I doubt whether the Cubans would do very well in the line of self government," Roosevelt told his sister. But here he was, in the perfect spot, if he played it right, to help strengthen presidential resolve and do so much more. This might be Theodore's chance to help put a little steel in the American backbone and in its arsenal. The decade-old shipbuilding program was coming to a close—a premature close, as far as Roosevelt was concerned. He meant to exploit this Cuban moment to persuade Congress to fund a proper navy. The United States needed battleships—a lot of them, he figured—so that no nation but a "first class power" would ever again risk, as Theodore put it, "insulting us with impunity." It was hard to say what nation had actually done that, but this was beside the point for Roosevelt. The point was, maybe now the Senate and the House would stop dithering and pay up for real military firepower.

Even better, the United States of America might finally make bold to measure itself in real battle against a European power. Spain was a middling power at best, it had to be said, so this would be a warm-up bout in Roosevelt's reckoning. "I do not think a war with Spain would be serious enough to cause much strain on the country," he had written to a friend, "or much interruption to the revival of prosperity." The nation needed to fight *somebody*, Roosevelt was convinced, because it was high time for American manhood—representing as it did the glorious white Anglo-Saxon race—to pursue its destiny of greatness. Roosevelt still had Oliver Wendell Holmes's recent Memorial Day speech ringing in his ears. "In this snug, over-safe corner of the world we need [war], that we may realize that our comfortable routine is no eternal necessity of things, but merely a little space of calm in the midst of the tempestuous untamed streaming of the world, and in order that we may be ready for danger," the fifty-four-year-old and oft-wounded Civil War veteran had avowed that day, evading the fact that thirty years earlier Holmes himself had walked away from his war in disgust.

> We need it in this time of individualist negations, with its literature of French and American humor, revolting at discipline, loving flesh-pots, and denying that anything is worthy of reverence. . . . And perhaps it is not in vain for us to tell the new generation what we learned in our day, and what we still believe. That the joy of life is living, is to put all one's powers as far as they will go; that the measure of power is obstacles overcome; to ride boldly at what is in front of you, be it fence or enemy; to pray, not for comfort, but for combat.

Theodore Roosevelt, for one, was for combat, and for combat now—with Spain. He was all the way in. The problem was convincing his bosses, which he had been trying to do since before he took office.

JOHN HAY COULD imagine how William McKinley must have dreaded to see the toothy assistant secretary stride manfully into his presence; but the Major could not say he hadn't been warned about Theodore Roosevelt, both early and often. McKinley had been well briefed on the young man's superhuman excitability and his difficulty in following orders that were not to his liking. "I want peace," McKinley had told one man who suggested Roosevelt for the assistant secretaryship, "and I am told that your friend Theodore—whom I know only slightly—is always getting into rows with everybody. I am afraid he is too pugnacious." But Henry Cabot Lodge had been a relentless partisan on Roosevelt's behalf, persuading House Speaker Reed, Harry White, key senators, and even the normally reticent John Hay to talk up Theodore to the president.

Roosevelt himself had provided this advance guard with points of argument to carry to McKinley and to the man who would be running the Navy

Department, John D. Long. "Of course I have no preconceived policy of any kind which I wish to push through, and I think [the president] would find that I would not be in any way a marplot or agitator," Roosevelt assured Cabot. "I would take the position understanding thoroughly that I was there, not to carry out my own course, but to help to the best of my ability Secretary Long to carry out his," he wrote to Harry White, "and to make his administration a success, and this I should certainly try to do."

Few besides Roosevelt believed he could remain coolheaded and rational, and nobody but Roosevelt believed he could be subservient, but it had to be admitted that he had qualifications for the navy job—his trouble with seasickness notwithstanding. Roosevelt had written a popular and well-received history of the naval engagements in the War of 1812, and he enjoyed the unqualified support of Alfred Thayer Mahan, a retired captain in the US Navy whose recent work made him *the* recognized authority on naval power around the world. Mahan's book—*The Influence of Sea Power upon History*—was bedside reading for Kaiser Wilhelm of Germany and the emperor of Japan. Both men had made Mahan's book a required text for their own admirals, and both men were following Mahan's oceanic blueprint in building a powerful naval force to help increase their commercial and political power around the world. Theodore Roosevelt was Mahan's chief confidant and most loyal acolyte. Then, too, Secretary Long had finally come around to the idea of Mr. Roosevelt as his assistant, and he assured the president that he could keep the younger man's bursting enthusiasm and energy in harness.

A few days after McKinley sent Roosevelt's nomination as assistant secretary of the navy to the Senate for confirmation, Secretary Long received a letter from yet another of Roosevelt's supporters—a Civil War general who had known Theodore for years and had not stopped campaigning when the battle for the assistant secretaryship was won. "You will find it a constant delight to have his cooperation," the general assured Long. "And he will be as loyal and obedient as the stupidest man you could find!"

By the middle of spring 1897, Theodore Roosevelt was settled into his new post in Washington, having left his wife and children behind in New York. The thirty-eight-year-old dynamo took lunch most days with Cabot and Mahan at the Metropolitan Club, a few blocks away, and bunked down at Cabot's house. The assistant secretary was also in the glow of his budding friendship with his boss. He "really wanted me," Roosevelt said, and he told his friends that Secretary Long was "a perfect dear." John Hay must have been feeling better about his decision to advocate Theodore's appointment to high national office; his impetuous friend seemed to be playing nice. A *New York Tribune* article cheered Roosevelt for having gone nearly a month without breaking any bureaucratic china at the Navy Department. "Oh, you know, my friends told the President I had got past the follies of youth, and had become sedate," Roosevelt explained. "I really think it is so. At any rate, I am sedate now."

Roosevelt was about as sedate as William McKinley had expected him to be. The assistant secretary of the navy was already peppering the president with letters about what must be done to protect American interests around the globe. Theodore was no longer suggesting the seizure of Canada, now that things had simmered down with Great Britain, but he saw dangers clear and present on both big oceans. First there was Hawaii: Congress was finally making its slow move toward annexation of the islands, which had caused the nervous Japanese to dispatch a well-armed cruiser there. The US Navy, Roosevelt realized with a start, had only one ship in the vicinity, and "as her bottom is foul," the assistant secretary warned McKinley, "she is probably not quite so swift; and moreover, she has no torpedoes, while the Japanese vessel has." He ran through a series of possibilities for shoring up the US naval contingent near Hawaii, winding up with an unsubtle reminder to the president that time was of the essence and that putting the new battleship *Oregon* near Honolulu would send a stern message to the Japanese to back off. "She would be an overmatch for half the entire Japanese Navy, although they have two battleships of the same class now on the point of completion."

The other big cause for worry, as Roosevelt judged it, was in not keeping a sufficient and able fleet of warships within striking distance of Cuba. When McKinley asked the Navy Department what ships might be available to help protect Crete, Assistant Secretary Roosevelt sent a letter explaining that it would be folly to send a formidable squadron of US ships to the Mediterranean. "We should keep the battleships on our own coast, and in readiness for action should any complications arise in Cuba," he reminded the president.

In the middle of making an inventory of the meager contingent of second-class battleships and gunboats and monitors and armored cruisers at his disposal (Theodore was not happy about giving over one of his best cruisers to parade around for Queen Victoria!), Assistant Secretary Roosevelt got himself wrought up near panic with the awesome import of his job. A weekend with his family in New York filled Theodore with terror and caused him to renounce any further holiday travel. "I wasn't easy a single hour I was away, and never again shall I leave this city when you are not here, unless you expressly order me to," he reported to a nonplussed Long. "I told Mrs. Roosevelt that I guessed I should have to give up even the thing I care for most—seeing her and the children at all until next fall when they come on here; this because I don't wish again to be away when there is the slightest chance that anything may turn up."

Just a few months into the job, and Theodore Roosevelt's frustration at the two men he was obliged to serve was already on the rise. He had not yet figured out where the blank-faced McKinley drew the line on receiving advice from subordinates, and he briefly worried that his own urgency, which McKinley seemed to regard as a sign of disrespect, might alienate him from the president. But the issues were simply too momentous, in Theodore's judgment; he couldn't cavil. So Roosevelt (with Cabot's help, of course) kept pressing. He counseled McKinley to seize Hawaii immediately, before Japan finished fitting out their new battleships! He wanted him to put through the canal in Nicaragua so that American vessels—commercial and military—could move quickly and easily from the Atlantic to the Pacific! He wanted McKinley and Long to tell Congress to quit whining about the national bank accounts and get to the business of funding warships. Roosevelt believed the United States needed at least a dozen new battleships, half for the Pacific, half for the Atlantic.

Theodore grew increasingly agitated because neither McKinley nor Long seemed to grasp the enormity of the present situation. "I wish to Heaven we were more jingo about Cuba and Hawaii!" Roosevelt complained in a letter to Harry White. "The trouble with our nation is that we incline to fall into mere animal sloth and ease, and tend to venture too little instead of too much."

Theodore hammered at his themes—action, movement, expansion, risk. He even managed to weave this starch and snap into the most mundane reports to Secretary Long. After his first official run on an accident-prone torpedo boat, Roosevelt sent Long an assessment that traveled far beyond damage and repair. "It is more important that our officers should handle these boats with dash and daring than that the boats should be kept unscratched," Roosevelt explained. "The business of a naval officer is one which, above all others, needs daring and decision and if he must err on either side the nation can best afford to have him err on the side of too much daring rather than too much caution."

MCKINLEY AND LONG remained, in Theodore's appraisal, maddeningly cautious on all matters naval and military, but the United States Senate's new resolve on Cuban independence added a heap of coal to the Roosevelt engines. In the last weeks of May—with the deployment of US battleships being seriously talked about on the Senate floor—the assistant secretary of the navy was manic: lobbying Congress for the big buildup of battleships (he was *pretty* sure that was what Secretary Long wanted); making plans to talk to German naval experts about the gun placements in their new battleships; arranging with the commander of the *Indiana* to spend some time on a shakedown cruise. He was anxious to see the guns in operation. He was also in a lather about his first address as an officer of the national government. Roosevelt had happily accepted an invitation, which Cabot had been forced to decline, to make a speech at the opening of a new term of the Naval War College in Newport, Rhode Island, in early June. He was working furiously on his message, "hot with indignation," he said, "at the seeming utter decadence of national spirit among us, and the craven policy which actuates the peace dilettante and the man to whom making money is all there is to life."

In off hours, he polished up his new article about the British navy's performance in the War of 1812, tracked a pair of calfskin lace-up boots that were lost in transit to his home in New York City, wrote letters to friends like John Hay and Harry White and Cecil Spring Rice, reviewed books, and then used those same books, no matter how "unhinged" he believed the author to be, as a springboard for his own grandiloquent philosophizing on subjects remote from his own experience. "There seems good ground for believing that France is decadent," he explained to Springy, as he called Spring Rice. "In France, as in the later Roman world, population is decreasing, and there is gross sensuality and licentiousness. . . . I quite agree with you that the main cause of Rome's fall was a failure of population which was accompanied by a change in the population itself, caused by the immense importation of slaves, usually of inferior races."

Assistant Secretary Roosevelt also found time to draw maps of the American West for a British hunter friend who was looking for suitable spots to find big game. And he spent hours penning a rebuttal of a recent article in *Science* magazine titled "Suggestions for a New Method of Discriminating between Species and Subspecies." While Roosevelt did "entirely agree" with the main thesis, he had plenty to say about the biologist-author's insistence on dividing up creatures into more specific categories. Theodore took particular umbrage at Dr. Merriam's desire to separate (in terms of nomenclature) northern wolves from southern wolves and northern coyotes from southern coyotes. "Now I happen to have hunted over the habitats of the four animals in question," Roosevelt wrote to the editors of *Science*.

> I have shot and poisoned them, and hunted them with dogs, and noticed their ways of life. In each case the animal decreases greatly in size, according to its habitat. . . . The northern wolf will hamstring a horse, the southern carry off a sheep; the northern coyote will tackle a sheep, when the southern will only rob a hen-roost. In each place the two animals have two different voices, and as far as I could tell, the voices were not much changed from north to south. Now, it seems to me that in using a term of convenience, which is all that the term species is, it is more convenient and

> essentially more true to speak of this pair of varying animals as wolf and coyote rather than by a score of different names which serve to indicate a score of different sets of rather minute characteristics.

Point taken! Secretary Long had been watching his deputy from afar, wondering whether young Theodore might soon burn himself out with all this furious activity, but there was nary a sign. The men who told Long about Roosevelt's remarkable industriousness had not been exaggerating after all. Long was only beginning to realize that this trait might be something other than a selling point. The mild-mannered and even-tempered Long grew weary just watching his assistant in action. Theodore, in this state, let nothing drop. He could juggle morning rides through Rock Creek Parkway, lunches with Captain Mahan, a few rounds of boxing or a game of tennis, and hours spent writing personal letters and articles and still tackle his job. On his visits to naval yards, Roosevelt was never shy to offer detailed instructions on the proper construction of the turrets in new ships. "I have been told he considers himself an expert in many lines," said one technical specialist who had to endure one of his lectures. "Now I know he thinks he's an expert in naval architecture." The assistant secretary also jumped at the invitation to pose a "Special Confidential Problem" to the staff and students of the Naval War College. He presented the college with one that would keep them on their toes in case of "certain contingencies."

> Japan makes demands on Hawaiian Islands. This country intervenes. What force will be necessary to uphold the intervention, and how shall it be employed? Keeping in mind possible complications with another Power on the Atlantic Coast (Cuba).

At the beginning of June, while Secretary Long readied the commencement address he was to deliver at the United States Naval Academy, Roosevelt was already on his way to the Naval War College in Newport for his first big speech.

As Long prepared to leave for Annapolis and Roosevelt motored across the open waters of Long Island Sound in a tired old torpedo boat—"a good boat in her day," Teddy offered—a group of citizens in Washington gathered for a mass meeting, occasioned by the recent killing of an American volunteer nurse by Spanish soldiers near Havana. The outdoor meeting in a Washington park was being styled the Cuban Indignation Meeting by the local newspapers. "The appalling warfare which has been and is being waged by Spanish soldiers on defenseless women and helpless children . . . was the theme," reported the *Washington Evening Times*. A series of speakers whipped the rally goers to a frothy indignation about how the House of Representatives, unlike the Senate, still dawdled on the issue of Cuban independence. "The Cubans have been subjected to agonies and miseries untold," said the lead speaker. "Now who shall say to [Spain], 'Release your grip'? One ship of war sent to Havana would do the work. Are we afraid? If Congress would not do that, then there is one more final appeal, and that is to the American people themselves." There followed a resolution, adopted unanimously by the crowd, to push the House to stand tall for Cuba and to "implore the President to put into action that which will secure the freedom of the island, the sympathy which our whole nation feels for the struggling patriots of Cuba."

Secretary Long steered well clear of the Cuba business in his commencement address at Annapolis. He gave an earnest yawner of a speech about the importance of honor and duty and character. "This was what the mother meant who told her son to be a good boy," the secretary said. "This is what the father meant when he told him to be an honest man. And this is what is meant by the country in expecting every man to be loyal to duty." Four hundred miles north in Newport, Roosevelt upstaged his boss and unleashed a corker.

The assistant secretary spoke for an hour and fifteen minutes that day to a handful of naval officers, in a ratty little auditorium at the War College, but he made certain the remarks were available to the press so that they could be printed in newspapers across America—which they were. Roosevelt didn't mention the reported depredations of the Spanish troops in Cuba, or Spain itself, but he beat the drums for war all the same. "The United States have never once in the course of its history suffered because of preparation for war, or because of entering into war," he asserted. More important, said Roosevelt, the nation had best be properly prepared to conduct a war. "The enemies we may have to face will come from over sea; they may come from Europe, or they may come from Asia." What we needed to face this imminent peril, he claimed, was a big navy. He told Americans it was time for the nation to step up and defend the Monroe Doctrine (which he believed in with all his heart, by the way) with more than talk. "Diplomacy is utterly useless where there is no force behind it," he said.

America's continued safety, Roosevelt said, depended on the battleship.

> In war the mere defensive never pays, and can never result in anything but disaster. It is not enough to parry a blow. The surest way to prevent its repetition is to return it. No master of the prize ring ever fought his way to supremacy by mere dexterity of avoiding punishment. He had to win by inflicting punishment. . . .
>
> We must rely mainly, as all great nations always have relied, on the battle-ship, the fighting ship of the line. . . . We must trust to the ships whose business it is to fight and not to run, and who can themselves go to

> sea and strike at the enemy when they choose, instead of waiting peacefully to receive his blow when and where he deems it best to deliver it. . . . If we mean to protect the people of the lands who look to us for protection from tyranny and aggression; if we mean to uphold our interests in the teeth of the formidable Old World powers, we can only do it by being ready at any time, if the provocation is sufficient, to meet them on the seas, where the battle for supremacy must be fought.

Roosevelt then called for a fleet of twenty battleships, nearly double the number he had been pushing for just a month earlier. "We ask for a great navy, partly because we think a great navy is the surest guarantee of peace, and partly because we feel that no national life is worth having if the nation is not willing, when the need shall arise, to stake everything on the supreme arbitrament of war, and to pour out its blood, its treasure and tears like water, rather than submit to the loss of honor and renown."

Who exactly constituted this "we" was hard to say, maybe Roosevelt and Cabot, maybe Roosevelt and Poseidon, but it certainly wasn't the administration Roosevelt was supposed to be serving. McKinley did not join Theodore's chorus that week. He wasn't touching anything that hinted at war preparations. The president was busy selling economic protectionism and patience in the face of a slowing economic recovery. "Let me tell you, my countrymen, resuscitation will not be promoted by recrimination," the president offered wanly. "The patriot makes a better citizen than the pessimist." John Long did take the rare step of making sure his displeasure was known to his rhino-hided young charge. He also took the time to acquaint Assistant Secretary Roosevelt with the current policy of the Navy Department. "Indeed," Roosevelt wrote afterward to Captain Mahan, with some apparent surprise, "[Secretary Long] is against adding to our battleships."

CHAPTER TWELVE

I Will Do without the Monument

Sam Clemens wasn't keeping close tabs on geopolitical events at the beginning of June 1897. Pouring out blood and treasure and tears to secure national honor wasn't exactly Clemens's cup of tea. Honor was a luxury reserved for the wealthy and the dead, as far as he was concerned, and Clemens's immediate prospects were not good for either contingency. Nor was Teddy Roosevelt high on his list of public speakers worth auditing. All in all, Sam Clemens found Roosevelt's budding statesmanship about as comforting as his new hernia; he had already started to form a definite opinion of the younger man. "He would go to Halifax for half a chance to show off," Clemens would later say of him, "and he would go to hell for a whole one."

Clemens did take note of the item in the London papers about Whitelaw Reid's departure for his grand mission to England, and on June 3, 1897, he wrote a melancholy little entry in his diary: "Hay and W Reid—friends of mine of 31 years ago when we were comparatively obscure. I being known for my virtues & they for their talents. Alas, that is all changed now." Clemens was coming off a very strange week just then; for one thing, he had suddenly been getting a lot of attention—more, anyway, than he had asked for.

The interest had started, oddly enough, with Ambassador John Hay's first public speaking engagement in London, at which he offered a bracing little tip of the cap on behalf of his countrymen on the occasion of the unveiling at Westminster Abbey of a bust of the beloved author Sir Walter Scott. "The romances of courts and castles were specially appreciated in the woods and prairies of the [American] frontier," Hay had told the crowd in the abbey. "[Scott's] work is a clear, high voice, from a simpler age than ours, breathing a song of lofty and unclouded purpose, of sincere and powerful passion to which the world, however weary and preoccupied, must needs still listen and attend."

Sam Clemens had remained home in Tedworth Square on the evening of that speech, but one Scottish newspaper decided to take the opportunity to pick a fight between him and Hay. Where Hay testified to the "wholesomeness of the influence" exercised by Scott in America, the paper noted, Clemens had previously taken a much more jaundiced view of Scott, and his "grotesque 'chivalry' doings and romantic juvenilities, . . . its inflated language and other windy humbuggeries."

The Scottish scribe didn't know the half of it. Clemens liked to say that Scott's novels were exhibit A in the case for keeping foreign literature out of the United States. "Can you read him? And keep your respect for him?" Clemens would ask a critic friend after his own heroic effort to scale Scott's novels. "Of course a person could in his day—an era of sentimentality and sloppy romantics—but land! can a body do it today?" Not that Sam Clemens was going to go after Sir Walter, especially that particular week. Clemens fancied himself a man of fair diplomatic skills, and he had more sense than to publicly run down a celebrated local favorite. Moreover, he and Sir Walter were something akin to brothers in arms, to hear the papers tell it. Not only were they both self-made men, but Scott had suffered his own legendary bankruptcy. The Scottish writer had labored for five years to dig himself out of his financial hole; he had failed, sadly, and the effort was said to have killed him. Scott's struggle was deemed valiant, of course, even chivalrous, and Clemens was gaining a new appreciation for his predecessor's personal courage, although he also understood well enough that public esteem and a monument in Westminster seventy years after death did precious little for the people who had counted on Walter Scott in life.

A few days after that strange newspaper interlude, Clemens found a reporter scratching at his door, there on a business assignment. Frank Marshall White had come over on behalf of his newspaper, the *New York Journal*, to ask if "Mark Twain" might be willing to write an article about the queen's jubilee parade next month. Clemens hemmed and hawed, White would later recall of the meeting. Clemens wasn't that busy, now that the manuscript of his new travel book was complete, but he had good reasons not to take the assignment: he didn't like to be rushed, and he worried that the *Journal* editors would muck with his copy like every other newspaperman he had worked with lately. "They put words into my mouth," he told the young American reporter that morning. "I'd rather they had put street sweepings there." He did not intend to be forced to file under any strict deadline, because he wouldn't ship any story without Livy's approving every word, and she wasn't well enough to accompany him to the parade.

Maybe the *Journal* could just drop the entire thing and do a nice little piece promoting his upcoming travel book instead, Clemens suggested. He would gladly sit for an interview or even write it up himself if that was more convenient. White held his ground on the jubilee piece, and Clemens finally started to come around to the possibility. "Now if you can offer me sufficient inducement," he drawled out to White, fully cognizant that the *Journal*'s boy proprietor, William Randolph Hearst, was paying big money for big names, "I might consider writing a newspaper article in a hurry, without my wife seeing it, and allowing a cable operator to have the first hack at it, and the printer to mangle what the operator left of it."

White named a price beyond which Hearst's *Journal*—or any other paper he had worked for—had ever paid. Clemens demurred. White had taken stock of Clemens at close range by now. The air of sadness in the house was unmistakable and the author's hair had turned almost entirely white, but Clemens was hardly decrepit. His health seemed fine, and he was clearly able to maintain a fine house in a nice neighborhood with a large staff. Surely the old man was good for a few thousand words. White doubled his offer. Sam Clemens wouldn't show it, but he was jollied by this little transaction. He made it his business to keep up with the going word rate, too. Clemens shook his head in a little nod of agreement, then leaned in conspiratorially and told White that he might just be able to pull this off, but that they should not tell Mrs. Clemens just yet. Clemens shooed the young reporter out his front door and into the square, with the promise that he would look for the right time to talk it over with her.

Sam was hiding a lot from Livy. He certainly wasn't going to tell her, in the face of her continuing anguish over Susy, that he'd just received by telegram the news of another blow to the family. Their old butler, George Griffin, had died unexpectedly in New York City. He had gone to bed at his new place of employment, the Union League Club, and had never woken up. How could Sam tell his wife there would now be two empty spaces at the family hearth in Hartford, if they ever did get back to the old house? Neither had he told her about his attempt to wrest control of a deluxe edition of his work from his longtime publisher Bliss, or about his grand vision for the $1,000-a-seat lecture in New York to clear their debt in one heroic fell swoop. And he certainly, certainly, certainly was not going to tell her—or anybody else—about the other scheme being cooked up on behalf of the Clemens family (and with Clemens's tacit approval), by James Gordon Bennett Jr. and his editors at the *New York Herald*.

The *Herald* gambit started in earnest a few days after White made his visit to Tedworth, and without any real warning to Clemens, with a multidecker headline at the top of an inside page, meant to excite sympathy for the author and lay the groundwork for a relief fund in his name.

MARK TWAIN IS

ILL IN LONDON.

Sad News About the Great Humorist's

Mental and Physical Collapse

AFTER A HARD STRUGGLE

"The sad news comes from London that Mark Twain is grievously ill and possibly dying," was the lead in the *Herald*. "Worse still, we are told that his brilliant intellect is shattered and that he is sorely in need of money. Bravely and sturdily he fought up to the last, endeavoring to regain some portion of his lost fortune, and now it seems that his indomitable energy has at last left him." The story, accompanied by a line drawing and a little aphorism in Mark Twain's own hand—"Be good & you will be lonesome"—was hardly a revelation to American readers, given the reporting of the previous five months, but it rippled out into papers across the country just the same. It traveled clear down into the hollows of Kentucky, for instance, adding pathos as it went: "Mark Twain is . . . utterly broken down, mentally and physically, his once brilliant mind incapable of further effort and almost penniless, his life is drawing to a close. Friends . . . say his physical condition is brought about by a broken heart."

American news bureaus in London received urgent cables of instruction from back home: *Go find out, yet again, if "Mark Twain" is dead! or dying! or in poverty!* And so newsmen headed for Tedworth Square to beg a response from the author. Frank Marshall White, though he had seen a very robust and savvy Sam Clemens just a few days earlier, felt nevertheless duty-bound to dispatch a man to Tedworth Square to get an answer for the *Journal* desk back in New York. White's man returned to the office not long after leaving and explained that he had not actually been allowed to see the great man, who was still in bed, but he did have a note Clemens had scrawled out and sent downstairs with a servant. "James Ross Clemens, a cousin of mine, was seriously ill two or three weeks ago in London, but is well now," it read. "The report of my illness grew out of his illness, the report of my death was an exaggeration."

Clemens would describe the morning's commotion for years after: "The London representatives of the American papers began to flock in, with American cables in their hands, to inquire into my condition. . . . Each in his turn was astonished, and disappointed to find me reading and smoking in my study and worth next to nothing as a text for transatlantic news. One of these was a gentle and kindly and grave and sympathetic Irishman, who hid his sorrow the best he could, and tried to look glad."

When the Irishman asked him what he should tell his editors, Clemens recalled, Clemens suggested the exaggeration line again. "He never smiled, but went solemnly away."

The next reporter arrived, Clemens remembered, with "his New York cablegram in his hand—from the New York *World*—and he was so evidently trying to get around that cable with invented softnesses and palliations that my curiosity was aroused and I wanted to see what it did really say. So when occasion offered I slipped it out of his hand. It said, 'If Mark Twain dying send five hundred words. If dead send a thousand.'"

This was a Sir Walter equation, to be sure—Sam Clemens had become worth more dead than alive.

Frank Marshall White showed up later that day to get the real story, and Clemens of course agreed to talk to the man who was helping him shake the change out of Willie Hearst's pockets. The interview was not entirely successful from Clemens's point of view, partly because this was a delicate dance he was attempting, especially with Livy in the next room, and he did not do it well. White's story in the *Journal* the next day took the wind out of the *New York Herald* story's sails right at the start line.

White rereported the "exaggeration" telegram verbatim and mentioned the new "Mark Twain" travel book, to be titled *Another Innocent Abroad*; he reported Clemens's good health and allowed the author to deftly evade the question of his poverty. The line from the *Journal* that nagged at Clemens, though, went like this: "He is living in comfort and even luxury in a handsomely furnished house in a beautiful square in Chelsea with his wife and children." Livy would appreciate the reference to their happy household situation, but this account did not altogether serve Sam's purposes.

Still and all, Clemens appeared surprisingly buoyant by the end of the two-day to-do. He officially accepted the assignment to write a jubilee piece for the *Journal.* He invited his newfound and newly healthy cousin out to the theater the next evening. He wrote a long letter of instruction to Henry Rogers about how to shake free from his numbskull publisher Bliss. He wrote to Frank Fuller to remind him to keep his name out of the $1,000-a-seat lecture scheme, and then crowed about having finished his book, "and just in time, too, for by reports I am now dead," adding, "Posthumous works always sell better than others." He even invited Clara and Jean to accompany him on a prospecting run along the jubilee parade route, boasting loudly to his daughters that he had privileged inside information on the timing of a secret rehearsal.

On June 11, he wrote Frank Marshall White to see whether they would have room to take Clara and Jean on the scouting run next week to help him "notice details." The next day, Clemens sent a cryptic invitation to White, asking him to the house. "Let us see if we can invent some way," Clemens wrote, "to repair the enormous damage which your cablegram has done me." White was a reporter of well-earned reputation and no babe in the woods; he was onto "Mark Twain" and why he wanted to see him. That very morning, White had received a telegram from the home office informing him that a competing paper, the *New York Herald*, was preparing to announce the advent of a relief fund to help the impoverished and indebted Clemens pay off his creditors.

White arrived at Clemens's Tedworth Square house with a strict charge from his bosses at the *Journal*: find out whether Clemens himself was behind the fund or had approved it. The wily old author did manage to put one thing over on White when they met that day; Clemens feigned astonishment at the news, as if he'd been blindsided. But he also assured White that he was neither offended nor embarrassed by this act of begging in his name. "You can say in reply that if it is true, it is pleasanter news than I have been accustomed to receive for some time past," he told the reporter. "I was expecting a monument by and by, but if my friends wish to pay my debts I will do without the monument."

Sam Clemens had been working over that line and others, judging from the next day's big fat Sunday edition of the *New York Herald*, which devoted an entire page to an exclusive interview with the author, the major purpose being to kick off the paper's relief fund in his name. "Of course I am dying," was Clemens's opening line, spoken through a grim smile, according to the *Herald*. "But I do not know that I am doing it any faster than anybody else. As for dying in poverty, I had just as soon die in poverty here in London as anywhere. But it would be a little more difficult, because I have got quite a number of friends, any one of whom I believe would be good for a month's provision, and that would drag out the agony a fairly long time."

The *Herald* and its man in London made no mention of the Clemenses' comfortable London town house with its multiple servants. The article noted, most improbably, the author's discomfort in laying his financial woes before the public. And it plucked hard on the sympathy chords: "There was a species of hopeless resignation in his bearing that was in painful contrast to his one time easy going carelessness; and in spite of his disclaimer, in spite of his assertion that he was perfectly well, I was convinced that if his physical health were of the best he was, nevertheless, so disturbed by mental worries that the report of his failing condition was practically well founded." "His air . . . seemed," according to the *Herald* reporter, "dreadfully like that of a man trying to keep his head above water and not succeeding too well." The *Herald* story described the strain of attempting to work off the enormous debt incurred by the failure of "Mark Twain's" publishing house—a collapse for which the celebrated author, by the way, was blameless—and the miserable isolation Sam Clemens had endured since the shattering thunderclap of his daughter's unexpected death.

There was a second story announcing the newspaper's sponsorship of a charity fund to lift "Mark Twain's" undeserved financial burden. "The HERALD begins the goodly work by opening a subscription for him with the sum of one thousand dollars. And the HERALD does this with the earnest hope and with full confidence that in every part of our broad republic the newspapers of all creeds and politics will open their columns for subscriptions to swell a fund that shall testify the feeling of esteem, gratitude and sympathy which we all feel for one who made life lighter with laughter and who, we trust, will live long enough to know that republics are not ungrateful."

The establishment of the fund had been no surprise to Clemens, and he badly wanted it to work, whatever the cost to his personal honor. He was so weary of being in debt, he admitted to a friend, he would "part with my skin and my teeth to get out."

COMPLICATIONS AROSE IMMEDIATELY, chiefly because his friends were more protective of his dignity than he was. Frank Bliss gave an interview to the Hartford paper explaining that the city's (and his own publishing house's) most celebrated author was healthy and solvent and, withal, too proud to accept what amounted to charity. The publisher suggested that proceeds from the upcoming travel book alone were likely to clear Clemens's debts, and that the family could expect a continuing stream of income from reissues of his copyrighted works and still claimed "two or three handsome residences." Bliss had already cabled Clemens a warning that the *Herald* campaign was tarring his reputation—that he should stand up and disavow it.

Discounting Bliss's advice was simple enough for Clemens. His publisher had always been more concerned with the firm's bank accounts than with Clemens's reputation. The dispirited look in Livy's eyes when she learned of the fund was not so easily dismissed; nor was the cable from his friend and protector, Henry Rogers, three days after the subscription was announced: "All friends think Herald movement mistake withdraw graciously." Clemens sat down to answer Rogers as soon as that cablegram arrived. He had got himself into another tremendous pickle, he admitted.

"I can't retire gracefully from the matter," Clemens wrote Rogers, "because three months ago when I was down in the depths & everything was looking black & hopeless a friend of mine approached me upon this thing & over-persuaded me & I finally gave him my word that if it was ever put before the public I would stand by it & not repudiate it." Clemens claimed that he had forgotten about the entire episode in the interim, that the relief fund was "objectionable," but that his hands were tied and he would have to let it go forward. "The project may end in a humiliating failure, & show me that I am not very popular, after all; but no matter, I am used to humiliations these years, & they do not come so hard now as once they did." Livy, he wrote, "is troubled about it now, but is good & kind, since I have told her I can't alter the matter now."

Livy Clemens's embarrassment edged toward horror in the next few days, and she made it known to her husband that she wanted him to put a stop to the fund. Sam kept telling himself that maybe his wife would relent, but this was a tall tale to tell—especially to the person who knew her best. He could have consulted his own recent notebook entries for the answer to how this campaign for her acquiescence would go. He had had a dream a few months earlier, on the eve of Susy's birthday, which he had recorded: "I dreamed I caught a beautiful slender white fish 14 inches and thought what a fine meal it would make. I was very hungry. Then came the feeling of disappointment and sorrow; it was Sunday, and I could not take the fish home, for it would deeply grieve Livy to know that I had been fishing on the Sabbath. Then it occurred to me to catch a fish for *her* and *that* would disarm her. The dream was a perfect reflection of my character and hers, down to that last detail—there it suddenly breaks down. But in the dream it seemed quite natural that her religious loyalty should be bought for a fish."

CLEMENS HAD NOT yet decided what to do about the *Herald* relief fund when Frank Marshall White showed up at Tedworth Square on June 19, 1897, at three thirty in the morning, just before sunrise in London. He was there by appointment. In the soft first light of one of the last days of spring, Sam Clemens, along with Clara and Jean, clambered aboard the hired carriage to tour the jubilee route with White. The party believed themselves to be operating on inside information, a special privilege of being with "Mark Twain." Clemens had it on good authority from a well-placed source that the rehearsal of the jubilee parade would be happening at daybreak that morning.

The author had already begun to gather string for his jubilee article, facts both exalted and otherwise. He had figured, for instance, the rate of territorial gain in the sixty years of Queen Victoria's reign—165 miles of territory per day. He also had it on the good authority of a neighbor familiar with officials at the army, navy, and excise departments that on any given night of the festival month, something near a third of the ten million people in London were drunk, or "jubilated"—the term now common in the police courts.

Sam, Clara, Jean, and Frank Marshall White rode the route that morning, in near darkness at first, past Buckingham Palace and London Tower, and by the sleeping Carlton House Terrace, searching for the secret dress rehearsal. Even in the new dawn, they saw no signs. They were out for an hour, then two, then three, and still nothing. Clemens had by then begun to fling increasingly sharp asides at his absent "informant." Livy was still home in bed or maybe sitting at her mirror while Katy combed out her hair, so it was up to the girls to calm the gathering storm: "Mind yourself, Papa. It does nobody any good if you lose your temper."

"I don't know about that," White heard him answer. "Sometimes when a man is in a thoroughgoing temper he finds things to say that are worth preserving." He didn't seem particularly incensed; in fact, Sam Clemens appeared to White more resigned than angry. It was as if he was finally coming to terms with something Livy had been trying to impress on him for years: celebrity was all well and good, but he should not expect it to bring him special privilege.

WHITE DROPPED THE family back at Tedworth later that morning, and Clemens sat down not long after to write a sad little letter to James Gordon Bennett Jr., the editor of the *New York Herald*. He owed it to Livy. He had been laboring for three days to make his wife see the upside of the subscription effort, but she would not be moved. She was mortified when their friend, Grace King, had enclosed a check for £10 4s. in a recent letter. Livy Clemens would not be a party to begging. "I hoped & believed, & I still believe, that a sufficient fund could be raised to lighten my debt very greatly & possibly even discharge it," Clemens wrote to Bennett, "but the family are not willing, convinced me that I have no right to take your money & other men's to smooth my road with, & so I have to come to you & ask you to cable the enclosed letter to the *Herald* to the end that I may once more stand well with the household. I shall be grateful if you will do me this favor. And I am already grateful to you for wanting to help me out of my slavery of debt." A follow-up letter requested that the *Herald* retire from the fund drive and return any money already raised.

It took another week to get the subscription fund shut down officially, and Clemens took a beating in the interim. "The only refuge," wrote one magazine, "seems to be in the belief that his health is really broken, that he has lost his grip on himself, and that the present false position is due to an act for which he is as little accountable as a sick child which escapes its nurse." The actual fact still remained, buried in Sam Clemens's own breast: if it were up to him alone, he would trade flagonfuls of Sir Walter's "honor" to make certain his wife and surviving daughters were provided for, in all ways and always, if they would just let him.

"Honesty is often the best policy," Sam Clemens had recently written, "but sometimes the appearance of it is worth six of it."

CHAPTER THIRTEEN

A Panorama of Power Unequaled in History

Whitelaw Reid landed in England the second week of June and headed straight for his temporary quarters in London, a palatial abode at Carlton House Terrace—which meant John Hay had three key presidential appointees to mind that summer. The other two wouldn't settle down in town until after the big jubilee had played itself out. McKinley's chosen fur seal envoy, General John Foster, had scuttled through London on his way to St. Petersburg to confer with the czar. He wasn't expected back at Hay's desk until early July, with greetings and word from on high about how the Russians wished to proceed in protecting the fruit of the Bering Sea. General Foster's reputation would precede him in London. He was fairly roundly despised in the British press and not much liked in official Britain; Hay would have to find a way to carry Foster's points to the Foreign Office himself, without offending.

Then there was Senator Edward O. Wolcott, who was heading a three-man commission that McKinley had dispatched to Europe to negotiate a deal on bimetallism. Wolcott and his two cohorts were in Paris already, trying to bring the French on board so that they could make a two-nation plea to the Brits, also in early July. Wolcott was straightforward, no bluster, and thoroughly agreeable. Hay could trust him to brace Lord Salisbury with serious currency proposals and not leave hard feelings in the wake. Wolcott, however, was an enthusiast on this issue, and his optimism for achieving a happy settlement seemed certain to outrun any realistic possibility. He was also blessedly innocent with regard to the maddening stripes of obstinacy and disregard that passed for diplomacy at the British Foreign Office. So Wolcott's bruising in London was inevitable, and Hay felt obliged to be ready to provide what balm he could. These two charges—Foster and Wolcott—were no unnecessary burdens as far as Ambassador Hay was concerned. They would be conducting real state business—real business high up on the president's agenda. Whitelaw Reid, though, was another matter. Whitelaw Reid was on his way to London for the greater glory of Whitelaw Reid, ready to run amok in the fields of royal Britain.

Whitelaw had a comfortable and auspicious entry. "Lord Lonsdale's house, as you probably know, is one of the great houses of London—being just double the size of that occupied by the Ambassador [Hay], and in the same vicinity," Reid reported to President McKinley. Lonsdale had left at the special ambassador's disposal his various carriages and the full servant staff of his Carlton House Terrace mansion. Within hours of Whitelaw's arrival, the special equerry assigned by the queen attached himself to Reid's London household; Colonel Henry Hallam Parr's job was to look after Reid and his family (the in-laws were well represented) as well as the rest of the special American mission. Colonel Parr was instructed to keep his charges informed as the official schedules were perfected, and to attend to their daily requirements.

The editors of the *New York Tribune*, too, were already at work clearing the path for Reid. Whitelaw's newspaper was diligently softening the field for his London ground campaign with a series of paeans to the British monarch's general *good*ness, noting her personal regard of the working classes, and the remarkable scientific flowering that grew from the soil of her sixty-year reign. (*All hail, Bessemer Steel!*) The *Tribune* even defended her sovereign honor from the attacks launched by some of its unseemly brethren back home.

John Hay, too, was performing social contortions on Reid's behalf, making dinners for the special ambassador and introducing him to all the English nobles he wanted to know. Reid, however, had unfortunately lost sight of the quid pro quo of his lofty appointment and was not executing reciprocity, editorially speaking. President McKinley had just completed his 180-degree turn on the Cleveland administration's policy and forwarded to the Senate a newly signed treaty of annexation between the United States and the "Republic of Hawaii"—along with a note explaining that the decision to take the islands "is not a change; it is a consummation." The good old Republican *New York Tribune*, meanwhile, had failed to stand up and back McKinley's call for ratification of the treaty, as Reid had promised it would. Reid's memory should have been jarred by newspaper coverage in London and by the wire reports from America and the Continent. "This American grab is a breach of good faith, if not a violation of treaty rights, and there is all the more reason for anticipating a prompt and watchful attitude upon the part of Lord Salisbury now, when it is remembered what a flabby appearance England presented to a contemptuous world in the case of Venezuela," London's hometown *Globe* editorialized. "Lord Salisbury and his colleagues should stiffen their backs and tell President McKinley politely, but plainly, that Great Britain claims the right to be consulted before the annexation of Hawaii is finally decided upon." French papers worried in print that when the United

States ate up Hawaii it would only increase the American appetite for Cuba, while the Germans wondered whether they should keep a closer eye on their commercial interests in the Pacific.

And still, it was left to Hay to prod Whitelaw. "I had a talk with Mr. Reid today about Hawaii," Hay wrote to the president. "He has been so busy that he had neglected giving orders about that subject, but he has this afternoon given confidential instructions that the *Tribune* is to support the treaty with energy."

Whitelaw's forgetfulness was not the only headache for Hay that week; the entire special embassy presented issues. Rear Admiral Miller's daughter had been stricken with typhoid fever on the Atlantic crossing and was in dire condition, so Hay's regular embassy had to arrange for doctors and nurses. Two of the commission's special secretaries became disgruntled and surly when they found out the third, Whitelaw's brother-in-law, started presenting himself, on his card of calling, as "*first* secretary of the special embassy." The two military envoys, Admiral Miller and Major General Miles, skirmished over the size of their respective hotel accommodations. And all that week, Americans who were just sure the ambassador could supply them with tickets to the jubilee parade were overrunning Hay's cramped Victoria Street embassy. One importuner from upstate New York whined aloud that Canadian citizens need only stop by the Colonial Office to secure *their* tickets, and demanded to know why the citizens of the United States were not being treated with equal respect. Hay and his small staff had no time for *that* kind of civics lesson.

While Hay toiled, Whitelaw was immersed in an orgy of happy days and nights. Hay presented his longtime friend to the Marquess of Salisbury, whom Reid found "unusually cordial" and ready to converse at length. Hay also saw his friend to the races at Ascot, where Reid was presented once again to the Prince and Princess of Wales and was then invited to remain in the royal enclosure all afternoon, among the well-wishers who cheered Bertie's own horse, Persimmon, to victory in the Gold Cup. Whitelaw even managed to wheedle what amounted to an official membership—alongside his friend Willie Astor—in the prince's Marlborough Club. "Unquestionably the person that can get lowest down in cringing before royalty and nobility, and can get most satisfaction out of crawling on his belly before them, is an American," Sam Clemens would jot in his notebook in the aftermath of Whitelaw's London visit. "Not all Americans, but when an American does it he makes competition impossible."

Reid was among the queen's special guests at a military tattoo at Windsor Castle and then was formally presented to her two days later, on the eve of the jubilee procession, in the box rooms at Buckingham Palace. The queen was a bit ragged from her trip from Windsor that afternoon, but somewhat cheered by her carriage ride from Paddington Station to the palace. "Hyde Park corner

& Constitution Hill were densely crowded," the sovereign wrote in her diary that night. "All vied with one another to give me a heartfelt, loyal & affectionate welcome."

Whitelaw stood by for presentation as regally as a man could in his dull black evening dress—a sign of virtuous Republican simplicity, remarked his *Tribune*—while the queen sat in her wheeled chair and received plumed royalty and colorfully uniformed special ambassadors from around the world. America's special ambassador had to wait out *every* royal, and then the two senior members of the *special* envoy corps, France's Duke of Auerstadt and Spain's Duke of Sotomayor, before his presentation to Her Royal Highness by his new friend, Lord Salisbury. This is where Whitelaw's chief official act began and ended. He handed over a message of congratulations and goodwill from the president, on behalf of himself and the American people: "It is pleasing to acknowledge the debt of gratitude and respect due to your personal virtues. May your life be prolonged, and peace, honor, and prosperity bless the people over whom you have been called to rule. May liberty flourish throughout your Empire, under just and equal laws, and your Government continue strong in the affections of all who live under it. And I pray to God to have Your Majesty in His Holy keeping."

It was difficult to ascertain exactly what the queen made of the day; she had already asked for God to protect her through the arduous ceremonies, but she was no less brittle for having made the prayer. She was, at the presentation ceremonies, "obviously in need of a little prompting on account of defective eyesight," Reid would remark. But he also liked to tell people how charmed the queen had been by *His* Excellency. "Of course I took my opportunity in the various turns of the conversation to say some of the things personally to her which I had been saying in my Fourth of July speech and elsewhere, about the friendly interest of America, and our great pride in the achievements of her reign," Whitelaw later explained. "Her face lit up constantly with smiles, and once or twice she laughed with great heartiness over something which I mentioned." The *Tribune* did not report how many little bows of the queenly head it took for Whitelaw to catch the royal drift and take his leave.

Whitelaw was only too pleased to be among the scores of royals and emissaries invited to ride in Her Highness's six-mile parade through the streets of London the next morning. Reid's carriage for the jubilee parade held an esteemed threesome: himself and the envoys from France and Spain. Whitelaw judged his own little part in the parade a ringing success. The cheers directed at this trio of international heavyweights began as soon as their carriage rolled through the Buckingham Palace gate, and Reid's carriage mates pointed out to him how much of the cheering was for the United States. Reid's special equerry was riding alongside the carriage, watching a fellow escort "sweating from every pore and on a fidgety chestnut and several other horses were giving trouble, having their nerves upset by the crowd." Whitelaw fought his natural instinct and refused at first to acknowledge the loud greetings. This was not, after all, a celebration of America, he kept reminding himself. "But the crowd would not have it so," he later reported to McKinley, "and after continuing the cheers, one resolute fellow shouted out my name in a loud voice. Nothing seemed left then but to lift my hat in acknowledgement, when the cheers were renewed. The same kind of thing went on at frequent intervals all the way along Constitution Hill, down Piccadilly."

The Canadian prime minister, reporters noted, got louder cheers than the American representative, but then it was an express political purpose of this Diamond Jubilee to snuggle the empire's colonies and dominions to the British breast, and Sir Wilfrid Laurier was a most honored member of the family. Still, all were agreed (all the Americans anyway) that the crowds gave Whitelaw a much warmer welcome than they gave the representatives from France and Italy, and a much, much warmer one than they gave the German envoy, who was hissed.

John Hay, with Clara and Helen and staff and friends, stood watch on the procession well above the crowd, on his private balcony at Carlton House Terrace, beneath the large decorative honorifics emblazoned on his residence: a large crown with the royal initials and the dates 1837–1897 centered between two large American shields sporting an eagle and thirteen stars on the field.

Hay and his well wishing party didn't get a good look at Victoria as she passed by, enveloped as she was by the prominent British war heroes who rode ahead and behind, and by the chosen male relatives who rode on horseback at her side, and by the little white parasol she used to block the overhead sun, so it was hard for John Hay to tell how Victoria was holding up. Hay knew the planners of this procession had taken every precaution to protect the queen's arthritic old bones; she was encouraged to stay put in her open horse-drawn landau while the archbishop of Canterbury led the prayer in her honor outside the St. Paul's Cathedral.

The aged queen had spent a hot and sleepless night, but she rallied on her day, energized along the way by thunderous hurrahs. "No one ever I believe, has met with such an ovation as was given to me," she wrote in her diary later that night. "The denseness of the crowds was immense." And yet, she noted, order was wonderfully well maintained.

There was much ado in the viewing stand outside the Hotel Cecil, where Sam Clemens sat quietly among the waiting crowd, making notes in the enormous pad that rested on his knee, being as inconspicuous as he knew how to be. "Mark Twain," noted his minder from the *New York Journal*, for which the author was on assignment, drew more interest among his viewing-stand mates than did the long line of dignitaries riding in advance of Victoria. Clemens tried to discourage the local newsmen who begged him for a humorous statement, a little copy for their readers back home. "No, no," he insisted. "We reporters mustn't quote one another." He wasn't interested in giving them good material for free.

The crowds in the grandstands near Clemens were anxious to see the queen and grew restless in anticipation and then wearied at all the two-bit dignitaries who preceded Her Majesty. Who wanted to see Whitelaw Reid? Then finally the eight creams pulling the state carriage came into sight. "All the world rose to its feet and uncovered," Sam Clemens would write of the moment. "The Queen Empress was come. She was received with great enthusiasm. It was realizable that she was the procession herself; that all the rest of it was mere embroidery; that in her the public saw the British Empire itself."

Soon after Her (mostly hidden) Majesty passed and the cheering ebbed away from in front of the Hotel Cecil, a phalanx of friendly Englishmen and Australians escorted Clemens across the crowded Strand and into a private house in Covent Garden, where the writer could work in peace to put the final touches on a few thousand words to be cabled *tout de suite* to New York.

He was already putting his jubilee article to bed as the queen and her guard glided through the parted crowd on the other side of the river, along Borough Road. "There is a very poor population, but just as enthusiastic & orderly as elsewhere," Victoria would remember. The only wrinkle in the entire program, as far as the queen could see, was the increasing afternoon heat, which caused the bearer of the ceremonial gilt rod, Lord Howe, to lose consciousness, fall off his horse, and land on the pavement with a muffled but alarming thud.

The day was, all in all, a grand success for queen and empire and for the American officials in attendance. "Personally I am highly gratified by their reception and also mine to-day," was John Hay's modest little statement to the press. "Everything was done to treat the special embassy well. The procession as a pictorial pageant was certainly one of the most wonderful things seen in modern times, both for the brilliancy and splendor and the marvelous organization which carried it through without accident." Whitelaw professed himself elated by the cheers he had personally received along the route and "amused by the delighted enthusiasm of the masses." He expressed his joy also on behalf of his wife, who had been allowed to kiss the queen's hand in the ballroom after the procession landed back at the palace, but Reid otherwise, and uncharacteristically, demurred. "Etiquette forbids me to discuss the Jubilee ceremonial," he told newsmen, "but you may say that it was extraordinarily successful in every way."

Chauncey Depew, another of the hopefuls passed over in favor of John Hay for the post of ambassador to the Court of St. James's, and then passed over for Whitelaw as special envoy, did not feel so bound by diplomatic convention. He had been the honored guest that day of a famous baroness, who had secured him a seat in front of St. Paul's. Chauncey and Chauncey Jr. were the *only* Americans in the alderman's stand at the churchyard, Depew explained to reporters, and this privilege made him more voluble even than usual about what he had witnessed. "I have often seen the Queen on state occasions, but to-day she seemed to be a deeply affected friend of mine," Depew offered. "I was close to her and saw her eyes suffused with tears." The pageant was full of drama; the entire citizenry was united for a radiant moment of fellow feeling for their common monarch and thrilled by the display of British supremacy—a "panorama of power unequalled in history." Among the American spectators," Chauncey said, "there was no jealousy nor stint of praise and applause. We could both glory in the vitality and virility of the mother country and rejoice mightily."

Chauncey was still talking, to anybody who would listen, when Sam Clemens cabled his uninspired little jubilee story, most of which he had written in advance, including the amusing factoid about the remarkable amount of territory gained per day in the queen's sixty-year reign, while noting the nonappearance at the party of so many of the national figures who had actually done the pirating of so much far-off land. The value of Clemens's effort was mostly in what the "Mark Twain" byline might do for William Randolph Hearst's circulation the next day, and not in the prose itself. "It was a memorable display and must live in history," Twain had cabled to New York. "It suggested the material glories of the reign finely and adequately. The absence of the chief creators of these was perhaps not a serious disadvantage. One could supply the vacancies by imagination, and thus fill out the procession very effectively. One can enjoy a rainbow without necessarily forgetting the forces that made it."

Clemens's newspaper story was a few meager drops in the journalistic rivers that flowed from the six-mile jubilee jaunt. The coverage of the queen's big party was unprecedented, especially the coverage by the hometown newspapers. "Perhaps the triumph around the walls of Rome when a Consul drove back to the capital after a victorious campaign would be the nearest approach to it," the *Standard* said of the parade itself. The least sentimental description, and perhaps the most reliable eyewitness account of the day, issued from the Clemens family maid, Katy Leary, who had grabbed discount seats along with Clara and Jean, in Trafalgar Square.

Katy was much impressed with the pomp and the "glittering royal carriages," but she was clear eyed about the mortal woman at the center of the event. "Queen Victoria looked pretty old and feeble," Katy would remember. "[She] sat there like a little mummy in the back of her carriage."

THE LONDON AND South Western Railway laid on thirty-seven special trains, beginning at five o'clock in the morning on June 26, four days after the big London parade, to carry passengers from Waterloo Station in London to Portsmouth, in advance of the naval review. The Prince of Wales had ordered two *additional* special trains—a full five hundred feet of passenger cars—for himself and his most honored guests, like Whitelaw Reid and his wife. By the time the temporary exodus of foreign royals and special ambassadors commenced, the queen was happy to see them go. The heat was suffocating, and she was sleeping poorly. Her Majesty had had enough and chose to stay behind.

Whitelaw Reid, still buoyant, was treated with continuing royal courtesy. (The Prince of Wales knew a wealthy mark when he saw one.) On arrival in Portsmouth, Whitelaw and his wife were ushered off the royal train and onto the royal yacht, the *Victoria and Albert*, where they were among the elect at Bertie's luncheon, at which his guests talked over the dinner they had enjoyed with the prince the evening before, at Lord Lansdowne's. John Hay and Clara were relegated that day to a "regular diplomatic boat," where they remained, to follow in the wake of the *Victoria and Albert* on the sail to Spithead to see the warships.

As the naval review began that afternoon with a thunderous volley of the big guns, the Prince of Wales, in his full naval regalia, summoned Whitelaw to join him on the bridge. "When I happened to say at the Naval Review in answer to some question from the Duke of Cambridge," Reid wrote to the president a few days later, "that we took as much pride in the magnificent display as they took themselves, and after all it was partly ours, since we sprang from the same stock, he turned and grasped both my hands in his with warmth, saying, 'I do hope that is the feeling of the majority of your countrymen,—and I am sure it ought to be—that is what we want.'"

Reid had the greater part of renown that day, but Hay had already pocketed a letter of heartfelt thanks from the president. "My Dear Ambassador, . . . the papers have already given us the particulars of Mr. Reid's gratifying reception, many of the arrangements for which I am sure were thoughtfully provided by yourself," McKinley's private secretary had written to Hay. "The *Tribune*'s editorial references to the administration have seemed to take on a new color."

John Hay knew what master he served, and it was not himself. He did not need to be on the bridge with a prince to grasp the dark diplomatic portents suggested by the naval review on the rainy summer night at the end of June. That night on the water, in the gathering darkness, when a barrage of friendly rockets illuminated the jewels of a dozen other foreign navies—the European powers, Japan, and the United States of America each had a warship on display—the *Brooklyn* held her own in every explosion of light. The crew of *Vizcaya* of Spain must have taken the measure of the new American cruiser, which would soon be back home, just off the coast of Cuba. It was the host empire, however, that showed itself the biggest gun on the water that night, perhaps the greatest single power the world had ever known. Twenty-one British battleships floated like proud Minotaurs before the gathered dignitaries, along with forty-four cruisers and seventy other gunboats, torpedo boats, and destroyers. No navy like it had ever existed, because no navy had ever had so much to protect. Where the mighty Romans had ruled 120 million people and a few million square miles, Britain had triple the number of subjects in 1897 and four times the landmass. Her Majesty's sailors held sway on the Atlantic and Indian Oceans, the Mediterranean, the Nile River, and any shipping lane it chose.

The considered consensus among the Americans who were on hand that day was pretty simple: *We really would do well to follow the lead of our mother country. And who says the Brits are destined to rule in perpetuity?* The *Gazette* in London, Americans noted with pride, was already warning that the annexation of Hawaii could mark the event that encouraged the United States to become, finally, a sea power capable of defending its Monroe Doctrine and much more besides. The cut of *Brooklyn* alone proved that the United States belonged in a small group of nations that might one day command oceans. "Swanlike," was how one British naval officer described the newly commissioned armored cruiser. "She is modern, fast and generally effective," bragged one American reporter on hand that night, "and her motto, 'Right Makes Might,' is peculiarly fitting."

The loquacious Chauncey Depew, still talking without pause, gave voice to the prevailing American sentiment that night. "I admit that when [the British] grab they give people better government, but Americans fear they will not be content with grabbing the land of the Old World and are going to try to grab in the New World," he said. "Anything of that kind done in our hemisphere we want to do ourselves."

JOHN HAY WOULD not soon forget the night at Spithead. Whatever were his dozens of tiny annoyances concerning Whitelaw that evening, John Hay did not miss the main point: the American republic, already possessed of spectacular wealth, had flashed its potential as a commercial and military match for the British Empire, maybe even a threat, and that simple fact meant he would have to manage the relationship with Britain with extreme caution. This was a friendship that mattered if the United States was truly going to push itself onto the world stage.

The ambassador still had that night of the glorious warships in mind many months later, when he agreed to deliver an Easter speech in London.

> On the evening of that memorable day, when all the ships lay enshrouded in darkness, the commander of the *Brooklyn* ran up the British and American colors, and then at a given signal turned upon those two kindred flags the brilliant rays of her searchlights. In that high illumination shrined in clear radiance far above the obscurity that hid the engines of destruction and preparations for war, those friendly banners fluttered, proclaiming to the navies of the world their message of good will. The beauty of the scene lasted but a moment; it passed away with much of the splendor and magnificence that adorned the historic day; but may we not hope that the lesson and the inspiration of that spectacle may last as long as those banners shall float over the seven seas, carrying always in their shadow freedom and civilization?

CHAPTER FOURTEEN

The Warm Afterglow of a Diamond Jubilee

And then the jubilee was over, evaporated like a nightmare—"gone like a Welsh-rabbit dream," was Hay's description—but with casualties and lingering aches. The first free Saturday after the jubilee, he and Mrs. Hay were preparing to host an Independence Day reception at their home, open to any American living in London or just passing through, when they received word that Rear Admiral Miller's ailing daughter had succumbed to typhoid. So in the middle of the Fourth of July celebration, Hay's embassy had to help the admiral and his wife find an appropriate church for the funeral and also help secure permission for the *Brooklyn* to stand in port in England a few extra days so that its commander could stow his daughter's body on board for the sad trip home.

The ambassador still had Reid on his hands, too, even after the rest of the special embassy left town. Whitelaw was intent on staying on for the entire month of July. He had a full calendar already: another state ball at Buckingham Palace; a banquet in honor of the colonial premiers; the Duchess of Buccleuch's ball; and a dine-and-sleep at Windsor Castle, at the invitation of Queen Victoria and the Prince of Wales. Whitelaw had Bertie on the hook to attend a private dinner in honor of His Royal Highness, hosted by Reid at his temporary residence. He had already rented some tapestries for the dining hall and had contracted for electric lights to be installed for the occasion. Whitelaw also made a number of public addresses, which Hay was forced to watch and sometimes to follow. At a dinner for the colonial premiers, Whitelaw pointed out to the Australians that the United States was about to become something like a neighbor—now that Honolulu was ready to fly the Stars and Stripes. At an Independence Day celebration on July 5, Whitelaw slathered tribute, rather unbecomingly, all over the current standard bearers of Britain's house of Hanover. "Possibly, if the wise and good Queen who reigns over British dominions had been in her grandfather's place, or if that Queen's son had been there, things might have been very different [in the American rebellion]," Reid said to a slightly disoriented crowd. "But they are far better as they are. The colossal development of the American Republic would have been impossible on colonial lines."

Whitelaw, amid his many London doings, had done very little of the one favor McKinley had *personally* asked of him: to see what he could do about heading off a war over Cuba. At their one private meeting at the White House before the jubilee mission, McKinley had tasked Reid—who had contacts among the Spanish diplomats he had known while ambassador to France—with opening lines of communications with his friend, the Duke of Sotomayor. The president wanted Reid to deliver the message sotto voce that the United States might be willing to pay Spain a fair price for Cuba. If Reid got any encouragement in that direction, McKinley told him, he wanted Reid to continue on to Madrid to try to make the deal.

Reid claimed later to have raised this point, albeit gingerly, but told the president he had received an unequivocal reply, not unlike what Prime Minister Cánovas had been saying in the newspapers: "Spain is not a nation of merchants capable of selling its honor." Sotomayor had told Reid that his country would never agree to sell "the brightest jewel in her crown." This was just what Whitelaw had hoped to hear; he had no interest in being consigned even temporarily to the dusty backwater of Madrid. Reid had bigger plans, which John Hay began to understand when he heard whispers that Whitelaw was interested in leasing Hay's town house in Washington—long term.

He knew Whitelaw well enough to know what that was about. The addlepated John Sherman couldn't survive as secretary of state much longer, Reid would be thinking, and now, coming off his London success—they called his name in the streets!—who was better positioned to take the reins of the State Department? Hay had had a bellyful of his old friend by then; Hay and his wife had already begun collecting little barbs from the Marlborough crowd, and he was unable to keep dissatisfaction with Whitelaw entirely within the immediate family. "Reid is winding up his commission in a blaze of glory," he reported to the president. "You have been the cause of great happiness to a worthy fellow-being. I only wonder whether this experience may not whet his appetite." And the president answered, with a wink: "Mr. Reid will I suppose soon be back here and will probably tell me personally of his experience." He didn't have to say *at length.*

McKinley had already received long dispatches from his special ambassador, who detailed some of his strenuous diplomatic efforts involving the Prince of Wales, the Duke of Edinburgh, the Duke of Connaught, the Duke of York, the Duke of Cambridge, Prince Christian, the Duke of Teck, the Marquess of Lorne, the blind Grand Duke of Mecklenburg-Strelitz, and Prince Edward of

President William McKinley

Saxe-Weimar. Whitelaw expressed great satisfaction at his success in calming their concerns that Americans "do not like them," which had grown as a result of the fight over Venezuela. Just how crucial it was to minimize anxiety among a gaggle of uniformed European nobles, who had very little to say in the running of the country, was unclear to President McKinley. The point Whitelaw wished to convey was this: Whitelaw had been busy.

HAY WAS RELIEVED when he finally had a chance to get back to the business of his ambassadorship. Lost for a time amid all the pomp and hideous circumstance of the jubilee was the fact that McKinley was still relying on him to secure British acquiescence on two issues he deemed important—saving the fur seals and negotiating, or at least appearing to negotiate, an international agreement on bimetallism. The fur seal guru John Foster arrived back in London from St. Petersburg on July 6, having seen Czar Nicholas II. The czar was disappointed that the American envoy was decidedly unenthusiastic about the idea of the world's two great wheat producers—the United States and Russia—colluding to keep the price nice and high, but he nevertheless professed his eagerness to send his representative to an international conference in Washington on pelagic sealing. Hay had meanwhile got a solid "maybe" from the Japanese minister in London. So on the hot and muggy day after Foster's return, John Hay strode through the still-crowded streets of London, where the last of the jubilee grandstands were being cleared, en route to another audience with Lord Salisbury. The prospects for success were beyond Hay's reckoning.

When Hay had delivered Foster's sharply worded message on the seals to the prime minister back in May, he had been certain that it would rankle His Lordship. He had even waited nearly two weeks in hopes that cooler heads would prevail at the State Department, but when Hay finally did make the formal presentation, essentially accusing Her Majesty's government of obstructing the international effort to protect the sealing industry, and of something close to outright and purposeful prevarication, Salisbury had let it float by without attempting even a minimal glancing blow. Hay was pleased to note that when he got in front of the marquess again that July day, that earlier uncomfortable meeting seemed forgotten.

The proposition Hay made to Salisbury on behalf of the American government was simple enough: a conference in Washington in October, after this year's seal-hunting season had closed, attended by the interested powers. The United States and Russia had committed to the conference; Japan was likely to attend. President McKinley desired especially the participation of Great Britain. Salisbury was his old inscrutable self. He wondered what might be the explicit *purpose* of such a meeting. Hay begged the marquess to understand that no specific instructions would bind the participants and no "positive line of action" would be required. "The meeting," Hay explained, "would be merely consultation as to the best means of preserving seal life in Bering Sea."

Of course, Salisbury explained, he could make no commitment without consulting with Chamberlain at the Colonial Office. "England was in this respect," Hay reported the prime minister as saying, "rather the trustee for Canada than the principal." Perhaps, Salisbury said, he would be able to give a more definite answer at, well, another time. And by the way, Salisbury mentioned, Her Majesty's government still believed that the American assertion that the fur seals were near extinction lacked solid foundation.

Hay suggested that perhaps a direct conversation about the issue should take place between the Americans and Chamberlain, and when Salisbury assented, Hay asked for the first available opening in the colonial secretary's schedule, which was that Saturday. "As I have observed before to you in this correspondence," Hay cabled Sherman, explaining why Chamberlain's compliance was the key, "the attention of the Government seems to be devoted exclusively this year to the cultivation of the imperial idea in the colonies, and nothing will be done which will militate against this sentiment."

Ambassador Hay was in a hurry to get Chamberlain on board, because he had begun to see rumors in Fleet Street newspapers that the US State Department might be on the verge of releasing to the public the entire text of Foster's shrill cable, which would ring ugly in English ears. The bullish Foster even sent a quick message back to the White House that it might be best to withhold the indignant missive he had written two months earlier. In the afterglow of the jubilee, the Brits seemed remarkably pliable, so why offend? Chamberlain was encouraging at the Saturday meeting. Hay's friend Julian Pauncefote, the British ambassador to the United States, was similarly hopeful of a settlement on the seals. And the Canadians had gone on record saying they "regard the latest proposals of the United States as entirely reasonable."

By Monday, July 12, less than a week into the postjubilee labors, it looked as if a deal for the conference was all but certain. The Canadian minister of marine and fisheries was talking up the idea of fair compensation for keeping the British Columbian sealers onshore for a season or two; and Lord Salisbury, it was reported, was "showing more disposition to reopen the question."

Later that same day, Hay, along with Senator Wolcott and the two other American commissioners, met with Prime Minister Salisbury and his government moneymen to make a presentation on the outlook for an international agreement on bimetallism. The American commission had just returned from Paris, Hay explained to the British contingent, where they had worked out a set of agreed-upon guidelines with the French, and if Great Britain would enter the talks, the prospects for successfully integrating silver into the international money system looked promising. Lord Salisbury, surprisingly, engaged. He wanted to know whether the French would consent to opening their mints to free coinage of silver, and what fixed ratio of gold to silver was being contemplated by the two other nations, and how they would make sure it *remained* fixed.

Wolcott made what might have seemed in earlier American administrations a presumptuous presentation to Salisbury. He actually laid out what would be asked of the British government: reopening the Indian mints to coin both gold and silver; placing 20 percent of the bullion in the Bank of England in silver; coining a specific amount of silver each year, the actual amount to be decided later; and so forth. Perhaps it was the afterglow of the jubilee again, or the soothing memory of the fifteen-mile-long flotilla of Royal Navy battleships floating by at Spithead, but neither Salisbury nor his chancellor of the Exchequer cut Wolcott short. They let him make his case in full. They did, however, remind the Americans that this discussion could not be considered official or formal until the French ambassador was present to speak for his own country. The group set a new meeting for three days later, when the Frenchman would be able to attend.

That's when things started to get crumbly. Hay's carriage, en route that evening to another in a series of London balls, was accidentally rammed by a public omnibus, and a pole slashed into the interior of the ambassador's elegant conveyance. Clara Hay was saved from serious injury, or even death, only because she was leaning forward to talk to her husband. Two days later, Foster's ignoble instructions to John Hay on the question of the fur seals did hit the press—and not just a pithy little digest of the instructions, but the instructions in full, taking up a half page, prefaced with this ditty: "They show at length England's policy of procrastination, her continued failure and refusal to support this Government in its efforts to prevent the extermination of the seal herd." The publication wasn't in just any newspaper but ran as an exclusive in the Great Moral Organ, the *New York Tribune*, owned by Whitelaw Reid, who happened to be on his way to his royal dine-and-sleep at Windsor.

Hay read the next-day editions of the London newspapers and could only shake his head. Americans were taking heavy fire already, much of it aimed at poor John Sherman, whose signature was affixed to Foster's cable. "It is a manifest attempt, in offensive language, to fasten upon England a charge of bad faith," said the *Times*. "If this was not Secretary Sherman's intention, he has shown himself singularly unfitted for the delicate and responsible duties of his office; if it was, then the statement he recently made repudiating the charge of bad faith was deliberately misleading. When he was first appointed to his present office, doubts were expressed as to the wisdom of the choice. If he really sent this dispatch, they will be fully confirmed."

The *Post* was more dramatic: "Every indication points to the certainty that Great Britain will be compelled to fight for her existence against the United States as soon as an American Government believes that war can be safely begun."

A war over sealskin coats and accessories, fashionable though they were, seemed far fetched, and Hay retained his capacity for amusement. He knew Salisbury and Chamberlain well enough to know they didn't give a tinker's damn about the editorialists on Fleet Street. These politicians were playing to an audience of one: their "white dominion" in North America—"Our Lady of the Snows," as Hay called it—Canada. They were terribly close to enticing Prime Minister Laurier into signing a trade deal giving British products preferential treatment. So they had to *appear* to stand tough for those poor, mistreated, and misunderstood sealers out of British Columbia until their trade deal was done. And Hay was secretly gleeful about one other thing: Whitelaw was caught in the wringer. Reid, as the American newspapers reported it, had finally managed to get himself into the McKinley cabinet, which had as its chief topic of discussion at its next meeting the unfortunate and unauthorized publication of the fur seal instruction. Secretary of State Sherman told his fellow cabinet members he had not approved its release; the culprit, according to cabinet consensus, was the president's special ambassador in London.

The third assistant secretary of state walked out that day and told reporters that the fur seal document had not come from official channels, officially. "I think it came from England, and was probably sent to the *Tribune* by WHITELAW REID. There was ample time to send the letter by mail to the *Tribune*." One of Reid's rival papers ran with the story, accusing the *Tribune* of embarrassing the president; the *New York Sun* also suggested probable cause for suspecting Whitelaw. Number one, he was the owner of the *Tribune*; number two, he was in London with "friendly access to JOHN HAY's mail bag"; and number three, Reid's father-in-law was a major owner in the company that held the sealing rights on the Pribilof Islands.

Reid came back from his royal supper at Windsor Castle and began harrumphing right away. Whitelaw's venerable *Tribune* called the *Sun* a journalistic ragpicker, but the *Tribune* did not exactly deny that Reid was the source of the leak. The charge that he "cabled or sent the instructions to his paper," the *Tribune* asserted, "is too absurd to demand either refutation or denial."

The secretary of state was taking it on the chin, too. John Sherman was initially reported to be clueless as to how a document from his department became public. Then came the revelation that General Foster was the real author of the dispatch and that Sherman had signed the document without so much as skimming it, followed by the pathetic report that everybody in the Foreign Office in London believed Sherman could be forgiven because nobody there took him seriously anyway. They regarded him, as a well-placed London correspondent for a New York paper described it, as "a doddering old man, who even in his virile days, veered round to every possible wind that blew, and now really recalls with difficulty what yesterday's attitude on any subject was."

The day that story came out, Secretary Sherman stayed home from the office; the State Department announced he was suffering from "some slight stomach derangement." He would have been at work the next day, his family said, but for the weather. A few days later, the secretary was found making a dash for the far end of Long Island to escape the Washington heat. "In seeking a cool resort by the sea," he told reporters, "I learned something about geography. I had never heard of Amagansett before." By the time Sherman had settled into the remote wagon-rutted little beach town of Amagansett, reporters were running down new rumors. Was Sherman stepping down? Was Whitelaw Reid taking his place? They had heard Reid would be leasing John Hay's house, a short walk from the State Department offices. Reid's friends could not deny that he wanted a place in the McKinley cabinet! "The story is without foundation," Sherman answered, somewhat feebly. "If my health holds out I shall see the Hawaiian annexation question to a settlement."

ON JULY 24, finally, Hay and the special equerry escorted Reid and his suite to Waterloo Station and out of town for good. The next day, Hay wrote Henry Adams in Paris: "I have seen my friend Whitelaw sitting between two princesses at supper every night, a week running, and I now may intone my *nunc dimittis* [Simeon has seen the baby Jesus, the savior, and now he may die in peace]. His rapture had the *aliquid amari* that the end must come, but the memory of it will soothe many an hour of ennui at [Reid's country home] Ophir Farm. As for Mrs. Oddie [Reid's mother-in-law], her tiaras got heavier and higher by the hour, till the ceilings were all too low. . . . I do not know why, in your presence, I naturally run to slanderous gossip."

The regular ambassador also complained to his friend about being stuck in London to push the limp strings on fur seals and more silver while Adams was sitting happy in Paris, in the company of their darling friend, Lizzie Cameron, and while Hay's wife and children were headed back home to their summer retreat in New Hampshire. "I cannot leave this blessed Isle," Hay complained to Adams. " 'Come again next week!' says my Lord of Salisbury, or, by preference, 'Wait till I send for thee, when I have a more convenient season.' "

Salisbury had waited two weeks after the publication of the Foster directive to let the press cool down, and the question of the seal conference was still hanging fire. The talks on bimetallism were going even less well. Her Majesty's government had made no official reply to any of the American proposals and offered no encouragement; the French were already in retreat. From what Hay could glean from friends like the head of the Rothschild banking house, who was vaguely sympathetic to silver, the consensus among the financial powers in London and the Continent was fairly settled: the economy was finally and firmly swinging up from the crash of 1893. Everybody they knew was prospering once again. Their own free-silver agitators were quieting down. Why change things now? The gold standard seemed peachy. Best to take a wait-and-see approach.

McKinley's chief bimetallist emissary, Senator Wolcott, was predictably downhearted, and there was little Hay could do to cheer him. "I was able to expedite the earlier stages of the negotiation," Hay reported to the president, "but there comes a period when [the British] will not be hurried and we must wait their pleasure." The line out of Whitehall was that experts were making a careful examination. Hay would joke, without laughter, "The British want a couple of months to study the silver question—none too much."

WHITELAW REID ARRIVED by steamship in New York Harbor on the last day of July, wondering what laurels and plaudits awaited. He had official tidings to report, which meant another audience with the president. Reid was most anxious to see the Major, who had just that week signed the piece of legislation he had most wanted out of the now closed congressional session, the Dingley Tariff, that beautiful and stalwart Republican shield for American industrialists. The president would probably be in a receptive mood. The tide was running Whitelaw's way, he figured, as he sat on deck scanning the newspapers while a tugboat hauled his ship to port.

What *actually* awaited Whitelaw Reid in the harbor that steamy summer morning was an unfriendly reporter, who had hitched a ride on the tug and got himself in front of Whitelaw before the ship came in. Reid was happy to talk at first, as the intrepid newsman reported the interview. The published account of the talk with Reid may have been 90 percent invention, but the broad burlesque hit the mark nonetheless. "Of course, I would rather not go into details about our dining with the Queen on July 15," said Reid, at least according to the report.

"Let me see," the correspondent reportedly replied, "that was the day after the *Tribune* here beat all the other papers by publishing, before it had been released, the official correspondence of Secretary Sherman to Ambassador Hay relative to the Bering Sea seal controversy, was it not?"

"I don't remember."

"Was any comment made at dinner by any of the English nobility on the enterprise of your paper in being able to publish official correspondence ahead of your contemporaries?"

"I didn't hear any. But you must excuse me. I can't talk for the newspapers until after I have made my report to the President at Washington."

"You knew, of course, that Mr. Thomas W. Cridler, Mr. Sherman's Third Assistant Secretary, had said that neither he nor Mr. Hamlin gave out that correspondence, and that he thought that it must have come direct from you from England?"

"I have heard some such talk, but of course I have nothing to say about it now."

"Were you not afraid that it would look a little personal for this seal fishery correspondence in favor of your father-in-law's company to come out first in your paper before the authorities at Washington had authorized its publication?"

"I have told you before that I can't say anything on this subject for the newspapers."

"Do you not think that the Tribune's premature publication of this diplomatic correspondence, which so much concerned your father-in-law's financial interests, has had a tendency to defeat your chances of being appointed to succeed Secretary Sherman?"

"Well, really, young man, you don't seem to understand that I have refused to talk shop."

"By that do you mean about the *Tribune*'s premature publication or about your chances of succeeding Secretary Sherman?"

"I'm not going to say anything more to anybody for publication, until after I make my official report as special ambassador to the jubilee."

"When do you expect to make that report to Washington?"

"In a day or two, after I have a chance to rest from the voyage."

"Shall we be able to read it in the *Tribune* the day before it is made public in Washington?"

WHEN JOHN HAY at last received the official word from Lord Salisbury that Her Majesty's government was willing to attend the proposed conference on the fur seals, the note was a tad vague. The prime minister mentioned only three parties to the conference, Great Britain, Canada, and the United States. His note of acceptance minimized the purpose of this conference to near uselessness: "The object of the meeting would be to arrive, if possible, at correct conclusions respecting the numbers, conditions, and habits of the seals frequenting the Pribilof Islands at the present time, as compared with the several seasons previous." Hay was certain he had been explicit about the details of the conference, which would include not just the three parties the marquess had named but Russia and Japan as well, and which, while not finally binding, would strive for a consensus on the facts *and* on what regulations might be put in place to preserve the fur seals and the fur seal industry. Hay sent a message over to the prime minister gently reminding him of at least one of these details: "It may not be out of place for me to recall to your lordship that, as I have already had occasion to mention, the President expects the Governments of Russia and Japan, powers interested in the preservation of the seal herds of Bering Sea, to be represented at the conference."

No answer was made and no objection was lodged, which Hay took as a victory. "I hope you will be pleased with this disposition, for the time being, of a matter which looked for a while as if it might have serious consequences," he reported to McKinley.

Hay's private correspondence with the president had picked up since the strange special appointment of Whitelaw Reid; Hay no longer felt constrained to hold the topics of discussion to seals and silver. He kept his eyes and ears open for anything the president might find useful. The Japanese minister in London,

Hay reported in one private letter, had assured him there would be no hard feelings over the annexation of Hawaii, provided the twenty-five thousand Japanese citizens living on the islands were treated with dignity and respect. "I hear that the Japanese government is displaying a feverish activity in naval preparation in England," Hay wrote to the president. "They are contracting for no less than eighteen war vessels of different kinds. They are building four battleships of the first class and two very swift cruisers. Some people think the preparations are intended for us. I am by no means certain of this. There is more immediate promise of difficulty with Russia and Japan, or between Japan and Spain on the Philippines matter than with us. But they are full of ambition and ardor since their victory over the Chinese, and want to be ready for anything that turns up."

"My dear Colonel Hay: Your last letter to me was delightful as all your letters are," McKinley wrote in a crossing correspondence. "I do not need to be reassured that you are using untiring energy and tact to help along two of the administration's greatest efforts—Bimetallism and Bering Sea Negotiations—but the details which you present are interesting and instructive. . . . The generosity and delicacy with which you have treated [Mr. Reid] could not have been exceeded by any one and will in the end I am sure strengthen your own position with the people of both countries, if this were possible, or needed, which it is not."

CHAPTER FIFTEEN

Repose and Restfulness and Superb Scenery

The summer exodus was on in early August 1897, in capitals around the world. The queen regent of Spain and her court decamped for San Sebastián; her loyal prime minister, Cánovas del Castillo, and his wife were already at the healing baths in Santa Águeda. Kaiser Wilhelm, having just finished the taxing business of centralizing government and ministerial power in his own God-selected self, was sailing his imperial yacht to a family conference with his cousin, Czar Nicholas, in St. Petersburg, then back to his summer retreat at Schloss Wilhelmshöhe. His inner circle was already busy planning special entertainments, as they did every year, for the kaiser's delectation at the annual hunt. "I'll parade you like a clipped poodle!" one imperial intimate, Georg, had written to another imperial favorite, Emil, some seasons earlier. "That'll be a hit like nothing else. Just think: behind SHAVED, in front long bangs out of black and white wool, in the back, under a real poodle's tail, a noticeable rectal opening, and, as soon as you stand up on your hind feet, in FRONT a fig leaf.... I already see it in my mind's eye, H[is] M[ajesty] laughing like us—and I'm counting on a *succès fou.*"

President McKinley was recreating in slightly more staid and republican fashion up near the Canadian border in Vermont—reports had it that his bowling was improving. United States secretary of the navy John Long was nursing his digestive difficulties with custard pies and tending his gardens at his summer home in Maine. Long had entrusted the operations of the department to Assistant Secretary Roosevelt, who vowed to man his post the entire summer if necessary, the crushing Washington heat be damned. He wrote his boss that "there isn't the slightest earthly reason for you to come back for six weeks or more." Henry Cabot Lodge was resting at the ancestral family retreat in Nahant, trying to settle a sour stomach and shaky nerves; he had, as at every session of Congress, worked himself into psychic and physical prostration and without a lot to show for it. His pet projects—the annexation of Hawaii, Spain's ouster from Cuba, and the canal in Nicaragua connecting the Atlantic and the Pacific—were still uncompleted, and Cabot had left Washington worn and discouraged. "I am very much pleased that you are loafing, and I am sure that you will very soon be yourself again," Roosevelt wrote his friend Cabot. "Any man who throws himself with such intense energy into his work as you do, and who therefore accomplishes so much, must pay the penalty in one way or another, especially if he not only *does* things, but *feels* them. . . . That good times are coming is now beyond doubt." John Hay's boss, John Sherman, was the exception to the rule of respite; he arrived back in Washington from Amagansett "fresh and improved," the newspapers reported, just after Congress adjourned, to make sure that nobody took his job away while he wasn't looking.

Ambassador Hay, still in London, was enduring annoying little eddies of senators and congressmen in the normal stream of visitors at his embassy; they were already beginning to pass through London for brief shopping sprees on their way to trout fishing in the countryside, looking for advice on how to beat the new Dingley Tariff. Should they mark their Harrods-bought pajamas down under the hundred-dollar limit? "They are all in a blue funk about the inspector on the New York docks," Hay wrote to Adams. "It was gentle and joyous sport to pass the Tariff Bill, but when it comes to paying duty on their London dittoes it is another story."

The streets of London in August were still teeming with proles who had nowhere to go. "A big hopeless hell of common people to whom all doors are shut save the grave and America," Hay's friend Clarence King said of England. But Hay didn't pay the working folks much mind. What he saw was *his* London neighborhood, which was quieting considerably. The great and noble households were packing up and moving to their deer forests and grouse moors in Wales or Scotland. "The stag-hunting season on Exmoor is to commence next week," announced the *Pall Mall Gazette* (now owned by Willie Astor). Lord and Lady Wolverton had arrived at Cowes to board the steam yacht they had engaged for a two-month holiday. They were likely to run into Bertie there. The governing classes in London were idling down also. The diplomatic corps was scattering to the Continent and beyond; Canadian officials were heading home with their pockets stuffed with most of what they had come for.

Lord Salisbury had promised his ailing wife another vacation at their home in the South of France as soon as he could get free, but for now he was busy trying to herd the European powers into a reasonable peace treaty between the German-sponsored Turks and the Greeks over Crete. The marquess was also enduring a little kicking from the London press about the regrettable deal he had made with Colonel Hay about the fur seal conference. "Apparently, then, Lord SALISBURY has once more been successfully bullied," the *Morning Post* scolded. "That matters should wear this appearance is humiliating to this country, and that the temper of the public should endure this kind of humiliation is deeply to be deplored. The consequence will inevitably be that the method of bullying, once more successfully used, will rise in favour with other nations, and especially with the United States Government, while our own people, thus accustomed to yielding without reason, must become less and less sensitive in regard to the national honour."

Hay and the marquess were both in a position, for now, to sit back and let the editorialists exhaust themselves on the subject of national honor. The American ambassador, too, was planning a month-long relay of visits to the deer forests and grouse moors and trout preserves of the Scottish countryside, the chief enticement being a few days with his old friend Sir John Clark at Tillypronie, near the queen's summer castle. John Hay was easier in his skin than he had been in years. The rest of his family was headed back to the doldrums of New Hampshire, and he was not. He could envision the scene at the Fells as it would shortly be: Clara picking her blackberries, and tending her flower beds, and trying to calm little Clarence after his thug of an older brother, Del, had cuffed him one too many times, and scolding their daughters for going out in the sun without their hats. John Hay was glad to be where he was and not sitting on his porch at "the Place-Where-Nothing-Happens," but on the dearest residential street on the planet, held fast once again, for the first time in more than thirty years, by the momentous turn of the world.

John Hay effaced the notion that he might alter in any significant way the world's path, but he delighted in his close-in view of the passing events and the parade of folks he saw. The American diplomatic corps was always good for amusement. "Woodfords came—eight strong—in the evening," Hay reported to Clara when America's new minister to Spain, Stewart Woodford, passed through on his way to Madrid at the beginning of August. "Mr. Sherman [the secretary of state] has broken loose again in the *World*, saying 'England would rather quarrel than fight' & that if she wanted to fight Russia & Japan would help us whip her. Woodford, to whom it's all new, was blushing & cringing with shame over it last night."

President McKinley had handed Woodford the difficult mission of persuading the Cánovas government in Madrid to call a cease-fire in Cuba and cede some measure of political autonomy to the insurgents. Hay already sympathized with the sad-eyed Woodford, who still sported the same old-fashioned muttonchop sideburns he had worn as an officer in the Union army. The Cánovas government had recently announced its commitment to giving its military commanders in Cuba another six months to "pacify" the island. The Spaniards appeared intent on ruling the "shining jewel" of their colonies, along with nearby

Puerto Rico, at their pleasure, for as long as they pleased. Even among the Spanish politicians who favored political reform in Cuba, American interference was deeply resented. The Spanish government had just that week answered Secretary Sherman's official communication to Spain deploring its inhumane policy of *reconcentrado* and its complete disregard for American economic interests in Cuba. The answer from official Spain was that Secretary Sherman must be misinformed; the state of affairs on the island was not nearly as grim as the Americans believed, and besides, the Spanish ambassador noted by way of gratuitous aside, the counterinsurgency program was no less humane than the one put into effect in the Civil War by the US secretary of state's own brother, William Tecumseh Sherman.

Hay could offer little useful advice to Woodford. Hay had been stationed three decades earlier in the US Embassy in Spain, where he quickly learned that fact and reason held little sway in Spanish politics. Cánovas, whom Hay had seen in action then, was still rabidly antidemocratic and would be preternaturally antipathetic to any American proposals Woodford might deliver. And the new American minister would be unwise to depend on more liberal politicians in Madrid to align themselves with a free Cuba. They had never been much interested in a *free Spain*. "I was one day talking with a most cultivated and enlightened gentleman, who spoke with great warmth and admiration of the liberal representative systems of England and America," Hay had written in his first book, *Castilian Days*. "'We shall have it here finally, I suppose'; then added with bitter sadness, 'The only trouble will be for the first five or six hundred years.' Even the reactionists appear, in conversation, to have a platonic regard for freedom, and speak of it as younger sons speak of the rose that all are praising, which is not the rose for them."

All Hay could do was squire Woodford around to British government officials and help him make the case that the United States had a special interest in Cuba—that "the sugar of Cuba is as vital to our people as are the wheat and cotton of India and Egypt to Great Britain," Woodford and Hay explained. They didn't run into much resistance at Whitehall to Woodford's assertion that the island would be better off under American protection. Woodford could report back to the president, as Hay already had, the likelihood of Britain's quiet acquiescence in whatever course the United States took in Cuba.

The two American diplomats were still making these rounds when the news hit the papers in London: the Spanish prime minister, Señor Cánovas del Castillo, had been murdered by an Italian anarchist in the resort town of Santa Águeda. The assassin's bullet left Spain without a permanent prime minister until the fall, at least; muddied the mission for Woodford; and gave Hay a new bit of work to attend to. There were official condolences to prepare and deliver to Spain's ambassador in London, the Count of Casa Valencia, with a special personal note to the ambassador's wife, whose sister was married to the fallen Spanish prime minister. Hay also had to attend the memorial service in Westminster, where he sat uncomfortably in the alien incense-permeated air and observed the rituals of the Catholic Mass, which had always suggested, to his prim Protestant nose, the occult.

The London papers filled with details of the murder in the next few days. When Señora Cánovas had berated her husband's twenty-six-year-old assassin at the scene, the man spoke calmly: "I respect you because you are an honorable lady, but I have done my duty." He told officials the killing was nothing personal; he was merely avenging fellow anarchists who had been executed in Barcelona.

The Cuban freedom fighters issued a statement denouncing the assassin and offering sympathy to the widow. "[We] are carrying on a fair and open warfare against the Spanish Government, and not a war of treachery and secret assassination," was the official release. "The Cuban Insurgent is fighting against the Spanish Government and against what he honestly believes to be tyranny and oppression. He is fighting for his independence and the freedom of that Cuba he loves so well." Unofficially, the talk among Cubans was that the Cánovas assassination would shatter the monarchy in Madrid and beyond. "I expect to see Cuba free in 90 days hence, and a Republic established in Spain shortly afterwards," said the head of one of Cuba's leading revolutionary families.

President McKinley and his cabinet were careful not to overencourage the rebels or the loud contingent of Americans already calling for US military action in Cuba. The president emerged from his lakeside retreat to say he was horrified by the murder of another head of state, but he declined to say anything further. Secretary Sherman suggested that the assassination, from the American point of view, was of little consequence. "Señor Cánovas was a strong partisan and a chief exponent of the element which is determined to keep the island at all hazards, and seemingly Spain forms almost a unit on this point," Sherman said. "The political effects of such events are not essentially far-reaching, and do not always produce radical developments."

By the time John Hay shipped Woodford and his family out of London to meet the queen regent in San Sebastián, he was beginning to wilt. Three days after the assassination, Hay found himself padding around his "lonesome and chilly structure" on Carlton House Terrace, pining for his family, and ready for a vacation. "I tried an excellent experience last night," Hay reported to Henry Adams. "I had nobody to dine with me, and a dinner alone is too gruesome. I was too lazy to go across the street to a club. So I ate no dinner at all, spent the evening reading accumulations of American newspapers, and then went to sleep and put in ten hours without a groan. . . . I spend the coming week in Hampshire and Somersetshire; then I come back here and sign some papers, and then I spread my snow-white wings for the North, which, like me, is cold, and true, and tender."

THE CLEMENS FAMILY, meanwhile, was settled into their summer lakeside retreat in Weggis, Switzerland, happy to be out of London and away from the site of their long gray mourning. The Clemens home at Tedworth Square had grown more dark and more tense every day at the end of their stay in London; the Diamond Jubilee had worn Clemens ragged and made him anxious. Then Livy caught a cinder in the eye on a rare outing, requiring surgery, which terrified Sam and delayed their departure from London an extra week; then Clara Clemens was nearly dragged underneath a team of horses in a hansom cab accident. Sam's hernia bulged so badly that he was afraid that he, too, would have to go under the knife, and his gout started acting up. Could a new run of carbuncles be far behind? He described himself to Henry Rogers as "old & played-out & pretty nearly callous."

Even the reports of John Hay's Independence Day celebration at Carlton House Terrace had set him off. That cur, Bret Harte, was there looking on as Whitelaw Reid and other notables reminded their countrymen how God had blessed and inspired and kept their Christian nation. "A man can be a [Christ] ian *or* a patriot, but he can't legally be a [Christ]ian *and* a patriot," Clemens wrote in his notebook a few days later. "Word it as softly as you please, the spirit of patriotism is the spirit of the dog & wolf. The moment there is a misunderstanding about a boundary line or a hamper of fish or some other squalid matter, see Patriotism rise, & hear him split the universe with his war-whoop. The spirit of Patriotism being in its nature jealous & selfish, is just in man's line, it comes natural to him—he can live up to all its requirements to the letter." This little essay was not offered for public consumption, of course. He didn't dare tempt public scorn. Whatever else he was, Sam Clemens remained alert to the dangers of advertising an idea like that, especially in his current predicament. Debt, he would say, makes a man a coward.

The move from London to Switzerland was just a deeper (and more affordable) retreat. Economies had to be maintained until Clemens had dug his family out of its financial hole, a task Livy was not making any easier. Sam had twice turned down Major Pond's guarantee of $50,000 *plus* expenses for a lecture tour in America that fall and winter because Livy was no longer willing to allow even a temporary breakup of the family. She also refused to consent to her husband's scheme for a small series of $1,000-a-seat lectures, which seemed to her another unbecoming instance of begging charity. The family would make do relatively cheaply that summer on Lake Lucerne, Livy had decided, and then move to Vienna, where Clara wanted to be. The family would hole up in Austria for as long as it took Sam to write them out of debt. Livy did not care to be seen gallivanting around Europe with a retinue of servants while their creditors twiddled their thumbs in America.

Their rented cottage in Weggis was plenty big, and for a few extra francs every week the landlady included all family meals and afternoon tea served in their rooms. "They feed us lavishly," Clemens wrote. "How do they manage it at these prices?" The lair was perched a hundred feet above Lake Lucerne and looked out onto distant mountains still snow-tipped in August. The first Sunday in Weggis, Clemens sat facing the big bay windows in the sunroom, admiring the scene: the long, graceful steamboats ferrying tourists across the lake, voices flashing off water and rock (a little German, a little French, and the sudden and unmistakable hard, sharp rasp of American English cutting through birdsong) and the liquid plash of paddle wheel; summer residents with fishing rods resting on their shoulders, ambling down to the lake; a lone bicycle rider passing noiselessly along a smooth path below; peasants returning from church in their Sunday finery; and, across the lake, the mountains.

The town of Lucerne was a smooth thirty-minute steamboat ride across the lake, and the family took turns at the daily shopping there. There was nothing you couldn't get in town, from salt mackerel to sheet music to anvils. When it was his turn, Clemens would hie himself off with his shopping list: mineral water for his gout, saccharin, tea, tea*pots*, fresh fruit, Clara's hair wash. He would even manage to surprise Livy and come back with much of the list completed. Nobody needed to remind him of cigars, of course; and Lucerne turned out to be well stocked with his favorite kind—cheap.

Clemens found a rental piano in Lucerne and had it shipped across the lake for Clara's daily practice; he also secured bikes for both girls, and he hired them a rowboat. Jean, who had her seventeenth birthday the week after they arrived in Weggis, was tall and sturdy and more self-sufficient than ever; she had gone so long without suffering an epileptic seizure that the doctors were ready to pronounce her cured. She was determined to improve her French and her German that summer. Clara practiced her piano without worry of mewling neighbors, shoring up her shaky confidence for Vienna, where she hoped to study with the world-renowned Leschetizky, mentor and guide of recent prodigies like Paderewski and Ossip Gabrilowitsch. She meant to step out of the family-imposed exile, as soon as she felt ready, and onto the concert stage. Sam Clemens had not seen his daughters this healthful and carefree since the debt siege had begun five years earlier. "[Our niece] Julia Langdon is staying with us," Clemens wrote to a friend, "& she & our two girls bike 20 & 30 miles a day & row us old people about the lake in the evenings, & are tanned like a meerschaum, & wholesome to look at."

Clemens was content to be cut off from the world that summer; by his own count he saw three days' worth of newspapers in ten weeks. What was happening with Cuba and Hawaii and the sultan of Turkey and free silver and fur seals, he couldn't say and didn't much care. He had grown bone weary of the international news by then—Cuban women and children starving to death under the watch of Spanish troops in the concentration camps, and suspected rebels in the Philippines being executed en masse by Spanish overlords. "After the volley the bodies are examined by doctors, and any one still showing a sign of life is given '*tiro de caridad*' (a charity shot) at close distance, to finish the work," explained one British journal. "In most cases there is some mutilation from the heavy Remington bullets used."

The war news from Crete had been just as ugly. Muslim soldiers there had cut off the nose and ears of one Christian monk and roasted him alive, then beheaded two others. The Christian side had reportedly done its fair share of burning, mutilating, and woman and child killing as well. "Of all the animals, man is the only one that is cruel. He is the only one that inflicts pain for the pleasure of it," Clemens had written on reading this news, in another not-for-publication essay. "Man is the only animal that deals in that atrocity of atrocities, War. He is the only one that gathers his brethren about him and goes forth in cold blood and with calm pulse to exterminate his kind. He is the only animal that for sordid wages will march out . . . and help to slaughter strangers of his own species who have done him no harm and with whom he has no quarrel. Man is the only animal that robs his helpless fellow of his country—takes possession of it and drives him out of it or destroys him."

But all this ugliness had receded from his view in Weggis, and life in general made fewer demands. The travel book was nearly behind him; he had only to approve and amend the final page proofs, which were due to arrive any day. And for the first time in years, Sam Clemens found his head swimming with ideas for new novels and short stories and articles. He rented a writing cabin a mile's walk along the lake from their cottage, determined to churn out work for fun and profit. He was at his writing desk before eleven every day, and hard at it seven days a week. Clemens worked on more than a half-dozen different pieces: sketches of Satan's boyhood, of an incident of found treasure's corrupting every heretofore honest person in a town, and of a tomcat who wanted to reform; an elegy to his friend George Griffin; an essay about the world as a living creature and people as microbes—"the little stinking human race, with its little stinking kings and popes & his bishops & prostitutes & peddlers." He jotted little notes and reminders to himself: "must keep working this patriotism racket."

He made time for only one friend, Robert Barr, a magazine editor and novelist who had also left London to spend a summer writing in Weggis. Clemens and Barr occasionally set aside an hour or two for an evening constitutional, so as the sun was beginning to drop in the early evening, Barr would come knocking at the office door and find his new friend still at the desk amid a haze of smoke, a cigar in one hand, a fountain pen in the other, tearing out another sheet of notepaper, which marked another 150 words done and laid aside.

Clemens told Barr, one writer to another, that he expected to be able to work from 11:00 to 4:30 every day that summer and make 1,800 words worth keeping at every sitting. But it didn't matter whether Barr showed up at 4:30 or 5:30 or 7:30 for their walk, the same scene played out. "Is time up already?" Clemens would say. "Just let me finish this sentence, and I'll be with you." Then he'd turn back and lose himself in some sketch of a new Tom Sawyer and Huck Finn adventure, until finally, maybe half an hour later, Barr would drag him away from his desk and into the gloaming.

On those walks through the grassy Swiss countryside, while he offered professional advice to the younger author, Sam Clemens was starting to feel easy in his shoes again, and happy to be living in his own head. "You can't depend on your judgment when your imagination is out of focus," he would say. There was extra comfort in knowing that Henry Rogers finally had in hand the $10,000 that Bliss had paid for the delivery of the travel book manuscript. Add to Bliss's ten thousand the other moneys Rogers had been holding for him—payments from earlier serializations, royalties from Frank Mayo's new theatrical adaptation of *Pudd'nhead Wilson*, the net receipts from the round-the-world lecture tour, and the unexpected boon of dividends and profits from wise investments Rogers had made on Clemens's behalf—and Sam Clemens, from his mountain perch, was beginning to see a possibility, at some not-so-distant day, of clearing his debt and restoring his good name.

But by the time the page proofs of the new book arrived at his doorstep—they had finally settled on *Following the Equator* as a title—a darkness had started to seep back in. He tried to keep himself occupied reading the proofs and making corrections, but the family's new anniversary kept creeping into his head. He could almost sense its approach, like a storm crossing the lake. When the day finally arrived, August 18, 1897, a year to the day after Susy's death, Sam watched Livy leave the house without speaking a word. She walked out into an already warm dawn and took a steamer alone to a separate village across the lake. Sam didn't try to follow, but neither did he go to his office that morning or even try to work. He spent the day wandering distractedly along the edge of the mountain, stopping to compose another line or two of the ode he was writing to his dead daughter. The next dawn was a relief. "The 18th of August has come and gone, Joe," he wrote to Reverend Twichell, "and we still seem to live."

Three days after the anniversary, Clemens traveled to Lucerne to send off the proofs of *Following the Equator.* The short trip across the lake, and the final release of the now publishable book, he told himself, were a milestone; they marked an end, at last, to the buccaneering, honor-gathering, round-the-world Clemens family adventure that had turned into a monstrous, costly two-year nightmare. "I would rather hang myself than do the like again," Clemens wrote a friend about the final leg, the travel book. "It was a contract, & couldn't be helped. But the slavery is over. I have mapped out four books this morning, & will begin an emancipated life this afternoon & shift back & forth among them & make them furnish me recreation & entertainment for three or four years to come, if I last so long. . . . I am hoping that the cold will hang back long enough to let us stay here till October. It promises very well."

CHAPTER SIXTEEN

Smoke and Fog

Theodore Roosevelt could feel his pulse quicken as he rode the deck of the USS *Dolphin* toward the rising sun. The spray of the Atlantic Ocean freshened the hot end-of-summer morning; the winds turned east, at Theodore's trim back; and as the gunboat sailed toward the southern drill grounds, the last whisper of land, the Virginia Capes, slid beneath the horizon. Theodore had broken free. He was in open water. It didn't get much better than this. In just a few hours he would be the honored observer of the most spectacular exercises the United States Navy had ever undertaken in peacetime, performed by a fleet unmatched in American history. The North Atlantic Squadron as outfitted that September comprised a half mile's worth of armor-plated warship, sixty-two thousand long tons of displacement, and nearly three thousand officers and men; the squadron included two armored cruisers—one was the *Brooklyn*, back from its naval review duty at the queen's jubilee—and five hulking battleships, including the most expensive and the most powerful the United States had ever built, the USS *Iowa.* The fleet had already embarked on its exercises but was ready to wheel at any moment and dance to the tune of the snappy young assistant secretary.

When the tiny *Dolphin* pulled in among the big bulls at the drill grounds a little before noon that day, the fleet's commander left his flagship to bid welcome to his thirty-eight-year-old civilian boss and to inquire as to his particular pleasure. Roosevelt would finish luncheon first, he said, but then he wanted to see the *Iowa*'s eight-inch guns and its twelve-inch guns in action. So Rear Admiral Sicard sent the message down the line: subcaliber practice was suspended. They were to get the assistant secretary aboard the *Iowa* and unloose the big guns.

This two-day jaunt out into the Atlantic was shaping up as the capper of a bully summer for Theodore. Navy Secretary John Long had decided to stay put at his retreat in Maine, which left the day-to-day doings of the department to his eager assistant, who feigned the occasional insincere fret over just how closely he should keep his boss informed of his summer program. "I have at times been a little nervous in the effort to steer the exact course between bothering him on the one hand, and going ahead with something too widely divergent from his views, on the other," Roosevelt wrote to Cabot. But mainly he decided to err on the side of not bothering, because, for one thing, he still wasn't really clear about just what his boss's views were on the subject of the navy. So *Acting* Secretary of the Navy Roosevelt just put his head down and acted, trusting to his own judgment, which, after all, he had never had reason to doubt. "I am having immense fun running the Navy," he crowed to one friend.

He meant to make sure, above all, that his navy was prepared for a war with Spain and maybe for a side skirmish with Japan, whose navy was believed to have impressive new submarine technology. Roosevelt had been poring over the various "war with Spain" strategies drawn up by the Naval War College in Newport and by his own department in Washington. He liked that the navy was taking the lead role in the war as planned, and he was particularly fond of the suggestion of an attack on the Spanish-owned Philippine Islands in the far-off Pacific. Give the Japanese a show to remember—two birds and all. Roosevelt had a man in mind to command the fleet in the Pacific, too, and hoped he could get him assigned there before Secretary Long came back and got all conventional about seniority and naval tradition. If America was going to war, it would be a new kind of war, Theodore reckoned, and tradition be damned.

Roosevelt had a frightful lot to do to put his force in order for modern sea battle. The US Navy was distressingly undermanned, he believed, top to bottom. The torpedo boat flotilla, in the acting secretary's judgment, had only two sufficiently buccaneering commanders on its six vessels. The others were known mostly for efficiency in their paperwork. There were likewise not nearly enough regular enlisted men to carry out the navy's ambitious war plans, even against the creaky Spanish navy. Roosevelt made a whirlwind tour of naval militia installations to drive home the message that commanders needed to make sure these reserve sailors became proficient enough to plug holes in the regular navy, and in a hurry—just in case. The reserves had to be ready to run signal stations, haul torpedoes and mines, man auxiliary gunships, and help defend the American seacoast from foreign invaders. Roosevelt was scrambling to supply militia officers with old monitors and armed vessels so that these reserves could finally get offshore and train on real boats, with real guns, in deep water.

Then, too, the greedy American suppliers who were reportedly gouging the United States Navy on its armor contracts—and stoking congressional outrage in the bargain—had to be brought to heel, or there might not be votes enough for the big buildup of the navy that Theodore was pushing. "We may have some trouble about getting more ships," he confided, "but if the President stands firm, we shall come out all right." Roosevelt was also looking to improve the scandalous condition of the navy's dry docks. The United States of America did not have a single facility on the East Coast fitted out to do serious repair and maintenance on the big new battleships just now coming on line. The newly constructed dry dock at the New York Navy Yard, which was supposed to answer to that problem, had already been deemed unsafe because of a breach in the piling. The Navy Department had suffered the embarrassment of having to run the USS *Indiana* up to Halifax—in Canada!—to have her bottom scraped.

The acting secretary commissioned a new board to look into a "radical revision" of the dry docks and dispatched a naval constructor overseas to look into the best practices of European navies. He had intended to have information and proposals on Secretary Long's desk when the boss returned from his summer vacation, but Theodore got itchy and started talking to reporters and pretty soon he was on record, in public, calling for three new docks on the Atlantic coast and one on the Pacific.

For all his headlong activity, Theodore got himself out over his water skis only once that summer—when he got overexcited while lecturing naval militiamen on Lake Erie, near Sandusky, Ohio, after having read newspaper reports suggesting that Japan might try to block the US annexation of Hawaii. "The United States is not in a position which requires her to ask Japan or any other foreign power what she shall or shall not acquire," Roosevelt told the boys in Sandusky that day, as well as the newspapermen he always invited along on these trips. "It is upon you, gentlemen, and upon organizations of your kind, that this nation depends to uphold her dignity in whatever misunderstanding we may have with foreign nations." Just how big a threat the Japanese navy posed to Sandusky and surrounding environs like John Hay's duck blind was not easily calculated, but that wasn't the point. Roosevelt's point was that the navy was in the business of upholding the national honor, wherever it was threatened, even if it meant war.

Secretary Long did not much appreciate Theodore's picking a fight with Japan, and after months of being poked and worried by his second-in-command, he could no longer hold his tongue. The secretary gave Theodore, as Theodore would describe it to Cabot, "as heavy a wigging as his invariable courtesy and kindness would permit." Long's reprimand was no match for Roosevelt's impenetrable self-regard. "I told him of course," said Theodore, explaining the scene, "that I was extremely sorry to have said anything of which he disapproved, and that I would not do so under any consideration, but that at the same time I thought what I said was, or ought to be, true, for most certainly the United States ought to decide whether or not it will annex Hawaii wholly without regard to the attitude of Japan or any other Power." Oh, and just by the by, Theodore mentioned to Cabot, all the folks he talked to out in Ohio were champing at the bit to free those Cubans from Spanish rule.

Roosevelt did exhibit a little grace in sending to the secretary for comment and approval a new pamphlet he had been preparing—a disquisition on the urgent necessity of a strong American navy (more battleships, of course), accompanied by messages on the subject by presidents from George Washington up to the present commander in chief. Long asked his assistant, please, to strike the part urging a *bigger* navy, and please, by all means, somewhere, put in the phrase "in my opinion." The secretary knew better than to suggest "in my *humble* opinion."

Even edited and softened according to Secretary Long's dictates, the pamphlet got such good play in the press that President McKinley, who had tucked it away unread when Roosevelt sent it to him weeks earlier, decided to pull it out and have a look. "Especial attention should be paid to the second quotation from Andrew Jackson," Roosevelt had written. "The victor of New Orleans had that 'instinct for the jugular' which is possessed by every great fighter. All that he says applies to the present day, for, as he points out so clearly, the only effective defensive is the offensive; the only way to defend our own seacoast properly is to attack our enemy instead of waiting for him to attack us."

THOSE STIRRING WORDS were fresh in the minds of newspaper readers across the nation that September afternoon as Assistant Secretary Roosevelt was ferried from the USS *Dolphin* to the USS *Iowa* and then ushered to the bridge to see just what his navy could do by way of attack. Preparations were already under way when Roosevelt, his two aides, and a gaggle of demonstrably "patriotic" newspaper reporters he had invited along stuffed the proffered cotton in their ears and took heed of instructions from the ship's medical staff: "Open your mouth, stand on your toes, and let your frame hang loosely." Apparently there was a substantial concussive force to be expected when the big guns fired. The crewmen had already screwed tight the battle plates and secured the hatch coamings; they had made sure the window sashes were open, left the doors ajar to swing free (doors closed tight were likely to be blown off their hinges), and removed any freestanding or breakable item from the shelves. The men in the officers' mess made certain to open the doors on the cabinet holding the silver service.

Up on the bridge, high above the glassy Atlantic, Roosevelt and the other guest observers scanned the horizon to sight the target, which had been dragged into place by two whaleboats and was now bobbing gently and innocently twenty-five hundred yards away. The sun was still high and bright when the ringing gong announced the start of target practice, and the five-hundred-man crew scrambled to battle stations in the gun turrets, in the handling rooms below, and deep in the bowels of the engine room. Earnest young Annapolis cadets stood on the bridge with clipboards in hand, ready to track the *Iowa*'s distance from the stationary target as the ship surged through the ocean and to tally the hits on that defenseless little faux enemy ship—a long piece of canvas wrapped around wooden uprights.

Theodore was already approaching naval nirvana when a steam whistle rent the calm skies and a bugle sounded and the first shots—from the eight-inch guns—flashed forth, loosing a great cloud of smoke, a *whoo-whoo-whoosh*, and a distant rumbling like a train in a tunnel. The smoke cleared in time for Roosevelt to see a terrific spray rise up out of the water as the shell landed fifty feet in front of the target and then ricocheted well off to the right of its mark. *Oh hell!* was the reaction from the turrets. Officers on the bridge agreed the shot was respectably *close*.

When the twelve-inch guns opened up, the first concussion sent two reporters who had roamed too far to one side of the bridge flying into the air, mouths open, frames hanging very, very loose. The sailors down below just kept swinging their 320 pounds of explosive material into place—*Hurry up that powder!*— The crew in the engine room boiled in the rising heat but kept the 360-foot-long *Iowa* moving at pace, slicing through the water—*2,600 yards! 2,500 yards! 2,700 yards!* The shots hit short, and wide, and long. Then the ship swung around and retraced its line to give the gunners on the other side their crack at the enemy target. The shots hit short, and wide, and long.

When it was over, the *Iowa* had suffered a few casualties: the concussions had splintered a whaleboat lying peacefully on deck, exploded skylights, sprung clocks, and blasted off a number of doors that had fallen shut. The men in the turrets emerged coughing and sputtering from the smoke and fumes, the engineers came to the deck with burns on their hands from touching the overheated railings down in their coal-fired sauna, and the powder men stood limp, wrung out from physical exertion. The smoke hung thick in the air for a long time, and everybody on the shaken ship seemed to be yelling, in hopes of being able once again to hear *something*. The men on board, right down to the Japanese cooks and waiters, squinted out to sea, looking for the target, which was no longer afloat. Officers on the bridge pronounced the target practice a grand success: the enemy ship was destroyed. It was likely, however—judged in hindsight by the fact that when the *Iowa* went into actual battle some months later, its squadron achieved hits on exactly 1.3 percent of its shots fired—that the floating banner of a target had drowned itself out of pity for the poor worn crew of America's most powerful warship.

Theodore was in a state of quivering euphoria when it was over; it was a *dee*-lightful performance all the way around. Acting Secretary Roosevelt remained out in open ocean to observe the signal and target practice that night and was still there the next day to watch the seven big warships make their arcing synchronized sea maneuvers, at cruising speed—wheels to the right, wheels to the left, single formation, double formation, in echelon. These gargantuan ships were like the William Howard Taft of the Atlantic: for a big man, it was said, he plied the dance floor with remarkable grace. Roosevelt lunched with the captains of the various ships and supped on the rear admiral's flagship. "Think of it," he wrote to Cabot, "on the Atlantic Ocean, out of sight of land, going out to dinner to a battleship in evening dress without an overcoat!"

The fleet's carrier pigeons had been delivering from the deck of the flagship to the Navy Department terse updates about the fleet maneuvers: "Ship New York, 9 a.m. September 8, southern drill grounds, fifty miles from Norfolk. . . . The squadron getting under way for evolutions before assistant secretary, who remains on Dolphin. Very successful target practice by Iowa and Brooklyn yesterday. Search light last night and attack on drifting target by six and one-pounders with aid of four search lights. Weather hazy, light airs from east; sea smooth." The pigeons deferred to the assistant secretary to carry a final and official assessment of American naval capability. "In short," Roosevelt told reporters on his return to land at Fort Monroe, Virginia, "there is every reason to be satisfied with every detail of the management of the huge warships, from the conning towers to the engine rooms and gun turrets. . . . At last we are beginning to have a navy fit to uphold the interests of our people, a navy, which though too small in size, need fear comparison with no other as regards the quality of its ships and men."

Theodore was more romantic, more himself, when he portrayed his swashbuckling adventure for his wife, Edith, who was seven months pregnant and gamely manning the home front, which involved five skirmishing children at their compound in Oyster Bay, New York. "I can not begin to describe the wonderful power and beauty of these giant warships, with their white hulls and towering superstructures," Roosevelt wrote to Edith. "At night each was a blaze of light. . . . The effect was as wildly beautiful as anything Turner ever dreamed. . . . It was almost as exciting as if we had been going into action."

Theodore Roosevelt had been atop those immense, throbbing war engines, and the feeling of potency had confirmed his own steely certainty: 1897 was a bully time to be an American! Roosevelt had felt the great machine's rumble in his vitals and walked away believing he had stood astride, for a brief moment, the new propulsive force of the white race—of civilization itself. The assistant secretary of the navy had been preparing his entire life to hop on this epic wave of history. As a boy reading the sagas of Norse kings and legendary Viking sea conquests, and then as an undergraduate at Harvard University, and briefly as a law student at Columbia University, Theodore had been simmering in a boiling academic stew whose signature ingredient was the immutable scientific *fact* that the history of man had been a history of race struggle. "It is in the deep traits of race that the fortunes of nations are written," the crown prince of American letters, Ralph Waldo Emerson, had said. Nature itself had decreed it, he declared from the cozy comfort of his frame house in Concord, Massachusetts: "Let buffalo gore buffalo, and the pasture to the strongest!"

The Sage of Concord had written a series of essays and jottings in which he analyzed and ordered the various "races." The Celts, the Jews, the Negroes (and any other dark-skinned peoples), all received inferior marks in the Emersonian grade book. The modern-day Germans (not to be confused with the proud Teutons and Saxons of ancient Germania) were not destined for world dominion, according to Emerson; like the Asian races, they lacked sufficient resolve. "It is race, is it not? that puts the hundred millions of India under the dominion of a remote island in the north of Europe," Emerson had written just before Theodore Roosevelt was born. For Emerson, the "English," or "Anglo-Saxon," race—which traced from the liberty-loving Germanic Teutons, who cracked Roman heads, and then added a smattering of brutish vigor from the best stock of Danish, Swedish, and Norse warriors—was, in all its purity and glorious whiteness, the head buffalo in the world pasture.

THEODORE ROOSEVELT HAD absorbed these lessons whole—from Emerson and from the self-worshipping historians and anthropologists at Harvard College—and he added his own modern and thoroughly optimistic twist. While Emerson thought his American countrymen "saplings" as compared to the empire-building English "pasture-oaks," Theodore believed otherwise. In Roosevelt's telling, in his book *The Winning of the West*, Americans—New World fruit of the Anglo-Saxon mother country—had proved their racial mettle by conquering a vast continent, sea to shining sea, in a manly battle against the savage Indian tribes. This continental march extended the march of civilization and self-government that had begun in those dark forests of northern Europe. "It was the crowning and greatest achievement of a series of mighty movements, and it must be taken in connection with them," Roosevelt wrote. "Its true significance will be lost unless we grasp, however roughly, the past race-history of the nations who took part therein."

Roosevelt believed, as he had been taught at Columbia University by Professor John Burgess (recent author of advice to the new Republic of Hawaii on how to keep the native Hawaiians and Japanese and Chinese immigrants off the voting rolls and how to "place the government in the hands of Teutons, and preserve it there"), that the world's superior political system evolved from the system of governing of the freedom-worshipping democratically inclined light-skinned killers in Germania to the Magna Carta and then to the apotheosis, the American Constitution, which formed a government of, by, and for the people who were white and men and, as Theodore's southern ancestors would have it, worthy. Uncle Jimmie Bulloch, a naval officer (US and Confederate) and a Georgia cotton planter, had apparently schooled his nephew in the "lower orders" of white men in the South—"people drawn from the worst immigrants that perhaps ever were brought to America . . . who formed such an excessively undesirable substratum to the otherwise excellent population of the tidewater regions in Virginia and the Carolinas," Theodore wrote in *The Winning of the West*. "Many of the Southern crackers or poor whites spring from this class, which also in the backwoods gave birth to generations of violent and hardened criminals, and to an even greater number of shiftless, lazy, cowardly cucumbers of the earth's surface."

IN THAT THRILLING summer of 1897, Theodore Roosevelt's obsession with race was no longer merely academic or literary—not given his position of national responsibility. He believed himself to be engaged in the actual and current innings of history's long-running race struggle. It was all well and good for his friend Cabot to stand up in the Senate and implore Americans to grab Hawaii, and to free Cuba from the papist monarchy, and to drive a canal through Nicaragua, but it was Roosevelt's duty to foresee any foreign naval and military obstacles that might present themselves in the doing. Even while devoting his time and energy to dry docks and naval manpower and submarine technology and armor prices, the acting secretary kept his eyes peeled for prospective enemies. Spain had to be considered first, but the Spaniards, in Roosevelt's understanding, were so blood-thinned, given their long tradition of intermarriage with inferior Latin American races, that they could not possibly present a manly impediment to American imperatives. At least the Spaniards were doing Roosevelt a favor: "Cuba Libre" fever gave Theodore the perfect excuse to put the navy on a war footing and keep it there.

The acting secretary of the navy was also keeping watch on the British, race brother or no, and on the Japanese, the way they were skulking around the Hawaiian Islands, and most especially he had his sights trained on the Germans and Russians—"the Slavs." His good friend the British diplomat-in-training Cecil Spring Rice was newly stationed at the queen's legation in Berlin, where he was writing up official reports about Kaiser Wilhelm's most ardent desire: a navy big enough to match Britain's. Springy believed Kaiser Wilhelm, inspired in no small part by his reading of Captain Mahan's treatise on naval power, wanted a fleet powerful enough to grab up and to defend new German colonies and commerce all over Africa, the Pacific, and South America. "His policy has been laid down pretty clearly; that is, advancement of German trade interests of every kind, agricultural and industrial—in order to pay for a big navy with which to face a possible enemy on the sea," Springy wrote to the British Foreign Office that summer. "One can't help being alarmist here, especially in view of the Emperor's deep irritation at not being asked to the Jubilee."

Springy and Theodore kept up a vigorous colloquy that summer, in which Roosevelt assured Springy that he, for one, was begging President McKinley and Congress to keep the navy "at a pitch that will enable us to interfere promptly if Germany ventures to touch a foot of American soil." "I would not go into the abstract rights or wrongs of it; I would simply say that we did not intend to have the Germans on this continent, excepting as immigrants, whose children would become Americans of one sort or another," he wrote, "and if Germany intended to extend her empire here, she would have to whip us first."

Roosevelt evinced slightly less concern regarding the Russians: "[American and English] men would outbuild, out-administer, and out-fight any Russians you could find from St. Petersburg to Sebastopol or Vladivostock—if that's the way you spell it. . . . Of course both the English and the Americans are less ruthless, and have the disadvantages of civilisation. It may be that we are going the way of France, but just at present I doubt it."

This was Theodore's overarching worry in those days: had the men of the United States grown too soft to fight mean, too "over-civilized," as he put it, to let "the wolf rise in the heart"? He fretted that the vicious war-making capability was being bled out of the American character by the ease of living in what Oliver Wendell Holmes had called this "snug, safe corner of the world." And the timidity went right to the top, near as Roosevelt could see. President William McKinley seemed too intent on protecting the national treasure, and enfolding American merchants and manufacturers in the skirts of his protective tariff, and running away from anything that might threaten the growing economic recovery—like a righteous war to free Cuba from Spanish control.

WHEN WILLIAM MCKINLEY rolled back into the capital in the middle of September, Roosevelt got the message that the president had been pleased with his performance that summer, and that he was also prepared to take Theodore's side over Long's and ask Congress to loose funds for a few more battleships and torpedo boats. McKinley even surprised the younger man by telling him he had not been bothered by the little elbow Roosevelt had given the Japanese in his speech out on Lake Erie. "Of course the President is a bit of a jollier," Theodore wrote Cabot, "but I think his words did represent a substratum of satisfaction."

Roosevelt spent one dinner and two carriage rides in a four-day period trying to convince the president that whether the country wanted war or no, the navy must be ready, at any moment, to face Spain and maybe even Japan. He presented McKinley with a map of the world showing the current deployment of all US Navy warships, drew out the moves he would make if tensions with Spain escalated, and urged on him the necessity of a vigorous initial attack "if we wished to avoid the chance of some serious trouble, and of the Japs chipping in." Roosevelt traced out for the nonplussed president how he could scramble a main fleet to Cuban waters in forty-eight hours, send a "flying squadron" to worry the Spanish coast, and throw a small group of marines onto the Cuban mainland to join the local rebels and make quick work of the tired and yellow-fever-depleted troops from Spain. He showed the president how he would maneuver the Asiatic Squadron into Philippine waters, where they would blockade Manila and perhaps even take the city. Not that anybody wanted the Philippines, but the navy planners thought it would make a fine bargaining chip when Spain came begging for a treaty of peace.

Theodore was still in full cry in his last few weeks of Long's extended absence. The acting secretary tried to scramble US gunboats to the Canadian border in Alaska and to the Great Lakes, and to convince McKinley that Commodore George Dewey was the right man to take over the fleet in the Pacific, seniority be damned. John Hay got a strange little missive in the mail after Theodore caught wind of the rumor that Her Majesty's government was prepared to return an American warship captured in the War of 1812. "I earnestly hope that you will refuse to have anything to do with so preposterous and undignified an effort," he explained to Hay. "To beg to be given back, as a favor, what was taken from us by superior prowess, would be to put us in a position of intolerable humiliation. When the British ask us to give back the flags and guns of the frigates and sloops which we took in the War of 1812, then it will be quite time enough for us to get [our ship] back."

Two days later, the acting secretary made spectacular headlines in the *Los Angeles Herald* by summoning a group of naval militia commanders to Washington and telling them the country was "on the verge of war with Spain." He denied the quote in public but still hoped it to be true. "In strict confidence," he told an old friend and professional military man, "I should welcome almost any war, for I think this country needs one."

Theodore had found a new "playmate" by then, a medical man and regular army officer named Leonard Wood. Wood had helped subdue Geronimo and the fighting Apaches before becoming personal physician to the president. On long walks in the countryside outside the capital, Wood and Roosevelt talked anxiously about how to make sure they both "had their parts in it" when the battle for Cuba commenced. "I had always felt that if there were a serious war I wished to be in a position to explain to my children why I did take part in it, and not why I did not take part in it," Roosevelt would say. "Moreover, I had very deeply felt that it was our duty to free Cuba, and I had publicly expressed this feeling; and when a man takes such a position, he ought to be willing to make his words good by his deeds unless there is some very strong reason to the contrary. He should pay with his body."

On one of his evening carriage rides with the president, Roosevelt, unbidden, told McKinley that while he would make sure his department was prepared to win in battle, he would probably not stick around Washington to oversee the effort. He would rather head to Cuba to join the fight. When McKinley asked Theodore what his pregnant wife might think of the thirty-eight-year-old father of her children running off to the rifle pits, Roosevelt said he had no doubts that both his wife and his best friend, Henry Cabot Lodge, would regret his decision, but his mind was made up. He would be consulting no one but himself.

AND THEN IT started to unravel for Theodore: Spain seemed to be going weak in the knees. The prime minister who replaced the assassinated Cánovas yanked the most infamous and hated Spanish commander out of Havana, made noises about political autonomy in Cuba, and sent a less combative reply to American demands to ease off the wanton destruction on the island. "It is in the direction of a better understanding," McKinley would report to the United States Congress. "It appreciates the friendly purposes of this Government. It admits that our country is deeply affected by the war in Cuba and that its desires for peace are just. It declares that the present Spanish government is bound by every consideration to a change of policy that should satisfy the United States and pacify Cuba within a reasonable time." McKinley was cheered by the new thaw, and the pink and jowly American bankers breathed a big sigh of relief, while Theodore watched another chance at war glory begin to fade away. He was not happy about it. Reports of the president's wry little asides to Leonard Wood—"Have you and Theodore declared war yet?"—were less and less amusing.

Roosevelt did finally allow himself a brief holiday when Secretary Long returned to Washington, but war was never far from his thoughts, even when he went to sermonize on the occasion of the two hundredth anniversary of the Old Dutch Church of Sleepy Hollow that October. "There are classes much worse, but not much more contemptible, than the class of the timid," he told the small and peaceful congregation.

> There are very nice refined people who wish well, but who wish feebly, who possess that kind of morality which seems to accompany a poverty of blood. . . . We have built up a marvelous material prosperity. Woe to us if we build nothing else. Woe to us if we are content only with the pride of riches. Woe to us if we do not feel within us a lift to what is higher and nobler. . . . Above all we must cultivate the rugged, forceful virtues, the virtues that tell in combat; for no nation can rise save through strife or readiness for strife. . . . No refinement, no business capacity, no mercantile success will atone for the lack of the virile virtues.

JOHN HAY GROPED his way home along a London sidewalk, his only guideposts the uneven rows of flaring orange gas jets floating disembodied in the dark. Sunset was still hours away on this warm midautumn day in 1897, but a soupy fog had seeped across the whole of Britain, and it would hang there for another twenty-four hours, gathering in its loose weave the settling residue and particulates from the coal-fired furnaces of London and Manchester and beyond. Hay's eyes burned as he walked, which made it all the more difficult to see where he was going. He could hear the eerie blasts from distant foghorns and the rhythmic *thock-thock-thock* on cobblestone as omnibus conductors led their horses gingerly down the darkened city streets.

Hay was adrift in one of Her Majesty's spectacular weather events, a fog of peril the likes of which the British Isles hadn't experienced in six years. As the ambassador inched through the murk, he was hopeful, but not optimistic, that he was heading in the right direction. This disorientation seemed an appropriate capstone to a very trying month following John Hay's return from a restful and sunny four-week holiday visiting Scottish castles and estates of old friends and new ones. The day after Hay's return to Carlton House Terrace, Prime Minister Salisbury had dispatched a new and unexpected message to Hay's boss, Secretary of State Sherman, rescinding his earlier pledge to send a representative to the fur seal conference in Washington. The marquess was making a public point of refusing, on behalf of Great Britain, and more particularly on behalf of Canada, to be party to any convention that included Russia and

Japan. The British Foreign Office had also published the earlier correspondence regarding the fur seals that ran between Ambassador Hay and Her Majesty's government, including Lord Salisbury's communication agreeing to participate in a conference of scientific experts from Canada, Great Britain, and the United States only. Her Majesty's officials had purposely omitted Hay's letter reminding the prime minister of President McKinley's long-stated intention to invite Russia and Japan as well.

Hay turned the other cheek at first and made light. "My own dear Salisbury has gone back on me," he wrote to Henry Adams, "and says he was joking when he agreed to a conference." The ambassador was perfectly aware that the prime minster had domestic political considerations; Britain's hometown press was beating the stuffing out of Salisbury for being too accommodating to American interests. "I do not think the British Government is very stiff in its attitude about the conference," Hay informed McKinley a few days after Salisbury's new note. "I hope you will excuse me for talking about it—but in the present state of our relations with England the *form* is of unusual importance. The tone of the press betrays quite uncommon sensitiveness; they think Lord Salisbury did not sufficiently resent our note of the 10th of May [the one Whitelaw's *Tribune* had printed in full]. It would be seriously embarrassing for him to yield to any demand of ours . . . not most courteously expressed."

Hay requested meetings at the Foreign Office to see whether he could salvage the conference, while at the same time moonlighting at the job of calming the most excitable government official on either side of the Atlantic, Theodore Roosevelt. Theodore's hair-on-fire letter about the old American frigate captured in the War of 1812, which arrived at the London embassy in the same week, was easy to ignore, but the assistant secretary was making real mischief for Hay. Theodore was threatening to send an American warship to the Great Lakes (by way of Montreal, of all places), in violation of a long-standing treaty between the United States and Britain, and then to send another gunship up the Yukon River in Alaska, where a gold rush in the Klondike promised to begin a contentious boundary dispute between the United States and Canada.

Hay had known of Roosevelt a long time, that knowledge going back to Hay's many friendly Civil War–era meetings with Theodore Roosevelt Sr., when Teedie, as he was then called, was just five years old. Theodore junior was still something of the little boy playing at soldier back then. Even thirty-five years later, Hay understood, Roosevelt needed reminding that real wars had real consequences and were to be avoided if possible, especially between nations as potentially mutually destructive as Great Britain and the United States. "It is a curious fact that while no Englishman, not a madman, wants to fight us, and no American, not an idiot, wants to fight England, there is never a civil word about England printed in America, and rarely a civil word about us printed in England," Hay wrote to Theodore in subtle admonishment. "Whether this ill-will is all historical, or partly prophetical, I cannot say. I implore my friends at Washington not to be too nasty in their talk about John Bull; for every idle word of theirs *I* get banged about the lot, till I am all colors of the rainbow."

Then Hay went back to the seals and, after putting the question with all courtesy, got the Foreign Office to agree to reconsider the conference, which allowed the prime minister's minions at Whitehall to string Hay along with their usual aplomb. The Honorable Francis Hyde Villiers, who had been overseeing the seal question for Lord Salisbury, admitted that, yes, Great Britain was *partially* at fault for not answering his communication six weeks earlier, before the formal invitations went out to Russia and Japan. And he let it be known, for Hay's ears only, that the Foreign Office was rather in agreement that the fur seal population had been much diminished by pelagic hunting. (Hay had new statistics suggesting that the Canadian catch was as much as 80 percent female seals and the majority killed by gunshot, which was illegal.) But Canada was not willing to concede anything, Villiers explained—those gunshot wounds found on the seals might have been from earlier hunts—and whined that including Russia and Japan was just a ploy to make sure the United States could outvote God's chosen empire. Joe Chamberlain at the Colonial Office made it clear from his vacation in Italy that he was going to be standing firm in the Canadian corner, so, said Villiers, well, sorry for your troubles, Ambassador Hay. When the prime minister made it official, in public, that the Washington conference was unworthy of British participation, sniffing that Japan and Russia had no "experts" on the seal population and no standing either—so what if they were seal hunters? —Hay was unsurprised but terrifically exasperated, especially by the accusations in British newspapers that Hay had tried to pull a fast one by including Russia and Japan.

The bimetal business was equally maddening. "I think nothing will be accomplished," Hay fretted to his wife. "England is very cross about the Bering Sea—the more especially because this time they are in the wrong, and they know it." England's chancellor of the Exchequer took another three weeks meandering toward the inevitable final answer. "I have been wrestling with England and getting a disgust with human nature that will last me long," Hay wrote to Henry Adams as the communication was being prepared at the Foreign Office. "We have not yet received our answer on silver, but I *know* what it is to contain: some sinuosity of words, but the substance a categorical negative." Her Majesty's government, as Hay expected, prated on about "having as great an interest as the United States and France in securing a stable par exchange for gold and silver and an enlarged use of silver" and offered, disingenuously, to consider any other proposals the United States and France might make in the future, but would not now be entertaining any changes to the status quo. The reason, of course, was colonial pushback—this time from India, whose governors claimed it would be put near death by unpredictable currency fluctuations. The colony, they asserted, was sure to lapse into a long-term industrial paralysis and endure a precipitous decline in export revenues, "accompanied by acute individual suffering."

The big problem, Lord Salisbury pointed out, was that the risk was simply too great, given the unsubstantial nature of the two prospective partners—the United States and France—who could not be counted on to keep the gold-to-silver ratio at a stable rate. "We doubt whether any two or three nations in the world, unless one of them were Great Britain, could establish the required stability," British colonial officials had warned Salisbury. "It is certain that France, the United States, and India could not."

Hay refrained from making any public statements about the bimetal commission and the fur seals. But he sent to McKinley the kind of tart little personal letter the president was beginning to appreciate from his ambassador in London. "*The Times* this morning prints the documents in the bimetallic negotiation, and in a leader utters a shout of triumph at having repulsed the attack upon its monetary virtue, and of course could not wind up without a gratuitous insult to the United States," Hay wrote. "I cannot help addressing the capacity these English have of shutting their eyes to all facts or arguments which do not go to sustain their own side of the case. They have, up to this moment, suppressed my note of the 29th July in the Bering Sea matter, and not a paper, even of the opposition, ever alludes to it, though it is the essential fact which convicts them of double dealing."

JOHN HAY HAD made only one real success for President McKinley in the entire month: a few discreet instances of informal intelligence gathering allowed Hay to present to McKinley some useful facts concerning Spain and Cuba. One was the result of the ambassador's social visit to the estate of his friend Lord Rothschild, London's most powerful international financier. ("I find that an Englishman will talk to you with far greater freedom in his own house than anywhere else," Hay explained to the president.) Hay had gone there to talk bimetallism, but the conversation drifted to the problems the revolution in Cuba had visited on Spain. The Spanish government was in a worse financial fix than the Prince of Wales, Rothschild had explained. No bank outside Spain was willing to make them more loans. He certainly wasn't. "They have wasted in

Cuba $400,000,000 and 200,000 men," Rothschild told Hay, "and the condition of things is worse than ever."

Ambassador Hay had also persuaded the prime minister to pledge backing for the restoration of peace and commercial viability in Cuba. Any "energetic measures" the United States deemed necessary to put things in order, Salisbury privately assured Hay, would not meet with interference from Her Majesty's government or Her Majesty's navy.

Hay knew to be careful in his assessment of the cagey Salisbury; whenever the marquess decided that he was being too acquiescent, or that Americans were being too ornery, all bets were off. And the *St. James's Gazette* had already issued a stern editorial warning that permitting the United States to have its way in Cuba could set a dangerous, and terribly un-British, precedent: "If the United States think they have a 'right' to intervene in a West Indian island because some of their subjects choose to incite a rebellion, or suffer commercial losses because of a rebellion which they have not incited, how far does that 'right' extend? Is its application confined to Cuba? We will put a case: There are American citizens in Jamaica. Suppose the negroes of that island revolt, take to the mountains . . . and defy us? Suppose, further, that we could not suppress the rising—say, within a week. Would the United States send Colonel Hay to Lord Salisbury to tell him that unless within a fortnight the island was pacified, steps would be taken to 'assure its independence'? And if it did, what would England say and do? . . . We would seriously warn Englishmen against United States aggression in the western tropics."

So this was how Hay stood on that fog-shrouded afternoon in October of 1897: he had come to London six months earlier with the clear and simple task of effecting international concord, and instead he was wandering in the disorienting murk of empire, enveloped by the singularly noxious British atmosphere, spun round by Salisburian pettifogging, crouched in readiness for another strong gust of ad hominem attack. "But for a good-natured schoolteacher I struck in the dark," Hay wrote to his old friend John Nicolay when he finally made it back to Carlton House Terrace, "I might have been wandering yet or in the Thames."

THE PROSPECT OF slogging through a long London winter and the thorny brambles of Lord Salisbury's British Foreign Office began to weigh on John Hay. He was suffering a recurrence of old bodily ailments, and a few new ones, such as the sharp pains in his lower back. He was already planning his winter escape, confident that Harry White could handle anything that came up at the embassy in his absence. Ambassador Hay entered delicate negotiations with the London office of Thomas Cook & Son even before Thanksgiving, selecting the stock of gustatory provisions for his steam-powered luxury houseboat—a *dahabeeyah*—combing through *Cook's Tourists' Handbook for Egypt, the Nile, and the Desert*, and sending personal handwritten notes asking a few close friends to join him, his wife, and their two daughters on a two-month journey on the great river. The recently widowed Sir John Clark took a pass, as did Henry James, and Clarence King was silent on the question for more than a month before finally declining. Henry Adams alone accepted John Hay's invitation.

"I want to know what kind of fizz you are drinking now, as I must give my order to Cook," he wrote to Adams as the start date neared. "The rest of us don't care, so it will simplify matters if you will say what champagne I shall lay in. Now don't be a dodo and say you don't care. . . . Most of my chores are over here. I have harvested a fine crop of Apples of Sodom, but as I look back on my failures I cannot see how anyone if he were Hercules and Mercury rolled into one could have pulled off a success."

CHAPTER SEVENTEEN

Proportionately Delighted

Life was too short, he figured, or at least what was left of his *particular* life was too short. John Hay might not possess a healthy corpus, but he had a robust sense of self-preservation, or thought he did. The ambassador was determined to have his nice long vacation at the start of 1898, and to leave behind the demands of his public office—the silver question, the fur seals, the relentless petitions to banquet and speechify, and the growing number of requests from Washington to gauge English attitudes toward whatever "energetic measures" the American military might undertake in Cuba. Hay's naval attaché in London had been assigned the task (and a nice little pot of discretionary money along with it) of running a stable of secret informants who could keep the Department of the Navy current on the movement of the Spanish fleet and its troops as well as any new armament purchases Madrid was making in Europe. This spy network was Assistant Secretary Theodore Roosevelt's personal initiative—he had not yet told his bosses much about it. Hay, on the other hand, did not share in the excitement over the possibilities of a battle with Spain to free Cuba. He trusted William McKinley to avert war.

The president had doused the fire-eaters in Congress (and in his own administration) in his annual address a month earlier, counseling against intemperate action in Cuba, such as official legislative recognition of the political legitimacy of the insurgents in Cuba. The rebels in the field there—and the president didn't have to point out that most were nonwhite—were, as McKinley said, quoting President Grant from a message twenty years earlier, hardly "capable of the ordinary functions of government toward its own people and to other states," and it would be imprudent to elevate them to the noble standing of the American revolutionaries of the previous century. McKinley cautioned also against simply grabbing the island. "I speak not of forcible annexation, for that can not be thought of," he reminded Congress. "That, by our code of morality, would be criminal aggression."

The Major likewise assured Congress that the policies put forward by the newly installed Práxedes Mateo Sagasta in Spain portended a new day in Cuba. "The first acts of the new [Spanish] government lie in these honorable paths. The policy of cruel rapine and extermination that so long shocked the universal sentiment of humanity has been reversed," McKinley told Congress and the nation. "I shall not impugn its sincerity, nor should impatience be suffered to embarrass it in the task it has undertaken. It is honestly due to Spain and to our friendly relations with Spain that she should be given a reasonable chance to realize her expectations and to prove the asserted efficacy of the new order of things to which she stands irrevocably committed."

Hay had sent the president a note of warm congratulation for his caution and forbearance. The ambassador was convinced that Spain's troops in Cuba were so ravaged by fatigue and failure and yellow fever, and its bank accounts so hideously drained, that Sagasta and his ministers would let go of Cuba regardless of all their talk about Spanish dignity and honor. So with war talk cooling, Hay determined it was no dereliction of duty to take his long vacation and leave it to the estimable Harry White to keep the State Department informed of the British thinking on Cuba.

Lord Salisbury was too busy keeping *his* eye on Asia, where it was increasingly clear that the Russian czar and the German kaiser—in order to glorify Christian civilization and, as absolute and God-appointed monarchs, their own two sacred persons—were going to use their newly seized seaports in China to start carving up that country like a Christmas goose. Cuba was small beer by comparison to the commercial potential of China and its *four hundred million* consumers, er, inhabitants. Where Cuba was concerned, Lord Salisbury's posture was mostly of the hands-off, what-do-we-care variety.

So three weeks into the new year, Ambassador John Hay, joined by Clara and their two grown daughters, and by his own private secretary, Spencer Eddy, packed up and left behind Carlton House Terrace, and his shoddy little office on Victoria Street, and the dull, gray fog bank that was London. The Hays dined with Henry Adams and his brother Brooks in the Latin Quarter the first evening in Paris and then went to the theater to see the exotically plumed Coquelin the Elder as Cyrano de Bergerac. Next was Genoa, for a brief visit, before the party headed to Naples to catch the boat to Egypt. "We have had two beautiful days here—the sky deeply blue and the air just cool enough for enjoyment," Hay reported to White from northern Italy, on the same day President McKinley sent a battleship, the USS *Maine*, to Cuba, as a friendly gesture to the Spanish government there, in case they needed any assistance keeping the peace or protecting private property or anything. While Spain bowed courteously at its diplomatic waist and, in a gesture of like friendship, its ambassador in Washington explained, dispatched its own warship, the *Vizcaya*, to New York, Hay maintained a distant man-on-leave uninterest. He would not let world events intrude on his much-needed break. "We have had thus far a most enchanting journey," Hay reported to White on February 2, after the traveling party alighted at their hotel in Cairo. "It has been slow, but exquisitely fine weather; there was not a pitch or roll during the whole week we were on board the vessel [from Naples to Egypt], and though we have met no one till we got here, we have got on very well amongst ourselves. Adams is, of course, delightful."

THEY STEAMED UPRIVER the next day, out of the present and into five thousand years of epic Egyptian history, beyond reach of newspapers and the diplomatic pouch. It was just the six of them in the Hay party, in their private *dahabeeyah*, with a cook and porters and waitstaff dancing attendance. Thomas Cook & Son had long since cleared a safe avenue for Western tourists who wished to see the ruins and relics of a once-great empire, studded by the occasional gas-lit sugar manufactory or a viceregal palace rising up on the riverbank. (Cook agents had also recently persuaded the Coptic patriarch at Gebel-el-Tayr to stop the half-naked charges at his little orphanage from swimming up to every passing riverboat to beg baksheesh.) Cook-sponsored donkeys waited "in readiness" at most ports, to carry the seekers to pyramids and temples and burial grounds. For those less adventuresome or athletic, the Cook company could make other arrangements. "Yesterday morning we all rode across to Saqquarah," Adams reported back to Lizzie Cameron, "us young people on donkeys, and Mrs. Hay like Cleopatra, on a throne borne by strong Nubians, and visible from miles across the plain, like Memnon."

The afternoon of February 9, a week into John Hay's float on the Nile, his engineer laid on some extra coal and the *dahabeeyah* sped toward Luxor so that the party might make it to the seat of power of ancient Thebes before sunset. The Hay boat had already made 450 miles upriver in the week, even with the donkey rides to ancient Memphis and the false pyramid at Wasta, the ruined tombs of Beni-Hassan and the old slave market at Assiout and the Temple of Denderah. No news had got through to puncture the calm of this voyage or to disturb the peaceful slumber of the heroic Egyptian rulers who had once held sway in the world. The desert weather had been dry and temperate and a tad chilly of an evening, and so had Adams, for the most part.

For Hay's old friend, this trip presented itself not necessarily as a carefree jaunt into the distant past but as a potentially harrowing psychic journey into his own personal history, which was, as Adams would style it, simply too, too utter. "Indeed," Adams confessed in a letter to Lizzie Cameron the first day out with the Hays,

> the sudden return to the boat came near knocking me quite off my perch. I knew it would be a risky thing, but it came so suddenly that before I could catch myself, I was unconsciously wringing my hands and the tears rolled down in the old way, and I had to get off by myself for a few minutes to prevent Helen, who was with me, from thinking me more mad than usual. She could hardly know what it meant, in any case, and it would not have been worthwhile to tell her. A few hours wore off the nervous effect . . . although of course there is hardly a moment when some memory of twenty-five years ago is not brought to my mind.

Henry Adams had seen this Egyptian landscape a quarter century earlier, in the middle of his own year-long honeymoon, which began to get wobbly on the Nile. His new bride, Clover, had suffered a frightening nervous collapse on the river, which, looking back now, Adams might have regarded as an event worth noting. Thirteen years later, behind the curtain of one of the many dark depressions that descended on her, Clover Adams had committed suicide by drinking the potassium cyanide she had on hand for use in the developing fluids in her home photography studio.

A strange cast of extras peopled Adams's memory as he retraced his honeymoon journey; a few other Americans had been out on the river in the winter of 1872–73, such as Ralph Waldo Emerson, sad and seventy and diminished by the recent destruction by fire of his beloved home in Concord. Emerson had been overpowered by the vastness and splendor of Egyptian history, which perhaps did not accord with his theories of Teutonic superiority. He had left the river and turned early for home. "The obelisks, the temple walls, defy us with their histories we cannot spell," Emerson noted in his diary. Clover could not make sense of the old scholar's lack of interest in the powerful and impressive ancient civilization revealed in the antiquities of North Africa, but she was sympathetic. "How true it is," Clover Adams wrote at the time, "that the mind sees what it has means of seeing."

The most vital and rambunctious figure on the river in that long-ago winter was a stick-thin, asthmatic, nearsighted American adolescent who stood out on the private *dahabeeyah* he shared with his wealthy parents, his three siblings, and a foursome of Harvard football players who had joined the family adventure. Emerson's daughter noted the fourteen-year-old Theodore Roosevelt's sunburnished cheeks, his sparking blue eyes, and his prodigious set of "perfectly brilliant teeth." Young Teedie was just then getting used to his new pince-nez spectacles, which sharpened his sights on a new and vivid world. He professed disappointment in the tombs at Beni-Hassan: "interesting in subject but not in execution."

Having just read Charles Darwin's *On the Origin of Species*, and armed with his spanking new spectacles and a *second* gun his father had given him on Christmas morning, Theodore set off on a rampage of collecting and cataloging wild birds. Every day but Sabbath Sunday, as soon as his parents released him from a morning's study of French and English, Theodore would make for the riverbanks and the desert interior to track and bag his quarry. Adams might not see the Roosevelt boat for days, but he could hear young Theodore's gunfire cracking in the distance almost any afternoon. Teedie made his first kill on the banks of the Nile, a tiny warbler, and pronounced himself, as he had no doubt read in a recent story of British huntsmen, "proportionately delighted." He gunned down plovers, desert larks, red-throated pipits, sandpipers, kestrels, pigeons, grosbeaks, a greater white-fronted goose, and a handful of Egypt's sacred bird, the gracefully regal ibis.

On the deck of the boat in the evenings, while the servants prepared supper and ironed the linen, and Teedie's sister Bamie mooned over the college boys, and Theodore senior smoked his cigar and read his Egyptian history, and Mrs. Roosevelt wrote letters to the family back home, Teedie unsheathed his knife and practiced the lessons of his taxidermy tutor—*gut and stuff, gut and stuff*—while making his field notes. The next day he would be back on the hunt. Bamie described her younger brother, spectacles on the end of his nose, loaded gun slung over his shoulder, spurring his braying donkey ahead, splitting groups of slower-moving riders as he pushed by, "ruthlessly" pursuing his quarry. The Harvard boys, increasingly fearful of accidental gunshot wounds, made it a point to give young Theodore a wide berth. The youngster's kill count soon neared two hundred, including thirty-seven doves, eighty-one pigeons, and two innocent squirrels. Close observers might be forgiven for suspecting that this seemingly serious scientific inquiry was actually a useful fig leaf for something approaching wanton bloodlust. His mother wrote home from Thebes, in the middle of February 1873, describing the scene of her older son's returning to the *dahabeeyah* cradling in his arms his largest kill ever, a crane. His blue eyes were, Mrs. Roosevelt said, "sparkling with delight."

JOHN DAVIS LONG could see his assistant secretary's bespectacled blue eyes flashing with ruthless purpose as the young man strode toward Long's office at the Department of the Navy on a cold day in January of 1898. Theodore Roosevelt approached with his chest forward, jaw working, big white teeth grinding.

When Roosevelt stopped long enough to close the door behind him, signaling a private conference of uncommon import, Secretary Long found himself, as always and against increasing odds, charmed by the younger man. Part of it was Theodore's natural animal way of *displaying* affection, of bodily showing Long he really liked him. And part of it was his singular ability, much like static electricity, to rearrange the elements in the air of any room he entered. Long always sat up a little in his chair when Theodore walked in.

Whatever Roosevelt's faults—and they were also hard to miss—Long was still glad to have the younger man careering around the department. Theodore Roosevelt brought a vitality and a sharp bristle to official Washington that John Long didn't often observe in his daily business: not when a United States senator came in to make the plea for some favored constituent to get the lousy two-dollar-a-day slot at some naval yard in his state; not when he went to testify before the inert members of the House Naval Affairs Committee about the conditions of the docks in New York. "It is fair to say, with entire justice to them, that not more than two of them have anything more than a general confused notion that there is a dock there, and that it is out of repair and in process of reconstruction," Long had recently recorded in his daily diary. "Probably not more than one has ever seen it."

The secretary of the navy certainly didn't see much vigorous thought or action in the highest council of the nation, President William McKinley's cabinet, which had regular business meetings twice a week in the first months of 1898 and formal or informal dinners nearly as often. They were old men all, some nearing obsolescence, some already passed it. Their official meetings and their social meetings were a snore. Vice President Hobart, Long saw, was "inclined to be humorous" at the cabinet dinners; it was a shame he generally fell short. There was fleeting evidence that John Sherman had once been an accomplished raconteur, but those days were long gone. "The Secretary of State is getting a little forgetful and tells the same story twice. The rest of us sit around in the usual fashion, of rather dull commonplace," read another of Long's diary entries.

Long himself had a little extra bounce in his step that winter morning when Roosevelt burst into his office to conference. The secretary recalled with some pleasure the scene at the Russian reception the night before, when he had taken his daughter onto the dance floor for a waltz and espied two other aged and venerable cabinet members, Postmaster General Gary and Secretary of Agriculture Wilson, standing off to the side drinking their punch. He had lorded his somewhat laughable turn on the dance floor over his two colleagues the rest of the night, "intimating to them that they were old fellows while I was still a youth." Long had come to believe that some of his renewed life force owed to his proximity to the electrically charged Theodore.

And Roosevelt was in fine fettle just then, in spite of the harrowing scenes at his own home. Theodore's wife had been dangerously ill since the birth of their sixth child two months earlier, and his oldest son was suffering debilitating headaches of uncertain origin. Roosevelt, meanwhile, had thrown himself all the more energetically into his official government work and was "proportionately delighted." The possibilities of a shooting war with Spain seemed to be on the upswing again in the middle of January. President McKinley's efforts to find some diplomatic conclusion to the problem in Cuba had been so slow and disheartening—while the *reconcentrados* on the island continued to starve to death by the thousands—that the administration had finally admitted the necessity of putting the United States military in a position to execute a real live war plan if need be. The Asiatic Squadron—led by Theodore's personal choice, Commodore Dewey—was already in the South China Sea, within range of the Spanish-owned Philippines and its restless population. And Long had given the OK to Theodore's scheme of gathering a large and *impresionante* fleet near Cuba.

The secretary had just ordered most of the North Atlantic Squadron—including the big, beautiful *Iowa* and four other battleships—for two months' training at Roosevelt's suggested drill grounds, off the Dry Tortugas, near the midway point between the southern tip of Florida and Cuba, a quick hundred-mile cruise from the Cuban port of Havana. Long was happy to see his young deputy so pleased and had learned to overlook Theodore's relentless hobby-horsing on the need for a larger navy, with *more battleships*!

Long watched Roosevelt as he finished closing the door behind him that late-January morning and turned, characteristically, already in midsentence. The secretary could reasonably expect from his pushy subordinate a plea for getting more torpedoes to both the Atlantic and the Pacific gunships, or for more smokeless powder; he expected a request from Theodore to rush the repairs on the *Brooklyn* so that it could join the drills in the Dry Tortugas, or a request to buy and fit out for battle more merchant ships, or a demand that Congress pass legislation allowing the department to call up militiamen and enlist new sailors. But Long got something unexpected from Roosevelt that day.

Hours later, when Long sat down at home to make his diary entry, he could not get the scene out of his head. Theodore Roosevelt, as anybody on the Nile River years earlier could have attested, was nothing if not entertaining. Roosevelt just wanted Long to be aware, in case of a declaration of war, that he would be resigning his navy post to join the ground force invading Cuba. He had already informed the president, who promised to help Theodore get his commission! "[Roosevelt] has gone so far daft in the matter that he evidently regards it as a sacred duty which he owes to his own character, to improve every opportunity of dying with malaria, or being played out with a hospital fever in this bushwhacking fight in Cuba. I tried to persuade him that if it was his country which was at stake, or his home should be defended, such a course would be worthwhile," Long recalled, with some real amusement. "I called him a crank, and ridiculed him to the best of my ability, but all in vain. The funny part of it is, that he actually takes the thing seriously."

LONG DID APPRECIATE Roosevelt's "honesty." Try as Theodore might, he was an artless dissembler. He couldn't hide his true desires even if he desired to. The assistant secretary of the United States Navy admitted three days after his conversation with Long—and somewhat injudiciously, as it was to a friend who was then serving in the German government—that he had been "working ardently to bring about our interference in Cuba." "If we could get the seven Spanish ironclads together against our seven seagoing ironclads on this coast," he wrote, "we would have a very pretty fight; and I think more could be learned from it."

Theodore was winched tighter and tighter as the possibility of his war neared, and he was driven near mad by a series of self-inflicted indignities suffered by his navy. The *Brooklyn* was stuck in the New York Navy Yard for repairs, which made it impossible for the ship to get to the Florida drill grounds. The torpedo boat flotilla also due in the Dry Tortugas couldn't answer the bell either. Two of the boats had broken propeller struts and another had a cracked driveshaft. A fourth was simply "shaken up" because of rough service in the Gulf of Mexico.

Word got out in the newspapers that the battleship *Indiana* had blown tubing in its boilers on the first day en route to the Dry Tortugas and it took every boilermaker in the squadron to get her moving again. Worse news leaked out a few days later: the *Texas* and the *Iowa* had both run aground in a poorly charted channel less than a week after the fleet's arrival in the Dry Tortugas. When other boats were dragging the *Iowa* off the bottom, a cable had snapped free and taken down a piece of Rear Admiral Montgomery Sicard's flagship; casualties included the fleet's morale and its readiness. "It created too a nervous distrust of the whole place [Dry Tortugas] and even now we are all shy of discolored water whether shoal or sunshine," the captain of the as-yet-uninjured *Massachusetts* reported to Roosevelt. "No one in the navy is much surprised at anything the *Texas* may do, even if she struck bottom in one hundred fathoms of water, because that is her history and reputation, but to have our pride and delight the *Iowa* come to grief was disheartening. . . . The *Texas* and *Iowa* will I think last until there is a chance to go north and repair. I sincerely hope that while these vessels are in dock under repair that no foreign complication will arise. Can not you stay the hand of war until we are prepared?"

Roosevelt waved off the request for extra time—events were moving too fast for dallying—as he waved off the news reports that damages to the big new battleships were a serious matter. "It is just such an accident as will happen at any time, and but little damage was done, not enough to be worth a mention," the assistant secretary told reporters on February 7, 1898, explaining why the navy had withheld the information from the public. There was rather more interesting and rather more embarrassing news that day. A two-month-old letter from the head of the Spanish Embassy in Washington, Enrique Dupuy de Lôme, had been passed to the Cuban junta in New York and then to the warmongering editors of William Randolph Hearst's *New York Journal*. It was a private and personal letter to a Spanish friend who was on a fact-finding trip in Havana. Minister Dupuy de Lôme had lashed out at McKinley's most recent message to Congress, which wasn't nearly as friendly to Spain as the president and his minister in Madrid liked to claim. And he had taken a nasty slap at the president himself, calling McKinley "weak and a bidder for the admiration of the crowd, besides being a cheap politician who tries to leave a door open behind himself while keeping on good terms with the jingoes of his party."

WORST INSULT TO THE UNITED STATES IN ITS HISTORY! was the headline in the *Journal*. And what did the offended party do, after being on the receiving end of this historic impertinence? McKinley conferred with his friend and confidante Judge Day at the State Department, and with Secretary Long, and with his best friend and campaign guru, Senator Mark Hanna, and decided to turn the other cheek. The government in Madrid agreed to force Dupuy de Lôme to make a formal apology and to step down. Negotiations between the United States and Spain for a peaceful settlement in Cuba continued. The worst insult in American history would be pardoned.

Theodore Roosevelt was beside himself at William McKinley's unwillingness to stand up and defend his personal dignity at a time when his person was *the* personification of the entire nation. When Roosevelt found himself at a reception with Senator Hanna that night, he went on the attack. Theodore didn't think much of Hanna to begin with, and he had been angered by the "weakness" Hanna had exhibited in opposing that "friendly" gesture of sending the *Maine* to Havana. "Like waving a match in an oil well for fun," Hanna had said.

At the reception that night, Roosevelt laid into Hanna about the importance of defending the national honor, leaning in closer and closer, growing more and more animated as he talked, pounding his fist harder and harder into his palm, flailing his arms until he accidentally ripped the dress of a poor unoffending Frenchwoman standing nearby. *Mon dieu!* she cried out, and Roosevelt didn't miss a beat, continuing his harangue in French, for the distressed woman's edification no doubt. When she offered that perhaps, just from the European point of view, France and Germany might have an objection to the United States'

Theodore Roosevelt

adjudicating all imperial questions in the Americas, Roosevelt felt compelled to defend the muscular new Monroe Doctrine, as interpreted by him and Lodge. "I hope to see the Spanish flag, and the English flag gone from the map of North America before I am sixty!"

"You're crazy, Roosevelt," said Mark Hanna.

Six days later, Hanna's oil well went up in flames. The *Maine*, still in the harbor at Havana, exploded in a spectacular fireball and sunk in its place. Spanish ships and sailors rushed to the aid of the *Maine*, but well over half its crew was lost. Nobody could be sure whether an accident on board had detonated the ship's magazines or an outside mine had caused the explosion. Assistant

Secretary Roosevelt was aware of reports concerning the possible construction folly of putting the gunpowder magazines too near the white-hot boiler room in new battleships like the *Maine*, but he wasn't going to let that be known. It was embarrassing enough to be caught off guard by an unexpected attack, but the public embarrassment of stupidity or incompetence was something Roosevelt would not allow his navy to suffer.

While the Hearst newspapers and a slew of others cried for an immediate declaration of war to avenge the *Maine*, Secretary Long followed McKinley's careful lead; he set up a board of inquiry into the explosion and counseled patience among his subordinates in the Navy Department and in the country at large. "There is an intense difference of opinion as to the cause of the blowing up of the *Maine*," Long wrote in his diary.

> In this, as in everything else, the opinion of the individual is determined by his original bias. If he is a conservative, he is sure that it was an accident; if he is a jingo, he is equally sure that it was by design. . . . My own judgment is, so far as any information has been received, that it was the result of an accident, such as every ship of war, with the tremendously high and powerful explosives which we now have on board, is liable to encounter.
>
> The occurrence suggests one important thing—and that is the frightful destruction of life and property which will hereafter accompany any naval or military engagement. In the old days a war vessel could be peppered all day long with comparatively little damage to ship or to crew. Now a battleship with five hundred men on board, fairly struck by one of the great projectiles, will probably go to the bottom and every life will be lost. This reflection ought to have weight with those who talk lightly of going to war. The illustration now afforded by this accident to the *Maine* gives food for sober reflection.

Roosevelt never set much stock in sober reflection; he made sense of the world while in motion. He set himself to a flurry of correspondence the morning after the explosion of the *Maine*, some of it official, some of it personal venting, some of it both. "I will say, to relieve my feelings, that I would give anything if President McKinley would order the fleet to Havana tomorrow," he wrote to an old Harvard clubman. "The *Maine* was sunk by an act of dirty treachery on the part of the Spaniards *I* believe." Roosevelt remained pathologically unable to think for a minute about the burdens on the president's head; neither was he able to refrain from using the disaster as a fresh opportunity to bull-rush John Long. "I venture again to point out how these events emphasize the need that we should have an ample navy," Roosevelt wrote to his boss the next morning. "The question of economy is very important; but it is wholly secondary when compared with the question of national honor and national defense. . . . It may be held against us for all time to come, not merely by the men of to-day, but by those who read history in the future, if we fail to point out what the naval needs of the nation are, and how they should be met."

Long was driven into the ground for the next week; his always tender stomach churned at every letter to the department from family of the crew members of the *Maine* asking for nothing more than information or, in the case of death, begging that their loved one's body be recovered and shipped home. President McKinley summoned Long to the White House nearly every day in the weeks after the *Maine* disaster. The Spanish, for instance, had asked to be a full and equal partner in the investigation to determine the cause of the accident, so Long was needed to confer on that question and to craft an answer, which was in the negative. McKinley asked Long for updates on the investigation day by day, though it would be weeks before the board could report on the cause, if it could in fact *ever* be known. The toll of the dead stood at 253 men and 2 officers—with a few more to come. After four days, only 142 bodies had been hauled up from the underwater wreckage; newspapermen reported scores of vultures circling the site of the explosion or perching on the few masts poking up above the waterline.

Spain made official and seemingly heartfelt apologies, including from Prime Minister Sagasta and the queen regent, who professed horror, but relations were not easy. When Henry White met the Spanish ambassador at the queen's levee in London, the Spaniard began the conversation with an offer of sympathy, but the more he talked the more it sounded like a veiled threat. He assured White that his government was keen to keep the peace, but if the Spanish people decided on war, the government ministers would not be able to turn back the tide. White was sympathetic to the political situation in Spain, he said, as a very similar one applied in the United States. President McKinley was personally still willing to allow time for Spain to get control of the chaos in Cuba, but if US citizens became intent on kicking Spain out of the Caribbean, no president could prevent the war.

The Spanish did not seem to be interested in meeting McKinley halfway. When the understandably sensitive United States Navy and the city of New York welcomed the Spanish armor-clad *Vizcaya* into port, a recently retired Spanish naval attaché was quoted as saying that the carnage on the *Maine* "was the result of an explosion inside the ship, which took place in one of the forward magazines." "The fact of the matter is," he continued, "that the discipline and watch observed on the ship were very lax."

McKinley just kept turning the other cheek. He graciously accepted all

Spanish apologies and ignored all incitement-to-war tabloid reports. "The country can afford to withhold its judgment and not strike an avenging blow until the truth is known," McKinley explained to the excited American public.

John Long watched as the president's deep-set eyes appeared to darken and recede; he found McKinley "more oppressed and careworn" than he'd ever seen him, and he could sympathize. Like the president, the secretary of the navy had been unable to sleep through a night since the disaster; newspaper reporters were at him day and night. He had trouble staying on his feet for long stretches because his corns were acting up. He began to suspect he was on the brink of a nervous collapse and could not foresee a time when the pace of events would let up. Long worried that some new thing outside the administration's control would spark a war with Spain, or that Congress would lose all patience and declare one—which meant that Long's new navy could be shoved into an unfathomable future. "Our great battleships are experiments which have never yet been tried," the secretary recorded in his diary, "and in the friction of a fight have almost as much to fear from some disarrangement of their own delicate machinery or some explosion of their own tremendous ammunition as from the foe."

While Long fretted, his right-hand man mounted another vigorous attack, pummeling the weakened older man with a relentless blizzard of memoranda jabs. "This is in reference to additional warships," Roosevelt wrote his boss four days after the *Maine* explosion.

> I was informed that both Speaker Reed and Senator Hale had stated that we must cease building any more battleships, in view of the disaster to the *Maine*. I can not believe that the statement is true, for of course such an attitude, if supported by the people, would mean that we had reached the last pitch of national cowardice and baseness. . . . I earnestly wish you could see your way clear now, without waiting a day, to send in a special message, stating that in view of the disaster to the *Maine* (and perhaps in view of the possible needs of this country) instead of recommending one battleship, you ask that two, or better still, four battleships be authorized immediately by Congress.

Long broke under the strain. He needed some space. He appointed Roosevelt *temporary* acting secretary in the early afternoon of February 25, 1898, and headed home to get a real night's sleep and maybe take the next day off before returning to duty. But when Theodore swung by Long's house that evening, the light of God in his eyes, the older man began to get worried. Long decided he wasn't going to stay at home the next day after all.

When Long arrived at his office that next morning, his suspicions were confirmed. "The very devil seemed to possess [Roosevelt] yesterday afternoon," Long would write.

> He immediately began to launch peremptory orders: distributing ships; ordering ammunition, which there is no means to move, to places where there is no means to store it; . . . sending messages to Congress for immediate legislation, authorizing enlistment of an unlimited number of seamen; and ordering guns from the Navy Yard at Washington to New York, with a view to arming auxiliary cruisers which are now in peaceful commercial pursuit. The only effect of this last order would be to take guns which are now carefully stored, ready for shipment any moment, and which could be shipped in ample time, to be put on any vessel, and dump them in open weather in the New York Navy Yard, where they would be only in the way and under no proper care.
>
> He has gone at things like a bull in a china shop.

Long spent much of that day reversing and redirecting his assistant secretary's spectacularly misguided managerial slalom, but there were a few orders he did let stand, including one that accorded with the Navy Department's agreed-upon plans—in case of war: "Dewey, Hong Kong. Order the Squadron, except the Monocacy, to Hong Kong. Keep full of coal. In the event of a declaration of war with Spain, your duty will be to see that the Spanish squadron does not leave the Asiatic Coast. And then offensive operation in the Philippine Islands."

CHAPTER EIGHTEEN

The Demands of His Conscience

While his country was heading toward war, Sam Clemens was across an ocean in Vienna, Austria, minding personal matters. Besides a new round of physical infirmities—gout, bronchitis, rheumatism in his writing hand—he had also been suffering an ongoing case of wounded pride. All through the fall of 1897, his publisher's agents had been using his continuing financial woe to boost sales of *Following the Equator*. "Mark Twain" remained an object of public pity, and Clemens was, he admitted to Rogers, "a little tired of being traded on as the only real living, unrivaled, genuwyne marketable pauper."

To make matters worse, Clemens's spectacular financial failure remained a punishing fact of life for his wife and his two remaining daughters. Sam took some solace in telling himself that the move to Vienna was for his daughter Clara, for her professional piano training. But the suite of rooms at the fashionable Hotel Metropole near the Danube Canal (he struck a deal to get 40 percent off the room tariff) and the lessons with Leschetizky, Sam knew, were just more in a line of consolation prizes for the Clemens women. They were all of them exiled from their former lives, and his wife was still an unhappy shut-in. "Constantly [Susy] visits me in my dreams," Livy wrote from Vienna to an old neighbor in Connecticut. "Friends say that time softens trouble: I do not know, I hope it may be so."

Clemens was pained that Livy missed so much of Vienna in the first months of 1898. The Austrian capital was alive with the mellifluous thrum of its salon talk, with the chatter of scientific inquiry, with eccentric royalty—the princesses smoked pipes!—with exhilarating musicianship, erotic painting, and raucous political intrigue, but Livy kept her eye fixed on her own nest. She worried over Clara, who sat at her piano four hours a day in the hopes of one day performing to the exacting standards of the great maestro-tyrant Theodor Leschetizky. "My, but Leschetizky used to be nervous!" Katy Leary remembered of the student recitals she attended. "He would be rushing all around the room, fit to kill himself, if [a protégé] didn't play right."

Jean was Livy's chief concern at the family's winter residence in Vienna. After a year without a grand mal epileptic seizure, the youngest Clemens daughter had in the summer of 1897 suffered another of the violent convulsions, the first one her parents ever witnessed. Three others followed in the span of a month. Doctors put Jean on a strict regimen of vegetable-heavy meals, preventive purgatives, and a daily dose of a sedative that slowed her nervous system to a low idle, but Livy was constantly on guard, anticipating Jean's next unconscious body spasm, ready to loosen her clothing and shove a spoon between her teeth so that she didn't accidentally bite off a hunk of her own tongue.

Sam and Livy communicated the news of Jean's affliction to no one—not to old friends back in America and not to new friends they made in Europe. They would not even disclose to Jean the severity of her medical condition. Jean "thinks herself subject to merely ordinary attacks of fainting," Sam Clemens wrote to one doctor, "& we prefer to keep her in ignorance regarding their true character."

Sam Clemens was shaken by the wrenching physical drama of the seizures, and when the worst of it was over and things in the house settled again, the unjustness of his daughter's affliction ate at him. Jean Clemens was among the most tenderhearted spirits he had ever known, and she had always been the jolliest, the healthiest, and the most physically capable of the three Clemens girls, so these seizures seemed like a taunt from above, like God striking lightning blows at Sam Clemens's most powerful issue for no better reason than his own amusement or just to prove he could.

Sam Clemens had lately begun to worry also that his own vital powers were beginning to erode. He had had such high hopes at Weggis the previous summer, but every piece of story or essay he started in his office above Lake Lucerne had turned to dust, and when he settled the family in Vienna, the change of scenery did him little good. He could not afford to prolong his debt agony any longer, he decided; he wanted it *over*, it had to be over. He was going to pay off his creditors in full, just as Livy had always wanted, if it took every penny he had in the bank.

"I have lost three entire months, now. In that time I have begun twenty magazine articles & books—& flung every one of them aside in turn," he wrote to Henry Rogers after six profitless weeks in Vienna. "The debts interfered every time, & took the spirit out of the work. And yet I have worked like a bond slave, & wasted no time & spared no effort. A man can't possibly write the kind of stuff that is required of me unless he have an unharassed mind. My stuff is worth more in the market to-day than it ever was before—& yet in 3 months I have not succeeded in turning out fifty acceptable pages. Peace of mind is easily attainable—& let's go for it."

Rogers's financial ministrations had put this peace of mind within reach. What money Clemens had accumulated in the bank over the previous three years was not chiefly the take from his own fevered efforts; it was the burgeoning dividends and paper profits that had accrued to him from shrewd investments Henry Rogers had made on his behalf, and from the new deals for reissues of old work that Rogers had struck with his publishers. Even factoring in this unearned windfall, however, Clemens knew that paying off his debt all at once was a risk, that it would leave him little margin for the future. He had no great literary prospects at just that moment. *Joan of Arc* had been a commercial bust, and *Following the Equator* wasn't promising significantly better returns. But with the $10,000 advance from Bliss and the royalties from the *Pudd'nhead Wilson* play and, most of all, the investment profits, Clemens figured he had enough banked to pay his creditors in full and still have a little money to live on while he regained enough of his wits to finish something and get paid for it. He would be starting over again, at age sixty-two, but at least it would be a fresh start.

So Sam Clemens sent instructions to Henry Rogers's personal assistant, Katharine Harrison, up in her new Standard Oil offices eleven floors above Lower Broadway in New York, asking her to start writing checks to the Clemens creditors. He suggested that Miss Harrison make three separate payments on his behalf, on December 1, 1897, on January 1, 1898, and on February 1, 1898, and to clear all but a few disputable debts, if Mr. Rogers signed off. "If the paying of this money at this time is going to be a fatal mistake, of course we must abide by your judgment & not do it," Clemens wrote to Rogers. "But I hope you will not regard it so."

When word of the first payment hit the newspapers, it was, given the way the press had been writing about "Mark Twain's" dire financial predicament, something of a sensation. And nobody was more delighted than his creditors. Miss Harrison shipped to the Clemens's suite of rooms at the Hotel Metropole a bundle of thank-you notes suggesting that the payees, in the aggregate, were both surprised that he had managed to plow up the cash and shocked that he still meant to honor his earlier (and extralegal) vow to pay to the final penny. "For the first time in my life I am getting more pleasure out of paying money out than pulling it in," he reported to Rogers after reading the first of the notes.

"I hope you will never get the like of the load saddled onto you that was saddled onto me 3 years ago," Clemens wrote to William Dean Howells in January of 1898. "And yet there is such a solid pleasure in *paying* the things that I reckon maybe it is worth while to get into that kind of a hobble, after all. Mrs. Clemens gets millions of delight out of it."

CLEMENS COULD ALREADY sense a return of his old focus. He got busy writing an article about the recent devolution of the Austrian parliament from ordinary, everyday disorderliness to name-shouting mob scene accompanied by "such a wild and frantic and deafening clamor as has not been heard on this planet since the last time the Comanches surprised a white settlement at midnight." He had a difficult time making much sense of the issues at hand, but it made for gaudy political drama nonetheless. Certain of the parliamentary cross talk he refused to translate to its fullest measure. "Its flavor is pretty high, in any case, but it becomes particularly gamey when you remember that the first gallery was well stocked with ladies," he wrote.

He was also chipping away at a few of the stories and articles he had started in Weggis. And he found himself absorbed, all of a sudden, in writing for the stage. He was burning through pages on a comedy he titled *Is He Dead?* about a painter who fakes his death to increase the asking price of his artwork. "Work is become a pleasure again—it is not labor, any longer," he told Rogers as his financial liabilities began to shrink. "I am into it up to my ears, these last 3 or 4 weeks—and all *dramatic.* (I always believed I couldn't write a play that would *play*, but this one will. . . .) And there's another one—a joint production. An Austrian playwright is plotting it out, & we are to write it together. . . . I shall want seven rooms in the eleventh story of the new [Standard Oil] building next year, to conduct my dramatic business in. Please have them frescoed. Put in a billiard table. I will send you further details as they occur to me."

Sam Clemens's mood remained the dominant weather pattern in the household, so his sunny spirits and the prideful way in which he had presented all those appreciative letters from their creditors even rallied Livy. She was able again to perform her wifely burlesque—*Youth!*—without hitting sharp notes of bitterness and disappointment. Her husband remained full of sweet juices all through that January and into February. Sam Clemens told Katy Leary that he "felt just like a boy again—free and out of school."

Livy still refused to venture out except for an occasional concert at Leschetizky's atelier, but she did agree to receive guests in the drawing-room of their corner suite at the Metropole, evenings, after five. Painters and composers and newspaper correspondents and Zionists and diplomats and royalty came to sit at the feet of the great American author. "They were just falling all over each other to know him," Katy Leary remembered years later. "There was a sofa right by the fireplace in the drawing room and it was the rule that the highest-ranked person in the room was to sit on this sofa." Loie Fuller, an ambitious girl from the American Midwest whose athletic, voluptuous, garment-billowing, and dramatically lit *Danse serpentine* had made her a preferred muse of art nouveau Paris, wriggled into the Clemenses' drawing room for a visit one evening that winter and caused a stir. Clemens had always recognized a kindred flame in Loie, another redhead in hot pursuit of applause and fortune. She had "the stuff," Clemens liked to say of her—maybe too much of it. "Well," Katy Leary remembered, "[Loie Fuller] came in and sat right down on the top seat of that sofa when the Princess was there! Oh, my! How Mrs. Clemens had to work to manage to get her off that seat and not let her know, or hurt her feelings."

Between his morning shave and haircut and his evening frolic on the Hotel Metropole's cushy sofas, Clemens was absorbed in work. Some rare mornings he played hooky and lounged in his bedroom; most days he had his working pages and his ink pen carried to his bedside, where he would prop himself up on his pillows, still in his nightshirt, and go to work. And a comfy Viennese bed turned out to be a fabulous place to write. He finished a draft of *Is He Dead?* in just three weeks. Livy sat and *laughed* and nodded approval when he read it aloud to her. He wasn't shy to herald its prospects to the wider world either. Newspapers announced the birth of the new "Mark Twain" play that same week, reporting the likelihood of a theatrical rarity: simultaneous debuts in New York and London. "I think, myself, that for an ignorant first attempt it lacks a good deal of being bad," he reported to Rogers. "I am learning the trade pretty fast—I shall get the hang of it yet, I believe." Clemens and his Austrian writing partner had already started in on an original comedy for the American stage and an English translation of some newly successful Austrian plays. Bram Stoker, manager of Henry Irving's Lyceum Theatre in London and author of the sensational but not yet best-selling horror novel *Dracula*, had agreed to act as worldwide agent for "Mark Twain" stage productions.

Some afternoons, Clemens gave a few hours over to sittings for a young Russian sculptor who was making a bust of his head. While at her studio, he became fascinated by Fräulein Ries's recently finished sculpture of Lucifer, especially when she described its creation. She had started the work as the Virgin Mary, but when it began to shy toward the masculine, Ries had made the switch—mother of Jesus was transformed into Satan. Clemens approved! "The Mother and Son have been overworked," he told her. The Prince of Darkness was much on his mind when in Vienna. He had been sketching out his story of a youthful Satan for months, but in the city where Goethe's soul-selling *Faust* was a well-worn stage play, the devil had snuggled deeper into Clemens's subconscious. "Dream," he noted one morning. "Tried to sell my soul to Satan. His polite objections and evasions. Certain lines of goods he was overstocked with. Never *had* paid the prices attributed to him by lying priests. (Lit his pipe with the end of his tail—made me shrink.)"

KATHARINE HARRISON WAS still figuring the exact final payment amount for each Webster creditor at the beginning of February, when Sam Clemens made a rare charity lecture at one of Vienna's most popular concert halls, the six-hundred-seat Bösendorfer-Saal. He noted with pride that he was still a big draw. There was far from enough room in the hall for all that applied for tickets—at four dollars a head! "Six members of the Imperial family present and four princes of lesser degree," he reported to Rogers, "& I taught the whole of them how to steal watermelons. Now all this sounds like brag, but that's what it *is*."

Among the attendees that evening was a perceptive forty-one-year-old Viennese neurologist who was so struck by Clemens's telling of the stolen watermelon story that he included it in one of his later classic studies. "[Mark Twain] stopped and asked himself as though he was in doubt: 'Was it the first?'" Sigmund Freud would write in *Civilization and Its Discontents*. "With this, everything had been said. The first melon was evidently not the only one." This was a mere Freudian footnote slipped into an interesting little discussion of how hard times and "ill-luck" have a tendency to overstimulate the conscience of an honorable man. "As long as things go well with a man," Freud wrote, "his conscience is lenient and lets the ego do all sorts of things; but when misfortune befalls him, he searches his soul, acknowledges his sinfulness, heightens the demands of his conscience, imposes abstinences on himself and punishes himself with penances." Even for men with the most supple and evolved minds, Freud observed, this was a tough habit to shake. Sam Clemens would not have argued the point.

THE CONFIRMATION OF his final release—one might even say triumph—arrived the third week in February, in the form of a letter from Henry Rogers's personal assistant. "I wish I could shout it across the water to you so that you would get it ten days ahead of this letter, but I'm afraid my lungs are not strong enough," Katharine Harrison had written. The debt burden was officially lifted. But for the ethics-shy Mount Morris Bank and one individual whose demand for preferential treatment irked Clemens, every creditor had been satisfied to the final dollar. More notes of thanks followed. "Your check just came to me for $3.35," a book and woodcut printer had written to Miss Harrison. "No words can express the good feeling towards him that I have to know there are some honest people left." Livy would not stop reading the letters. She spent nearly one full day poring over them, then pronounced it, as Clemens reported to Rogers, "the only really happy day she has had since Susy died."

SAM CLEMENS TOLD no one but family and close friends that he had finally wriggled free of debt, but news got out, loosing a flood of editorial encomium. "We are proud to congratulate him on a noble achievement," the London Academy announced. "It will be remembered that early last year, when sick at heart and in poor health, Mark Twain accepted the offer of a public subscription which was made by a New York paper. But in the course of a few days that acceptance was revoked, and he determined that not from without but from within should the debt be paid. Honor be to him for such a decision." Newspapers in England wrote of his genuine probity and "his high-minded" accomplishment. The *Salt Lake Herald*, like many other American journals, slathered it on: "The whole English-speaking world will rejoice over his great triumph, and wish him long years full of happiness and prosperity. His country is proud of him as an author, but prouder of him as a man."

Hollow talk, was the way Clemens read it, as counterfeit as one of Sir Walter Scott's turgid little honor-and-duty pageants. Sam Clemens's conscience was still at full steam. He had been keeping the real score of this battle he had been engaged in—had been counting the casualties and the collateral damage—and in his darker moments, he had doubts that a single noble thought or impulse had driven his three-year quest for "honor." Clemens was already testing and refining his "sinister doctrine" of human nature, as Clara called it, and he was exhibit A: "The human being—with not a single exception in the whole earth—is a fool. And to his very marrow he is a hypocrite and a humbug." Hadn't he embarked on this mad debt-defying expedition, at bottom, to raise himself up in the eyes of the world and to assuage his own guilty conscience? "The foundation-stone of the [human] race," Clemens wrote to a friend as the praise began to pour forth, "is shabbiness & selfishness."

CHAPTER NINETEEN

No Back Down

Theodor Leschetizky—the Grand Mogul, as Clara called him, but only behind his back—agreed to come to dinner at the Hotel Metropole in the first bloom of the Viennese spring. It was to be a full table that night; Livy's brother and his son, Charley and Jervis Langdon, were visiting from America, and Clara was anxious that they meet her master. Clara's desired beau of the moment, an art student named George Townsend Cole, had also accepted an invitation, along with a handful of American pianists, and two of Leschetizky's prize European students, Mark Hambourg and Ossip Gabrilowitsch. Young piano geniuses, much like young authors, never passed up a free meal—not in Sam Clemens's observation.

Leschetizky's willingness to present himself at the Clemens home was a special treat, for the master was generally wary of socializing with his student's parents. He found them a nuisance as a rule; they were always certain their issue was possessed of rare genius, often stunned by Leschetizky's cutting critiques, and given to questioning his pedagogical methods, if not in front of him, then in front of their precious child. He did not seek intimacy *mit den Eltern*—no matter how renowned. Leschetizky had treated the famous American author as he would all other fathers on first meeting. When Sam Clemens showed up at the piano instructor's home and studio in the fall of 1897 and sat in silent moral support while Clara Clemens tried to play and talk her way into Leschetizky's class, he was forced to endure a long lecture regarding Clara's shortcomings in strength and technique and tone and prior training. If Leschetizky did agree to take Miss Clemens as a student, he explained, it might require a year of hard and steady work with his underinstructors before she qualified for a private lesson with the Grand Mogul himself. Clara thought she saw her father shrink under this "German cataclysm," but he did not argue. "Are we to remain in Vienna, or not?" was all he asked.

Sam Clemens's fondness for the Grand Mogul grew over time. After hearing him play, Clemens judged Leschetizky the greatest living pianist on the planet. And Clemens, who was nothing if not competitive in the talking arts, also judged the wiry seventy-year-old Russian Jew a gifted raconteur—with stories to tell. Leschetizky had become the world's most famous teacher just as the piano was becoming an instrument of drama and power and warmth and sustain, and had been part of a golden age of Viennese music and musicians. Leschetizky had known Bruckner and Johann Strauss the Younger and Johannes Brahms, with whom he had a prickly friendship. He liked to tell the story of the morning Brahms walked into his studio, peered over his shoulder, and sniffed. "Ha! What sort of things are you writing this morning? I see—quite *little* things, *little* things, of course, yes."

"*Little* things? Yes," Leschetizky answered, at least in his own telling, "but ten times more amusing than yours, I can tell you."

LESCHETIZKY DID MUCH of the talking at dinner in the Clemens's Hotel Metropole suite that early spring evening in Vienna. His talk meandered on until well after midnight, and the Viennese master ranged as always, but he did give way at times to the other guests. Livy's brother, Charley Langdon, had just arrived from America, so everybody wanted to know what he thought of the situation in Cuba, especially after the *Maine* debacle. Would the United States go to war with Spain? Livy for one was happy to have an American to talk to about this touchy subject. She had recently started to feel as if she were living behind enemy lines. The Austrians who came to visit almost always supported Spain and wondered how Americans could presume to interfere with the sovereign rights of another nation—especially an established European power! They were also quick to suggest that America would be no match for the Spanish navy or its army, which, after all, had been perfecting its military science for centuries.

Livy felt compelled to defend her home country, but on exactly what grounds she was not sure. Her husband found the anti-American banter convivial and appreciated the placid manner in which he and his Austrian friends could "disagree without harmful results." Nobody in Vienna, Clemens included, was much invested in the matter.

Charley Langdon offered to his tablemates the opinion that a war against Spain, if it came to that, would be fought in the just cause of freedom and independence for the Cuban people. America had no imperial designs and no desire to seize the island or any other foreign state. The Senate, by way of illustration, was continuing to block the annexation of Hawaii. And nearly every member of that legislative body was on record renouncing American ownership of Cuba.

Leschetizky disagreed. He did so calmly but, after the fashion of the aristocratic European circles he served, peremptorily. All the talk about a righteous war to free the weak and mistreated Cubans was a sham, he said. There was a self-serving impulse at the bottom of all this rhetoric. The United States was as rapacious as any other world power: it would swallow Cuba whole if it got the chance, along with whatever else it could get.

Clemens did not put up a real argument about American motives that night. Maybe it was because his German was spotty, and maybe it was because Leschetizky was pretty seriously outnumbered by patriotic Americans, and maybe it was because he wasn't quite sure where he stood on war with Spain. But the subject was beginning to be more and more on Sam Clemens's mind.

WAR TALK WAS everywhere in Vienna at the beginning of spring. The odds that the United States and Spain would avoid organized bloodletting thinned by the day. The reports Sam Clemens was getting—from his American diplomat friends and from the erudite and bookish young secretary in the Spanish legation in Vienna—pointed *nach Krieg*. Clemens had even heard about Harry White's chesty exchange with the Spanish diplomat in London.

American newspapers and the American wire stories were easy to get in Vienna, so Clemens had for months been aware of the insistent martial prodding of his countrymen back home. William Randolph Hearst and other sensation-driven publishers discovered that screaming for revenge against Spain did wonders for sales. Hearst already had a war slogan: "Remember the *Maine*, To hell with Spain!" And even one of the least excitable Republicans in the United States Senate, Redfield Proctor, having just returned from an unofficial fact-finding trip through Cuba, was reportedly ready to stir the pot.

McKinley's patience in allowing the new Spanish government more time to "pacify" the islands, as far as Senator Proctor had seen, had been cynically exploited by the Spanish overlords in Cuba. Prime Minister Sagasta had talked a good game about reforms in Cuba, but dismal and deadly conditions prevailed among the *reconcentrados*. These Cubans were still penned at gunpoint in dingy makeshift villages, ringed with trenches, barbed wire, and armed guards. In the western rural provinces where the Cuban insurrection had begun, Proctor observed, entire populations were living in captivity.

When Proctor reported his findings in a private meeting with the president, McKinley tried to caution his fellow Republican. "If you read that to the Senate," McKinley warned, "our negotiations end and war is inevitable." Proctor, a man with the kindly eyes of a Mennonite pastor and the aura of ease that came from enormous private wealth, would not be dissuaded. "I doubt if any senator could have resisted this rare opportunity not only to be the center of the stage but to occupy the whole platform," Chauncey Depew said of Proctor. The senator from Vermont made no prior announcement of his presentation, but when word began to circulate around the Capitol that Proctor was heading to the Senate floor to make a report on the conditions in Cuba, every member in the vicinity made a beeline for the chamber, and civilians crowded into the galleries.

Proctor did not play to the growing crowd that day but kept his eyes fixed on his paper and limited his remarks to his prepared text. The chamber remained silent and rapt as the senator droned on in a bloodless, matter-of-fact cadence. "A form of dropsy is a common disorder," Proctor read. "Little children are still walking about with arms and chests terribly emaciated, eyes swollen and abdomen bloated to three times the natural size. The physicians say these cases are hopeless. . . . Deaths in the streets have not been uncommon. I was told by one of our consuls that people have been found dead about the markets in the morning where they had crawled hoping to get some stray bits of food." And all this, Redfield explained, in spite of the hundreds of thousands of dollars in food and supplies American citizens had donated to succor Spain's victims in rural Cuba. Generosity and humanity were insufficient to the task.

Proctor warned against annexation of the island "because it is not wise policy to take in any people of foreign tongue and training, and without any strong guiding American element," but he did not see how a Christian nation like the United States could permit the hateful Spanish rule to continue. The strongest case for war, according to Senator Proctor, was "the spectacle of a million and a half people, the entire native population of Cuba, struggling for freedom and deliverance from the worst misgovernment of which I ever had knowledge." Proctor said he was willing to leave it to the president and the American people to find the proper remedy, then turned calmly on his heels and left the chamber to its chapel-like silence.

THEODORE ROOSEVELT WAS in a hot rage after Senator Proctor's presentation. "The blood of the Cubans, the blood of women and children who have perished by the hundred thousands in hideous misery, lies at our door; and the blood of the murdered men of the *Maine* calls not for indemnity but for the full measure of atonement which can only come by driving the Spaniard from the New World," he reported in a personal letter to Henry Adams's brother. "I have said this to the President before his Cabinet; I have said it to Judge Day, the real head of the State Department; and to my own Chief. I cannot say it publicly, for I am of course merely a minor official in the Administration." But then—and who could have imagined this?—Teddy's private recommendations went public.

"Mr. President," was how the newspapers quoted him, "I not only think [the American people want war], I know positively that fully 85 percent of the population of the country is for immediate war. They think that peace has ceased to be a virtue, and that we must fight in order to preserve our honor."

A FEW DAYS later, on a chill Friday morning at the end of March, navy secretary John Long delivered to President McKinley the report from the just-completed investigation into the explosion of the USS *Maine* in Havana's harbor. The conclusions of the American commission appointed by the United States Navy preserved the honor and dignity of the United States Navy: the explosion had been no accident, and no matter of faulty design, and no matter of negligence on the part of the ship's officers. An outside submarine mine, and not an internal explosion, had without a doubt been the cause. The investigators did not, however, claim sufficient evidence to definitely fix final responsibility for the deaths of 266 Americans and the loss of $5 million worth of battleship on anybody in the Spanish military or government. McKinley withheld this report from Congress over the weekend, but he knew the window for making a peaceful settlement with Spain was closing fast. Word that the McKinley administration was twisting itself in knots to find a way to avoid war reached diplomatic circles and salons as far off as Vienna; the United States was even rumored to be willing to make a secret deal to *buy* the damned island.

McKinley was up late into the night through the weekend with his assistant secretary of state, William Day, nudging the Sagasta government to meet the United States halfway. Secretary of State Sherman was too sclerotic to be entrusted with any real responsibility, so the instructions that burned the wires between Washington and Spain went straight from Day's desk to Stewart Woodford's office in Madrid. "[The president] can not look upon the suffering and starvation in Cuba save with horror," read one cable from Day to Woodford. "All this has shocked and inflamed the American mind, as it has the civilized world, where its extent and character are known."

The president's demands to Madrid that weekend were direct and final: an immediate cease-fire to allow for negotiations between Spain and the insurgents, with McKinley himself as the preferred umpire, and an immediate revocation of the *reconcentrado* order. The president offered his "friendly offices" to ensure that the insurgents in Cuba honored the armistice, but he wanted Woodford to explain to the Sagasta government that time was running out. The *Maine* report was about to be made public, and it was going to incite the US citizenry. A large majority of the United States Congress, which was vested with the exclusive power to declare war, was in the mood for a fight. That body had already appropriated a stunning $50 million just to *prepare* for military action against Spain, and there was plenty more in the US Treasury if needed. American agents had been buying up and refitting gunships by the score. The president explained to Sagasta that he could not hold back the war party on Capitol Hill without serious concessions from Spain.

The government officials in Madrid stuck to their practice of evasion, four centuries of habit being hard to break. They begged extra patience from the president and the American people and asked the American minister in Madrid to be sensitive to the imperatives of Spanish politics: if the royal family and its government gave away Cuba now, its own rule would probably be over. The Sagasta government preferred to let the newly forming congress in Cuba make the political deal with the insurgents, and this body would not be meeting for six weeks.

McKinley had no good answer from Madrid by Monday, when he presented the findings of the *Maine* investigation to Congress, but he still made no call for military retaliation in his accompanying letter. The Major had already sent the report to the Spanish government, he explained, and expected them to pay a proper indemnity. "I do not permit myself to doubt that the sense of justice of the Spanish nation will dictate a course of action suggested by honor and the friendly relations of the two governments." McKinley's message landed in Congress—as in the nation at large—with an ugly thud. *Was the president joking?* The passwords in the halls of Congress the next day, the *Washington Evening Star* reported, were "action" and "no back down."

The combative Theodore Roosevelt scrambled cruisers and torpedo boats and begged Secretary Long to permit him to "smash" any Spanish warships heading west toward the Americas, and he privately complained that McKinley had "no more backbone than an chocolate éclair." The president was hanged in effigy, as a traitor and a coward, in Newport, Rhode Island; Richmond, Virginia; and Buffalo, New York. But William McKinley still refused to be forced down the warpath. He had been on hand at the bloodiest battle Americans had ever fought, at Antietam, in 1862. The romance of battle held no appeal. "I have been through one war," he told friends. "I have seen the dead piled up; and I do not want to see another."

JOHN HAY, JUST returned to England from his Nile cruise, had similar misgivings about a new war, but he could report excellent and surprising tidings from Her Majesty's government. He noticed at a recent levee at the Court of St. James's that the British royal family had received the Spanish ambassador with cool and formal bows. Hay wrote to Henry Cabot Lodge:

> For the first time in my life I find the "drawing room" sentiment altogether with us. If we wanted it,—which, of course we do not, we could have the practical assistance of the British Navy,—on the *do ut des* principle [you scratch my back, I'll scratch yours], naturally. . . .
>
> The commonest phrase is here:—"I wish you would take Cuba at once. We wouldn't have stood it this long." And of course no power on earth would have shown such patience, and such scrupulous regard for law.

But the ambassador was a bit unnerved by the domestic political risk McKinley was taking in attempting to restrain the inflamed American polity. "You and I better have no opinion about the Spanish War except the President's," Hay wrote to his wife. "He has done everything a man could do to avert it—If it comes now, it is not his fault."

THE SAGASTA GOVERNMENT did finally make an answer to McKinley's weekend cable, but it was not what the president needed to hear. The Spanish offered a partial lifting only of the *reconcentrado* policy and made it clear, as a nonnegotiable matter of pride, that there would be no cease-fire unless and until the armed revolutionaries in Cuba begged for it. Oh, and by the way, they thought it best to turn the question of an indemnity for the *Maine* over to disinterested arbitrators. They still believed the explosion was set off by an action inside the battleship. When the Spanish suggested that the president apply to a higher power, in the person of Pope Leo XIII, to help make the peace, the good Methodist workhorse McKinley spit the bit.

The Major began work on a war message to send to Congress, but his first try was a limp rag. "He has been robbed of sleep, overworked; and I fancy that I can see that his mind does not work clearly and directly and as self-reliantly as it otherwise would," Secretary of the Navy Long recorded in his diary after McKinley read his first draft to his cabinet. The president delayed the rewritten address long enough for the US Consulates in Cuba to get American citizens safely off the island, and then he handed Congress an invitation to open a debate on a declaration of war, which Congress accepted with aplomb.

THERE WERE VOICES against, both inside Congress and out, and even forty-five hundred miles away Sam Clemens could note in the newspapers that his friend and confidant William Dean Howells was among the most stalwart. As Congress debated war, Howells signed on as an avowed supporter of a resolution to be presented to the Central Labor Union in New York. The argument offered by Howells and his copresenters showed wit, intelligence, and uncommon logic—"a masterly arraignment of war and a plea for peace," was how one discriminating newspaperman described it—but it also betrayed a paucity of good political sense. "Honesty compels us to acknowledge that it is not the Spanish race especially, but the human race at large, that is cruel, and that our crusade in this matter should begin at home," read the resolution.

> We see every day the vast injustice prevailing in our own land, the hopeless toil, the wretched poverty, the armies of unemployed, and until we remove these beams from our own eyes we should not presume to take the mote from our brother's. . . . The real evil, which is hatred between men, we extend all over our own land, and we hand down to our own children a legacy of hate against people who differ in no wise from ourselves. We are in a position in which, by moral interference, we can insist on justice for the oppressed Cubans. . . . Finally we believe that all questions should be settled by reason and, as man is the only creature endowed with reason, the reasonable way is the manly way. Now, how can a war settle questions reasonably?

When the honorary treasurer of the Longshoreman's Union introduced the resolution for the approval of the assembled labor delegates, he was shouted down. "We are the government and the sailors are our servants," one delegate declared. "We should avenge the murdered men of the *Maine*."

Another delegate stood and suggested that any working man who would allow Spanish rule to continue in Cuba should be shot.

"[Mr. Hall] has brought his pigs to the wrong market," said another delegate from the ironworkers.

The labor delegates voted down the peace resolution two to one. Members of the American Longshoreman's Union called on newspapers the next day with a statement distancing themselves from their softheaded treasurer. "The longshoremen," reported the *New York Sun*, "are in favor of war with Spain."

Sam Clemens had always kept common cause with his friend Howells, and he certainly would have felt right at home on the "one" side of a two-to-one vote. "In a crowd," Clemens explained to a gathering in Vienna, "[men] don't think for themselves, but become impregnated by the contagious sentiment uppermost in the minds of all who happen to be *en masse*." He had always been on guard against "the mob talking through his mouth." But Sam Clemens was not in New York or Boston or Hartford. He was in Vienna, Austria, where the population sided with their European brothers from Spain, and Clemens was a genetic contrarian, and a practiced one, and he never felt more alive than when he was swimming against the tide. So these were bracing days for him in Vienna, where public sentiment ran hard and fast against the United States.

The day after Howells made his antiwar argument, Clemens was already beginning to build a case against the Spanish. "Are there any supremely illustrious Spaniards?" he jotted in his notebook, from his study three stories above an elegant stone-paved Viennese square. "Call to mind at the moment none but Duke of Alva, Torquemada, Satan."

Chapter Twenty

You May Fire When You Are Ready

John Hay dodged a big bullet, thanks to Harry White, who happened to be on a monthlong leave in the United States in April 1898, while the Senate debated committing the country to war. Hay's trusted deputy had been called into a number of conferences with the president during his stay in the American capital, in no small part so that William McKinley could bring White into his confidence on a touchy personnel subject: the question of who should be the next secretary of state. The current secretary, John Sherman, seemed more senile by the day. Sherman was no longer able to function at cabinet meetings without a department handler in tow, and his short-term memory was so questionable (e.g., the president's plan to annex Hawaii had slipped his mind) that his infrequent private dealings with foreign envoys in Washington left them either confounded or scandalized. Senators who had served for decades with Sherman said the secretary of state no longer recognized them.

Sherman's deficiencies had been a poorly kept secret from the beginning of his term and an ongoing embarrassment to the administration. The consensus in political circles was that McKinley had appointed the seventy-three-year-old Ohio native to the State Department only in order to clear his Senate seat for the Major's friend and campaign manager, Mark Hanna. McKinley, who may have had a twinge of conscience about wheedling the Senate seat away from Sherman, had stood by the failing man as long as he could, but with a war now on the horizon the president decided the prudent move would be to dump the secretary, and in a hurry. McKinley's first choice to replace Sherman was his close friend William Day, who had been doing much of Sherman's job for a year anyway. But the Major was not entirely confident in the wisdom of the appointment, because Day was a novice in the field of international law and diplomacy. So McKinley put the question to Harry White before he made his final decision: wouldn't John Hay, perhaps, be the best man for the job?

White was diplomatic as ever and let it be known in the subtlest possible manner that his boss and dear friend might not—at present—possess the physical vigor required of a wartime secretary of state. McKinley decided in the end to tap Day and to leave John Hay in London to focus on the job of promoting good relations with the world's most powerful empire.

HAY HAD NO ambition to run the nation's foreign affairs, especially now, in the middle of the march toward war. The payout of victory hardly seemed worth the effort: A free Cuba, and then what? Would the United States have to take ownership and run it as an island colony? Or make it a US territory and thus eligible one day for statehood? Hay's old boss John Bigelow had waved away Spain's offer to sell Cuba thirty years earlier—with just that complication in mind. "It would have resulted," Bigelow wrote to a friend in 1898, "in sending probably six senators and twice as many members to the lower House of Congress with whom we have not one single bond of sympathy except such as we have with the beasts of the field."

John Hay was also wary of the cost of war. He had seen the ugly side of a real fight close-up during the Civil War—the endless lists of casualties, the execution orders handed down on terrified deserters, men desperately wounded and dying in pus-and-blood medical hovels—and he detested it. The experience of that war made him immune to the fever that accompanied the run-up to any new fight; he didn't care to look on as his countrymen's reason and judgment went walkabout. The ambassador was growing weary of being called on to referee disputes between his embassy's naval attaché and its military attaché, who nearly began throwing punches in Hay's Carlton House Terrace dining room one evening that April. Alfred Bates, lieutenant colonel, US Army, had innocently predicted that there would be no war, and John C. Colwell, lieutenant, US Navy, told him he best keep his peace ideas to himself, especially in front of any Englishmen who might think Americans cowardly. The more time Colwell spent away from the office running Theodore's spy ring or buying up new gunboats, John Hay had come to believe, the better. "They are unequally matched," Hay explained. "Colwell is a quarrelsome fellow . . . and Bates is feeble folk."

The war babble was not limited to Americans and their champions; everybody had an opinion. Hay had to endure European newspapermen extolling the fighting prowess of the Spaniards, as well as naval experts in England who pulled him aside to offer friendly warnings. The Spanish navy had better ships and munitions than the Americans, they told Hay, their sailors were more professional and better drilled, and they were the far superior gunners.

Hay nodded quietly at all the talk and stuck to his ambassadorial duties. The

United States of America was headed, alone, into the first full-scale transoceanic foreign war in its history, and it was his duty to solicit sympathy and approval from the world's dominant empire. When the lord mayor of London toasted his American guest at the Easter banquet, Hay answered it with a nod to the enterprise and enlightenment that had characterized the rise of the British Empire. He had to wait for the loud huzzahs to fade before starting in again. "Perhaps I may be pardoned if I say a word about my own country," Hay said.

> We [Americans] hear sometimes that we are thought to be somewhat eager and pertinacious in pursuit of our own interests. If that is so, I can say, I hope with no impertinence, and in a spirit rather of pride than of contrition, that it merely goes to show of what stock we are. All of us who think cannot but see that there is a sanction like that of religion which binds us to a sort of partnership in the beneficent work of the world. . . . We are bound by a tie which we did not forge and which we cannot break; we are joint ministers of the same sacred mission of liberty and progress.

THE UNITED STATES Congress made its official and expected declaration of war on April 25, 1898, and every day that followed brought Hay a mail pouch stuffed with new news of enraptured young American heroes in the making. Two of his Illinois nephews enlisted. Henry Cabot Lodge's son, Bay, a promising young poet, signed himself into the navy. Then came the news that Theodore Roosevelt had officially tendered his resignation from the Department of the Navy and won permission from President McKinley to raise and train a volunteer cavalry unit.

"[Roosevelt] has lost his head to this unutterable folly of deserting the post where he is of the most service and running off to ride a horse and, probably, brush mosquitoes from his neck on the Florida sands," Secretary Long wrote the morning his assistant secretary resigned. "He thinks he is following his highest ideal, whereas, in fact, as without exception every one of his friends is telling him, he is acting like a fool. And yet, how absurd all this will sound if, by some turn of fortune, he should accomplish some great thing and strike a very high mark!"

The report of Theodore's new venture was not entirely unexpected to Hay, but it was somewhat surprising under the circumstances. Last Hay had heard from Nannie Lodge, just a few weeks earlier, Assistant Secretary Roosevelt's wife had just been cut open by surgeons in an attempt to clean out the life-threatening abscess that had been growing in her groin since she had given birth the previous fall. Edith Roosevelt was still on her sickbed, and her recovery was no sure thing. And now Theodore was headed off to meet the Spanish army and its Gatling guns and Mausers and machetes. "It was my one chance to do something for my country and for my family and my one chance to cut my little notch on the stick that stands as a measuring rod in every family," Roosevelt later said. "I know that I would have turned from my wife's deathbed to have answered that call."

"I wish we could all be chloroformed for a few months, and begin life again in October," Hay lamented in the spring of 1898. "I do not so much mind my friends going into battle, but the fever is a grizzly thing to encounter."

THE WAR NEWS was received with either extreme dudgeon or glum resignation in most quarters of Vienna, Sam Clemens's own household included. "I cannot help feeling that we are wrong," Livy Clemens wrote to her brother, Charley, who had just returned home. "I, the more, want to say it to you because here I must say that America is right—I know in one way she is, but I wish she could have tried still longer to bring about a new state of things in Cuba peaceably." Livy's husband was the exception in the Austrian capital; he found himself strangely invigorated by the entire business. "Old as I am, I want to go to war myself," he wrote to his old lecture agent, Major James B. Pond. "And I should do it, too, if it were not for the danger."

THE US ARMY brass was not entirely sanguine about coming up to the scratch line of this battle with Spain. The call for volunteers had swelled the ranks, but the War Department wanted a few months to prepare these new recruits to fight alongside the regular army enlistees. In any case, US Army honchos explained to the president, they thought it a mistake to invade Cuba until the Spanish naval fleet had been eradicated. The generals were just full of ideas about how *not* to prosecute the war.

The rest of America, however, embarked on this martial escapade with jaunty and heedless naïveté. "[War] is a God-send to all the young men in America," Henry Adams observed. "Even the Bostonians have at last a chance to show that they have emotions." The president asked for a hundred thousand men to fill out the American fighting ranks, and ten times that number volunteered; college boys formed their own units, and campus quadrangles rang with songs that generally ended in "to hell with Spain!" Jay Gould's daughter pledged $100,000 to the war effort. John Jacob Astor IV donated his private yacht to the navy and funded his own artillery battery. All he wanted in return was an officer's commission and a crack at the Spaniards. Henry Cabot Lodge handed over his family estate in Nahant to be used as an army signal station—"free gratis for nothing," he reported with pride.

Roosevelt's volunteer cavalry unit was already taking shape; Theodore was to be second-in-command, subordinate to his great friend Colonel Leonard Wood. The two men were calling their new unit the Rough Riders, and Theodore had already fired off his first order, this one to Brooks Brothers, requisitioning a lieutenant colonel's uniform, waterproof and in blue, "without yellow on the collar, and with leggings."

THE DASHING YOUNG war correspondent Richard Harding Davis, who had managed with Roosevelt's help to secure a berth on the USS *New York*, embarked to report on the first move against Spain, the blockade of Cuba. "It is grand to see the line of battleships five miles out like dogs in a leash puffing and straining," Davis wrote home from aboard the armored cruiser. He wrote again a few days later, once the siege of the Cuban ports had begun: "We drift around in the sun or the moonlight, and when we see a light, chase after it. There is a band on board that plays twice a day. . . . The other night, when we were heading off a steamer and firing six-pounders across her bows, the band was playing the 'star' song from the Meistersinger. Wagner and War struck me as the most fin de siècle idea of war that I had ever heard of. The nights have been perfectly beautiful, full of moonlight, when we sit on deck and smoke. It is like looking down from the roof of a high building."

On the other side of the globe, the strains of John Philip Sousa's stirring new march "El Capitan" rang out over the South China Sea, compliments of Commodore George Dewey's marine band, as his squadron steamed toward its destiny: "Proceed at once to Philippine Islands," were his orders from Secretary Long. "Commence operations at once, particularly against the Spanish fleet. You must capture vessels or destroy. Use utmost endeavors."

As it neared the archipelago, Dewey sent to the other eight ships in the squadron the recent message of the Spanish governor-general of the Philippines to his own soldiers and sailors there. The captain of each American ship was ordered to read it aloud to his entire crew, apparently to get the blood up: "Pretending to be inspired by a courage of which they are incapable," the Spanish message concluded,

> the North American seamen undertake . . . to take your riches, as if they are unacquainted with property rights, and to kidnap those persons whom they consider useful to man their ships or to be exploited in agricultural or industrial labor. Vain design! Ridiculous boasting! . . . The aggressors shall

> not profane the tombs of your fathers; they shall not gratify their lustful passions at the cost of your wives' and daughters' honor. . . . Your valor and patriotism will punish and abase the people that, claiming to be civilized and cultivated, have exterminated the natives of North America, instead of bringing to them the life of civilization and progress.

Dewey and his excited squadron went first to Subic Bay, where any capable Spanish admiral would have arrayed his ships to cut off the American approach to the port city and colonial capital, Manila. The commodore found the bay empty of Spanish gunships, and a path open to him. Not long after midnight on May 1, 1898, under the cover of darkness, Dewey's squadron steamed into Manila Bay. The squadron's guns were loaded and ready to fire. The sailors had already covered the wooden decks with sand, to afford traction for the crew once the blood began to spill; Dewey's flagship *Olympia* led the way forward. "I have waited sixty years for this opportunity," the commodore told a subordinate who tried to warn him off. "Mines or no mines, I am leading the squadron in myself."

The outlines of a Spanish flotilla moored just offshore began to come clear in the morning's first light, and Dewey hoisted the "Prepare for general action" signal. The Spanish batteries opened fire a few minutes later. "Apparently every Spanish gun had been turned loose and the shore line was one blaze of fire," the paymaster of one boat would remember of that first moment of battle terror. "The din was simply indescribable. Tons of shot fell over our ships, and enough steel to have sunk the entire fleet." Shells fired from the shore batteries arced and whistled overhead, while the smaller projectiles raked nearer the waterline. One shell ripped through the foremast of the USS *Boston*, and fires broke out on that ship. Another shot sailed into the *Baltimore*, ricocheting through the ship, exploding a cache of small ammunition, and wounding eight men. A few officers aboard the American ships were recalling the remarks at a farewell dinner given them by the British military men on their last evening in Hong Kong. "A fine set of fellows," the Brits had said, "but unhappily we will never see them again."

In the face of the Spanish barrage, the American squadron, as ordered, pushed to within fifty-five hundred yards of the enemy ships before Dewey finally turned to the captain of the *Olympia*: "You may fire when you are ready, Gridley."

✥ CHAPTER TWENTY-ONE ✥

What Is Our Next Duty?

Like most of the rest of the world, John Hay was anxious to know the outcome of the naval battle at Manila Bay, but news of Dewey and his ships was all rumor and guesswork in the first few days. The commodore had ordered his men to cut the underwater telegraph wires between Manila and Hong Kong as a war precaution before sailing to the Philippines, so even if there were American ships still afloat to carry a message, it was a six-hundred-nautical-mile trip from Manila back to British-controlled Hong Kong, and the world was left to wait and wonder as to the score of the first serious engagement of the Spanish-American War.

On the third morning after the Battle of Manila Bay, Hay could already sense a change in the air. American visitors were trickling into the embassy on Victoria Street to ask Ambassador Hay to please pass along to the president congratulations on a Dewey victory. Later that day, as Hay made his way through a crowd of fellow envoys, all eyes were on the representative of the United States of America, and not without apparent envy. "The quadrangle of the Foreign Office was yesterday afternoon crowded with Ambassadors' and Ministers' carriages, and in the building itself there were continuous visitors at Lord Salisbury's first reception since his illness," the *Daily News of* London reported of the May 4 event. "Among the most important of the visitors was the Hon. John Hay, the United States Ambassador, who had a long interview."

Three days later, on May 7, 1898, the US Department of the Navy finally received Commodore Dewey's much-anticipated official report, which he had scrawled out from the bridge of his flagship off the coast of Manila on the afternoon of May 1, just hours after the battle had concluded. "SECRETARY OF THE NAVY, Washington: The squadron arrived at Manila at daybreak this morning. Immediately engaged enemy and destroyed the following Spanish vessels: *Reina Christina [*sic*], Castillia, Don Antonio de Biloa*, *Don Juan de Austria*, *Isla de Luzon*, *Isla de Cuba*, *General Lezo*, *Marquis del Duaro*, *El Curreo*, *Velasco*, one transport, *Isla de Mandano*, water battery at Cavite. I shall destroy Cavite arsenal dispensatory. The squadron is uninjured. Few men were slightly wounded. . . . Dewey." A second telegram arrived at the Navy Department that day also, written three days later. "I have taken possession of the naval station at Cavite, Philippine Islands, and destroyed its fortifications. . . . The squadron excellent health and spirits. The Spanish loss not fully known; very heavy; 150 killed, including captain, on *Reina Cristina*, alone. I am assisting and protecting Spanish sick and wounded, 250 in number, in this hospital, within our lines. . . . Much excitement at Manila. Scarcity of provisions on account of not having economized stores. Will protect foreign residents."

"How Dewey did wallop them!" Hay wrote to Henry Adams, finally getting in the spirit of things. "His luck was so monstrous that it really detracts from his glory. And don't you go making mistakes about McKinley! He is no tenderfoot—he has a habit of getting there."

The European newspapers were heaping no great praise on Commodore Dewey and the United States Navy—their commonest practice was to caricature Americans as swine—but British response ran toward respect for an impressive display of naval power. Dewey had destroyed or captured the entire Spanish fleet at Manila Bay in a single morning, without losing a ship or sustaining a single serious injury among his crew. And he had even paused to offer his men breakfast in the middle of the engagement! "It is one of the most brilliant Naval combats in history," an admiral in the Royal Navy told newspapermen. "It was formerly my opinion that the warships of the United States would not fulfill all the necessary conditions for successful warfare in a crucial test, but now I believe that the American Navy is equal to any of its size in the world."

HAY WAS SCHEDULED to dine that evening at Joseph Chamberlain's house, and he arrived there anticipating much discussion of the British preoccupation of the moment: the threatening moves the German kaiser and the Russian czar were making in China. But after dinner that evening, when Chamberlain pulled John Hay aside to talk, the colonial secretary wanted to know whether Hay thought that an offer from Spain to cede Cuba ("through some neutral power, England for instance") might bring a quick end to the war. "There could be little question of indemnity," Chamberlain told Hay. "Spain is incapable of paying one." Hay explained, as Chamberlain must have known, that he could make no definite answer, as he had no official instructions on these points. "The sooner Spain should offer terms of peace including the independence of Cuba," Hay did say, "the more favorable would be the disposition of the President."

Hay reported this interesting conversation to the new secretary of state, Judge Day, first thing the next morning. "Mr. Chamberlain did not give me the impression that he was speaking with any mandate from his colleagues, nor with any authority from the government of Spain," Hay cabled. "At the same time I felt I ought not to withhold from you the fact of the question having been asked. The significance of it consists in the indication it gives of the state of mind of the men at the head of affairs here, their wish for a speedy termination of the war in the independence of Cuba, their certainty of our success, and their willingness to take a prominent part, if desired, in the work of pacification."

McKinley and Day were both struck by Hay's discretion and by his scrupulous modesty. Another and more ambitious ambassador—say, Whitelaw Reid, who had been peppering the president with unsolicited war advice—might have pushed the issue beyond good sense just to see his name in the papers. Not Hay, who understood that he was in his official seat to do McKinley's bidding and that the president would not wish to give the slightest appearance that he was *asking* for quick settlement, not while the US Navy was kicking the stuffing out of Spain. It was up to the Sagasta government to come begging now.

John Hay had, however, gone to work on a different diplomatic front that evening, which bore surprising and unexpected fruit a few days later, when the Right Honorable Joseph Chamberlain, his monocle and orchid in place, gave a Friday evening speech in Birmingham. The colonial secretary had given neither Hay nor anyone else warning of his remarks, but Chamberlain's address to his hometown crowd would reverberate through all of Britain and into the capitals of Europe.

"A new situation has arisen," Chamberlain said. British commercial success, he went on to say, had engendered much jealousy and a fair measure of simple spite, and there were great powers allied in their hatred of the British who might see the value of working in combination to knock Her Majesty's empire from its lofty perch. Germany, Russia, and France came to mind. Chamberlain had already been at work welding the dominions and colonies into a bulwark of imperial defense, he explained, but perhaps this was not enough. "What is our next duty?" Chamberlain asked. "It is to establish and to maintain bonds of permanent amity with our kinsmen across the Atlantic." And here he paused, for the cheering was loud. And when he continued, his words rhymed perfectly with the expression of goodwill US ambassador John Hay had made at the recent Easter banquet. "They are a powerful and generous nation. They speak our language, they are bred of our race." Chamberlain was forced to pause again here, until more loud cheers faded away. "Their laws, their literature, their standpoint upon every question are the same as ours; their feeling, their interest in the cause of humanity and the peaceful development of the world are identical with ours."

Chamberlain did not have to remind the crowd that the American navy had recently shown itself to be a fighting force worth having on the British side of the skirmish line.

> I do not know what arrangements may be possible with [the United States], but this I know and feel—that the closer, the more cordial, the fuller, and the more definite these arrangements are, with the consent of both peoples, the better it will be for both and for the world. And I even go so far as to say that, terrible as war may be, even war itself would be cheaply purchased if in a great and noble cause the Stars and Stripes and the Union Jack should wave together—over an Anglo-Saxon alliance. Now, it is one of the most satisfactory results of Lord Salisbury's policy that at the present time these two great nations understand each other better than they have ever done since more than a century ago, when they were separated by the blunder of the British Government.

Americans all over London must have rubbed their eyes as they read the transcript of the speech on Saturday morning. Had he apologized for King George? The French were miffed at Chamberlain and feeling the wounds of a jilting. "If England had remained true to the French alliance, which is indispensible to her if she would retain her rank as the premier commercial, industrial, financial, and maritime Power, she would not have that concern to worry her," *La Liberté* pointed out. The Germans received the secretary's speech with "displeasure and contempt," correspondents reported. "They are astonished at Mr. Chamberlain's indiscretions; they despise his almost piteous appeals for help." Prime Minister Sagasta and his cabinet conferred and decided the speech was offensive to Spain and impudent. "Should an Anglo-American Alliance be brought about," they were reported to have said, "Spain will not be without friends in Europe."

There was a range of reaction in America and in England, but nobody could doubt where Chamberlain believed Britain's best interests lay and where America's did also. "That France, Germany, and Austria support Spain means less in this connection than that they impugn, and England alone credits, the sincerity of the United States motives," the *London Standard* observed three days after the speech, after reprinting a slew of cordial American editorial responses. "Mr. Chamberlain spoke at a juncture when events combine to convince Americans that their national morality has neither appreciation nor counterpart except in England."

Hay had by then started privately telling his friends—though never his bosses— that he deserved some credit for pushing Chamberlain. "It is hardly too much to say the interests of civilization are bound up in the direction the relations of England and America are to take in the next few months," Hay wrote in a private letter to Henry Cabot Lodge, a man he had been nudging toward a more charitable view of England. "Chamberlain's startling speech was partly due to a conversation I had with him, in which I hoped he would not let the opposition have a monopoly of expressions of good-will to America. He is greatly pleased with the reception his speech met with on our side, and says 'he don't care a hang what they say about it on the Continent.'"

Hay understood that the happy sentiments expressed by Joe Chamberlain owed in part also to Commodore Dewey's great show in the Far East, so near to China, where Her Majesty's government was looking for a little extra leverage to counter the strange intrigues of Kaiser Willie and Czar Nicky. He also understood that British men of affairs respected the display of power the American squadron had made at Manila Bay, which was why Hay was impatient for the United States to win this just-begun war in a hurry, before the major bleeding began. "A smashing blow in the Caribbean would help wonderfully," he told Cabot. "But an enemy determined not to fight can elude a battle a long time. And our hair is growing gray while we wait."

THE WAR WAS little more than a thousand shivers of anticipation for the weeks that followed. The United States Pacific Squadron was sitting in Manila Bay, waiting for a second Spanish flotilla to cruise through the Suez Canal for another run at Dewey. Meanwhile, Spanish admiral Pascual Cervera y Topete's squadron, recently stationed in Cuban waters, had disappeared into the Caribbean and could not be found. WHERE IS CERVERA? was a headline in newspapers across America. Nervous citizens up and down the Eastern Seaboard screamed for protection, in case Cervera's ships suddenly steamed up on the coast and started lobbing shells onto, say, Commercial Street in Boston. Cervera, for his own part, was not about to expose his depleted little fleet to enemy guns and had begun a pretty nifty game of keep-away from Admiral William T. Sampson's big battleships. Was Cervera in Haiti? The Dutch West Indies? The Gulf of Mexico? The Straits of Florida? US Navy ships went on the hunt, stopping on the way to pound on the Spanish fortifications at Puerto Rico, where the enemy put up no resistance worthy of newsprint. "The Spanish aim was so astoundingly bad," one reporter observed, "that absolutely no anxiety was felt for our ships." The whereabouts of Cervera's squadron, meanwhile, remained a mystery to the United States Navy.

The American military embarked on its own game of cat and mouse. Secretary Long played coy about the location of the biggest, baddest new battleship in the American fleet, the USS *Oregon*. Nobody could report for sure which hemisphere the *Oregon* was in. Then the War Department announced it was readying transport boats to haul infantry, artillery, and cavalry from Tampa, Florida, to Cuba. (Lieutenant Colonel Roosevelt was reported to have hugged Colonel Wood and danced a spirited jig when he got the happy news that his Rough Riders were to be in the first wave of invaders.) But the department intentionally exaggerated by double the size of the initial invasion force. And then, not much happened.

The war lull gave overstimulated watchers ample opportunity to celebrate the Battle of Manila Bay and all that it portended. As fuel for the hero machine, the victory was bunkerfuls of coal. Dewey was held up as a naval executive on par with men who already had statues, like Farragut and Nelson, and as an exemplar of "Anglo-Saxon valor." Congress fast-tracked special legislation raising the commodore to the rank of rear admiral, effective immediately—forget the usual knotty bureaucratic rigging.

SAM CLEMENS WAS beginning to be caught up in the national mission. He refused in spite of himself to believe that this war with Spain was propelled by nothing more than shabby selfishness. He showed no patience for ditherers back home like his old friend Charles Dudley Warner, who had become agitated at the Reverend Joe Twichell's sermon about the selflessness of a soldier fighting for a higher cause. Twichell had reported to Clemens that Warner told him afterward that he had been tempted to rise from his seat in the middle of the sermon and offer a motion to the congregation: "That, in consonance with the views just presented, we postpone the Christian religion to a more convenient season."

Clemens surprised his reverend friend by writing back that he was on Twichell's side all the way. "I have never enjoyed a war—even in written history—as I am enjoying this one," Clemens wrote to Twichell. "For this is the worthiest one that was ever fought, so far as my knowledge goes. It is a worthy thing to fight for one's own freedom; it is another sight finer to fight for another man's. And I think this is the first time it has been done."

"Mark Twain" popped up unexpectedly from Vienna with a note of praise for American military courage past, present, and future. While regretting that he could not attend a Decoration Day celebration in honor of the Civil War dead, America's best-known author made his thoughts on the current war public for the first time. "I thank you very much for your invitation, and I would accept it if I were foot-free," read his note, when it was published in the newspapers. "For I should value the privilege of helping you do honor to the men who re-welded our broken Union and consecrated their great work with their lives; and also I should like to be there to do homage to our soldiers and sailors of to-day who are enlisted for another most righteous war, and utter the hope that they may make short and decisive work of it and leave Cuba free and fed when they face for home again."

This statement brought a hail of editorial seconds. "Mark Twain, in his serious moments, has common-sense carried out to a high power," wrote an expatriate American in Europe, "however incapably he may have managed his commercial ventures."

THE BATTLE OF Manila Bay, as the *Washington Evening Star* noted, "put a new aspect on things," but it was a milky star with which to reckon a national future. Dewey's great victory had given the United States of America a grasp on a Spanish property seven thousand ocean miles away, but could the rear admiral hold it? The naval planners hadn't exactly thought through the aftermath of a sea battle in the Philippines. No American soldiers had accompanied the Asiatic Squadron across the Pacific, so Dewey had no troops to land in the colonial capital of the Philippines. "All the city at our Mercy," was how the rear admiral explained the situation in a personal letter to Ambassador John Hay. "If we had had five thousand troops we would have occupied Manila." All he could do was float in the bay, cut off supplies to the port of Manila, and await further developments. Instructions from the US capital about what to do next, or what to expect in the way of support, were few and far between, as was information from the rear admiral to the bosses back home about the condition of the squadron. How much ammunition did Dewey have left after the battle, they wondered, and how much coal? How long could he safely keep watch on his nation's first bargaining chip of the new war, especially considering the number of great powers who had important naval assets in the Far East?

England, Russia, and Germany each controlled a port on the nearby China coast. Japan had a powerful navy right next door. The nearest South Pacific port the United States could access was in Honolulu, which was more than five thousand miles away, twice as close to San Francisco as it was to Manila. And besides, America did not yet really *control* Hawaii. Nearly a year after McKinley's new treaty of annexation was signed by the *haoles* who had (with the help of the US Marines) grabbed the Hawaiian government from the elected queen, that treaty had not yet been reported out of the Senate Foreign Relations Committee for a floor vote, because McKinley's backers knew they didn't yet have the votes for ratification.

So with Dewey in his watery postvictory purgatory, McKinley and his war council made it plain that the United States needed the Hawaiian Islands as a place from which to recoal and resupply the Asiatic Squadron, and he threatened to seize them as a war measure if Congress wouldn't stand up and do its duty. McKinley's friends in the Senate were trying everything they could think of. They ran a work-around to the doomed treaty ratification vote, trying to attach annexation to a revenue bill, and then introducing a "Joint Resolution to Provide for Annexing the Hawaiian Islands to the United States." The opposition stood firm, but McKinley's backers did not relent, and there was no more ardent advocate for the annexation of Hawaii than Senator Henry Cabot Lodge, who had been thwarted in this tropical property transaction for more than three years.

Now, with the exigencies of war crystallizing the political atmosphere, Cabot could almost see the glorious vision of his "large policy" become real. The United States could have Hawaii, the Philippines, and a few other coal-bunkered stepping-stones to that greatest of all potential consumer markets, China, Cabot argued, then would come the canal through Nicaragua to join the two great oceans, and, voilà, the United States would be the central way station for the commerce of the entire globe. Taking Hawaii had always been a sound business proposition, Cabot had reminded his fellow senators on hearing the first rumors of Dewey's triumph, but now it was a matter of national dignity. "Here is our gallant Asiatic squadron fighting successfully to uphold the national standard in that faraway eastern country," Cabot had lamented on the floor of the Senate. "With all the foreign ports closed against us our only recourse is to ship a coal supply from San Francisco. How different would be the condition if Hawaii had been annexed to the United States before this war with Spain came on."

Cabot had to fight off some stark and logical arguments against his insistence on taking ownership of Hawaii right away as a matter of intelligent war strategy: there was no actual coaling station in the Hawaiian Islands, his opponents pointed out, and Pearl Harbor could not yet accommodate big warships; add to that, the United States already had a perfectly acceptable harbor in Unalaska, which was *five hundred miles closer* to Manila than was Honolulu. Cabot, up against the wall, was a bit incautious in divulging private intelligence provided to him about a particular European nation that was already intriguing to upset US plans in the Pacific. Kaiser Wilhelm was on the hunt, he insisted, and the United States just didn't have time to waste.

The legislative fight over Hawaii got hotter and hotter the longer Dewey sat stranded in his sultry bay half a world away, and pretty soon the debate on the Senate floor spiraled off into a discussion of the wide variety of territorial acquisitions that might soon come available. Ordinary caution against truth telling on the Senate floor boiled away under sun-beaten skylights; men exhibited a refreshing frankness, revealing a motive force in this war somewhat outside compassion and fellow feeling for those poor souls living under the yoke of Spanish rule—as when a gimlet-eyed senator from Alabama began totting up potential receipts.

> We shall have a good deal of [money], for the income of the government at Manila from importations alone is over $13,000,000 a year—a large sum to neglect. . . .
>
> When you get to Cuba what are you going to do, sir? We have been receiving from Cuba $90,000,000 a year of her productions. It may not be two years until she will get back to the point of production, when she can again supply us with $90,000,000, after we get possession and restore peace and order and that country is open to the migration of our people, who will go there in swarms.

And while we're speaking of Cuba, said Senator Stephen Benton Elkins of West Virginia, "We *are* going to take the Island of Cuba, and not pay any debts to anybody or for anybody, not to the Cuban Junta in New York either, and we are going to keep the island, I hope we will."

"We said we would not keep it," interrupted another senator, who had the record of earlier proceedings and the war resolution to back him up on that point.

"I know we did, but we did not mean it—not one of us. Er, two or three meant it."

"It was a lie?"

"I do not know," said Senator Elkins, "whether the Senate understands such language."

WHITELAW REID, WHOSE eye was focused on the spoils due a deserving nation, gave a talk in New York that same week and sent his friend John Hay a bound pamphlet containing his speech. "The war is upon us," Whitelaw had said, before implying that it was time for Americans to start learning how to be colonial masters, like our fine cousins in Great Britain. "Whether we are right or wrong, at any rate we are at war for our institutions and must face the future, whether we like it or not. We cannot exert, we cannot possess our power and evade its responsibilities, whether in Cuba or the Philippines."

Hay answered Reid right away, praising his old friend for his wisdom and his eloquence, but suggesting that maybe the United States did not lack for income-generating properties as things stood. “It seems to me we are in a tide of enormous prosperity—greater than anybody has any idea of,” Hay suggested to Reid. “We quarrel and row among ourselves so that it is hard to recognize how well we are governed, what a portentous prosperity we present to the rest of the world. Europe can hardly owe us today less than four hundred million dollars. Our Treasury overflows. We carry without staggering the awful and scandalous weight of our pensions—the marvel of nations. Heaven grant we do not lose our heads.”

CHAPTER TWENTY-TWO

You Hold the Game in Your Own Hands

John Hay hoped to help end the war before it took a serious toll, which seemed doable at the beginning of June. The US Navy had taken the main harbors of the Philippines and Puerto Rico without losing a single ship and had finally located Admiral Cervera's fleet bobbing gently off the southeastern corner of Cuba, outside the city of Santiago de Cuba, in Guantánamo Bay. Those Spanish ships were now in the vice of Admiral Sampson's big battleships and Commodore Winfield Scott Schley's Flying Squadron. Theodore and his volunteers, along with the rest of the American invasion force, were still onshore in Tampa, tucked away safe and sound but for the perils of thunderstorms, mosquitoes, putrefied meat, and liquored-up comrades with government-issue weapons.

The Spanish army in Cuba, after three years of tangling with yellow fever and *insurrectos*, was a ragged bunch. The soldiers hadn't received proper rations or pay for nine months, and it looked as if things would only get worse for those troops. The first tremors of war had cleaved the Spanish political factions in Madrid; they were now feuding openly and were unable to supply resources to their soldiers in the field.

The pressure on Spain was made worse by a new fighting force around Manila, where Dewey's sea victory had inspired a restart of the Philippine Revolution. Led by the charismatic young Emilio Aguinaldo, whom Dewey had supplied with extra guns and ammunition, the revolutionaries were already closing in on the city. Hay could track the Filipino movements in the London newspapers every day. The rebels were mauling Spanish outposts around Manila, killing colonial soldiers by the hundreds, and taking thousands more as prisoners. The *insurrectos* were within seven miles of the city and fighting with increasing ferocity as they neared Manila. "There was sharp hand-to-hand fighting for seventy hours, despite a typhoon which was blowing," according to wire reports in the London papers. "A violent gale is blowing to-day and torrents of rain are falling, rendering rifles of the troops almost useless. The natives easily get into close quarters with the Spaniards, and win at every step, slashing fiercely with their knives."

The Spanish military governor, according to the newspapers, was worried enough to put a $25,000 bounty on Aguinaldo's head. "Aguinaldo has succeeded in raising the country," read an official dispatch from General Basilio Augustin y Dávila in Manila back home to Madrid. "I am trying to keep up the courage of the inhabitants, and I shall employ every means to urge them to resist. But I distrust the natives and the Volunteers, for numbers of desertions have already taken place. The Insurrection is powerful, and if I cannot rely on the country's support, the Forces at my disposal will not be sufficient to cope with two enemies." If the Spanish had any sense, McKinley and his State Department figured, they would ask for peace terms within the week.

HAY FORESAW COMPLICATIONS beyond bloody casualties if the war was prolonged. Kaiser Wilhelm was his biggest concern. Hay had been taking the measure of the German emperor for a few years now. John Bigelow's son Poultney, who had been a boyhood classmate of the kaiser's in Germany and remained in touch, had plenty to say. "The Prussians were trained to believe that courtesy was synonym for weakness and that it was the duty of a strong man to beat and rob a weaker one," Poultney would write in his study of the kaiser.

Wilhelm was just beginning to extend his imperial wingspread in 1898. He had grabbed his first port in China and was in the market for more property in the Far East, and no one in the German government was strong enough to check him. *Regis voluntas suprema lex*, the kaiser liked to say. "I recognize no Constitution or Parliament—my word alone is law!" was how Poultney translated it. "He was never weary of reminding his subjects that *his* will was law, because *he* was divine; and therefore disobedience to his will was tantamount to sacrilege."

Hay was also getting reports of Wilhelm from his friend Cecil Spring Rice, now the second secretary of the British Embassy in Berlin. Springy was watching the German government in operation from his office on Kaiser Wilhelm Strasse and full of confidential warnings for Ambassador Hay. The kaiser had been speaking scathingly of McKinley and the United States behind closed doors and, as Springy confided, had been intriguing with other European powers since before the war began. "He has also been saying that England should lead a continental alliance to punish the Transatlantics for their insolence," Spring Rice wrote to Hay. Springy also educated Hay on the German practice of skulking around the edges of other people's wars in hopes of grabbing off a piece of the spoils for themselves, calling it compensation for commercial losses. They had done this with success in the Sino-Japanese War and in the more recent fight, which the kaiser had encouraged, between the Turks and the Greeks in Crete.

The German navy was already preparing to send a contingent of warships out to the Philippines and neighboring islands. The kaiser would not pick a fight with the United States unless Dewey's squadron was in dire straits, Spring Rice assured Hay, but they would be out there trolling the waters, just to see what they could get. And watch out for a move by Germany to try to draw France, Russia, and even Japan into a combination capable of checking any show of American power in the Pacific. The United States had better hurry up and annex Hawaii while there was no serious international opposition, Spring Rice advised.

Hay made it a rule to pass the information contained in private letters from Spring Rice ("an excellent authority," Hay called him) to President McKinley and Secretary Day almost verbatim. On a cool, gray Saturday morning in early June, Hay sat down at his desk at Carlton House Terrace to recapitulate for Judge Day Springy's most recent epistle.

> [The Germans] are very much occupied about the distribution of spoil which they imagine will take place after the war is won. Germany is very jealous lest France or England should get the Philippines. . . . Germany is very restive under the Monroe Doctrine. They would like a foothold in South America—in Brazil or Argentina—& might suggest it, if we kept the Philippines.
>
> One of the unfortunate results of the action of the Senate in regard to Hawaii will be that when—sooner or later—we do annex the islands, Germany will want Samoa, or something else, as compensation. Hawaii has always been regarded in Europe as within our sphere of influence, as ultimately ours. The opposition in the Senate is teaching them how to think otherwise.

Hay might have ended the letter there, but this was no time to be circumspect. The newspapers in London that morning contained reports out of New York that American troops had been dispatched to Santiago de Cuba; from Jamaica came rumors that a fleet of Spanish battleships and torpedo boats—sixteen vessels in all—had left Cádiz to reinforce Cervera's squadron in Cuba. He had no business sticking his nose into war strategy, Hay confessed to Day, but he did it anyway. He suggested that Day tell the president it would be best to hold off on the ground invasion in Cuba and let the navy pick off a few more of Spain's haphazardly defended island colonies, like the Canary Islands, until the Spanish Treasury was bled so dry that they would voluntarily walk away from Cuba. This might, Hay told Day,

> save us the terrible expense of life and money which the conquest of the island would cost. Our advices from Madrid show that the intelligent men in the government are anxious for peace, if they can see their way to making it without personal and political harm.
>
> Please excuse the personal letter. I wanted to say these things to you and they are hardly suited to a formal dispatch.

The ambassador was just finishing his letter when Spencer Eddy came in with a new cable from Secretary Day in Washington. The president wanted Hay to know, confidentially, what terms of peace might be acceptable if Spain got the notion to propose them. McKinley expected Spain to get out of Cuba and leave the protection of the Cuban people to the United States; he also wanted the Sagasta government to hand over Puerto Rico, in lieu of the cash indemnity Spain would be unable to pay. The president was willing to give the Philippines back to Spain, except for a port and coaling station, but he also wanted Spain to cede a second naval port and coaling station somewhere between Honolulu and Manila.

Hay scrawled a hasty PS on top of his morning's letter: "I have this instant received your cable dispatch about terms. I have no time to express my admiration. They are, to my mind, perfectly wise and noble. They do honor to us and to civilization." Then he went to work to see whether he could make peace happen.

First thing Monday morning, the ambassador called on Prime Minister Salisbury at the Foreign Office. Hay assured the marquess he was speaking unofficially and hypothetically only and presented the outlines of the president's thoughts regarding a peace proposal. Hay assured him that McKinley, as commander in chief of the armed forces, could stop war operations whenever he desired, and he was prepared to do so if Spain asked for mercy. But, Hay added, the president might not be in this magnanimous mood for long.

Lord Salisbury made discreet inquiries of Spain through the Austrian Foreign Ministry and received scant encouragement. Spanish honor, the prime minister was told, prevented their asking for any terms.

WHEN VICE ADMIRAL Otto von Diederichs sailed for Manila Bay in early June 1898 to keep watch on German citizens and German property in the Philippines, he carried orders from Kaiser Wilhelm to observe strict neutrality and to refrain from interfering with American military operations. The German presence, the kaiser believed, should not be a cause of undue alarm in Washington. Germany and the other neutrals had the right, acknowledged by the United States, to provide protection for their nationals in the Philippines and to stand ready to evacuate them in the case of serious military action. The British, the Japanese, the Austro-Hungarians, and the French had all sent ships in and out of Manila Bay in the six weeks since Dewey had set up his blockade. But the kaiser, whatever the substance of his orders, stood apart from the others. Wilhelm had dispatched to the war zone of the Philippines not only an officer who outranked the American commander in charge of the bay but also *five* armored cruisers. The German fleet steaming toward the bay was potentially stronger than Dewey's and capable many times over of defending the single German commercial house in Manila. When Dewey noted this strange fact on first meeting, von Diederichs's curt answer—"I am here by order of the Kaiser, sir"—did not sound particularly amicable.

Dewey's nerves were already frayed. He and his men had been living on their ships in Manila Bay for six long weeks, suffering in the unrelenting, sweltering heat, short on fuel, food, and matériel. Dewey's gunners had expended six thousand shots to make 141 hits on Spanish targets in their great victory, leaving him, as he noted, "without sufficient ammunition to meet the emergencies of an engagement." The asked-for contingent of US soldiers and a resupply of coal and ammunition were still weeks away. Meanwhile, Washington had just sent warning to Dewey that a Spanish squadron of "two armored cruisers, six converted cruisers, four destroyers" might be headed his way. Dewey's fast-track promotion to rear admiral was a welcome honor, but it did nothing to alter the fact that his head was in a tropical vice. He and his men were seven thousand miles from home, information from Washington was out of date by the time it arrived, and the admiral still lacked specific instructions as to how to proceed in the Philippines. He was in desperate need of guidance. Basilio Augustin y Dávila, the Spanish governor-general in Manila, had grown so embarrassed by the success of Aguinaldo's rebels that he had begun begging Dewey to hurry up and take charge of the city. Failing that, officials in Madrid wanted England to take over in Manila—anything to keep Aguinaldo and his men from overrunning the capital. President McKinley, meanwhile, had only recently been able to find the Philippines on a map and was not yet capable of telling Dewey what the United States meant to do with the Spanish colony.

The arrival of Vice Admiral von Diederichs and his German flotilla churned the Philippine waters anew. The besieged governor-general in Manila began suggesting to his new friend Otto that Germany take over the protection of the city, and even though von Diederichs wisely demurred, Augustin started to show a little backbone. He made a surprising public U-turn and pronounced his colonial forces ready to face the thirty thousand rifles and one hundred thousand clubs in rebel hands. "An emissary from Aguinaldo has been sent to me to urge surrender of the city in order to avoid the sacrifice of life," Augustin cabled back to Madrid, "but I refused to listen to his message, as I am determined to maintain the sovereignty of Spain and the honour of the Flag."

JOHN HAY SUSPECTED the kaiser would never risk a real fight, especially with the British navy nearby, but he didn't much like what he was reading in the morning newspapers. "Once again such influential papers as the *Heraldo*, *Imparcial*, *El Liberal*, and *Correspondencia* are doing their best to make the people believe that a German naval demonstration at Manila against an American bombardment, or a landing in concert with Aguinaldo, is imminent," the Madrid correspondent of the *London Standard* reported shortly after von Diederichs's arrival. "It is supposed that Germany will invoke the necessity of protecting the lives, properties, and commercial interests of her subjects in the Spanish Archipelagoes."

The situation in the Pacific occasioned a new set of instructions from Washington to Hay in the second week of June, which sent him back to the Foreign Office to confer again with Lord Salisbury. Conditions in the Philippines had changed and so had the president's unspoken peace terms, Hay explained to the prime minister. McKinley wished to reserve the right to dispose of the Philippines however he saw fit. Salisbury continued to assure Hay that the United States could do as it wished in the Philippines and that the kaiser would get no help or encouragement from anybody at Whitehall. Her Majesty's government only wanted to help, so Hay's job was getting easy. But there was an interesting new turn in the president's thinking with regard to the Philippines, and one Hay had noted. "[Aguinaldo's] insurgents," read the updated instruction from the State Department, "have become an important factor in the situation and must have just consideration in any settlement."

IT DID NOT surprise John Hay to learn that his closest friend at the State Department in Washington, Second Assistant Secretary Alvey Adee, was spending most nights at his office at the State, War, and Navy Building, one door down from the White House. Adee was a twenty-year fixture at the State Department by 1898. Though he had never had any personal champions or backers with significant political pull, Alvey had, through a long and consistent display of competence, made himself indispensible. He was the institutional memory, keeper of all state protocol, and possessor of much of the brainpower in the thinly staffed department. Secretaries of state had come and gone in Adee's tenure, and even in a crisis the bosses generally slept fairly soundly in their own beds, because they knew Alvey would be on the case, as he was, yet again. Poor put-upon Adee had planned to be on his annual European bicycle trip that June, taking a leisurely spin along the Swiss Rhine, but he was instead at his desk day and night while the country was at war, sleeping fitfully on a cot in his office, ready at all hours to decipher incoming cables from any and all embassies.

This meant that Alvey Adee was the closest thing the United States foreign service had to a national nerve center. He knew the contours of American military movements and of American diplomacy across the globe at a given moment better than any man, and what he told John Hay about the near future was disheartening. "I have not shared the popular delusion that the present troubles will be of briefer duration, or as General Sickles expressed himself one day last winter that it would be a 'damned short war!'" Adee wrote to Hay on June 23, 1898, the day after American soldiers landed near Santiago de Cuba. "On the other hand, I hardly go so far as the Swedish Minister, Mr. Grip, who, in condoling with me the other day upon the loss of my summer vacation, said, 'Ferry vell, you vill not be too olt to dake it fife years hence.'"

NOTHING ABOUT THE preparation for the ground war in Cuba had promised clean and easy victory; even without harassment from an enemy, the invading force appeared a senseless lot to the veteran war correspondents at the training camps in Florida. "In no army of Europe, not even in Spain, have I seen troops so badly treated through the incompetence of staff officers, who to-day are strutting about in new uniforms, when they ought to be whistled out of camps as frauds," Poultney Bigelow wrote for publication from camp, about the numerous politically appointed commanders. "To-day, thirty days after the declaration of war, there has not been held at Tampa a single military field exercise likely to be of service to generals of brigade or division, let alone an army corps. The main reason is, no doubt, that there are no brigadiers or major-generals in Tampa who would know how to go to work in the matter."

Lieutenant Colonel Roosevelt's correspondent friend Richard Harding Davis took the War Department line, attacking Poultney as a malcontent who might be subject to official punishment: "This is no time to print news of such a nature, and it is certainly not the time now, or later, to print reckless and untrue statements concerning our regular army."

In private letters home, though, Davis was singing Poultney's tune. "The Greek army, at which I made such sport, is a fine organization in comparison as far as outfit goes," he wrote the week before Bigelow's article appeared in print.

> One colonel of the Florida regiment told us that one-third of his men had never fired a gun. They live on the ground; there are no rain trenches around tents, or gutters along the company streets; the latrines are dug to *windward* of the camp, and all the refuse is burned to windward. Half of the men have no uniform or shoes.
>
> I pointed out some of the unnecessary discomforts the men were undergoing through ignorance, and one colonel, a Michigan politician, said, "Oh, well, they'll learn. It will be a good lesson for them." Instead of telling them, or telling their captains, he thinks it best that they should find things out by suffering.

The embarkation of the American troops bound for southeast Cuba was no more confidence inspiring. American transport ships—full of suffering soldiers—sat idle in the steamy weather off Tampa for a few extra days, held up by rumors of Spanish warships lying in wait. The holds of the ships were so overheated that *mules* keeled over and died. "It is worse than the French at Sedan," Davis wrote, again privately. "We are just amateurs at war and about like the Indians Columbus discovered."

Early press dispatches that followed the US landing at Daiquirí, Cuba, which was a twenty-mile hike from the target city of Santiago de Cuba, suggested the beginning of what John Hay feared: a long and wasteful slog through a tropical hell. Theodore and his Rough Riders got a lot of newspaper ink the first day out, June 24, 1898, on the initial push toward Santiago de Cuba—not all of it good. Lieutenant Colonel Roosevelt had apparently put his mark on his line officers and his troopers. "With careless disregard of Military precautions Roosevelt's Rough Riders, who headed the party, noisily went forward, talking volubly as they made their way along a narrow woodland road," the *Morning Post* of London reported. "Suddenly a withering fire was poured into them from both sides by the Spaniards, who had carefully prepared an ambush."

Ten of the Rough Riders were mowed down in a few curdling and disorienting minutes. Roosevelt's were bailed out by some regular army outfits, and after a few hours' hard fighting, the Americans had cleared the enemy gun positions on the high ground and set the Spanish to a hasty retreat. When the day was done, American soldiers could sight Santiago de Cuba from the heights they now held. But they were still five miles out, the Spanish defenses were only going to be stronger as they neared the city, and the first little victory had cost plenty.

Richard Harding Davis had been along for the ride with Theodore's unit that day; he heard all around him during the battle the dull suck of bullets in flesh, and later that afternoon he came across a dead American whose eyes and lips had been plucked away by vultures. There were reports of numerous hurried amputations, a bloody restaging of the old Civil War limb toss Hay had witnessed thirty-five years earlier. At least fifty Americans had been wounded in the ambush and the fight that followed; ten of those were expected to die. More than a dozen US soldiers had died on the battlefield. The ground war was only a few hours old.

TORRENTIAL DOWNPOURS STARTED in Cuba a few days later, three inches of rain an hour every afternoon. Hot and itchy uniforms became hot, itchy, and wet. The muddied wagon roads into Santiago de Cuba turned treacherous. Nervous soldiers took to smoking a confection of grass, roots, and dried horse turds. The American army seemed to Hay and most other observers in London to be in danger of sliding down a slippery slope in Cuba—and evidence suggested a long slide. The ambassador's son was graduating from Yale that week, and Hay had made a temporary and unofficial place for him to work at the embassy in London. But what if the war dragged on? Would Del Hay catch the war fever like some of his friends and classmates who had already volunteered for service?

John Hay was doing what little he could for American soldiers and sailors on his visits to the Foreign Office in London. Would the British consul in Havana, Hay asked, be willing to inquire as to the treatment of American navy men held prisoner in Cuba? Would Great Britain permit passage of American warships through the Suez Canal? Would Her Majesty's government see to it that the Spanish fleet now in Port Said, Egypt, was not supplied with coal enough to make it to the Philippines? And how about refusing coal to any Spanish ships that might try to get fuel in British Jamaica?

Hay was suffering stabbing pains in his lower back those last few days of June and was uncharacteristically prickly. Henry Adams, back in London, found him distracted and distant. When the ambassador made it plain that he was not interested in advice on diplomacy and treaty making from his old friend, Adams bolted for the estate Lizzie Cameron and her now reconciled husband were renting in the English countryside—a two-hour journey from the action in London. So Adams would be spending the next month in the company of the darling Lizzie Cameron, and Hay would be stuck at his desk in the London heat.

As American Independence Day approached, and the Hays prepared for another reception at Carlton House Terrace, the happenings in the advance on Santiago de Cuba filled the newspaper columns in London. US regulars and volunteers had started an attack around dawn on July 1, 1898, and the first reports, which came from American command headquarters twelve miles behind the action, were hopeful: US soldiers had fought to within three-quarters of a mile of the city; more than fourteen thousand Americans and four thousand of their Cuban allies were on the line and preparing another day's push; US gunboats had pummeled the Spanish fortifications near the city; the American flag, it was predicted, would be flying over Santiago de Cuba in forty-eight hours.

When the actual details from the front lines began to emerge, the situation seemed far less rosy. A "storm of shot" from the Spanish army's rapid-fire artillery guns and "murderous hail from Mauser rifles" had felled hundreds of advancing US soldiers. A member of the Twenty-Fourth Infantry Regiment had been hacked to death with a machete. Two commanding generals had come unglued and were packing it in for a while; a third had been shot in the foot by Spanish raiders. The corpulent walrus-faced commander of the invasion force, General William Rufus Shafter, was finally forced to admit that the first day was a "drawn battle." He reported four hundred casualties, though with the happy caveat that there had been few deaths. Less than twelve hours later, Shafter sent an update. "I fear I have under-estimated to-day's casualties," he wrote. "A large and thoroughly equipped hospital ship should be sent here at once to care for the wounded." There were more than a thousand dead or wounded. An addition of forty or fifty extra army surgeons, Shafter said, might be a welcome thing.

THE STORY OF that ugly day, July 1, 1898, would become the central chapter of the Teddy Roosevelt myth. Later accounts of the rough-riding Roosevelt's courage under fire would be stirring. He did stand out. When Theodore led the charge against a lightly defended and minor strategic position called Kettle Hill, first on horseback and then on foot, he was, thanks largely to the tailors at Brooks Brothers, exceptionally well accessorized. "Roosevelt, mounted high on horseback, and charging the rifle-pits at a gallop and quite alone, made you feel that you would like to cheer," wrote Richard Harding Davis, whom Theodore had hosted and fed in style in his troop camp. "He wore on his sombrero a blue polka-dot handkerchief, *à la* Havelock, which, as he advanced, floated out straight behind his head, like a guidon."

Davis's initial reporting had done much for Theodore's reputation, but Roosevelt would set down his own chronicle of that day, too; Theodore was actually a much better writer and storyteller than he ever was a soldier or public servant or racial theorist, and he deftly rendered the seduction of battle: the sound of bullets cutting the air around him, "like the ripping of a silk dress," the exalted feeling of sending men "where death might smite them." He boasted in print of being the highest-ranking American officer to have bagged a Spanish soldier, though in the immediate sweaty aftermath of the fight he had been uncertain about the propriety of taking credit for shooting a fleeing man in the back.

He would also take the opportunity in various tellings to aggrandize the white soldier at the expense of African American cavalrymen (some of whom had saved his Anglo-Saxon ass) and also went out of his way to disparage Cuban soldiers, who had been living off the land and getting the better of the Spanish military for nearly three years. "A crew of as utter tatterdemalions as human eyes ever looked on," Theodore said of the island's rebel forces. "It was evident, at a glance, that they would be no use in serious fighting."

One of Theodore's troopers would describe the scene of his lieutenant colonel standing triumphantly over the dead Spaniards at the end of the fighting on July 1. "Theodore," he wrote in a letter to Mrs. Roosevelt, "was just reveling in victory and gore." Another would recall Roosevelt's spirited dash earlier that day. Dismounted and on the run with his sword slapping uncomfortably at his legs, the lieutenant colonel had turned to the soldier running beside him: "Holy Godfrey," he wailed, "what fun!"

Theodore's contemporaneous letters, however, were of a different stripe, especially in the two days that followed his charge up Kettle Hill. Pinned down in trenches a mile from Santiago de Cuba, lacking food and clean water, under fire from secluded and entrenched enemy gunners, Roosevelt, sensing a "terrible military disaster" unfolding around him, was near panic. "For God's sake," he scrawled out in a note to Henry Cabot Lodge on July 3, "have heavy reinforcements sent us instantly."

Lieutenant Colonel Roosevelt could see but a small, wet pointillist's dot of the Santiago de Cuba campaign, but it was suggestive of the bigger picture of the ground war. General Shafter's same-day dispatch to his bosses in Washington, which hit the London papers on the morning of July 4, said it all. "The gloomy forebodings which have been depressing everybody here for the past twenty-four hours were fulfilled early this afternoon," wrote the American correspondent of the *Daily News*, "when the War Department received the message from General Shafter saying that he would be unable to take Santiago by storm with his present forces. This is regarded as a virtual repulse, instead of the speedy victory which was so confidently anticipated. Every effort will be made to hurry reinforcements to General Shafter, but a delay of several days is regarded as inevitable."

THE DOWNHEARTED TENOR of the far-off news changed on a dime later that Independence Day, when the word came of another great United States naval rout. It had happened on the same morning Roosevelt sat panicking in his muddy trench, a few miles from the scene of victory. The Spanish admiral Cervera, under orders from General Blanco in Havana to *do something*, had noticed a small change in the US blockade line on the morning of July 3. The USS *Massachusetts* was already off-line getting a resupply of coal, and then Cervera saw Admiral Sampson's *New York* steam away. (Sampson had been called to a meeting with Shafter and decided to go over in his flagship instead of hopping on a smaller conveyance.) Cervera, noting the rare instance of having two of the biggest US warships off-line, made a break for open waters.

So shocked was the US squadron at Cervera's sudden and unexpected move that the American ships got crosswise. When Commodore Schley set the *Brooklyn* on a wide, arcing circle to give himself sea room for the fight, he narrowly missed colliding his armored cruiser with the maneuvering *Texas*. The only US ship to have taken the precaution of keeping her steam up and ready for battle at all times, the mighty *Oregon*, made its own quick turn to chase Cervera's four cruisers and two torpedo boats and nearly ran through both the *Iowa* and the *Texas*.

Once the American ships managed to get settled into an improvised battle formation, though, they made short work of Cervera's little contingent. Admiral Sampson watched the battle commence at a distance, and by the time he got the *New York* turned around and back to the action, the fight was all but finished. The four Spanish cruisers had been driven aground and were aflame; Cervera's two torpedo boats were sinking to the ocean floor. Sampson's latecoming flagship managed to get off only three of the nine thousand shots fired at Spanish ships, but the squadron commander did get to sign and send the dispatch announcing the great victory: "The fleet under my command offers the nation as a Fourth of July present the whole of Cervera's fleet."

The day's casualty figures were similar to Dewey's at Manila Bay: nearly every one of Cervera's twenty-two hundred officers and crewmen were killed, wounded, or captured. Only one American sailor had been killed; two were wounded. Captain Mahan, now serving on Secretary Long's naval war board in Washington, was almost embarrassed by the rout. "It is not likely," he said, "that the United States will ever again be confronted with an enemy as inapt as Spain proved to be." But John Hay, for one, was able to stand up in London on Independence Day and shout victory.

> To how many people today the thought must have occurred—how fortune seems to favor this day of all days in the year; how history seems determined to regild it from time to time, consecrating it anew to glory and use. First in Philadelphia in 1776; then in 1863 a double splendor lighted upon it, illuminating a continent from Vicksburg to Gettysburg; and now

the world is spanned with its brilliancy from Santiago to Manila, from the Antilles to the Antipodes.

This year all omens are with us.

THE SPANISH ARMY in Santiago de Cuba had no real heart for a fight after the squadron defending Cuba had been wasted. Less than two weeks later, after a short truce to allow foreigners time to leave the city and the Havana-to-Madrid-to-Washington-to-Madrid-to-Santiago dickering that delayed capitulation, the Spanish laid down their arms. The American army waltzed undisturbed into Santiago de Cuba on July 17, 1898, to take part in the surrender ceremony. The Cuban revolutionary forces, however, were not invited to this fete, which was a tad insulting to them, because the ceremony seemed to mark, at least nominally, the beginning of Cuban independence, for which some of these men had been fighting for decades. This insult drew the ire of Cuban general Calixto García. "A rumor, too absurd to be believed, ascribes the reason for your measure and of the orders forbidding my army to enter Santiago, to fear of massacres and revenge against the Spaniards," he wrote to General Shafter. "Allow me, sir, to protest against even the shadow of such an idea. We are not savages ignoring the rules of civilized warfare. We are a poor, ragged Army, as ragged and poor as the Army of your forefathers in their noble war for the Independence, but as [did] the heroes of Saratoga and Yorktown, we respect too deeply our cause to disgrace it with barbarism and cowardice." This plea had little effect; neither the Cuban general nor his soldiers were allowed into Santiago de Cuba to witness the Spanish surrender.

The next day the Sagasta government in Madrid asked for a halt to the fighting everywhere—including in Puerto Rico and the Philippines—to begin peace negotiations. McKinley said he would take it under consideration. The fight was all but over; the ground war had lasted a few weeks.

THERE WERE MANY glad tidings for Ambassador Hay that week. On the strictly personal front, he had just received a delicious letter from Lizzie Cameron, a secret crush of John Hay's. Lizzie's latest epistle displayed coquettishness and a breathily solicitous prose beyond Mrs. Hay's matronly ambit. Mrs. Cameron had clearly been keeping tabs on Hay. "[I] thought about your cold, which worries me," she wrote. "I do not like a summer cold to establish itself if it's too serious. Come down here. The country is sweet, the air pure, there is nothing to think of and nothing to do and we will all charm you and delight in you and serve you. Judge [Oliver Wendell] Holmes has made himself delightful, and his visit was too short. Abigail is here, and we are looking in every direction for Brooks [Adams, Henry's brother]—But the one person we really want is *you*. Do come."

On the business front, Hay was intrigued by a summons to a rare meeting with the reclusive German ambassador in London, who was himself surprisingly coquettish and solicitous that day. So it was with growing pleasure and amusement that Ambassador Hay sat quietly and listened as Count von Hatzfeldt tried to convince him of the German government's friendly attitude and intentions toward the United States, most particularly in the vicinity of the Philippines. All the kaiser desired, the count insisted, was a few little coaling stations here and there and maybe a naval base somewhere.

Hay cabled an official account of his meeting with the count to Judge Day and then sent a separate private letter to McKinley. Germany was no concern, Hay assured him. So long as the president adopted a friendly tone in his language toward Germany, they would take whatever scraps the United States deigned to give them. "In fact I am rejoiced to say that you hold the game in your own hands," Hay wrote to the president. "Your wisdom, prudence, and political sense have steered us safely through all the initial dangers of our position. You can now make war, or make peace, without danger of disturbing the equilibrium of the world. I congratulate you with all my heart on this great and bloodless victory at Santiago. It is your work, and you and your friends have the right to be proud of it. That we have escaped the double peril of disease through delay and of needless slaughter by assault, is due, as everyone said, to your wisdom and your courage. . . . As to the coming parley of peace I am sure you will keep the golden mean between too much liberality and too much rapacity, and will make a peace as glorious as the war has been."

THE OTHER PLEASING follow-up to the sea victory in Cuba was the fixing of President McKinley's signature, on July 7, 1898, to the "Joint Resolution to Provide for Annexing the Hawaiian Islands to the United States." The McKinley administration and its backers simply elided the Senate's inconvenient failure to ratify the proposed treaty of annexation. The joint resolution only required a majority, not the two-thirds vote necessary for a treaty. So Hawaii was now the property of the United States of America, signed, sealed, and delivered. The British Empire tipped its cap in respect. Japan acceded without argument once the United States promised to respect the rights of its citizens in the islands and to force the expiring Republic of Hawaii to make good on its debts to the Japanese government. The Germans kept their traps shut. The only formal complaint came from the disenfranchised Native Hawaiians and the many other supporters of a democratically elected queen who had been overthrown five and a half years earlier—with the help of the United States minister in Honolulu, an American gunship, and the cannon-wielding US Marines:

> WHEREAS: By memorial the people of Hawaii have protested against the consummation of an invasion of their political rights, and have fervently appealed to the President, the Congress and the People of the United States to refrain from further participating in the wrongful annexation of Hawaii; and
>
> WHEREAS: The Declaration of American Independence expresses that Governments derive their just powers from the consent of the governed; Therefore, Be it
>
> RESOLVED: That as the representatives of a large and influential body of native Hawaiians, we solemnly protest against annexation in the manner proposed and without reference to or obtaining the consent of the people of the Hawaiian Islands.

This Hawaiian protest, like the protest from General Calixto García at Santiago de Cuba, was waved away as inconsequential in most quarters of official Washington and laughed at in others. Who had time for these shenanigans? The Cuban army invoking the American Revolutionary War heroes of Saratoga and Yorktown? Native Hawaiians quoting the Declaration of Independence about the consent of the governed? If the best argument these poor benighted souls could make for just treatment from America was based on American history and American ideals, they had already lost the case.

CHAPTER TWENTY-THREE

A Larger Orbe Than My Ambition Doth Stretch Unto

John Hay had learned to live with the dull generalities of his physical afflictions—malaise, blurred vision, ringing in the ears, headaches—but the slicing pains in his lower back and hips were a disturbing new wrinkle. These searing spasms were draining him of strength and stamina, as were the demands of his ambassadorship, which were not so much difficult as they were unrelenting. His Vandyke was a little whiter; the creases in his forehead were a little deeper. "I am afraid that just now your official duties are no sinecure," an English friend told Hay. The doctors in London suspected the ambassador's ailment was located in the kidneys, or the lower spine, or the prostate. The best treatment in any case was rest, which was exactly what John Hay intended to get in the late summer and early fall of 1898, now that the Spanish seemed to be resigned to defeat.

Hay would not repeat his holiday itinerary of the previous September, a full month in the Scottish Highlands, courtesy of a dozen or more dine-and-sleep invitations from dukes and earls and baronets. John Hay was seeking instead a respite that might truly refresh and restore, while promising minimal movement and even less arranging. His entire family was on hand, having gathered at Carlton House Terrace at the end of July. Clara and his two daughters had been under foot since the return from the Nile, and Clarence and Del, his new Yale baccalaureate in hand, had sailed into England that month. Hay much preferred the ease of a quiet retreat in the nearby countryside to the complications of dragging the five of them all over the British Isles or onto the Continent.

The official line as given to the newspapers in London was that the ambassador felt obliged to remain within a few hours' journey of his embassy and the British Foreign Office. "His Excellency's position," it was noted, "may be important in the negotiations that may take place for peace with Spain, and he will not go far afield on that account." The matter was, in point of fact, as much personal as professional. "I am a ghastly wreck and nothing but Surrenden air will bring me round," Hay wrote to Lizzie Cameron, who had been begging him to move into her grand summer rental—an enormous country estate just a few hours by train from London. Lizzie and her husband, now retired from his Senate seat, and Henry Adams, not yet retired from his campaign of wooing Mrs. Cameron, had set up their odd little household at the seat of one of the oldest baronetcies of the county of Kent at the end of June. Mrs. Cameron, *La Dona*, the bewitching temporary chatelaine of Surrenden Dering, was the true air and atmosphere Hay was seeking. He had been itching to be in Lizzie's company since her earliest entreaty, though it was August before he finally felt it safe to be away from the office.

Hay planned to settle in at Surrenden Dering for a month, doing what work was required of him in the library of the manor house and using the telegraph office up the road at Pluckley for urgent communications with his embassy or the State Department or the White House. The ambassador sent his family down early, and on Friday, August 12, the day the British Parliament decamped and Prime Minister Salisbury settled in for another of his "cures" in France, John Hay headed out for what was to be a long, peaceful, and restorative country sojourn.

The place held promise, Hay could tell as they drove him inside the Surrenden Park walls, past the ivy-covered hunting lodge and stables and through the sculpted hedgerows and gardens and spreading oaks to the magnificent redbrick Elizabethan manse. The beauty of the estate had been chronicled across the previous three centuries, starting with John Weever, best known for his 1631 study, *Antient Funerall Monuments*. Speculation among visitors to Surrenden Dering was that the main house itself held more than a hundred discrete rooms, thirty of them suitable for private bedchambers. "About the size of Versailles," Adams had judged when they took the place. The secret escape tunnel from the cellar to an exit beyond the park walls was still passable. The hops fields were well tended. The forests and meadows abounded with game. A small hunting party at Dering Wood had a few years earlier bagged 1,167 pheasants, sixteen partridges, two woodcocks, four hares, and ninety-four rabbits in just five hours' work. The estate was also distant enough from the parish to keep its inhabitants clear of intercourse with the local townsmen and tenant farmers.

For all its charms, however, Surrenden had a way of infecting its residents with acute torpor. Henry Adams, who had taken on the duties of "cellarer and chaplain," the historic lot of the noninheriting sons of the estate, had grown bored of the place by the time Hay arrived in mid-August. "One is obliged all day to look at sheep," he complained. Henry James, who lived down the road at

Rye and made frequent visits to Surrenden Dering that summer, found Lizzie Cameron restored to her previous good health, Donald Cameron drunk and ornery as always, and Adams and Hay both shaky and wan.

On Saturday morning, August 13, the first day Ambassador Hay awoke on the premises, a cable arrived for him with big news: President McKinley and the French ambassador in Washington, who was acting as representative of the Sagasta government in Spain, had signed the temporary peace protocols they had been negotiating in the previous weeks. The final treaty was to be worked out at a conference of five American commissioners and five Spanish commissioners beginning in October, in Paris.

The terms of the temporary peace were less generous than those McKinley had offered back in June, before the United States started burying citizen-soldiers in Cuba, but Spain could hardly object, given the weakness of its military position. The American army had landed its soldiers in both the Philippines and Puerto Rico, and US warships patrolled their coasts unchallenged, prepared to open the big guns on capitals, harbors, and major cities. The situation in Cuba was the same. Spain had wisely agreed to give up sovereignty and title in Cuba immediately and to hand over Puerto Rico and every remaining Spanish colony in the West Indies, as well as a Spanish-owned island between Hawaii and the Philippines "to be selected by the United States." The future of the Philippines itself was not entirely worked out.

In its discussions during the negotiations of the peace protocols, McKinley's cabinet had split on the question of the Philippines. Two members salivated over the commercial possibilities of a property close enough to serve as a gateway to those glorious Chinese markets and wanted the entire archipelago; so did the secretary of agriculture, a staunch Presbyterian who saw a great and fertile field for Christianizing the natives. "Yes," McKinley had joked at one cabinet meeting, "you Scotch favor keeping everything including the Sabbath." Three members, including Secretary of State Day, wanted to keep only the port of Manila for a naval base—"a hitching-post," McKinley called it. Day was a modest man, and wary of expansion; he had argued that the imposition of "sound government" on millions of Filipinos half a world away was beyond the nation's capacity and far outside the nation's interest. Two cabinet members were simply too confused to take a side.

Ambassador Hay, at the president's request, had weighed in from London. He was with Day: the oceanic hitching post was all the United States needed. Hay did, as a matter of full disclosure, advise McKinley that the leading British statesmen, concerned as they were about the Russians' and the Germans' carving off pieces of China as their private commercial domains, preferred that the United States keep a strong naval presence in the area, with the Philippines as a bulwark. "If we give up the Philippines it will be a considerable disappointment to our English friends," Hay had written to McKinley, "—but of course we can consider nothing but our own interests; and the more I hear about the state of the Tagálog population [in the Philippines] and their leaders the more I am convinced of the seriousness which would devolve upon us if we made ourselves permanently responsible for them."

McKinley, in mid-August of 1898, was not yet ready to make any final decision regarding the Philippines. Point three of the protocol, Hay noted as he read that morning at Surrenden Dering, left it for McKinley to do as *he* desired, and not just in Manila, which the United States had surrounded though not yet entered, but anywhere on the thousands of islands and islets that made up the enormous archipelago of the Philippines. "The United States," it read, "will occupy and hold the city, bay and harbor of Manila, pending the conclusion of the treaty of peace which shall determine the control, disposition and government of the Philippines."

John Hay had some trepidation, the day the telegram arrived, that McKinley would name him to the Paris Peace Commission to help settle the treaty with Spain, but those meetings were at least six weeks away, he knew, which meant he could still have his long rest at Surrenden Dering, near Lizzie. And if that call never came, which was the more likely scenario, he would have his month of ease and then head back to London, where the American war triumph had clarified the diplomatic atmosphere—and improved his bargaining power.

The men who made up Her Majesty's government might not need or want friends among other nations, but they loved a winner, because winners were useful. They took pride in riding the right horse. Lord Salisbury was in the market for a useful horse just then, to help him keep Russia and Germany at bay in China. His Foreign Office was promoting the "Open Door" there—free and fair trade throughout that vast country. He had already made it clear to Hay that he wanted to partner with the United States, the newest power in the Far East, to push that door open and keep it open. If Hay could help make that happen, it would bind the United States and Great Britain as never before. Monetary policy, fur seals in Alaska, and boundaries in the Klondike would be much less sticky wickets in this new iteration of Anglo-American relations. Hay could retire his ambassadorship in a year, maybe two, as the man who cemented the most important international alliance in the modern world. He could go back home to Washington, DC, and gaze out on the White House, or loll at his mountainside retreat in New Hampshire, and be satisfied. He could finish his life in the quiet contentment of knowing that he had done his duty to the fullest and had been able, as the long-ago newspaper clipping challenged, to "make his mark in the world as a bright and shining light."

JOHN HAY KNEW something was afoot when Harry White presented himself in the great gallery at Surrenden Dering the next day, Sunday, August 14. Hay had left White in charge of the embassy in his absence, confident that the first secretary was capable of handling almost any issue without advice or instruction. Even in an emergency, a telegram to Pluckley would be faster than a two-hour train ride. But here in the great gallery was Harry White, whom everyone at Surrenden was pleased to see—except for John Hay. White did not make much small talk and wasted no time in handing the ambassador a cable from Washington. He watched Hay's face fall as he read: "It gives me exceptional pleasure to tender to you the office of Secretary of State, [succeeding] Day, who will resign to take service on the Paris Commission, to negotiate peace. It is important that you should assume duties here not later than the first of September. Cable answer. William McKinley."

This was cause for despair. John Hay knew that Judge Day wanted out of the State Department, that he had taken the position only because his friend McKinley had begged him to do the job at least as long as the war lasted. And Hay had even seen it conjectured in the newspapers that he would be the replacement. But he had regarded this chatter as uninformed speculation. The newspapers were usually wrong, after all, and the president had never so much as intimated to John Hay that his appointment as secretary of state was under consideration. Hay's first instinct when he read the cable was to decline McKinley's offer.

He remembered the last time he had disappointed a president, seventeen years earlier, when James Garfield had asked him to come back to the White House as private secretary with a much-expanded portfolio. The reasons Hay cited in refusing that job pertained as well to the office of secretary of state. "To do a thing well a man must take some pleasure in it, and . . . half of the work, the contact with the greed and selfishness of office-seekers and bulldozing Congressmen, is unspeakably repulsive to me," he had written to Garfield on Christmas Day, 1880. "The constant contact with envy, meanness, ignorance, and the swinish selfishness which ignorance breeds, needs a stronger heart and a more obedient nervous system than I can boast."

As secretary of state, Hay would have human swine snuffling around his office every day, competing for every two-bit consulship and second secretary job that came open. Hay was "utterly depressed" by the offer, White would later tell friends, and clearly torn about how to respond. John Hay was no shirker. His duty as ambassador, as he saw it, was to take whatever load off the president he could. Wouldn't this new office involve the same simple task in a different location? Then again, he had no *desire* for the job, which was, as the first baronet of Surrenden Dering once said of an office tendered him, "a larger Orbe than my ambition doth stretch unto." Without desire for it, Hay was sure, the secretaryship would drain him dry. The office, Hay told Harry White that day, "will kill me in six months."

HAY'S FIRST DRAFT of an answer to McKinley was an act of self-preservation. "I received your dispatch with mingled emotions of affection, gratitude and sorrow," Hay wrote out in his own hand. "It would have been the dearest wish of my heart to be associated with you in that way, but my health will not permit it. I will hold [the ambassadorship] through the winter or resign it immediately, whichever will be most convenient for you."

Hay could not bring himself to send the dispatch, and by the end of the afternoon he had involved the entire house in his agonizing deliberation. Henry Adams took up the question with grave solemnity, though he later betrayed peevishness at the fact that Hay's choice, one way or the other, would come out all right for his friend. "Hay needed no office in order to wield influence," he would write. "For him, influence lay about the streets, waiting for him to stoop to it." In spite of Adams's jumbled emotions of pride in his friend, fear for his physical well-being, and actual envy, he duly recorded the proceedings at Surrenden Dering that August day: "The discussion on both sides was earnest, but the decided voice of the conclave was that, though if he were a mere office-seeker he might certainly decline promotion, if he were a member of the Government he could not. No serious statesman could accept a favor and refuse a service."

John Hay sent a wire to the president later that day, reporting himself "most gratefully at your disposition." He did leave himself an out, however, explaining that his shaky health would necessarily delay his arrival in Washington to the beginning of October. "If the need of a change is urgent and it would be inconvenient to wait for me," he concluded, "I hope you will act without reference to me."

Later that day a second telegram arrived in Washington, also in cipher, from London, addressed to Secretary Day, marked "PERSONAL AND CONFIDENTIAL":

> I think it my duty to let the President and you know that it is very doubtful whether the Ambassador's present condition of health is equal to the onerous duties of your office. In fact, certain it is not but such are his devotion to and desire to be with the President that he will not tell him—So he has been in the country for the past few days and still is resting there. Could not immediate vacancy be avoided by your going to Paris as Sec of State

> for which there are several precedents, notably Casterleigh at Vienna and Beaconsfield and Lord Salisbury at Berlin. Time would thus be allowed for careful consultation with [Hay's] doctor, who is not now in London and you could satisfy yourself as to his condition when you are over here which might then have greatly improved. He does not know I am sending you this. I will write you fully by next mail. White.

William McKinley had by then, as all presidents must, grown accustomed to having things go his way and would not be frightened off his choice by Harry White's warning; the Major immediately cabled Hay that he wanted him there as soon as he was physically able. Day would be resigning on his way out of town to Paris in about four weeks. The department could muddle along with Alvey Adee as temporary head for a short time, but John Hay would be the new secretary of state.

MRS. HAY TOOK Clarence and the Hay girls and headed for the Continent to have a final "whack at the French vittles" and at Paris's finest jewelry cases. Hay spent much of the next month back in London trying to put the office in order and to disassemble his household. He escaped to the seclusion of Surrenden Dering when time permitted, which wasn't often enough for his taste. There were dozens of invitations to decline and *already* a host of office seekers to put off, and he still had ambassadorial duties to tend. He had to arrange for permission from Her Majesty's government for Admiral Dewey to dock and clean his warships at the British-controlled port of Hong Kong. And always, he complained to Clara, there was the "mountain of letters" to work through, including dozens of notes of congratulations to be answered. There was one consistent note in all his replies to well-wishers: he was damned sorry to be leaving London so soon.

The ambassador counted the year and a half in England as among the greatest and most rewarding adventures of his life, but it was obvious that it would not be his last. Three weeks shy of sixty, John Hay found himself headed into deep water—"worried by every wind of destiny," as he explained in a letter to a friend, the last letter he wrote on his way out of London. "You can imagine with what solemn and anxious feelings I am starting for home. Never, even in war times, did I feel anything like it. But then I was young and now I am old."

CHAPTER TWENTY-FOUR

As Becomes a Great Nation

"We have had a foggy & miserable voyage thus far," John Hay wrote from his oak-paneled stateroom on September 18, 1898, another dark and soupy night at sea. "We are 80 miles short of our schedule time." The RMS *Teutonic* had carried him little more than halfway home by then, and Hay was feeling anxious. It wasn't just that the big ship had accidentally run up against an unseen fishing smack earlier that evening, somewhere off the coast of Newfoundland. What most unsettled John Hay was the realization that his long years of ease and freedom were coming to an end; he found himself once more the prisoner of presidential prerogative—and with no honorable means of escape. Secretary of State William Day had handed in his official resignation the day before and headed off with the delegation of peacemakers he was to lead in Paris. Hay's commission was already being engraved on steel plate: "Reposing confidence in the patriotism, integrity and abilities of John Hay of the District of Columbia, I have appointed him . . ."

President McKinley was impatient to have John Hay on the job, but he had remained solicitous of his new appointee; the Major had made a point not to hurry him into office. "Consult your own pleasure and convenience," McKinley had written when Hay asked for a few days' leave to rest and recuperate at his farm in New Hampshire after his ship docked. The decision on replacing the first assistant at the department could await Hay's arrival, the president had assured him: "I want you to have the man of your choice."

John Hay would be McKinley's third try at a secretary of state in just eighteen months. John Sherman was too senile to do the work; William Day was uncertain and unhappy in it. The president had done much of the job himself in that time, but now, at this moment of prodigious national reckoning, McKinley knew he needed a firm hand on the ship of state. He was expecting in John Hay a partner familiar with the conventions and intricacies of international diplomacy and a man he could trust to put the best face on America's increasing presence around the world. The war with Spain might be winding down, but the war *aims* were still in a state of expansion, mostly because of the unexpectedly spectacular display of US naval power. There was no precedent for this sort of military triumph (or for the spoil taking that came with it) in the adult life of anyone in the McKinley administration. Little distinction or dignity had been won in kicking a gaggle of depleted Indian tribes across the plains of North America, and not much loot was gained either. But the victory over Spain had been a stunning rout of a once-great European nation, and the other powers had taken notice.

The American military masterpiece had already swelled national pride and influence, and now perhaps the national Treasury. What had begun as a noble humanitarian mission to remove the venal Spanish colonialists from the island of Cuba—"A good war with a dignified cause to fight for," Sam Clemens had said of it, adding, "A thing not to be said of the average war"—had branched without considered thought or planning (Manila was just supposed to be a bargaining chip, right?) into a shopping spree in *both* hemispheres. American businessmen and financiers who had despaired at what a war might do to their holdings in stocks and bonds had been enormously cheered by the pecuniary advantages of its happy aftermath: a cut of the profits from sugar manufacturing in Cuba and Puerto Rico in the Atlantic, and Hawaii in the Pacific; millions of islanders who would be obliged to buy American *stuff*; the long-dreamed-of Chinese market finally within the nation's commercial grasp! Even Theodore Roosevelt's conservative old boss, Navy Secretary John Long, was showing a stout willingness to protect the nation's new-won prerogatives, especially in the East. Long's naval planners had reportedly asked Congress to fund construction of fifteen new warships, including three *Oregon*-size battleships and three first-class cruisers bigger than any the United States now deployed. And Congress stood ready to sign the check. "It is significantly stated that the ships are to be adapted to the Pacific, rather than Atlantic, service," the *London Standard* had observed while Hay was still at Carlton House Terrace. "A fleet of this kind, operating from Manila as a base, will be able to exercise a considerable influence on the progress of events in Chinese waters."

There were voices of caution, such as the steel magnate Andrew Carnegie, who had made it his business to send John Hay, secretary of state in waiting, his essay in the August 1898 issue of the *North American Review*. As a purely financial proposition, the acquisition of the Spanish colonies in the Americas (and maybe the Philippines, too) was a loser by Carnegie's icy calculation. He could not see how these faraway territories could generate enough profit to justify the terrific expenditure needed to defend them. He wanted no part of the cost of joining the European powers in divvying up among themselves what was left of the globe. And he feared the grip of Treasury-depleting militarism, which the United States had so long avoided. But Carnegie had a bigger concern, speaking as a patriotic American. "Is the Republic to remain one homogeneous whole, one united people, or to become a scattered and disjointed aggregate of widely separated and alien races?" Carnegie asked. Then he answered himself, and without a scintilla of the humility that might accompany the statement of a man who had never been to the place whereof he spoke: "The Philippines have about seven and a half millions of people, composed of races bitterly hostile to one another, alien races, ignorant of our language and institutions. Americans cannot be grown there."

Republican Speaker of the House Tom Reed wasn't as worried about the bottom line or racial purity as he was about simple practicality: "Isn't [the president] trying to make the world better in more spots than he can visit and oversee?" he had been saying for more than a year.

William McKinley, in the warm glow of his martial success, was not much concerned with the dissenters. The president was always less excitable than the general run of his countrymen, but he was nonetheless intoxicated by the possibilities offered up by winning at war. He was keeping his own counsel and inventing a new narrative to suit himself as the days went along. The burdens of war and acquisition had been thrust upon him by the indecencies and immoralities of the Spanish, he reminded himself, and by their stupid insistence on inviting America's holy wrath. McKinley believed in his Methodist heart he had done all he could to avoid the fight; he was still annoyed that the Sagasta government had refused to meet him halfway before things got bloody.

While McKinley deprecated wars of conquest, which his moral crusade of a war *was not*, he was no longer interested in handing back what was won. "The march of events rules and overrules human action," he wrote in his instructions to the peace commissioners as he shipped them off to Paris. "The war has brought us new duties and responsibilities which we must meet and discharge as becomes a great nation on whose growth and career from the beginning the Ruler of nations has plainly written the high command and pledge of civilization." Upon further review, McKinley told his commissioners, he had decided he wanted more than just a hitching post in Manila Bay; he wanted control of the entire island of Luzon. "Incidental to our tenure in the Philippines," he noted, "is the commercial opportunity to which American statesmanship cannot be indifferent."

When those peace commissioners scudded past John Hay and the *Teutonic* on September 18, 1898, crossing the Atlantic in the opposite direction, four of these men retained a somewhat open mind about the disposition of the Philippines: who might own it, and who might govern it, and how. The fifth, Whitelaw

Reid, was solidly on record—in public—for taking hold of the entire archipelago for the good of all involved. Reid had written Hay that he was not fool enough to think ruling the islands in the Far East would be easy, but he was certain it would be worth it. And one needn't get all worked up about providing niceties like self-government there, he assured Hay. Whitelaw was even more expansive in private. "The constitution interposed no obstacles and there would be little difficulty in so modifying our present territorial system as to adapt it to any of these islands whenever it might be thought best to relieve them from military rule," he had counseled the president. "But they should be governed permanently as colonies, never with the remotest idea of permitting them admission as states in the Union."

HOW IT WOULD all turn out in the Philippines, or anywhere else, John Hay could not know on that foggy night in the North Atlantic—nor did he expect to have a significant role in the final outcome. Hay's new position in the cabinet would make him, on paper anyway, the second-most-powerful man in the Republic, and third in line to the presidency, behind only Vice President Hobart, who reportedly had a foot in the grave already. But John Hay knew better than to expect deference from any quarter. And he knew better than to expect to have any real sway over final decisions. He had seen how it worked the last time he had been in the White House, more than thirty years before. Even Abraham Lincoln's trusted and brilliant secretary of state, William Henry Seward, was more sounding board and backroom adviser than he was a force in Civil War–era policy. President Lincoln had always been the first word and the last. And unlike Seward, a popular New York senator who had nearly won the Republican nomination over Lincoln, John Hay came to office with no real political base or backing.

Hay understood that he would be serving at the president's pleasure and that he was there to support McKinley in whatever action he chose to take. John Hay would commit himself to nothing, and offer no opinion in public on any subject, until a presidential decision had been made. "You are going to do a most important piece of work at Paris, and I know it will be well done," he wrote blandly to the empire-minded Reid. And to the anti-imperialist Carnegie he wrote: "I am not allowed to say in my present fix how much I agree with you. The only question in my mind is how far it is now *possible* for us to withdraw from the Philippines. I am rather thankful it is not given to me to solve that momentous question."

ON WEDNESDAY NIGHT, September 21, 1898, the *Teutonic* passed the entrance of the Swash Channel, in the Lower Bay of New York Harbor, and was steaming toward the Narrows, when Captain John G. Cameron saw the lights of another steamship appear all of a sudden out of the darkness. A military transport packed with doctors, nurses, hospital corpsmen, and enough gear and supplies for a five-hundred-bed hospital, headed to minister to one of the newest US possessions, Puerto Rico, was on a collision course with Cameron's ship. The *Teutonic* shrieked out two sharp whistles, but the *Berlin* gave no answer and just kept plowing toward a cold, wet disaster. Cameron threw an electric signal to his men in the bowels of the ship, and the crew reversed engines at full speed. Hay and the rest of the passengers heard the muted roar and felt the *Teutonic* shudder and tremble as it churned up foamy torrents from its twin propellers. Captain Cameron wasn't yet sure if he had made his signal in time. The two mighty ships came together at an acute angle and met with a sickening screech that lasted for a full minute before the *Teutonic* managed to back clear. Neither of the behemoths suffered more than a paint scrape. One newspaperman on scene would describe it as "a touch of almost feathery lightness." But it had required the practiced hand of an experienced sea captain to avert a deadly disaster.

Two hours later, just after nine o'clock that night, the *Teutonic* pulled into Pier 48 in Lower Manhattan, where a gaggle of reporters waited. They wanted the story of the near wreck from Captain Cameron, but they wanted something approaching news from the incoming secretary of state as well. John Hay, somewhat shaken by the evening's events, begged their indulgence. He was happy to talk about America's improving relationship with Great Britain but said he was absolutely unwilling to answer questions about the Philippines or any other future diplomatic business. "You must excuse me from talking on international subjects," he said. "The trip over has not been a pleasant one, and I am glad to be on solid ground again."

Cleared through quarantine, Hay and his family headed for Fifth Avenue and Thirtieth Street, to the Holland House, where, he had told reporters, there might well be a communication from the president summoning him to the White House.

McKinley, however, was as good as his word. Hay was not expected in Washington for a week. He could spend a few days in New York, then go to his farm in New Hampshire to shake off the effects of his journey and to acquaint himself with the changing political landscape. Senator Henry Cabot Lodge was already bellowing to Hay about "what a wonderful war it has been" and to Harry White that "we have risen to be one of the great world powers." Cabot's near neighbor at his Massachusetts Bay summer retreat wanted Hay to see evidence of this transformation for himself. "Visit Nahant (near Boston) and stop at the elegant home of Senator Lodge, who has the scalp of Spain hanging in his front entry in the shape of the flag of Ponce which [his son] Bay hauled down and judiciously looted," William Sturgis Bigelow had written in a note that awaited Hay on his arrival in New York. "Cabot says he is going to make every d——d Dago in Washington walk under that flag. . . . Theodore R. is going to be Governor at once and President as soon as he can get around to it."

Theodore was all the talk at the end of September, having made it back from the battlefields of Cuba to attend to his own public glorification. John Hay had been among the many friends who doubted the perspicacity of Theodore Roosevelt's abandoning his ill wife and his place at the Navy Department to run off to the war, but he was forthright and generous in his praise when it was all over. "I imagine we older fellows will all have to confess that you were in the right," Hay had said in his note to Colonel Roosevelt.

> As Sir Walter wrote:—
>
> "One crowded hour of glorious life
> Is worth an age without a name."
>
> You have written your name on several pages of your country's history, and they are all honorable to you and comfortable to your friends.

But while Hay was pleased to flatter his young friend, he had also hoped to fashion for him a gentle reminder that this war had not been a true test of national (or personal) mettle. He knew that Theodore had not seen enough of the *real carnage* of war to be properly humbled by it. The fight with Spain had been a walk through the lilies as compared to the conflagration John Hay had witnessed while at President Lincoln's side. The American Civil War had lasted four years; the ground war against Spain a few weeks. The combat deaths in Cuba, Puerto Rico, and the Philippines were two-tenths of 1 percent of the Civil War's. Ten times the number of men had died in a single day at Antietam as in the entirety of the fight with Spain. "It has been a splendid little war," Hay wrote to Theodore—and it was a phrase aimed to deflate—"begun with the highest motives, carried on with magnificent intelligence and spirit, favored by that Fortune which loves the brave. It is now to be concluded, I hope, with that fine good nature, which is, after all, the distinguishing trait of the American character." This invitation to humility and grace in victory was, of course, an unequal match to Colonel Roosevelt's personal fabulousness.

Theodore was all over the New York papers when Hay awoke at the Holland House the morning of September 22, 1898. The media-styled "Hero of

San Juan Hill" (he had not actually stormed that critical hill, but it sounded so much better than *Kettle* Hill) had the day before made his first public speech since his return from Cuba, out near his home on Long Island. The colonel had spent the afternoon of the Peace Jubilee and Roosevelt Reception at Oyster Bay telling tall tales about himself and his Rough Riders, who were so esteemed in New York that they had been given, as the newspapers reported, "a good deal of latitude" when they had, on a recent visit, fired their revolvers off the Brooklyn Bridge. President McKinley himself was just then hosting another small cohort of Rough Riders at the Executive Mansion in Washington. "Roosevelt is going to be the next governor of New York," the president told the men, "and it was you boys who made him so hard to beat."

Good fortune and good press notwithstanding, Theodore was not in the best state of mind that week. The governorship sounded like the correct next step, and he suspected his war fame needed to be cashed in while it was still the coin of the political realm. But he wasn't sure he was ready for the contest. "I have, literally, hardly been able to eat or sleep during the last week, because of the pressure upon me," he complained to Cabot. Now that the war he had dreamed of for so long was behind him, Theodore found himself not proportionately delighted with his personal tally in the Cuban escapade. The War Department had resolutely refused to bestow upon him the nation's highest award for valor, even though he had been telling anyone who would listen how much he deserved it, if anybody did, and even though he had plenty of help in high places. "I do wish you would get the Medal of Honor for me anyhow," he had written Senator Henry Cabot Lodge, back when he was not sure he would make it out of Cuba alive. "I should awfully like the children to have it and I think I earned it." Colonel Roosevelt *could* boast, and did, that his volunteer cavalry suffered far greater casualties than the ordinary run of regiments [illegible] certain that this was a product of regimental valor and not suspect leadership. But he would always be disappointed that he wasn't himself grievously, visibly, obviously wounded. He had been fascinated as a young boy by the strange, visceral thrill of seeing the Civil War veteran's "empty sleeve," and he was sure a missing limb, or any similar war-made physical deformity would have been a most welcome asset in his future political campaigns.

But whatever his disappointments in the battle and its aftermath, Theodore had done enough in Cuba to assure himself the governorship of New York that November if he wanted it—no matter that most of the men in Boss Platt's Republican machine could not abide Theodore Roosevelt and were working behind the scenes to unhorse him. They harried him by contesting his New York residency (there was no record of his paying taxes in the state that year) and belittled him in public. "Roosevelt would run like a scared dog, and as governor he would be as crazy as a scared dog," Platt's men joked to reporters. But the party machine was no match for Roosevelt's Rough Rider renown, which had been so joyously inflated by Richard Harding Davis that it was big enough to knock aside all obstacles. Theodore was nominated for the governorship in a landslide at the New York State Republican Convention just five days after his first public appearance. His opening campaign speech traveled far afield of the meager issues that might cross his desk in Albany, New York, and far afield of the modesty John Hay had hoped to instill in his young friend. "There comes a time in the life of a nation, as in the life of an individual, when it must face great responsibilities, whether it will or no," Roosevelt told an overflow crowd at his opening campaign event.

> We cannot avoid facing the fact that we occupy a new place among the peoples of the world and have entered upon a new career. . . .
>
> The guns of our warships in the tropic seas of the West and the remote East have awakened us to the knowledge of new duties. Our flag is a proud flag, and it stands for liberty and civilization. Where it has once floated there must and shall be no return to tyranny or savagery. We are face to face with our destiny, and we must meet it with a high and resolute courage. For us is the life of action, of strenuous performance of duty; let us live in the harness, striving mightily; let us rather run the risk of wearing out than of rusting out.

SO THIS WAS the sluicing course of the river John Hay was to run, with wild men like Cabot and Theodore grabbing at the ship's wheel while he himself was already "rusting out." The newspaper coverage of Hay's return was enough to make him laugh out loud. Whitelaw's *Tribune* described the next secretary of state as a man in "robust health" and "exceedingly animated in spirits," which was news to John Hay. "Men of his caliber are badly needed just now, and we are glad he has been called home into the field of action . . . in which he is so eminently fitted," one of Hay's hometown newspapers editorialized. "No one doubts that the gravest necessity exists for a man at the lever of Colonel Hay's ability, courage and devotion."

Alvey Adee, who was holding Hay's place as secretary of state until his arrival and who knew his old friend well, penned a quick note to his new boss. "Your commission is signed, sealed, and recorded, awaiting only the filling in of the date in order to effect its delivery," he wrote to Hay on September 23. "The cuss-words await your pleasure." The notion of any pleasure—even the pleasure of cursing his fate—was beyond John Hay's powers of imagination. "I have never been so oppressed by a sense of inadequacy before," he wrote to his brother-in-law from his three-day vacation in New Hampshire. "I look forward to the next year with gloomy forebodings."

FELIPE AGONCILLO AND his interpreter, José "Sixto" Lopez, arrived in San Francisco on a US Army transport ship on September 22, 1898, in the company of Major General Francis V. Greene, full of high hopes, and with a story sure to inspire the fellow feeling and respect of the American people. Agoncillo, a thirty-nine-year-old attorney from the Philippine province of Batangas and for the past two years an invited guest at the home of the United States consul in Hong Kong, was the official emissary of the newly forming Republic of the Philippines, representing its revolutionary leader, Emilio Aguinaldo. The existence of this nascent democracy, the first in the Far East, owed to the best intentions and military power of the United States of America and to the stamina and courage of the Filipino *insurrectos* under Aguinaldo's command. The combination had made quick work of Spanish authority in Manila and the entire island of Luzon. Spain appeared to be on its way out of Agoncillo's native land after more than 350 years of colonial rule, and something new was on its way in. More than eighty of the Filipino people's chosen representatives, including attorneys, doctors, painters, businessmen, farmers, and a priest, had already gathered at the first Philippine Congress in the city of Malolos, where members were in the process of ratifying an earlier declaration of independence and fashioning a constitution for their new country. This was the beautiful tale Agoncillo had to tell, one that recalled America's own world-shaking revolution a century before, and one that gave Americans their due as magnanimous and heroic liberators of nearly nine million oppressed Filipinos.

Agoncillo understood there was a careful balance to be struck between conveying the gratitude of the Filipino people on the one hand and expressing their strong desire to exercise sovereignty in their own homeland on the other. He understood it was a delicate diplomatic task, gentling the leading men in the United States into recognizing the independent personality of the *self-governing* Filipino people. A group of Hawaiians had been too bold in their postannexation demands, and according to newspaper reports Agoncillo had seen on his way through Honolulu a week earlier, "This action has so thoroughly convinced [American] Commissioners of the complete lack of political sense and sagacity of the native Hawaiians that it is believed they will make no recommendation to give the natives the right of suffrage."

Don Felipe also understood that it would require care and political agility to advance the first request of the new republic: a place at the negotiating table in Paris, where the "disposition" of the Philippines was to be settled. But the first-ever Filipino envoy on US soil went to work without hesitation, the minute he walked off the SS *China*, stating forthrightly to newsmen on hand in San Francisco that the Filipino people believed they had earned the right to govern themselves, that they were fully capable of doing so, and that they had received tacit assurances from American officials that this was the future of the Philippines. The *New York Times* praised the two Filipinos for their shrewdness and for their surprising fluency in English.

Agoncillo was at something of a disadvantage at the start; he was expecting instructions from General Aguinaldo as to the exact message he was to deliver to the White House, but none awaited him in San Francisco. Aguinaldo, for his part, was growing less certain of the actual intentions of the United States. The American military leaders on the ground sounded less and less interested in being anybody's liberator. A week into Agoncillo's month-long sea journey aboard the US transport, Aguinaldo had been ordered by the American military governor in the Philippines to remove all Filipino troops from the vicinity of Manila—*or else*. "You and your associates could not regret more than I any conflict between our forces which would tend to excite the citizens of my country, who are always a unit in action when its sovereignty is attacked or when its right to fulfill its international obligations is called into question," General Elwell S. Otis had written to Aguinaldo. "Then they never count the cost; and, as you are fully aware, resources are abundant."

Even lacking official instructions, Agoncillo exhibited a flair for political theater on the five-day rail journey from San Francisco to Washington. During his short stay in Chicago, Don Felipe made a public visit to Lincoln Park, where he removed his stylish silk hat and bowed his bared head before the bronze statue of Abraham Lincoln. "In all my historical studies," Agoncillo told the reporters who followed him there, "I have paid the most attention to the growth of the power and influence of the United States Government. It is my ideal of a Government, and it is the pattern which the Philippine people will follow when they are independent. This is the land that we have looked up to for many years, and the one in whose footsteps we have tried to follow." He then made a direct plea for Filipino representation at the peace conference in Paris. "It is justice that the Philippine people should not be undefended, for it might happen that the representatives of Spain would make formidable charges against the Filipinos and in the absence of representation from the Filipinos these charges might be credited," he said. "Therefore, it is inadmissible, under the most rudimentary beginnings of natural or written law and sound reason, that the Filipinos should be without a hearing." He went on to express the Filipino people's willingness to live for a time under American protection and control, so long as the United

States continued to disavow any plan to make the archipelago a permanent colony. "If the Filipinos are not to govern themselves," he offered, "there is no nation they would wish to be governed by more than the United States."

General Greene, who was headed for a meeting with President McKinley, proved a most companionable escort for Agoncillo in his journey across the United States. The general had been in the Philippines for more than six weeks and had made a study of the citizenry in and around Manila. He accorded Agoncillo and Lopez respect both in public and in private and he seemed at times to be a true advocate of Filipino independence. Greene "expressed a very high opinion of the Filipinos as men and fighters," wrote one correspondent in Chicago. "The inhabitants of the islands, he says, are superior in every way to the Cubans and to the North American Indians, and once they are freed from Spanish oppression have a magnificent future before them."

Sad to say, Agoncillo did not find many other champions of the Filipino cause in the United States. He ended up expending much of his time and energy parrying the rumor, innuendo, and outright falsehood that awaited him at every station stop on his trip. The tenor of the American press was an eye-opener for Agoncillo: General Aguinaldo was an illiterate jungle fighter whose only real purpose had been to rob Spanish civil officers, newspapers in the States asserted. He was a dangerous threat to private property rights. His support in the archipelago was thin, and limited to the poorer and less educated members of his fellow Tagalogs. The Visayans, the wealthy Filipino business class, the Chinese and Japanese laborers, and the Muslims in the Philippines had little use for General Aguinaldo. "The truth is," said one anonymous source, "Aguinaldo's revolt and his supposed recognition by the Filipinos as their chief are mythical."

That Aguinaldo and Agoncillo and the rest of their comrades had accepted a "petty bribe" to walk away from the Filipino cause before Dewey showed up in Manila Bay, and would happily do so again, was the most damaging lie on the march in American newspapers. It suggested that the leaders of the Filipino insurgency did not truly want independence; they simply wanted to extort money and position from their coming American governors. If that failed, one nameless source offered, the duplicitous Aguinaldo had another great power at his disposal. The revolutionary general, it was reported the day Agoncillo arrived in Utah, had been intriguing with the kaiser to bring the Philippines under the control of Germany. "The Salt Lake newspapers contained stories to the effect that the Germans had entered into an alliance offensive and defensive with the Aguinaldo government and would furnish equipments for an army of 150,000 men," noted Murat Halstead, who had just signed on as the War Department's official historian of the American military campaign in the Philippines. "We were on the Union Pacific Railroad at the time, and I called the attention of

Don Felipe Agoncillo to this remarkable intelligence and asked him what he thought of it. He said emphatically that it was 'Nothing,' 'Not true,' 'Nothing at all,' and he laughed at the comic idea." Agoncillo, however, was beginning to get worried about the prospects for success on behalf of Filipino independence.

As Agoncillo neared Washington, President McKinley announced that he would be happy to receive Don Felipe as a private individual, but not as a credentialed ambassador of the "so-called Filipino republic," a government no nation recognized as legitimate. And neither would the president entertain any request for Filipino representation at the peace conference in Paris. The future of the Philippines would be worked out between the two interested parties—the United States of America and Spain. The Filipinos, by McKinley's reckoning, needed to exhibit political sense and sagacity by putting their faith in the integrity of the United States.

By the time Agoncillo finally settled into the finest hotel in Washington, the Arlington—half a block from John Hay's regal house on Lafayette Square and within sight of the White House—the effort to push back at the thundering herd of bad press had worn him down. He was beginning to feel, as General Greene had described him for newspaper readers, "small in stature." Agoncillo released an official statement on his arrival in Washington, asking the American people to respect the dignity of the Filipino people, who were more like them in culture and outlook than they had been told, but he left it to Sixto Lopez to do the talking that evening. "He is very, very tired—much fatigued—after his long journey," the interpreter said of his boss. Lopez, whose English was now being described as tortured and halting, wasn't sure when Don Felipe might confer with the president or what his message would be. Lopez judiciously avoided anything that sounded like a demand for freedom and independence. "If the United States is unwilling to accord us that from the first," Lopez told reporters on Lafayette Square, "then the next thing which would meet with favor by our people would be the establishment of a protectorate by the United States, and, third, to become a colonial possession of this country."

JOHN HAY EMERGED from his house on Lafayette Square shortly before eleven o'clock the next morning and into exquisitely temperate weather, a rarity for late September in the nation's capital. The temperature was just then pushing up toward seventy, and as Hay walked south across Lafayette Square toward the White House, a gentle breeze rustled the overhead leaves of magnolias and elms and beeches. The warm balm of sunshine brushed his left cheek. Hay read no special good omen in the felicitous weather, just as he read no ill omen in the news that the body of the man who had preceded him as ambassador to the Court of St. James's had just that morning been presented to an embalmer. All Hay could really say was that in comparison to poor dead Bayard, he felt right spry.

He had enjoyed a cigar beneath the high coffered ceiling of his own library the night before, then slept in his own bed for the first time in nearly eighteen months. And he slept well in spite of the clangor and keening of nearby cable cars and the glare of the new arc lights from the square. He had breakfasted on ham and eggs plated and served by his household staff and had plenty of time that morning to inspect the interior of his residence, which had been repainted and filled with the fresh-cut flowers Mrs. McKinley had sent over from the White House conservatory. He was home, and his home was more pleasant and more beautiful than he had remembered.

Reporters who had not seen the ambassador since he left town eighteen months earlier noted an uncommon bounce in his step as he crossed Lafayette Square that morning—"the picture of vigorous good health," wrote one. The newsmen did not press when Hay politely but firmly refused to answer any questions about the big issues facing his State Department until he had seen the president. He was not sure who would be his first assistant secretary. And he certainly was not going to make any statement about the Philippines or the mission of the Filipino "ambassador" now domiciled a few doors down from the Hay residence, on the other side of St. John's Episcopal Church.

Ahead of Hay as he walked, in a direct line, was the White House, where the president awaited him, and a hundred yards to its west, in the gaudy Second Empire building, Alvey Adee and the rest of the State Department staff were busy preparing Hay's new office. Receding slowly behind Hay was his own house, the most pleasing of the three buildings by far, if he did say so himself. This quarter-mile-long track from Hay's big redbrick Romanesque Revival mansion to the White House to the State Department and back home again formed a tight right triangle, the closed circuit of his new life, which was about to snap shut.

When John Hay passed beneath the ungainly porte cochere and into the vestibule of the White House, it was like walking through a wrinkle in time, where ghosts roamed. The first person he recognized was the chief doorkeeper, Thomas Pendel, who had been manning various doors of the White House since 1864. It was Pendel who had pushed open this same front door to see Abraham Lincoln away from the White House on the evening of April 14, 1865. And it was Pendel who had walked into John Hay's bedchamber some hours later to deliver the message that the president had been shot. "He was a handsome young man with a bloom on his cheeks just like that of a beautiful young lady," was how Pendel remembered Hay that night. "When I told him the news, he turned deathly pale, the color entirely leaving his cheeks. He said to me, 'Don't allow anybody to enter the house.'"

More than thirty years later, in spite of the new electric lighting and telephones and an elevator, and the gay profusion of hothouse flora in every nook and cranny, the bones of the old house still creaked under the enormous and growing weight of its public load. To the left of the vestibule, in the East Room, Hay could see a gaggle of uninvited but not unwelcome citizens milling about, surveying the yellow ottomans and the rest of the surprisingly threadbare furnishings and hoping the president might descend from his office above for a quick hello. Those elect visitors who had cards to present were allowed to wander at will through the State Dining Room and the Red Room and the big oval Blue Room, where they could peer out the curved windows onto the South Lawn and the Washington Monument beyond.

Hay pivoted quickly away from the hoi polloi and made for the stairway to his left. At the top of those stairs, and also to his left, was the room he and his coworker and best friend, John Nicolay, used as a bedchamber, where Abraham Lincoln, unable to sleep, would rock Hay awake for middle-of-the-night talks and reading sessions. President McKinley's private secretary and his staff of clerks manned the dozen or more desks in that room now.

Hay could see the favor seekers lining the benches in the main corridor at the top of the stairs, and newspapermen crawling all through William McKinley's executive offices, trying to make sense of the latest press release, which noted that the president was considering the wisdom of initiating joint military-civil commissions to govern America's newest possessions—however many that might be. This would be a governing body similar to the one operating in Washington, DC, where residents had no vote or voice in local or national government. "Such commissioners have, to a certain extent, absolute power, and this, the President believes, would operate to an excellent advantage in Manila, Havana, Honolulu, and other places which are so far removed from the central government, that their governors should have extraordinary powers to act without consulting the home authorities in every emergency," read the official release. "The military commissioner could also be the commanding general of the army of occupation."

Hay could feel the give of the weight-bearing rafters beneath his feet as he was ushered through the throng and into the Cabinet Room, where he found President McKinley in a leather-sheathed swivel chair at a corner of the room's big conference table. The president had ceded his private office as an annex to the waiting corridor and retreated into this room as a sanctuary where he was actually able to perform the labors of his office. In front of the nation's chief magistrate were an array of pens and inkstands, a blotter, a sheaf of stationery with the heading "EXECUTIVE MANSION," and a bouquet of flowers Mrs. McKinley had had sent over, which did not, alas, provide much cheer to the room. This "might have been the director's room in an old-fashioned and not very flourishing bank," one of McKinley's biographers would write. Drab oil paintings of past presidents lined the walls. A brass chandelier hung at a slight melancholy tilt beneath a tangle of electrical wires. Dust and discarded paper gathered behind the radiators and cabinets, where the housekeeper, who was a cheerful soul but not diligent in his work, swept much of the daily detritus. Among the furnishings was a rosewood desk and a marble-topped table that had been in the room back when Lincoln and Seward were swapping stories in front of a young John Hay.

McKinley rose from his chair and greeted Hay with sincere and unexpected ardor. He then startled Hay by saying he was now, for the first time in his presidency, unworried about the leadership at the State Department. The only other person in the room that morning was Major General Francis V. Greene, just then ending an interview with the president, and McKinley suggested that Hay and Greene have lunch that day so that the general could bring Hay up to speed on the situation in the Philippines.

Hay had come over simply to pay his respects; he wasn't going to be sworn in and put in harness until the next day. But McKinley seemed hungry for the company of a man who didn't *want* something from him, and he kept Hay in the room for more than an hour. The president confided his fatigue; he complained of sleepless nights and eyestrain made worse from mountains of daily reading material shoved at him. But the president's appearance belied his talk. The nation's chief executive, unlike the nation's tattered old Executive Mansion, hardly seemed unequal to his load. McKinley looked better than Hay had seen him in years. The president's tailored clothing—adorned with a pink carnation from the White House conservatory—was not on a par with Hay's own bespoke suits from Henry Poole & Co. on Savile Row in London, but it was a cut above anything he had seen McKinley wear before. The Major had put on a little weight, but he wore it well; he had been neatly shaved and barbered and buffed to a high gloss. His face showed a pleasing summer brown, a happy consequence of his hours in the afternoon sun during his daily walk or his ride with Mrs. McKinley in their new carriage. He was unhurried in speech, and when he twirled his eyeglasses in his right hand the smooth motion appeared less a nervous tic than a manifestation of mastery.

The Major had long ago—in training himself to calm his invalid and epilepsy-plagued wife—perfected the ability to show the world what Hay called his "ecclesiastical mask" of complaisance. And it served him well as chief magistrate. He lived within the maddeningly narrow physical constraints of the White House with unprecedented equanimity. Newspapermen crawling all over McKinley's suite of offices wondered that they had never—even in the nettlesome run-up to war with Spain—seen the slightest hint of passion or anger or unease from William McKinley.

The mask, however, did not obscure the president's recently acquired magisterial confidence or his growing belief in America's rising place among nations. He wasn't advertising it, like Henry Cabot Lodge, but he was no less certain of it . . . or of himself. The Major had come by it honestly, too. He had personally directed many of the recent battles from the first War Room in the White House, complete with maps decorated with colored pins marking the movements of troops and ships in Cuba, Puerto Rico, and the Philippines, and telephones, and telegraph hookups to commanders in the field. He was the first president to be able to pick up a telephone and bark out orders to War, Navy, State, Treasury, Interior, and every other department he oversaw. In the past few months, McKinley had cleared the Caribbean of the Spanish; Cuba and Puerto Rico were already under American control. And he had taken Hawaii despite the Senate's inability to ratify the annexation treaty.

The president seemed to be riding safely to shore on the long wave of national destiny. The *Sun*, a popular and politically independent paper in New York, had just that week reprinted a breathless reminiscence of separate private auguries made by two previous secretaries of state, both of whom Hay had served and liked, William Henry Seward and William Maxwell Evarts. The first, by Seward, was a remembrance of an informal colloquy with Americans living in Europe at the end of his long trip abroad in 1871. "The fact is the Americans are the only nation that has and understands liberty," Seward had said almost three decades earlier.

> I had all my life talked in public and private of the greatness of our mission of civilization and progress, of the ideas we represented and the lessons we were teaching the world, but I never realized how true it was that we were of all others the representatives of human progress. Now I know it. I am sure now, from what I have myself seen, that nothing I have ever said, or others have said, as to the destiny of our country was exaggerated. . . . Some of you boys may live to see American ideas and principles and civilization spread around the world, and lift up and regenerate mankind.

Seward's sentiment still tracked, even these many years later, with John Hay's single deeply held belief: that the great hope of the future was government by free men of means and ability and training—true republics. The Evarts prophecy, as recalled by the *Sun*, added a rousing righteousness to Seward's mission statement. "Gentlemen, God has America in his direct keeping, and lets it work out its destinies in accordance with His own wishes and for His own purpose," Evarts had told a group of his countrymen in Geneva in 1872. "He will lead the people to its final destiny as the advance guard of civilization, progress and the upbuilding and elevation of mankind, and in good time the bars will be again let down for the benefit of humanity—when or why we know not, but He knows."

God's plan was about as clear to John Hay as a dark and soupy night in the middle of the North Atlantic, and he suspected it would remain so always. Then again, Hay's new job did not require him to interpret the Divine's desires as to the Philippines or any other issue. His only duty was to understand the plan of the man sitting in front of him that sunlit Washington morning—the man the American people had seen fit to put in the White House—and to help him in perfecting its execution.

CHAPTER TWENTY-FIVE

The United States Is God's Country

Arested and restored Felipe Agoncillo crossed Lafayette Square with high hopes, and his entrance into the White House did little to dampen his spirits. Nothing about the rickety interior of this government building suggested a nation bent on empire; the informal and slightly down-at-the-heels seat of American executive power literally reeked of republican modesty. When General Francis V. Greene escorted Agoncillo and Sixto Lopez into the Cabinet Room, the president rose from his chair at the corner of the long table and greeted the two Filipinos with genuine interest and regard. Agoncillo, fashionable silk top hat in hand, noted with some disappointment that the new secretary of state, John Hay, was not in the room. Don Felipe did not present his official commission as the ministry plenipotentiary from the new Republic of the Philippines, because he had got the message about the president's desire that this meeting be regarded as an unofficial private affair only. Felipe Agoncillo was being careful not to antagonize the man with the power to dictate the future of the Filipino people. He was just happy to have the president's ear, though it became clear at the start of the meeting that the ear he was to speak into belonged to the near-deaf assistant secretary of state, Alvey Adee, who was on hand to act as translator. The diminutive Adee spoke first, in his cheerful little falsetto, asking in Spanish, on behalf of the president, after the purpose of the visit.

Agoncillo understood this interview would not be long and leisurely, and he started talking fast. He thanked the president and the American people for aiding in the liberation of the Filipinos and then asked permission to provide some background about his country and a brief report on the current state of domestic politics there. When McKinley nodded assent, Don Felipe launched into a story of the long Spanish depredations in the Philippines, the Filipino insurgency that preceded Dewey's arrival in Manila Bay by more than two years, the peace treaty negotiated between Emilio Aguinaldo's insurgency and Spain, and Spain's unwillingness to honor the explicit provisions of that treaty, which led Aguinaldo and his army back into the fight.

Agoncillo, stopping at intervals to give Adee a chance to translate, then explained to President McKinley the Filipino understanding of the special relationship between the United States and the Philippine insurgents. "At the outbreak of hostilities between the United States and Spain, General Aguinaldo was invited by Admiral Dewey to proceed to the Philippines and renew the revolution," Adee translated for William McKinley. "Aguinaldo returned and faithfully fulfilled his part of the agreement, operating with his forces against the Spaniards and referring all matters to the superior judgment of Admiral Dewey, his sole desire being to cooperate with him in establishing the independence of the Filipinos."

The president said nothing and betrayed no emotion at the mention of Philippine independence. He simply asked, through Adee, if Agoncillo had anything else to say. Agoncillo took the opportunity to request Filipino representation on the peace commission in Paris. The president dismissed the idea as impossible. The commission was set, and the Spanish could not be forced to assent to Philippine representation. Even a simple hearing in front of the American commissioners in Paris was unlikely. McKinley suggested, given the obvious language barriers, that Agoncillo take a few days to compose a formal written statement for the commission and present it to him through the State Department. But the president promised nothing. And in a parting shot, Agoncillo and Lopez were given to understand that they had been a little too energetic in making their case for Filipino independence to the American newspapers. Perhaps, it was suggested, their cause would be best advanced by discretion or even outright silence.

When Agoncillo and Lopez emerged into the crowded main corridor after a little less than thirty minutes in the Cabinet Room, reporters on scene thought the two men looked rattled. Agoncillo refused to answer their questions and then appeared flustered when the president's doorkeeper, an avid and slightly unseemly collector of autographs, asked for Agoncillo's signature. The Filipino diplomat was understandably reluctant to sign anything for an American working in an official capacity, even when this innocent hobby was explained to him. "Hasta mañana," Agoncillo said as he hurried down the stairs toward the front door. "It is believed that their talk with the President was not altogether satisfactory," that evening's newspapers reported. "The visit was practically without significance, except as showing that the President was extremely cautious in not giving any official status to his callers or any standing to their alleged government."

The Filipino envoys retreated back to their hotel across the square, left to mull the brief strange history of the dealings with the United States of America in the previous six months, dealings instigated by Americans. The history as they knew it went like this: The US consul in Singapore had tracked down Emilio Aguinaldo a few days after the American declaration of war against Spain and made a direct appeal for assistance. "Now is the time for you to strike," Consul E. Spencer Pratt told Aguinaldo. "Ally yourselves with America and you will surely defeat the Spaniards! America will help you if you will help America." Aguinaldo had been wary and requested from Pratt a formal agreement—in writing: General Aguinaldo and his revolutionary army would fight alongside the United States military in exchange for an American commitment to the independence of the Filipinos.

Pratt explained that the best he could do was to talk it over with Commodore Dewey. "You need not have any worry about America," the US consul assured Aguinaldo, citing the Teller Amendment in the recent declaration of war against Spain. "The American Congress and President have just made a solemn declaration disclaiming any desire to possess Cuba and promising to leave the country to the Cubans after having driven away the Spaniards and pacified the country. As in Cuba, so in the Philippines. Even more so, if possible; Cuba is at our door while the Philippines is 10,000 miles away."

It wasn't until a few weeks later, after the naval battle at Manila Bay and Dewey's promotion to rear admiral, that Aguinaldo and Dewey finally met. The rear admiral had by then signaled his willingness to give Filipino independence all due consideration, and when Aguinaldo arrived at Manila Bay on the USS *McCulloch*, Dewey brought the Filipino general straightaway to his flagship, where he made a personal pitch for something akin to an alliance. Dewey offered to give Aguinaldo all the small arms he had captured from the Spanish arsenal in Cavite and to ferry him and his men to shore if they would begin harassing what was left of the Spanish military on the main island of Luzon.

Aguinaldo was struck by Dewey's personal warmth and by his "honest and benevolent" face. But the Filipino leader did not want to fly under false colors at the initial meetings. He told Dewey that some of his fellow rebels feared that the United States would refuse to recognize Filipino independence and that they *knew* the American military was powerful enough to recolonize the Philippines as its own if it so desired. Aguinaldo begged forgiveness for speaking so frankly to Rear Admiral Dewey, but he needed to know whether his countrymen's fears were founded.

The rear admiral, as Aguinaldo recorded that day, believed "earnestness and frankness" were required in any exchange between true allies: "He then stated that, as he had already indicated, the United States would unquestionably recognize the independence of the people of the Philippines, guaranteed as it was by the word of honor of Americans which, he said, was more positive, more irrevocable, than a written agreement which might not be regarded as binding when there is an intention or desire to repudiate it, as was the case with the pact we had made with the Spaniards."

So Aguinaldo had gone ashore on an American warship, carrying a message for the Filipino people that he had already shared with officials of the United States government. "Compatriots, Divine Providence is about to place independence within our reach, and in a way that the most free and independent nation could hardly wish for," was how US diplomats translated it for the State Department.

> The Americans—not from mercenary motives, but for the sake of humanity and the lamentations of so many persecuted people—have considered it opportune to extend their protecting mantle to our beloved country, now that they have been obliged to sever relations with Spain, owing to the tyranny this nation is exercising in Cuba, causing enormous injury to the Americans, who have such large commercial and other interests there.... Do not fire on Americans, who are our liberators, but rather on the Spaniards, who are our natural enemies. The Americans will attack by sea, therefore the insurgents must attack by land. Assemble where you see the American flag flying.

As Filipino fighters gathered to his standard, Aguinaldo issued a guiding proclamation—as suggested by the American consul in Hong Kong—commanding his followers to respect the lives and property of all foreigners and all unarmed soldiers. The Philippine army was to ensure the safety of all enemy hospitals and ambulances and to refrain from assassination, arson, robbery, and looting. Those who disobeyed would be put to death. "The great nation, North America, cradle of true liberty and friendly on that account to the liberty of our people, oppressed and subjugated by the tyranny and despotism of those who have governed us, has come to manifest even here a protection which is decisive, as well as disinterested toward us, considering us endowed with sufficient civilization to govern by ourselves in this our unhappy land. To maintain this so lofty idea, which we deserve from the now very powerful nation, North America, it is our duty to detest all those acts which belie such an idea."

The Filipino fighters did impressive work in and around Manila. They invested the city by land, cutting off its freshwater supply and leaving the Spanish colony to starve. "Insurgents have practically surrounded Manila," Dewey reported to Navy Secretary Long just a few weeks after Aguinaldo landed. "They have taken 2,500 prisoners whom they treat most humanely." That same day, Aguinaldo signed the Philippine Declaration of Independence in a ceremony witnessed by the highest-ranking American military officer on hand at the nearby Cavite naval station. And when Dewey asked Aguinaldo to delay the taking of Manila until American ground troops arrived, "I beg for you to wait for [them] and let them take part in the final battle," was the translation Aguinaldo got from Dewey. "Let them share your final victory." Aguinaldo waited, as a show of respect for an ally.

Six weeks later, as it became clear Spain could not put up a real fight, the alliance between Aguinaldo and the Americans began to unravel. American commanders cut a deal with the Spanish governor-general in Manila to allow US troops to take the city in a bloodless Kabuki-theater assault, so long as no soldier from the Philippine army was allowed within the city walls. So after doing almost all the fighting on land, decimating the Spanish forces, investing the entire city of Manila and cutting off its water supply, making prisoners of nearly nine thousand Spanish soldiers, and sacrificing thousands of native men to the cause of Filipino independence, Aguinaldo noted, "Our reward was our exclusion and snubbing in the hour of final triumph. It was an insult and a betrayal hard to take." As American army units filed into Manila in a fairly calm procession on August 13, 1898, almost all their gunfire was aimed at the few Filipino troops who followed along in the expectation of taking part in the victory.

Most of Aguinaldo's fighters sat idle in their trenches outside town and watched at a distance as the Spanish flags came down and American flags rose high above the city, while a British warship in Manila Bay fired a twenty-gun salute in honor of the Stars and Stripes, irking a nearby German admiral. A young American private described the scene: "The tears filled my eyes and I choked up so that I could not shout for a moment . . . for the happiest moment in all my life was when I saw that flag on high. You ought to have heard the sailors cheer when it went up—that beautiful banner. . . . The United States is God's country." Nearly two months later, as Agoncillo and Lopez sat in their Washington hotel, Filipino soldiers were still unwelcome inside the city.

LAFAYETTE SQUARE WAS near tropical that first weekend in October; the temperature just kept rising, unbroken even by sudden bursts of rainfall. "Postage stamps melt into a liquid mass," John Hay complained. "Envelopes gum themselves together. The town steams like a tropical forest." The wet heat suited Don Felipe Agoncillo fine; he remained in his suite at the Arlington, working on his memorial for the US peace commissioners so that he might deliver the document, as the president had suggested, into the hands of John Hay at the State

Emilio Aguinaldo

Department. Agoncillo's task in presenting the Filipino case was to execute a dexterous piece of political jujitsu—using the compelling force of America's idea of itself to nudge it toward the cause of Filipino independence. He meant to echo Aguinaldo's own recent letter to the once-friendly US consul who was now dismissing as absurd the idea of self-government in the Philippines. "I am fully persuaded that the Filipinos will arrive at the height of happiness and glory if in the future they can show with raised heads the rights which to-day are shown by the free citizens of North America," Aguinaldo had argued. "I have full confidence in the generosity and philanthropy which shine in characters of gold in the history of the privileged people of the United States."

DON FELIPE AND Sixto Lopez maneuvered their horse-drawn coupe up to the steps of the building housing the Departments of State, War, and Navy shortly before noon on Tuesday, October 4, with their official ten-point memorial in hand. The two envoys bounded up the steps of the "wedding cake" edifice, each man wearing a well-tailored morning suit with striped pants, a patterned vest, a high silk hat, and a deep red carnation on his lapel. They meant to present the face of friendship and good cheer. This meeting with the chief diplomat of their powerful ally was as close to official recognition as they could expect, and they proceeded directly to the private office of the new secretary of state, who was, alas, absent. Agoncillo instead paid his respects to Alvey Adee, and when he learned that John Hay was at the White House for a regularly scheduled cabinet meeting, that his time of return could not be predicted, and that the secretary was unlikely to have the time for a personal meeting anyway, Don Felipe handed over his memorial to Adee and suggested he would try to call on the secretary again before he left town. "As the Filipinos left the State Department and entered the coupe," a reporter noted, "their faces wore an expression of acute disappointment."

HAY WAS HAPPY to have dodged the visit. He didn't relish another unwelcome hassle, his first week on the job having been one snag after another. He had already had to parry McKinley's request that he accompany him on a two-week campaign trip to the Midwest. But he could not wriggle free from the "invitation" to a full-dress White House party for the Episcopal bishops and honored laymen who had gathered in Washington that week for their triennial meeting. His main difficulty in attending the White House reception would be finding proper attire. The family steamer trunks were still piled in the back hallway of his house a week after Hay's arrival, and not only could he not find a key to any of them, but he had yet to *locate* the trunk that held his considerable wardrobe. The secretary of state of the United States of America had been living in the same two suits since he landed, buying new shirts, ties, undergarments, and socks as the need arose.

John Hay's domestic affairs were a shambles, mainly because he was living a bachelor existence, waiting for his wife to complete a three-week visit with her mother in Cleveland. And in spite of its comforting initial welcome, his house was not without its bothers: the Hamilton clock seemed broken beyond repair, a casualty of the capital's humidity, and the *once*-valuable Tanagra figurines were now in shards. The household staff was makeshift at best. Hay had never paid much attention to the anonymous faces who served him, but the ad hoc staff manning the long-empty Washington residence was a notably underwhelming assemblage. The kitchen maid was filling in admirably for the missing cook, but Hay's attempts to engage a new butler to run the household operation were disheartening. "A drunkard is inevitable," he complained in a letter to his wife.

Meanwhile, the daily mail drop added to the mountain of letters—from dozens of friends and acquaintances—begging Secretary of State Hay for a job at his department, or a consulship, or a place in some embassy or legation, which caused him no end of personal embarrassment. The president, it was now apparent, had promised away every position that might come up in the next year. Hay was pained to write in the negative to his friend William Dean Howells, whose bronze bust held a place of prominence in Hay's private library, in response to Howells's request for a spot for his brother, who actually was an experienced diplomat: "I got your letter in due time & have been waiting ever since, first to find time to write with mine own hand and second, to ransack the department & see what, if any, are my powers. I find that there is not a place vacant at this moment. Judge Day cleaned off the shelf before going to Paris: worse than that, for the one or two prospective vacancies in sight, the entire Senate has entered its caveats, and the President has ordered appointments."

The personnel John Hay did control at his department, he found, had been worked near to mental tatters in the previous year. Few had been able to get their thirty days' vacation, and there was whining aplenty. On the day of Hay's arrival at the department, the chief of the consular bureau absented himself for a month-long leave to get married at his fiancée's home in San Francisco. Poor Adee, chipper and cheerful in spite of it all, was in dire need of a rest, and soon; but how could Hay spare the second assistant secretary when the third assistant secretary was begging for six weeks off to take his eighteen-year-old Prussian bride—wife number three—on a honeymoon tour of Europe? "Both Adee & Cridler want to go away on leave & they are pulling hair over it to the Queen's taste," Hay reported to his wife.

The department, even with a full complement on deck, was woefully insufficient, especially now that Hay and his team might be asked to govern a new crop of territories or protectorates or colonies or some new invention in the Caribbean and the Pacific and the Far East, or to rewrite a fifty-year-old treaty with Great Britain to allow for Senator Lodge's dream—or was it a crucial national security *necessity* now?—of a canal through Nicaragua to connect the Atlantic and Pacific Oceans.

There were fewer than eighty professionals on the job and under Hay's direction in Washington, many of them hoary civil servants who quaked at newfangled technologies like the typewriter and the telephone. With this meager cohort, Hay was expected to reckon with the entire globe, and he was without power to add new positions or to make improvements in the ones he had. Hay was unable to persuade President McKinley to pick his trusted friend (and a needed Asian expert) William Woodville Rockhill for first assistant secretary. The president gave the job instead to a tariff-happy Republican committeeman from upstate New York to whom he owed political favors. Adee, Thomas W. Cridler, and two other long-suffering employees in the department were especially unhappy to get this news, because each had put in a plea for the first assistant's job, which meant, as Hay explained to Henry White, "there are many kickers under one roof."

Then, too, the torturous drip of daily chores at the State Department made Hay pine for the quiet of his ambassadorial desk at 5 Carlton House Terrace in London. After just two working days in Washington, Hay decided to push up his regular arrival time at the office by half an hour, and he still felt as if he was playing catch-up from start to finish, while enduring constant unnecessary interruption. "I receive twenty or thirty worrying visits a day; all from people wanting something," he confided to his wife. "Two or three chargés d'affaires call; from fifty to a hundred dispatches must be read and signed. (I will not sign without reading, as Mr. Sherman did.) . . . I do not know how long I can stand it but certainly there is no fun or comfort in it."

And again to Mrs. Hay: "Adee has just come in with the request of a pen-maker that the Spanish treaty be signed with his pen; also that we shall send him a photo of McKinley shaking hands with the Queen of Spain! These are some of the daily tasks."

"I can only do my best till I drop in my tracks," he wrote to a friend.

Why would he add to his list of these stupid complications a nonofficial visitor from a government the United States had deemed unworthy of recognition? He had no appetite for small talk with somebody named Felipe Agoncillo, and as for Agoncillo's document, he had neither the time nor the inclination to read it. The native memorial on the Philippines and its "so-called Republic" was not, after all, among the operative documents on file at the State Department and the White House that particular week. The reports that mattered, the ones the White House had shipped over for John Hay's consideration, were General Francis V. Greene's blandly titled "Memoranda Concerning the Situation in the Philippine Islands," along with the written testimony and memoranda General Wesley Merritt, who had been Greene's superior officer in the Philippines, was presenting to the American peace commissioners in Paris that same morning. These US Army reports were settling the issue of the Philippines.

The main source of information in these memoranda comprised the observations of the two generals, along with an army engineer and a judge advocate, none of whom had logged more than six weeks in the Philippines; Rear Admiral Dewey, who had been living in splendid isolation in Manila Bay, in the world's most ferociously armed houseboats; a surgeon in the US volunteer forces in the Philippines who had spent three years on various scientific expeditions on the archipelago and had "always talked freely with the people of whatever place I have visited"; and a Belgian consul general in Manila who was very intent on maintaining stability in the commerce of the Philippines. (The Belgian had been so terrified of the Americans' bombing Manila that he had almost personally engineered Spain's property-sensitive and face-saving capitulation of the city, because, as he explained to Dewey, "all the property I have in the world is in Manila.")

The various personal estimations and opinions in the reports tracked to the same not particularly accurate or charitable conclusions, to wit: The small "copper colored" natives were pliant and capable of hard and sustained labor, though not as vigorous as the Chinese. The Filipinos—whether the Christianized Tagalogs and Visayans, or the Muslims of the southern islands, or the primitive hill people—were "docile." "The people are for the most part easily controlled by proper methods, the essence of which can be expressed in two words—justice and firmness," the surgeon noted. Filipinos en masse lacked understanding of political autonomy, had no desire for it, and were not capable of it. "They belong to an inferior race," offered the Belgian consul, "unfitted to rule a country." Even the most generous American witness, to his regret, concluded that the Filipinos did not possess a sufficiently developed sense of equity to govern the country with fairness to all citizens.

The only possible complications to simply taking and running the whole of the Philippines, the reports offered, were popular Tagolog rebel leaders like Aguinaldo, who had nursed and succored the rebellion among the poor and uneducated country people and now wanted to rule. General Greene, who had so cordially escorted Felipe Agoncillo from the San Francisco pier to the White House Cabinet Room, was blunt in his disdain for Aguinaldo's leadership of the temporary revolutionary government. It was "a dictatorship of the familiar South American type," Greene wrote, eliding the fact that an American consul had requested that Aguinaldo create just this sort of government to control his army. "Pure despotism," Greene called it. "Aguinaldo himself never failed to claim all the prerogatives due to his alleged position as the de facto ruler of the country."

Worse still, according to the consensus of the US reports, Aguinaldo had stirred up a dangerous and disorganized pack of wild young marauders with no property and nothing to lose, who sat menacing the outskirts of Manila, waiting for their chance to loot the city. "If the United States does not take these islands under their protection, the country will be utterly ruined and all the foreign merchants will leave these islands," warned the Belgian consul/foreign merchant.

Well, anybody who was reading these reports closely, and whose sense of irony had not been put in total eclipse by American pride and prerogative, had to recognize with amusement the invitation to a looting expedition after the most modern and organized fashion—and not just in Manila, or Luzon, but in the whole of the Philippines. The naturalist-surgeon included in his write-up a shopping list of the natural resources in the various islands. Cebu held sugar and hemp, as well as deposits of coal and petroleum. Panay had the second-most-important commercial port, Iloilo, and great swaths of farmland under cultivation. Palawan had another fine harbor and untouched forests of the "most valuable woods" (the German kaiser had his eye on that). Negros produced sugar; Samar and Leyte had hemp of the highest quality.

General Greene, a practicing capitalist himself, was more businesslike and much more specific in his reporting. He noted the $882,451.39 seized from the Spanish authorities when the US Army took Manila. "I believe that the law in such cases was clearly defined in decisions made by the United States Supreme Court in 1815," the general explained. "We captured Manila, and the capitulation (under which these funds became United States property) was signed by both parties." The American military government in Manila pocketed $100,000 in customs fees in the first three weeks after the takeover, Greene reported. Spain's $30 million of bonded debt the Americans left in Spanish hands. The general dug into the colonial account books, figured the income and the expenses of the islands to the dollar, and noted a most favorable import-export balance: $23,558,552 in imports as against $33,149,984 in exports. He itemized $12 million worth of hemp exported from the Philippines, $11 million worth of sugarcane, $2.4 million in coconuts, and $1.75 million in tobacco. "Manila cigars of the best quality are unknown in America; they are but little inferior to the best of Cuba and cost only one-third as much." He suspected the coffee industry could be reinvigorated, sugar production enlarged, and the mineral resources exploited. "With these islands in our possession and the construction of railways in the interior of Luzon, it is possible that an enormous extension could be given to this commerce," Greene concluded. "We ought to be able to secure the greater part of the trade which now goes to Spain in textile fabrics, and a considerable portion of that with England in the same goods and in iron."

Even Dewey, who still occasionally exhibited some remorse about his dealings with Aguinaldo, and still insisted the local population was fit for self-rule, saw the pecuniary upside of grabbing, at the very least, Luzon and Manila. "Were railroads and highways built—and labor is very cheap—there is little doubt that this island would rapidly increase in productiveness and wealth," he reported. "[Luzon] is nearest the great centers of trade in the far East, such as Hongkong, Canton, Shanghai, Pekin, Nagasaki and Yokohama, and nearest the trade routes from the United States and Honolulu to those centers; consequently its influence would be greater if held by us."

FELIPE AGONCILLO WAS not privy to the reports circulating through the White House and the various cabinet departments around Washington, but neither was he insensitive to the gale force of the diplomatic winds now blowing into his own face. In the days after Agoncillo's abortive visit to the State Department, Agoncillo and Lopez had become, in a flash, caricatures to delight American newspaper readers: little brown men in ill-fitting suits, spouting malapropisms: "We have had a cock good time.... Ah, we proceed much.... We observe much with the eye."

Don Felipe did not lose heart. He had spent much of his legal career in the Spanish-held Philippines advocating for people with no resources and no political standing. He wasn't going to surrender now. On his way out of Washington to board a ship to Paris, Agoncillo stopped long enough to deliver a message to the conclave of Episcopalians meeting in the city. His note was accepted in Christian brotherhood, then translated and read to the assembly at large: "We fulfill our purpose in supplicating you to offer your prayers to the Most High on behalf of the natives of the Philippine Islands," Agoncillo had written, "and in asking you to do all that can be done to protect and help them in this supreme moment of their history, and to assure them their liberty and protected personality, to which they are entitled by their loyalty and their services to the American cause."

Two days later, however, after the two Filipinos had left town, Agoncillo's message underwent some editing. The translation "was not an absolutely correct one," it was noted in the Episcopal assembly, "the appeal to the convention not being that it do something to give the Philippines their rights, but that the prayers to the Almighty might be that the people have a true religion." The convention's board of missions also had something to say that day. "What will occur with regard to Cuba, the Philippines and one or more of the Ladrone Islands, it is premature to say. It is certain, however, that the accession of territory means increased missionary responsibility."

Agoncillo left Washington without ever having laid eyes on the secretary of state, who was, the day of the Filipino envoy's departure, hosting his first formal reception for the *official and recognized* Washington diplomatic corps. Hay was disappointed that his great friend and the dean of the ambassadorial contingent, the Brit Julian Pauncefote, was not there to lead the procession into the diplomatic anteroom. Sir Julian was suffering an attack of gout and had decided to extend his summer's retreat from the American capital, so he sent his regrets. Neither were the French, the German, or the Russian envoys on hand, though this was not entirely unexpected, as Hay had already heard grumblings from their embassies about his reputed favoritism for all things British.

Still, half a hundred souls filed into the anteroom, and it took a full thirty minutes for Alvey Adee to escort Secretary Hay down the line. The all-knowing Adee presented his new boss to various ministers and chargés d'affaires, who then wanted to present to John Hay their own assistants and attachés, which meant Hay found himself suffering through the first of the heap of unwelcome public duties he would be obliged to perform as long as he held office. He complained privately, but he was determined to shoulder the load for the country, for the administration, and for his friend the president. He would do his duty in all ways. This was who he was, who he had always been: a man who would not shirk when needed, whatever the personal cost.

There was little in the way of immediate recompense for the new secretary of state at the reception that day. He was pleased to find a few old friends among the callers, but most of the diplomats were of the non-European, nonwhite persuasion. Why, he wondered, did he have to make nice with the minister from Nicaragua or Colombia or Costa Rica, or, as he described him, "that bright little nig" from Haiti? "They were mostly dagoes & chargés," Hay complained in a letter to his wife a few hours after the reception ended. But he had done his duty, had stuck it out, had made nice with the various international personalities and personages and peons, right down to the end of the line.

CHAPTER TWENTY-SIX

Planned and Designed by the Master of Men

YOUNG MAN: What do you say of duty for duty's sake?

OLD MAN: That *it does not exist.* Duties are not performed for duty's *sake*, but because their *neglect* would make the man *uncomfortable.* A man performs but *one* duty—the duty of contenting his spirit, the duty of making himself agreeable to himself. . . . Men pretend to self-sacrifices, but this is a thing which, in the ordinary value of the phrase, *does not exist and has not existed.*

This sardonic little exchange was tucked among the hundreds of new manuscript pages Sam Clemens was about to haul back to Vienna after the family's quiet summer in the salubrious air of a little resort town in the foothills twenty kilometers outside the city. The chief objective of the retreat had been for Livy Clemens to have the benefit of Kaltenleutgeben's cold-water cure. Sam Clemens had heard the cure praised in the finest salons of Vienna, and he had arrived at the resort with hopes that the waters might buoy his wife, who was suffering bouts of rheumatism and generalized grief-induced lassitude. He had not been much cheered by the early results. Livy had seemed weaker in spite of the treatment. "It may be that the benefit comes *after* the course," he wrote to Henry Rogers. "I hope so."

Livy's main comfort that summer had been in watching her husband, unyoked as he was from the social pull of Vienna and, now that the debtor's ransom had been paid in full, from the weight of financial distress. The family had a little money on deposit in London and with Henry Rogers in New York; income was trickling in from the *Equator* book, and there was the promise of more money from the compilation of Sam's earlier work into a multivolume uniform set; Rogers had managed to clear the Webster debts while preserving Livy's ownership of the "Mark Twain" copyrights, as well as her inheritance from her father, which was throwing off still more income for the family. Livy was pleased to see her husband engaged and happy, working as he had in the old days at their summer retreat in upstate New York, when he was writing *Tom Sawyer* and *Huck Finn* and *Connecticut Yankee*. "Summer is the time!" Clemens would rhapsodize, "—wish there were more of it."

And still, Livy refused to let herself believe that the bounce in her husband's work step heralded the return to high cotton for the Clemens family. "Sometimes I have felt almost frightened lest it be his swan song," Livy wrote to a friend as she was packing up the household to move her husband and daughters back to Vienna, "but it continues & he seems well."

Actually, he had had a tremendous lark at his desk in Kaltenleutgeben, using the time to amuse himself by fiendishly whittling down tales and essays into sharp instruments aimed at deserving targets. He had continued sketching his tale of a visit to Earth from a fun-loving, earnest, and charming young son of Satan, the most popular boy in town; and he reworked an earlier short story inspired by his days as a young husband and patriarch-in-training in Hartford. "Wapping Alice" was a fictionalized retelling of an incident in which Sam Clemens forced a housemaid and a local carpenter into marriage after he discovered them trysting in the Clemens house. He gave this new iteration another strange turn by remaking the maid, young Alice—a native of the Wapping section of London—as a man *passing* for a woman, and without offering any rational explanation. "Why he unsexed himself," Clemens wrote, "was his own affair."

Clemens had produced as many pages of "philosophy" as he had pages of story that summer. He spent hours on end writing about the nature of the human race and the preposterous untruths it was in the habit of telling itself, such as, for instance, about the God who was keeping such a jealous and obsessive eye on mankind. If the Omnipotent Being truly wanted to win all of humanity to the glory of Christianity, Sam Clemens reasoned, would the divine plan really be to outsource the job to priests and missionaries for nineteen hundred years and then blame the wiles of Satan for God's own inability to haul in more than a sorry one-fifth of all humanity? Was Satan more powerful than God by a factor of four? Was God playing possum, waiting for a big strike? The answer, plainly observable as a fact of nature, Clemens believed, was that God didn't really give a tinker's damn about humankind. Man, as far as Clemens could see, was an invisible and unheeded mass of bacteria to the creator of all things. All the unjust pain and suffering visited upon the righteous and innocent, all the worldly rewards bestowed upon the wicked—they were just accidents and outcomes of divine lack of interest. The hand of God was simply not available to man, even for hire.

"He cares nothing for men's flatteries, compliments, praises, prayers—it is impossible that He should value them, impossible that He should listen to them, these mouthings of microbes," Clemens wrote in his notebook in Kaltenleutgeben.

> He is not ignorant; He does not mistake his myriad great suns, swimming the measureless ocean of space, for tallow candles hung in the roof to light this forgotten potato which we call the earth & name His footstool. He cannot see it except under His microscope. . . .
>
> The Bible of Nature tells us no word about any future life, but only about this present one. It does not promise a future life, it does not even vaguely indicate one. It is not intended as a message to us, any more than the scientist intends a message to surviving microbes when he boils the life out of a billion of them in a thimble. The microbes discover the message in it; this is certain—if they have a pulpit.

He did not present this work to Livy for editing and emendation—didn't care to have his wings clipped in the middle of such joyous flight. The most fulfilling work he had done that summer he also did on the sly. He hadn't quite decided what to call it—his "gospel," his "bible," his "private philosophy"—but he knew what he meant to say, and he had worked out a form also: a Socratic bull session between Young Man and Old Man. The older man serves as mouthpiece for Clemens as he spools out his observations on human nature—those humbuggeries of duty and self-sacrifice, for instance—to the scandalized and increasingly disoriented Young Man, who mounts a mealy defense of humankind: "Now look here—let us call a halt," cries the youth.

> "I have stood the other infamies and insanities and that is enough; I am not going to have man and the other animals put on the same level morally."
>
> "I wasn't going to hoist man up to that."
>
> "This is too much! I think it is not right to jest about such things."
>
> "I am not jesting, I am merely reflecting a plain and simple truth—and without uncharitableness. The fact that man knows right from wrong proves his *intellectual* superiority to the other creatures; but the fact that he can *do* wrong proves his *moral* inferiority to any creatures that *cannot*."

Clemens had been constructing this philosophy in his head for years, and he rested it on one bedrock principle, based on a lifetime of observable proofs, with himself as the alpha exhibit. Nobody, he had concluded, could escape the one immutable fact of human nature, the root cause of all human action: "This is the law, keep it in your mind. *From his cradle to his grave a man never does a single thing which has any* FIRST AND FOREMOST *object but one—to secure peace of mind, spiritual comfort, for* HIMSELF." He liked that line and clothed it in italics and caps to stand it apart. This was an idea to reckon with.

Sam Clemens was, of course, aware that publicizing his private philosophy was a fool's errand. The microbe who introduced an uncomfortable thought-mutation into an otherwise contented culture, he knew, would be the most unwelcome member of the petri dish. "Many a man will examine Selfishness & apply the tests, & (to himself) confess judgment," he had recorded in his notebook that summer, "but to confess it in public! He would not be a man if he had that much pluck. I have no pluck to publish it, the outside influences (my wife, the risk of destroying my reputation & my family's bread) being dead against it & stronger than my desire to print. To print it would do thousands of men a real service I do believe, but I am too selfish to damage *my* comfort to promote theirs."

As he wrote to Rogers at the close of the summer sojourn: "It has been a good peace for me; I have written a raft of stuff—for publication when I am dead, mainly."

SAM CLEMENS DID allow that maybe there was something about attaching one's self to an institution, of subsuming the self in a larger cause, that expanded a man's generosity muscle or gave him an escape hatch from the destiny of self-interest. Clemens had plenty of friends for whom he would gladly cede that point. William Dean Howells had labored through two decades to build the *Atlantic Monthly* magazine and increase its sway in the world of thinking men and women, and there wasn't a more generous man on the planet; blessed Joe Twichell had spent his entire adult life growing and tending his church in Hartford, and his parishioners were all better for it. And consider John Hay: He had served President Lincoln night and day for four years, then worked in US consulates all over Europe. And now here he was, on the job again as secretary of state, earning a lousy $8,000 a year—the cost of one of his wife's necklace-and-tiara sets, most likely—because he believed in the consecrated mission of the American republic and the pledge he had heard Lincoln make over the dead at Gettysburg: "It is for us, the living, rather to be dedicated here to the unfinished work which they have, thus far, so nobly carried on. . . . We here highly resolve that these dead shall not have died in vain; . . . that this government of the people, by the people, for the people, shall not perish from the earth." Hay liked to remind the overly righteous that he was suffering a mighty hairy hangover that morning in Pennsylvania in 1863, but the message stuck just the same. And as far as Clemens could tell, Hay had not been able to shake it.

Sam Clemens didn't put much stock in institutions or larger causes, made up as they were of the human race, by the human race, for the human race.

Everything was *personal* for him, including the American republic itself. He might not always agree with the actions of its governors, might find them—as in what he'd seen of the coming Spanish-American War settlements—equal parts grasping and moronic, but he still thought of his native country as a friend. "The proper office of a friend is to side with you when you are wrong," he had jotted in his notebook in Austria. "Nearly anybody will side with you when you are in the right."

There was really only one institution in which Sam Clemens had invested his energy and his faith; it could fairly be said he had spent nearly *all* his energy and faith on that one. And that was the institution Clemens had organized himself, and funded, reinvented, refurbished, and polished with vigor: his creation and his crutch, "Mark Twain." He had done a pretty fair job of keeping its value on a steady upward trajectory. Fifteen years earlier, even before the publication of *Adventures of Huckleberry Finn*, "Mark Twain" had polled in the top fifteen in a popular vote to select "Forty Immortals" for inclusion in a new literary pantheon, the American Academy of Letters. And "Mark" was still on the rise. A new poll was about to name him first runner-up in America's literary beauty pageant. The previous top three—Oliver Wendell Holmes, James Russell Lowell, and John Greenleaf Whittier—had exhausted their eligibility by dying, but "Mark Twain" had leapfrogged over living authors like Thomas Bailey Aldrich, George Washington Cable, Henry James, and (most happily) the despicable Bret Harte. Only Howells stood above him now in the hearts of reading Americans, and even Howells bowed down before his old friend. "You have pervaded our century almost more than any other man of letters," he had just written to Clemens, "if not quite more; and it is astonishing how you keep spreading." Turns out "Mark Twain's" well-publicized slog through the mire of bankruptcy had only increased his fame.

Sam Clemens was not shy to exploit this celebrity right up to its full value; take, for instance, the new residence the Clemens family settled into in Vienna in the middle of October 1898—a suite of rooms at the just-completed, modern, and splendidly appointed Hotel Krantz. When the Clemenses had taken their brief leave of the city in May, Sam had reconciled himself to moving the family back to the Hotel Metropole for the following winter, but then Livy had ventured into the Krantz on one of her day trips from Kaltenleutgeben to Vienna and found a large oil painting of her husband hanging in the lobby. Neither Livy nor Sam was sure of the provenance of this portrait, but as Sam reported to Rogers, its public display suggested that the Krantz was "a hotel that has taste."

The painting inspired Clemens to commence a campaign for a large discount on a suite of rooms there, playing the Hotel Krantz against the Hotel Metropole, which was already giving him a cut-rate deal—probably half the cost charged to a normal and uncelebrated guest. "The [Krantz] dropped another [forty dollars]," Clemens bragged to Rogers,

> & indicated that they were ready to come lower still; but really it was already robbery, & we surrendered & said [the offer] would answer.
>
> The Krantz is a fine building & is completely & richly furnished like the Waldorf. . . . We have a dining room, a parlor, a music-parlor, a study, & 4 bedrooms—& there are bathrooms attached to 3 of the bedrooms. . . . I used to be a little ashamed when Ambassadors & dukes & such called on us in that rusty & rather shabby Metropole, but they'll mistake us for millionaires next fall & will probably lend us money.

The proprietors of the Krantz liked their deal with Clemens just fine; they got what they needed, too. Newspapers around Europe and the United States announced the arrival of "Mark Twain" at his new winter home in Vienna, and the hotel itself was soon advertising in the *New York Tribune*, among other American papers:

HOTEL KRANTZ
"Newest and Most Modern in the City"
First Class Family House
"The Home of Mark Twain"

Sam Clemens understood the transaction: with discounts come responsibilities. He had to sing for his supper. The hotel? "There is nothing approaching it in France, Germany or Austria," he assured friends. The elixir of the local cafés? "That unapproachable luxury," he wrote for publication the week he returned to Vienna, "that sumptuous coffee-house coffee, compared with which all European coffee and all American hotel coffee is mere fluid poverty." He made a point to be seen around the neighborhood also. "In connection with this custom which the Austrians have of working over a cup of coffee, the Viennese relate that Mark Twain may frequently be found in a certain large café on the Ringstrasse plying his pencil over page after page of his fat notebook," reported the Vienna correspondent of the *New York Times*. "From this the Austrians strongly suspect that the American humorist is preparing some fun of which they will be the subject."

Clemens felt obliged to accept as many social invitations as he could, including a summons to the Ronacher ballroom just four days after his return to Vienna, to bear witness to a meeting hosted by the Austrian Society of the Friends of Peace. The purpose of the event was to enlarge popular support for Czar Nicholas II's surprising new manifesto calling for worldwide disarmament.

The czar was becoming worried that the hundreds of millions of rubles and francs and deutschmarks and pounds and dollars expended in the arms race was a threat to prosperity, productivity, and peace. "It is the supreme duty . . . of all States to put some limit to these unceasing armaments and to find means of averting the calamities which threaten the whole world," the Russian minister of foreign affairs had written. "Impressed by this feeling, his Majesty the Emperor has been pleased to command me to propose to all Governments accredited to the Imperial Court the meeting of a conference to discuss this grave problem."

The head dame of the peace movement in Vienna, Baroness Bertha von Suttner, had engaged a Prussian military officer turned Christian-based peace advocate—and the author of *Ernste Gedanken* (*Serious Thoughts*)—to expound and defend the czar's manifesto at the Ronacher that Wednesday evening. But when the Prussian had finished his talk and other luminaries had had their say, members of the audience pressed "Mark Twain" to weigh in.

He shambled up onto the stage, and as he began to talk, the baroness grew nervous. Clemens had already explained to von Suttner months earlier that while he was in sympathy with her peace aims, he didn't think much of their chances for success. "[The movement] can appeal to the selfishness of nations, possibly," he had written to her, "but nations have no command over their governments, & in fact no influence over them, except of a fleeting & rather ineffectual sort." And to another of her friends and colleagues, he had been harsher: "Peace by persuasion has a pleasant sound, but I think we should not be able to work it. We should have to tame the human race first, and history seems to show that that cannot be done."

Sam Clemens, though, saw no margin in making a head-on challenge to the crowd of eager peacemongers that night at the Ronacher. He had long been skeptical of this universal peace movement, he slowly drawled out to the crowd, but the czar's recent statement had "made a convert of him." The baroness drew a great sigh of relief when the American author, after searching his pockets for an uncomfortably long interval, finally pulled out a prop and held it aloft. "As far as I am concerned," she heard him say, "having only a penknife on me, I am ready to disarm."

THIS WAS AS close as Sam Clemens got to commenting on the state of world affairs that autumn. He was happy to boom Viennese accommodations and libation but had no opinion to offer about the big story on the Continent in his first weeks at the Krantz—the treaty conference in Paris between the Spanish and the Americans (whose number included that turd Whitelaw Reid). The American commissioners seemed to be kicking hell out of the Spanish, who could mount little in the way of defense even at the negotiating table. But dodging comment was a pretty simple thing for Clemens to do in Vienna that fall. The Austrians were not paying much attention to treaty negotiations in Paris, the ignominious rout of the Spanish having taken the starch out of the America bashing in the salons of Vienna. And Austrian newspapers were much more interested in the recent assassination of their empress and the state of the Viennese theater than in the future of the Philippines.

PRESIDENT WILLIAM MCKINLEY, as his friends and acquaintances and later biographers would tell it, was rending his magisterial garments over the question of the Philippines as the peace commission began its work. "I walked the floor of the White House night after night until midnight," was how an official of the missionary committee of the Methodist Episcopal Church would later quote the president, "and I am not ashamed to tell you that I went down on my knees and prayed Almighty God for light and guidance more than one night." In the secular version of the tale, the president decided the best course was to defer to the judgment and wisdom of the American people, which was why, at just after seven o'clock on the morning of October 11, 1898, as the sun burned off the last of the previous night's heavy rain, the Presidential Express was chuffing west at fifty miles an hour across Illinois on the Chicago and North Western Railway.

The president was headed for a date at the Trans-Mississippi and International Exposition in Omaha, carrying with him friends and family, a few cabinet members, and officials from the War Department and the State Department. A separate train of Wagner sleepers trailed the president's with a handful of the best-celebrated heroes from the recent overseas battles (along with their wives, aides, valets, and attachés), a dozen or more news correspondents, and diplomatic representatives from China, Korea, Brazil, Argentina, and newly liberated Cuba. The trip to the near edge of Nebraska and back had a twelve-day itinerary, with half a dozen major speeches—in Omaha, Chicago, St. Louis, and Springfield, Illinois—as well as dozens of announced and advertised whistlestops where the president would show himself, make a few remarks, campaign for fellow Republicans on the ballot in the upcoming midterm elections, and afford himself (as the story went) the opportunity to tap into that vast reservoir of wisdom that is the American citizenry, to look for guidance on the complicated question of what to do with the Philippines.

William McKinley had been anxious and excited before his first presidential trip west of the Mississippi and had asked John Hay, with uncharacteristic eagerness, to accompany him. When Hay declined the offer—there was too much work to do at the State Department and he was still getting his feet under him, he had explained—McKinley insisted on sitting down with his new secretary of state in the Cabinet Room and reading him the full text of the speech he had prepared for the exposition in Omaha. And even when the president received the shocking news, on the eve of departure, that Mrs. McKinley's brother had been shot to death in their hometown of Canton, Ohio, in what was reported to be exceedingly tawdry circumstances, the president refused to alter his speaking schedule. "I imagine [Mrs. McKinley] will not care much about it," John Hay theorized to his own wife. "She is very feeble, both in body and mind. . . . The vulgarity and disgrace of it will not affect her." The president simply added to Ida McKinley's normal dose of daily sedatives, detoured his party through Canton, and kept the press apprised of his grieving wife's state of mind. After attending the private services and the burial, McKinley had left his wife behind in Canton, hopped back onto his private railroad car, enjoyed a predeparture cigar, and woke the next day to find himself in Illinois and pointed toward the rolling hills of Iowa.

What surprised the president that day was the *excitement* his approach created at the depot of every little town along the route. Townsfolk lined the track at each stop and crowded rows-deep into every station, all to see the first victory-leading war president since Abraham Lincoln. The cheering began when the presidential engine, draped in red, white, and blue decoration, first specked the horizon and did not cease until long after the Major stepped onto the open-air platform of his private car. He always had to stand silent until the noise subsided enough for him to begin his remarks. "I appreciate your generous welcome, and share with you in the congratulations to our country and to your army and navy for the successful issues of the last four months," he said at the first stop, at just after nine o'clock in the morning. "I am sure there has never been a time in our history when patriotism has been more marked or more universal than it is to-day."

His successive stops were always brief, and the people in attendance loath to let him move on. As McKinley's train pulled away from the crowd in Dixon, Illinois, a young man jumped up onto the presidential car, caught hold of the railing, and reached for McKinley. "Give us a shake, please." McKinley grabbed the teenager's hand as the train gathered speed, and advised him to jump while it was still safe. In Sterling, Illinois, a reporter on the presidential train noted that every man, woman, and child in town appeared to be on hand. In Clinton, Iowa, the same man wrote, an enormous American flag hung from an electric line kept swinging over toward the president as he spoke. "We have, too, a good national conscience, and we have the courage of destiny," McKinley said under that enormous waving Old Glory. "Our achievements on land and sea are without parallel in the world's history."

McKinley seemed to gain confidence as the day went on, and pumped up the sum and substance of his talk so that it might match the thunderous roar of the audience. "This war, that was so speedily closed through the valor and intrepidity of our soldiers, will bring us, I trust, blessings that are now beyond calculation. It will bring also burdens, but the American people never shirk a responsibility and never unload a burden that carries forward civilization. . . . Out of the bitterness and woe, the privations and sufferings and anxieties of the past five months, will flow the benefits to the nation which may be more important than we can now realize." He even managed the unlikely feat of swelling patriotic pride in the American genius for merging a selfless and virtuous cause with good business sense. "You will be glad to be reminded," he told the crowd at Marshalltown, Iowa, "that when it was necessary to raise money for the prosecution of the war, and a loan was sought of two hundred millions of dollars, more than fourteen hundred millions were subscribed by the people of the United States, and for the first time in our history your government, my government, sells a three percent bond, a bond which sold at par, which is now worth a premium of five cents on every dollar, which profit has gone to the people."

For fifteen hours, across 490 miles, at fifteen different stops, McKinley's train of thought barreled unimpeded through throngs of what looked like happy, prosperity-plumped midwesterners. The president extended his brief stays only long enough to accept small gifts, like the gold-topped walking cane presented to him by high school students from the central Iowa town of Boone.

By the time he was welcomed into Omaha by two hundred thousand cheering citizens, on streets illuminated by a glow of electric lights the power of which had never before been seen on the American plains, and then marched through downtown, beneath dozens of pictures of himself plastered onto the buildings, amid unceasing undulations of applause, William McKinley felt sure he was plugged into the great reservoir. The American people, in the glow of what seemed more like lusty desire than wisdom and sober judgment, evidenced by their loud and prolonged shows of approval, had backed everything their president had to say that day. "Providence has been extremely kind to the American people—kind not only in the recent conflict of arms, but in every step and stage of our history from its very beginning until now. We have been singularly blessed and favored. The past of our country is secure, and it is glorious," William McKinley had extemporized as the day's journey wound to its conclusion. "We have a great country—we will be excused if we say the greatest country in the world; great in possibilities, great in its opportunities. And with these rest upon all of us great responsibilities. I trust that we will be able to meet them and to measure up to every opportunity of honor and duty."

FOR THE NEXT full week in the mellifluous early-autumn weather, as the presidential train swung around and headed back toward the capital, McKinley kept sharpening his talk: a divine blessing was upon the nation; America's aims were noble and selfless; rewards necessarily follow duties manfully performed. "Shall we deny to ourselves what the rest of the world so freely and so justly accords us?" he asked. And the crowds shouted, *No!* "Territory sometimes comes to us when we go to war in a holy cause, and whenever it does the banner of liberty will float over it and bring, I trust, blessings and benefits to all the people."

Through scores of whistle-stop speeches in scores of cities and towns, McKinley preached duty and selflessness and spoke reverently of the new world markets for the surplus broomcorn produced in places like *right here* in Arcola, Illinois. He did not, however, talk of the people America had successfully liberated—the Cubans or the Puerto Ricans. The words "Philippines" and "Filipinos" never passed his lips. But nobody doubted his meaning when he talked about responsibilities and *rewards.* They got the drift even across the Atlantic. "It is clear there will be no abatement of the American minimum demands [at the Paris Peace Conference]," commented the *Speaker* in London. "President McKinley's speeches, indeed, indicate that those demands are likely to become more rather than less extensive."

The president was rallying a crowd in Chicago on October 18, when the United States, by an earlier agreement with Spain, officially assumed sovereignty over Puerto Rico. "The currents of destiny flow through the hearts of the people," the president said that day in Chicago. "Who will check them? Who will divert them? Who will stop them? And the movements of men, planned and designed by the Master of men, will never be interrupted by the American people."

THE TRIP TURNED out to be all that the president had hoped. He had known when he left Washington exactly what he meant to do about the Philippines, and his travels had convinced him that he could do as he saw fit, and with the full backing of the American people. Even Mrs. McKinley had caught the imperial bug by the time the First Couple arrived back at the White House. She certainly needed something to keep her occupied in the aftermath of her brother's murder. The papers were beginning to give a full accounting of the dissolute life and salacious career of the forty-nine-year-old George Saxton. He had been shot dead, it was supposed, by a jealous lover on the front steps of another of his many paramours. A female suspect—a tall, slender woman dressed in black—had already been charged with his murder, but her attorney insisted there was a large pool of possible suspects, and all with plausible motives. Behind George Saxton, going back more than a quarter century, was a trail of jilted women, angry fathers, and distraught husbands, at least one of whom had brought suit against Saxton for the "alienation of the wife's affections." On the evening of Saxton's death, there were at least three separate women who believed they were secretly betrothed to him. As one of the more intrepid newsmen on the ground in Canton reported, "The best friend that George Saxton ever had told him time and time again that some woman would kill him some day, and that the jury who tried her would release her on the plea of justifiable homicide."

Ida McKinley told her friends that while she loved her brother deeply, she was entirely unfamiliar with his personal affairs. She had seen her brother into his proper Christian grave, but she eschewed the conventions of mourning and was, quite literally, sticking to her knitting. She sat in her comfy old rocking chair in the Executive Mansion, fashioning bedroom slippers for friends and black satin neckties for her husband. She gulped down her doctor-prescribed sedatives, braved nights out at the theater, and entertained private guests in the parlor of the White House residence for games of euchre, which she always insisted on winning. But the First Lady seemed to have picked up a new public cause near the end of the western swing, after she had rejoined her husband's traveling party. Ida McKinley was now professing herself intensely interested in the Christianization of some of the interior tribesmen of northern Luzon in the Philippines. "Mrs. McKinley talked ten to the minute about converting the Igorrotes," one friend remembered of a visit soon after her return. She asked that his children pray for them.

ON OCTOBER 23, 1898, President McKinley rode through the rich autumn crimsons and golds to the high ground above Washington, at Mount St. Alban, to help the Episcopal bishops unveil a peace cross. The skies were clear and the president could see the slanting sun glint off the white Capitol dome and silver the Potomac River as he climbed the hill. "His step was firm and elastic," one newspaperman noted of the president, "his eyes were bright and he manifested a reverent interest in the proceedings." After a hymn and a recitation of the Apostles' Creed, and lessons and collections, the bishop of Washington offered a solemn prayer. "Today we face the glowing future with the divine conviction that as this country was born of God in the beginning of its history, so it has a great mission, given by God, to bear fruit among nations," intoned Bishop Satterlee. "Our country has awakened to a realization that there must be a divine purpose in it all; awakened to hear above the noise and tumult the angels' song of peace, goodwill. It has been truly said that in those one hundred days of war God carried this dear country forward one hundred years."

JOHN HAY WAS hardly surprised when the president presented him a few days later with a new set of instructions to send to the peace commissioners in Paris. They were to insist on the cession from Spain to the United States of America of *every square mile* of the Philippines. "Grave as are the responsibilities and unforeseen as are the difficulties which are before us," Hay's cable read, "the President can see but one plain path of duty—the acceptance of the archipelago." Hay knew Whitelaw would be in a tremor of ecstasy at this news; this was what he had been advocating all along.

The president was more worried about the reaction of his friend William Day, who had always believed the question of grabbing up territory like the Philippines was of a more juridical nature than a divine one. William McKinley had already sent a note to his old friend, who was leading the peace commission in Paris. "There is a very general feeling that the United States, whatever it might prefer as to the Philippines, is in a situation where it cannot let go," McKinley wired. "It is my judgment that the well-considered opinion of the majority would be that duty requires we should take the archipelago."

CHAPTER TWENTY-SEVEN

Back into the Great Happy River of Life

It had been a long time since any good bit of Clemens family planning had come out right or on schedule. Sam Clemens had not exactly grown accustomed to this obvious fact of his life, but he had resigned himself to it. And yet he did have hope for the new itinerary. Herr Professor Leschetizky had assured Sam and Livy back in the springtime of 1898 that Clara was only a year away from completing her instruction at his private conservatory and would then be capable of continuing her studies on her own, wherever the family desired. The Clemenses knew that Leschetizky was not one to shade the truth, not where students were involved. So Sam and Livy held fast to this expert assessment and began to plan accordingly. Sam left the timing to his wife. "The madam says that now that we have endured this Austrian exile a year for Clara's sake, she must complete the job, not leave it half finished," he explained to Rogers. "Well, I robbed the family to feed my speculations, & so I am willing to accommodate myself to their preferences."

Clemens had no great hankering to be neck-deep in the American political current just then—"Everything literary here is filled with the din of arms," William Dean Howells reported to him from New York, "but Providence has turned our war for humanity into a war for coaling-stations"—and yet he was ready to be home. "We are hoping that Clara can complete her piano-education next spring & end our exile," he confided to a friend. After that, the family would "be content to burn the trunks & stay home," he reported. "I like Europe—I like it very much indeed—but I am two or three thousand years old sometimes, & don't like so much paddling around."

The idea was to ride out the winter of 1898–99 in the luxury of Vienna's Hotel Krantz and then pack up in the spring and sail for New York, where they would rent a house and live near friends like Henry Rogers and William Dean Howells. If New York prices didn't suit, there was always Washington, DC, or even Richmond, Virginia. One thing was certain, though they were not telling Jean: Connecticut was out of the running for now. Livy was still in dread of a return to the Hartford house, where she was sure she would be haunted by the memory of Susy's lonesome end. The move to New York was a way to take into account Susy's own long-ago preferences. Reuniting the family in that city had become her great desire after a visit to the Howells family, just before she died. "I think I never had so perfectly delightful a time as those three weeks in New York, and I came away from there a full fledged lover of society, at least of N.Y. Society," read one of the last letters Clara had received from Susy. "The life there *can* be ideal, . . . [and] I am sure we would all *love* it. The way the Howells live seems to me quite perfect."

And then came the thunderbolt, right there in the friendly Austrian salon of Madame von Dutschka. Clara did a little singing at the salon one day, and another of Madame's guests took her aside. "Why do you go on with the piano when you have a voice?" the woman asked. "The piano is so much less recompensing than singing and the work is so very much heavier." Clara was struck giddy, not so much by the speech as by the speaker—Alice Barbi. Miss Barbi was a celebrated Italian mezzo-soprano, known throughout Europe as the adored muse of Johannes Brahms. The raven-haired thirty-six-year-old beauty was just coming out of mourning for the great composer, who had been her constant companion as well as her great champion. Clara was understandably enchanted, not only by Miss Barbi, but by the possibilities suggested by this recognition of her previously unseen talent. Clara went off to see a professional voice teacher in Vienna, who told her she would be well advised to give up the rigors of the piano and make a serious effort to train her voice. The Viennese teacher would be happy to take her on as a student.

Livy reported the "great change" to friends in Hartford and confessed relief that Clara would no longer be draining her strength and stamina in pursuit of the piano virtuosity. The voice training, however, necessarily meant the extension of the family's European exile. Sam Clemens's letters to friends in America suddenly shifted the family's estimated arrival in New York to the autumn of 1899. Another full year at the Hotel Krantz was fairly benign, as purgatories go, and eminently affordable, especially given "Mark Twain's" preferred-customer status, but it was purgatory nonetheless.

CLEMENS WAS BACK to his old habit of reading all the newspapers he could get hold of, and plenty of papers landed at the Hotel Krantz each morning and afternoon in the fall of 1898. One carried a little news brief about the Paige typesetter. The current owner of the patent and the two machines extant, P. T. Dodge, of the Mergenthaler Linotype Company, had just *donated* a Paige typesetter to Cornell University's college of engineering—as a museum piece. The report of the donation spoke admiringly of the typesetter's *nineteen thousand* moving parts and the surprising delicacy of the 5,500-pound machine, which stood nearly seven feet high and took up thirty-five square feet of museum floor space. "It runs without perceptible vibration," read Cornell's press release. "One of the most remarkable of all mechanical productions," Mr. Dodge himself styled the machine. "Considering its great complexity, its perfection of design and workmanship, the many novel mechanical movements contained in it and the precision with which it runs, I think it has no equal." It was also, Mr. Dodge noted, "valueless from a commercial standpoint because of its great expense."

Dodge estimated the cost for the production of the Paige typesetter—a production phase that spanned a generation—to have been $2 million. Sam Clemens, sitting in his Viennese parlor, couldn't vouch for the final number, but he knew exactly what he had put into it, without a penny of return: $170,000, two-thirds of it Livy's money, enough to have scrabbled out of the Webster publishing house debt with cash to spare, enough to have saved him the task of circling the earth begging money for talk. The story noted in the first paragraph "Mark Twain's" spectacularly ill-advised and increasingly hopeless investment, and all he could do was stare, defenseless, at the charge. "A monument of human ingenuity and stupidity," he would later write of it, "—the ingenuity was Paige's, the stupidity was mine."

Clemens found himself surprisingly calm in spite of having the old typesetter folly flung in his face; he was, after all, in pretty sound financial shape again. New royalties were rolling in, he was producing new words by the thousands for paying magazines, and he even suspected he had learned his lesson—to a degree anyway. He was as greedy as ever for the kind of fortune that would put Livy and Clara and Jean in the clover for the rest of their lives—still hopeful of quick strikes, and big ones. Within weeks of paying off his debts the previous spring, Clemens had tried to get himself in business with the most celebrated young inventor in Vienna, Jan Szczepanik, and his banker-patron.

The twenty-six-year-old Szczepanik was hard at work in his new laboratory in 1898 and rumor had it that he was close to perfecting the automated production of expertly designed tapestries, carpets, napkins, tablecloths , handkerchiefs, and anything else fit for the loom. Szczepanik's machine, using a process of specialized photography, would produce a perfect design plate, capable of guiding mass production; as Clemens saw it, this new machine would be a leap forward from the industry standard, the Jacquard loom, and an enormous money saver for any textile manufacturer.

Clemens spent days researching the finances of the textile industry (and talking to his new friend Jan), and by the time he was finished, he had formed a scheme to sew up controlling interest of the new textile trust in America—and then worldwide. He had still been in a reverie over the colossal, envy-inspiring riches he was about to acquire, when Rogers (who was to provide the lion's share of the investment money, courtesy of Standard Oil and its friends) cut him off. "A cursory examination," Rogers wrote, "leads me to place no very high value upon the invention, from a practical standpoint."

And hadn't he learned his lesson? Hadn't he acted with becoming caution? When Henry Rogers had warned him off, he had held his powder. Sam Clemens was never again going to leave his financial fortunes to soothsayers and celestial alignment and his own blind luck, and yet (how could he not?) he remained on the lookout. "I was born with the speculative instinct," he said with unmistakable pride.

Sam Clemens knew he had hit on a main chance the minute he read the news that fall: a powerful new industrial and financial consortium had just announced its incorporation in New Jersey. Clemens couldn't help noticing the impressive lineup of directors of Federal Steel. Henry Rogers was among them, but it also included Whitelaw Reid's filthy-rich father-in-law, D. O. Mills; John Hay's brother-in-law, Samuel Mather (of the Cleveland Iron Mining Company); the Chicago department store magnate Marshall Field; and the biggest and strongest money machine in the American engine house, the banker J. Pierpont Morgan. The business mission sounded like a winner. "We decided," one of the directors later explained, "to organize a corporation to own the stock of these various companies and thereby to have one controlling power for producing iron and steel from the ore to the finished product."

By the time Clemens and the rest of the world got the news, Federal Steel had gathered in the Illinois Steel Company, the Lorain Steel Company, the Minnesota Iron Company, and the Elgin, Joliet & Eastern Railway. The corporation was valued in the neighborhood of $200 million, and even after earmarking funds to build a major new steel plant on the South Side of Chicago, Morgan, Mills, Rogers, and company still had $9 million cash on hand. The directors appeared to be preparing to make a run at the industrial colossus, Carnegie Steel. And here was the beauty part, where Sam Clemens was concerned: unlike Carnegie's privately held company, the public was being invited to feed at the Federal Steel trough. The directors announced an offering of 532,610 shares of preferred stock (at a healthy 6 percent dividend per annum) and 464,843 shares of common stock.

Clemens, sitting in Vienna, decided his future depended on coupling himself to the bright, gleaming engine of Federal Steel. And he knew he wouldn't even have to send a check. He already had in excess of $18,000 cash on account with

Henry Rogers (corporate director, Federal Steel), and he cabled his wishes to his friend Henry's office in New York, leaving the details of the transaction to the experts. On November 2, 1898, Rogers's secretary, Miss Harrison, cabled back confirmation that Sam Clemens was the owner of 201.7 preferred shares at $69, and 249.3 shares of common stock at $28. "This is immense news," he wrote that afternoon to Rogers. "For 24 hours I have been trying to calm down and cool off and get sane over it, but I don't succeed very well. I would rather have that stock than be free from sin. . . . Many many thousands of thanks to you—and may you live forever! (Partly here, and partly in the other place.) Which place are you going to? . . . Let's make up a party, and go together. I can work you in at either place; I've got pull."

For the next five days, Sam Clemens was busy looking for ways to raise money to buy *more* shares and ciphering how much Federal Steel he would have to own—supposing an annual dividend of 5 percent—to allow him to retire from the pitiful grind of earning his living by producing literary matter for the magazines. He would mortgage the house in Hartford to buy more Federal Steel stock, Clemens decided, and take a cash advance on his as-yet-unwritten autobiography, and take up Pond on his offer to trail-boss a new "Mark Twain" lecture tour. On the fifth day, however, Sam Clemens got nervous and decided to play it safe. He would *not* ask Rogers to invest him deeper, he decided, even while kicking himself for being so timid. "A man who is in debt once," he lamented, "is afraid to venture it again."

HIS MOOD GREW jollier that autumn in Vienna, the delay of the Clemenses' return to America notwithstanding. And why not? The Federal Steel common stock he did have climbed almost 20 percent in just two weeks. "It makes me lazy, the way the Steel stock is rising," he reported to Rogers. He was already flush enough to toss into the fire his try at a commercial play, *Is He Dead?* and to withdraw some of the stories he had recently offered for sale in the American magazine market but found beneath his standard. For the few things he did leave on the market, like "The Man That Corrupted Hadleyburg," Clemens demanded top dollar.

Rogers, in the meantime, while running Standard Oil and keeping an eye on his new steel enterprise, was moonlighting as the sales agent for the "Mark Twain" magazine articles and also found time to wrestle down an agreement between Clemens's longtime publisher Frank Bliss, of American Publishing Company, and his new suitor, Harper & Brothers. Harper would produce any new "Mark Twain" trade books, and Bliss the subscription books. Bliss was also taking hold of the forthcoming multivolume Uniform Edition, which he had wrested free from Harper & Brothers in the negotiations. And he was taking hold with uncharacteristic vigor and purpose. "I have had two letters from Bliss since you signed the contract, but they contain not a whimper of dissatisfaction with the bargain—seems only delighted to be footloose & free to get to work on the Uniform," Clemens chortled to Rogers by way of thanks. "I couldn't *give* the books to him 3 years ago; now he is glad to get them on any hard terms. It's the same old human nature; Adam was the original Bliss; if God had told him to help himself, the crop would have rotted on the trees; but as soon as He loaded the apples up with extra-territorial royalties & other wanton exactions & obstructions, Adam was bound to sample the orchard if it cost him his shirt-tail. Bliss is happy, now, & I am, too."

He got his top-dollar price for "Hadleyburg" in late November, and some extra income on the serialization of *Following the Equator*, and then, out of the blue, Frank Mayo's son decided to take over the stage role of *Pudd'nhead Wilson* in honor of his recently deceased father and was making, to Clemens's absolute astonishment, a bona fide commercial hit of the play. The royalties would be on the way soon. When Clemens found himself unable to write for nearly two weeks running—general malaise, he suspected, or a "touch of malaria or piety or something like that"—he was unable to work up any authentic worry. Hell, he was making money *not working*. He spent his days lolling around his Viennese study, smoking, reading, composing and recomposing letters. "If I could afford it I would be like this all the time; merely lie around and manage the Steel Company & never do any work," he wrote to Rogers.

He was having a rollicking good time in Vienna, where, at one dinner in his honor that fall, an American attorney rose, with his hands in his pockets, and offered a toast meant to be amusing. "Doesn't it strike you as unusual that a professional humorist should be funny?" the visiting American asked. Clemens interrupted in a growling drawl, without missing a beat: "Or that a lawyer should have his hands in his *own* pockets!"

LIVY CLEMENS EMERGED from her long, self-imposed hibernation for the first time since the awful season of Susy's death. Mrs. Clemens was once again an active and willing participant in society. She attended the American minister's Thanksgiving reception and dinner at his home at Palais Springer, where, newspaper reporters noted, the Clemenses stood out among the two hundred guests milling around the giant red-marble pillars or walking through the lush Louis XIV–inspired drawing room and the adjoining Japanese-style salon. Then Livy surprised her husband by taking the lead in designing costumes for a fancy Christmastime costume ball—one of her daughters would be going as Night and the other as a Hindu princess. She spent days in the shops hunting for Christmas presents for friends in Vienna. And on Christmas Eve, Sam, Clara, Jean, *and* Livy left the Hotel Krantz to attend a special performance of William Dean Howells's play *The Mouse-Trap* at the home of an English friend. "I thought the house would kill itself with laughter," Clemens reported to Howells. "By George they played with life!"

When the Christmas fun faded away, Livy sat down and allowed herself another of her occasional thorough accountings of the family assets and bankbooks, which she duly reported to her husband; in the two or three years past, Livy had presented her findings chiefly to raise her husband's spirits when he looked to be at his lowest. But there seemed to be a finality to her latest accounting. They had the Hartford house and its furnishings; the "Mark Twain" copyrights, valued somewhere around $200,000; $107,000 in the bank; and the investments, which were throwing off a sizable income. She didn't have to mention the growing majesty of the Federal Steel stock. This report from Livy was the finest gift Sam Clemens could have received. "Here lately the dread of leaving the children in difficult circumstances has died down and disappeared and I am now having peace from that long, long nightmare, and can sleep as well as anyone," he wrote to Howells. "I have been out and bought a box of 6-cent cigars; I was smoking 4 ½ centers before."

The day after New Year's, 1899, a holiday letter arrived from Rogers with more glad tidings: the $18,000 investment in Federal Steel had nearly doubled in less than two months. Sam Clemens's first instinct was to reply with the horse-pill dose of Twainian humor Rogers had come to expect, a transatlantic poke in the ribs. But sitting in his plush private study at the Hotel Krantz, pen in hand, Clemens managed to carry off only one meager laugh line—one short sentence. This was not the time for high hilarity. Something else needed saying, and in perfect earnest. Sam Clemens had always taken a stubborn personal pride in "paddling his own canoe," but after the past five years, he had a hard time sustaining that image of himself. He had not made his last hard trip alone. "Hell hound" Henry Rogers, out of pure friendship, had portaged Sam Clemens and those he held dear across the dreadful and searing desert of boils and plague and slid them back into the great happy river of life. Clemens would not let this go unsaid. "By grace of you," he wrote to Rogers, "we have had a Christmas & a New Year this time which knocked the gloom out of a season which we have grown accustomed to anticipate with dread. There has been no dismalness—we have been gay. . . . We are resembling the long-vanished Clemenses of 10 years ago. God knows what we should be resembling if it had not been for you."

CHAPTER TWENTY-EIGHT

I Have Never Felt So Absolutely Alone

A couple of interesting rumors made their way—a few weeks after their American advent—into the European newspapers in the first week of January. The first bore a direct relationship to Sam Clemens and his fellow steel capitalists:

Chicago, Dec 25—A combination of steel manufacturing interests with the object of ultimate control of armor plate and heavy ammunition manufacture in the United States is rumored among Chicago men interested in the output of steel. Two plants, one at South Chicago for the manufacture of steel shells and projectiles by a new process, and the other at Kensington for the production of patent hollow steel car axles, it is said, will shortly be built by a syndicate of Europeans, represented by Carl and Adolph Mannesman, in conjunction with the Federal Steel Company at South Chicago.

Another report that week suggested that Federal Steel was in line to win $3 million worth of United States War Department contracts for the manufacture of "projectiles," which put the three-month-old corporation in line to challenge Carnegie Steel in the field of armaments and armor plating. So Sam Clemens found himself quite unexpectedly invested in the mass production of the weapons and tools of war, which, when considered from the rational calculus of profit and loss, was probably a much better bet just then than the mass production of sweaters and drapes and tapestries.

The second rumor, which caught his eye, was this:

Washington, Dec. 19—Inquiry was made at the State Department today in regard to the report that Judge Day and Mr. Whitelaw Reid are each to receive $100,000 for their services as members of the Paris Peace

> Commission. . . . At the State Department it was said today in the most positive terms that the question of the compensation of the members and officer of the Peace Commission is entirely in the hands of the President of the United States, and so far as is known he has not indicated to anybody his plans in the matter.
>
> Washington, Dec. 20—The report that Judge Day and Whitelaw Reid would receive $100,000 each for their services as peace commissioners has raised a storm of indignation among Senators and Congressmen.

Sam Clemens could work up plenty of indignation about Uncle Sam's stuffing yet more American ducat into Whitelaw Reid's open maw, but his recent good fortune had widened Clemens's natural generosity of spirit so vastly that even an outlier like Reid could find gentle protection in it. Clemens was moreover tired of Congress's starving the American diplomatic team. Sam Clemens had been around the world capitals and courts enough to know the score. The British government was currently paying its men in Paris, Berlin, Rome, and St. Petersburg about three times the salary the United States ambassador could expect in those cities. British ambassadors also lived rent-free in their country of service in palatial British-owned residences, while Americans had to hire on local rental agents to find lodgings at the unlikely intersection of presentable and affordable.

Clemens sat down the same day he read the Whitelaw Reid rumor to tackle the subject. "If we are to maintain present salaries, let us make no more ambassadors; and let us unmake those we have already made," he wrote in "Diplomatic Pay and Clothes."

> The great position, without the means of respectably maintaining it—there could be no wisdom in that. A foreign representative, to be valuable to his country, must be on good terms with the officials of the capital and with the rest of the influential folk. He must mingle with this society; he cannot sit at home—it is not business, it butters no commercial parsnips. He must attend the dinners, banquets, suppers, balls, receptions, and must *return* these hospitalities. He should return as good as he gets, too, for the sake of dignity of his country, and for the sake of Business. . . .
>
> If our Government has really paid representatives of ours on the Paris Commission $100,000 apiece for six weeks' work, I feel sure that it is the best cash investment the nation has made in many years. For it seems quite impossible that, with that precedent on the books, the Government will be able to find excuses for continuing its diplomatic salaries at the present mean figure.

Clemens made sure to ship a copy of the article to his friend the new secretary of state.

JOHN HAY COULD feel his dread rising the morning before Christmas, 1898, as the hour of Whitelaw Reid's expected arrival neared. The secretary of state had been fighting a wicked case of the grippe for more than a week already. He had climbed out of his sickbed only two days earlier and was still unsteady on his pins; he was suffering waves of light-headedness and could muster only a dull croak of a voice. Hay's debility was apparent to all who saw him. Alvey Adee had supplied him with doctors and nostrums and had efficiently shoveled through the paperwork on Hay's office desk in his boss's absence. Henry Adams had sat for days at Hay's bedside to commiserate and sympathize. Would Whitelaw take note later that day and allow his ailing friend a little peace on Christmas Eve? Well, having known Whitelaw a long, long time, John Hay was not optimistic. Whitelaw Reid would be coming for his.

Reid and his four fellow peace commissioners were just then disembarking from the *St. Louis* at the pier in New York, where they were hailed as conquerors. They held in their hands the fruits of two months labor, the Treaty of Paris, which was less treaty than bloodless plunder. By the time they got around to the final agreement with their Spanish counterparts, Reid and his fellow American commissioners had taken Cuba, Puerto Rico, Guam, and the Philippines; the Spanish retained nothing save whatever shred of honor they could feign and the $500 million Cuban debt. "It was really a dramatic spectacle, [at] which these provisions for deeding away the last vestige of their possessions in the world they had discovered and conquered were slowly read and translated," Whitelaw later bragged, about watching the sad-faced Spanish commissioner, Montero Ríos, whom he counted as an old friend. "[The Spanish] were all visibly moved; and old Montero looked as a Roman Senator might, when told that the Goths were at the gates."

A brass band was playing "The Star-Spangled Banner" on New York's Fulton Street pier that late-December morning and a special train with four private cars was rumbling in place across the Hudson River in Jersey City, waiting to haul the commissioners and their wives and their steamer trunks to Washington. The men were expected to present their treaty to President McKinley that afternoon, and John Hay's twenty-two-year-old son had been dispatched by the president to escort the traveling party out of New York. Del Hay had a time herding the group to the Hudson River ferry. Reid and his fellow commissioners had made a pact not to talk to reporters, but there were so many there, and they were so insistent, and the men were feeling understandably expansive.

Senator William P. Frye wanted the newsmen to understand how stoutly he and his team had battled to win the American points, and how stubbornly the Spanish commissioners had fought back. Senator Cushman K. Davis explained that the Filipino, Agoncillo, had pestered the commissioners outside their suites in Paris, demanding to be heard, but was never heard, which was his own fault, because he had never made a formal request *in writing*.

"Did he let you know what Aguinaldo desired?" one reporter asked.

"He never got that far," Davis answered.

Senator George Gray admitted he was aware that certain parties in the United States were already voicing opposition to the treaty, especially with regard to the acquisition of sovereignty in the Philippines. "I have no doubt there is a sober thoughtful opinion in this country against expansion. There must be. The treaty merely gives us control of the situation. We can now do as we please with the islands. We can keep the Philippines or not, as may be determined by us in the future."

William Day was busy answering questions about the rumored $100,000 fee the president was ready to hand over to him and Reid. "The report is utterly silly," Day told the inquiring reporter. "If I were to receive $100,000 for doing my duty, I'd give you half of it."

Reid backed him: "Such a proposal would be absurd."

Mrs. Day, who had stood by her husband while his service at the State Department and in Paris drained her household of much of its meager wealth, blurted out, in a spasm of unguarded candor apparently inspired by the rousing hero's welcome, "I only wish it were true!"

The Days needed the money; the Reids did not.

Not that Whitelaw Reid expected to go *un*rewarded, and the prize Whitelaw had his eye on was Hay's old place as ambassador to England. He had begged McKinley before he left for Paris—"with tears in his eyes," as the president told Hay—to hold the place for him until he returned. Hay had advocated for Reid's appointment, as he had for Henry Adams's and Harry White's, out of personal loyalty and friendship, but without any conviction that he could win the day. Hay was admittedly still chafed by Reid's behavior at the queen's jubilee, and he took a measure of private glee when Harry White described the scene of the peace commissioners' passing through the London embassy on their way to Paris back in September. "Mrs. Cushman Davis took quite a shine to [White] & said to him in Reid's presence that she was going to use her influence to have him made Ambassador," Hay wrote to his wife. "Reid grinned a ghastly smile & said he approved."

President McKinley had, in fact, already settled on another New Yorker for the London ambassadorship, the attorney Joseph Choate, but had yet to make an announcement, which meant Reid still thought he had a chance at London—which meant Hay was certain to hear about it. Hay had already been at work on Whitelaw. He had peppered Reid's suites at the Hotel Continental in Paris with fawning notes of congratulations: "Your talk with the Spanish Ambassador was to my mind the turning point of the negotiation. . . . The treaty can only be made on your lines. . . . We are to have a Republican Senator from New York. I wish with all my heart it might be you," and "It is comfortable to feel we have a man on deck who knows what to do and how to do it."

The thing was, Hay knew he had to keep Whitelaw Reid happy, because the president needed Whitelaw and his *New York Tribune* to help sell the new treaty.

The ratification of the Treaty of Paris would be Hay's first major test as secretary of state. The blame for a failure to secure ratification would fall largely on him, and requiring as it did the vote of two-thirds of the Senate, ratification was no sure thing. Corralling two-thirds of the Senate on *any* issue was difficult, and even Cabot, Hay noted, was edgy about the prospects for the treaty. A double-barreled argument was forming against it: The first point was that the acquisitions set forth in the treaty put the United States of America, for the first time in its history, in the position of master of overseas colonies. Whether British-style imperialism was the right path for the United States to follow seemed a perfectly legitimate question to contemplate, Hay conceded, and a profound one, especially for a nation built on the principle of human liberty and self-government. It needed to be met head-on. The second point of opposition was rather less ennobled, to wit: if the nation admitted Puerto Rico and Guam and especially the Philippines as political entities capable of achieving statehood, it would have, as one opposing senator put it, "frightful results in mongrelizing our citizenship."

"If the Philippines are annexed, what is to prevent the Chinese, the Negritos and the Malays coming to our country?" the head of America's most powerful labor organization was already asking. "How can we prevent the Chinese coolies from going to the Philippines and from there swarming into the United States and engulfing our people and our civilization?"

The solons of the South—and oh, how they had struggled with the "Negro problem" in their own states, they explained—were already working themselves and their constituents into a hydrophobic froth over the Philippines or, more to the point, the Filipinos. "We are asked to annex to the United States a witches' caldron—black spirits and white, red spirits and gray," Virginia senator John W. Daniel said.

> We are not only asked to annex the caldron and make it a part of our great, broad, Christian, Anglo-Saxon, American land, but we are asked also to annex the contents and take this brew—mixed races, Chinese, Japanese, Malay Negritos. . . . This mess of Asiatic pottage, 7,000 miles from the United States, in a land that we can not colonize and can not inhabit, we are told today by the fortune of a righteous war waged for liberty, for the ascendency of the Declaration of Independence, for the gift of freedom to an adjourning State, we must take up and annex and combine with our own blood and with our own people, and consecrate them with the oil of American citizenship.

As secretary of state, Hay, who would need to win other big votes down the line—on the interoceanic canal issues, tariffs, China markets, contemplated territorial acquisitions in the Caribbean and the South Pacific, a dozen different issues now in arbitration regarding Canada—would have to be gentle in answering opposition to the Paris treaty in the Senate. Whitelaw Reid had no such fetters—and very little natural inclination to consider somebody else's argument. Reid had already worked up a stalwart defense of his treaty against both points of opposition: The Constitution, he asserted, had proved flexible enough to permit the national government to take and rule possessions as it saw fit and for as long as it saw fit. Neither was the United States of America under any constitutional obligation to enfranchise or admit into citizenship the inhabitants of these possessions. "Still further," Reid would write, "it is insisted not only that Congress is under no obligations to prepare these territories for Statehood, or admit them to it, but that, at least as to the Philippines, it is prevented from doing so by the very terms of the preamble to the Constitution itself—concluding as it does with the words 'do ordain and establish this Constitution for the United States of *America*.' There is no place here for States of Asia."

Hay was anxious to have Reid's outspoken public advocacy, because it would take one small thing off his very full plate. He was at that moment trying to convince a handful of senators of the wisdom of appropriating funds to pay the soldiers of the Cuban Liberation Army to give up their guns and go home; keeping an eye on the Russians and the Germans in China (Great Britain was still asking for Hay's help in maintaining free and open trade in that spectacular commercial plum); and working to close a new agreement with England that would allow for the building of a canal through Nicaragua to join the Atlantic and Pacific Oceans. Hay had anywhere from fifty to one hundred official outgoing dispatches to work through each day. Adee or another assistant drafted most of them, but Hay insisted on reading and emending each one before he affixed his signature. He did not wish to end his public career an embarrassment like John Sherman, who had only vague acquaintance with many of the instructions that went out under his own name. And occasionally a White House messenger would arrive carrying a draft of a letter or note McKinley was working on: "Add or take away," was the president's request of John Hay. "I want it put right." Hay's office hours had expanded by the day, and his good humor had shriveled in proportion.

The administration of the department, *his* department, was not much fun. The sixty or so clerical workers at the department seemed, to Hay, nameless drudges in dark, ill-fitting suits. With the notable exception of Alvey Adee, Hay found his assistant secretaries and bureau chiefs to be glorified clerks, promoted above their abilities, and dullards to boot. The president's choice for first assistant secretary was a political hack, and Hay did not trust the man. The third assistant secretary, while celebrated around Capitol Hill for his blunt manner and his willingness to cut through red tape, was in Hay's estimation merely boorish. "I have never in my life, not even in a foreign country, felt so absolutely alone," Hay told his wife at the beginning of his tour at the State Department. "There is not a soul in the place I care to speak to. Dear old Adee comes fluttering around twenty times a day at the Department to see that I don't overwork, or to tell me a new joke he has thought of, but with that exception I know nothing of human companionship."

The agenda of the State Department was bigger than ever, already beyond its capacity and still growing. Hay knew what needed to be done at the department—knew it from the bottom up. He knew the department's faults, which were many, and he knew its virtues, which were few. Alvey Adee carried the place on his small tweed-covered back. He did all the dirty jobs, big and small, like Cinderella, Hay joked, and got little rest and less reward. Hay would have happily disassembled the entire machine down to his second assistant secretary and built it anew, with horsepower to meet any job, but he knew enough not to waste time or energy on any such rehabilitation project. Sam Clemens could vent his spleen in print about diplomatic pay and republican wardrobe, but Congress would not be listening. Hay didn't even bother to ask for money to increase diplomatic salaries. "As to the appropriations for necessary expenses of the Embassies," Hay wrote to the American ambassador in France, "I am afraid that is a mirage which will float before us all our lives, and never be caught up with." Presidents would just have to keep appointing wealthy men who could maintain extravagant households on their own dime. Secretary Hay had made bold on just one issue: he had started to lobby Cabot and a few other senators about the possibility of adding an extra secretary to the embassy staff in London, Paris, and Berlin, at a total cost of less than $4,000 per annum. "No other first class power would be satisfied with less than twice that number of Secretaries,"

Hay reminded them. But he got little encouragement, except, perhaps, that they could see their way to sponsoring the amendment *if* they might be allowed to put forward their own men to fill one of the new paid positions.

This was Hay's daily plunge, the petty, grasping quid pro quo, the constant tide of senators and congressmen washing up in his office to suck a place for some bright young constituent, or former business partner, or son-in-law, or nephew. Sometimes it was one of Hay's old friends presenting herself at Hay's office or seeking him out at home, in dire need of a sinecure. "You have only to ask," they would implore. "The President will do anything for you." Hay would sit in his chair, smiling wanly, powerless to help, thinking, *How I do want to kill them.* He did not hide it well. Cabot even suggested through mutual friends that the secretary try to "not look so exceedingly tired when approached on business at the department."

IT WAS AFTER dark, Christmas Eve, when Whitelaw Reid, having detoured with his peace party to the White House to deliver what the newspapers reported to be a "good-sized satchel" stuffed full of treaty, found his way into John Hay's warm and inviting library. Hay tried to congratulate his old friend once more on his great diplomatic triumph in Paris, but Whitelaw waved him away. He wanted to talk about the embassy in London: Had the president made up his mind? There had been no announcement. Whitelaw still had a chance, did he not? He could not believe he would be passed over once again. The other peace commissioners were unanimous in supporting him for the ambassadorship in England. What would be Hay's next move on his behalf? Hay, already pale with illness, blanched. He felt bound by honor and loyalty to express nothing as to President McKinley's actions or his motives. He was wary of so much as hinting that the president seemed to have already made up his mind. Hay let his visitor hold forth instead and tried to keep up as Reid sledded through the names of prominent Republicans who would speak to the president on his behalf. Hay tried to enlighten Reid as to which of those men had really been in his corner and which were only telling Whitelaw what he wanted to hear. But the secretary of state was unequal to the task and worn by the effort.

An hour or so into Whitelaw's filibuster, when Henry Adams stopped by for tea, he found Reid still wailing away: "Poor Hay had to bear the brunt of Whitelaw's insane voracity for plunder, at a moment when he was barely able to walk." Reid did stay for Christmas Eve dinner, but he took the late train back to New York.

When Hay awoke Christmas morning, he could not get the previous night's uncomfortable scene with Whitelaw out of his head. "I fear he will never forgive me for not having been able to get him the English Embassy," he wrote to his sister-in-law.

THE PRESIDENT DID finally announce the appointment of a new ambassador to England a few weeks later, and Hay wrote to Harry White in London with the news. White had been doing the ambassador's job for three months and doing it well, but he would be stepping back into his role as first secretary of the embassy to make way for the new appointee. It was a shame, in a way. There was no more skilled or valuable man in the foreign service than Harry White, but White had no political champions in the Senate or the House or among the state party nabobs. His appointment as ambassador would have been politically worthless to McKinley. "The President has decided to appoint Mr. Choate to London," Hay wrote. "It will be a great blow to Reid. . . . I have no idea what course he will take towards the President. Probably no overt opposition, but merely an attitude of cold support and covert criticism. I am sick and tired of this constant play of selfish interests. No human being ever approaches me but to work me for some purpose or other. But why whimper about it—it is all in the day's work."

CHAPTER TWENTY-NINE

Winter and Discontent

John Hay was determined to be useful to the president and to the Republic. His best chance, as he saw it, was to help clear the way for the vital national initiative of the day: the building of a shipping canal through Nicaragua, which would provide for a quick transit between the Atlantic Ocean and the Pacific and relegate to oblivion the wasteful month-long journey around the tip of South America every commercial and military ship was forced to endure. "That the construction of such a maritime highway," William McKinley told Congress, "is now more than ever indispensible to that intimate and ready intercommunication between our eastern and western seaboards demanded by the annexation of the Hawaiian Islands and the prospective expansion of our influence and commerce in the Pacific, and that our national policy now more imperatively than ever calls for its control by this Government, are propositions which I doubt not the Congress will duly appreciate and wisely act upon." The Major need not have wasted his executive breath. Congress was already in a hot lather for the canal, especially Alabama senator John Tyler Morgan, whose big dream seemed suddenly within reach.

For twenty years, Morgan had been leading the call for an American-built and American-controlled canal across Nicaragua. His motivations had been more parochial than national: he believed the canal would remake his beloved and war-ravaged South. He had long believed the shortcut would allow fast delivery of raw cotton from southern ports like Mobile and New Orleans to the faraway and fabulous markets in China and the rest of the Far East, and the recent war acquisitions had doubled his possible pleasure in the project. A former Grand Dragon of the Ku Klux Klan in Alabama, United States senator John Morgan now thrilled to the vision of a million Alabama "Negroes" being gathered up at Mobile Bay and off-loaded into the new American possessions of Hawaii and the Philippines. Morgan was increasingly nervous about the threat to white supremacy in the old Confederacy, especially because black men, representing more than 40 percent of his own state's population, had got it in their heads that they should vote. The senator was ready to fight the black man's right to vote tooth and nail, and he made no apologies. But he saw blessed respite in the removal of this (unwanted, by his lights) population to the distant islands of the Pacific. Senator Morgan would no longer have to waste time and effort, for instance, arguing for legislation legalizing vigilante lynching, and his fellow white-sheeted Klansmen could stop the torch-and-terror runs on black families and carpetbagging missionaries and maybe get a proper night's rest. So the canal had become an extremely enticing proposition for Senator Morgan, and he wanted to get cracking on it.

There was one international sticking point with the canal project, even if Congress gave the go-ahead and loosed the money: the United States and Great Britain had signed a treaty half a century earlier agreeing that neither country would take exclusive control of any canal across Latin America. Many members of Congress would have been happy to see the United States unilaterally abrogate this moldy old neutrality agreement, especially now that the Monroe Doctrine, in the wake of the routing of Spain, was gaining international currency. McKinley didn't seem particularly mindful of the earlier treaty either; he had not even bothered to mention the agreement with England when he asked Congress to act.

John Hay, for his part, had certain scruples about treaties—for example, that unilateral abrogation was beneath the dignity of the American republic—but he knew he would have to move fast to persuade Britain to agree to a new set of terms concerning a canal in Nicaragua. Once the senators got back to business in early January of 1899 and started bloviating about US dominion in the Americas, they could be counted on to offend Her Majesty's government. So Hay began by calling in British correspondents working in Washington and insisting that the president had no intention of flouting *any* provision of the historic Clayton-Bulwer Treaty. And he dispatched Harry White to the Foreign Office in London to gauge the prospects for a mutually agreeable amendment to Clayton-Bulwer, one that might afford the United States some leeway.

White went his boss one better in the holiday season of 1898, after accepting Lord Salisbury's invitation for a weekend visit at his country home. Harry spent the long weekend shooting and dining and commiserating with the prime minister, and by the time he took his leave of the marquess's home, the American chargé d'affaires was satisfied in all ways. White reported back to Hay that Lord Salisbury believed the canal was better left to the control of one country, the Clayton-Bulwer Treaty notwithstanding, and he also said, *privately, of course*, that now that England controlled the Suez Canal in Egypt, the Nicaraguan canal was "of comparatively little" interest to the British Empire. The prime minister told White he was confident in leaving it to his ambassador to the United States, Julian Pauncefote, to work out the details with John Hay. Hay and Pauncefote were fine friends, after all, and would make congenial coadjutants.

So Hay's first big initiative at State looked as if it was nearly in the bag as New Year's, 1899, approached, and he was confident enough to whisper it to a select few. "Dear Senator Morgan," Hay wrote two days after Christmas. "I do not look forward to any protracted negotiations; we ought to know before long what we are to expect, but I cannot fix a date. Meanwhile there is, to my mind, no reason why your work on the Canal Bill should be checked or retarded in the least on account of any such negotiation. We are striving for the same object, on parallel lines, and I do not see how we are to interfere with each other. For my part I shall always be glad of any suggestions you may feel inclined to make." Hay also took the opportunity to tell Morgan how much he valued his "wisdom and experience" in all matters pertaining to this crucial national undertaking.

AN ARCTIC BLAST of snow and cold blew down from Canada on New Year's Eve. Thermometers in Washington read zero at the first dawn of 1899, having dropped fifty-four degrees in less than twenty-four hours, making it the coldest New Year's Day in the national capital in nearly twenty years. The temperature held in the single digits all that Sunday and into the next morning, when John and Clara Hay and their children buttoned their furs against the chill and climbed into their carriage for the short ride to the White House. The sky was crystal blue that morning, and the sun bounced harshly, almost painfully, off the fresh snow blanketing Lafayette Square; the Hays could hear the far-off trill of sleigh bells and the crunch of carriage wheels on the roads packed hard with snow. All of official Washington—senators and representatives, cabinet members and staff, Supreme Court justices, and the diplomatic corps, wives included—was descending on the White House to shake the president's hand at the annual New Year's reception.

The Hays were expected early, to take their places in the receiving line, where it would be John Hay's job to introduce the foreign ambassadors and ministers and chargés d'affaires to President and Mrs. McKinley. Mrs. Hay would be doing double duty, substituting for the ailing wife of Vice President Hobart, who usually kept watch on the invalided and high-strung Ida McKinley and made sure the First Lady did not say or *do* anything untoward. The Hays would then have to hustle back to their own home, where the two-hundred-member diplomatic corps would soon arrive for the annual breakfast given by the secretary of state. The other cabinet officers had their own official repasts to tend.

This all-day entertaining marked the opening of the compulsory social season in the national capital. The next six weeks promised a rondo of diplomatic receptions, state dinners, cabinet dinners, bachelor's germans, military balls, daily open houses, and freelance private dinners and cotillions given by cabinet members, foreign diplomats, and the recognized first families of Washington society. The descendants of old lions of the Republic like John Adams, Thomas Jefferson, and John Marshall, unable to foot the bill for lavish parties, had faded down to the small print in the city's society columns, topped by new governmental potentates and nouveaux riches like the Leiters and the Warders and the Boardmans. The Hays were the rare Washington family who boasted august official standing *and* the multimillion-dollar fortune required to entertain in a style befitting a newly powerful nation. But if the long, cold slog of New Year's Day receptioning was any indication, the next six weeks were shaping up to be an unhappy season for the Hay family.

Del had the least to worry about, his father figured; the newspapers generally ignored the young swains, even if they misbehaved. Mrs. Hay would be watched like never before, as was made clear by the description of the family's arrival as they hurried under the portico of the White House that morning. "It was the first official appearance of the wife of the new Secretary of State," offered the capital's *Evening Times*, "and there were many eager eyes among the mass of humanity on the outer side of the golden gate to study her appearance and her gown." John Hay did not worry much about their daughter Helen. She had debuted in Washington to great acclaim two years earlier. Helen could count on good press; she was described as vivacious and clever, a fine dancer, and a passable sportswoman. Helen's younger sister, Alice, who had made her own social debut the previous fall, drew the hurtful slings. One reporter at the New Year's morning reception pointed out that Miss Alice, while "radiant," was wearing the *same* dress she had worn at her debut. And that was tame compared to a report in the *New York Times* that winter, which would describe Alice as "tall and inclined to develop an amplitude of figure inherited from the maternal side."

BY THE TIME the cabinet convened for its first meeting of the year the next morning McKinley's official family seemed already drained. They were none of them young men, and none of them particularly well. Hay himself was not yet fully recovered from his own recent illness, and he had plenty of company on the sick list, all over town. Local pharmacists, counting store traffic and prescriptions filled, figured the current influenza epidemic had hit more than 10 percent of the city. One in ten policemen called in sick that Tuesday morning; one justice of the Supreme Court and several lower court judges were in bed under a doctor's care. Representative Nelson Dingley was in critical condition at his home a few blocks away. He was struggling to breathe, and one lung, according to his attending physician, was "entirely consolidated." Julian Pauncefote was sick in bed and unable to work; Chinese minister Wu Ting-fang had not risen from his bed for five days. The poor old Mexican minister Matías Romero, who had been about to be named his country's first-ever ambassador to the United States, was already a fatality. "Our social season opens here in general gloom," Hay reported to a friend. "Some of us are dead, some of us are dying, and most of us have a touch of the grip, and all something which in the last century it was fashionable to call spleen. I think I never saw a more silent and gloomy assemblage of respectable gentlemen than met around the Cabinet table this morning. But the ground is covered with snow, and snow always chills our spirits in Washington."

The next evening the entire cabinet was back at the White House for a command performance at a state dinner in their honor, an intimate little sit-down for seventy. And they would be back again and again and again in the coming weeks: the diplomatic reception, the diplomatic dinner, the judicial reception, the Supreme Court dinner, the congressional reception, the army and navy reception, were all on the schedule. The official social calendar was a miserable trial for Hay, in no small part because the White House was simply unfit for state affairs. No matter how many waxy camellias and poinsettias and garlands of asparagus and carnations and palms the White House staff used to cover the creaky bones of the place, close inspection drew pity. The nation's seat of executive power lacked a sufficient amount of matching china for the large dinners, so there was always a mix of place settings at the back tables. "A nice country house," the newly arrived Russian ambassador had sniffed on first sight, and that was before he went inside.

When Count Arthur Cassini did gain entrance, he and his sixteen-year-old daughter, who had just come from the silk-and-jade splendor of the imperial palaces of China, were aghast at the East Room, where the president chose to receive his most esteemed visitors. Marguerite Cassini noted the ugly mustard-yellow carpet, the strange clumps of circular seating, with potted palms rising through the center, and the upholstery that shone with the wear of age. "Ugly Victorian," was Marguerite's frank assessment. The room could handle the crowd for a dinner, but the big receptions were frightful, with people bumping and lurching in the crush, and the floorboards succumbing to a worrying sag, and the heat rising until women started to keel over in faints. At that point the White House ushers would throw open the windows and turn a sharp eye on the First Lady.

Mrs. McKinley was the other wild card at any White House affair, and accommodations to her infirmities set the pace and protocol of any evening. Ida

McKinley did not stand on line to receive visitors. She sat instead, next to the president, on a little blue-and-gold couch, and she did not shake anyone's hand. William McKinley kept a close watch on his wife at these public functions. Official usage dictated that the president escort the wife of the guest of honor into the dining room and seat her at his right. He had done this at first, but had been so distracted with worry about Ida, who was seated across the table from him, out of reach, that he asked Mrs. Hobart if she thought it could possibly offend anyone if he sat his wife at his right hand instead. She allowed he could do as he pleased; this was *his* home. The president still escorted the proper female guest (though long in the habit of supporting Ida with his left arm, the Major once mistakenly offered his arm to the president of Costa Rica), but he made a point to seat the lady of honor at his left and then seat his wife at his right, leaving it to John Hay to smooth any ruffled international feathers.

These minor insults and embarrassments suffered by visiting dignitaries were accepted with increasing graciousness as the reasons for these breaches of decorum became more widely known. The fact was not trafficked in public, even by the opposition newspapers, but Mrs. McKinley suffered from epilepsy, and the stress of a state dinner made a seizure more likely. William McKinley was always on the lookout for a medical disaster at these events; he would hear the familiar hissing begin to escape his wife's lips and see Ida go stiff and convulse, and then he would calmly and casually pull his napkin from his lap and veil his wife's face. Nobody could be sure if he was sheltering her or the onlookers. Mrs. McKinley's maid stood ready to leap from the shadows and escort her by prearranged escape route out of the dining room and to her private quarters. The president carried on as if nothing whatever had happened, while the nearest dining companions sat by, slack jawed.

"What an evening! What a dinner! What a household!" Count Cassini reported after one of his first social events at the White House. "For entertainment a series of contretemps; for refreshments an open window and a glass of water!"

John Hay much preferred the one less formal event in the first week of the 1899 social season, when Mrs. Warder threw a reception and cotillion in honor of her two daughters, Alice and Elizabeth. Youth be served; John Hay was happy to attend. Elizabeth Warder, after all, had been one of the Hays' young traveling companions on their slalom through the sites and museums of England, France, and Italy a few years earlier. And Mrs. Warder exhibited good instincts for entertaining. "The hostess," one local society column reported, "never permits her guest list to overtax the capacity of her home, thus avoiding the unpleasant phase of so many otherwise faultless entertainments—a crush." This was the subtle way of suggesting exclusivity in extremis.

Two hundred of Mrs. Warder's closest friends (she had a *big* house) enjoyed a late reception that January evening, followed by a midnight supper and dancing on a floor polished to high sheen, with music provided by a live orchestra. "Patriotism was the dominant spirit of the dance," the *Washington Times* noted the day after. "The favors were flags, shields and tin soldiers, and the figures included a sham battle, in which a screen painted to represent a stone fortress played a thrilling part. A band of pretty heroines defended its walls from a bombarding enemy that stormed it desperately with pop-guns. . . . 'Our New Possessions' were introduced in the dance by comical and distinctly unique favors, consisting of tiny black dolls, dressed to represent Columbia's new daughters of Porto Rico, Hawaii and the Philippines."

JULIAN PAUNCEFOTE WAS well enough to be back at his post the following Monday and happy to speed through the finalization of the new agreement to replace Clayton-Bulwer. Sir Julian and his family already appeared to be caught up in the expansive mood in the United States capital; his daughter Maude had designed one of the figures at the Warder Ball, in honor of the American victory in Cuba, called the "Storming of Morro Castle." Then, too, Pauncefote's instructions from Lord Salisbury clearly leaned toward conciliation of American interests in Nicaragua. The British ambassador was confident that the prime minister would be pleased with the treaty proposal he and Hay had worked out. The agreement was determinedly vague, at Hay's insistence. The secretary of state was worried that the Senate, given a whack at too detailed a treaty, would load it up with a slew of undesirable amendments. The proposed treaty language gave the United States the right to build the canal on its own hook, as long as the Americans granted passage to vessels of all nations. And while the canal zone itself would remain demilitarized, both Hay and Pauncefote took it as a given that the operation and defense of the Nicaraguan canal zone would follow that of the Suez—"neutral" in name only. As the British unilaterally controlled the Suez Canal, the Americans would unilaterally control the Nicaraguan.

Sir Julian sent the new Hay-Pauncefote Treaty project off to Lord Salisbury on the second Friday of January, just before he dressed for that evening's affair, the annual diplomatic dinner at the White House. Hay sent an informational copy to Harry White that same afternoon, in case Salisbury wanted to discuss any particulars in person. Hay also instructed White to do what he could to goad the Brits to take up the treaty project with some semblance of urgency. "It is a matter of the utmost importance that if we are to make such an arrangement, it should be done at once," Hay warned White. "In the usual reckless manner of our Senate, they are discussing the matter with open doors every day, and are getting themselves so balled up with their own eloquence that it is greatly to be feared they will so commit themselves as to consider themselves bound to reject any arrangement that may be made."

Hay expected help from the prime minister, because Her Majesty's government was still asking for assistance from the US in China: the Russians, the French, and the Germans seemed intent on cutting it up into "spheres of influence," which the Anglos took to mean provinces of commercial exclusivity.

The one little wrinkle that concerned Hay as to this improving relationship with Great Britain was the strange goings-on at the commission attempting to settle a dozen or so issues between the United States of America and Canada—from fur seals and fishing to lumber tariffs and boundaries. After months at the table in Washington, the American commissioners—in spite of orders from President McKinley to be as yielding as was honorably possible—were unable to tie up a deal. Almost every point was harmoniously decided, but the Canadian side, led by a British jurist, the Right Honorable Lord Herschell, was unwilling to give way on its very questionable boundary demand in the Klondike. (The big gold strike there was the chief consideration.) "In the case of Alaska, it is hard to treat with patience the claim set up by Lord Herschell that virtually the whole coast belongs to England, leaving us only a few jutting promontories without communication with each other," Hay reported to Harry White in early January, asking him to suggest to their friends at the Colonial Office and the Foreign Office that it might be best to try to tame their advocate in Washington. "We are absolutely driven to the conclusion that Lord Herschell put forward a claim that he had no belief or confidence in, for the mere purpose of trading it off for something substantial. And yet, the slightest suggestion that his claim is unfounded throws him into a fury."

Whatever Lord Herschell heard from the home office after White started lobbying in London, he remained petty, argumentative, and whiny, complaining—"with oily sobs," one of Hay's friends reported—that the American commissioners had hurt his feelings.

JOHN HAY HAD certain domestic duties to tend to as well that winter, chief among them figuring out what to do about Del. The young man had decided, after his brief stint as an unpaid secretary at the London embassy, that he would never again chain himself to desk work. And he continued to disregard his father's suggestion that he might profit from law school, even if he chose not to practice.

At age twenty-two, and less than a year removed from his Yale graduation, Adelbert Stone Hay was looking for adventure. Hay's older son had a streak of

John Hay with his son
Adelbert "Del" Hay

the Dionysian in him and, as he prized activity over thought, a tendency toward recklessness. John Hay worried that Del could get himself into real trouble. This did not diminish the wide and embracing love he felt for his grown son, but the two men shared little of the natural affinity that existed between Hay and his poet daughter Helen. This left John Hay uncertain about how best to steer his son; and since his reputation among his children as the softest touch in the household was well earned, his attempts to rein Del in had little bite. Hay admonished and then backpedaled. "You must not think I am cross with you," he had written to Del a few months earlier. "Your welfare and happiness is more to me than anything else in life. I would give up all I have got to insure your happiness & that of your sisters and brother."

Judging from the bills that had trailed Del back to Washington from Europe, Hay's gentle chidings had little effect. While Del danced his way through the cotillion season and wooed Marguerite Cassini, Hay was forced to send a check to Harry White in London to clear the remaining family debts. A few days later, John Hay acceded to his son's latest adventure scheme and secured passage for

Del and his friend Jimmy Wadsworth on a troop ship full of reinforcements being sent to the Philippines. Del and Jimmy would be making an inspection of the newest American possession to assess possible business opportunities. The papers reported that the two young men were scheduled to steam out February 9, 1899, with temporary ratings as clerks in the service of a colonel of the Third Infantry. When Eugene Hale got wind of the trip, the senator from Maine asked Hay to secure a berth for his own son, Eugene junior, who had been Elizabeth Warder's mad knitting partner on the Hay-Adams European tour of 1896. So it was settled: the three young men would be steaming off to Manila, though exactly what they would find there was hard to guess.

THE QUESTION OF the Philippines was jangling all of Washington by the end of January. Even before presenting the Treaty of Paris to the Senate for ratification, the president had already issued a message to the Filipino people claiming absolute American sovereignty in all the islands. The mission of the United States—Benevolent Assimilation, he called it—was "the bestowal of the blessings of good and stable government upon the people of the Philippine Islands under the free flag of the United States." William McKinley alerted the inhabitants that he meant to "maintain the strong arm of authority to suppress disturbance, and to overcome all obstacles" to this noble cause. Aguinaldo and his revolutionary forces were indignant at this proclamation, and threatened trouble, but they did not veer from their own mission of establishing an independent government in the Philippines. The Filipinos wrote and ratified their new Constitution and stood up a new, democratically elected government at the end of January 1899 and then sent instructions to Felipe Agoncillo, who was back at the Arlington Hotel, to argue the Filipino case against the Treaty of Paris. Aguinaldo tasked Agoncillo with tracking down John Hay at the State Department to ask for recognition of this new, independent, self-governing Republic of the Philippines.

Hay had already spent the entire month of January dodging Agoncillo's insistent pleas and his letters and his memorials. The department was sticking to the White House line, as elucidated by the pen of Alvey Adee. "We hold the territory by cession and evacuation and it is our right and duty to protect the inhabitants of the ceded territory from insurgent aggression," Alvey had written to Hay. "It is not necessary to wait for the exchange of ratifications of the treaty to confirm our rights. They are as complete now as they were at Santiago after the total capitulation. I strongly favor immediate coercive action against Aguinaldo as a disturber of *our* peace."

Agoncillo would not back down in the face of the ongoing ridicule about his "pretend" republic. Don Felipe continued to insist that the United States live up to the honor and integrity of its founding principles and to its word. Neither the president nor the secretary of state was willing to meet with Agoncillo, but he did manage an unofficial parlay with Hay's nightly walking companion, Henry Adams, an early and enthusiastic champion of the old Cuban junta, who really did want to be of help in avoiding a shooting war with the Filipinos but could feign little actual interest in the "usual worthless Malay type."

"I am getting up to my neck in Agoncillo's affairs, and every hairy traitor and murderer in the islands of ocean seems to gravitate towards me," Adams complained. "Cubans and Philippinos [*sic*] are now running in harness together, and I'm trying to get them all off our hands, and let them murder each other instead of us."

THE MCKINLEY ADMINISTRATION badly needed the Treaty of Paris to be ratified, quickly and quietly, but it got neither. The floor vote was pushed to early February, and the debate inside the Senate was loud and open. Democrats demanded an amendment that left the islanders to their own devices. "The Philippines are tenanted by a very peculiar mass, a heterogeneous compound of inefficient oriental humanity," California senator Stephen M. White argued on the floor. "I care not, for the purposes of my argument, whether these islanders are fit for free government as you and I understand it." Senator White suspected they were not. "We do not in that event want them," he went on to say. "Those who are incompetent to control themselves should not be one of us. We do not seek the irresponsible."

The more generous argument against the treaty went all the way back to first principles. "The question is this," said Senator George Hoar, a fellow Republican. "Have we the right, as doubtless we have the physical power, to enter upon the government of ten or twelve million subject people without constitutional constraint?" May Congress "conquer," Hoar asked, and

> govern, without their consent and against their will, a foreign nation, a separate, distinct and numerous people? . . . Now, I claim that under the Declaration of Independence you cannot govern a foreign territory, a foreign people, another people than your own; that you cannot subjugate them and govern them against their will, because you think it is for their good, when they do not; because you think you are going to give them the blessing of liberty. You have no right at the cannon's mouth to impose on an unwilling people your Declaration of Independence and your Constitution and your notions of freedom and notion of what is good.

Just for effect, Senator Hoar offered his head on the chopping block if it would prevent ratification of the treaty. The most vital argument on the other side was no less dramatic, summoning as it did a higher authority than the Constitution and the Declaration of Independence. *God* wanted us to bestow our blessings on the Philippines. It was time for the United States, as Rudyard Kipling's new poem in the latest issue of *McClure's* read, to "take up the White Man's burden," this burden apparently being the Filipinos, which he described as

> Your new-caught sullen peoples,
> Half devil and half child.

"Rather poor poetry," was New York governor Theodore Roosevelt's judgment, "but good sense from the expansion standpoint." Senator Henry Cabot Lodge thought Theodore too harsh a critic of the poetics, and he certainly agreed with Kipling's worldview. "To the American people and their Government, I am ready to intrust my life, my liberty, my honor; and what is far dearer to me than anything personal to myself, the lives and liberty of my children and my children's children," Cabot announced on the Senate floor. "If I am ready thus to trust my children to the Government which the American public create and sustain, am I to shrink from intrusting to the same people the fate and fortune of the Philippine Islands?"

In the few days leading up to the vote, though, Senator Henry Cabot Lodge's tummy was in a twist. What with Republican defections, Cabot was terrified that they would not be able to come up with the number of aye votes needed to ratify. He took to staying in the Senate cloakroom late into the night, trying to cut deals for votes; he even took a brief respite from the time-consuming task of seconding Theodore Roosevelt in his campaign to shame the War Department into conferring on him the Medal of Honor. ("If I didn't earn it, then no commissioned officer ever can earn it," Theodore had written to Cabot. "I am entitled to the Medal of Honor, and I want it.") Theodore *was* understanding of Cabot's need to temporarily suspend the Medal of Honor campaign. "I confess I am utterly disheartened and cast down at the thought that the treaty is in such serious danger," Theodore wrote from the governor's mansion in Albany. "It is difficult for me to speak with moderation of such men as Hoar."

Meanwhile, the treaty debate was gumming up the rest of the nation's business. John Hay couldn't even be sure of getting his lousy little appropriation for additional secretaries at the large embassies in Europe. The only certain movement in Washington was the steady flow of job seekers, even though they had to trudge through the late-January snow to get to Hay's office. Further souring the secretary's milk, official Britain had gone silent on the Hay-Pauncefote Treaty.

All the pulling of strings attached to nothing, the entertaining of "dago" diplomats, the smoothing of difficulties caused by Mrs. McKinley's infirmities, had taken its toll on John Hay. His closest friends could tell, and so could his new acquaintances. "Although I think the Tartar Cassini rather exaggerated in saying the other day that he never saw such a change for the worse in any man in so short a time as two months," Adams wrote to Lizzie Cameron, "still I do see deterioration especially in irritability of temper." A week later, Adams pronounced his friend still worse. "John Hay's temper," he noted, "is quite savage."

SNOW WAS FALLING hard at first light on February 6, 1899, and didn't let up all day, but hundreds of Washingtonians made their way to the Senate gallery in the Capitol to watch the ratification vote on the Treaty of Paris. The outcome was still in doubt as the galleries began to fill, and Cabot was still working the undecideds in the cloakroom as the roll call began. Senators Hoar and Hale both broke with the Republican Party line and voted against, but the other skeptical Republicans held their noses and stuck by the president. There proved to be enough expansion-minded Democrats, like the Klansman John Tyler Morgan for instance, to squeak the treaty through by a single vote. The close-run ratification of the treaty did not do much to improve the mood of the secretary of state, and it wasn't just the new snowdrifts banking the Washington streetscape that irked him. The other event in the news was likely to last well beyond the melt: A battle on the outskirts of Manila had broken out between the American occupation army and the Filipino freedom fighters. It appeared to have been an unintended outbreak between a couple of small hair-trigger units on each side. Aguinaldo was furiously trying to walk back the conflict before it turned into an all-out war. He asked the American military commander for a quick cease-fire to talk things over. General Otis, with the United States Congress now on the record for full American control of the islands, told Aguinaldo the time for negotiating had passed. "The fighting having begun," the message to Aguinaldo read, "it must go on to the grim end."

DEL AND HIS two friends steamed off on the troop transport the day of General Otis's challenge to Aguinaldo, so the young men were headed for a war zone. And the three recent Yale graduates were already, to John Hay's regret, drawing fire at home. Democratic newspapers attacked the president in specific and the Republican Party in general for granting these millionaires' sons free passage on a military transport, and simply for the purpose of making a private inspection of the new American possession. "This incident emphasizes the gradual advancement of the spirit of governmental aristocracy and the development of an office-holding class with superior, but unwarranted privileges which are inimical to the well being of a democratic republic," was the take in one newspaper syndicate. "The practice of official favoritism is becoming abominable and should be checked."

THE WASHINGTON SOCIAL season, meanwhile, wound down in ominous fashion. Another frigid blast roared in from Canada the day before Valentine's Day, blizzard included. The Hays were expected that evening at the climactic ball of the year, the Assembly Ball, just a few doors down at the Arlington Hotel, but it was wait-and-see all through the day. The roads in Washington were deemed impassable by early that afternoon; the streetcars stopped running and would not run again for two more days. The president was already considering cancellation of the next day's public reception at the White House.

Three feet of snow was piled at the Hays' front door by nightfall, and their horses and carriage were barricaded in the stable. Clara Hay was scheduled to receive at the Assembly that night, so Hay started calling around in hopes of finding a working carriage or sleigh. None was available, and Mrs. Hay could not be expected to make the walk in her finery. The Hays never made it out their front door that night. Neither did anybody else in Washington. The Assembly ballroom was a cavernous, howling wasteland, attended by only a few score of guests who were already staying at the Arlington.

HAY WAS LUCKY to make it across the square to the State Department the next morning, though once there, he could do little to advance his chief concern. It was now more than a month since Sir Julian had presented the projected Hay-Pauncefote Treaty to Lord Salisbury, and the prospects for a timely resolution were dimming.

The British cabinet was finally out in the open on the matter, or at least on the reasons for stalling the treaty. The prime minister and his advisers had begun to think more closely about the difficulties of selling Parliament on the wisdom of another conciliation of US interests. "There is a certain feeling here of late we have usually got the best of any arrangement between the United States and this country," White had reported to Hay after a talk with Colonial Secretary Joseph Chamberlain, "and [Chamberlain] feared that this feeling might be aggravated if so large a concession without any *quid pro quo* were to be announced." The

Salisbury cabinet determined instead that it would not be recommending the signing of the Hay-Pauncefote Treaty until the Canadian Commission in Washington had been concluded to their satisfaction. Quid pro quo.

This intelligence greatly increased Hay's already savage temper because Lord Herschell remained a towering menace in the business of the Canadian Commission; the Brit was still unwilling to let go of his ridiculous make-believe map of the Klondike, which meant any final agreement was impossible. "I think it deplorable," Hay complained in a Valentine's Day letter to White,

> that the British Government insists on making the arrangement in the Clayton-Bulwer matter depend on the successful issue of the Canadian negotiations. The two questions have nothing to do with each other.
>
> Every intelligent Englishman is ready to admit that the Canal ought to be built, that the United States alone will build it, that it cannot be built except as a Government enterprise, that nobody else wants to build it, that when built it will be to the advantage of the entire civilized world, and, this being the case, it is hard to see why the settlement of the matter ought to depend on the lumber duty or the Alaska boundary.

Hay dropped this splenetic letter in the mail of the day.

Lord Herschell was a casualty of the latest blizzard; he slipped on a patch of ice that Valentine's Day and broke his femur. And yet, even with Herschell laid up in his suite at the Shoreham Hotel, it appeared to Hay there was little hope for a successful conclusion to the Canadian negotiations and consequently little hope for a quick signing of the Hay-Pauncefote Treaty. All the secretary of state could do was put his head down and try to keep other possible antagonisms at bay. He sent a short note to Senator Morgan in response to his recent introduction of a Canal bill: "It seems to me," Hay suggested, "that the word 'defend' in the second line page 92, and the words 'and such fortifications for defense' should be omitted from the bill. If they are omitted there is nothing in the way of our taking such measures for defense as may seem to be necessary hereafter, while their presence in the bill would seem to foreign governments a negation of the principle of neutrality, on which we have said that the Canal was to be constructed. I defer to your superior knowledge and judgment on this as on most other matters, but since you have been so kind to ask my opinion I can only say what I have indicated above. I thank you for your promise to keep this matter entirely confidential."

THE CANADIAN COMMISSION adjourned without reaching a final agreement a week later, so the Alaska boundary and the Hay-Pauncefote Treaty would be put over for another season. Lord Herschell expired unexpectedly in his bed at the Shoreham a week after that, forcing Hay to convey both official and personal sympathies to the British embassy. There wasn't much more to be said. Herschell had come to Washington, had worked himself, literally, to death, and had less than nothing to show for his final effort. Hay sympathized on one very real level: except for the ratification of a peace treaty that had precipitated a new shooting war in the Philippines, where his own son was about to disembark, Hay had very little to show for his first half year on the job. "Except three Third Secretaries of Embassy which Hay obtained by bribing Cabot with two of them," Adams reported to Lizzie Cameron, "I believe Hay has accomplished nothing."

A LETTER ARRIVED for John Hay at the State Department a few days later, in a familiar hand, from the Hotel Krantz in Vienna. "Dear Excellency," it began, dispensing with niceties and hellos in typical Sam Clemens style, as if he and Hay had been corresponding every day instead of, well, almost never in the past ten years.

> Now then—listen! For a year, off & on I have been thinking out a simple scheme for the betterment of the Post Office revenues, & now it is finished & for sale. If it were a new & particularly comprehensive way of killing Christians I know the War Department would buy the idea, but I know that governments have sometimes bought ideas of purely commercial value—like the £20,000 paid by the British government for an improved chronometer, for instance. So, there's a chance! I am serious. But the government needn't take any risk; I merely want a royalty for a while—no lump sum. I only want the government to issue & sell a thing which is as simple as a post-card, & pay me a royalty of *one per cent* on the sales *for twelve years.* The government would derive other revenues from this scheme but in those I could not share. I have explained the scheme in detail confidentially to [the US minister in Vienna] Mr. [Charlemagne] Tower, & at first he thought there were weak places in it, but he ended by conceding that it was not so, & that the scheme was sound & valuable. He was surprised that it had not been thought of earlier.
>
> Don't you see? Suppose the sales were only $5,000,000 a year, & brought an additional revenue of $5,000,000; I shouldn't receive a royalty on both sums, but only on the first-mentioned. *That* wouldn't make me any richer than I ought to be—you know it yourself.
>
> Can't you get the government to instruct you to say to me that it will grant me that royalty if upon examining the idea it concludes to use it?

Then I will send you the thing clearly written out so that you will have no difficulty in understanding it. I am sorry to bother an over-worked man in this way. I am very sorry indeed; but honestly I don't know any way to help it.

Well, not much had changed. Clemens always did like commercial opportunities. And Hay knew his old friend was in deadly earnest, as he always was where money was involved. John Hay was mildly curious to see just what Clemens had in mind, and it was generally amusing to be carried into one of his strange adventures, especially if it could be done at a safe distance. So Hay marked off the sentence, "Can't you get the government to instruct you to say to me that it will grant me that royalty if upon examining the idea it concludes to use it?" and sent the letter over to the postmaster general with a typewritten note: "What sort of answer do you think I ought to send Clemens?"

The official government response to Sam Clemens's postal project was about what Hay expected; it was meant to discourage. But when Hay forwarded it to Vienna, Clemens was mainly heartened to have heard again from his old friend. So he sat down right away and addressed another letter to the secretary of state, who, he suspected, could use some cheering up.

Dear Excellency:

This is only a line to thank you. It was fine of you to do that for me when your hands were so full. In fact I did not foresee how particularly full . . . they were going to be, or I should have waited a little. I am going to let the P.O. Department rest & strengthen-up until I come in the fall; & meantime I will arrange to make myself the pet of the War Department. I am perfecting a scheme whereby I can cheaply & thoroughly exhaust the life-principle of the atmosphere and instantly kill the massed armies of the world & every living thing within a radius of three hundred thousand miles around them. In fact I am *already* able to do this. I have made all my preparations, & was expecting to touch the button and abolish the race this afternoon as an experiment, but must postpone it & think further, for I do not know what to do with my family.

There had been more to the correspondence than that, but before it left the Hotel Krantz, Mrs. Clemens had hacked half a page out of the letter. Hay suspected it had been too ribald for Livy to let pass. Clemens had scrawled a note under his signature before he sent it on to Washington. "The omission was poetry—& good, too, I think—but it has been edited out. *I* didn't do it."

CHAPTER THIRTY

Daaaaaam-*nation*!

The Clemens family's stay in Vienna rose to its glorious crescendo in the last week of May 1899. The grand old master of Vienna, the composer Johann Strauss, summoned Sam to his house for a talk and a smoke; then came an invitation for a private audience with Austrian emperor Franz Joseph, who insisted on meeting "Mark Twain" before the American author left town. The emperor was so informal and so inviting that Clemens forgot the little German speech he had prepared and the two men chatted breezily for twenty minutes. The emperor was up on Clemens's work and felt obliged also to congratulate the American on his country's recent display of military might and efficiency. Clemens mentioned that he was currently perfecting a plan to ensure "universal peace" with their mutual friend the inventor Jan Szczepanik, who could keep the sovereign posted on the details.

When Clemens returned from the meeting to his suite at the Hotel Krantz, where trunks and travel bags were packed and waiting, he wrote a quick note to his friend the Viennese humorist Eduard Pötzl.

> The New York papers have asked me about my audience, & I have telegraphed the following, which I consider quite nice because it is dignified & does not give any information: It was only a pleasant unconstrained private conversation on matters unconnected with international policy. I was very much wanting to explain my plan, now in the hands of the Secretary of State in Washington, for insuring universal peace [i.e., exterminating the human race], but I feared his majesty would laugh, or else consider it too radical. Print that, if you think it worth it & this also: All the papers in American will telegraph the Secretary of State to ask what that plan *is*.

The next day, when the family headed for its train out of Vienna, Sam Clemens was anxious and excited to be—finally, blessedly, thankfully—heading *toward* home. He had managed to convince Livy and his daughters to forgo a planned month in another resort in the Austrian mountains and move to London, where they could loaf around a hotel suite while Clara did a quick few months of voice study with Madame Blanche Marchesi, or maybe they would find a nice little country inn where they could spend a part of the summer. If the plan held, they would sail for America that autumn.

When the Clemenses arrived at the railway station for their departure, they found awaiting them a farewell party of nearly thirty, including the usually gruff and standoffish old genius Professor Leschetizky. (Sam had grown to love Herr Professor, even if he still could not correctly spell his name.) The well-wishers presented Livy with a silver vinaigrette vessel and Clara with a ring. The ladies surrounded the family in a scrum of hugs, while Madame de Laszowska and one little countess sobbed so deeply that the Clemenses had to be pushed up into the train—"get in, get in"—with tears in their eyes. The train had already whistled and started its forward lurch by the time the four got settled in their compartment. "And so we moved out of Vienna," Livy wrote to her sister, "with a coupe so filled [with flowers] that we were obliged to pile them at one end in order to get sitting room and looking out on 27 faces, many of whom had become very dear to us. Most of them we shall probably never again see in this world."

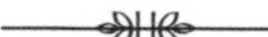

THE FIRST FRIEND they saw in London was Poultney Bigelow, who came charging into their rooms at the Prince of Wales Hotel only hours after their arrival. Clemens was struck dumb at the hearty bounce in Poultney's step; he figured on finding his young friend near death. Poultney had returned from a reporting trip in the Philippines with a case of dysentery that defied all medical ministrations. Clemens had been begging Poultney to try his homegrown cure. "Eat 3 slices of a ripe fresh water melon and bid your dysentery a prompt and sudden good-bye," he had counseled from Vienna earlier in the year. But watermelon was no easy thing to find in late-winter London, and when last Clemens had heard from the Bigelows, only a month earlier, Poultney was so weak and dehydrated he was unable to walk or to turn over in his bed without severe pain. But here he was, three weeks later, full of howling talk, ready to take Clemens out for a night on the town. Poultney's savior had been Mr. Kellgren (he pronounced it CHELL-gren) and his Swedish movement method, he explained. Mrs. Bigelow had heard about this "doctor" from a friend and, figuring they had nothing to lose, sought his help. Kellgren had tossed out all of Poultney's medicines and worked him back to perfect alimentary health in a matter of days. Poultney swore by his new physician's Swedish movement method and offered to take Clemens to see it in action at the nearby London clinic.

This was a welcome invitation. The Clemenses were not a physically robust family when they arrived in London. Livy was suffering from rheumatism in her back and her hip, or maybe it was gout. Clara had a sinus infection and cough so pronounced that a London doctor ordered her out of the city smog to take some fresh seaside air. Sam, as he had been for the previous seven years, was prone to rheumatism, gout, intestinal woes, hernias, and bronchitis.

These various afflictions paled in comparison to Jean's. Her epilepsy had become a frightening fact of the family's life. The petit mal seizures had become a common occurrence, sometimes daily for days on end. Sam and Livy euphemistically referred to these spells as Jean's "absentmindedness," as if she were simply struggling to call up a memorized fact. But these events were actual electrical disturbances in Jean's brain, which caused a near-total suspension of her mental faculties, lasting for minutes at a time and leaving her woozy and unfocused for hours afterward. Jean's grand mal seizures were far less common, but they took a much greater toll and left all who witnessed them terrorized. Jean would begin seizing and convulsing, first losing control of her own body and then losing consciousness. Her muscles contorted, her face flushed to purple, her teeth clenched, and in the most savage occurrences she lost control of her bladder and bowels. Jean would regain herself five or ten or even twenty minutes later with a slashing headache and an understandable sense of fear and shame. The brain fog and exhaustion that followed a grand mal seizure could last for days in Jean, while her parents lived in constant dread, anticipating the next harrowing event.

The medical specialists had been treating Jean in the accepted way: monitoring her diet and lifestyle—red meat, alcohol, strenuous intellectual effort, and masturbation were frowned upon—and prescribing daily doses of bromides that might include potassium, lithium, and oxide of zinc. This drug therapy, the same prescribed to Ida McKinley, kept the patient in a state of mild but constant sedation. The daily dosage of the bromide increased as the seizures became more frequent or more violent. This treatment would soon go out of common favor, though veterinarians a century later would still be using low doses of potassium bromide, judiciously and cautiously, to treat epileptic dogs.

Clemens took Poultney's suggestion and went straightaway to scout Mr. Kellgren's London clinic. The core treatment of the Swedish movement method, regardless of the ailment, was a series of manipulations, massages, and vibrations of the spinal column, the joints, the major organs, and the major nerve groupings. As practiced by the Kellgren team, all of whom had trained as medical doctors and walked the rounds in London hospitals, the sessions were intimate and physical wrestling matches. Clemens saw right away why this clinic was called a gymnasium and the professionals were called gymnasts. "It is vigorous exercise," he reported to a friend, "& *other people do it for you*."

The patient was meant to emerge from this exercise realigned and retuned: spinal column bent back into proper shape, joints loosened for a freer articulation, nerves uncompressed, air passages unclogged, and arteries and vessels dilated to allow for healthy and unimpeded blood flow. Clemens was not entirely convinced that the movement method could have much effect on disease, but given the way he felt for days after his own earliest treatments, he thought it was worth a try. He put it to Kellgren bluntly: could the movement method cure epilepsy? Kellgren admitted he had only ever cured "nonhereditary" epilepsy, but as there was no history of the disease in the Clemens family, and all previous doctors believed Jean's case had presented only after a hard knock to the head, Miss Clemens *might* be a candidate for a real and lasting cure. This was a mere glimmer of hope, but Sam grabbed it.

When Kellgren suggested the family go for a minimum of three weeks to his sanatorium in Sanna, Sweden, where Jean could begin intensive therapy, Sam Clemens paid the deposit. He had a way of hearing what he wanted to hear, and the way he heard it, Jean could be cured in a matter of months, which meant there was time to repair his youngest daughter and still sail for home, happy and healthy, that fall.

The Clemens family arrived at Sanna in the middle of July 1899, and the gymnasts there immediately insisted that Jean forgo the bromides she had been taking for the past three years. These clinicians believed, and with good reason, that most of the good they had done in the previous decades was simply in halting the flow of poisons the regular physicians were shoving down their patients' throats. Sam concurred and felt confirmed in this concurrence by what he witnessed in his daughter in the first seven days in Sweden. Jean was more physically able and mentally sharp than she had been in years. She suffered only two minor spells of "absentmindedness," where he would have counted on fifteen or twenty in the worst of weeks. Sam and Livy didn't dare speak aloud of Jean's apparent improvement. Livy was terrified that her daughter was off her long-prescribed medication, and little surprised when Jean suffered three major seizures in the next five days—two in a single afternoon. "It's all right." the doctor assured a skeptical Livy, "Keep your grip."

And then the apparent miracle began to unfold. Jean went a week, then two weeks, then *three* weeks and more without a seizure. Her father kept score as the streak of seizure-free days grew longer: no bromide for fifty-seven days; no major seizures for thirty-five. The family decided to extend Jean's already extended therapy to the end of September. Sam was happy to do it and willing to pay the price. "An outsider would think Jean is already cured," he wrote to

Henry Rogers and Sam Clemens

Rogers. "[Jean's] health has blossomed out in the most extraordinary way, & she is full of life & go & energy & activity." Call it Sanna Syndrome: Sam Clemens had become a believer, and a partisan one. He began referring to Jean's previous drug regimen as the "deadly poisons" that had been "destroying her." And he was quick to *testify*, citing his own daily treatment, which knocked out one of his normally insistent bronchial episodes in less than a week. "We shall have some more frights [over Jean], but they will be light," Sam wrote. "And by & by Jean will be cured. That, I quite believe."

Livy remained wary. She worried about her husband's unrealistic expectations and felt compelled to sit him down and have a talk. "[Livy] has been correcting me this morning," Clemens explained in a letter to Henry Rogers. "I thought it was held that Jean could be cured in six months, but she says no, it was to be six months *possibly*, but it might take 9 & even 12. It puts off America a good while, & makes me tired to think of it."

MAYBE IT WAS the eighteen hours of Swedish daylight, but Sam Clemens did not stop believing: Jean would be cured! They would soon be back in America! Three days after Livy's little talk, he was moved to write Twichell a cheerier note. "I have seen about 60 sunsets here; and a good 40 of them were clear &

away beyond anything I had ever imagined before for dainty and exquisite and marvelous beauty and infinite change and variety. America? Italy? The tropics? They have no notion of what a sunset ought to be. And this one—this unspeakable wonder! It discounts all the rest. It brings the tears, it is so unutterably beautiful."

He had the time and the energy to write most days also, and in mid-September he finished a little magazine sketch called "My Boyhood Dreams." The essay was a sentimental make-believe about a long-ago meeting of Sam Clemens and a few friends, then a happy little secret society, who were all now (separately) nearing the end of long careers in the public eye. "I remember it so well—that night we met together," he wrote, ". . . and under the seal of confidence revealed to each other what our boyhood dreams had been: dreams which had not as yet been blighted, but over which was stealing the gray of the night that was to come—a night which we prophetically *felt*, and this feeling oppressed us and made us sad." The celebrated poet Thomas Bailey Aldrich dreamed of being a horse doctor; the acclaimed novelists William Dean Howells and George Washington Cable, an auctioneer and a circus ringmaster; the author of the best-selling *Uncle Remus* stories, Joel Chandler Harris, a pirate; Professor Brander Matthews, a cowboy. "At that time," Clemens wrote,

> [John] Hay's boyhood dream was not yet past hope of realization, but it was fading, dimming, wasting away, and the wind of a growing apprehension was blowing cold over the perishing summer of his life. In the pride of his young ambition he had aspired to be a steamboat mate; and in fancy saw himself dominating a forecastle some day on the Mississippi and dictating terms to roustabouts in high and wounding tones. I look back now, from this far distance of seventy years, and note with sorrow the stages of that dream's destruction. . . . Hay climbed high toward his ideal; when success seemed almost sure, his foot upon the very gang-plank, his eye upon the capstan, misfortune came and his fall began. Down—down—down—ever down: Private Secretary to the President; Colonel in the field; Chargé d'Affaires in Paris; Chargé d'Affaires in Vienna; Poet; Editor of the "Tribune"; Biographer of Lincoln; Ambassador to England; and now at last there he lies—Secretary of State, Head of Foreign Affairs. And he has fallen like Lucifer, never to rise again. And his dream—where now his dream? Gone down in blood and tears. . . .
>
> We were under oath never to tell any of these things, and I have always kept that oath inviolate when speaking with persons whom I thought not worthy to hear them.
>
> Oh, our lost Youth—God keep its memory green in our hearts!

THEY GOT BACK to London on the last day of September and started looking for a temporary residence that put them within walking distance of Mr. Kellgren's London gymnasium. Clemens found a respectable flat and signed a lease that committed them until the next May. "We must remain in London & continue Jean's cure till it is perfected, if it takes a year," he wrote to a business acquaintance. "She will come out all right by & by & then we shall go home & stay there."

He could have been perfectly content in London. Jean *was* better. The end of the exile *was* in sight. But so much of the news he read was about the new US war in the Philippines. Reports of America's efforts to put down the Filipino freedom fighters had been ugly and demoralizing from the first, and after eight long months, they were just getting worse. For every Filipino wounded or captured by the US military, four were killed—a near-complete reversal of the five-to-one ratio of wounded or captured to killed that prevailed in the meat grinder of the Civil War. General Arthur MacArthur explained that this was because men of "inferior races" (in this case, Filipinos) were less likely to survive their wounds. Letters from American soldiers reprinted in their hometown newspapers told a more sickening story, and a more plausible one, given the casualty statistics. "We do not take prisoners. . . . [Company I] had four prisoners, and didn't know what to do with them. They asked Captain Bishop what to do, and he said, 'You know the orders,' and four natives fell dead. . . . One company of the Tennessee boys was sent into headquarters with thirty prisoners, and got there with about a hundred chickens and no prisoners."

Others' letters home revealed the terror campaign the United States military was waging against Filipino civilians.

> If they fire a shot from the house we burn the house down and every house near it, and shoot the natives. . . . We burned hundreds of houses and looted hundreds more. . . . You have no idea what a mania for destruction the average man has when the fear of the law is removed. . . . We bombarded a place called Malabon, and then we went in and killed every native we met, men, women and children. . . . I am probably growing hard-hearted, for I am in my glory when I can sight my gun on some dark skin and pull the trigger.

The US terror campaign did not seem to be having the intended effect; Emilio Aguinaldo and his freedom fighters did not lie down, even after American soldiers leveled the town of Malolos, capital of the new Republic of the Philippines. The Philippine republicans would not be cowed, even by more than thirty thousand United States troops, a force larger than the entire regular American army before the war with Spain. American commanders began calling for more men. Reinforcements trickled in by the thousands, including one "Negro unit" whose men, when asked on arrival, "What are you coons doing here?" replied with some evident relish, "We have come to take up the White Man's Burden."

By the fall of 1899, as Sam Clemens was settling his family into its new London flat, General MacArthur was begging for an increase in force to one hundred thousand men—and he would get it. The McKinley administration was not going to be embarrassed. As the war dragged on—the US Army, it was reported, controlled an area 117 miles square, about one-tenth of 1 percent of the archipelago—the supporters of the president's Benevolent Assimilation policy became louder. War was a rough business, they asserted, especially when battling an "uncivilized" enemy. "They are, as a rule, an illiterate, semi-savage people, who are waging war, not against tyranny, but against Anglo-Saxon order and decency," wrote Frederick Funston, who had gained the reputation as one of the most vicious American commanders in the Philippines.

"There is no use dilly-dallying with these uncircumcised, uncivilized, unthankful and treacherous cutthroats," one California newspaper editorialized. "The sooner soldiers are sent there in sufficient numbers to finish up the business, the better it will be for Christianity and human progress."

The main message to the American people was *Buck up!* A few practiced British colonialists were offering advice and suggesting their own tried-and-true methods: "Americans do not seem to understand the game, which is to use one set of natives against the other. This would not be a difficult matter in the Philippines; the suspicion of some tribes against the dominating Tagals could easily be aroused." And Whitelaw Reid (among many others) was reminding his fellow countrymen of the benefits that would accrue to them if they stayed the difficult course. "The two richest archipelagoes in the world are practically at our disposal," Reid said in a speech at Princeton University in October of 1899. "The greatest ocean on the globe has been put in our hands, the ocean that is to bear the commerce of the Twentieth Century."

OTHER WAR NEWS hit closer to Clemens's London home in the middle of October 1899, as Great Britain's own simmering donnybrook with the Boers in South Africa was about to become a declared and official fight. Sam Clemens, given his time in South Africa and his reporting on the Jameson Raid a few years earlier, believed he knew the root and the cause of this conflict: Her Majesty's government was not about to give up their quest for the treasure of the Transvaal after just one failed attempt. He would have a hard time backing his English neighbors in this new fight. Sam's heart was with the Boers, who were defending their homeland. His head was with England, which was then in lockstep with America in the great march of civilization. "Poor as it is, [our civilization] is better than *real* savagery," he wrote to Twichell, "therefore we must stand by it, extend it, & (in public) praise it. And so we must not utter any hurtful word about England in these days, nor fail to hope that she will win in this war, for her defeat & fall would be an irremediable disaster for the mangy human race. Naturally, then, I am for England; but she is profoundly in the wrong, Joe, & no (instructed) Englishman doubts it. At least that is my belief."

Once the shooting began in early October of 1899, Sam Clemens did not trust himself to hold his tongue. So as England went war mad, Clemens socialized among intimate friends only and avoided talk of *any* war. He told Poultney once again to safeguard his new address. "I don't intend to go to any Club dinners nor speech-making places this winter, nor get into the hands of any interviewers," he explained to his friend, "and if anyone asks about me I require you to lie loyally, and say I have gone to the Continent for a few months."

LONDON WAS DRENCHED in a record-breaking rainfall the first nine days of November. Clara was still attending her daily voice lessons with Madame Marchesi, and Jean still marching through the dull, smoggy mornings for her treatments at the Kellgren gymnasium, when the bombshell arrived—a letter from Sam's sister Pamela Moffett. He had written to his sister to sing the praises of the Swedish movement method and all the great good it was doing Jean, and in her return letter Pamela said she was not at all surprised. She had just had a similar and very successful two-month treatment with a Dr. Steele, in Buffalo. This Swedish method seemed exactly like Dr. Steele's osteopathy, which had been spreading across the United States for twenty years. Clemens immediately located three osteopathic offices in New York alone: on Fifth Avenue, East Twenty-Third Street, and East Thirty-First.

Daaaaaam-*nation*!

"My temper is under a heavy strain this morning, for I find the Kellgren system . . . is being practiced all over America!" he wrote to Henry Rogers on November 9. "If I had only found this out in September, instead of yesterday, we should have located in New York the 1st of October . . . & now we are tied here till April or May."

THE APPROACH OF the Christmas season lacked the great good cheer they had rediscovered in Vienna the year before—and then Livy got sick with influenza and bronchitis. She begged for a standard medical doctor, but her husband reminded her that they knew of no good one in all of London and sent for Kellgren. Sam's stubborn insistence on the genius of the movement method was already beginning to rankle Livy, and Kellgren's manipulations didn't help. "The terrible treatment has been nearly unendurable for violence," Clemens admitted in a letter to Livy's sister, Susie Crane, "& has made her sore & lame, & filled her mind with black thoughts & antagonisms toward the system." In her weakened state, Livy was no longer able to even feign hope about Jean's prognosis. Her younger daughter *was* in better physical condition after all these months, but the seizures continued, and Livy was starting to believe the Swedish method had not truly cured the epilepsy and never would.

The war reporting out of the Transvaal grew dark. The London papers were filled with news of the worst week the British had suffered since the charge of the Light Brigade. They had endured three spectacular setbacks at three major battles in the span of four days. From December 11 to December 15, reports said, the British army counted as many as 450 men killed in action, 1,500 wounded in action, 700 captured, and 340 missing. Boer casualties were reported as "slight" or "trivial."

"It's awful here!" Clemens reported home, while Livy lay in her sickbed in the next room, "—half of our friends are in mourning, & the hearts of the other half stop beating when they see a newsboy. And the fogs & the day-long darkness! & my dreary attempts to feel cheerful, & the people's attempts—on the street—to *look* so—it's dismal times! . . . This is no place for merriment."

THE NEW YEAR, 1900, blew into London with a chill wind, which settled into a dull gray mist, and Clemens's bitter private reverie continued largely unbroken into February—"days of fog & rain & influenza & war." Among the few cheery little notes was a letter forwarded to Clemens from *McClure's Magazine*, which had just published "My Boyhood Dreams."

> My dear Clemens:
>
> There have been some newspaper paragraphs indicating that I "resented" your allusion to me in that most delightful article of yours. . . . As these idiotic paragraphs may have reached even you and as the inherent improbability of a lie is not always sufficient to take the poison from it, I write now to tell you how I was moved and delighted by your article, not only for its exquisite skill and delicacy of touch, which I really think increases with you year by year, but for its proof of your inveterate goodness and friendship towards me, which I assure you I hold as a most precious possession.
>
> Yours faithfully,
> John Hay

CHAPTER THIRTY-ONE

Et Tu, Theodore?

The winter so far had turned into a happy reversal from John Hay's season of misery the previous year. The weather in Washington had been mild and sometimes even pleasant, and except for his department's minor misstep of offending the wife of the Austrian minister, and a malfunction of a White House furnace that caused a wave of heat stroke at the annual diplomatic dinner, the social season was going along smoothly.

Hay's family was well also. Del had come safely through his trip to the war zone in the Philippines—"He was shot through the hat at Caloocan, and has not yet told us about it,—showing a lucidity of intellect which astonishes his dad," Hay reported to a friend—and had impressed enough military men that President McKinley decided to ship him off to fill an unexpected vacancy as the United States consul in Pretoria, South Africa, in the middle of the Boer War. Hay was hesitant to give his blessing to this dangerous assignment, but as he wrote to his son that February, "I could not resist your earnest desire to go, and I am sure that such a test of character and of endurance, if you come happily out of it, will be of advantage to you all your life."

John Hay also seemed to have begun to master the job of secretary of state or had at least grown more comfortable in it. It had helped that William McKinley, sufficiently concerned at his secretary of state's darkening mien, had occasionally pulled Hay aside and told him to trust in his own judgment and work to negotiate the most honorable treaties he could—with Canada or England or Germany or any other nation—and he would back him with all the power of the presidency.

The Senate, meanwhile, had been exhibiting an uncommon respect for the Department of State, which was the most dramatic turnaround of the year. When Hay had negotiated a treaty with Germany and England to carve up Samoa, the Senate Foreign Relations Committee reported it to the floor unmolested, and it was ratified in less than two hours. Hay had secured for the United

States another useful coaling station in the Pacific and exclusive rule over the islanders on Tutuila. The opposition didn't put up much of a fight. "I'm opposed to this whole business," "Pitchfork" Ben Tillman said on the Senate floor, "but I don't see the use of making a fuss over this one little speck of coral down there by itself when we've got islands to burn in the Philippines."

By the time John Hay and Sir Julian signed the Hay-Pauncefote Treaty at 11:00 a.m. on February 5, 1900, Hay appeared as close as he ever got to buoyant, as if he were channeling the mood of the nation. "I find America so cheerful, and so full of swagger and self-satisfaction, that I hardly know it," was how Henry Adams described it. Hay was also feeling more than usually solicitous of his British counterpart that morning. The surprising reports of the Boer War were splashed across newspapers in America and Europe: the mightiest empire the world had ever known, along with its commanding general, Sir Redvers Henry Buller, was being run ragged by a bunch of farmers with guns. GLOOM IN LADYSMITH WHEN BULLER DRIVEN BACK was one headline in the papers that morning, accompanied by large photographs of strapping mustachioed young British officers (one photographed in evening wear) who had been wasted in recent battles.

Hay suspected these recent setbacks in South Africa, and the fact that all of Europe seemed to have joined the kaiser's cheering section for the Boers, were the main reasons Prime Minister Salisbury had recently decided to decouple the canal treaty from the US-Canadian dispute over the Alaska boundary. Lord Salisbury and his cabinet would not wish to be caught in the shameful position of soliciting friends and allies, of course, but they were pleased that the McKinley administration, with the memory of Britain's quietly pro-American stance in the late US war with Spain still fresh, was returning that favor in South Africa now. Hay was also, to the increasing discomfort of the Russians, the French, and the Germans, willing to carry water for Great Britain's main policy initiative in the Far East—the "Open Door" in China. The prime minister's decision to move on the canal treaty also factored in the new gold strike in Nome, Alaska, deep in the American-owned territory, over a thousand miles distant from the US-Canadian borderline. This new fact on the Alaskan ground made it much less interesting or profitable to continue the wrangling over Lord Herschell's phantom boundary line in the Klondike. "We are all agog about Nome," said Henry Adams, who was apt to measure nations by their gold supplies. "Klondike is nowhere. The miners are all rushing out of it, and hurrying to Nome."

Hay had constructed this canal treaty, even before the Boer War had begun, with an eye toward the Salisbury cabinet's need to avoid any appearance of weakness, and he assured Sir Julian Pauncefote, as the hot wax seals hardened on the new-signed official documents that morning, that the United States Senate would certainly ratify the treaty and without any invasive amendments that could offend in London. In fact, he was certain the treaty would sail through the upper chamber untouched. The advantage was all to the United States without calling attention to it, Hay believed; the Senate could not fail to miss this bald fact. The secretary of state was already beginning to think of the canal treaty as the capstone of his long public service.

Hay "actually trembles for fear that he should wake up and find that he dreamt it," Henry Adams wrote to a friend of theirs, after one of his daily constitutionals with the secretary of state. "He has given nothing for what a dozen Presidents have broken their necks to get. . . . He beams with content, and says he is now ready to go."

IF THIS HAY-PAUNCEFOTE Treaty was to be the final triumphant stroke of his career, Hay was well satisfied. He did not mean to be in office much longer in any case, and Mrs. Hay concurred. Clara's resolve to have her husband returned to private life had hardened in the two months since Vice President Hobart's death put John Hay first in line for the presidency. She had no choice but to live with the terrifying possibility of her husband's ascension, but she was more insistent than ever that his tenure in the cabinet would not extend beyond McKinley's first term.

This seemed very sensible thinking to John Hay as well, though he had yet to confess his plan to William McKinley. His hesitation owed mainly to genuine sympathy for the Major. The president, too, was prone to his own private fantasies of escape, which he occasionally confided to his personal secretary and to members of his cabinet. The Major had confessed to Hay that he looked forward to another term as president with "unaffected dread and distaste," that he did not expect to accomplish much worthwhile in a second term, and that he was weary of the whole business. Hay considered the consequences of McKinley's early retirement: the Republican Party would find itself suddenly running around looking for a new man, and the party's nominee could very well be the popular new Rough Rider governor of New York—*Theodore Roosevelt*! McKinley could not in good conscience step away from his duty to the country and to the party, Hay told his boss.

"If I could only keep my present Cabinet about me," the president finally said to Hay, "I should not so much mind."

Hay had nodded in silent acknowledgment, knowing that most of that cabinet was already making plans for a return to various private law and banking practices. "I have never had yet the evil courage to tell [the president] I shall not stay," Hay told Harry White after the discussion. "I shall wait till after the elections."

PRESIDENT MCKINLEY SENT the Hay-Pauncefote Treaty to the Senate for ratification with a short but muscular note of his absolute approval and waited for the members of that august body—the Republicans, at least—to begin to fashion the laurels to wreath on John Hay's head. The initial reaction was disconcertingly at odds with the administration's expectations. There were whiffs of praise: Reid's *Tribune* called the treaty, without having seen it, John Hay's triumph and foresaw little opposition. But when the critics got down to the details, Hay's confidence began to soften. He stood accused of disregarding the shiny, new controlling tenet of American foreign policy—the revitalized Monroe Doctrine. It was well and good, these expansionists argued, that the Hay-Pauncefote Treaty ceded to the United States the right to build, manage, and maintain the canal, as well as the power to police it. But they could not understand why Secretary Hay had permitted the United States to be barred from building military fortifications there, or to be obligated to allow free and equal passage of ships of all nations, even in time of war. Did this mean enemy ships could pass through a US-made canal? And why did his treaty invite other European nations to sign on to the accord? There was much talk in the Senate about amending the treaty, in spite of the secretary of state's insistence that any tinkering would surely kill the deal in England.

The prospects for quick and easy ratification flickered and dimmed in the first few days, as opposition to the treaty grew louder and wider. On February 9, a member of the House called for the immediate passage of canal legislation without regard to the pending treaty. "We should build the canal and own it and control it without waiting for the consent of Great Britain or any other power on earth," the Tammany Democrat "Plain Bill" Sulzer told reporters. Hay waved this off as election-year politicking—another craven attempt to excite the growing blocs of German and Irish voters who hated all things British. What followed three days later was not so easy to slough off.

ROOSEVELT IS AGAINST IT, read the front page of the *Sun*, a normally reliable Republican paper in New York. Hay had been warned the night before the story ran, and he had tried to take Theodore's chest-thumping in stride. He understood that his friend now had certain political bases to cover as the sitting (and about-to-be-running-again) governor of New York and that Theodore was probably also positioning himself for a shot at the vice presidential nomination, but it pained the secretary of state to see the story in black and white. "I most earnestly hope that the pending treaty concerning the Isthmian canal will not be ratified unless amended so as to provide that the canal, when built, shall be wholly under the control of the United States, alike in peace and war," Roosevelt had told reporters called to the steps of his sister's New York City brownstone. "This seems to me vital, no less from the standpoint of our sea power than from the standpoint of the Monroe doctrine." The governor said he might have something more substantive to add when he returned to his office the next day.

"Et tu!" Hay wrote in a personal letter to Theodore the day the story appeared. "Cannot you leave a few things to the President and the Senate, who are charged with them by the Constitution? As to 'Sea Power' and the Monroe Doctrine, we did not act without consulting the best living authorities on those subjects." Perhaps, in his anger, Hay forgot for a moment that Theodore Roosevelt recognized no authority greater than his own on the questions of sea power and the Monroe Doctrine or on pretty much any other issue under the sun.

Hay got a reminder in the form of a private letter from Governor Roosevelt a few days later, in which Theodore told Hay how agonizing it had been to cross him but then made another hot slap across the secretary's face. "I cannot, try as I may, see that you are right," Roosevelt wrote.

> Understand me. When the treaty is adopted, as I suppose it will be, I shall put the best face possible on it, and shall back the Administration as heartily as ever; but oh, how I wish you and the President would drop the treaty and push through a bill to build *and fortify* our own canal! . . . If that canal is open to the warships of an enemy, it is a menace to us in time of war; it is an added burden, an additional strategic point—to be guarded by our fleet. If fortified by us, it becomes one of the most potent sources of our possible sea strength. . . . One prime reason for fortifying our great seaports is to unfetter our fleet, to release it for offensive purposes; and the proposed canal would fetter it again, for our fleet would have to watch it, and therefore do the work which a fort should do; and which it could do much better. . . . As for existing treaties—I do not admit the "dead hand" of the treaty-making power in the past. A treaty can always be honorably abrogated—though it must never be abrogated in dishonest fashion.

By the time Hay had read that nasty little epistle, the attacks in the *Sun* had become personal. The newspaper's Valentine's Day editorial accused Hay of inviting "national calamity" with his "stupendous blunder."

A few days later, Senator Henry Cabot Lodge told Henry Adams—which was Cabot's way of telling Hay—that the treaty would be strangled in the Senate crib. Politics made ratification too dangerous in an election year, he told Adams. Then Cabot declared his opposition. Hay was furious at his old friend and began privately accusing Cabot of cowardice ("the first to flop") and then charging the Senate in general with cowardice, stupidity, and, most generously, mere indolence. "It is a curious state of things. The howling lunatics, like Mason and Allen and Pettigrew, are always on hand, while our friends are cumbered with other cares and most of the time away," he wrote in a private letter to the US ambassador in England. He added up who was suffering delirium tremens, who was back home trying to save his seat, who was having a romantic rendezvous in another city or falling over and breaking ribs when he should have been in town ratifying his treaty. "I have never struck a subject so full of psychological interest as the official mind of a Senator."

Hay's initial fury receded to passive disgust and private remorse and finally to something like relief: a defeat of his canal treaty might be his best chance for an early exit from the cabinet, even before William McKinley's first term was up. This outcome had its allure for Hay. Once out of office, he would have time to improve his art collection or to write more poetry. He could have long, uninterrupted summers of leisure at the Fells, or he could run off to London for another round of holidays with his friends in the Scottish moors.

"If I were he, I should stay in, just to pay back my little debts, and take out the change," Henry Adams reported to Lizzie Cameron, "but if he does not choose to stand kicking, it is his affair, not mine; and it is not my administration that Cabot is kicking, or my treaty or my canal."

SECRETARY HAY WAS tending toward self-pity the first week of March, when he received a note posted from a London address unknown to him—Wellington Court, Albert Gate. It was an answer to the "Boyhood Dreams" letter he had sent a few weeks earlier, on the day the *Sun* trashed him: "Dear Mr. Hay," Sam Clemens's letter began, rather formally.

> No, if I had seen the paragraphs they would not have deceived me into the superstition that your large mould had shrunken with age & a wide experience of life. I should have known much better than that. You would easily see that I was trying to pay well-intended compliments to the distinguished careers of old old friends of mine & that the feeling back of it was pride & affection, not envy and malice. . . . As for the public—oh, bother the public!
>
> I watch your onward & upward career with the interest & pride of one with a personal stake in it, & when you say you value my friendship you give me a pleasure which is complete, & which you could add nothing to.

ON FRIDAY, MARCH 9, 1900, the Committee on Foreign Relations moved the Hay-Pauncefote Treaty to the Senate floor. The committee report commended the secretary of state and recommended ratification. Hay saw this commendation for what it was: the committee members were putting on their bright public smiles while sticking their shivs deep into his ribs. On the treaty's way out the committee door, the members had attached an amendment giving the United States wide berth to defend its interests in the canal. Two or three other amendments, all with much sharper points, awaited the treaty's arrival on the floor. The next Tuesday, an anonymously sourced story in the morning papers suggested that John Hay had been shamefully outmaneuvered in his negotiations with Sir Julian Pauncefote: the British had fooled the unwitting secretary of state into giving away the store, and it was up to the Senate to clean up his mess. The president was also implicated in Hay's fecklessness.

There was not much to be done or said about the treaty in the regular meeting of the cabinet at the White House that day, and when it ended, John Hay walked over and pressed a note into William McKinley's hand. "Mr. President," he said, "here are some communications which I hope you will read at your leisure." It wasn't until later in the evening, as he was disposing of the last bits of his daily paperwork, that McKinley opened the envelope from Hay. "Dear Mr. President," read the note.

> The action of the Senate indicates views so widely divergent from mine in matters affecting, as I think, the national welfare and honor, that I fear my power to serve you in business requiring the concurrence of that body is at an end. I cannot help fearing also that the newspaper attacks upon the State Department which have so strongly influenced the Senate, may be an injury to you if I remain in the Cabinet.
>
> I therefore hand you my resignation as Secretary of State.

Hay was at home that evening, anticipating his coming freedom, when the White House messenger arrived at his door bearing tidings from the president.

> Dear Mr. Secretary Hay,—
>
> I return your resignation. Had I known the contents of the letter which you handed me this morning, I would have declined to receive or consider it. Nothing could be more unfortunate than to have you retire from the Cabinet. The personal loss would be great, but the public loss even greater. Your administration of the State Department has had my warm approval. As in all matters you have taken my counsel, I will cheerfully bear whatever criticism or condemnation may come. Your record constitutes one of the most important and interesting pages of our diplomatic history.

If John Hay still had a flicker of hope that he might wriggle free from the cabinet, it was extinguished by what followed. "We must bear the atmosphere of the hour. It will pass," McKinley's message continued. It was as if Abraham Lincoln himself was speaking to Hay from the grave. "We must continue working on the lines of duty and honor. Conscious of high purpose and honorable effort, we cannot yield our posts however the storm may rage. With hearty assurance of appreciation and confidence I am, Yours devotedly.

SECRETARY OF STATE John Hay rose the next morning, donned one of his many dark Savile Row suits, hauled himself back to his desk at the State Department, and dutifully and devotedly shouldered his responsibilities. Hay found a communication from Lord Salisbury awaiting him in his office that morning. The prime minister's message was direct and firm. Her Majesty's government had received the communication forwarded to it by way of the American consul in the South African capital of Pretoria—a communication that amounted to a plea from Boer president Kruger for third-party mediation and an honorable peace in South Africa. The prime minister was having none of it. The United States (and every other nation on the planet) was best advised to keep its nose out of the British Empire's war in South Africa, he wrote. Hay knew this meant the bloodletting there would continue until one side was crushed, and the fight was probably headed toward Pretoria, where Adelbert Hay had settled into the US consul's office.

Del was in a particularly awkward and perhaps even dangerous position. The United States was a neutral country in this war but had agreed to look after British interests in Boer-controlled Pretoria, just as the British consuls had seen to American interests in Havana and Madrid during the Spanish-American War. Del had been the victim of some unfair and nasty press there; newspaper accounts that preceded his arrival in Pretoria suggested the younger Hay was no friend of the Boers, but a pro-British agent whose instructions came from London and not Washington. John Hay had watched Del's work in South Africa with fatherly pride; his son had quickly won the favor of President Kruger and the trust of his Boer government, even while pressing the interests of British subjects and prisoners of war. His reports to his bosses at the Department of State were lucid and informative. John Hay's firstborn son might never share his interest in painting and poetry, but at age twenty-three he was showing remarkable diplomatic skills.

That Saturday, when John Hay's long, eventful week was done, he sat down in his library at home and composed a four-page letter to his son: "My dear boy, I feel very remote from you when I sit down to write. . . . It is hard to give you any advice at this distance. In case the theatre of war should be shifted to Pretoria and the city should be closely besieged, it is probable that the consuls will all think it proper to go to Lourenço Marquez. I know you will do what is right and honorable. If you are able to communicate with me, do so; if not, act without orders, as you may think best." After he had laid out all the fatherly advice and support and official instruction, Hay offered his son a rare private confidence. "[I] am having, now in my old age, my first experience of filthy newspaper abuse," he wrote. "I have made some mistakes, but they have not got onto them. The things they blackguard me for are the ones where I am absolutely sure I am right. But all this will pass away."

THE ELECTION OF 1900 was on the horizon now, and the question everybody was asking was who would replace the dead vice president Hobart as William McKinley's running mate. McKinley was dodging the issue in public and in private. "The utmost artesian boring has not availed to elicit from the President his choice," Hay joked. The simple fact was, McKinley was having trouble roping a running mate. His closest political allies in the Senate and in the cabinet had all turned him down. The most talked-about and recognizable of the other possible candidates had issued an early and unequivocal communication to the country at large. "In view of the continued statements in the press," New York's first-term governor, Theodore Roosevelt, said, "and in view of the many letters that reach me advising for and against such a course, it is proper for me to state definitely that under no circumstances could I or would I accept the nomination for the Vice Presidency." Theodore had managed to keep himself in the conversation by repeating this assertion over and over and over.

Governor Roosevelt might have actually walked away early in the process had the McKinley people simply *acknowledged* his public refusal of the vice presidential nomination. But for three maddening weeks after his first statement, Theodore heard not a peep from Pennsylvania Avenue. So what else could he do but send a special emissary to the White House to tell the president, to his face, that Theodore Roosevelt could not accept the vice presidential nomination? McKinley had a big laugh with the governor's messenger, a Mr. Butler, and told him some aromatic tales about Theodore's tenure as assistant secretary of the navy. He then sent Butler to deliver the governor's message to McKinley's key political manager, Senator Mark Hanna. Hanna barked and growled and told Butler that Roosevelt needn't bother stepping aside yet again. Butler *could*, however, explain to the governor that Mark Hanna would be running the nominating convention and that Governor Roosevelt would have a place on the ticket over his dead body.

Butler's report from Washington was not exactly what Roosevelt had expected to hear. Theodore sat and stewed, and reiterated his love for the governorship of New York, where they were just getting a start on solving all the big problems facing the state, and manfully explained to anybody who would listen that the vice presidency was not well suited to a figure of his bursting energy and myriad abilities. And still he heard nothing from the White House. So finally, just days before the nominating convention, seeing there was no possible way to avoid it, Theodore took the train down to Washington. He would have to declare himself to McKinley, personally, as uninterested in the vice presidency, which would of course give the president ample opportunity to recruit him.

Hay and Elihu Root, the new secretary of war and an old friend of Roosevelt's, were among the few men at the White House when Theodore arrived that June morning. "It was more fun than a goat," Hay wrote to Adams when it was over.

> [Roosevelt] came down, with a somber resolution throned on his strenuous brow, to let McKinley and Hanna know, once and for all, that he would not be Vice President, and found to his stupefaction that nobody in Washington, except Platt, had ever dreamed of such a thing. He did not even have a chance to launch his *nolo episcopari* at the Major. That statesman said he did not want him on the ticket—that he would be far more valuable in New York—and Root said, "Of course not—you are not fit for it." And so [Theodore] went back, quite eased in his mind, but considerably bruised in his *amour-propre*.

Hay had actually done a little of the bruising himself, when he pulled the governor aside for a brief chat. "I think you are unduly alarmed," Hay told his old friend. "There is no instance of an election of a Vice President by violence."

THEODORE ROOSEVELT ARRIVED at the Republican nominating convention in Philadelphia in the middle of June, with the air of someone much greater than a mere delegate from New York. Cabot was already there, visiting state delegations to encourage a Teddy-for-veep boomlet. Roosevelt meant to be noticed. "The Governor was in a state of rare excitement," said one of his traveling companions, "even for him." The "empty sleeve" war wound would have come in handy for Theodore just then, but he grabbed the best he had and came bouncing into the convention waving his Rough Rider headgear. "Gentlemen," said one onlooker, "that's an acceptance hat."

McKinley was in a pickle: no one he wanted as his vice president was willing to sign on to the ticket, but how could he admit that? "The President has no choice for Vice President," was McKinley's official statement to the delegates.

"Any of the distinguished names suggested would be satisfactory to him. The choice of the convention will be his choice; he has no advice to give." The statement electrified the Exposition Auditorium and every hotel, bar, and restaurant in the neighborhood. Everybody knew an open floor vote meant Roosevelt in a sweep, if only the rough-riding governor would, finally, *consent*.

"I cannot disappoint my Western friends, if they insist," was among Theodore's many final, long-awaited capitulations. "I cannot seem to be bigger than my party." Arthritic Mark Hanna almost spit out his teeth. "I'm through!" he was overheard screaming in his private suites that day. "I won't have anything more to do with the convention! I won't take charge of the campaign! I won't be chairman of the national committee again! . . . Don't any of you realize that there's only one life between that madman and the Presidency?"

When the question of the vice presidential nomination was moved to the floor for a decision, Roosevelt won every delegate but one. Theodore's was the lone dissenting vote, which must have appeared extraordinarily magnanimous to anybody who did not know him well. To those who did know him well, it was just one more spectacular instance of *Look at me!*

John Hay was not there at the conclave on the Schuylkill to see it happen. He kept his distance from elections and politicking as a hard-and-fast rule and did not care to hear the jingoes in the Republican Party trash his canal treaty to score political points. Conveniently, there was also an international crisis brewing in China, and he said it was better for him to monitor the action from his office in Washington. Hay did read the accounts of Theodore's rousing landslide victory and was quick to send off a note of congratulations. "The week has been a racking one to you," Hay wrote. "But I have no doubt the future will make amends. You have received the greatest compliment the country could pay you, and although it was not precisely what you and your friends desire, I have no doubt it is all for the best. Nothing can keep you from doing good work wherever you are—nor from getting lots of fun out of it. We Washingtonians of course have our own little point of view. You can't lose us; and we shall be uncommonly glad to see you here again."

John Hay did *like* Theodore. Who didn't? He really was more fun than a goat, if slightly more destructive. And maybe McKinley would keep a tighter rein on him inside the White House than he had at the Navy Department. But Hay was sympathetic to Mark Hanna's heartfelt, and very rational, concern. "Your *duty* to the country," Senator Hanna wrote to McKinley when the convention was over, "is to *live* for four years from next March."

CHAPTER THIRTY-TWO

And Just beyond the Philippines . . .

He knew the siege would pass, but when the gout flared—a searing-hot pain like a fireplace poker jabbing into his left big toe—Sam Clemens was unable to get out of bed or get dressed. This lasted for days, and when he did feel well enough to rise, he was still compelled to go clumping around the house with only his right foot shod. He found himself not much minding this disarrangement, other than the damned excruciating hurt, because it kept his days quiet. Sam Clemens had no great interest in civilization or society in the summer of 1900. He did have an itch to be home, though, and he was now counting down the weeks to the voyage back to America. Kellgren had assured Sam and Livy that Jean had "turned the corner," and Clemens had located an osteopath in New York who could continue her treatments. The family would be home before the elections that fall; there was no doubt about that now.

The household had meanwhile removed itself to a country cottage just the right distance from London: Jean could make it to her daily therapy at the Kellgren gymnasium, but nobody could be offended when "Mark Twain" begged off social engagements in town. Sam, Livy, and the girls were whiling away the summer on six green acres walled off by proper English hedgerows, amid the satisfying yeoman's aroma of summer hay and sheep, the regal broad-leaved shade trees, a tennis court, and a sweep of lawn fit for an earl.

Clemens had been wary of the sudden cease of noise and tumult when the family first arrived at Dollis Hill House, and rankled by the afternoon delivery of his *morning* newspaper. But as he settled into a summer of lordly remove, Sam Clemens grew content to let the lives of others march by, a half turn of the planet ahead of him. He did follow along, though, because even a few hours stale, the news of the world *was* compelling.

The elections in America filled the papers that summer of 1900, and one of the big issues of the campaign was the US Army's eighteen-month-old pacification and Benevolent Assimilation project in the Philippines. The Democrats, with William Jennings Bryan back at the top of the ticket, were taking the hide off the McKinley administration, accusing them of getting the country into a dishonorable and deadly fight with no end in sight. McKinley's Republican backers were on the offensive, with their rough-riding Roosevelt as the spear's point. Roosevelt and others were charging Bryan's Democrats and the Anti-Imperialist League with prolonging the fight in the Philippines by encouraging General Aguinaldo and his army. The US military commander Frederick Funston claimed he could produce evidence that Aguinaldo and his followers were rooting for William Jennings Bryan to win the White House and call a halt to the war and even had assurances from the Democrats. "The insurrection still goes on because the allies in this country of the bloody insurrectionary oligarchy in Luzon have taught their foolish dupes to believe that Democratic success at the polls next November means the abandonment of the islands to the savages," Roosevelt had said in his nomination speech. He was screaming similar sentiments at his whistle-stops across America: "To grant self-government to Luzon under Aguinaldo would be like granting self-government to an Apache reservation under some local chief."

Sober elders in the Republican Party had long been claiming that the war was waning and that the United States would soon emerge victorious—and with the national balance sheet on the side of profit. "This is a practical age," said one Republican senator. "We are going to deal with the question on the basis of dollars and cents." But the true motive force in America's ruling party that election season was not its sober, hardheaded businessmen but its buccaneering evangelical voices. "The Philippines are ours forever," thirty-seven-year-old first-term senator Albert Beveridge had asserted earlier that year.

> And just beyond the Philippines are China's illimitable markets. We will not retreat from either. . . . This question is deeper than any question of party politics, deeper than any question of isolated policy of our country even; deeper even than any question of constitutional power. It is elemental. It is racial. God has not been preparing the English speaking and Teutonic peoples for a thousand years for nothing but vain and idle self-contemplation and self-admiration. No! He has made us the master organizers of the world to establish a system where chaos reigns. . . . He has made us adepts in government that we may administer government among savage and senile peoples. Were it not for such a force as this, the world would relapse into barbarism and night. And of all our race, He has marked the American people as His chosen nation to finally lead the regeneration of the world. This is the divine mission of America, and it holds for us all the profit, all the glory, all the happiness possible to man.

The London papers were just beginning to speculate on the possible dissolution of Great Britain's ruling government and the call for a new national election, which would be, as far as Clemens could tell, a looking-glass image of the American political scene. Like McKinley and the Republicans, Lord Salisbury and Joseph Chamberlain would be standing to defend their own war of conquest against the Boers in South Africa. Their Conservative and Liberal Unionist backers were already at full volume, and Sam Clemens took particular note of one dazzling new light on the British political landscape, a man just back from an eventful tour as a briefly imprisoned war correspondent in the Transvaal. The would-be candidate was already working an impressive double bill, hawking his new book about the war (and his dramatic escape from the Boer prison camp) while trying to win back for the Conservatives his dead father's seat in the House of Commons. "Winston Churchill is only twenty-five," read one newspaper editorial. "He is a boy to look at, red-faced, chubby, wholesome; he is a boy to talk to, joyous, cheery, a trifle irresponsible; but he is a man in ambition, a man in talent, and a very old one in worldly wisdom . . . and he inherits from his mother that 'cuteness' which is so essentially American. In fact he is a perfect little marvel."

While Clemens was still hopping around in one shoe, Churchill was bursting into a mass political convocation on his home turf in Oldham to thunderous applause and a brassy, thumping rendition of "See, the conqu'ring hero comes!" The dough-faced politician was forthright in his admission to his townsmen that the war in South Africa had been a dire and sometimes disheartening muddle and would, on some occasions, continue to be. But! he proclaimed, the tide had turned now that General Buller and his men had captured the Boer capital of Pretoria. The British Empire must now unite as one in its effort to destroy the Republic of South Africa. "Surely the people of England will never allow that British flag to be hauled down again?" Churchill said, and he was loudly cheered.

When young Winston told the crowd in Oldham that an early peace could be had whenever Lord Salisbury was "prepared to give the Boers back their independence," his auditors roared in knowing laughter. *Boer independence! How droll.* "If we allowed the Boers a republic the size of a shilling, it would constitute a national rallying point, a centre for all discordant and disaffected forces in South Africa, and we would therefore have no true union between the British and the Dutch races in that country," Churchill concluded. "The only hope of a permanent peace in South Africa lay in the absolute destruction of all semblance of Republican government and aspirations."

The blood and thunder of domestic politics and colonial wars, however, was thin gruel to Clemens as compared to the meaty drama of midsummer 1900, which was taking place in China. A Chinese nationalist group called the Righteous Harmony Society (or Boxers by the Westerners) was reportedly on a rampage that threatened the life and limb of every foreigner in the country. This conflagration had come on suddenly, but it had not been a complete surprise. Anger in China had been building for years against the foreign merchants and Christian missionaries who were crawling all over the treaty ports and into the interior. The kaiser and his admiral von Diederichs had used the murder of two Catholic missionaries in 1897 as a pretense to extort from the empress dowager a large cash settlement, a deepwater port, and absolute sovereignty over more than two hundred square miles of Chinese territory and nearly a hundred thousand Chinese citizens. "China had been oppressed, trampled upon, coerced, cajoled, her territory taken, her usages flouted," said one Chinese official who was no sympathizer of the Boxers.

Drought and famine wracked China and inflamed hard feelings toward all foreigners, particularly against the foreign missionaries and their converts, who stood accused by the Boxers of the defilement and destruction of Buddhism. "[They] have irritated heaven and in consequence no rain has fallen," Boxer leaders cried. "If foreigners are not swept away no rain will fall."

When the sweeping began, to the chagrin of the foreign governments and foreign businesses with valuable property and growing financial prospects in the country, the imperial Chinese government did little to dissuade the Boxers. "The various powers," the empress dowager remarked in private, "cast upon us looks of tigerlike voracity, hustling each other in their endeavors to be the first to seize upon our innermost territories."

The Righteous Harmony Society burned churches, chapels, and cathedrals and terrorized and murdered foreign missionaries. Christian converts among the Chinese were burned out of their homes and in some cases killed. The depredations moved from the countryside into the capital city of Peking. By the third week of June—in the terror-stricken aftermath of the assassination of the German minister—every Western diplomat, merchant, and missionary and every Chinese convert ran for cover behind the barbwired and barricaded walls of the British legation building. The Chinese army in Peking surrounded the legation immediately, and the Westerners could not be sure whether the empress dowager's army had taken up the position to protect them or to prepare to attack them. The British legation remained in this strange state of siege for two months, without means to communicate with the outside, while the great powers sent warships, bombed the port of Tientsin, landed marines, and prepared for war. "*What* a world tumult is on hand just now!" Joe Twichell, who had friends among the missionaries in China, wrote to Sam Clemens. "And what a black appalling cloud Pekin lies under! . . . I dread the tale of shuddering horrors presently to unfold."

"It is all China, now, and my sympathies are with Chinese," Clemens replied to his reverend friend. "They have been villainously dealt with by the sceptered thieves of Europe, and I hope they will drive all the foreigners out and keep them out for good. I only wish it; of course I don't really expect it." He had already shipped an essay to a friend at the *Times* of London and suggested he publish it in his paper straightaway. "Try to get up a squabble," Clemens told him, "for the weather is just suitable." But Sam Clemens also asked that his name be kept out of it, and the editor, after reading the letter, had no trouble understanding Clemens's insistence on anonymity. "Wherever the missionary goes," Clemens had written,

> he not only proclaims that his religion is the best one, but that it is a true one while his hearer's religion is a false one; that the pagan's gods are inventions of the imagination; that the things & the names which are sacred to him are not worthy of his reverence; that his fathers are all in hell, & the dead darlings of his nursery also, because the word which saves had not been brought to them; that he must now desert his ancient religion & give allegiance to the new one or he will follow his fathers & his lost darlings to the eternal fires. . . . The missionary has no wish to be an insulter, but how is he to help it? All his propositions are insults.

The *Times* man declined to publish, anonymous or no, and kept the letter folded safely in his desk. The author did not push him on it. While the fate of the foreigners in China drew more and more panicked public attention, Sam Clemens decided to remain calm and hold his tongue and his pen. He kept his thoughts and feelings inside the home circle.

A MONTH INTO the siege, with no word still from Peking, newspaper correspondents from distant Shanghai began shipping off fanciful and detailed accounts of a final "massacre" and "butchery" in the imperial city. The "revolutionary horde," one reported, "turned its sole attention on the doomed Europeans in the Legation. . . . Standing together, as the sun rose fully, the little remaining band, all Europeans, met death stubbornly. There was a desperate hand-to-hand encounter . . . and finally, by overwhelming odds, every one of the Europeans remaining was put to the sword in a most atrocious manner." The women and children, reports averred, were spared no brutality.

"This is the greatest blow Western civilization has sustained in modern times," said one British paper. And it well might have been, were reports of the "butchery" at the legation true, but nobody, even in the highest levels of government, knew for sure what was happening inside that city. "God! What a strain this suspense is," Alvey Adee exclaimed as the relief force neared Peking in early August. When a force of Russian, German, Japanese, British, and American soldiers, with help from the Chinese army, finally fought its way into Peking on August 14, the soldiers found the Western "hostages" worn and rattled but well fed and unharmed.

Much of the public credit for the successful relief went to John Hay, who managed at the beginning of the crisis to persuade the Europeans to confine their attacks to the small group of brigands—the Boxer rebels—and to avoid making an all-out war on China itself. He had also persuaded the Chinese government to forsake the Boxers in order to save itself from extermination. "The Secretary of State is the recipient of such praise in the United States," reported papers in London, "as to make it appear that his record has never been surpassed by any of his predecessors."

By the time Peking was made safe again for foreigners, however, John Hay had absented himself from his post, and all official State Department pronouncements were issuing from Acting Secretary Alvey Adee. The newspapers were suggesting that John Hay's extraordinary and selfless efforts might have put him at death's doorsill. "Col. Hay's condition was so alarming," said one breathless report at the end of August, "that the eldest son, now in Pretoria, Adelbert Hay, was cabled to come home at once."

Kaiser Wilhelm, meanwhile, announced that he was dispatching nine German warships to the China coast and that he did not mean to leave the punishment of the Boxers (or any government officials who had aided the Boxers) to the imperial authorities in China but would reserve that privilege for himself and whichever of the great powers wished to join him in the revenge game. The empress dowager of China protested. The United States Department of State protested. Russia protested. England—reflected "in the brain of Salisbury," deadpanned Adee—wavered. Japan wavered. The leading American missionary in China, however, was on board with the kaiser. "Boxer leaders must be sought out and punished so far as possible," the Reverend W. S. Ament wrote home. "I shall begin in that line soon." The reverend, to his credit, was sickened by the indiscriminate murder, rape, and arson committed by the European soldiers in the weeks after the siege, but he was more forgiving of property theft. As missionary chair of the Committee on Confiscated Goods, Reverend Ament was already arranging to auction off porcelains, furs, silks, and furniture from the palace the American Board of Foreign Missions had occupied in Peking. "I have just had the Christian commandments read to me and I think they need revising," a Chinese government official in Peking told reporters on hearing this news. "The eighth commandment should be made to read, 'Thou shalt not steal, but thou mayest loot.' "

Sam Clemens remained silent. He had more pleasant things to ponder: he had finally booked the passage to New York—October 6, 1900, on the *Minnehaha*. The Clemens family was going home.

NEWSPAPER CORRESPONDENTS TRACKED Clemens to his London hotel a few days before he was to leave, and found the sixty-four-year-old author a happy and carefree man. His only complaint was a little soreness in his back, which did nothing to dampen his ebullience or his general good humor. "I've got the lumbago," he explained. "It isn't the ordinary kind. It's what's called 'private hotel' lumbago. One gets it from the beds. They're unnecessarily firm. Their main interest is geological. They're old Silurian superimposed upon red sandstone and they still contain the print of pre-historic man." Even the finest of London's private hotels was "lingering along upon its bygone honorable reputation," Clemens continued. "Many elderly English people still cling to it from inherited habit and arrested development. Rich Americans frequent it through ignorance and superstition."

The lumbago joke was all a fine lark, but newspapermen were after something a tad more topical. Didn't "Mark Twain" have something to say about the American elections? "Well, you see, I have only read scraps and snatches of news in the papers here, not sufficient to stir my prejudices and partialities," Clemens responded, dissembling. He knew he would have to answer for anything he said once he arrived at the pier in New York in ten days' time.

When the *New York World* reporter pressed the great man for his views on American imperialism, Clemens waded in very, very cautiously. The entire issue, he said, was a head-scratcher. "There is the case of the Philippines," he began.

> I have tried hard, and yet I cannot for the life of me comprehend how we got into that mess. Perhaps we could have avoided it—perhaps it was inevitable that we should come to be fighting the natives of those islands—but I cannot understand it, and never have been able to get at the bottom of the origin of our antagonism to the natives. . . . But now—why, we have got into a mess, a quagmire from which each fresh step renders the difficulty of extrication immensely greater. I'm sure I wish I could see what we were getting out of it, and all it means to us as a nation.

CHAPTER THIRTY-THREE

How Much Truth to Tell?

They were there waiting for him when the *Minnehaha* glided into the pier on West Houston Street in New York City at just after ten o'clock on the night of October 15—must have been twenty reporters milling around on the cobblestones below. Sam Clemens was in no great hurry; he intended to take the final few steps of his return to his native land on his terms. *He* was the story, after all. "This homecoming is as great a compliment as has been paid to us as a people for a long time," was how the *Brooklyn Eagle*, edited by his old friend St. Clair McKelway, had already put it. "Mark Twain holds more of the popular good will and affection than any author among us." The newsmen would wait, Clemens reckoned. And they did, nervously scanning the parade of arriving passengers, wondering among themselves whether there was any other way off the ship.

A half hour later, when the line of disembarkation had thinned to a trickle, the reporters finally caught sight of their quarry coming down the gangway. The small crowd onshore broke into applause. "Welcome!" they cried out. "Welcome!" He did not look much different from the "Mark Twain" who had last lived in America nine years earlier. "His hair and mustache are a shade whiter, and his form is a little more bowed, but he seems to be in better health than he was in 1891," one reporter noted. "Ruddy but composed as always," said another.

A handful of intimate friends were also there at the West Houston Street pier to greet Sam and Livy and their daughters as they stepped off the gangway, and these folks gently patted Sam's shoulder and his back, and tugged at his elbow, as he nodded and smiled and whispered conspiratorially to the select few and generally tried to get his land legs underneath him. But he was unable to devote much time to his friends because the reporters had gathered around, too, and all he had to do was nod and they started firing off questions. His answers were a stubbornly calm counterpoint, rolling out in the long, slow drawl the reporters had all heard, or heard about, already.

Where will you live?

"I shall spend the winter in New York. . . . I expect to keep close and devote my time to reading, smoking, and as little work as possible. In the spring I shall return to Hartford, Connecticut, where Mrs. Clemens, my daughters and myself will settle down for some home life, after nine years of wandering up and down the earth."

Do you plan to do a lecture tour?

"I don't want to lecture again, and will not unless forced to do so. I am tired of it and want to rest."

So you're part of the leisure class?

"I was born into the leisure class, but that is the most courteous name I have ever heard it called by. Usually it is called by a pretty rude name. I have been charged with being lazy, but from this time forth I shall claim my place in the ranks of the leisure class."

Were you just joking in England about writing your autobiography and delaying publication for a hundred years?

"I was in dead earnest, but of course the English set it down as a great joke. . . . Fate has its revenge on a humorist. Now, I have lied so much, in a genial, good-natured way, of course, that people won't believe me when I speak the truth. I may add that I have stopped speaking the truth. It is no longer appreciated—in me."

Are you an imperialist?

"It is most too grave a question for one of any temperament, but I have taken a try at it. I have thought of it, and it has got the best of me."

He did not stop there but kept talking it through, as if he were still gathering his thoughts on the matter. He had been a "red-hot imperialist" five years earlier, he said, and had wanted the country to stretch itself and its freedoms out into the Pacific.

> But I have thought some more, since then, and I have read carefully the treaty of Paris, and I have seen that we do not intend to free but to subjugate the people of the Philippines. We have gone there to conquer, not to redeem. . . .
>
> It should, it seems to me, be our pleasure and duty to make [the Filipinos] free and let them deal with their own domestic questions in their own way. And so I am an anti-imperialist.

The reporter from the *Sun* was startled by this candor but would recover his wits in time to make copy for the next morning's edition of that pro-expansionist newspaper: "It was remembered afterward that [Mark Twain] was also a humorist."

"WE ARE ALL pretty well & 'Mark' unusually so," Livy reported to a friend from the Clemens's temporary quarters at the Hotel Earlington in New York. "He looks like a fighting cock." But even in his fine cut and trim, Sam wasn't sure how to be or what to do first, now that he was finally back on home ground. "I am crowded for time," he wrote to a friend back in London. "I don't get a moment to myself." He needed to make arrangements to get Jean in to see the new osteopath, Dr. Helmer; Clara was ready to make her professional stage debut as a mezzo-soprano, and he owed her his help; the Red Cross wanted a message of greeting to the new century—to be read in public on New Year's Eve, 1901. Apparently almost all the celebrities of the world were contributing a hello, and so were half the kings and queens of Europe and Asia, excepting Kaiser Wilhelm, who felt debarred because he had already, by imperial fiat, decreed January 1, *1900*, the official start of the twentieth century.

Clemens also had to get snapping on his newest financial speculation, the American Plasmon Company, which had secured the exclusive US rights to manufacture and sell a dietary supplement he had discovered in Austria. He had already shipped some samples of plasmon to Andrew Carnegie's castle in Scotland. Clemens swore by it; it had cured *his* chronic indigestion. He had even tried to start a little word-of-mouth on the *Minnehaha* by plasmoning every passenger who started to look a little green, but he was stymied by the steamship itself, which rode so smooth and level that there was hardly any seasickness to speak of. He ended up treating only Livy's temporary maid and one drunk. Clemens did make a convert of Henry Rogers in the first week in New York and was angling for a meeting with John D. Rockefeller so that he could "tell him how to beat his indigestion." He was in constant and excited communication with his partner back in London, J. Y. W. MacAlister. Plasmon, he crowed to MacAlister, would soon be like Vaseline, "which pays a monster income."

Every day, correspondence that had to be answered poured in, and so, too, did invitations to dinners and banquets in his honor and to an endless array of benefits for worthy causes. His old friends at the Lotos Club wanted to welcome him as a returning member, and so did the Aldine Association. Would he speak to the Press Club? The Authors Club? Would he talk at the benefit for the victims of the Galveston hurricane? Would he expound on Milton and Walter Scott at the Nineteenth Century Club? Would he preside over the fund-raising celebration of President Lincoln's birthday? Would he act as master of ceremonies for Winston Churchill's first speech in the United States? He tried to be judicious, hoping to gentle his way back into the daily lives of his countrymen. "I don't wish to destroy my welcome with my tongue," he said.

There were new living arrangements to consider, too. The Clemens family could not go on living at the Earlington all winter, but Sam wasn't sure just where they should settle in the city or how soon they might consider a move back to their house in Connecticut. Besides Jean, they were none of them anxious to be back in Hartford. Sam himself was certain of it after a brief trip there a few days after they arrived. "There was a pathetic pleasure in seeing Hartford and the house again; but I realize that if we ever enter the house again to live, our hearts will break," he wrote to a friend after his return to the Earlington. "I am not sure that we shall ever be strong enough to endure that strain."

Clemens started harrying acquaintances and business associates to find him a house in New York where his family could be comfortable for the long haul. A friendly publisher, Frank Doubleday, located for Clemens a furnished town house just north of Washington Square and fixed it up with the leasing agent for Sam to sign the papers and move in as soon as he desired. Clemens did not get around to signing the lease. He did move in. Which was why Katy Leary found a very agitated Doubleday at the front door a few days later. "You can't move into a house until you've signed the lease!" Doubleday said to Clemens. But young Doubleday had clearly not grasped the key piece of evidence at 14 West Tenth Street. "Well, I *have* moved in, haven't I? And that's all there is to it," Clemens answered, before dropping into one of his painfully long rhetorical pauses. "But bring along your lease, Doubleday," he said finally. "I'll sign it."

Livy was pleased on all counts. "It is large & bright & sunny," she reported, "& being down town the rent is not as high as it would be up town."

THE ELECTION SEASON of 1900 came to an end just as Clemens was signing his new lease, and the results were as expected. William McKinley won by a comfortable margin over William Jennings Bryan. The Republicans emerged with a 56–32 edge in the Senate and added a dozen seats to their already commanding majority in the House of Representatives. Theodore Roosevelt was headed for Washington as McKinley's new understudy. The president and the key men in his administration accepted this victory as a vindication of their policies in general and of their policy in the Philippines in specific. The gloves were coming off. ADMINISTRATION WEARY OF PROTRACTED HOSTILITIES! rang the headlines in the days after the election. REAL WAR AHEAD FOR FILIPINO REBELS! WILL SHOW NO MERCY! Commanders in the field received the orders from on high, and by the time the word filtered down to the privates, the message they got, according to one young soldier, was this: "The people of the United States want us to kill all the men, fuck all the women, and raise up a new race in these islands."

Sam Clemens remained silent in the immediate aftermath of the election.

He knew what he wanted to say, but he hadn't quite figured out *how* to say it. "Now it is an art—a high art," he had mused to a newspaperwoman who had found him down at the Earlington dining room one morning in the final weeks of the campaign, "to speak the truth so that the object does not object, does not become offended."

THEY CAME BANGING at his door just after seven on that Saturday night, four days after Election Day, and found Sam Clemens, cigar in hand, slouched in his easy chair in front of a nice warm fire, reading the evening newspapers. Was he aware, someone in the small group inquired, that there were 150 gentlemen awaiting him at the Lotos Club? "That so!" Clemens exclaimed, jumping to his feet. "It's Saturday night, isn't it? I'd forgotten all about it. I thought it was Friday. Tell them I'll be there in fifteen minutes."

The expedition from the Lotos put him in their carriage and rode him up Fifth Avenue to the clubhouse, where the banqueters were cooling their heels. He *was* sorry, he explained on arrival, but his audience was understanding. They had known him a long time. St. Clair McKelway forgave him without hesitation. "He has enough excess and versatility of ability to be a genius," McKelway offered that night. "He has enough quality and quantity of virtues to be a saint. . . . And he has preferred warm fellowship to cold perfection, so that sinners love him and saints are content to wait for him . . . and long may he remain to brighten, to broaden, and to better our souls with the magic mirth and with the mirthful magic of his incomparable spell."

Clemens was demonstrably happy to be with his friends at the Lotos Club, at the first of a series of welcome-home dinners in his honor. He had turned down plenty, but he had accepted plenty, too. "I like compliments," he would say after listening to a long string of encomiums. "I like to go home and tell them all over again to the members of my family. They don't believe them, but I like to tell them in the home circle all the same. I like to dream of them if I can."

The Lotos Club was first because it was family; he had been one of the earliest joiners of the club nearly thirty years before, along with other newsmen and literati like Poultney's father, John Bigelow, and Whitelaw Reid and John Hay. None of that august triumvirate could be there that night, but Chauncey Depew, the new senator from New York, was there to roast Clemens, and so was Henry Rogers, and William Dean Howells, and the recently retired Speaker of the House, Thomas Brackett Reed. Reed, one of the few loud Republican voices against the recent war, tried to bait Clemens into discussing politics. "[Sam] came to Washington with a lot of those literary fellows with a vague idea that they were going to prove their rights to some of their own property [by a copyright law]," Reed said in his welcome speech. "I explained to him that he and his friends were absolutely incapable of self-government. We intended to let him keep some small percentage of right to his property but we were going to benevolently assimilate his property, or most of it. Apparently he behaved most creditably, but after he left me he had gone around town telling people the thing he would have said to me if he hadn't been scared."

When Clemens got up from his banquet chair to address the gathering, he had to stand for three minutes while the manly cheering and loud applause washed over him. When the room finally quieted enough for him to be heard, he wished only to be pleasing to his friends and to avoid stirring up trouble for his fellow clubmen. "How many things have happened in the seven years I have been away from home," Clemens said.

> We have fought a righteous war, and a righteous war is a rare thing in history. We have turned aside from our own comfort and seen to it that freedom should exist not only within our own gates, but in our own neighborhood. We have set Cuba free and placed her among the galaxy of free nations of the world. We started out to set those poor Filipinos free, but why that righteous plan miscarried perhaps I shall never know. We have also been making a creditable showing in China, and that is more than all of the powers can say.

He did have a little sport with the newly elected vice president, whose uncle Robert Roosevelt was an early member at Lotos. "[Governor Roosevelt] is widely known and in some places favorably," Clemens said. "I am a little afraid that these fulsome compliments may be misunderstood; I have been away a long time, and I am not used to this complimentary business; I merely want to testify to my old admiration for my friend the Governor. If you give him enough rope—" Here the men in the room roared in knowing laughter. "I meant to say—well, it is not necessary for me to say any more; you know him."

CLEMENS WAS UNCERTAIN as to how much truth to tell at the tail end of 1900. He wasn't sure he could trust himself. When he sat down in the privacy of his new office and wrote by hand his Red Cross message, for instance, it came out hot: "A salutation-speech from the Nineteenth Century to the Twentieth Century, taken down in short-hand by Mark Twain: I bring you the stately matron named Christendom, returning bedraggled, besmirched and dishonored from pirate-raids in Kiao-chow, Manchuria, South Africa & the Philippines, with her soul full of meanness, her pocket full of boodle, and her mouth full of pious hypocrisies. Give her soap & a towel, but hide the looking glass."

He shipped it off and then decided to withdraw it. He did not wish to disavow the statement, but he thought it best to conduct his political business, for the time being anyway, sotto voce. "My sense of duty," he admitted to a new acquaintance on his sixty-fifth birthday, November 30, 1900, "is getting spongy."

Much as he tried to be placid and unoffending, it was not easy. He was obliged to speak at all manner of dinners and fund-raisers, and things started to leak out. In a speech in support of public education he somehow wandered off into the China question. "Why should not China be free from foreigners, who are only making trouble on her soil?" he asked. "We do not allow Chinamen to come here, and I say in all seriousness that it would be a graceful thing to let China decide who shall go there. China never wanted foreigners any more than foreigners wanted Chinamen, and on this question I am with the Boxers every time. The Boxer is a patriot. He loves his country better than he does the countries of other people. I wish him success."

Two weeks later the St. Nicholas Society dragged him out of his sickbed—gout, toothache, bronchial cough—to toast the city of New York at their annual banquet at Delmonico's. Maybe it was the gout pain that caused him to stray, but he found himself limping out into dangerous political boondocks, pointing out that the temporary Dewey Arch in Madison Square Park was turning out to be the perfect symbol of America's war in the Philippines. "We owe him [a monument]," Clemens said of Dewey. "Not a permanent one, maybe. We might build it of plaster, and, after gazing upon it for a while, tear it down."

By the middle of December, when young Winston Spencer Churchill arrived in New York to sell Americans on the Boer War and on his book about it, Clemens was becoming bolder. William Dean Howells, Tom Reed, and a few other avowed anti-imperialists had refused Major Pond's plea to act as patrons for the Churchill event; most refused even to attend. But Clemens always liked to see an *infant phenomenon* up close, so he accepted the invitation to introduce Churchill in the grand ballroom of the Waldorf-Astoria. It was to be the young man's first-ever American speech.

The snowy sixty-five-year-old American and the patrician twenty-six-year-old British Conservative met backstage before the program that night and began arguing good-naturedly about the righteousness of the British Empire's war in South Africa. Churchill found himself in an uncharacteristically hasty retreat to his national ramparts, finally blurting out to Clemens, just to stop the older man's onslaught, "My country right or wrong."

"Ah, when the poor country is fighting for its life, I agree," Clemens answered. "But this was not your case."

They agreed to disagree, and Clemens was happy to autograph the "Mark Twain" volumes Churchill had carried to the Waldorf. "To do good is noble,"

Clemens wrote in the first volume; "to teach others to do good is nobler, and no trouble."

When the two men walked onstage, the grand and glorious ten-thousand-square-foot Waldorf ballroom was full to capacity. Churchill was the undisputed draw of the evening and would have the last word, but Sam Clemens had his say. "Although he and I do not agree on the righteousness of the South African war, that is a matter of no consequence," he began in his slow drawl.

> There is no place where people all think alike.
>
> For years I've been a self-appointed missionary to bring about the union of America and the motherland. . . . They ought to be united. Behold America, the refuge of the oppressed from everywhere (who can pay fifty dollars' admission)—any one except a Chinaman—standing up for human rights everywhere. . . . And how unselfishly England has wrought the open door for all! . . . How generous England and America have been in not compelling China to pay exorbitantly for extinguished missionaries. . . . And how gallantly we went to the rescue of Cuba, struck the chains off and set her free—with England at our back. . . .
>
> Yes, as a missionary I've sung my songs of praise; and yet I think that England sinned when she got herself in a war in South Africa which she could have avoided, just as we have sinned in getting into a similar war in the Philippines. Mr. Churchill, by his father, is an Englishman; by his mother he is an American; no doubt a blend that makes the perfect man. England and America; yes, we are kin. And now that we are also kin in sin, there is nothing more to be desired. The harmony is complete, the blend is perfect—like Mr. Churchill himself, whom I now have the honor to present to you.

The *Sun* reporter noted, as Clemens retreated to his chairman's seat, a "mystified cerebration in some quarters of the room."

THE STORY IN the *Sun* on Christmas Eve, 1900, broke the Clemens floodgates. It was a dispatch from China, where Westerners were mopping up in the aftermath of the Boxer Rebellion. "The Rev. Mr. Ament of the American Board of Foreign Missions has returned from a trip which he made for the purposes of collecting indemnities for damages done by Boxers," read the wire report. "Everywhere he went he compelled the Chinese to pay. He says that all his native Christians are now provided for. He had 700 of them under his charge and 300 were killed. He has collected 300 taels for each of these murders, and has compelled full payment for all the property belonging to Christians that was destroyed. He also assessed fines amounting to thirteen times the amount of the indemnity. This money will be used for the propagation of the Gospel." The story didn't stop there. "In the course of a conversation Mr. Ament referred to the attitude of the missionaries toward the Chinese. He said: 'I deny emphatically that the missionaries are vindictive, that they generally looted or that they have done anything since the siege that the circumstances did not demand. I criticize the Americans. The soft hand of the Americans is not as good as the mailed fist of the Germans. If you deal with the Chinese with a soft hand they will take advantage of it.' "

Sam Clemens went to his desk, picked up his pen, and spent most of the holiday season composing an article he called "To the Person Sitting in Darkness," rolling up the ugly recent blunders in China and South Africa and the Philippines into one untidy ball. And when his New Year's slap at "the stately matron named Christendom . . . bedraggled, besmirched and dishonored" did go public on the eve of the new century, he made no effort to walk it back. Four days later, at the tail end of a speech to the City Club, which was supposed to be devoted to the topic of "The Causes of Our Present Municipal Degradation," he gave his auditors a brief little sample of what was coming. "Not long ago we had two men running for President. There was Mr. McKinley on the one hand and Mr. Bryan on the other," Clemens said to 130 of New York City's esteemed civic leaders. "I didn't know much about finance, but I knew some pretty shrewd financiers, and they told me that Bryan was all wrong on the money question, so I didn't vote for him. [As for McKinley], I knew enough about the Philippines to have a strong aversion to sending our bright boys out there to fight with a disgraced musket under a polluted flag."

There was a chill silence in the room as his words hung in the smoke-filled air. Did "Mark Twain" just take a slap at the president of the United States? Did the nation's most celebrated and beloved author just call the American flag "polluted"?

St. Clair McKelway was invited to follow his old friend, though he was not in the announced speaker lineup for the evening. "I have listened to Mr. Clemens as we all invariably do, with attention and pleasure," McKelway said. "And he must bear with me while I say—and I may be the only one in this room of this opinion, although I don't believe it—that I cannot agree with him. Candidly and absolutely, I protest against his estimate of the able and dignified soldier and statesman who is the President of the United States, and I believe that our gallant Army is fighting behind no dishonored muskets and under no polluted, but under a glorious flag."

New York's good-government assembly rose almost as one to applaud the brushback pitch aimed at Sam Clemens. The clapping continued for minutes; shouts of assent and cheering echoed off the ceilings, again and again and again. Clemens remained in his seat throughout, expressionless, working the stub of his cigar. He knew they were watching him, but he betrayed no concern and no consternation. He would be *goddamned* if he was going to give them the satisfaction.

CHAPTER THIRTY-FOUR

I Am Expecting a Diminution of My Bread and Butter

Clemens's City Club talk got big play in the newspapers. "No American may thus refer to his flag with impunity thinking to escape censure, if not actual condemnation," was a typical editorial comment. Sam Clemens was hardly surprised. "The standard of honor is shrinking pretty fast every where," he wrote to a Massachusetts historian who sent a private letter of support. "I find but few men who disapprove of our theft of the Philippines & our assassination of the liberties of the people of the Archipelago."

He knew what he would be facing if he pushed his luck, and he knew what he stood to lose. His popularity had never been higher than it was at the start of the new century. Strangers crowded Clemens whenever he ambled up and down Fifth Avenue; fire captains invited him to pass through the mobs of watchers for a privileged look at the latest neighborhood disaster. When a Columbia University classics specialist published an essay calling "Mark Twain" nothing but a funnyman grown stale—"A hundred years from now it is very likely that 'The Jumping Frog' alone will be remembered"—authors and fans shoved his words back down his professorial throat. Clemens's pen name, meanwhile, was money in the bank. Harper & Brothers had mounted an aggressive holiday season push for *The Man That Corrupted Hadleyburg and Other Stories and Essays* and was advertising the fact that "Mark Twain" had signed an exclusive contract to write for its magazines. "[He] can choose any subject he pleases, write as much or as little as he thinks fit, and there his worry and responsibility ends," the president of the company, George Harvey, would say. "Talent ought not be hobbled with orders and instructions."

Well, give me enough rope . . .

THEIR COMFY RENTED redbrick house on Tenth Street turned out to be a tad loose in the joints, and Livy had no easy time keeping it heated. Sam Clemens didn't take much notice of his drafty work quarters; it was like stopping to eat lunch: who had time to think about that? Clemens was on fire to finish "To the Person Sitting in Darkness" for the February number of Harvey's *North American Review*. The newspapers delivered a steady lot of fuel for his righteous blaze. The legality of the US acquisition of Puerto Rico and the Philippines, along with the attendant question of the rights due the inhabitants under the Constitution, was being argued in front of the Supreme Court in early January. William McKinley sent his attorney general to present the legal justification for ruling those islands by executive fiat. "When, as commander-in-chief, he exercises government over conquered territory, he has, by the undoubted law of nations, the right not only to govern but to make laws for the territory so occupied," the attorney general told the justices. "They are merely incidents under the public law of belligerent rights, vested by the constitution in the president as commander-in-chief of the army and navy. They are not unconstitutional but are exercised by virtue of the constitution, not by any express clause which confers them, but are implied in the functions and duties of the commander-in-chief." As to the question of any rights due the natives living under American government, the attorney general said they had none.

There were older texts to reconsider also, like the previous January's issue of *Scribner's Magazine*, which had an article about the fine art of American war making in the Philippines. "If any criticism could be offered, it was that we were humane to the point of military weakness," the reporter explained. "The campaign in the Philippines is not war, but a chase where the prey, more cunning than a fox, leaves neither track nor scent. . . . The hunted one is a barefooted, little brown man, in cotton shirt and trousers. . . . 'Come out, Mister Aguinaldo!' [a private near the enemy's trench] exclaimed. 'Come out in the open and bring your whole army! If our regiment can't lick you before dinner you can have our rifles and the Islands, and we'll quit. H-m, yes, but you know better, don't you.'"

Clemens was ready to have his say on all of it, including those "humane" tactics the United States Army had been using to civilize the poor benighted Filipinos: "Of course," he wrote in the manuscript for the *North American Review* article, "we must not venture to ignore our General MacArthur's reports—oh, why do they keep on printing those embarrassing things?—We must drop them trippingly from the tongue and take the chances: 'During the last ten months our losses have been 268 killed and 750 wounded; Filipino loss, three thousand two hundred and twenty-seven killed and 694 wounded.' We must stand ready to grab the Person Sitting in Darkness, for he will swoon away at this confession, saying: 'Good God, those "niggers" spare their wounded [enemies], and the Americans massacre theirs!'"

Clemens was planning to call out his villains by name, under the umbrella of the Blessings-of-Civilization Trust: Joe Chamberlain in South Africa, the German kaiser and the American missionary Reverend Ament in China, William McKinley in the Philippines. Clemens did not care to repeat himself, so he left out any reference to the polluted American flag and instead recommended that the United States make up a new one to be flown over its Philippine possession. "We can have just our usual flag," he wrote, "but with white stripes painted black and the stars replaced by the skull and cross-bones."

Sam Clemens knew the publication of this article would have consequences. He wrote a quick note to the chairman of the upcoming Abraham Lincoln birthday celebration, agreeing to act as master of ceremonies. "I'm venturing to accept—*on condition* that you will be frank & disinvite me if you find you don't want a person of my stripe after you read my article in the next North American Review," he offered. "I give you my word I shall not take offence."

THERE WERE so many compelling reasons to do what he had always done in these instances: have a number of good splenetic sessions at his writing desk and hand the pages over to Livy so that she could put them in the fire—"*Youth!*"—or even just skip the intermediate step and burn them himself. The best argument for self-censorship was the well-being of his wife and daughters. Clara was just then trying, finally, to step out into her own spotlight, and while Sam was wary of his daughter's ambition to court public fancy, he did not voice opposition, nor did he intend to do anything that might complicate her effort. Clara had some sterling advance notices in a few papers, occasionally accompanied by an enormous full-length photograph. The articles spoke of Miss Clemens's long training in Europe, her command of foreign languages, "her rich mezzo soprano," and her beauty. "She does not intend, she says, to make use of her father's name at all, for she believes that she can win success solely by her merits." Even so, Clara's debut as a professional singer got off to a very bumpy start.

Clara did not have her father's steel nerves or his native good luck. She backed out of a command performance for the Women's Press Club in New York City after suffering an "access of modesty at the last moment." Her debut in Washington was postponed by the unfortunate illness of the headline performer, a celebrated baritone and cousin of the king of Portugal. The concert came off four days later, on the same afternoon the city got word of the death of Queen Victoria, which thinned the audience considerably. Sam and Livy sat watching, in pain, while Clara, who had had doctors tending to her cold all that morning, stumbled and croaked through her opening set of songs. The reviews were as kind as they could be. "While she was evidently undergoing the sufferings of a newcomer to the stage yesterday, after her first numbers, her singing was in every way delightful," the *Washington Times* reported. "She is programmed as a mezzo, but in truth her work shows more of the contralto quality." Clara soldiered on. Even as her cold grew into a full-blown bronchial infection, she kept going, traveling to Hartford and Boston with Sam and Livy to give concerts for friends.

LIVY WAS FELLED by her own bronchial attack at the end of January, and a few of her friend's noted that her illnesses seemed to be more frequent. William Dean Howells, who was spending his first extended time with the Clemens family in a decade, wondered later if Sam's profane rants—"The damned human race! . . . Filthier today than it ever was before! And that is saying much!"—had something to do with Livy's indisposition. "I could quite understand why Mrs. Clemens should have found some compensation, when kept to her room by sickness. . . . The contrast of the lurid blasphemy with her heavenly whiteness should have been enough to cure any one less grounded than he in what must be owned was as fixed a habit as smoking with him."

The fact was, *God-dammit*, there were times when it could not be helped, Clemens would argue, times when a man had to *let it out*!

The Reverend Joe Twichell, who was Clemens's chief spiritual guide and counsel and a trusted reader of Sam's meanest private musings, had been trying for months to jolly his friend out of his indignant fits. By the end of January 1901, Twichell's concern had grown. He was worried his friend was about to do serious harm to his reputation, and he tried to use Clemens's own long-standing private philosophy to pull him back from a dangerous precipice. If Clemens truly believed, as he had been saying over and over through the years, that the human race was hopelessly lost, incapable of improvement, beyond salvation, why was he wasting his breath? Why was he willing to risk his reputation howling in the wind?

Clemens did not take the counsel well. "To the Person Sitting in Darkness" was about to go public, and its author was spoiling for a fight. "I'm not expecting anything but kicks for scoffing at McKinley, that conscienceless thief & traitor, & *am* expecting a diminution of my bread & butter by it, but if Livy will let me I will have my say," he answered Twichell.

> This nation is like all the others that have been spewed upon the earth—ready to shout for any cause that will tickle its vanity or fill its pocket.

> What a hell of a heaven it will be, when they get all these sons of bitches assembled there! . . . I *can't* understand it! You are a public guide and teacher, Joe, & are under a heavy responsibility to men, young and old; if you teach your people—as you teach me—to hide their opinions when they believe their flag is being abused & dishonored, lest the utterance do them & a publisher a damage, how do you answer for it to your conscience?

THE NEW "MARK Twain" literary bomb exploded in public a few days after the note to Twichell. "The Blessings-of-Civilization Trust, wisely and cautiously administered, is a Daisy," read Clemens's essay in the esteemed *North American Review*.

> There is more money in it, more territory, more sovereignty, and other kinds of emolument, than there is in any other game that is played. But Christendom has been playing it badly of late years, and must certainly suffer by it, in my opinion. She has been so eager to get every stake that appeared on the green cloth, that the People who Sit in Darkness have noticed it— they have noticed it, and have begun to show alarm. They have become suspicious of the Blessings of Civilization. . . . Perhaps he is saying to himself: "It is yet *another* Civilized power, with its banner of the Prince of Peace in one hand and its loot-basket and its butcher-knife in the other."

Clemens took his shots at the kaiser and the Russians, and though he noted with some real pride the selfless scruples the American government had displayed in Cuba and in China, he indicted the American missionary who bragged of looting and revenge taking in China (including indemnities thirteen times actual damages) and spent about a third of his 6,500-word article arraigning the president on his performance in the Philippines. Clemens laid out in simple, stark detail the long, sad, unplanned march of events in the Philippines as it must have looked and *felt* to the Filipinos. "The Person Sitting in Darkness is almost sure to say: 'There is something curious about this —curious and unaccountable. There must be two Americas: one that sets the captive free, and one that takes a once-captive's new freedom away from him, and picks a quarrel with him with nothing to found it on; then kills him to get his land.'"

By the end of the article, Clemens's sarcasm had turned acid and unsparing. The Blessings-of-Civilizations Trust would be well advised to make a full and frank explanation to its many and potential beneficiaries, he wrote.

> We should say to him: . . . "There have been lies; yes, but they were told in a good cause. We have been treacherous; but that was only in order

that real good might come out of apparent evil. True, we have crushed a deceived and confiding people; we have turned against the weak and the friendless who trusted us; we have stamped out a just and intelligent and well-ordered republic; we have stabbed an ally in the back and slapped the face of a guest; we have bought a Shadow from an enemy that hadn't it to sell; we have robbed a trusting friend of his land and liberty; we have invited our clean young men to shoulder a discredited musket and do bandit's work under a flag which bandits have been accustomed to fear, not to follow; we have debauched America's honor and blackened her face before the world; but each detail was for the best. We know this."

HE DIDN'T HAVE to wait long for the editorial reviews.

"[Mark Twain] is in a state of mortifying intoxication from an overdraught of seriousness, something to which his head has not been hardened."

"A man who sees nothing in our endeavors to carry the blessings of freedom and civilization to the Filipinos is lacking in moral sense."

"Utter disregard of truth and fact . . . disgraceful exhibition of the prostitution of Clemens' mental apparatus to the base purpose of slander and indecency."

The *New York Times* accused him of "tumbling in among us from the clouds of exile and discarding the grin of the funny man for the sour visage of the austere moralist." "Mark Twain draws a grotesque picture of the Philippine transaction," the *Times* continued, "true at no point and faithful in no detail." The newspaper went on to urge any readers whose thinking might have been infected by the Twain article to read the original authorities, the official sources, so that they might understand that the Twain-made portrait of the US relationship with the "Filipino insurgents . . . is a travesty of the truth, a reckless travesty." The *Times* neglected to mention that this official US history had been scrubbed of testimony from General Aguinaldo or Felipe Agoncillo or any other Filipino independence fighter. And a reader would have to dig deep to find the report of the two naval officers who spent six weeks after the Spanish overthrow traveling in Luzon and there encountered an impressive young republic with a newly ratified constitution based largely on that of the United States, a democratically elected legislature, a chief executive, and a judicial system capable of fairly enforcing an impressive body of law.

When a letter writer calling himself "A Christian Patriot" had the temerity to defend Twain's article, the *Times* attacked him as softheaded. "We have determined that our Christian Patriot should be delivered out of the meshes of Twain," replied the *Times,* giving itself the last word. "Mr. Twain's statements are untrue and his views perverted." Vice president elect Theodore Roosevelt, incensed that one of his favorite authors had joined the treasonous anti-imperialists, was privately calling Mark Twain a "prize idiot."

The Reverend Judson Smith, DD, head of the American Board of Foreign Missions, accused Clemens of slandering Reverend Ament. Dr. Smith demanded a retraction and a very public apology from "Mark Twain." Clemens warned the missionary men not to pick the fight. "If required by circumstances," Clemens announced, "I will respond to Dr. Smith's letter at some length in *The North American Review*."

Retreating in the face of verbal fire was not his custom, and he spent the morning of Valentine's Day working up some new lyrics for "The Battle Hymn of the Republic," which he sent out for circulation among special friends:

> I have read his bandit gospel writ in burnished rows of steel:
> "As ye deal with my pretentions, so with you my wrath shall deal;
> Let the faithless sons of freedom, crush the patriot with his heel;
> Lo, Greed is Marching on!"

The rest of the West Tenth Street household was wobbly. Jean was pining for the Hartford house. Clara, who had been forced by ill health to give up her winter tour, insisted the city was best for her new career. "I feel much pulled & very unsettled as to what we are to do," Livy wrote to her old friend Grace King. Livy also voiced disappointment that so many of their other friends disapproved of Sam's new commentaries. Her husband didn't seem to notice, though, or to care. Sam Clemens was back where he felt most alive—swimming against the swift and powerful currents of convention. Two months into his public battle, he remained in fighting trim; he spent long days at his writing desk and still had energy for evening entertainments. He certainly wasn't hiding from the public, and he accepted its criticisms as a "valuable compliment."

He received plenty of letters of support, but few interested him. What gratified him most were the deeply strange letters from the outer edges of society. These he would send over to his wife with a note in the margin: "Read it Livy & return to me." "In the black darkness I saw many *things* and dreamed dreams that I knew did not belong to me and I ought to go out and tell them to the world," an old man from California had written.

> Then I would turn over and *listen* to *you*, and you would tell me nice stories, and I would laugh and then stop to ask God if there was really a *man* behind the mask, for I knew you had the *ear* of the *great audience* and if you saw the *things* I did may-be some day you would tell them and they could not help hearing and their conscience would smite them unawares.

After a while the mask dropped; I saw the *man*; I knew he saw the *things* and he *said* so.

HE WAS HAVING a good bit of fun and found himself steadily engaged. He had causes and he had work that paid him well. He was putting the finishing touches on "Extracts from Adam's Diary" for *Harper's Magazine*: "TUESDAY.—She has taken up with a snake now. The other animals are glad, for she was always experimenting with them and bothering them; and I am glad, because the snake talks, and this enables me to get a rest." He ran up to the state capital in Albany to offer his support for a bill legalizing the practice of osteopathy. He accepted the office of honorary vice president of the Anti-Imperialist League of New York, which wanted him as a main speaker at its rally in opposition to McKinley's Army Appropriations Bill, which had riders handing the president free rein in Cuba and the Philippines. And Clemens was still fighting off the Christian missionaries, who would not give it up.

Dr. Smith had turned up new information! He had just discovered that the *real* problem was an error in the transmission of the cable to the *Sun* containing that Christmas Eve story about Ament's tour of retribution. Reverend Ament *had* secured punitive damages on behalf of the Chinese Christians, but at only one-third the actual damages and not thirteen times, as was originally reported. The fractional line was accidentally dropped. "The whole procedure [of demanding punitive damages] is in accordance with the custom among the Chinese of holding a village responsible for wrongs suffered in that village," Smith explained in an open letter printed in, among other periodicals, Whitelaw Reid's *New York Tribune*. Dr. Smith believed this sewed up his argument. "So collapses—and convulsively—Mark Twain's sensational and ugly bombardment of a missionary whose character and services should have exempted him from such an assault. . . . To Dr. Ament Mr. Clemens has done an injustice which is gross but unintentional. If Mark Twain is the man we take him to be he won't be long in filing a retraction, plus an apology."

That cut it for Sam Clemens. "Personally, I have nothing against Mr. Ament," Clemens wrote in a private letter to Smith. "You will remember I tried to save him from your—pardon me for saying it—disastrous championship of his cause. . . . He has twice confessed. And you have exposed the fact that the American Board approved of his substitution of Chinese morals for Christian. I sincerely hope you are satisfied with these remarkable results. . . . I believe poor Ament has the unwisest set of friends & about the unkindest, that ever a man in trouble had."

Clemens made his public answer in another 6,500-word essay in the *North*

American Review. He apologized for nothing and retracted nothing. "[Dr. Smith] manifestly thinks that when it got scaled away down to a mere 'one-third,' a little thing like that was something other than 'theft and extortion,'" he wrote. "Why? Only the Board knows! I will try to explain this difficult problem, so that the Board can get an idea of it. If a pauper owes me a dollar, and I catch him unprotected and make him pay me fourteen dollars, thirteen of it is 'theft and extortion'; if I make him pay only a dollar and thirty-three and a third cents the thirty-three and a third cents are 'theft and extortion' just the same."

He also quoted liberally from the recent dispatches of war correspondents who had marched into Peking with the international relief column:

> A day or two after the relief, when looking for a place to sleep in, I met Rev. Mr. Ament. . . . He told me he was going to take possession of the house of a wealthy Chinaman who was an old enemy of his, as he had interfered much in the past with his missionary labors in Pekin. A couple of days afterward he did so, and held a great sale of his enemy's effects. I bought a sable cloak at it for $125, and a couple of statues of Buddha. As the stock became depleted it was replenished by the efforts of his converts, who were ransacking the houses in the neighborhood.

Ament came back to the States to defend himself in person later that spring, and the more he talked—*Everybody was looting!*—the deeper was his disgrace. "I am enjoying Ament. He is doing my work for me—damaging his nefarious cause," Clemens wrote to Twichell. "If ever he shows signs of quieting down I will stir him up again. He is doing good, & must be kept at it. I believe China can be saved yet, from Christianity of the American Board breed, & I think that that old mud-turtle, Smith, & the talky Ament will accomplish it if some traitor doesn't gag them."

AS A PRACTICAL matter, Clemens's double-barreled diatribe against the missionaries made little difference. The American Board of Foreign Missions remained in China, and six months later it reported an annual income of $697,370, including an increase in church and private donations of nearly $10,000 from the previous year. The missionaries were taking care of themselves just fine, thank you very much.

William McKinley and his policies were likewise running fast and free with the popular current. Congress passed the president's Army Appropriations Bill, along with the amendment giving McKinley near-dictatorial powers in the Philippines. Also attached was an amendment grabbing for the United States the de facto sovereign power in Cuba. "There is, of course, little or no independence left in Cuba after the Platt amendment," Brigadier General Leonard Wood, the US military governor on the island, explained to his old pal Vice President Roosevelt.

The Supreme Court, in a 5–4 decision, had backed the administration's assertion that the president was within his constitutional rights to own, occupy, and govern the Philippines while denying the natives there the rights of citizenship. "Yes, as near as I can make out the Constitution follows the flag," said Secretary of War Elihu Root on hearing the first decision, "but it doesn't quite catch up with it."

The administration was also growing confident that the cause of independence in the Philippines was about to collapse now, thanks to Brigadier General Frederick Funston, US Volunteers. More than eighty Filipinos under Funston's command had marched into Emilio Aguinaldo's camp as friends, wearing the uniforms of the revolutionaries, and then quickly turned their guns on the "rebel leader" and his much smaller force. Aguinaldo was captured, hauled to Manila, and forced to swear public allegiance to the United States of America and to "recognize and accept the supreme authority of the United States" in his native country.

Admiral Dewey came forward to hurrah the capture and denied that the Filipino general had played any great part in the war with Spain. "Aguinaldo was in no sense an ally," Dewey told reporters as news of the capture hit the cables. "We made use of the Filipinos just as the Union forces in the Civil War made use of the negroes. We used anybody that we could to aid us, but there was nothing whatever upon which to base the declaration that they were our allies in a technical sense."

Funston was hailed a national hero for his gallant deed and rewarded with a coveted slot as brigadier general in the regular army. "You have given us one of those careers which must necessarily be an inspiration for all Americans who value courage, resolution and soldierly devotion," Vice President Theodore Roosevelt wrote to Funston a few days after the capture became public. When a few sticklers for military niceties suggested that the "little Kansas general" had violated the rules of war by dressing his soldiers in enemy uniforms, the defense was quick and furious. Professor Theodore Woolsey of Yale, an expert in international law, explained that the rules of war simply did not pertain. The United States was not at war with a "civilized power" and "the Aguinaldo party was not a signatory of the Hague convention." This meant, according to Woolsey, that Funston's men were under no obligation to adhere to the rule barring them from disguising themselves in enemy uniforms. It was small potatoes anyway, the good professor explained, in an argument right out of the Blessings-of-Civilization Trust handbook: "Contrast the good likely to flow from the hastening of the end of the insurrection by means of it with the offense of the use of enemy uniforms—a stratagem illegal in war only with a lawful belligerent—and you have the measure of the justice of the criticism."

SAM CLEMENS TRIED to keep the faith. "It is my belief that the things which I have been saying tally with the feelings and opinions which reside in the hearts of all the intelligent men in the nation," he wrote in answer to a downhearted supporter. "They will confess bye-and-bye, when the tide turns and they feel sure they are swimming with the majority. That day will come, and I am content to wait for it, and be comfortable while waiting."

By late March of 1901, however, Sam Clemens was flagging. Maybe it was the constant lousy news. *Filthy goddamned human race!* Maybe he had given a few too many speeches. Why, Livy wondered, did he feel compelled to accept the invitation of the Eastman Business College of Poughkeepsie, New York? Maybe it was his social schedule. He made the mistake of accepting an invitation to a small private lunch with Vice President Roosevelt and was nearly pummeled by Teddy talk. "He dragged San Juan Hill in three or four times, in spite of all attempts of the judicious to abolish the subject and introduce an interesting one in its place," Clemens would write of that luncheon. "I think [Roosevelt] is clearly insane in several ways, and the insanest upon war and its supreme glories."

Finally and inevitably, at the tail end of the long and eventful winter of his return home, Sam Clemens collapsed into a sickbed for two full weeks. "I am wrecked with rheumatism," he explained. "I have temporarily broken myself down with trying to do too many things."

CHAPTER THIRTY-FIVE

The Sorrow of One Who Knows

The Washington constabularies were on the sidewalk, holding back a crowd of expectant onlookers, when the secretary of state and his family climbed down out of their carriage at the railway depot. John Hay could feel the gentle breeze and the warm late-April sun on his face as he worked his way past the voluble well-wishers and through the station doors. The interior waiting room was also filled a half dozen deep with American plebeians, who patted Secretary Hay on the back and shook his hand and wished him Godspeed as he and Clara and Helen and Del worked their way down the police-protected passageway and out onto the platform, where the seven-car Presidential Special awaited. There was already talk of adding an eighth car, just for the baggage. The trip was to last seven weeks, with only a handful of extended stops, which meant there was no guarantee of laundry service. Everybody boarding that morning had been encouraged to pack forty-plus days' worth of collars and undergarments. There were a lot of bags.

The notion of this trip had begun with an invitation proffered to William McKinley to attend the launch of the new battleship *Ohio* in San Francisco; the itinerary expanded to fill an enormous vacuum in the executive schedule and became the most ambitious single tour a sitting president had ever contemplated—10,581 miles, through twenty-five states and two territories. The president's train, it had been announced to the world, would be the moving seat of national government for the duration of the trip. The Major had seen the results of leaving Theodore Roosevelt in temporary charge of the Navy Department a few years earlier and wanted it explicitly understood that his vice president would not be permitted to apply his considerable personal force to the levers of government. McKinley had persuaded most of his cabinet officers to ride along on the trip, where they would enjoy the passing scenery of the nation they served, dine together under the care of the finest culinary artists employed in the Pennsylvania Railroad commissary, and attend regular cabinet meetings in the president's private Pullman car.

The train would loop McKinley and his traveling party into the Deep South, across Texas and the Southwest, up the coast of California and into the Pacific Northwest, then back east through the Great Basin, the Colorado Rockies, the plains of Kansas, Missouri, Illinois, and into the Great Lakes region. The last major stop would be on June 13, in Buffalo, for President's Day at the Pan-American Exposition, where he would help fair organizers in their mission to "illustrate the progress and civilization of the nations of the Western Hemisphere, and strengthen their friendships and inaugurate a new era of social and commercial intercourse with the beginning of the new century."

Hay had been the first of the dignitaries to arrive at the depot in Washington, so once on the platform he could hear behind him the smattering of cheering and applause that greeted the arrival of the other cabinet officers; then, just five minutes before the scheduled departure, came a roar to shake the rafters of the old depot. A few minutes later President and Mrs. McKinley, flanked by their security men, arrived at the platform, ready to climb aboard their imperially appointed private car. No president had ever traveled in such mahogany-and-gilt luxury. The seventy-foot-long Olympia—trimmed with onyx and marble and maple—had its own private dining room, an observation room, a sofa room, an office, and two bedrooms furnished with brass beds, mirrors, and armoires. The McKinleys' quarters at the Executive Mansion paled by comparison. The First Couple had their own chef, a brace of private servants, and a certified electrician to keep the lighting and power circuits up and running.

The Major was in a jolly mood that morning, as evidenced by the bright pink carnation on his lapel. He tipped his hat to the screaming crowd and smiled broadly. Even Mrs. McKinley seemed hale and happy and inordinately pleased with the floral display. There was a cut-glass vase with an 'American Beauty' rose in every window of the dining car, and the McKinleys' private car was filled with farewell bouquets from the White House conservatories and from their many friends around town. Messenger boys were still arriving at short, irregular intervals with more, and more spectacular, arrangements, so that the entire platform was perfumed with a sweet fragrance of lilies and roses.

John Hay was ready to get on the road already. He had spent much of the previous day accepting cloying adieus from ambassadors, ministers, and chargés d'affaires. It was an amazing and sometimes laugh-provoking thing, how the balance of power in the world was tilting to the humble acreage of Lafayette Square. "I am singularly impressed by the change of tone and attitude in our Court," Henry Adams wrote after watching the procession of foreign diplomats that afternoon. "Not only is it now the biggest, most numerous, Court in the world, but there is an eagerness to attract favor such as no one ever saw here in happier days of heroism. The whole pirate crew tumble over each other to catch a favor." The next morning, at the depot, it was Hay's fellow citizens—the "chattering idiots," he called them—who were bon-voyaging him on the platform. "What a good time you are going to have," they insisted.

And then there was Del, who had truly shown his father something in the past few years, standing manfully on the platform to see his parents away. Del had always had a kind of animal and electric bonhomie, but he had matured of late into an unexpectedly calming presence. The old tensions between father and son had faded in the younger man's long absence abroad. The two men had become surprisingly solicitous of each other. Del had returned to Washington from his successful consulship in South Africa only a few weeks before, and though he was not sure what was next for him, his father told him to take some time and catch his breath. He did not have to be in a hurry; he could figure it out toward the end of the year. Hay was sure his son would have options. The president seemed anxious to find Del a new place in government, and Hay had already made an offer to buy him a good property to manage if he wanted to pursue private business instead.

As the waiting engine whistled off its steam, Del turned to his much smaller father and looked down at him with understanding and empathy. "Perhaps," he said, "it won't be so rotten after all."

THE TRIP HAD been a contentious subject in the Hay household. Hay did not want to make this journey; his wife had insisted on it. Clara had not been pleased when her husband had acceded to the president's plea that he stay on as secretary of state in the second term. She had watched, helpless, as the complications at the end of the first term had worn her husband to a raw nub. And there had been no more irritating complication than their friend Senator Henry Cabot Lodge. Cabot had presented himself to Hay at the State Department as soon as the November 1900 election results were in, "yelping for loot like a Christian in China," Hay wrote to Adams, demanding jobs for family and constituents—this while Cabot was still engaged in extensive diddling with the Hay-Pauncefote Treaty, leading expansionist senators in what Hay called "a ghost dance around it with tomahawks drawn." The full Senate *did* finally end up ratifying the treaty in December of 1900, eight months after it was delivered into its hands, but not before attaching three amendments that Hay had warned again and again and again were too odious for acceptance in London.

Cabot had not merely shamed John Hay with the amendments but also managed in the normal course of his ongoing public utterance to insult the office of secretary of state and demean the function of the State Department. "Lodge has now come out in a carefully prepared interview, saying that a treaty, when sent to the Senate, is not properly speaking a treaty—it is merely a project," Hay complained to Harry White. Hay had to keep quiet through that and also while Cabot suggested that he and his fellow senators were simply doing their duty by patching over all of Secretary Hay's mistakes with amendments, thus making a *proper* treaty—from the American point of view. Hay was at the end of his thin rope where Cabot was concerned, and was expecting worse. "Neither you nor I would weight a feather weight with [Cabot] as against any selfish advantage," he wrote to White. "He would cut my throat or yours for a favorable notice in a newspaper."

Cabot did speak publicly of Hay's good intentions and his patriotism, and the two remained social friends, but the senator continued to lecture Hay privately about what the American people would and would not stand for, and how international law, even as embodied in treaties between nations, was "fluid," and how the United States was perfectly within its rights to opt out of earlier treaty agreements when they no longer fit the practical requirements of the situation, such as, for instance, the greater glory of the Monroe Doctrine. Cabot had essentially managed to negate much of the already overtaxed State Department's work on the canal treaty, which, coupled with the continuing crisis in China, had nearly broken Hay's already brittle health. The secretary of state had spent about a third of the previous nine months confined to his sickbed, dosing on strychnine and quinine and consulting doctors who offered the normal run of vague and useless diagnoses. Hay suspected obstruction in his circulation and thought his heart was probably failing. There were days he was sure he was dying.

The Brits rejected the much-amended Hay-Pauncefote Treaty, of course. But by the beginning of William McKinley's second term, in March of 1901, Hay had decided to ignore the embarrassment of the situation and began consulting with a few key senators (Cabot was *not* one of them) and with Ambassador Pauncefote to come up with acceptable language for an entirely new treaty, er, project. He put Adee to work on language for an early draft, which was ready in mid-April 1901, just as Hay began suffering unsettling episodes of temporary paralysis on one side of his body and haloed vision. These symptoms kept him in nervous anticipation of a final, fatal brain hemorrhage.

This was John Hay's general state when the president had suggested that the cabinet officers and their wives accompany him on the nationwide tour. Hay balked, but Clara grabbed at the trip as her best hope to save her husband: it would get him away from the State Department offices, and the loathsome and illiterate creatures who worked for him, and the difficulties caused him by their ineptitude. Hay could see her point. Congress was out of session. Ambassador Pauncefote was decamping to London to sell the new treaty project to Lord Salisbury and his cabinet. This might be the Hays' only chance to see the Pacific Ocean. They would travel in luxury, rest and relax, feed on the finest victuals. Hay finally nodded assent to his wife, but not before asking, and only half-jokingly, if he could add a silk-lined coffin to the baggage car, just in case he needed it for the ride home.

HAY WAS HAPPY enough in the Presidential Special that first week, when the party was on the move. He spent uninterrupted hours reading and writing and loafing in his private quarters or lounging in the smoking car. He didn't even much mind the alkali dust and heat of West Texas and New Mexico and Arizona, but the frequent stops for public display were a drain on his already low reserves. He groaned under the daily imperative of being hauled off the train and driven with the rest of the presidential party to an overexcited and overdecorated town square for hours of speech making and banqueting. He dreaded the moment some burgher would ask what he thought of his fair city. "I hastily run over all the advantages of London and Paris and Tadmor in the wilderness, and say their town combines all their charms and none of their faults,—which is swallowed even as a turkey gobbles a June-bug," he joked to Adams.

On the occasions he and the other cabinet members were introduced and asked to make a few remarks, Hay spoke in a flat, uninflected tone, and could tend toward the morbid. "I am glad to get even this slight glimpse of this state," he said of Texas, "and would like further only that we are at the mercy of that common fiend, the calendar and time tables."

The cabinet was the undercard anyway, unrecognizable by name or face to most Americans. But the presidential presence drew noisy and affectionate crowds all across the West, especially in New Mexico and Arizona, where the citizens of those territories waved their little American flags and shouted their eager desire for statehood. "What can they mean by it," Hay joked, "except that all the adult males want to be Senators?"

McKinley's speeches rarely inspired, however, because it was hard to follow exactly what he was trying to say. The political purpose of the trip was to sell the second-term agenda, which was, in a nutshell, to do God's work in lifting up the American economy, to protect those deserving sorts in American business and industry (he could offer the tariffs *and* that big new military), and to crack open new foreign markets for *all* American product. The thing was, American business didn't appear to be in any dire need of assistance, presidential or otherwise. The country was enjoying an enormous and growing trade surplus with the home base of the British Empire; the stock exchange in New York was setting new records in volume and threatening to unseat London as the capital of global financial markets; J. P. Morgan had just got up the first *billion-dollar* corporation. Still and all, McKinley stumped his vision of prosperity. "There is nothing in this world that brings people so close together as commerce," was the Major's big line on the trip, and what could his audiences do but cheer the sentiment? "There is nothing in this world that so much promotes the universal brotherhood of man as commerce and we want to encourage commerce." Well, anyway, wasn't it amazing for any citizen—once in a lifetime, probably—just to see the president of the United States of America? Nobody seemed to mind that he had nothing much to say.

HAY WAS A little annoyed after that first week (and still a month to go!) and started joking about having "grown quite adept at saying a word or two absolutely without meaning and without cerebral expense." But in the early-morning dark of May 8, 1901, the train passed through the last western desert and the Hays and their fellow travelers awoke to find themselves in the enchanting verdure of Southern California—the American Oz. Soon after sunrise, after the train pulled into the station in Redlands, President and Mrs. McKinley were escorted to the first in a line of waiting carriages, and with the Hays and other dignitaries in line behind, the First Couple rode through lanes of flowering fruit trees and down streets carpeted with fresh-cut roses to the Casa Loma Hotel. Thousands of men in their Sunday finery and women in bright summer dresses thronged the hotel court to greet the presidential party. "My fellow citizens, our triumphs are not the triumphs of war," McKinley told the crowd. "Our triumphs are those of a free, self-governing people, looking to the development and upbuilding and extension of liberty to the human race. . . .We will meet these problems in the fear of God, and will carry and maintain the blessings of liberty wherever our glorious banner floats."

The next morning they were in the Los Angeles Fiesta, with the president at the head of a rose parade, riding in a carriage drawn by six white horses, each cloaked in yellow satin. The Hays stood on the reviewing stand that day, up to their ankles in rose petals, looking out at the tens of thousands of happy Californians. The presidential group had by then had their first glimpse of the thunderous, rolling tides of the Pacific Ocean. John Hay was beginning to feel considerably better.

Mrs. McKinley, however, was beginning to feel considerably worse.

The president's doctor had early in the trip lanced a painful inflammation in one of Ida's fingers, and she had been up and down ever since. By the time the party arrived in San Francisco on May 14, the First Lady had developed a raging fever and diarrhea. The doctor feared blood poisoning; the next morning, he feared imminent death. McKinley's private secretary, after consulting with the medical man, was already making plans for a funeral train, and the president begged off his public schedule, leaving John Hay to fill in as commencement speaker across the bay at the University of California, Berkeley.

Mrs. McKinley made an unexpected recovery and was well enough to release her ever-vigilant husband from her bedside to launch his new battleship a few days later. But the president had been spooked by his wife's near-death experience. He scratched the rest of his itinerary and ordered the special train to haul east with all deliberate speed. He wanted his wife back to the known comforts of the White House.

HAY WAS STILL in the glow of California when he arrived home, and why not? Pauncefote was about to arrive in London, where he would work with Lord Salisbury's cabinet, Hay's trusted man Harry White, and US ambassador Joseph Choate to put the new canal treaty convention in shape for the prime minister's final approval. Hay was confident Sir Julian would return in the fall with a treaty even Cabot could love.

Both of Hay's daughters appeared headed toward happy betrothals to Del's closest friends from Yale. They were young men of wealth and standing and would keep the Hay girls nearby in New York or Washington. And after much tortured deliberation—while his father kept a studied silence on the matter—Del had finally accepted President McKinley's offer of a job in the White House starting in the fall. Del was going to have a final summer of play, maybe take a yachting trip with Helen's about-to-be fiancé, Payne Whitney, before taking up his post.

Other cabinet officers were nearly struck dumb when the secretary of state suggested they make a nod to the public desires and hold open the *possibility* of a third term for McKinley. The president himself was having none of it. "I will say now once and for all, expressing a long-settled conviction, that I not only am not and will not be a candidate for a third term, but would not accept a nomination for it if it were tendered to me," the Major emphatically announced to the press. "My only ambition is to serve through my second term to the acceptance of my countrymen."

The evening that statement hit the newspapers, June 11, 1901, John Hay was already heading west on a train to Buffalo. He had been deputized once again to fill a presidential bill, this time to help consecrate the Pan-American Exposition, which he did, two days later, in a speech of rare eloquence coming from a member of the McKinley administration. "Last night," Hay began, "as I looked from my window at this marvelous creation, lined in fire upon the evening sky, and to-day, as I have walked through the courts and the palaces of this incomparable exhibition, the words of the prophet have been constantly in my mind: 'Your old men shall dream dreams; your young men shall see visions.' We who are old have through many hopeful years dreamed this dream. . . . And now we share with you who are young the pleasures of beholding the vision, far nobler and more inspiring than the dream."

HAY RETURNED FROM Buffalo to an empty house in Washington; the family had scattered. Clara and the girls were already at the Fells for the summer. Clarence was finishing his school term in Connecticut. Del was heading to New York to bid adieu to the darling little Marguerite Cassini, who was sailing with her father for a summer tour in Europe. After that, he was going to New Haven to celebrate Class Day at Yale, where his consular success would make him the star of the class of '98. Hay found himself lonely in the most delicious of ways, happy to have so much to pine for. He decided first to write to Clarence King at the sanatorium in Prescott, Arizona, where he was being treated for tuberculosis.

Hay and King had been growing apart for years, and Hay did not entirely blame the press of his public duties or the press of King's financial woe. Neither did Hay believe King was embarrassed into silence by the many loans from Hay left unpaid. Something mysterious and unspoken had come between them, but Hay had not quit trying to break through. "My dear King," he wrote. "I have just returned from a very hurried visit to the exposition at Buffalo. . . . The electrical show at night is unquestionably the finest thing ever yet seen on earth. I don't believe that the show that Nero got up in Rome was any worthier of his fiddling. . . . Write me a letter whenever you can. I know you are excessively busy, but snatch a moment from other cares, and tell me how you are. Yours faithfully, John Hay."

He also dashed off a quick note to Harry White, to weigh in on the treaty talks in London and to make uncharacteristic little brags about his oration in Buffalo (he enclosed a proof of his speech) and about his son. "The President has appointed Del his assistant secretary," he wrote in closing, "the one through whom he communicates with Congress,—the place I held with Lincoln ages ago."

A NIGHT WATCHMAN saw the figure as it fell, soundlessly, then heard the awful thud of impact on the pavement in front of the hotel. He ran toward it in the darkness, shouting for help, the first to reach the body. There was no blood, nothing oozed, but neither was there any sign of life. He looked closer. The man was wearing pajamas. Next to the body was a broken opal ring, which must have cracked on impact. A crowd of the curious began to gather around the body in the next few minutes. People gazed up through the streetlamps, trying to determine the path of the fall, trying to find the open window. One young man pushed his way to the front of the crowd, then reeled back in shock and pain: "My God!" he screamed. He knew who it was.

John Hay was called out of his own bed an hour and a half later, at four o'clock in the morning. George Cortelyou, President McKinley's private secretary, was downstairs; he needed to speak with the secretary of state right away. Hay put on his robe and padded down his polished staircase, wondering what sort of international crisis could not wait until dawn. Cortelyou wasted no time: There had been an accident at the New Haven House. Del was dead. The words shot through Hay's body like electricity, and when their meaning had sunk in, he slumped in physical pain, not sure where to turn for relief. The big house was empty but for people paid to serve. Cortelyou stayed by John Hay's side as he recovered his wits; then Hay begged the president's secretary to get him on the first train to New Haven, so that just five hours later, the secretary of state was alone in a railcar heading north. The trip to New Haven took nine hours, slowed by increasingly agitating regular stops at stations along the way, and Hay did not arrive at his destination until nearly six o'clock that evening.

His son's body—if it was his son, and he still held faint hope that it wasn't—had already been taken from the medical examiner's office to the private home of the owner of the New Haven House. Hay knew he would be watched, closely, and prodded himself to maintain his dignity as he walked from the station to a waiting carriage, which drove him to the house on Wall Street. No other family member had arrived. Helen was on a train from Boston, but she wouldn't be there for hours. Clara and Alice were in New Hampshire awaiting instructions, and Clarence was in Connecticut. Clara's sister and her sister's husband, Sam Mather, were still a day away.

The first clue was the size of the body. Del was big, six-feet-two and more than two hundred pounds. And when Hay got close, his last little sliver of hope evanesced. The face, unmarked but for a bruise on the right side of his forehead, was his son's. John Hay crumpled into himself. The few people in the room thought Hay might be having a heart attack, and they yelled for a doctor. The best they could do for him was to carry him to a bed upstairs, which was where Helen Hay found her father when she arrived a few hours later. She was not allowed to linger over him. The doctor had ordered absolute solitude and left a lone nurse to attend at bedside. "Mr. Hay is simply overwhelmed," the attending physician told reporters, "and is suffering from a prostration which probably will be relieved by sufficient rest."

John Hay was up and around the next day, and with the help of Helen and her beau, Payne Whitney, and a few of Del's other friends, he began to make the necessary funeral and travel arrangements. Del's classmates were already gathered two hundred strong and asked if they might have a memorial service in New Haven, but Hay said no. Simple and dignified, was all he could think. Simple, dignified, and *private*. He and Helen would wait for Clara and the other two children to arrive, and then they would all head for Cleveland to bury Del in the family plot. Hay wondered whether he had the strength to carry his wife through the next few days. He would have to explain to her all the stupid, mundane details that added up to this spectacular life-altering tragedy: Del had spent a happy Saturday night with friends. He went around the corner from the hotel to the Hyperion Theater to see a vaudeville act, which was headlined by Cissy Loftus, one of Henry Irving's troupers whom Del had known in London and New York. He stopped by the flower store on the way to the theater to buy Cissy a few dozen roses. And after the show he went back to the New Haven House, picked up two bottles of champagne, and escorted Miss Loftus to the pier, where a boat would be ferrying her and the rest of the cast and crew back to New York. He arrived back at the New Haven House a few hours later, hung around the lobby for a while, and headed up to his room on the third floor. He undressed, pulled back the bedding, and then, it being such a hot and close night, perched himself on the windowsill to have his final smoke of the night. Del's friends had told investigators that he was always fussing with that opal ring, pulling it on and off his finger. They thought he might have dropped it and fallen out the window while lunging for it. They also told investigators he had not been drunk, in spite of the champagne. No matter how much or how little of this story Hay told his wife, he knew he could not answer the big question: why? "I dreaded to meet her," he wrote to a friend weeks later, "—but when she arrived and stood with me beside him, looking into his serene and smiling face,—he never looked so handsome and so happy,—I felt and have felt ever since that she had character enough for both of us."

Newspapermen reporting on the private family funeral in Cleveland a day later described Clara Hay as an understandably distraught mother in need of constant physical assistance from her husband. But they did not see her once the ceremony was over and her son was buried, when she drew the line. "We must act as if he were away on one of his long journeys, and as if we were to see him again in due time," Clara told her husband and her other children. "We must make no change whatever in our way of life." Hay noted the pure steel will in his wife's statement, and he suspected there was wisdom in it. "I hope for the best," he told Harry White.

CONDOLENCES PILED UP at Lafayette Square and at the Fells. Clara received all the sympathy due a grieving mother, and a few people shared their last sightings of the deceased: "I saw Dellie driving in Central Park in all his strength and beauty," wrote one young woman. "I think it was the 8th [of June], a young man of his own age with him." Mrs. Hay also received an occasional reminder of her duties as a wife and a US citizen: "We have all of us here watched with keen interest & much sympathy the great work which Mr. Hay has been doing . . . & we pray that strength may be given him to recover from this crushing blow, so that he may continue his good & patriotic work."

Foreign ambassadors and ministers called and telegraphed and wrote letters. The new king of England sent a personal note. The president telegraphed from the White House: "Besides the personal bereavement which I feel, I had counted so much upon having your noble son a member of my official household. May God give you and your family His consolation." Henry Cabot Lodge and his wife wrote separately, on their way out of the country to meet Henry Adams. "My heart is breaking with the knowledge of your anguish," Nannie wrote to Hay. "I only wish that you could read between these poor lines all that I long to say." Cabot was, well, Cabot. "In the presence of such sorrow as yours," he wrote, "I feel that the great proof of affection would be silence." Then he filled a page with his thoughts and feelings. "He seems such a loss to me," wrote Cabot.

Theodore Roosevelt tried to be helpful, too, in all his pitiless exuberance. "It must in the end be a satisfaction to know that among all the millions of our people, no other young man of his age had achieved so much," he wrote three days after Del's burial, "and in addition to the sum of achievement, gave promise of so much to come."

There were unexpected cards, including one from Sam Clemens: "Dear Hay," read the handwritten note. "Out of a heart hurt beyond healing five years ago by the death of my daughter, I offer you all that I have—the sorrow of one who knows. I will not torture you with words; they would help if they could, but in all the ages they have not availed."

Clemens was right; words did not avail. "If sympathy could help, our sorrow would be brief," Hay wrote to Harry White a week after Del's death. "But every word of praise and affection which we hear of our dead boy gives a keener edge to our grief. Why should he go, I stupidly ask, with his splendid health and strength, his courage, his hopes, his cheery smile which made everybody like him at sight; and I be left, with my short remnant of life, of little use to my friends and none to myself? Yet I know this is a wild and stupid way to rail at fate. I must face facts. My boy is gone, and the whole face of the world is changed in a moment."

THE HAYS RETREATED to the Fells after the burial and tried to adjust themselves to the *absence*. Helen and Payne Whitney agreed to postpone their engagement announcement in honor of Del. Alice and Jimmy Wadsworth did the same. Clara and Clarence feverishly tended to their gardening. Hay was buoyed by his family's strength. The children had their mother's temperament. They were Stones, after all, and made a foundation that would *not be moved.* Helen "was more of a man than I," Hay told a friend, "and Alice and Clarence are all I could wish." After less than two weeks of quiet mourning in New Hampshire, John Hay felt as if he had absorbed the full force of the blow and had withstood it. In fact, he convinced himself he was strong enough to leave the family for a trip down to Washington. The president had already sent Hay a second telegram by then, telling him to remain in New Hampshire to make sure his wife and family were OK, "then return to work, which will be the best avenue to bring you relief and strength." Hay figured he was not strong enough for a long stretch of office toil, but maybe he could do the ten hard days it would take to clear his desk, and then he would return to New Hampshire for the rest of the summer and leave Alvey Adee to superintend.

Hay was partly comforted by the demands of the affairs of state once he arrived back in Washington. The new Hay-Pauncefote treaty was still being put in shape for the Senate's consideration when it convened in December. The European powers were still threatening to carve China into their own little fiefdoms. An opportunity to purchase Denmark's colonial holdings in the West Indies had presented itself. And the president was anxious to find a way to transfer governance of Puerto Rico and the Philippines from the War Department to the State Department. These diversions did not change the central new fact of John Hay's existence, and after a week in Washington, he was wearying. "My sorrow grips me from time to time so that I can hardly bear it," he wrote to Clara. "Everybody seems to think that I will be better at work. I do not know whether they are right or wrong."

At home at night, Hay did the dispiriting work of winding down Del's affairs. He cleared Del's closets of clothes and sorted them so that he could make gifts to friends. He emptied his son's valises, where he found his bankbooks and checkbooks and divided the money evenly between Del's brother and sisters. He searched for Del's personal papers and official documents but got little satisfaction. He did find a shell from Pretoria marked for the war correspondent Richard Harding Davis, who had known Del in South Africa. Hay had received a photograph of Del and Davis outside the consulate in Pretoria just before it fell to the British, along with a letter from Davis. "The hill marked with a cross is occupied by the largest Boer guns," it read, "so when the English begin to bombard it Del will get all of the shells that the fort fails to catch en route. He is digging a cellar." Hay wondered where his son had come by this fearlessness—surely not from him. When Del's traveling trunks arrived from New Haven, it took Hay days to get up the courage just to open them.

The days in Washington grew lonelier after his first week back, and his mood soured whenever he contemplated the muted response of his three closest friends. John Nicolay, his boyhood classmate who had brought him into the Lincoln White House, had left it to his daughter to communicate. "My father is still very weak," Helen Nicolay wrote, "far too ill to write the message he would wish to." Henry Adams had sent from Europe a short telegram saying he was sorry he could not be with the family. When Hay did finally receive a longer letter of sympathy from Adams, Henry spoke of no immediate plans to return to America. And Hay had heard nothing from Clarence King, who was by all reports still out west in California or Arizona, fighting for his life. Hay could understand why his friend had not answered a letter or card for more than six months, but he was stung, and deeply, that King had not taken the time to acknowledge his loss.

The secretary of state was still in Washington on July 14, three weeks to the day after Del's death, when he was smacked in the face by an ugly front-page story in Washington's latest gossip rag, the *Sunday Globe*. The headline said it all.

ADELBERT S. HAY
Drunk When He Fell from the
Hotel Window

Hay was angry and hurt—and in need. He reached for his closest friends; most pathetically, he reached for the still unheard-from Clarence King. "Dear King: I wonder if I can write a word to you without going to pieces in the process. All my thoughts are with my dead boy. His face is always before me, always smiling and happy, never the least shadow of pain, or resentment against the cruelty of fate. I am growing to feel a little comfort in this. Perhaps it means all is well with him, that length of days is not so greatly to be desired. His little life was very happy. He had ease and variety; his family idolized him; everybody liked him and sought his company. . . . He was famous at twenty-four—his name well known in three continents. After all, is it not well with the boy?

These are things I try to think, but I mock myself. My grief seizes me like a bull dog and will not let me go. God help me!"

Two weeks later, and still without communication from King, Hay tried again. He didn't bother mentioning Del this time but sent a package with Zola's latest book and another plea. "I have heard nothing from you for ages," Hay wrote. "I don't want you to write if it bores you—but if you ever feel like it, we should like very much to have news of you. Henry, I suppose, has gone to Bayreuth with the Lodges. Edward Hooper [Henry's brother-in-law] died last month—but apparently he did not need to come home on that account."

CHAPTER THIRTY-SIX

No Answers but in Time

Clara Hay received her first long letter from Henry Adams more than a month after her son's death, and it bore little resemblance to a sympathy note. From his distant perch in the Bavarian mountains, Adams lectured Mrs. Hay on her responsibility to guard her husband's health ("All turns on you. If you break down, John will break down") and he reminded the grieving mother of his own constant, awful pain, which he had been living with for the fifteen years since his wife poisoned herself. Adams offered to return to Washington if needed, but he asked Clara to recognize the noble sacrifice he was making in keeping his distance from John. "As a matter of medical opinion, I should say that I was not altogether the best sort of help or tonic to persons needing strength and courage," he wrote. "It is so long since I have got the habit of thinking that nothing is worth while! That sort of habit is catching and I should not like to risk too close contact at a critical moment with a mind disposed to be affected by it."

Clara Hay had known Henry Adams a long time, and she knew better than to expect something beyond his capacity. Adams would keep to his own plans and maintain his safe transatlantic remove. He spent the rest of the summer traveling with the Lodges through Germany, Austria, Poland, and Russia, favoring his friends back home with the catty little observations he was certain they would find amusing: "Of all great European cities, Vienna is the most Amerianised, and the least amusing at first contact." "Warsaw is a big, bustling city, like all other cities, only mostly Jew. . . . The people are uglier than on Pennsylvania Avenue which is otherwise my lowest standard." "The Kremlin is more than half barbarous, but it is not strong." "Cabot is bored! for once he is not unreasonable."

Hay's other great friend, Clarence King, was Henry Adams's opposite in most ways, so full of heart and courage and possibility. Adams looked back, while King looked ahead. King liked to talk about the glories to come, when "flight through the upper air will be a daily matter of course" and people "shall whisper around the globe." He even wrote (for publication) of the strange, beautiful promise of miscegenation, "when the composite elements of the American populations are melted down into one race alloy, when there are no more Irish or Germans, Negroes and English, but only Americans."

King knew Hay tended toward Adams's way of seeing the world, but he had never stopped working on his friend. "People are looked at in only two ways," he had once written to Hay, "with the brain and with the heart. If you take the former method you initially classify and judge people by their *differences* with other people usually yourself. If you see them with the heart you have your conceptions on the *similarities* between them and some other people usually yourself."

Clara Hay knew how desperately her husband needed Clarence King's healing personal touch, so she beseeched a society matron in California to try to contact him. The woman found King in Pasadena, where his doctors were treating him for tuberculosis and a weakening heart. "He says he is a very sick man, but does not show his illness in his face," Clara's friend reported. "I think there might be great hope for him. What a charming man he is. He was very entertaining & told me to say to you that he was 'gay without— sad within.' . . . I should only be too glad to do anything I could for Mr. King; it is a pleasure to meet such a man."

A letter from Clarence King arrived shortly thereafter. Hay was struck by the natural grace of his old friend's ministrations—how King assured him that the worst pain would pass and that Hay could look forward to the time he would carry the memory of his son as a cherished companion. Hay found what he called "a beginning of comfort in them." King's parting words were not so heartening. "What would I give to be well and with you," King wrote. "But I am a poor, sick, old fellow, uncertain yet of life or of death, suffering more than my lot, and simply waiting till nature and the foe have done their struggle."

"There you have it in the face!" Hay wrote to Adams. "The best and brightest man of his generation, who with talents immeasurably beyond any of his contemporaries, with industry that has often sickened me to witness it, with everything in his favor but blind luck, hounded by disaster from his cradle, with none of the joy of life to which he was entitled, dying at last, with nameless suffering, alone and uncared-for in a California tavern."

JOHN HAY SPENT the first part of August in the sanctuary of the New Hampshire hills, trying to remind himself of his lifetime of unsought fortune. If his blind luck had finally run out, and surely it had, the balance was still far in his favor. Even his son's unjustifiable death had its comforts. *Del died well loved and without pain*, he told himself over and over, *famous at twenty-four, after a life of variety and adventure*. Some days, Hay simply felt numb to the world. "I cannot even find it in my heart to rail at the Senators," he wrote, temporarily adopting Sam Clemens's private philosophy. "They are as God made them, and they act according to the law of their being."

Other days he simply felt beside the point and doubtful of his own utility. President McKinley could handle the complications of US foreign policy with or without him. Adee was running the State Department with his usual efficiency in Hay's absence. Harry White and Joseph Choate were pulling the loose ends of the canal treaty with the powers in London. Why did he stay in the job? Was it sheer stubbornness, he asked himself, was it duty? "To take the best view of it," he confessed to Adams, "it may be the dregs of a puritan conscience which makes me stay simply because I don't want to."

He stayed in office anyway, took some solace in the diversion of the work and in the chance to make one final difference in the national fortunes. He was not without purpose. John Hay was not going to allow the United States to stain itself by unilaterally abrogating the old Clayton-Bulwer agreement with England on his watch. When the Senate came back in session that December, John Hay meant to present the members a canal treaty they could neither denigrate nor demagogue; whether it passed or failed, he could leave office without regret. "At least my course was clear," he told a friendly newspaper editor in New York. "I had to try again, to save us from a threatened dishonor. If I fail again, I shall know what my duty to myself requires."

The first week of September, as more happy reports came in from Choate and Harry White, Hay began to see the very real possibility of a final worthy triumph: "If Lord Pauncefote brings it back next month in the form we have indicated, I shall be ready to intone my *nunc dimittis*."

Now thou dost dismiss thy servant, O Lord.

JOHN HAY GOT the bulletin at the Fells on Friday afternoon of that same week, by telegram, even as the big special-edition type was being set in composing rooms of newspapers across the country.

PRESIDENT M'KINLEY SHOT DOWN BY AN ANARCHIST IN BUFFALO

HIS CONDITION IS VERY SERIOUS, BUT THERE IS HOPE

The president had just finished a speech at the Pan-American Exposition in Buffalo—a makeup date for his cancellation in June—when a lone "average looking" man walked through the milling crowd, pulled out a .32 caliber Iver

Johnson revolver, and, at a distance of two feet, gut-shot William McKinley. The news traveled fast and far. Adams read about it in Stockholm, Sweden. "I do not yet know how serious the case is, but I take for granted it is very bad, and I am much troubled about it," he wrote to Hay in a letter that would not reach him for nearly two weeks. "I see what an increase of responsibility it throws on you, and what an extra strain it may give your nerves."

Vice President Roosevelt had already been summoned, and he raced to McKinley's bedside at a private home in Buffalo, where he found the Major very much alive and remarkably alert in the first few days after the shooting. The entire cabinet eventually made its way to town to have a look at their convalescing leader. John Hay was the last to arrive, on the fourth day, and by the time his train rolled into Buffalo, the physicians' bulletins were pointing toward a swift recovery: "The President's condition steadily improves and he is comfortable and without pain or unfavorable symptoms. Bowel and Kidney functions normally performed. Pulse 113. Temperature 101. Respiration 26."

Hay was in Buffalo little more than a day, and McKinley was in good spirits throughout, able to take broth and sit up in bed. The physicians were so confident of the president's recovery that Vice President Theodore Roosevelt and the cabinet were released to carry on as normal. Hay sent a telegram to Clara that all was well and that he was heading for Washington and would probably be back at the Fells by the weekend. Hay was anxious to get to Washington so that he could reassure nervous governments around the world that William McKinley would survive the shooting and would be able to carry on as president. But the secretary of state wanted to be certain before he spoke, so on his way out of Buffalo, he made an arrangement with the president's private secretary, George Cortelyou.

The next day, as planned, Cortelyou sent a message to Hay at the State Department: doctors remained certain of the president's full recovery. As the secretary of state completed the text of his happy message promising glad tidings, an eerie foreboding settled on him, as if he had just tempted the Fates. He was immediately wary of transmitting the cable around the world and asked Alvey Adee for his advice. Both these men had lived through this sort of crisis before: Hay had a close-in spot at the gruesome vigil at Abraham Lincoln's deathbed in 1865, while Adee had suffered through the seventy-nine-day deathwatch following the shooting of President Garfield in 1881. Adee was shy to offer reassurance. "I distrust the eighth day," he said cryptically to Hay.

A STATEMENT UNDER John Hay's signature to the foreign diplomats serving in the United States was not released until two days later.

> It is my painful duty to announce to you the death of William McKinley, President of the United States, in the city of Buffalo, at fifteen minutes past 2 in the morning of today, September 14.
>
> Laid low by the act of an assassin, the week-long struggle to save his life has been watched with keen solicitude, not alone by the people of this country who raised him from their own ranks to the high office he filled, but by the people of all friendly nations, whose messages of sympathy, and of hope while hope was possible, have been most consolatory in this time of sore trial.
>
> Now that the end has come, I request you, sir, to be the medium of communicating the sad tidings to the Government of the honored nation you so worthily represent, and to announce that in obedience to the prescription of the Constitution, the office of President has devolved upon Theodore Roosevelt, Vice-President of the United States.

The president-to-be had raced that morning from the Adirondacks to Buffalo, where most of the cabinet was assembling; Hay remained in Washington and kept watch on the affairs of state for the hours the country was without a president, expecting this to be his final official duty. The newspapers were already speculating about who would replace John Hay in the new Roosevelt cabinet. Everybody remembered Theodore's vicious clubbing of Hay's first canal treaty. There seemed little doubt that Hay was out as secretary of state; the most likely successor appeared to be Theodore's best friend, Henry Cabot Lodge. Hay meanwhile sent the new president a handwritten note all but offering his resignation.

> My dear Roosevelt—If the Presidency had come to you in any other way, no one could have congratulated you with better heart than I. My sincere affection and esteem for you, and my old-time love for your Father—would he could have lived to see where you are!—would have been deeply gratified. And even from the depths of the sorrow where I sit, with my grief for the President mingled and confused with that for my boy, so that I scarcely know from hour to hour, the true source of my tears,—I do still congratulate you. . . . My official life is at an end—my natural life will not be long extended, and so, in the dawn of what I am sure will be a great and splendid future, I venture to give you the heartfelt benediction of the past.

Hay was waiting at the depot on Monday evening, September 16, when Roosevelt and the rest of the cabinet arrived in Washington aboard the McKinley funeral train. President Theodore Roosevelt saw John Hay on the platform and advanced on him with his usual animal vigor and a new jolt of presidential electricity. "You must stay with me," he told Hay. "You cannot decline, or even take the time to consider."

Hay was powerless before the press of this strapping new executive will. ("You must still call me Theodore in private," Roosevelt insisted.) "I saw of course, it was best for him to start off that way," Hay wrote to Adams a few days later, "& so said I would stay, forever of course, for it would be worse to say I would stay a while than it would be to go out at once. I can still go at any moment he gets tired of me, or when I collapse."

JOHN HAY WAS more deeply moved than he had expected by the solemn sight of the flag-draped cedar coffin holding another dead president being carried from the railway station on Sixth Street to the East Room of the White House a few blocks away. The East Room was kept clear of all visitors for the first few hours, and Mrs. McKinley sat alone there with her husband's body until Dr. Rixey finally pulled her away. He doubted the First Lady was fit to attend any of the coming public observances.

The next morning at nine o'clock, while the military band played McKinley's favorite hymn, "Nearer, My God, to Thee," the casket was loaded into a hearse and driven down Pennsylvania Avenue for a state funeral at the US Capitol, then hauled back up the avenue and placed on the lighted observation car for the Major's last journey home to Canton, Ohio. The new president, Theodore Roosevelt, rode along to pay his final respects.

THE DAY AFTER McKinley's remains left Washington, John Hay felt compelled to drive across town to B Street Southeast, on Capitol Hill, to visit John Nicolay. Nicolay had a malignancy of some sort obstructing his stomach and had been enduring a "long slow torture" for five months already. When Hay arrived he found his friend of fifty years in blinding pain. Nicolay did not even recognize Hay that day and would be dead in a week.

The next morning, Hay attended a prayer service for McKinley at a church in Washington and then walked over to a memorial for a near neighbor who had died unexpectedly, at age forty-nine, of appendicitis. "I have acquired the funeral habit," he lamented.

WILLIAM MCKINLEY'S BODY was entombed at the West Lawn Cemetery in Canton at two thirty in the afternoon, on September 19, 1901. For a full five minutes—even the telegraph wires were stilled—Americans observed a devout nationwide silence. Then the silence was over, and the national clangor recommenced, ushering in the Age of Theodore.

The new president was back in Washington the next morning, in time for his first cabinet meeting, and it went as John Hay expected. Theodore held forth in a series of long soliloquies broken by an occasional interjection from a cabinet officer, or more often by Roosevelt himself, who was prone to interrupting his own barreling train of thought to toss another of his personal notions into the hopper. In that first meeting, President Roosevelt talked himself out of authorizing the new Bureau of Insular Affairs, which had been in the works at the State Department for months and was to begin operations on October 1, 1901. The purpose of this new bureau was to allow the president's selected civil authorities to take over from the military commanders the governance of Hawaii, Puerto Rico, and the Philippines. "[The president] seemed to develop as he went along a fear that there might be a possibility of friction and complications between the civil and military authorities in the Philippines as a result of the establishment of the Bureau," Hay reported to the man who had been scheduled to take over the bureau, "and he hardly seemed to think it was worth while to establish it simply to deal with questions referring to Hawaii and Porto Rico." Theodore, kaiser-like, was more comfortable with the iron hand of military rule.

HAY HAD AGREED to stay on as Roosevelt's secretary of state because he thought it would offer a sign of stability in the new presidency. He was there to calm fears, he told himself, to do his duty. But the beaten-down secretary of state found himself unexpectedly invigorated by Theodore's youthful dash—ungovernable as it was. The two old friends had long working lunches together on two consecutive days. Theodore wanted to know *all* of Hay's views about the major US foreign policy initiatives. With no audience at hand, Roosevelt allowed Hay to talk his way around the globe and then pronounced himself on board with the secretary's judgments in every instance. There would be no changes in policy. The new Hay-Pauncefote Treaty sounded bully! We could militarize the canal zone if we desired, correct? Not that we *had* to. Theodore promised to use all his powers to push it through in the next session of the Senate. Hay walked away from those first meetings believing that if he could keep Theodore's expansive ardor within the bounds of acceptable international usage and honorable statesmanship, William McKinley's legacy (and Hay's own) would be safe.

Hay went back up to New Hampshire after those initial meetings for a final try at healing his health and his wits, but he stayed in touch with Roosevelt—even found himself presuming on the old intimacy and on his senior status in the personal relationship. "My dear Theodore: (As there is nothing official in this letter, I will use the familiar name which it is pleasant for me to write.)," he wrote at the beginning of October 1901. "I am ready to come to Washington at any moment if you want me. But . . . I should like to stay a week or two longer—say till about the 15th, if nothing happens to prevent. . . . Next week the greatest of all personal—this is, individual—misfortunes, is to happen to me—my 63rd birthday. On that day I become an old man—without possibility of denial or evasion, and there is nothing worse in the arsenal of evil that can happen to any man."

Roosevelt shot back an answer at once, after consulting with his wife. "Edith and I have held a solemn conclave on the matter, and we hope this is the right conclusion. I read your letter, and pronounced the last sentence, about your age, 'affectation,' whereupon she answered severely 'not at all! I know just what he means, and I feel exactly that way myself!' She is forty, and I do not think I deceive myself when I say that she neither looks nor acts or feels as if she was more than thirty. As for me, on the whole I have continued all my life to have a better time year after year."

Maddening as he could be, Roosevelt was pure oxygen for an old man like Hay, and Theodore's attempts to fit himself into his new office were amusing. He would not be "the slave of the tradition that forbids Presidents from seeing their friends," he insisted to Hay one day. "I am going to dine with you and Henry Adams and Cabot whenever I like." Hay reported to Adams that the new president was suddenly stopped by the enormity of what he had just said—"the shadow of the crown sobered him a little." "Of course," Roosevelt concluded, "I must preserve the prerogative of the initiative."

The ensuing Roosevelt-dominated cabinet meetings rated with the finest popular entertainments in all Washington. Hay wrote a long letter to Clara describing one of the earliest such meetings, when the question arose of who should be appointed the new governor of Oklahoma Territory. Somebody mentioned Mulhall. "Oh yes, I know the family," said Theodore.

> I met Miss Bossy Mulhall at a cow-roping competition. She was splendid: she rode up and shook hands with me at full speed. She roped three steers in fine style; broke the shoulder of one and whipped out her revolver and shot him dead. I would prefer not to have a controversy with Miss Bossy. They wanted me to come up to their ranch. There were two or three men hanging about her—men with greased hair and a homicidal grin. I saw them again as I went through the country stumping [for McKinley in 1900]. Miss Bossy said she had bet her last pony on me and if I was defeated I better never show my face in Oklahoma. She gave me a stuffed wolf for a mascot; her dogs had caught it and held it while she killed it with her spur.

"It is a gay family," he concluded, "but I would hardly think of Mulhall for Governor."

LORD PAUNCEFOTE ARRIVED in Washington with the new Hay-Pauncefote Treaty in early November; it was everything the United States Senate had thuggishly demanded, and then some. Hay and Pauncefote signed their new treaty in Hay's home on November 18, and then the secretary of state and Adee crafted a twelve-page letter to the chairman of the Senate Foreign Relations Committee detailing the triumph: Clayton-Bulwer was honorably abrogated by both England and the United States, and the British had granted the United States the exclusive right not only to build and maintain the canal but to defend that canal however it chose.

The day after the signing, Hay kept a speaking engagement President McKinley had made with the New York Chamber of Commerce before he died. Secretary of State John Hay came as close as he ever did to thumping his own chest about honorably clearing the way for unprecedented new possibilities of commercial expansion.

"We consider our interests in the Pacific Ocean as great now as those of any other power, and destined to indefinite development," he told these New York businessmen.

> We have opened our doors to the people of Hawaii; we have accepted the responsibility of the Philippines which Providence imposed upon us. . . . Next in order will come a Pacific cable, and an isthmian canal for the use of all well-disposed peoples, but under exclusive American ownership and American control—of both of which great enterprises President McKinley and President Roosevelt have been the energetic and consistent champions. . . .
>
> I can yet assure you that so long as the administration of your affairs remains in hands as strong and skillful as those to which they have been and are now confided, there will be no more surrender of our rights than there will be violation of the rights of others.

A week later, the Hays began to emerge from their family mourning. Payne Whitney and Helen Hay announced their wedding date—just three months away. John Hay's canal treaty got its judgment in the full Senate a few weeks after that, just days before the Christmas recess. "Cabot, who felt himself particularly responsible for the wreck of the last one, put his whole back into promoting this one," Hay reported gleefully to Harry White in London. "The President was likewise extremely zealous in rounding up the bunch of doubtful

Senators, and the treaty at last went through with no opposition, except from the irreclaimable cranks. Seventy-two to six was near enough unanimity."

THE END OF the year brought one final hard blow. The day before Christmas, Hay received the news that Clarence King, not quite sixty, had died of tuberculosis in Phoenix. Hay was assured that his letters and messages had been a source of great comfort in his friend's last days, but this did not change the awful fact of his friend's lonely death. "In some ways Clarence King's life seemed pathetic to those who really knew him," one of King's many friends, the poet Edmund Clarence Stedman, told the newspapers. "His devotion to his nearest kindred was beautiful, but there should have been even dearer ones to bear his name and mourn his loss."

So Hay's dearest friend had died alone, a continent away from his mother and two siblings, with no wife or children to call his own. Hay would go on helping to support Clarence King's mother and his half brother, as he had been doing for years already. "To love someone is the single medicine," Clarence King had written somewhat mysteriously to Henry Adams a few years earlier, "and God knows I have reason to love Hay as he will one day see."

JOHN HAY PUT an emphatic period on his dread year in February of 1902, when he rose to the invitation from Congress and pronounced the final word on his friend William McKinley. Hay's eulogy was not universally lauded; a few in the opposition party attacked it as partisan celebration of Republican policies. There was some truth in that criticism; how many eulogies intone the beauties of a nation's "excess of exports over imports." But there was a moment near the end of that address when John Hay rose above politics and brushed the poet he had once wished to be: "Every young and growing people has to meet, at moments, the problems of its destiny," Hay said.

> Whether the question comes, as in Egypt, from a sphinx, symbol of the hostile forces of omnipotent nature, who punishes with instant death our failure to understand her meaning; or whether it comes, as in Jerusalem, from the Lord of Hosts, who commands the building of His temple, it comes always with a warning that the past is past, and experience vain. "Your fathers, where are they? and the prophets, do they live forever?" The fathers are dead; the prophets are silent; the questions are new, and have no answers but in time.
>
> When the horny outside case which protects the infancy of a chrysalis

nation suddenly bursts, and, in a single abrupt shock, finds itself floating on wings which had not existed before, whose strength it has never tested, among dangers it cannot foresee and is without experience to measure, every motion is a problem, and every hesitation may be an error. The past gives no clue to the future. The fathers, where are they? And the prophets, do they live forever?

We are ourselves the fathers! We are ourselves the prophets!

CHAPTER THIRTY-SEVEN

The Prophet Samuel . . . Banished

He loved his commanding new perch on the bluffs above the Hudson River, loved the way he could gaze out across the long, sloping lawn and through the impressionist's cold-sleet haze to the whitecaps on the water below and the glistening Palisades rising across the river. He even loved the seventy-mile-an-hour winds that roared in out of the west that first week in February 1902, making the big leafless chestnuts bow and sway like willows. "We have the noblest roaring blasts here I have ever known on land," Sam Clemens would say of the gales.

Clemens and his daughters had been drawn to the sixty-year-old stone mansion the moment they saw it; they had to have the gardens and the big, open porches and the cavernous oval drawing room on the ground floor. The Appleton property in Riverdale was just forty minutes by train from Grand Central Depot in Manhattan, and it offered all the outdoor life Jean could want. Sam had rented the house and the acreage for a year, until October of 1902, dismissing Livy's mild cavil about the expense of running a property that size. They were entertaining again as they had in the old days in Hartford—guests at almost every meal, and afternoon tea, and overnighters two or three nights of the week.

Livy was trying to be hopeful—the household finances looked wonderful, she told herself—but she knew her husband too well. Sam had already put $5,000 into the American Plasmon Company, and Livy suspected he had not really broken the habit of upping the ante in his business ventures, no matter how far fetched. He was even trying to pull poor Howells into the plasmon scheme. *Think of Vaseline!*

Livy was suffering painful attacks of gout and rheumatism at closer intervals now, along with occasional unnerving flutters in her heart, and she could not rest easy where her daughters were concerned. Livy wished Clara would give up on her dream of a singing career, but she was too wary of alienating her daughter to make those wishes known. Jean was a constant, daily worry;

the incidence of seizure had not abated, osteopathy notwithstanding, and Livy had finally resigned herself to the fact that her daughter's epilepsy would be a lifelong challenge. Sam Clemens helped her with Jean as best he could—"after a man's fashion," he would offer by way of an alibi. He wasn't a lot of help.

Clemens was also beginning to feel pangs of regret about the big public fight he had picked over the ugliness in the Philippines. He knew he was inviting enemies and chancing damage to his good name, but he couldn't seem to help himself. He was mainly sorry it put him in violation of his long-standing contract with his wife. Sam Clemens had made bold promises during his long and avid pursuit of Olivia Langdon more than thirty years earlier. He had assured Livy he would try for devout Christian living, for instance, and not simply as a matter of faith, which was easy enough to counterfeit, but by acts. He cut down on his drinking, his smoking, his swearing, and his disorderly conduct. "These reforms were calculated to make a man fractious & irritable," he wrote to a friend a few weeks before the wedding day, "but bless you she has a way of instituting them that swindles one into the belief that she is doing him a *favor* instead of curtailing his freedom & doing him a fatal damage."

None of the reforms had held entirely; controlling his volcanic temper was especially difficult, but his efforts were heroic. He had tried hard, for Livy's sake, to dam up his most sacrilegious and corrosive rivers of thought and to forgo any public pronouncement that would make him, as he put it, "comprehensively and uncompromisingly odious" to his reading public.

He had, for instance, stood down on the Philippines issue for most of the second half of 1901, had even bitten his tongue when the new president, who took such pride in shooting a fleeing enemy soldier in the back, started talking tough. In the aftermath of a bloody ambush of US soldiers on the island of Samar, Roosevelt had begun telling callers that he would expect his commanders there to use the "most stern measures to pacify" Samar and the rest of the Philippines. The president stayed the course of vigorous "pacification" throughout the archipelago even as the viciousness of America's three-year program of Benevolent Assimilation was getting a fresh airing in the newspapers early in 1902.

Clemens was riled by the news reports and by President Roosevelt's idiotic pronouncements about the Filipinos' unfitness for self-government. "What has taken us thirty generations to achieve," Theodore had lectured in his first annual message to the nation, "we cannot expect to have another race accomplish out of hand, especially when large portions of that race start very far behind the point which our ancestors had reached even thirty generations ago." Clemens might have been prodded by Roosevelt's ugliness and stupidity—clearly shared by a lot of his fellow citizens—but he managed to refrain from voicing his opinions in public. His most strident sermons about the unsalvageable mass of humanity and its *damnable* character he preached within the privacy of the home circle. "Coldly received" by Livy and the girls Clemens reported after one harangue. "It seemed best not to try to take up a collection."

The one thing he did do, alongside the other famous and distinguished members of the Anti-Imperialist League, was to put his name on a public petition asking the United States government to call an immediate truce in the Philippines and to invite the leaders of the Filipino independence movement in for a peace conference. This petition hit the doorstep of the US Senate on February 4, 1902, which happened to be the thirty-third anniversary of Sam and Livy's engagement. February 4, 1902, was also the beginning of a very trying few weeks for anybody with a continuing interest in American operations in the Philippines. The highest US civil authority in Manila, William Howard Taft, admitted in his third day of testimony before a special Senate committee that murder and torture had been a part of the American arsenal in the pacification of the Philippines and "that cruelties have been inflicted."

The US military officer who followed Taft in the witness chair elucidated the justifications for common US Army practices like burning out an entire village if anybody within had previously sheltered Filipino freedom fighters. "The destruction was as a punishment," the general explained.

"The punishment in that case would fall, not upon the men, who could go elsewhere, but mainly upon the women and little children," suggested one senator on the investigating panel.

"The women and children are part of the family, and where you wish to inflict a punishment you can punish the man probably worse in that way than in any other way."

"But is that within the ordinary rules of civilized warfare? Of course you could exterminate the family, which would be still worse punishment."

"These people are not civilized," the general answered.

"Then I understand you to say it is not civilized warfare?"

"No, I think not."

At this point a friendly Republican senator jumped in to provide the general with some much-needed support: "In order to carry on civilized warfare," said Charles Dietrich, "both sides have to engage in such warfare."

"Yes, sir; certainly," the general said. "That is the point."

The daily deluge of testimony went on for months and put Clemens in a hot rage, but he kept plugging his leaky dam, partly by reminding himself that there was no point in his picking another fight. The last one had not done a lick of good, he told himself. He had just warned a crusading newspaper editor not to make the mistake of adopting "the superstition that Moral Courage and a Hankering to Learn the Truth are ingredients in the human being's make-up."

"Those two ingredients," Clemens told him, "are on vacation, in our race, & have been from the start."

Then came the news of another in a long line of smug denials from Brigadier General Frederick Funston, the celebrated captor of Emilio Aguinaldo. Funston had been dancing around the many and varied accusations of war crimes leveled against him by his own troops over the previous two years; these included looting Catholic churches in the Philippines, prodding his men to murder, torture, and rape; and promoting the officers who did the dirty work. On February 22, 1902, Funston was back in the news to deny the accusation that men in his command had subjected more than a hundred Filipinos to the "water cure" and that many of the victims had been killed. The general claimed he had never been witness to this queer form of torture, but he seemed to delight in describing it. "The victim is bound and a canteen forced into his mouth," Funston stated.

> His head is thrown upward and back, and his nose grasped by the fingers of the torturer. Strangulation follows as a matter of course. When the victim is about suffocated the application is released and he is given a chance to talk on recovery or take another dose of it. The operation is brutal beyond a doubt, but hardly fatal.
>
> The charge which I have just refuted at the request of the War Department was most vague. It was made by "a soldier," and to the effect that he had "helped administer the water cure on 160 natives." That is the kind of rot a soldier is apt to write home when business is dull and he has three or four beers under his jacket to help his imagination.

In related news, the *New York Tribune* reported, General Funston, newly returned to the United States, was embarking on a triumphal little speaking tour wherein he would expound his capture of Aguinaldo, among other war topics. One of Funston's first stops would be at Clemens's own Lotos Club in New York.

The general's lip flapping—along with the promise of more to come—occasioned a gusher on that high hill overlooking the Hudson; Clemens could not hold this one back. He began another bitter essay that same day, titled "A Defence of General Funston." Clemens gave over pages to Funston's own description of his famous capture of Aguinaldo, then took aim at the extraordinary tactics the general had admitted to employing: dressing his own native troops in enemy uniforms, making believe they were marching in to reinforce Aguinaldo's own army, forging documents, concealing himself and other US officers in the guise of prisoners. "By the custom of war, all these things are innocent, none of them is blameworthy, all of them justifiable; none of them is new," Clemens scrawled out by hand, "all of them have been done before, although not by a Brigadier-General. But there is one detail which is new, absolutely new. It has never been resorted to before in any age of the world, in any country, among any people, savage or civilized."

Near the end of the ninety-mile march through the jungle toward the enemy camp, Funston had explained, he and most of his men were on the verge of collapse, unable to go on. They sent messages begging food from the Filipino freedom fighters, and Aguinaldo's men hiked eight miles into the jungle with sustenance for the men they assumed to be their brothers in arms. Of this episode, Clemens wrote:

> When a man is exhausted by hunger to the point where he is "too weak to move," he has a right to make supplication to his enemy to save his failing life; but if he takes so much as one taste of that food—which is holy, by the precept of all ages and all nations—*he is barred from lifting his hand against that enemy for that time.*
>
> It was left to a Brigadier-General of Volunteers in the American army to put shame upon a custom which even degraded Spanish friars had respected. *We promoted him for it.*

Clemens compared Funston unfavorably with McKinley's assassin: "Bad as he was, [the assassin] had not—dying of starvation—begged food of the President to strengthen his failing forces for his treacherous work."

He stopped there and pigeonholed the document with a sheaf of other loose pages containing his most recent rants about the war in the Philippines. What would its publication accomplish besides inviting more opprobrium from the other side and vexation for his innocent wife? Then, too, and in spite of himself, Sam Clemens had not entirely given up hope on the future of the human race.

What he did choose to send off that day instead of the Funston screed was a small and *most private* piece of evidence of his most hidden faith—an invitation to a young Frenchwoman who had written him a sweet and knowing fan letter. He asked her to become the fifth lifetime member of his secret society, the Juggernaut Club. "One of my Members is a Princess of a royal house, another the daughter of a village book-seller on the continent of Europe," he wrote to Helene Picard. "For the only qualification for Membership is intellect and the spirit of good will; other distinctions, hereditary or acquired, do not count."

He gave Jean a handwritten memo so that she could type up a copy of the club's constitution and bylaws to send to the new initiate. "*From 'Indian Lore'* (*Burnet.*) 'The good Juggernauth (or Juggernaut) is the only deity among the two million gods of India who has no preferences, no partialities, no prejudices, no resentments, & sets no man higher than another, nor lower. He is the common friend of the human race; in his presence, master & slave, prince & peasant, banker & beggar, stand upon one level; at his temple's threshold rank & caste dissolve away."

He closed his letter with answers to Miss Picard's most pressing questions. "My favorite [of my books]? It is 'Joan of Arc.' My next is 'Huckleberry Finn,' but the family's next is 'The Prince and the Pauper.' (Yes, you are right—I am a moralist in disguise; it gets me into heaps of trouble when I go thrashing around in political questions.)"

SAM WAS TRYING hard to want what Livy wanted, which was to have a house of their own by the time their lease ran out in the fall of 1902. The Clemens family was done with Hartford, Livy had declared. They would sell the house there and look for a new place nearer Clara's music and concert scene in New York; it would be their first permanent home in ten years. Sam first suggested they simply buy the property in Riverdale and live there, but Livy still insisted it was beyond their means. So he went full tilt into the adventure of securing her a proper house, roping in Henry Rogers's son-in-law, William Benjamin, who knew the market and the brokers up the Hudson in Tarrytown, where a man could get more for his money. Clemens also liked the idea of being neighbor to John D. Rockefeller. Benjamin rode the train to Tarrytown with Clemens on the first Tuesday in March and introduced him around.

Clemens's noble quest lasted a single day. "I am killed," he reported to Poultney Bigelow. "Examined 12 county seats from garret to cellar, and it ended my usefulness, and my strength. I struck."

He jumped instead at Henry Rogers's offer of a six-week Caribbean cruise on Roger's private yacht, which was a very handy way of excusing himself (only somewhat honorably) from the immediate demands of the family's house hunt. "Mrs. Clemens will continue the raid, along with the daughters," he wrote to Benjamin, "& when she has finished her pilgrimage she will know all about the houses between here & the pole, & in addition will know *which one* she wants—& *that's* a fortunate make of mind."

Clemens tried to keep his thoughts on the warm Caribbean days to come—he was packing extra plasmon in case any of his fellow travelers got seasick—but General Funston was all over the newspapers. Fearless Freddie was on the publicity attack, even at the Lotos Club, and Clemens was starting to take some of it personally. The general had accused the anti-imperialists of giving both aid and false hope to the enemy in the Philippines, and thus prolonging the war. The blood of American soldiers was on their hands, Funston told the gathering at the Lotos.

On the day before Clemens's departure for the Caribbean, the newspapers quoted long passages from another of Funston's recent speeches. "Two negro soldiers deserted our army and for a time served in the insurgent army," the general had told the civic fathers of Chicago. "They were caught and hanged. It would have been more of an act of justice had we hanged some of the people who signed the recent petition to Congress asking that we confer with the Filipino leaders in an effort to secure peace. In the one case two ignorant beings were executed, while in the other people more guilty than they and in possession of their senses were allowed to go free."

SAM CLEMENS LET it all pass for the present. He was happy to be sailing off into the West Indies in Henry Rogers's elegant and powerful yacht, the *Kanawha*; the traveling party of a half dozen was the same convivial set of comrades who had enjoyed a sea trip together the previous summer—including Mr. Rogers and Thomas Brackett Reed, the former Speaker of the House. They would loll and smoke while Rogers's big crew handled the sailing and the serving; the men would eat when and what they wanted, drink expensive scotch whiskey, recite favorite passages from the books they were reading, and josh like schoolboys.

Tom Reed could have been a useful guide to Sam Clemens—or the Prophet Samuel, as Reed jokingly called him. Reed was as embarrassed and angered as Clemens was by the American performance in the Philippines. "They were—these Filipinos—only a short time ago our wards to whom we owed sacred duties, duties we could not abandon in the face of a censorious world without soiling our Christian faith," Reed said in 1902. "Now they are 'niggers' who must be punished for defending themselves. This is the history of the world with perhaps a stronger dash of hypocrisy than usual to soothe our feelings." But this was only talk among friends for Reed. The former Speaker of the House of Representatives and almost presidential nominee had nothing to say in public these days. Reed had retired to private life and was piling up a fortune in attorney's fees while representing officials of Standard Oil and US Steel, among others. Reed had come to appreciate smooth water, and on a floating vacation such as this, he preferred poetry and poker to political talk.

Clemens and the boys had a restorative journey into the Caribbean Sea, in spite of the heat. And the sixty-six-year-old author was pleased to point out to these titans of industry and politics that it was *he* who was recognized and greeted as the hero in even the remotest little isle in the Bahamas. "I cannot *believe* I am actually looking at 'Mark Twain,'" a young black minister on Rum Cay had said, grabbing his hand. "I was just talking about you *this very morning*—why it's as if you are God-sent, sir."

The yacht party kept a loose schedule and made few calls on local officialdom. They sailed past the wreckage of the USS *Maine* ("like a brobdingnagian tarantula in his death squirm," Clemens wrote to Livy). They walked the Prado in Havana on Palm Sunday, ogling the multiethnic pageant of men, women, and children in their billowing finery. They sucked the sweet tang of fresh-picked oranges and grapefruits, glided in a glass-bottomed boat above coral reefs, and stopped for idylls at isolated beaches.

Clemens's only complaint was about the pace of the Caribbean mail service; letters from home chased the *Kanawha* but were always a port or two behind. Clemens had not been away from Livy this long since Susy's death, so he was desperate for news from home by the third week of the trip and missing his wife badly. He was also growing anxious to collect huzzahs for the ring he had instructed Clara to purchase to replace one Livy had recently lost. "It will cost several hundred dollars, & will come out of the article which you sent to the *North American Review* a day or two ago," he had written to Clara just before the yacht sailed from Miami, "—the rest of which money your mother will spend in her own way, together with such sums as shall result from the article on Washington, Funston & Co. which I mean to finish presently & send home for supervision & acceptance or damnation by the head of the house." As it happened, he simply had too much fun on the *Kanawha* to spoil it with work, and let "Funston & Co." sit untouched for the whole of the trip.

THE TRAVELING PARTY decided to cut the six weeks down to four, and Clemens was ready to be home when the captain pointed the *Kanawha* north at the beginning of April and ran her up the Atlantic Seaboard at speed. The travelers took a brief rest at Charleston, waved at Fort Sumter, stopped to coal the boat in Virginia, then to drop Tom Reed in Washington. They were passing the coast of Delaware when the first big storm of the trip blew in, like a sign of Sam Clemens's return to the American scene. Rain lashed the yacht, flying almost parallel to the water. The winds howled. Lightning flashed, and the *Kanawha* pitched and yawed on the rough seas. The captain managed to duck the boat in behind a breakwater, where at midnight the old men sat silent in their staterooms and watched the lightning show out on the horizon. There was very little sound for all the fury, save one roll of thunder, distant and mellow—almost calming.

The *Kanawha* docked at East Twenty-Third Street in Manhattan at five o'clock the next afternoon, April 9, 1902. Clemens could still move fast for his age (and conductors were known to hold the train for him from time to time), so he was on the 5:45 train for Riverdale, and the carriage delivered him to his door before the sun dipped down below the Palisades. There was big news, he discovered when he walked into the house. Livy had bought a property in Tarrytown—nineteen acres and a river view—for $45,000. The house itself was not big enough for the family, not yet anyway, but Livy was already working on the addition. She wanted Howells's architect son, John, to draw the plans and oversee the work. Livy had settled it all. News of the purchase was on the front page in the *New York World* that day.

Another report on that front page, datelined from the court-martial in Manila of a US military officer named Major Littleton W. T. Waller, was a tad more eye catching. The major's legal counsel was just then mounting a final defense against the charge that his client had executed without trial eleven Filipino civilians. The defense was straightforward and explosive: Waller was just following the orders of his commanding officer, Brigadier General Jacob Hurd Smith. The story in the *World* described Waller's testimony: "Major Waller said Smith instructed him to kill and burn; said that the more he killed and burned the better pleased he would be; that it was no time to take prisoners, and that he was to make Samar a howling wilderness. Major Waller said he asked Gen. Smith to define the age limit for killing and he replied, 'Everything over ten.'"

Three days after Clemens's return to Riverdale, Waller was acquitted.

THE WALLER VERDICT was handed down as the daily drip of ugly news from the Senate investigation into the Philippine war neared its fourth month, with no end in sight. Theodore Roosevelt decided it was best to step in and take hold of the Waller story before it got out of control. The president wanted it known that he was not proportionately delighted with the verdict, and he went on record as being opposed to war crimes. Roosevelt instructed his staff to make sure that his new directive to General Jacob Smith's commanding officer got into the hands of the reporters: "Great as the provocation has been in dealing with foes who habitually resort to treachery, murder and torture against our men, nothing can justify, or will be held to justify, the use of torture or inhuman conduct of any kind on the part of the American army." Theodore Roosevelt also made public his instructions to the War Department to bring charges against General Smith in a military court, and promised to review the case personally. Theodore thought this a wise move, politically speaking.

The new president was a natural in office—which is to say, he knew where politics separated from policy. As a matter of policy, Theodore remained committed to cracking Filipino heads until they cried uncle. On the day the president made public his pronouncement against "torture and inhuman conduct," for example, another US field general in the Philippines brought one province to heel by explicitly ordering his soldiers to destroy "humans, crops, food stores, domestic animals, houses and boats." Roosevelt instructed his secretary of war to send the general congratulations.

General Funston, meanwhile, was winding down his cross-country speaking tour, telling banqueters in San Francisco that the antiwar writers and editors "ought to be strung up" and bragging about all the Filipino "savages" he had personally executed in the war. "Bully for Waller!" he shouted, and "Hooray for Smith!" The crowds bullied and hurrahed in answer.

SAM CLEMENS COULD not let it be. He hunted up the Funston article he had set aside back in February and went to work. "*April 14.* I have been absent several weeks in the West Indies: I will now resume this Defence. . . . Is Funston to blame? I think not." The bulwark of the defense was a riff on Clemens's unpublished private philosophy, the one Livy had deemed unprintable: the Little General was just a man, Clemens argued, and unable to alter the low-down character God had visited on him. "[Funston] did not make his own disposition, It was born with him. It chose his ideals for him, he did not choose them," he wrote. "It took as naturally to moral slag as [George] Washington's took to moral gold, but only It was to blame, not Funston. . . . [His disposition] had a native predilection for unsavory conduct, but it would be in the last degree unfair to hold Funston to blame for the outcome of his infirmity; as clearly unfair as it would be to blame him because his conscience leaked out through one of his pores when he was little—a thing which he could not help."

"A DEFENCE OF General Funston" was still in proofs when Clara left on a four-month trip to Europe with a $1,000 letter of credit her father had procured. Clara insisted she was simply heeding her voice teacher's recommendation to spend time studying German and Italian, but the trip was also a grab for independence. Clara Clemens was already twenty-seven, and she could feel her chances for a career of her own withering at home. Livy was not happy that Clara was abandoning her, what with all the complications of the new house, and the inability to find a buyer for the Hartford place, which made Livy suddenly fretful about money. On top of it all, Mr. Clemens would not quit thrashing around about the *G-d d——d human race*.

Livy was doing her normal workaday duty of vetting her husband's outgoing letters when his acid pen finally cracked her estimable reserve of patience. "Youth darling, have you forgotten your promise to me?" she wrote to him.

You said that I was constantly in your mind & that you knew what I would like & you *would not* publish what I would disapprove.

I am absolutely wretched on account of your state of mind—your state of intellect. Why don't you let the better side of you work? Your present attitude will do more harm than good. You go too far, much too far, in all you say, & . . . people forget the cause for it & remember the hateful manner in which it was said.

Do darling change your mental attitude, *try to change it*. . . . You can if you will—if you wish to. Think of the side I know; the sweet dear, tender side—that I love so. Why not show this more to the world? Does it help the world to always rail at it? There is great & noble work being done, why not sometimes recognize that? Why dwell on the evil until those who live beside you are crushed to earth & you seem almost like a monomaniac. Oh I love you so & wish you would listen & take heed.

THE FUNSTON ARTICLE was out in May of 1902 and elicited minimal fireworks. There was almost no direct response, largely because the men running the show in the Philippines were impervious to public shaming. General Smith was not even bothering to make a forceful denial of his orders to Waller to burn and loot and kill every Filipino over the age of ten. He had a better defense at his own trial: he was responding to a savage attack on his own soldiers, and the enemy needed to be taught a lesson. As General Smith's attorney said in his closing argument,

> The army's magnificent services . . . have reflected nothing but glory upon our flag and our country.
>
> While the campaigns in the Philippines have not been conducted to meet the views of the sentimentalists and troublesome busybodies in the United States, they have been conducted on the lines which have reflected credit upon the valor, pluck, humanity, and kindness of American soldiers.

Any reader who might have expected a sharp retort from "Mark Twain" was disappointed. He had plenty of material tucked away and ready to go, but he kept it tucked away. "In order not to seem eccentric I have swung around now and joined the nation in the conviction that nothing can sully a flag," read one completed manuscript. "I was not properly reared, and had the illusion that a flag was a thing which must be sacredly guarded against shameful uses and unclean contacts lest it suffer pollution; and so when it was sent out to the Philippines to float over a wanton war and a robbing expedition I supposed it was polluted, and in an ignorant moment I said so. But I stand corrected. I concede and acknowledge that it was only the government that sent it on such an errand that was polluted."

EARLY ONE MORNING in the middle of May, Livy awakened in the dark with a start. Her heart was beating rapidly and she kept saying she *could not breathe*. She spent the rest of the night agitated and frightened, propped in a sitting position to try to catch air. Clemens called the osteopath to come the next morning, but Livy insisted on making the trip to his office. "She wouldn't allow him to come here," Clemens complained to Henry Rogers, "—double rates & the Hartford house has not sold."

They took a place in York Harbor, Maine, for the summer, and by the time the Clemens family (except for Clara, who was still in Europe) was ready to head north at the end of June, Livy appeared to have regained herself. Sam accepted Rogers's offer to sail them to Maine in the *Kanawha*, and thank God, because once on board, Jean had one of her big seizures and Livy was up for two long and difficult nights tending to her daughter. They had just settled in the cottage among the pines when Jean suffered her next fit—one of the most violent her parents had witnessed. Sam thought this one had nearly killed Livy.

Clemens walked over to his writing cottage every day and worked—nothing political—while Livy seemed to curl into herself. She was suddenly terrorized by any downhill run in a carriage and begged off the family's driving outings. Her gout was flaring; her back pain, worse than ever. She could not seem to stop her racing heart, and the medicines the doctors gave her only made it worse. "I am alarmed about [Livy], & she suspects it, tho I lie the best I can in the circumstances, & so does the doctor," Sam wrote to Rogers. "In order to be able to breathe, she had to sit upright in bed last night from 9 o'clock almost all the time until 4 this morning. This is becoming a nightly experience."

GENERAL JACOB HURD Smith, US Army, retired, was due to arrive at his hometown of Portsmouth, New Hampshire, a few railroad stops south of York Harbor, on August 11, 1902. The general had been found guilty of "conduct to the prejudice of good order and military discipline," which was an umbrella charge covering offenses like drunkenness, or petty theft, or absence from drill. The court advised President Theodore Roosevelt to show leniency in sentencing. General Smith had been engaged in a "desperate struggle" with a "cruel and savage foe," the military judges noted, and as for his order to his troops to kill children, "the accused did not mean everything that his unexplained language implied."

The president followed the recommendation of the military court and ordered sixty-two-year-old General Jacob Smith struck from the active duty list, but with a pat on the back on the way out the door. "General Smith has behind him a long career distinguished for gallantry and on the whole for good conduct," Roosevelt had said in his sentencing statement. "Taken in full, his work has been such as to reflect credit upon the American army and therefore upon the nation."

When the retired general arrived at the station in Portsmouth that warm summer evening, ten thousand of his fellow citizens were waiting to greet him. *Hooray for Smith! Hooray for Smith!* An impromptu honor guard demanded a few words from the general, who was happy to oblige. "There are two beacons of light by which, if a man guide his life, he cannot fail to succeed—God and country," said the man who ordered the killing of eleven-year-old boys. "All my life these two have been my guiding stars. If a man devote himself to them, he cannot fail eventually to receive the approbation of his countrymen, even though at times the way may seem long and the path dark." HOORAY FOR SMITH!

Sam Clemens had no answer for that.

LIVY WOKE AT seven the next morning unable to breathe, her heart racing. She thought she has dying, and her husband was having a hard time convincing either of them otherwise. He summoned doctors, who worked on her until noon, when the acute danger seemed to have passed. Clara arrived home from Europe that night, but her return did little to revive her mother. Livy begged Sam to summon her sister, Sue Crane. Livy "says the rest of us are not valuable comforters," he told Sue. "The truth is, she won't *let* us be."

Clemens flailed. He wrote a nasty letter to Western Union about its lousy service. He accused Frederick Funston of forcing a public library in Denver (the Little General's new residence) to ban *Huckleberry Finn* as immoral: "If Satan's morals and Funston's are preferable to Huck's, let Huck's take a back seat; they can stand any ordinary competition, but not a combination like that." Clemens brought a tribe of doctors to Livy's bedside and then argued with them all or complained about them to friends. "It has been one continual guess, guess, guess, change, change, change, from one incompetent drug to another, & from one indigestible food to another," he wrote to Henry Rogers. "It seems a stupid idea to keep a student 4 years in medical college to merely learn how to guess—& guess wrong." He dosed his wife with plasmon until she doubled over with gas pains.

He wrote to his business agent in Hartford, telling him to sell the house—*now*!—for whatever they could get, "so that I can tell Mrs. Clemens that that burden upon her spirits is gone. She secretly reproaches herself for buying a new house before selling the old one," Clemens explained. He begged his landlord in Riverdale to extend their lease until the following June so that Livy could live in comfort on their return.

Livy did not get out of bed for forty-five straight days. There were days when she didn't even *sit up*. When Clemens called in his favorite osteopath, the treatment nearly killed Livy. Sam managed to find a specialist in Boston, and when this new doctor said there was no physical reason why his wife should not make a full recovery, Clemens installed him as the undisputed head of the medical team. A full-time trained nurse was hired, and then Clara, feeling guilty, pushed her father aside and took charge. "My trip to Paris was not done to gratify my thirst for study but also to overcome that weakness (which has possessed me for six years) of fearing to turn my back on the family for any length of time," Clara confessed to a friend. "I think my duty could not be more clearly pointed out to me than it has been and if it is not too late I shall be thankful that the question has been decided for me once & for all. My mother or art? The *sacrifices* will be made for the former."

The specialist from Boston announced that the patient required *absolute* calm and quiet—a single nurse at a time was allowed in Livy's bedroom, and no one else. Livy agreed it was for the best, and the Clemens patriarch, acknowledged instigator of much of the household's emotional drama, was ordered to go live next door. "[The doctor] banished us all," Sam Clemens wrote to his cousin, "—me out of the house entirely."

CHAPTER THIRTY-EIGHT

And Look Where We Are Now

Sam Clemens was in his best bib and tucker when he arrived that evening, November 28, 1902, at the most splendid private clubhouse in all New York, at the corner of Sixtieth Street and Fifth Avenue. Henry Rogers was at his side as Clemens, with his too-big head tilted slightly atop his hunched and boyishly narrow shoulders, stole in beneath a Palladian archway and entered into a new temple of American wealth—the Metropolitan Club. He had turned down almost every other invitation that came across the transom since the family's return to Riverdale from Maine. "I can't endure the buzz & confusion of a long dinner—it exhausts me like physical labor," he wrote. But this was an invitation he had not been able to refuse, because he, Samuel Langhorne Clemens, was to be the guest of honor. The event was his sixty-seventh birthday dinner, hosted by the president of Harper & Brothers, George Harvey, who was trying to induce Clemens to sign an exclusive lifetime contract with his publishing firm. Harvey had managed to secure the use of the Metropolitan through the good offices of the businessman who had saved Harper & Brothers a few years earlier—the most powerful financial force in the country, if not the world, J. Pierpont Morgan.

The Metropolitan Club, like US Steel, was among J. Pierpont's many fabulous new creations. Morgan had not had any real *need* for this club, and as the story around town went, it would not have existed at all except that the exclusive Union Club had blocked the banker king's effort to secure membership for a railroad-president friend of his ten years earlier. Morgan, mightily offended, had gathered a powerful group of industrialists and pols, and together they purchased a lot near the southeast corner of Central Park for their rump club. "Build a club fit for a gentleman!" Morgan told the society architect and art plunderer Stanford White. "Damn the expense."

White did what he did best, creating a facsimile collage of Old World masterpieces. The exterior of the four-story mansion (with a hundred feet of frontage on Fifth Avenue) was modeled on the Palazzo Pandolfini, a fifteenth-century pile redesigned by the painter Raphael for his Florentine patrons around 1514. In the West Lounge of the club, the nation's most energetic money chasers did a hushed daily business under the modern American version of the Sistine Chapel's ceiling: painted on one panel was the goddess of fortune, and on another the god of cheats and thieves.

SAM CLEMENS UNDERSTOOD he was entering the Metropolitan on a day pass; owning a few hundred shares in Union Pacific and US Steel didn't exactly make him a commercial titan. But he was about to enter his sixty-eighth year, which put him on the cusp of realizing the spectacular fortune the fortune-teller Cheiro had foretold. And he had put another $25,000 into the American Plasmon Company just a few weeks earlier. Might finally be his big jackpot.

America's most famous author looked a little fragile that evening, and the cavernous reception hall at the Metropolitan Club didn't help. Harvey had ordered covers for about fifty-two that night, so the crowd did not fill the space. The first murmurs of the predinner chat echoed faintly off thousands of tons of dark-veined marble and off the white-and-burgundy coffered ceiling forty-five feet above.

Many of the evening's celebrants were authors who were part of Harper's stable, from the talented young novelist Booth Tarkington to the corporate lawyer who had just written a book on the joy of autograph collecting. This was all great publicity for them: they would have their names in the newspapers the next day alongside "Mark Twain." Clemens was happy to help. He remembered what it was to be young and on the make, and he was naturally generous to up-and-comers. Each man in attendance found waiting for him on his seat a memento of the evening: a letter-size gilt-edged leather folder with his own name embossed on the front. Inside, etched on an electrotype plate, was a self-portrait of the honored guest, and beneath it a personalized inscription. "For financial advice apply without diffidence to Mark Twain," Clemens wrote to J. Pierpont Morgan. To Harper's young humorist du jour, Twain had offered some friendly advice: "To John Kendrick Bangs. It is more convenient to be rich than good."

The crowd included men of import and national renown, including Senator Chauncey Depew; Wayne MacVeagh, the former attorney general of the United States who had just helped negotiate a truce in the dangerous labor strikes in the anthracite coal region; the industrialist August Belmont Jr.; and W. B. Leeds, whose tinplate company was now a wholly owned subsidiary of Morgan's US Steel. The tin plate king's personal worth was estimated at $30 million. There were bank presidents, trustees of New York's Metropolitan Museum of Art, officers of Standard Oil.

A few men at the club that night—Joe Twichell, for instance—had been invited at Clemens's insistence, for no reason other than friendship. And then there was the handful of guests who were both men of national standing and men of intense personal feeling for the guest of honor: William Dean Howells and Henry Rogers, of course, and Tom Reed. The man whose attendance most pleased Clemens was the secretary of state, John Hay. Hay's presence, for Clemens, gave the dinner the warm glow of reunion. They had kept up through mutual friends and the occasional letter, but they had not really been together for years.

They were both so old now. It had been more than thirty years since Sam Clemens and John Hay—along with Bret Harte—had held forth to their distinguished elders at Horace Greeley's birthday celebration just a few blocks down on Fifty-Seventh Street. Old Man Greeley, who had been younger that night than Clemens and Hay were now, was long dead. Harte was dead, too, more than six months now, but the other two stood yet. Clemens's hair was just as ungovernable as it had been at Greeley's town house in 1872, but its fire of red had burned away. Hay was thicker through the middle, and his boyish face was wrinkled and masked with a heavy beard and mustache. But Clemens could see how his old friend's mouth still pulled down a touch at the corners, with the hint of melancholy. Hay's eyes were bright and alive as always and betrayed that "shade of pride," as someone once wrote of him, that deflected unwanted intimacy. Clemens could imagine how hard Hay's job must be, what with that wild man Roosevelt riding him. Clemens had also heard from their friends that Hay was frankly admitting that he was dying, and not joking around when he said it, which was why Clemens had been so pleased when George Harvey showed him Hay's note of acceptance to "Mark Twain's" birthday party.

"Dear Mr. Harvey," he had written in his own hand. "I never leave Washington and I never dine out. But all rules are subject to *force majeure*, and it is out of my power to decline your invitation to celebrate my old friend Clemens' birthday. But you will be merciful at my age and infirmities and not ask me to speak. Otherwise you would convert what I look forward to as a great pleasure into a vista of torment. John Hay"

Harvey had seated the secretary of state next to Clemens at the dinner, but there would be many speeches and little chance for the two to catch up. They did have a few minutes before the crowd moved into the dining arena, and they fell into talk about days gone by. They reminded each other about a conversation they had had when they were just passing the age of forty. Hay had prophesied back then, with his accustomed matter-of-fact lightness of touch, that life would be a tragedy the rest of the way; Clemens had vigorously refuted the assertion at the time.

Care to testify again? Hay asked that night at the Metropolitan Club, and Clemens had to admit the wisdom of Hay's pronouncement.

"I counted my graves," he would write of the moment, "and there was nothing for me to say."

THE EVENING PROCEEDED at an unhurried pace, with tributes from Depew, Howells, Reed, MacVeagh, and Harvey. Every time Clemens rose to protest a statement from the dais, somebody pulled him back into his seat. It was after midnight when "Mark Twain" finally stood to speak the final piece. "It is a proud thing to me, indeed, to see such a distinguished company gather here on such an occasion as this, when there is no foreign prince to be feted—when you have come here not to do honor to hereditary privilege and ancient lineage, but to do reverence to mere moral excellence and elemental veracity."

He bounced along like this, twitting his high and mighty friends: "I knew Chauncey before he could walk straight, and had learned to tell the truth. . . . Tom Reed has a good heart, and he has a good intellect, but he hasn't any judgment . . . and St. Clair McKelway and me from Missouri, and we are doing what we can to build up New York a little bit—to elevate it." And then finally he turned to John Hay. He paused. There were a few in the audience who held their breath for a moment and wondered whether Sam Clemens might unleash on the American secretary of state a sharp little tirade against the country's recent foreign entanglements. St. Clair McKelway, for one, had seen him do that sort of thing in the recent past. But it was the long-ago past that Sam Clemens was thinking about that night. He and the secretary of state shared a history.

John Hay was the *one person* among all those in the audience at the Metropolitan Club that night who understood the unlikelihood of Sam Clemens's emergence from the Mississippi River mud, understood the tremendous psychic distance he had traveled in his life, and understood the gnawing feeling in the gut that whatever he made of himself, it would not be *enough.* Here were two men, old men now, nearing seventy, who were still at it, still stoking the fire that had propelled them since boyhood, still trying to measure *up*.

"Look at John Hay and me," Clemens said.

> Consider the ladder which he has climbed, the illustrious vocations he has served; . . . he has in all those vocations acquitted himself with high credit and honor to his country and to the mother that bore him. Scholar, soldier, diplomat, poet, historian—now, see where we are. He is Secretary of State and I am a gentleman. It could not happen in any other country.
>
> Our institutions give men the positions that of right belong to them

through merit; all you men have won your places, not by heredities, and not by family influence or extraneous help, but by the natural gifts God gave you at your birth, made effective by your own energies; this is the country to live in.

Clemens could have closed there, but he did not. There was one final person he wished to acknowledge—"the invisible guest"—and he started talking about things few men in 1902 were comfortable revealing in public.

A part of me is present; the larger part, the better part, is yonder at home; that is my wife, and she has a good many personal friends here . . . and I think it quite appropriate that I should speak of her. I knew her for the first time just in the same year that I first knew John Hay and Tom Reed and Mr. Twichell—and she has been the best friend I have ever had, and that is saying a good deal; she has reared me, she and Twichell together—and what I am I owe to them. . . .

I wish I could return thanks in proper measure to you, gentlemen, who have spoken and violated your feelings to pay me compliments; some were merited and some you overlooked. . . . And now, my wife and I, out of our single heart, return to you our deepest and most grateful thanks, and—yesterday was her birthday.

HE WANTED so badly to tell Livy about his big night. John Hay had been there—*for him*. But Clemens, by doctor's orders, was still not permitted to see his wife, even for a moment. The last time he had got a glimpse of her was in the private railroad car he had hired for the long trip back from Maine. "She was only a shadow . . . & could hardly raise herself in bed," he explained before the birthday dinner. "Clara reveals to me she is still frailer now & weaker." It had been three months since he had been in his wife's presence, and the medical honchos refused to promise him a visit anytime soon. So he sent her a letter a few days after, like a schoolboy with a prize to show.

I must say a word about my birthday banquet. It was very grand & flatters one, & finely successful. . . . All through the various speeches there had been fine bursts of applausive approval; but it was the last name & the last praise (yours) uttered that night that brought the *mighty* burst. . . .

Howells said, "It's the best speech you've ever made"—that, or something like it—"& it was splendid to close, like that, with Mrs. Clemens." He, & John Hay, being closest to me, began it, & the others flocked by & they all said it—& many had to work their way half way round the great

> room to say it, but they were *bound* to say it. It would have shriveled Clara with jealousy. I'm a-loving you with all my might, Youth.

LIVY DID NOT improve in December, and Sam remained in exile. The doctors did grant him the privilege of sending little notes into her room—one in the morning, one before bed.

> Don't know the date or day. But anyway, it is a soft and pensive foggy morning, Livy darling, and the naked tree branches are tear-beaded, and Nature has the look of trying to keep from breaking down and sobbing, poor old thing. Good morning, dear heart, I love you dearly. Y.

Jean had her first seizure in four months, then slipped on the ice, which caused two seizures in quick succession; a few days before Christmas, she came down with an illness the doctors were unable to diagnose. Her fever raged—some afternoons her body temperature topped 104. The doctors hemmed and hawed and after a week they finally decided it was pneumonia; they could not assure Clemens that his youngest daughter would live. Sam and Clara made a pact to keep Jean's condition hidden from Livy, no matter what. "Clara & I are face to face with a tremendous emergency," Clemens wrote to Howells in the last week of 1902.

William Dean Howells was sympathetic to his friend's domestic woe, so he was not exactly *pushing*, but he wished Clemens would step a little more forcefully into the ongoing national debate about the Philippines. There were stories that the American people needed to hear, and they would listen if "Mark Twain" was telling them. Others from the Anti-Imperialist League were sending Clemens information about the "water cure" torture murders: one victim was a Spanish priest; another was an American private who ran afoul of his platoon mates. Clemens was torn. He had reasons to keep quiet. The chief one was "to keep from breaking my wife's heart, whose contentment I value above the salvation of the human race," he had explained in a letter written on Livy's birthday. "This is a confession that in building a wall across my Nile and damming my feelings and opinions behind it, and trying to caulk the leaks, I am not actuated by principle, but something much stronger—sentiment."

He was still debating the wisdom of another Philippines article when he received a letter from the Anti-Imperialist League the day after New Year's, 1903: the group was having terrible difficulties meeting its fund-raising goal and needed his help. "Hoping you can secure some assistance," was the closing line.

They wanted him to beg people for money. That cut it.

"At some cost in public approval (& consequently in money)," he responded,

> I contributed a Satanic magazine article which got the missionaries in my hair—also some politicians—& I was on the very point of repeating that sacrifice when your letter came, offering me another hod of bricks to carry. . . . I contributed that article, knowing quite well what I was going to catch. Must I pass the hat *besides*? . . .
>
> We have 5000 members? It is as many as that, I suppose. And can't raise the $2500 you need? What enthusiasm! . . . Let us go out of the Anti-Imperialist business & start a morgue; we have the material. . . .
>
> Now what is our League *for*? It has but one purpose; it has but one function; and that is, to stir up the nation in our holy cause. Why, by your own showing we can't even stir ourselves up. . . .
>
> But never mind, let it go. The League had an elegant chance & has gone to sleep over it.

He would not be contributing any money. He was out of the political-prophet business; the cost was too great. And the return was apparently nil.

JEAN SURVIVED PNEUMONIA, and at the beginning of January, Sam was allowed to start making fairly regular daily visits to Livy's sickroom, where he found his wife was still pale, bone weary, and *nervous*. The medical professionals warned him not to talk too much, but what exactly was *too* much?

Livy remained unable to rise from her bed all that winter, and there were days when the doctors thought it best for her husband to stay away. He sent in his notes morning and night, whether or not he was allowed his visits.

> Wedding-day Anniversary. It's a long time ago, my darling, but the 33 years have been richly profitable to us, through love—a love which has grown, not diminished, and is worth more each year than it was the year before. And so it will be always, dearest old Sweetheart of my youth. Good night, and sleep well.

> Feb 4. . . . Good morning sweetheart, it is bright & beautiful—& I love you most deeply.

> Feb 27—pm. . . . The day is done, it is time for reading, smoking, reflection, sleep—with you for text & undertone, dear sweetheart, whom I love—& so, with a kiss, & another, & others, beside, Good night & pleasant dreams. Y

Chapter Thirty-Nine

I Could Not Resign Now If I Wanted To

He passed the first days of July 1903 in splendid idleness in America's most splendid summer colony. "I am convinced of one thing which I always doubted," John Hay wrote to his wife. "You can be perfectly quiet in Newport if you want to be." It did take some effort. Mrs. Henry Clews was anxious to host a dinner in honor of the secretary of state, and so was Mrs. Vanderbilt, and so was Senator Wolcott. John Hay declined as politely as possible, though Mrs. Vanderbilt remained insistent. Most of Hay's time was spent in the simple contentment of being the guest of his daughter Helen and her new husband, Payne Whitney, in the big house the couple had rented from Harry and Daisy White. He ventured out on occasion for strolls along the cliffs to ogle the grand residential palaces that stood in stately remove above the crashing Atlantic, or downtown to post letters, or to the harbor to inspect Payne's new thirty-foot racing yacht.

The real reason for this visit, aside from a needed break from the grind of office, was to spend time with his first grandchild, Joan, who was just five months old. "She continues as sweet as honey, coos and kicks and laughs, not always, but often enough to appreciate," wrote the happy new grandpapa, who could not help worrying about the red rash on the baby's leg, occasioned by a recent vaccination. Payne pulled out his camera one day, ordered his father-in-law to the front steps, put Joan in the old man's lap, and snapped away while the baby broke into gleeful peals of laughter.

Hay did have to take a break from the family fun one morning, in order to fashion a small note to calm the president, who was making ominous noises about backing out of a tribunal Hay had set up with Britain to determine once and for all the disputed boundary line in Alaska. Hay had been dealing with Great Britain over Alaska's boundaries and its fur seals for more than six years now and wasn't keen to have Theodore muck it up just as a happy conclusion appeared within reach. Roosevelt had pronounced recent British efforts to delay the conference unacceptable and sent word to one of his handpicked American commissioners, Henry Cabot Lodge, that he was about ready to scotch the negotiations and run the boundary line to suit his own sense of justice. Theodore had a very definite sense of the justice of this matter. He had already warned the British military attaché in Washington that he was prepared to be "very disagreeable" and ready to send US soldiers to the Klondike to prove the point. Hardheaded Cabot, meanwhile, would not stop goading the president "with querulous complaints of the [State] Department being too easy with England," Hay complained to Harry White, "when the Lord knows we have been rigorous to the point of discourtesy."

"Dear Theodore," Hay wrote on July 2, begging him to stand down. "I do not think [the British] are acting in bad faith. They are availing themselves of every possible pretext the treaty gives them of demanding more time to patch up their deplorably weak case.... They are amazed at the strength of our case & the promptness with which it was made ready, and are trying to spar for wind. I do not think any threats are at this time advisable or needful. We shall be as hard on them as is decent and perhaps more so." Once Hay had dialed that presidential boil back to a low simmer, the press of international affairs melted into the background. Baby Joan was a welcome diversion in Newport that week—perhaps they should go downtown and buy her a sun hat!

By the fifth day of his visit, Independence Day, the secretary of state's only anxiety was for his daughter Alice, who was home with her new husband in western New York, attended by her mother, and due to give birth any day to the second Hay grandchild. The Newport clan was expecting a telegram of good news from the James Wadsworth Jr. household at any moment. John Hay was a satisfied man just then, physically stronger than he had been in years, and comforted by thoughts of the security his family was sure to enjoy for generations to come. Hay could claim little credit for this happy circumstance, but he was nonetheless pleased that his children and grandchildren would never have to worry about money.

Helen was the most comfortably swaddled of the Hay children. Her husband's bachelor uncle, the former Standard Oil treasurer Oliver Hazard Payne, had recently made his nephew the chief inheritor of his fortune, which would mean something near $100 million to the couple. Uncle Oliver had also, on his own dime, hired the architect Stanford White to build the Whitneys a mansion on upper Fifth Avenue in New York. The personal fortune of Hay's two remaining children might pale by comparison, but John and Clara's estate was hardly piddling. "There will be enough for a dearest living for the children," Hay could tell himself.

"I have reached my grand climacteric with no serious illness, no material bad luck," he had written to his brother-in-law. "My dear Del is safe, with a beloved memory and a bright young fame. The girls are well settled, with excellent men, fellows of heart and conscience. Clarence promises an honorable and tranquil life."

He was particularly pleased that his bequeathal to his progeny was as much about his own good name as it was about cash and property. Only six men in the history of the United States of America had served as secretary of state as long as had John Milton Hay; three of them had gone on to be president. Hay had run the ship with a steady hand, too, even as the undermanned State Department made its way out into uncharted waters. China was still intact and open for business to all comers, and Hay had managed to help slow Russia's move to take Manchuria for its own; he had dissuaded the kaiser from making a foolish land grab in Venezuela before Theodore seized the chance to open fire with one of his new battleships in defense of the Monroe Doctrine; the Alaska boundary (and the old fur seal extinction problem with it) seemed about to be settled in favor of the United States; latest reports out of Colombia were that the Congress there was ready to ratify the recently signed Hay-Herrán Treaty, which made way for the interoceanic canal through Colombia's Departamento de Panamá—a canal to be built, owned, militarized, and controlled by the United States government.

Hay was also personally funding the construction of a terra-cotta-faced apartment building that promised to add nine stories of Old World elegance and gravity to downtown Washington. Newspapers there were already rhapsodizing about the convenient carriage access provided by the central court and the "French renaissance" decorations. Helen and Alice would each have one of the ninety-three suites for the next winter season; Senator Dietrich had taken apartments there, and William Randolph Hearst an entire floor. The newly finished portrait of John Hay by John Singer Sargent, meanwhile, was about to be hung in the Hay family mansion on Lafayette Square. Henry Adams had been aghast at the streak of meanness Sargent brought forward in his picture of John Hay. Hay had joked with Adams that it was a good likeness, showing "only just the ornery bourgeois and average cad I am," but he was pleased by the steely personal resolve the painter had recognized and memorialized. "I think it is very good," Hay had told Helen when he first saw it. "It was an odd thought that the most of my reputation in after years will depend on this picture."

There was nothing more John Hay need do in July of 1903, nothing more he need prove. So he idled in the Newport heat, perfectly at ease, and awaited news of the second addition to the newest generation, content in the knowledge that he could hand down to his two grandchildren, and all those who came afterward, a family legacy worthy of pride. John Hay had met the long-ago challenge of his youth; he had made his mark on the world.

THE TELEGRAM ARRIVED that Saturday morning, the Fourth of July, just after Hay returned from another walk along the cliffs. The message did not bring the joyful family news Hay was expecting from the Wadsworth house in western New York; the telegram had originated at Sagamore Hill, in Oyster Bay, Long Island—the Summer White House. President Roosevelt wanted John Hay at his country residence in three days; there were things he needed to discuss with his secretary of state. Theodore had too much time on his hands, Hay figured, and just wanted him there to watch him grind his axes. The president would be on again about the Alaska tribunal and would probably try to reopen the question of sending to the czar a petition signed by thousands of American citizens condemning a recent massacre of Jewish citizens in Russia.

This summons would cost Hay two days of rest in Newport, and if things went as they usually did at these impromptu conferences, he would probably be forced to stay the night at Theodore's country estate. "As if he had not already upset my plans sufficiently this week," Hay complained in a letter to Clara. "When McKinley sent for me he gave me all his time till we got through; but I always find T.R. engaged with a dozen other people, and it is an hour's wait and a minute's talk—and a certainty that there was no necessity of my coming at all. Destroy this mutinous and disloyal letter as soon as you have read it."

The summons to Oyster Bay, once it became known to the public, did the further mischief of fanning the gossip already smoldering among the newspaper boys. Reporters in Newport even started bracing poor Payne about it. *Is it true the secretary is resigning? Aren't Secretary Hay and President Roosevelt at odds over the Russian massacre petition? Is he asked to Oyster Bay for his dismissal?*

HAY WAS MUCH buoyed by the message the president's valet handed him as he got off the train in Oyster Bay on Tuesday morning: Alice's baby had arrived, another girl, Evelyn Wadsworth. Hay was sure there would be a crowd at Sagamore Hill to help him celebrate. There were two senators in Hay's railcar to Long Island, and one of Theodore's favorite young poets was on his way. Senator Mark Hanna was scheduled to sail into Oyster Bay that afternoon on the private yacht of J. P. Morgan's partner in the new international shipping trust. Hanna's arrival added a spark of intrigue, from the newsmen's distant vantage anyway, and an unwanted complication for Hay. It was common knowledge that Hanna believed Theodore unfit for the presidency, and the *Sun*, whose editors had begun to get the idea that Theodore was not sufficiently appreciative of the nation's capitalists, was roiling the political waters now that the Republican nominating convention was less than a year away. "Somehow the Republicans who surrounded Senator Hanna at the Waldorf were recalling the services that Secretary Hay had performed for this Government in all the trials and tribulations of the last few years, and were speaking highly of his abilities and his popularity with the people of the United States," appeared on the front page, above the fold, in that morning's edition of the *Sun*. "Mr. Hay was one of the right-hand men of Abraham Lincoln." By the afternoon of Hay's arrival in Oyster Bay, other papers had picked up the story: "It is represented that the friends of Mr. Hanna in New York show a disposition to groom John Hay for the presidency."

The stories pointed out that the secretary of state was scrupulously loyal and unlikely to maneuver against his boss, but Hay knew politicians were a paranoid lot, and Theodore was more paranoid than most.

Theodore Roosevelt hosted a long luncheon for all the guests that day (at which Senator Hanna proposed a toast to the health of baby Evelyn), so Hay's meeting with the president was put off until later in the day. But when the guests finally scattered that afternoon, an old friend of Theodore's from Harvard appeared in the doorway. "Will you excuse me till I play a game of tennis with Winty Chanler," Roosevelt asked Hay. "I have had no exercise all day." Hay was disappointed but not surprised at the president's insistence on physical activity. He had recently taken to calling Theodore by a mock Indian name: Young Man Afraid of His Waistband.

Hay took a long walk across a few of Roosevelt's ninety-five acres of woods, marsh, and bay front. The property reminded him of his own estate in New Hampshire, where he would soon be, which calmed him greatly. Hay had been telling himself for years now that he was *not* an inmate of Theodore's asylum, that he could leave the job anytime he wanted, but the presidential talk, inane as it was, meant his leaving anytime soon would open a whole new inning of unwanted questions—like whether he would be challenging Roosevelt for the presidency—and was probably out of the question. Roosevelt certainly wasn't asking for his resignation, and Hay had always told Theodore he served at his pleasure. The president had lately made his pleasure known to his secretary of state. "I wonder if you realize how thankful I am to you for having stayed with me," Roosevelt had written Hay a few months earlier. "I owe you a great debt, old man."

Theodore evaded his conference with Hay until after dinner, and the two men stayed up well after dark talking over Alaska and Russia. Hay was direct on both points. It was best to be patient on the Alaska boundary question; justice was on the US side and against Canada's ridiculous claim. The British judge on the tribunal would have to see that and rule against his Canadian brethren, and even if the lord did not admit it in his decision, Roosevelt was no worse off than before. He could still run his boundary line as he saw it and defend it to the world.

The president agreed! It sounded bully.

As far as the Russia petition went, Hay said, a formal protest would only get the czar's back up when the United States and Great Britain were still trying to crowbar his army out of Manchuria. "What possible advantage would it be to the United States, and what possible advantage to the Jews of Russia, if we should make protest against these fiendish cruelties and be told that it was none of our business?" Hay had already told Theodore. Ugly as it was, no American citizens or property had been involved in the massacre at Kishinev, so it really was none of their business. How would the US government react if the Russian people stood up and formally denounced the more or less weekly practice of lynching black men in the United States?

The president agreed again! But it was late by the time Theodore finished agreeing, and Hay was forced to stay over at Sagamore Hill.

By the time he got back home to Washington the next night, changed into a more comfortable suit of clothes, and sat down to write to Clara, John Hay was feeling considerably more charitable toward Theodore. "The President was so cordial and hospitable that I felt ashamed of any surly crossness at having to go there," he wrote. But this letter to Clara turned out to be a difficult one to finish. Newspaper reporters came banging at John Hay's front door five different times in two hours. They all wanted to know whether he had resigned or was planning to. Hay told them the same thing he had been saying all along. The subject of his leaving had never come up. He had no plans to step down. He and the president, Hay insisted, "agree on all points of foreign policy."

"I could not resign now if I wanted to," Hay wrote to his wife after the reporters had left him in peace, "—I have denied it so emphatically."

HAY PLANNED TO stay at his desk in Washington for a week only before heading off for two months of solitude at the Fells. He had a new first assistant secretary, Francis B. Loomis, who could actually carry his weight, and there was always Adee. So as long as Theodore didn't husband any new and unexpected bees in his presidential bonnet, Hay could trust the department to run smoothly. The Alaska boundary tribunal was not meeting until the fall; things were quiet in China; the Colombian Congress in Bogotá had the canal treaty under consideration. The Russian government was even promising to punish the perpetrators of the massacre of the Jews in Kishinev, confirming in Hay's own mind the wisdom of not publicly shaming the czar.

Hay shipped his trunks off to New Hampshire as planned and sent ahead a few little treats of his trade—honey from the US consul in Athens, and tea leaves plucked from a monastery garden by one of the Asian consuls. On his way out of his office, Hay posted the president a last note. "I had an hour with [Colombian chargé d'affaires] Herrán yesterday," Hay wrote. "He seems to think there is a fairly good chance of the treaty passing [in the Colombian legislature] without amendment. He has most earnestly urged that course upon the Government, telling them that *any* amendment will imperil the life of the treaty when it returns here. From every other quarter of the sky things look quiet and peaceful."

THE CANAL TREATY with Colombia started to fall apart a month later, while Hay was in New Hampshire. This did not bode well for Hay's near future. The treaty might be an officious and ridiculous document from the Colombian point of view, but it was Theodore's pet. The president had chosen the Department of Panama, in Colombia, as the best location for the canal. The Nicaraguan route, he had decided, would be a much more costly and difficult engineering project than the Panama route, in part because there was already a forty-seven-mile railroad linking the two oceans in Panama. Roosevelt had persuaded the French company that had tried for more than twenty years—and failed—to build a canal in Panama to sell its rights and assets (including that railroad) for $40 million, which was a third of the original asking price. He had also instructed Hay to force a favorable treaty down the throat of the Colombian government. "The great bit of work of my administration, and from the material and constructive standpoint one of the greatest bits of work that the twentieth century will see, is the Isthmian Canal," he had told Hay back in 1902. "In the negotiations to start this straight I must trust you and [Attorney General Philander Chase] Knox. I hope you will take personal direction."

The first of Hay's Colombian negotiating partners had been scandalized by Roosevelt's demands: the US president was willing to pay Colombia only a quarter of what he was paying the French stockholders for their canal concession, and an annuity so meager it did not even make up for the revenue they were going to lose from the demise of the railroad. Roosevelt also expected Colombia to cede absolute sovereignty in the canal zone to the United States—and without a whimper. When Colombia's diplomatic representative in Washington, José Vicente Concha, realized that the president was not requesting these terms but dictating them as a finality, he fled the United States without even bothering to officially resign his post. Ambassador Concha knew what was coming, and he did not want to be a part of it. He did, however, as he wrote home, want to see how Secretary of State Hay handled his instructions from Roosevelt. He expected so honor-loving a man as Hay to suffer "some little mortification," at least privately. "One having jaws as powerful as this Uncle of ours," Concha wrote, "can settle it with a single crunch. The desire [of the United States] to make themselves appear as the nation most respectful of the rights of others forces these gentlemen to toy a little with their prey before devouring it, although when all is said and done they will do so in one way or another."

By the time the new Colombian chargé d' affaires, Tomás Herrán, took over the job of negotiating with Hay, Roosevelt had marked his territory. "The canal will be of great benefit to America, and of importance to all the world," the president had explained in his annual message to Congress in December of 1902.

> It will be of great advantage to the countries of tropical America. It is earnestly to be hoped that all of these countries will do as some of them have already done with signal success, and will invite to their shores commerce and improve their material conditions by recognizing that stability and order are the prerequisites of successful development. No independent nation in America need have the slightest fear of aggression from the United States. It behooves each one to maintain order within its own borders and to discharge its just obligations to foreigners. When this is done, they can rest assured that, be they strong or weak, they have nothing to dread from outside interference.

The implication was crystal clear. This was the first salvo of what would soon be overly dignified as the Roosevelt Corollary to the Monroe Doctrine: in return for the United States' keeping European colonists out of the Americas, the nations of the Americas would be expected to do as they were told. The United States government would be monitoring their behavior. "More and more," Roosevelt wrote, "the increasing interdependence and complexity of international, political and economic relations render it incumbent on all civilized and orderly powers to insist on the proper policing of the world."

Hay was not altogether behind Theodore's twist on settled American foreign policy, but the secretary of state had no compunction about pushing the Colombians around. He had something bordering on contempt for the "dago" countries, as he called them. They were, to Hay, like some of Payne and Helen's less genteel friends: while they were no harm to have around if they kept quiet, they were and would remain "nonentities." Hay had managed to browbeat Herrán into accepting Roosevelt's ultimatums. The Colombian chargé was convinced that if he refused to sign the Hay-Herrán Treaty as presented, the US president would build the canal in Nicaragua, or worse. Herrán feared Roosevelt might take the advice of the chairman of the Senate Foreign Relations Committee, who was on record suggesting that the United States simply seize the land in Panama as a "universal public utility" and worry later about what compensation might be due Colombia. There was even talk about backing a revolution in Panama, which would then become an independent nation under the protection of the United States. Lacking clear instructions from his government in Bogotá, Herrán signed the treaty and left it to the Colombian Congress to amend it into a more palatable document. Herrán had noticed from his years in Washington that the United States Senate was quite fond of this method of revision.

HAY WARNED THE Colombians in July of 1903 that Theodore Roosevelt would not stand for any amendments in this treaty, nor would the president permit the Colombian government to negotiate payment from the French canal company for the right to sell its concession to the United States. The special congress called to consider the treaty in Bogotá, however, got it into its collective head that it was duty-bound to protect the best interests of Colombia. This body unanimously rejected the treaty as written and formed a committee to come up with an acceptable set of principles on which their president could negotiate a new treaty with the United States. "This would be an ingenious device," Alvey Adee wrote to Hay in the middle of August, "quite within the reasoning capacities of the anthropoids."

Alvey also mentioned another likely scenario: a violent secession from Colombia by the Department of Panama. The citizens of Panama, many of whom were employed by the railroad owned by the canal company, did not want to miss their chance at the boom the building project would surely bring. "Such a [secession] scheme could, of course, have no countenance from us—our policy before the world should stand, like Mrs. Caesar, without suspicion," Alvey wrote to Hay. "Neither could we undertake to recognize and protect Panama as an independent state, like a second Texas. Such a state would have a hard time between Colombia on the one side and Costa Rica on the other."

Roosevelt was not happy that the Colombians were wavering. They had until September 22, the president warned, to ratify and sign the treaty—*as written*! Colombia's own position began to become clear in early September, after their Senate committee had weighed all the factors, such as the unconstitutionality of handing over sovereignty of a part of their own country. They suggested a bill to empower President José Manuel Marroquín to conclude a new agreement along more equitable and more honorable lines, making Colombia and the United

States coguarantors of the neutrality of the canal zone, but allowing Colombia to retain sovereignty over all territory and all inhabitants. The cities of Panama and Colón were not included in the canal zone and would therefore remain under the undisputed rule of Colombia. This would seem a reasonable request from a sovereign nation; it was not greeted as such at the Summer White House on Oyster Bay.

Roosevelt immediately started complaining about the Colombians: "contemptible little creatures!" he called them. Theodore Roosevelt would not be intimidated by greedy blackmailers! Hay cautioned the president to hold his fire until Colombia showed its final hand. Good options would still be open to him. "It is altogether likely that there will be an insurrection on the Isthmus against the regime of folly and graft that now rules at Bogota," Hay wrote to the president. "It is for you to decide whether you will (1) await the result of that movement (2) take a hand in rescuing the Isthmus from anarchy, . . . something we shall be forced to do in the case of a serious insurrectionary movement in Panama, to keep the transit clear. Our intervention should not be haphazard, nor this time should it be to the profit, as heretofore, of Bogota. I venture to suggest you let your mind play a little about the subject for two or three weeks, before finally deciding."

Encouraging Roosevelt to let his mind frolic in the fields of international diplomacy and law was something Hay rarely did. The secretary of state was in the habit of using all his guile to keep the fetters on Theodore's musings. His letters to the president often had subtle little hints about the necessity of honor in public dealings, and reminders that he had been "born a gentleman" and should act the part. So this was an uncharacteristically aggressive strategy. But the secretary of state was in an aggressive mood. The only thing worse than having one of his treaties second-guessed by the United States Senate was having one second-guessed by the nonentities in some Latin American congress. Like Adee, Hay had taken to referring to the Colombians as greedy little anthropoids.

At Oyster Bay, between reading Aristotle, Plutarch, and the early speeches of Abraham Lincoln, and between the tennis matches, the four-hour horseback rides, and the bouts of strenuous wood chopping, Theodore thought through the problem of Colombia. He noted the many times the United States had been obligated, by treaty, to help Colombia put down little insurrections in Panama in order to keep the railroad running, and he came up with a surprising strategy. The early results of his thinking got abroad in a hurry, for Theodore Roosevelt did not think quietly. His views—helped along enormously by a very interested party in France—were starting to get wide play by the middle of September: the president's privilege and his duty, according to a long-standing treaty with Colombia, was to protect the free flow of all US goods and all US citizens across the isthmus. "The right of way in the legal language of the United States is the right of passage in its highest sense; that is to say, not merely the right of bodily locomotion, but the right of making all the artificial works needed for locomotion in any shape whatsoever," recorded newspapers in the know.

> The right of way is in reality a right of establishing the works needed for the passage of trains, if it is a matter of a railroad, and for the passage of vessels, if it is a matter of vessels.
>
> If our information is correct . . . it is to this legal coercion exercised on the strength of a treaty, that President Roosevelt has decided to have recourse, in order to obtain from the Republic of Colombia the control which it is indispensable for him to have on the territory needed for the working of the canal. No one could blame President Roosevelt for making use even of force in order to obtain that which right secures to him and which cannot be obtained graciously.

Chapter Forty

I Pledge You My Honor

John Hay did not think of himself as an easy mark, but he was happy to have the resources available to ensure his personal honor, as when a laborer from the Stoneleigh Court construction site would show up at his door requesting compensation for bodily injury. Hay knew the Stoneleigh project was dangerous work: men had monkey wrenches dropped on their heads from two stories above, or tripped and fell off girders; one poor fellow accidentally walked into an empty elevator shaft, dropped eight floors, and died in the hospital a week later. But Hay was rarely anywhere near the construction project and had no way of knowing which claims were real and which were not. "I wish you would communicate with Mr. Parsons [the foreman], and tell him that in cases of men having suffered injuries on the Stoneleigh, I should be glad to have him bring the matter to my attention or to yours and I authorize you to give them any reasonable relief—payment of doctors' bills, &c.," he wrote to his banker on the project. "If there should be any case of genuine distress which commends itself to you and to Mr. Parsons, I should, of course, be glad to do something for the person in trouble."

Stoneleigh had turned out to be a million-dollar project, and Hay had paid nearly 80 percent of the costs out of his own pocket. His personal outlay was nearly double what he had budgeted, and his expectations of the annual return on his investment had fallen from nearly 20 percent down to around 2 percent. The labor unions had been no help. Hay had contempt for unions in general and union bosses in particular, but if the hod carriers demanded a raise of twenty-five cents a day—a very reasonable want—Hay was happy to shell out the extra pay to keep things running smoothly.

Money solved most problems. When merchants walked into the US Embassy in London and presented bills for little debts Del had incurred on his last visit there, Hay sent drafts to Harry White to settle them, even when he was sure the debts had already been settled. "I would rather, of course, pay it twice than have the man think I was trying to do him," Hay had written in one instance.

He was conscientious about protecting his reputation, and also the good name of those closest to him, which was not always painless. Not long after Del's death, Hay began to hear rumors that a young woman in Washington was making charges at downtown department stores in his son's name. Then he received a letter from her claiming that she and Del had been secretly married shortly before his death, and they had a child together. "If your story is true, it is my duty, as well as my wish, to provide for you and the child," Hay had answered. "If it is not true, it is equally my duty to defend the memory of my son from unjust aspersions." The woman's story proved demonstrably false, and Hay had managed to keep the allegations out of the newspapers and out of Clara's hearing.

Clarence King's legacy hit a similar snag in 1903: the estate's executor alerted Hay that there was a woman who claimed to be King's wife and the mother of his five children. This claim, unlike the one against Del, could not be disproved. She had proof that she had been married to King for nearly fifteen years, though none of King's closest friends knew anything about it. Ada King also had letters from Clarence written at the end of his life, including the promise of an $80,000 trust fund to provide for her and the children. King's cryptic note ("God knows I have reason to love John Hay as he will one day see") made more sense now. Those many loans from Hay were helping to support a secret family. King was apparently depending on Hay to do the honorable thing in the aftermath of his death.

By the time Ada King emerged, Hay had already forgiven all of Clarence King's debts to him and had made certain the assets from his estate were put in trust to provide for King's mother and two siblings. After Ada's claim was revealed to be true, Hay continued to do what he believed to be the honorable thing. He had no doubts as to his course of action, particularly in light of the fact that Mrs. Clarence King was a black woman, and their four surviving children were of mixed race. Hay's duty, as he saw it, was to protect the King family from scandal. He and King's executor kept the trust in place for King's mother and bought Ada's silence. John Hay paid $2,200 of his own money to buy a house for Clarence King's wife and children, covered the real estate taxes each year, and sent monthly checks of $50—all anonymously. John Hay never met or even saw Clarence King's wife and children, they being, in the Hay lexicon, "nonentities."

JOHN HAY WAS almost embarrassed to importune the most celebrated sculptor in America, but he did so in spite of himself. Augustus Saint-Gaudens, who had carved famous and celebrated statues of Abraham Lincoln and General Sherman, was a friend, after all. "I wonder if you could make anything of so philistine and insignificant a head as mine," Hay wrote to Saint-Gaudens on

September 30, 1903, as he was winding down his summer at the Fells. "I lack profile, size, and every other requisite of sculpture—but I have been an unusual length of time in office and I fear that, after I am dead, if not before, some blacksmith will try to bust me."

A week later, when John Hay turned sixty-five, Saint-Gaudens had not yet made a reply. Hay was not overly concerned, however, because the things that mattered most to him seemed to be turning his way again. The United States and China signed a wide-ranging new commercial treaty on October 8, 1903—"my birthday has been properly celebrated," Hay told his wife—and the Alaska boundary tribunal appeared to be days away from a decision exceedingly favorable to the United States.

Hay found himself clearing business off his desk in Washington with a vigor uncommon in a man his age, if he did say so himself, and had time to enjoy long carriage rides through the outskirts of the city in the cool of the evening. He preferred to ride alone but for his driver so that he could nap if he wanted, so he was bumping along on newly cut roadway one crisp mid-October evening, sound asleep, when he was jolted awake by a familiar voice cracking the sky. "HELLO JOHN!" Hay's vision cleared quickly enough to see Theodore and Edith Roosevelt gallop by on horseback, still waving as they disappeared from view.

The secretary of state got the answer he wanted two evenings later. "St-Gaudens is going to bust my head," he wrote to Clara the next morning, while waiting around for picture hangers and decorators to arrive at their house.

> It is a ruinous expense and folly, but . . . it may as well be done by the greatest artist of our time. It will be ugly but it will be an object of art; and perhaps the family will be no poorer for it. . . .
>
> [Today] will be a very important day I have come to a definite conclusion on two great subjects. The Alaska Tribunal have asked for new instructions—and Canal matters have reached a critical stage and yet I slept well last night.

HE STARTED TO get the unofficial word of the Alaska decision two days later. It appeared that the British judge was going to side with the United States against Canada. "We give up 30 square miles of our claim, which we don't want, and the Canadians have to give up 30,000 square miles of their claim, which is of enormous value," Hay confided to Clara. "It is an immense success—not a victory over England, because the English Chief Justice gave us the verdict, but an enormous success for our cause, and for honor and fair dealings among nations."

The decision of the Alaska tribunal was officially communicated the next day,

October 20, 1903, and it was as Hay had hoped. The secretary of state actually found himself stunned at "how perfectly all my ideas in this great transaction have been carried out." Roosevelt had forgotten all his earlier qualms about the tribunal, and he would not stop talking about the triumph in the regular cabinet meeting. "Nobody living could have done this work as John did," Hay remembered him saying. "It is the biggest success of his life!"

Hay more or less agreed; he calculated that he had dedicated more hours of work to this single issue than to any other in his career. "When I began everybody was against me, and it required an endless amount of individual solicitation before I could bring the matter to pass," he confided to an old mentor from Brown University. Not only had John Hay been vindicated, but his career now had its elegant and unshakable capstone. The happy outcome of the tribunal had bound the futures and fortunes of the United States and Great Britain closer than ever. Hadn't this binding been John Hay's chief ambition in his six years of service as ambassador and secretary of state? The Canadians could whine all they wanted about being bullied, but they had no case. "As Mr. Sherman used to say," he wrote to Clara, "'serves 'em right if they can't take a joke.'"

The secretary of state particularly enjoyed his regular drive and drowse on the Canal Road that evening, out along the Potomac River. He didn't sleep much on the ride. "One group of darky children cried out 'Hello President Roosevelt,'" Hay told Clara. "A little further on a woman said, 'I 'clare! Takes two hosses to ca'y one man.' A third group said, 'Thar goes President [Jefferson] Davis!' I must be getting to look like *some* kind of statesman!"

JOHN HAY WAS not sure what to make of the man he ushered into his library on another in a long string of pleasant mid-October afternoons. Philippe Bunau-Varilla was a sharp-featured man with the thick, bristling mustache of a stevedore, the sleek nose of a French aristocrat, the squared jaw of a Roman consul, and the watchful eyes of a matador. He had a bulbous and balding head and appeared to have an excess of energy tamped into his compact frame. Bunau-Varilla was an explosive personality. He boasted of having wanted to slap Senator John Morgan across the face during a heated argument about the better of the canal locations. Morgan was a committed partisan of the Nicaraguan route, to which he had dedicated nearly twenty years; Bunau-Varilla was a dedicated partisan of the Panamanian.

There were those who said Bunau-Varilla was driven almost entirely by Gallic pride and idealism. He had briefly, at age twenty-six, been the director general for the Compagnie universelle du canal interocéanique de Panama, and even after the French company went bankrupt and into receivership, Bunau-Varilla

Philippe Bunau-Varilla

continued to believe the canal project was a great gift to civilization that he was honor-bound to push toward completion. The Americans might be the ones to complete the canal across the wilds of Panama, but Bunau-Varilla and his fellow Frenchmen (and the twenty-thousand laborers who had already died during construction) could rightly claim a fair measure of credit if they did. Others said Bunau-Varilla's motivation was strictly mercenary: he was rumored to be one of the biggest individual stakeholders in the successor of the bankrupt canal enterprise, Compagnie nouvelle du canal de Panama, whose shareholders stood to pocket US$40 million worth in gold coin if the American government took over the project. For John Hay, however, Bunau-Varilla's motivations were beside the point. The point to him was this: Philippe Bunau-Varilla appeared to be a very useful man.

Bunau-Varilla was only a private citizen, but he was a very resourceful one; his spectacular one-man lobby had been largely responsible for the United States government's decision to turn away from the Nicaragua project and toward Colombia. And when the treaty began to unravel in Bogotá in the summer of 1903, the Frenchman had returned to the United States and thrown himself once again into the fray. A week before his visit to Hay's home, Bunau-Varilla had managed to get an audience at the White House, where he told President Roosevelt the Panamanians were furious at Bogotá for putting the canal in jeopardy. They were already making battle plans for a fight for their independence from Colombia. Roosevelt seemed pleased to have this intelligence, but he was circumspect. He could not be seen encouraging revolution in a friendly country in the Americas.

Bunau-Varilla did not get much more in the way of direct encouragement for breakaway Panama that pleasant October afternoon in John Hay's library. "But," Hay assured him, "we shall not be caught napping." And as Bunau-Varilla was taking his leave, Hay went over to his bookshelves to grab a novel, *Captain Macklin.* He had a personal connection to this book. The author was his longtime acquaintance and Del's friend from South Africa, Richard Harding Davis. The adventure novel had been mauled by the critics, but Hay had liked it and had said as much. "It was the first word I had heard about the book that was encouraging," the author had written to Hay. "I tell you as I told Mrs. Davis, if *you* think it is as good as that I do not care what the rest of them think . . . and I thank you a thousand times for saying so."

Hay found *Captain Macklin* right where he had shelved it, and handed it to Bunau-Varilla. "Take it with you," Hay told him. "It will interest you."

Bunau-Varilla would later say Secretary Hay described the novel as "the history of a West Point cadet, who leaves the military academy to become a soldier of fortune in Central America," where "he enlists under the orders of a General, a former officer in the French army, who commands a revolutionary army in Honduras." Bunau-Varilla tucked into the book right away and divined deep meaning from his reading assignment. "The chivalrous figure of the old French warrior who is the hero of the history, corresponded perfectly to the description given by Mr. Hay," he found. "At the head of his half-wild army, in the virgin forest, [the Frenchman] pursued undeviatingly the high aim of justice and progress. I could not help thinking that Mr. Hay, in giving me this volume, had meant to make a subtle allusion to my own efforts in the cause of justice and progress. . . . Did [Hay] not wish to tell me symbolically that he had understood that the revolution in preparation for the victory of the Idea, was taking shape under my direction?"

And by way of more practical and actionable intelligence, Bunau-Varilla had also heard the US secretary of state say that American naval forces had been ordered "to sail towards the Isthmus."

MUCH AS THEODORE Roosevelt was impressed by the "duelist's" mien of the Frenchman, the president refused to take an active role in the unfolding of

Bunau-Varilla's revolution scheme in Panama. "He had no assurances in any way, either from Hay or myself, or from any one authorized to speak for us," Roosevelt later said. "He is a very able fellow, and it was his business to find out what he thought our Government would do. I have no doubt that he was able to make a very accurate guess, and to advise his people accordingly. In fact, he would have been a very dull man had he been unable to make such a guess." Bunau-Varilla was a very interested observer, and by the last week in October, as the Frenchman had learned, Roosevelt had dispatched a half-dozen US warships to within striking distance of the two coasts of Panama. Bunau-Varilla was now convinced that a revolution would enjoy the energetic and weapon-rich backing of the United States of America.

The representative of the Panamanian revolutionaries sent to plead their case for independence in Washington had less luck in his efforts to determine American intent. John Hay refused to see Dr. Manuel Amador Guerrero, who had little choice but to use Bunau-Varilla as go-between. Bunau-Varilla assured Amador that the revolution would be successful, that President Roosevelt secretly supported an independent Republic of Panama, and that the United States would prevent the landing of any Colombian soldiers sent to Panama to interfere with the inevitable victory. He was also certain the Roosevelt administration would recognize and protect an independent Panama from the start.

Bunau-Varilla put money on it. He pledged $100,000 to Amador to be used as tribute to the general in charge of the Colombian soldiers garrisoned in Panama City. The officer and his men were almost all Panamanian, and the price of their loyalty to the cause of independence was expected to be reasonable. Bunau-Varilla demanded one thing in return from Amador: a crucial office in the new republic's government. "Nobody knows better than I the final aim, which is the completion of the Canal and the best way to attain it," he told Amador. "It will, therefore, be necessary to entrust me with the diplomatic representation of the new Republic at Washington."

COLOMBIA'S CHARGÉ D'AFFAIRES was among the many foreign diplomats who stopped in to see Hay on October 30, 1903, a regular Thursday reception day. Tomás Herrán could offer little hope for a reasonable treaty proposal anytime soon; he was being excoriated as a weakling and a traitor back home in Colombia for making such a lousy deal in the first instance. Herrán told the secretary of state that afternoon, "with a grim smile," that he expected to be assassinated when he returned to Bogotá. "And the worst of it is," Hay wrote to his wife, "he meant it."

THE REVOLUTION IN Panama was quick and peaceful, in spite of about five hundred Colombian troops who landed in Colón on November 3. The Panama Railroad Company executives stalled their trip to Panama City long enough for the first US gunship to arrive with its slightly out-of-date orders from the president: "Government force reported approaching the Isthmus in vessels. Prevent their landing if, in your judgment, it would precipitate a conflict."

The Colombians on the ground evidently thought better of making a fight. The White House received only one report detailing casualties, the result of a small barrage from a Colombian gunboat off Panama City, "killing a Chinaman in Salsipuedes Street," it said, "and mortally wounding an ass." By the time a US troopship carrying four hundred marines arrived in Colón on November 5, the Colombians had sailed for home. A new flag flew over Panama.

When word of the Colombian retreat reached the State Department the next day, Hay shipped off an official telegram to the US Consulate in Panama City, meant for all the world to see. The United States of America would recognize the newborn nation: "The people of Panama have, by an apparently unanimous movement, dissolved their political connection with the Republic of Colombia and resumed their independence. When you are satisfied that the *de facto* government, republican in form, and without substantial opposition from its own people, has been established in the State of Panama, you will enter into relations with it as a responsible government."

JOHN HAY WAS met with an unwelcome little complication involving the family honor the following day. That week's edition of the New York society scandal sheet, *Town Topics*, was out, and somebody directed Hay's attention to one of its society items. The extortionate editors of the gossip rag claimed that Del had fathered a daughter before he died, but that John Hay and his wife had refused to recognize the girl or her mother. The secretary of state fired off a two-page letter. "The story has been offered to the newspapers of this city for a year, but its falsity has been in every case immediately discovered," Hay wrote before going on to refute the charges. "I request that you will, without mentioning my name, print in your next number a statement, which I pledge you my honor is true, that you are informed on good authority that the story you have printed about the late Adelbert S. Hay has no foundation." The editor obliged.

PRESIDENT ROOSEVELT WAS a little nervous about the public response to the revolution in Panama, and he took up much of the cabinet's time and patience talking through the legal (and moral!) justifications for suddenly reversing the more than fifty-year history and policy of defending Colombian sovereignty over their Departamento de Panamá. The act of watching Roosevelt think out loud made certain members of his cabinet uneasy, and they tried to put the boss at ease. "Oh, Mr. President," Attorney General Philander Knox said at one point, "do not let so great an achievement suffer from any taint of legality!"

At another point, as Roosevelt begged assurances that he was on solid ground—"Have I answered the charges? Have I defended myself?"—the secretary of war suggested that silence might be golden in this particular instance. "Mr. President," Elihu Root said, "you have shown you were accused of seduction and you have conclusively proved that you were guilty of rape." There was no turning back now in any case—not for Roosevelt, and not for his secretary of state.

PHILIPPE BUNAU-VARILLA RETURNED to the Hay residence less than a week after the revolt in Panama, on November 9, 1903, with an original of a letter he had already cabled to Hay. The official letter, written by Bunau-Varilla, announced the appointment of Philippe Bunau-Varilla as the new Republic of Panama's envoy extraordinary and minister plenipotentiary.

Hay had reason to be skeptical of this "official" correspondence. News from Panama City was spotty, but there were reports that a delegation from Panama's new government was on its way to Washington to discuss the canal situation. Bunau-Varilla insisted there was nothing to the report, but he reminded Hay nonetheless of the need to move with "lightning rapidity of action" on the treaty before the Panamanians began making the sorts of demands the Colombians had made. Hay did not waste time. By the time the Panamanian delegation reached Washington on the night of November 18, a slightly reworked treaty had been signed by Philippe Bunau-Varilla and a very tired John Hay.

"I have never, I think, been so constantly and actively employed as during the last fortnight," Hay wrote to his daughter Helen the next morning.

> Yesterday morning the negotiations with Panama were far from complete. But by putting on all steam, getting Root and Knox and [Treasury Secretary Leslie M.] Shaw together at lunch, I went over my project line by line, and fought out every section of it; adopted a few good suggestions; hurried back to the Department, set everybody at work drawing up final drafts—sent for Bunau-Varilla, went over the whole treaty with him,

> explained all the changes, got his consent, and at seven o'clock signed the momentous document in the little blue drawing-room, out of Abraham Lincoln's inkstand, with Clarence's pen. Bunau-Varilla had no seal, so he used one of mine. So that great job is ended—at least that stage of it.

The Panamanian delegation arrived in Washington five hours after the signing and was not at all pleased with the terms of this treaty. But they were given to understand, most vociferously by Bunau-Varilla, that the United States (who was, after all, the sworn protector of their infant republic) would not countenance any changes to the Hay–Bunau-Varilla Treaty. The Panamanians got the message and did not care to test the crunching power of Uncle Sam's jaws. The treaty was unanimously ratified within twenty-four hours of its arrival by ship in Colón. Word was that the nervous provisional representatives of the people of Panama had not even taken the time to unwrap the document so that they might read it.

LIKE THEODORE ROOSEVELT, John Hay was convinced the United States had acted honorably in advance of and during Panama's "war" for independence. "The matter came on us with amazing celerity," Hay wrote a month after the event. "We had to decide on the instant whether we would take possession of the ends of the railroad and keep the traffic clear, or whether we should stand back and let these gentlemen cut each other's throats for an indefinite time, and destroy whatever remnant of our property and our interests we had there. I had no hesitation as to the proper course to take, and have had no doubt of the propriety of it since."

The hastily negotiated Hay–Bunau-Varilla Treaty was not so easily justified. Hay had first sent for Bunau-Varilla's consideration a treaty with terms equivalent to the ones offered Colombia, but Bunau-Varilla had insisted on changes. He was wary of anything that might hit snags in the United States Senate and rewrote Hay's treaty proposal to be *more* favorable to the United States. Bunau-Varilla's rewrite ceded to the United States absolute sovereignty in the canal zone "to the entire exclusion of the exercise by the Republic of Panama of any such sovereign rights, power and authority." It widened the canal zone under US control from six miles to ten miles, and it changed the term of the lease from a hundred years to "in perpetuity."

Hay had accepted all these changes and suggested another one. He asked that the phrase "leases in perpetuity" be changed to "grants to the United States in perpetuity the use, occupation and control." What did Bunau-Varilla care? The United States was getting its canal; the Compagnie nouvelle du canal de Panama was getting its $40 million in gold coin.

John Hay was a sick man in the run-up to Christmas, 1903; he suffered from bronchitis, then a painful attack of rheumatism and gout, then bronchitis again. His maladies continued well into the New Year, until he reckoned it the longest single sustained stretch of illness he had had in his long-suffering adult life. He had plenty of time in his sickbed and plenty of time to think about the Hay–Bunau-Varilla Treaty. Hay could tell himself, and did, that he was merely an officer of his government and obligated to carry out the policies of the president he served, who was, after all, elected by the entire nation.

But John Hay understood the line he had crossed, and he said as much in the letters he sent to senators in January of 1904, begging them to ratify the Hay–Bunau-Varilla Treaty without amendment so that the terms did not get any unwanted public airing. "[Panama's] *Junta*, in making their report to the present Constitutional Convention, said that, although many of the provisions seemed harsh and hard, yet it was judged for the public good to accept it as it was," he wrote to the chairman of the Senate Foreign Relations Committee. "When they get the amended treaty in their hands again, they will compare it with the treaty we made with Colombia and see how vastly more advantageous to us this treaty is than that one was."

If the Senate would just ratify the document as is, "we shall have a treaty in the main very satisfactory, vastly advantageous to the United States, and we must confess, with what face we can muster, not so advantageous to Panama," Hay wrote to another senator. "You and I know too well how many points there are in this treaty to which a Panama patriot could object."

The United States Senate ratified the Hay–Bunau-Varilla Treaty near the end of February 1904, without amendment. That same month, Secretary of State John Hay received a bill from a business concern in South Africa claiming Adelbert S. Hay had left Pretoria without making good on a debt for services provided. Hay wasted no time in sending off a draft for the full amount of the bill—£27 4s. It was an inconsequential sum of money, after all, and a question of honor.

CHAPTER FORTY-ONE

She Said She Wanted a Home

"John Hay was not afraid of Horace Greeley," Sam Clemens dictated to his new secretary, Miss Isabel Lyon, on the last day of January 1904, in the hills above Florence, Italy.

"I will leave that remark in a paragraph by itself; it cannot be made too conspicuous," he told her.

> John Hay was the only man who ever served Horace Greeley on the *Tribune* of whom that can be said. In the past few years, since Hay has been occupying the post of Secretary of State with a succession of foreign difficulties on his hands such as have not fallen to the share of any previous occupant of that chair, perhaps, when we consider the magnitude of the matters involved, we have seen that that courage of his youth is in his possession still, and that he is not any more scarable by kings and emperors and their fleets and armies than he was by Horace Greeley.

Clemens had to speak slowly and pause frequently to let Miss Lyon catch up with her longhand transcription. He drew on his cigar while he waited, and silently paced around his sun-flooded office, looking out onto his rented Italian gardens. If he stepped out his floor-to-ceiling doorway at Villa di Quarto, he could gaze down the hillside and onto the distant Duomo and the campanile and the spindly tower of the Palazzo Vecchio.

Clemens, just turned sixty-eight, wondered from time to time why he and Hay had grown so distant. He still kicked himself for correcting Hay's poem about the riverboat engineer, Jim Bludso, thirty years earlier. But he knew that did not account for the benign estrangement. He suspected it was Mrs. Hay, who had once caught the two men cutting up in her own parlor—and on the Sabbath—and had made her disapproval very apparent before abruptly taking her leave. Clemens described the scene to Miss Lyon: "There was an embarrassed pause—I may say a very embarrassed pause," Clemens said while Isabel Lyon transcribed.

> If Hay was waiting for me to speak, it was a mistake; I couldn't think of a word. It was soon plain to me that the bottom had fallen out of his vocabulary, too. When I was able to walk I started toward the door, and Hay, grown gray in a single night, so to speak, limped feebly at my side, making no moan, saying no word. At the door his ancient courtesy rose and bravely flickered for a moment, then went out. That is to say, he tried to ask me to call again, but at that point his ancient sincerity rose against the fiction and squelched it. Then he tried another remark, and that one he got through with. He said pathetically, and apologetically, "She is very strict about Sunday."

Clemens paused again, standing quiet in the late-morning light, while Miss Lyon rushed her pen across the page. She always seemed *very* anxious to hear what came next. "Twenty-five years have gone by since then, and through manifold experiences I have learned that no one's courage is absolutely perfect; that there is always some one who is able to modify his pluck."

These dictation sessions were part of a new scheme Sam Clemens had hit upon for his autobiography, which John Hay had first encouraged him to write, back when they were both nearing forty. Clemens had made at least half a dozen abortive starts on the book since then, but in January of 1904 he decided on a new plan: he would *talk* his autobiography, and it was working. He was already trying to sell the idea to William Dean Howells. "You will be astonished (& charmed) to see . . . how real it sounds, & how well & compactly & sequentially it constructs itself, & what a dewy & breezy & woodsy freshness it has, & what a darling & worshipful absence of the signs of starch, & flatiron, & labor & fuss & the other artificialities!" he told Howells. "Mrs. Clemens is an exacting critic, but I have not talked a sentence yet that she has wanted altered."

CLEMENS NEEDED SOMETHING to keep his mind from grinding, grinding, grinding, twenty hours a day, on his wife's miseries. Livy had not been back on her feet since her heart seizure in Maine eighteen months earlier. She had remained bedridden all through the next year in Riverdale, and only improved to sitting in her wheelchair after a few summer months spent at her sister's home in Elmira. When the doctors prescribed a mild winter climate, the family had chosen a village just outside Florence called Fiesole, where they had all been so happy together, ten years earlier, as Susy prodded her father toward the finish of *Joan of Arc*, the family's favorite book of all. And when they first arrived at their rented villa, Livy had seemed reinvigorated. She had sat up for hours at a time on the long terrace off her parlor in Villa di Quarto, or in the gardens, where the fountain sounded a calming burble and the roses were still in bloom, and wheeled the two hundred feet across the length of the villa from her bedroom to the dining room to sup with the rest of the family every night.

"The fact is, the place improves," Clemens wrote to Henry Rogers on November 12, 1903, a few days into their new lease, "with a prodigality of sunshine and stimulating air not findable elsewhere outside of heaven." A day later, Livy suffered her first attack of breathlessness in more than two months. She made a brief recovery in mid-December and began taking dinner with the family again; she was nowhere near able to climb the stairs to take the view of the Tuscan hills from Clara's bedroom, but she spent a few hours a day outside in the gardens, sitting up. This lasted a few days only, until she was downed again by an infection in her throat. Her fever spiked off and on for the next few days, and she was up through the night, delirious and suffering sweats. By the time the fever broke and the painful lesions in her throat healed, Livy was exhausted and discouraged. Any ground she had gained in the previous nine months was lost. She did not complain aloud, but as the Florentine winter turned gray, and the far-off city below disappeared in the fog, and the bloom came off the roses just outside her bedroom door, she, too, seemed to be fading.

Her days were long and slow and eerily quiet. She was lonesome for her husband, who was once again banished from Livy's room save for brief, intermittent visits when the patient was deemed strong enough. "Youth my own precious Darling," she wrote one day that winter. "Couldn't you write in my boudoir? then I could hear you clear your throat & it would be such joy to feel you so near. I miss you sadly sadly. Your note this morning gave me support for the day, the one at night peace for the night. With the deepest love of my heart, your Livy."

Peace for the night was a white lie; there was little peace for Livy in the dark, when the rest of the household was sleeping. She could not always catch her breath when she lay flat, so she propped in a sitting position all night long, too sore, or too frightened, to fall into a deep slumber. Clemens slept fitfully in his nearby room or paced the hallway, listening for any signs of his wife's condition and cursing the unfairness.

The entire family did what it could to put Livy at ease: Clara was at her mother's bedside all afternoon, and Katy Leary all through the night. Sam insisted his wife put money worries out of her mind; he reminded her of his fabulous new contract with Harper & Brothers, which promised the family absolute financial security (despite the $32,500 he had sunk into the American Plasmon Company disaster, which he did *not* divulge to Livy). He wrote like a madman and reached his annual goal of $10,000 worth of prose matter for the Harper magazines before 1904 was a quarter done; he begged Livy to remember that the Hartford house was finally sold and Tarrytown rented, which lifted the burden of the mortgage; he kept *two* doctors on the payroll, and others in backup, and put in a telephone system so that he could summon them from Florence anytime, day or night. But no matter what he did, Sam Clemens felt powerless to relieve his wife of her anguish or to put out of his mind the discomforting knowledge that her weak heart often raced at 120 beats a minute every day, all day, or to ease her dread anticipations of the next attack of airlessness, which might kill her. "Think of those lonely nights in the gloom of a taper, with Katy sleeping, & with no company but her fearsome thoughts & her pathetic longings," Clemens would confess to Twichell. "It makes my heart bleed." He had begun to curse himself for dragging Livy across the Atlantic.

HE TRIED TO keep himself occupied with work; he stayed busy perfecting those new magazine articles—"Italian with Grammar," "Sold to Satan," "You've Been a Dam Fool, Mary"—and spending an hour and a half a day, minimum, on the autobiographical transcriptions. He consulted with Livy's doctors and fueled his spreading brushfire of hate for the Villa di Quarto's overbearing landlady, the daughter of a Philadelphia coal broker and boardinghouse owner who had thrown off her first husband when she saw the chance to snag an Italian count working as the consul in that city. The Countess Massiglia had added to the Clemenses' misery from the moment the family arrived at Villa di Quarto. She had decided at the last moment to scotch her winter in Paris, grabbed some of the finer furniture from the villa, and moved into a room in one of the estate's outbuildings, where she could oversee her famous tenant's every move. She refused to allow Mrs. Clemens to occupy the bedroom Sam chose for her, because the rental agreement stipulated no sick person could reside in that room, so Livy was forced to use a bedroom over the stables.

The countess also demanded that the entrance gates of the villa, four hundred yards distant from the house itself and without a bell to afford notice of arrival, be locked every night at six o'clock. She did not bother to explain this to Clemens, so that the first doctor summoned on a nighttime emergency was unable to reach Livy. And when Clemens put in the telephone line so that he could make calls to these distant city doctors, the countess demanded he take it out immediately, then had the wires cut. ("I had her oral consent," Clemens complained, "but hadn't the wit to make her put it in writing.")

Things continued on their rocky downhill slide that February. One of the countess's donkeys attacked Isabel Lyon, and the fright nearly killed her, putting her out of commission for most of the month. Livy was unable to get out of her bed, and Clara cracked. For a year and a half, Clara had been acting as her mother's day nurse, as well as shielding her from anything that might upset her, while trying to prepare for singing engagements in Florence and acting as peacekeeper between her explosive father and the insane countess. She was also acting as peacekeeper between the Florentine heart specialist and her father, who was now screeching that the doctor had secretly been giving Mrs. Clemens bromides and electricity therapy—in flagrant contravention of their wishes. "Father dear, do not say anything to Mother about this [new fight] till I see how she feels," she begged. "Katy says she is very miserable."

Clemens heard the crash and the screaming from overhead on the afternoon of February 4, and he ran upstairs to find Clara in her room throwing furniture. "I hate you!" she yelled as her father approached. "I hate my mother! I wish you would all just die . . . and if you don't die soon, I may have to kill you." This was a new wrinkle in the household; Sam thought *he* had cornered the market on the family's irrational fits of rage. By the next day, Clara was calmed and apologetic, but Clemens was in a fighting mood.

He went to town to talk to an attorney about lawsuits he might file against the countess—"the American bitch." He fired the esteemed doctor Pietro Grocco and brought in a heart specialist named G. W. Kirch, who was recommended by the most famous American physician in Italy, William Wilberforce Baldwin, a man who had treated J. P. Morgan, Edith Wharton, and Henry James (Baldwin was the model for a character in James's novel *The Wings of the Dove*). He put Katy in charge of making Mrs. Clemens's meals. And he promised his wife he would scout the hills of Fiesole for a more comfortable villa, where they could be happy, and he would get an option to buy it. "Many a time, these months, she said she wanted a *home*—a house of her own, that she was tired & wanted rest, & could not rest & be in comfort & peace while she was homeless," he explained to Joe Twichell.

SAM CLEMENS WOKE on the morning of February 16, 1904, with the memory of a curious and vivid dream: the cook at the villa had come running to him in a fright, saying as he ran, "The Countess has bitten the murderous donkey & it is dead." The next day was less amusing, especially after he learned that the villa had an open and active cess-pool, repository of *all* the house sewage, sited almost directly underneath Livy's room. He brought in Dr. Kirch to investigate the cesspool and went back to consult an attorney; he was ready to start filing lawsuits against the countess. He would fund Miss Lyon's suit for the damage caused by Massiglia's mad donkey, and another on behalf of a local man who had his thumb bitten off by the same animal. "I got the weightiest lawyer in

Italy, and the game was called," he reported to Rogers. "The Countess is doing the sweating, now."

He was in a lather to find another villa to rent now—"I will make the change at any cost," he insisted—but was felled by bronchitis almost immediately, which put him in his own bed, flat on his back. He was there at midnight on February 22, when Katy sounded the alarm from Mrs. Clemens's room. Livy was unable to breathe, and her heart raced up to 192 beats per minute. They told Sam the next morning that Livy had been saved only by an injection of brandy under her skin.

Goddamn it all. He did not know what to do for his wife, but he was going to make someone else's life a living hell, too. The countess made the ill-timed mistake of trying to persuade him to drop the lawsuits. *Like hell I will!* He was ready to bring a new suit; he would have the place condemned on account of the open cesspool. "I expect to drive the Countess off this place," he reported to Rogers from his sickbed. "Her presence poisons the whole region. . . . She appealed to the priest, yesterday, to placate me and call me off—which he declined."

Sometimes Clemens managed to choke down his anger and to reflect on how many people were on his family's side. The old friends from back home were begging for reports of Livy and sending good wishes. New friends in and around Florence were no less concerned. That Catholic priest, Father Raffaello Stiattesi, who presided at the church up the hill from Villa di Quarto, was unfailingly solicitous of the Clemens household in general, and of Livy in particular; he made a point of lighting a candle for Mrs. Clemens in his church every morning and sent flowers down the hill to the patient, and when he learned how disturbed Livy was by the church bells, which rang in holy days and feast days at any time, night or day, he ordered them silenced.

SILENCE RULED THE cavernous Villa di Quarto at almost all hours. Sam, Clara, and Jean took their breakfast alone in their bedrooms every morning and spent the rest of the day in separate pursuits: Clara kept up with her voice lessons when she was not in with Livy; Jean spent hours riding her horse through the cedar and poplar-lined trails on the enormous property or snapping photographs with her new Kodak. When the three did finally gather for dinner, they were cautious in their talk. "I do not reveal my fears to them, they do not reveal theirs to me, if they have them," Sam wrote to Livy's sister. "No doubt we do *want* to disburden ourselves to some friendly ear, but we can't, we *mustn't*. We shall lose the courage that keeps us up if we ever open our mouths!" Even when the trio wrote to friends and family, they did not fully "disburden" themselves, which made Mrs. Clemens the only person in the house who was not playing pretend. Livy tired of listening to Katy read her the chain of platitudes in letters from back home: "We are so glad Livy is improving. . . . We are glad Livy is getting along so nicely."

"Youth," Livy asked her husband one morning when he came for a bedside visit, "what was in the cable you sent this morning?"

"I said you were doing well," he replied.

"It is not true," said Livy. "Has there ever been a time here when it was true?" Livy demanded with what breath she could muster. "Has there ever been a time when I was actually improving, since we left [home]?"

All Sam Clemens could do was hang his head in silence.

THE MOST ABSORBING extracurricular activity at Villa di Quarto in the early spring was the preparation for Clara's upcoming concert dates in Florence. Sam never spoke it aloud, but he was haunted by visions of a repeat of Clara's stage-frightened performance in Washington a few years earlier, and he grew more anxious as the first concert date approached. And then, on that beautiful Friday night in Florence, Clara was boffo, *di gran successo*! She "astonished the house—including me—with the richness and volume of her voice, and with her trained ability to handle it," Clemens wrote to a friend in America. "It was a lone hand quite triumphantly played. The congratulations have been abundant and cordial." Livy was still unable to rise from her bed—twelve weeks and counting—but she summoned her daughter for a report, and Clara was able to show her mother the notice in that day's *Italian Gazette*: "Miss Clemens possesses a very sympathetic contralto voice of considerable extension and of a remarkably sweet and touching quality."

At just after ten o'clock that same night, Clara found Livy gasping for breath, and she had to sit by and watch her mother battle for air for more than an hour. Livy *fought* for her life. She "came out of it white, haggard, exhausted, & quivering with fright," Clemens would remember, and he was not much better. A friend who drove up the hill from Florence to call at Villa di Quarto two days later found Clemens gaunt and drawn. He smoked nervously, three cigars in less than an hour; his right eye was red and irritated and his right cheek would not stop twitching.

Livy was taking morphia hypodermics for pain, and to ease her increasing panic, while Clemens blamed himself for his wife's morbid state. "I WISH—I WISH—but it is too late," he wrote to Livy. "I drove you to sorrow and heartbreak just to hear myself talk. If I ever do it again when you get well I hope the punishment will fall upon me the guilty, not upon you the innocent. The summer is here. Cheer up."

SAM CLEMENS REFUSED to permit his wife to lose courage. Visits from Dr. Kirch always buoyed her, and Sam brought in a new doctor in the middle of May, Henry James's man, and begged him to join the household's game of pretend. "Medicine has its office, it does its share & does it well," he wrote to Dr. William Wilberforce Baldwin, "but without hope back of it, its forces are crippled & only the physician's verdict can create that hope when the *facts* refuse to create it. You can lift the patient up again to where she was before, & I was to see you when you come, & conspire with you to drive her fatal imaginings out of her head."

Dr. Baldwin had a lot of practice at the game, and he played it so well that his new patient appeared to improve. On the afternoon of May 20, Livy had burst into something like giddy laughter—"an echo of the long-buried past," Clemens wrote to Livy's sister, Sue. "I hope it may mean a step toward recovery." Nobody in the house suspected that Livy was simply joining the household's game of pretending—nobody but Katy Leary.

Katy and Livy were awake in Livy's room late one night at the end of May, with the windows open and the smell of roses wafting in on a pleasant Tuscan breeze. The nightingales were chirruping softly outside until suddenly, for the first time of the season, they were drowned out by darker and more insistent tones from the hills above. Owls, Livy Clemens thought, a sign of death.

"Katy, I don't think I can live much longer," she said. Then she started giving instructions. She wanted to be buried in the lavender dress she had ordered when they were in Riverdale, she told Katy, the one trimmed with lace. Mr. Clemens always wanted her to be cheerfully dressed.

"Oh, Mrs. Clemens," Katy said. "*Don't* talk about death. It's too awful. You're not going to die."

Katy waited for words of assurance from her mistress of nearly twenty-five years, but none came. Livy lay in stubborn silence and left it to Katy to speak first. "I realize everything you're telling me, and what you want done," Katy finally said. "And I'll make everything just as you'd like it." Katy did not betray Livy's confidence, not even to Mr. Clemens.

SAM AND JEAN returned from an excursion on the first Sunday in June with news, and they rushed to Livy's room to share it. Clara met them in the corridor.

"She is better today than she has been for three months," Clara told them. "Unberufen."

"Unberufen," Sam and Jean repeated, which was the family's long-practiced shorthand for "don't tempt the Fates by exhibiting excessive cheerfulness." Then the pair went in to tell Livy of their triumph. They had found a villa, and if it suited Livy, Sam was going to *buy* it. It was beautiful; it was perfect. The family would have a home of its own again. Livy wanted to hear more; she wanted to hear all about it. So they flouted the house rules, and Sam stayed in her room for more than thirty minutes, telling her all the details, before finally taking his leave. "You will come back," Livy demanded.

"Yes," he promised, "to say good night."

KATY WOULD NOT remember hearing music when she returned to the Villa di Quarto that evening, having been gone all day to attend the Forty Hours' Adoration with Father Stiattesi's congregation. Katy had marched in the candlelight procession for miles, from church to nearby church, and by the time she arrived home she was spent, maybe too tired to hear anything. But Sam Clemens would sometimes recall what he was doing that night, around nine o'clock, as he would explain it to his chosen biographer. "He was moved to do a thing which he had seldom done since Susy died," Albert Bigelow Paine would write of that night.

> He went to the piano up-stairs and sang the old jubilee songs that Susy liked to hear him sing. Jean came in presently, listening. She had not done that before, that he could remember. He sang "Swing Low, Sweet Chariot," and "My Lord He Calls Me." . . .
>
> Mrs Clemens, in her room, heard the distant music, and said to her attendant: "He is singing a good-night carol to me."

BY THE TIME Katy got to Livy's room, the patient was done pretending. "She's having a bad spell," the attending nurse said, somewhat flummoxed. "I am going to give her some oxygen."

"Oh, I've been awful sick all the afternoon, Katy," Livy said.

"Well, you'll be all right now," Katy replied, and she moved in to help Livy sit up straight so that she could catch her breath. Katy sat holding Livy for a few moments, fanning her, before noting one oddly short little exhalation, and then . . . nothing. "She fell right over my shoulder," Katy would always remember.

Sam was called to the room, where he found Katy and the nurse on either side of the bed, and Clara and Jean standing at the foot. He bent in over Livy and saw no flicker of recognition in her eyes. He heard a voice from behind him. "Katy is it *true*?" It sounded like Clara's voice. "Katy, *is* it true?"

HE PACED THE empty corridors of the rented villa the rest of the night and found himself drawn back, again and again, to his wife's room, where he sat petting her unresponsive face and hands. "How sweet she was in death, how young, how beautiful, how like her girlish self of thirty years ago," he wrote to Reverend Twichell. "This rejuvenescence was noticeable within 2 hours after death; that was 11:30; when I went down again (2:30) it was complete; the same at 4, 5, 7, 8."

The embalmers came at five o'clock the next afternoon and put Livy's body in a horse-drawn carriage to take her on the long downhill journey into town, a journey that would have terrified her the day before. Sam and Clara and Jean were in no shape to leave the house, so Katy escorted the body alone, to see that Livy's last wishes were carried out.

Sympathy letters from all over the world began to arrive in the first days, including a number that arrived care of the US Consulate in Florence: "Dear Clemens," read one. "I wish I could say something to comfort you. But there is no use in trying. You have got to bear your burden alone. All we can say is that thousands of people are sorrowing with you—and that there are many friends who would divide your sufferings with you, if they could. Yours affectionately, John Hay."

Clemens had ordered black-bordered cards embossed with words in answer to the raft of sympathy notes: FOR WHAT YOU HAVE SAID, I THANK YOU MORE THAN I CAN TELL. He scrawled out a handwritten note at the bottom of the card addressed to John Hay: "I am grateful to you and Mrs. Hay for your love & sympathy, & I know it is as you say: that I must bear this burden alone. But I am grown old, & it is heavy—let the time be mercifully short."

CHAPTER FORTY-TWO

Without Danger to the Public Health

We shall carry her home and bury her with her dead, at Elmira," Sam Clemens wrote to Henry Rogers. "Beyond that, we have no plans." Clemens was in a daze for the first few days, but he noticed that Clara appeared strangely unperturbed. His oldest surviving daughter was affectless, had not wept a single tear. She locked herself away in her room, refusing all visitors and all meals. Jean was no better, but in her own peculiar way. She had wandered Villa di Quarto's mazelike corridors all through that death night. When the first light came in the morning, Jean was so exhausted and on edge that she suffered a crushing epileptic seizure—the first in thirteen months.

Clemens put it to his daughters that he wanted to take them back to the States right away, but the girls complained that they were not ready to leave Italy. Katy heard him begging one day. "I'm going home where I have friends I can talk to," he told Clara and Jean. "Where I can see Howells and [Richard Watson] Gilder and Twichell and Mr. Rogers—all those dear friends of mine. There's nobody here." He came armed with enticements on the second try: they could go spend the summer in one of the Gilders' summer cottages in the Berkshires. There was nobody on earth with whom Clara and Jean felt so comfortable; they could *talk* to them. There were good stables for the new riding horses Livy had just bought for the girls, and plenty of trails. The girls did not say no, so Clemens rushed off a cable: "Gilder we want your cottage next to your house for the summer all end june cable answer."

That first definite bit of planning rallied Jean, who took charge of executing her father's design. Jean was best suited to the task, as she was the only one of the three who was fluent in Italian. The first available passage from Naples to New York was on the big, fast *Prinzess Irene* on June 16, but they had come over on that boat and the associations were too painful, so instead they booked staterooms on the slower and smaller *Prinz Oskar,* sailing a few weeks later. The family contracted with a company in Florence to transport Livy's body to Genoa, where it would be stowed in the hold of the *Oskar* on June 25. The rest of the family and its traveling party would meet the boat in Naples on the morning of June 28 and sail for home that afternoon.

By the third day, the tickets home were purchased and Livy's body had been embalmed and made ready for travel. The paperwork for her final trip, including proper certification from the attending physician and the US consular office in Florence, was being prepared. Packing up their belongings at the Villa di Quarto had already begun by June 8, which was, Clemens noted, Clara's birthday. "Thirty years ago, to-day," he wrote to Livy's brother, Charley Langdon, "Clara lay in the hollow of her happy mother's arm—just the top of her head showing—& Susy was admitted to see the new wonder & said admiringly, 'Lat bay go to boofu hair.' And now Susy is gone, and the happy mother is gone, & Clara lies motionless & wordless—& has lain so ever since Sunday night."

There was nothing to do but wait. They would vacate Villa di Quarto on June 20, spend four days at a hotel in Florence, tying up loose ends, and a day in Rome, and then arrive in Naples with a few days to spare. So they sat in that big sun-drenched mausoleum of a villa and anticipated the day of departure. The people who came up to the villa on sympathy visits were a comfort of sorts, "but they are not the old old friends, the friends of the old, old times when we laughed," Clemens wrote to Howells. "Shall we ever laugh again? If I could only see a dog that I knew in the old times! and could put my arms around his neck and tell him all, everything." Clemens didn't talk much; Clara still had not emerged from her private sanctuary. "It is nearly two weeks since she died & I grow happier as the days pass," Clara wrote to a friend back in America. She was comfortable and healthy, she reported, feeling something like giddy release. Whenever she tried to think of her mother, her mind seemed to go walkabout.

They were scheduled to leave the house for their hotel in Florence at four o'clock on the afternoon of June 20, but Jean began to feel the signs of an incipient seizure just before the appointed hour, so Sam sent the rest of the party down the hill to the city, while he and Jean stayed at Villa di Quarto and rode out the attack together. They were able to get away and into town before the sun dropped down beyond the Arno. They were in the hotel for four days, awaiting the delivery of the mourning gowns. "Friends write me beautiful words of sympathy & I sit here feeling *nothing*," Clara wrote to Dorothea Gilder from their Florentine hotel. "I read all these letters expressing anguish which I should be feeling myself and no change takes place inside me." Sam was beginning to worry that Clara was headed for a crash, and he was having a hard time sleeping himself, and so he was exceedingly nerved up the day before they were to leave town, when Dr. Kirch's final bill arrived. *The hog! The thief!* Kirch had been gouging him for three months now, he was sure of it.

He sent for the doctor to meet him at his banker's office the next morning. Kirch wanted to talk in private, but Clemens insisted his trusted Florentine banker, Mr. Cecchi, sit in as witness. Clemens accused the doctor of robbery and refused to pay the final third of the bill. Kirch made the mistake of arguing his case, and Clemens refused to listen. If the doctor wanted to make an argument, he could do so in court, where he would have to make it in public. Clemens already had a *very* good Italian lawyer working for him.

A few hours later, Clemens loaded the remnants of his household (including his daughters' new black mourning gowns) onto a train and headed south toward Naples.

THE NEXT FOUR days turned into a harrowing chase to catch up to Livy and the *Prinz Oskar.* The family spent an extra day in Rome because Clara did not appear capable of travel, and when the time came to depart for Naples the next day, Jean was feeling odd, sure of another seizure to come. So the Clemens party stayed another night in Rome, which made Sam nervous enough to send a distress signal to Charley Langdon. "I hope to have these two safe on board the ship day after to-morrow," he wrote. "Unless the strain is removed from Clara she will go down with a crash and her present two-thirds nervous breakdown will take on an additional third & be complete. I set my hopes upon the journey to Naples to-morrow. If we fail to make it, poor Livy will make her pathetic voyage all alone—she has never had to do that before. Then, of course, I will cable you. . . . With love to you all, out of a heart that is full of bitterness & rebellion."

THEY MADE IT to the pier at Naples with a bit of time to spare and were assured that Livy's body was already safely stored on the *Prinz Oskar.* But when the three surviving Clemenses boarded the ship an hour before departure, the authorities asked Sam for the death certificate and the paperwork from the US Consulate in Florence permitting them to land Livy's coffin in New York. The ship's captain and the purser explained that these documents had not been presented in Genoa. If Mr. Clemens did not have them, Livy's body would have to remain in Naples. He did not have the paperwork, of course, because that was supposed to have been taken care of by others. *Kirch! The son of a bitch!* Clemens was sure he had withheld the certificates on purpose.

The captain of the *Oskar* and the United States consul were willing to do a favor for "Mark Twain." Fame had its perquisites. They allowed Sam Clemens to swear out a personal affidavit that afternoon and then have a friend in Florence chase down copies of the documents and ship them to New York on the next fast boat out of Italy. The consul in Naples wrote up the affidavit, but Clemens was forced to read this mournful and hastily manufactured little document before signing. "Mrs. Olivia Langdon Clemens late wife of Samuel Langhorne Clemens, born in Elmira, New York, Nov. 27, 1845, died in the Villa Di Quarto, Florence, Italy, June 5, 1904 after 22 months of nervous prostration—died finally of heart failure suddenly. The remains were embalmed by Dr. Kirch, naturalized American, now of Florence, and are contained in a leaden case hermetically sealed—also in an oaken coffin. Therefore the remains can be landed in the United States without danger to the public health."

THE *Prinz Oskar* was an annoyingly slow vessel, but the water voyage had its usual calming effect on Sam Clemens. Katy Leary thought he looked like a sorrowing old shadow, but Clemens did not feel tired or old. He didn't feel much of anything except lonely. He could not stop thinking about his wife. "I know one thing," he would write,

> & I get some poor small comfort out of it: that what little good was in me I gave to her to the utmost—full measure, the last grain & the last ounce—& poor as it was, it was my very best, & far beyond anything I could have given to any other person that ever lived. It was poverty, but it was all I had; & so it stood for wealth, & she so accounted it.
>
> I try not to think of the hurts I gave her, but oh, there are so many, so many!

Clemens was awake and staring through the fog at one o'clock in the morning on the third night out when the ship passed by Gibraltar and into the narrowing strait, which would lead them out into the Atlantic, and nothing but open water between himself and home. His notebook was tucked away in its place in his cabin, its newest entry still fresh: "I cannot reproduce Livy's face in my mind's eye—I was never able to reproduce a face. It is a curious infirmity—& now at last I realize it is a calamity."

Chapter Forty-Three

From the Political Point of View

The acceptance of such an honor was tempting on a strictly personal basis. The Grand Cross of the National Order of the Legion of Honor was among the very highest distinctions the French Republic bestowed on an individual, and something meaningful to pass down to his children and grandchildren. But when John Hay received the official offer from Paris at the end of June 1904, his first instinct was to decline, as he had already done twice before. The main reasons for denying himself this recognition of his six years' service in the interest of world peace still pertained, and humility was not at the top of the list. The Constitution forbade the acceptance by any elected or appointed officers of the United States of an award from a foreign government without the explicit approval of Congress. Legislation would have to be introduced on the floor of the Senate, which would mean a loud and contentious debate in the Capitol over the relative merits of John Hay. Hay did not care to see himself cartooned and caricatured in the press while the issue hung fire, though he had to admit it would be a refreshing change to be momentarily derided as a French tool as opposed to a secret British agent.

Hay would have written his letter of declination to the French government already if it were not for Theodore Roosevelt. The president had suggested there might be very good reasons for the secretary of state to accept the medal this time. For one thing, it might do Theodore some good in the coming election. The vote was only five months away, and Roosevelt would be on the ballot as the Republican presidential nominee. "For the first time in my life, I am in doubt what to do," Hay recorded in his diary on June 30. "I shall sleep on it."

Hay did not raise the issue of the Grand Cross at the cabinet meeting the next day, but he wrote Roosevelt a long letter afterward. "I do not see that accepting the proposed offer is going to be of any benefit to the canvass. I think the less that is said about any of us, except yourself, for the next four months the better," he wrote. "I have tried—and I think I have succeeded in the attempt—to divest my mind of any considerations of kudos or personal vanity. My wife entirely agrees with me, and the children, who would be most interested if they knew about it, need never know. I admit that I have no right to put upon you even so slight a burden as deciding this question, but my will is so absolutely neutral in the thing that I will gladly accept your judgment, whatever it is."

Roosevelt told Hay to come over to the White House that evening, and when he got there the president ushered him into the library to talk it over. The only other man in the room was George Cortelyou, William McKinley's former secretary, who had just become the chairman of the Republican Party, which made him head of the president's political team. Theodore talked, and talked, and talked, and the gist of the talk was that the honor would go a long way in answering charges that the Roosevelt administration was reckless and warmongering. There was little disadvantage to his administration or his campaign, as far as Theodore could see. "Cortelyou—looking at it from the political point of view—was strongly of the same mind," Hay remembered.

Hay cabled his acceptance to France the next day.

If John Hay was anybody's tool, he was the president's, and that was as it should be. Going back to his first real job, with Abraham Lincoln, Hay had accepted it as his duty and his privilege to make a little lighter the terrific burdens of the office. Lincoln and McKinley had accepted his help with a magnanimity and grace that permitted Hay to retain some shred of a sense of his own personal agency. Theodore was different; he absorbed, like a manic inversion of Walt Whitman's "Song of Myself": "For every atom belonging to *you* as good belongs to *me*." In Roosevelt's mind, John Hay was simply an extension of the presidential self. Theodore made it plain in offhand comments about Hay's future—"If you and I stay here four years more . . ."—and whenever Hay moved to interject, to suggest he could not possibly make it through another term at the State Department, Roosevelt would not let him finish the thought. "If I stay you will have to," Roosevelt said one day. "I say it not in compliment."

Theodore had also made it plain one afternoon when he invited himself to the studio to see the bust of Hay that Augustus Saint-Gaudens was working to finish. Hay and Saint-Gaudens watched as the president circled the sculpture, pronouncing it *dee*-lightful before stopping on one side. There was, the president proclaimed, "not power enough in the jaw."

Hay was worried that the remark had offended, and he tried to take some of the sting out after Theodore took his leave. Hay approved of the bust in all ways, he assured the artist, it was perfect as it was. But Saint-Gaudens just smiled. Theodore Roosevelt, the sculptor observed, "projected his own powerful jaw on the universe."

HAY HAD KNOWN Roosevelt long enough and well enough to know that the president was not an irremediable narcissist. Theodore showed big, lusty flashes of generosity and personal kindness. At a cabinet meeting a few weeks earlier, the president had instructed his Treasury secretary to send an order to the docks in New York to have poor Sam Clemens, along with his wife's coffin and his bereft traveling party, passed through US Customs without a single question or annoyance. This was the sort of kindness, Hay knew, that a man like Clemens was unlikely to discount—or to forget.

But this was the political season, and Theodore Roosevelt was about to be judged by the entire nation. Henry Adams recorded the notable fact that Theodore had even dropped the tales of his Cuba war heroics and his western wolf hunts from his dinner table filibusters. "Theodore thinks of nothing, talks of nothing, and lives for nothing but his political interests," Adams said. "If you remark to him that God is Great, he asks naïvely at once how that will affect his election."

Hay had sympathy for Roosevelt, whose irritable tummy always flared in the campaign season. Theodore was worried about his prospects on the Pacific Coast, where he had to convince Californians in particular that he was not going to give an inch on the Chinese immigration question. "Congress has done its work so well that even Confucius could not be made an American citizen—though he would seek it with prayer and tears," Hay assured his boss. Roosevelt was anxious about his chances in the recent Republican strongholds like Indiana, Wisconsin, Delaware, and Colorado. He was even nervous about his chances in his own home state. "Here in New York, where close on a million and a half votes will be cast, and where the difference may be a few thousand one way or another, it is simply out of the question to prophesy," he wrote to the equally skittish Henry Cabot Lodge. "The thing to do is to strain every nerve to bring the results right."

Roosevelt was demanding all the help he could get; he expected his cabinet officers, like his horses, to be "willing jumpers." Theodore had already dispatched his secretary of the navy, secretary of war, attorney general, and secretary of the Treasury out onto the stump. The postmaster general was given a pass only on account of his retirement to what looked to be his deathbed. When the president had started in on Hay to join the political parade in the early spring, the secretary of state resisted, just as he had resisted all through the midterms two years earlier. Screeching out partisan political platitudes was beneath the dignity of his office, Hay maintained. Hay had also promised his wife he would not put himself through an ordeal so disruptive to both his physical and his mental health.

Roosevelt was not easily dissuaded and renewed his pursuit of Hay at cabinet meetings, when reinforcements were at hand. "The motion was seconded by

Shaw and Moody with considerable eloquence," Hay noted in his diary. "I sat mute—fearing to speak lest I should lose my temper. It is intolerable that they should not see how much more advantageous to the administration it is that I should stay at home and do my work than that I should cavort around the country, making . . . jejune orations."

The next day a delegation from Michigan showed up begging Hay to give the keynote at the celebration of the fiftieth anniversary of the founding of the Republican Party. (The first state party convention had opened in Jackson, Michigan, in July of 1854.) They said they were there with the blessing of Theodore.

"All you have to do is *read* the speech," said one importuner.

"Yes!" called out a second. "You can sit in a chair and read it if you like."

Hay sent a note of surrender to Roosevelt that afternoon—a grudging note of surrender. "I have thus broken the promise made to myself for good and sufficient reasons, which still seem to me good and sufficient," it said. "Of course there is in all this an element of personal indolence and a desire to shirk, but leaving that out, I am convinced that if I am worth anything in the State Department, it is a waste of whatever I *am* worth, to go about the country making speeches."

JOHN HAY COULD rationalize like anyone else. He told himself that this Michigan event would be his one and only political speech of the campaign; he told himself he was on the right side of history, he told himself that the Democratic opposition (treacherous, cowardly, vulgar loafers that they were) was too dangerous to be trusted. And when he sat down to write his text for Michigan, he told himself he was fashioning not a stump speech but an ode to the entire epoch of the Republican Party, an institution to which he had dedicated most of his life.

When he showed the draft of his speech to Roosevelt, the president gushed. Theodore was "lyric," as Hay told it later that day. "He flowered out in superlatives: he would be willing to go to the country on that one speech alone; everything was said when one read it, &c. . . . I had not liked the speech; it had not seemed to fulfill my own intention. But if it so impressed the person most interested perhaps it will do."

THE EARLY-JULY SKY looked menacing on the morning of Hay's first (and he hoped only) election-season speech, but the sun burned away the clouds by the time the secretary of state climbed up onto the stage early that afternoon in Jackson, Michigan. The Republican vice presidential candidate and the Speaker of the House were on the docket that day as well, but John Hay was the featured guest. A crowd of thousands had already assembled in the wide, tree-lined meadow to hear what Hay had to tell them, and when he was finally called to the podium, a thunderous applause rose up through the treetops.

He stood at first, mute and nervous, and anxious for the noise to die away so that he could get started. "Under the oaks of Jackson, on the 6th of July, 1854, a party was brought into being and baptized, which ever since has answered the purposes of its existence with fewer follies and failures and more magnificent achievements than ordinarily fall to the lot of any institution of mortal origin," Hay began. He was surprised by the strength of his voice and by his ability to hold the attention of his audience. He spoke for more than an hour, starting with a reminder of the party's first principles, its central role in the abolition of slavery, its commitment to the protection of American business and industry, and its great North Star, Abraham Lincoln.

> I admit it would be little less than sacrilege to try to trade upon that benignant Renown, whose light "folds in this orb o' the earth." But we who have always tried to walk in the road he pointed out can not be deprived of the tender pride of calling ourselves his disciples, and of doing in his name the work allotted to us by Providence. And I hope I am violating neither the confidence of a friend nor the proprieties of an occasion like this when I refer to the ardent and able statesman who is now, and is to be, our President, to let you know that in times of doubt and difficulty the thought oftenest in his heart is, "What, in such a case, would Lincoln have done?"

He made no apologies for the party's recent doings—not for the Philippines, or Cuba, or Hawaii, or the tariffs, and not for Panama, and he returned to Washington happy with his effort on the stump, which was, as he wrote to Harry White, "unusually and unexpectedly pleasant."

HAY WAS BACK at his desk at the State Department the next Monday but a little worse for the recent wear. The work at the department had been unrelenting in the previous few months. All the ambassadors and ministers in Washington wanted Hay to advise them about their country's current rows—Costa Rica versus Panama, Brazil versus Peru, Paraguay versus Brazil—or pledge sympathy to their side. The biggest fight, Japan versus Russia, was a hot war in the Far East, and a demoralizing one for the Russians. It looked as if the Japanese had probably already won their points: they wanted Russia out of Manchuria, the Open Door in China preserved, and control of Korea. Russia was too proud to back down, and Count Cassini kept telling Hay the czar would not sue for peace or stand for mediation. Roosevelt, meanwhile, kept telling Hay they were not going to allow a coalition of European powers (led by Kaiser Wilhelm) to rob the Japanese of the war spoils they had rightfully won.

The good news, though, was that Thursday, three days after his return from the Michigan trip, was escape day. But when that day arrived, the day Secretary Hay was to flee Washington for the Fells, he suffered a vicious attack of vertigo and was so faint he had to lie down in the dark for half an hour. He was still at home on Lafayette Square, and a little fuzzy, when the letter from the chancellor of the French Embassy arrived. "To-day the 14th of July, the day of French national festival," the translation read, "I have the honor to make known to Your Excellency that the Government of the Republic . . . has decided to confer upon Your Excellency the dignity of the Grand Cross of the National Order of the Legion of Honor." His Excellency, the secretary of state, would be accepting the honor.

Hay wrote a quick note to Theodore Roosevelt that same day. "Now that it is all done, I am convinced, subtracting any personal interest in the matter, of your wisdom in insisting that I should accept this dignity. Offered as it is by the great Republic of Europe, it is the highest possible commendation that can come from outside our own borders of the work we have done in the interest of the world's peace, and it serves as a much more conclusive answer than anything we could say to the charges of the other side, who accuse us of breeding hostility and disorder throughout the world." Hay added, "I feel that I have about reached the end of my tether here, and, with [Dr.] Rixey's permission, I shall start to-morrow for Newbury, New Hampshire, where I shall be at your disposition until further orders."

HAY WAS LEAVING the day-to-day affairs of the office to Alvey Adee, but it was a busy time at the department and Alvey would have to keep Hay in the loop; the agenda was filled with issues of now ancient origin. Lord Salisbury was dead and gone, and the Alaska fur seal problem was still not settled. The British had not yet persuaded the Canadians to give up their rights to the decimating open-water hunts without a big and bloated payoff, and the American companies were showing little interest in halting the slaughter on the Pribilof Islands. "The sense of the Senate," Hay had moaned, is "that if some arrangement for the protection of seal life was not speedily adopted by the two countries, Congress would pass a law to kill off the whole herd at once."

Hay was obligated to circle back to Washington for some work in August, but he was happy to be five hundred miles from Lafayette Square (and well away from the noise of the presidential campaign) for the rest of that summer.

He rode over to the Saint-Gaudens home in nearby Cornish, New Hampshire, to sit for the last touch-ups and see his bust in final form, and to commiserate with the sculptor, who was in pain from the return of cancer in his spine. And Hay was cheered by the arrival of the Wadsworths. "[Our daughter Alice] has lent us for a few weeks her baby Evelyn, a singularly pretty and amusing child before whom my wife and I spend hours of idiotic adoration," Hay reported to Sir John Clark, his old friend in England, as the family was beginning its annual breakup in early September. "Clarence has just gone up to Harvard, grieved to the heart to leave his garden and his dogs and horses." A week later, he wrote another plaintive note to Sir John: "It seems a sin to leave this exquisite country in its autumnal bravery, and go back to the worries and bickerings of Washington."

The day before he left the Fells for the last time that year, John Hay sat on his porch and pulled out his diary. "I have never seen such splendor in the woods as today," he wrote. "Around the house the maples are blazing in every shade of color from scarlet and orange to pale yellow and delicate pink, while the beeches, birches, ashes, and poplars add their varying shades to the chorus and the evergreens form the green background." He left for Washington with real regret. And on the way to Washington, he was obliged to stop in Boston to give a talk to the Thirteen International Congress of Peace.

This was supposed to be a simple, nonpartisan address, but Hay took the opportunity to do a little politicking for Theodore. "No Presidents in our history have been so faithful and so efficient as the last two in the cause of arbitration and of every peaceful settlement of differences," he said in the middle of his talk. "I beg you to believe, it is not by way of boasting, . . . it is rather as a profession of faith in a cause which the present Administration has deeply at heart that I ask you to remember, in the deliberations upon which you are entering, the course to which the American Government is pledged and which it has steadily pursued for the last seven years."

SO MAYBE HAY had himself to blame for the next onslaught, which began soon after he stepped off the Federal Express and into the cabinet meeting of Tuesday, October 4. Roosevelt asked Hay to stay around for a private conference after the meeting and told Hay it might be well for him to make a few political speeches in New York. Hay replied frankly that he did not feel up to it, and Theodore didn't push. "I want you to keep well, John," Roosevelt said. "I am going to need you in the State Department—if I am elected, of course—for the next four years."

Roosevelt begged him again at lunch a few days later, while the steel magnate Henry Clay Frick looked on, probably happy that all he had to do was write checks to the campaign. "I told him if I could not convince him of the impolicy of my going," Hay sighed into his diary that evening, "I would go." He still had hopes that Theodore would see reason: a Republican sweep in next month's elections seemed a certainty. There was no real value in Hay's going on the stump, while there was potential harm. "I am not an easy or effective speaker," Hay told his old boss the Civil War general Dan Sickles, who was also asking him to campaign in New York, "and besides, whatever I say rouses antagonisms to me and to the State Department, which seriously interferes with the success of its work."

Theodore did not see it that way, so on Sunday, October 9, he came around to John Hay's front door, as he often did on his way back to the White House from church, and pleaded anew for Hay's help. Theodore was sure New York was slipping from his grasp, he told Hay. He could not face the ignominy of losing his own home state. The Democrats had the biggest financiers in New York, and Tammany was going to be passing their money around. The president *needed* Hay on the stump there. Hay recognized the "October scare" and he cataloged for the president all the practical reasons for declining, but he could tell by the set of Theodore's jaw that the younger man was not going to stop asking him. Hay buckled. "I will go," he finally said, by way of conclusion. "Of course."

The White House alerted the organizers in New York, who secured Carnegie Hall for October 26, less than two weeks before Election Day. Hay went to work on his speech and continued on with his regular duties, like lunching with Theodore and one of his friends from France. "The President talked with great energy and perfect ease the most curious French I ever listened to," Hay recalled that evening. "It was absolutely lawless as to grammar and occasionally bankrupt in substantives, but he had not the least difficulty in making himself understood, and one subject did not worry him more than another."

THE STREETS AND sidewalks around Carnegie Hall were mobbed on the evening of October 26, 1904. Tickets to the Republican rally—with Secretary of State John Hay as the headliner—had long ago sold out. There were four thousand seats available, and almost triple that number of people crowded around the hall in the hour before the doors were to open. The organizers were kicking themselves for not renting the much bigger Madison Square Garden for the event. The local police inspector had laid on a detail of three hundred men for crowd control, and it soon became clear it was not enough.

The organizers flung the doors open early in hopes of clearing the streets, but when the hall filled to capacity and the fire marshal closed the doors, there was still a crowd of disappointed thousands milling around outside. John Hay's carriage driver had to fight through this phalanx to get to the stage door.

The cheering began as soon as he was introduced, and continued as he stood and walked to the rostrum. Through the glare of lights, he could see the entire audience rise from their seats. The cheering and applause swelled. He could see people waving flags, or their handkerchiefs, or their hats, and he stood for almost five full minutes while the noise continued.

Hay started slowly and without apparent emotion. He was nervous as he began, and was also suffering from a cold that evening, so that his voice was scratchy and hoarse. Hay started with a brief nod to his fallen friend William McKinley, who had shown himself so worthy a leader. "In the classic myth, when the golden bough was torn away another immediately appeared in its place," Hay noted. "Theodore Roosevelt took up the burden our beloved chief laid down, and with incomparable courage and strength has carried it on."

Was there any fear that the country would step off its glorious path if the Republican Party was chosen to carry on? Hay asked his crowd, and a man in staid evening clothes rose from one of the reserved boxes and yelled, "Not while you're there!" The crowed roared its approval.

Hay spent the next half hour scoring the Democratic Party. "It is not campaign rhetoric, it is merely the simple fact, to say that nothing but disaster could follow the reversal of the policies to which we are indebted for the prosperity of the past few years," he said. Hay accused the Democrats of "base treachery" and an "instinct" for "blundering." He called their platform a mass of "turbid and evasive phrases" and defended the administration's record in foreign affairs, especially in Panama.

John Hay closed his speech with the boss's specific wishes in mind. "It quickens the pulses to think what splendid progress we are to make on every line of national welfare in the next four years with Theodore Roosevelt at the helm," Hay intoned to the now hushed thousands.

> In the strength of his young manhood, with lofty hopes and purposes, with large experience of life, with the country his only care and God his guide, he will fill his high office with reverence for the law and the Constitution "as ever in his great Taskmaster's eye." His just fame in history will add a new splendor to the glory of his native state.
>
> Men of New York! will you allow it to be said that while the rest of the country stood by him you fell away? When President Roosevelt ascends the steps of the Capitol next March shall it be said that his mother State has no part in his triumph? If that shall be so, yours will be the loss, not his.

HAY WAS STILL energized by the event when he returned to the Holland House late that night, surprised at his lack of fatigue, and he woke the next morning to blaring notices. JOHN HAY'S BRILLIANT SPEECH was the *New York Tribune*'s front-page headline. "A veritable masterpiece," it called the speech. The *Sun* had Hay on the front page above the fold also. "When the speaker sat down the pent up enthusiasm broke loose," the *Sun* reporter noted. "The hall echoed and reechoed with the cheers, the salute of the flags was given all over again, and the women were so delighted that many of them, knowing not what else to do, wept for joy."

SAM CLEMENS WAS living in New York City again that autumn, biding his time at the Grosvenor Hotel on lower Fifth Avenue while the workmen completed renovations on the nearby town house he had leased for the next three years. He wasn't sure what those three years would bring. Jean was still up in Massachusetts at the Gilder cottage, recovering from serious injuries suffered in a riding accident so violent it killed her horse. Clemens had managed to persuade his youngest daughter to give up this dangerous sport, but he wasn't sure how to make it up to her for this new loss. Clara had been trying to right herself in the months since Livy's death, but without much success. She had collapsed while overseeing the town house renovations and had to be confined to a private hospital uptown for a "rest cure." She was being shipped off for further treatment at a sanatorium in Connecticut, and Clemens had been told not to expect to see his older daughter for a year or more.

"Dearest little Marcus," Clara wrote to her father on the way out of town.

> I feel like sending you one more fluttering goodbye before the bars are bolted. I don't know why I call it fluttering except that a thing which flutters seems to be uncertain of its whereabouts. . . . You will daily be in my thoughts this long winter and . . . I shall be hoping all the time that nothing will go wrong with you in the smallest ways.
>
> You are a cunning little man and very touching with all your thoughtfulness. I hope that soon I shall hear you are beautifully situated with companionable friends about you.

Clemens had raged against his awful fate in the first months after Livy's death. "How life & the world—the past & the future—are looking to me?" he wrote in answer to a question from Joe Twichell.

> As they have been looking to me the past 7 years: as being NON-EXISTENT. That is, that there is *nothing*. That there is no God & no universe; that there

> is only empty space, & in it a lost & homeless & wandering & companionless & indestructible *thought*. And that I am that thought. And that God, & the universe, & Time, & Life, & death & Joy & Sorrow & pain only a grotesque & brutal *dream,* evolved from the frantic imagination of that insane thought.
>
> By this light, the absurdities that govern life & the universe lose their absurdity & become natural, & a thing to be expected. It reconciles everything, makes everything lucid & understandable: A God who has no morals, yet blandly sets Himself up as Head Sunday-school Superintendent of the Universe; Who has no idea of mercy, justice, or honesty.

Life had "lost color & zest," he wrote to another friend, "& I do not value it."

Clemens had dabbled at work through the late summer and autumn. He sketched ideas for "Eve's Diary," which Katy Leary was certain would be a memorial of Livy, and he started an essay on the genocide the Belgians were perpetrating in the Congo. "I am whetting up for King Leopold of Belgium," he warned Twichell. "By January I shall have all the material (& venom) I want."

He steered clear of the American political campaign; in fact, he maintained absolute silence on national affairs. The kindness Theodore Roosevelt had shown Clemens on his return from Italy with his wife's remains was not forgotten. Sam Clemens was paying attention, though, and occasionally tweaked Twichell for his public sermons in support of Roosevelt. And reading the full text of John Hay's speech in the New York papers on the morning of October 27th turned his stomach. "I am sorry for John Hay; sorry & ashamed," Clemens wrote to Twichell. "And yet I know he couldn't help it. He wears the collar, & he had to pay the penalty. Certainly he had no more desire to stand up before a mob of confiding human incapables & debauch them than you had. Certainly he took no more real pleasure in distorting history, concealing facts, propagating immoralities, & appealing to the sordid side of human nature than did you; but he was his party's property, & he had to climb away down & do it."

THE DEMOCRATIC PAPERS were predictably critical of Hay's jeremiad and invited the secretary of state to a political knife fight. SECRETARY HAY FLAYED ALIVE: SENATOR MORGAN SKINS ADMINISTRATION WINDBAG. When Theodore arrived at Hay's front door for his regular after-church visit four days after the Carnegie Hall speech, the president was clucking humorously at the attacks on his secretary of state and at his friend's obvious discomfort. Hay reminded Theodore that this was exactly why he had cautioned the president about sending him out to the stump. The Democrats, and Morgan especially, who was already angry about losing his canal in Nicaragua, would be sure to block every treaty Hay brought to the Senate. The Carnegie Hall performance had probably destroyed him as an asset of the administration, he told Roosevelt. Theodore laughed again, a sharp bellow of a laugh. "What would my assets avail me," the president said, "if the Administration and I [lost the election and] went out together?"

Hay was in his bed with a cold for much of the next workweek, but Theodore stopped by that Sunday, two days before Election Day. The president was in fine fettle and remarkably calm. He was fairly sure of victory, and *certain* he had waged a bully campaign, with no loss of personal honor. He said he was especially pleased by the speeches on his behalf by his cabinet members, including Hay himself—"though I had trouble enough," the president reminded John Hay, "to get you on the platform."

HAY STAYED AT his desk at the State Department on the big day and did not head over to the White House to check on the returns until after nine o'clock that night. John Hay had once spent an Election Day at the White House, back in 1864, and he still had his forty-year-old diary pages, which recalled the scene at the drafty and unusually empty old mansion. "Everybody in Washington, not at home voting, seems ashamed of it and stays away from the President," Hay had recorded in 1864. Abraham Lincoln was on his way to victory that afternoon, and yet he remained in a somber mood. "It is a little singular that I, who am not a vindictive man, should have always been before the people for election in canvasses marked for their bitterness," Lincoln mused aloud to his young secretary and confidant that gloomy, rain-soaked day.

The mood at the White House was ebullient when Hay walked in forty years later—to the day. Hay would record the events of that election night in 1904 in his new diary a few hours later.

> I found the Red Parlor full of people, the President in the midst of them with his hands full of telegrams. I asked him if he had anything decisive as yet. He said, "Yes. [Democratic nominee] Judge Parker has sent his congratulations." . . .
>
> "I am glad," said Roosevelt, "to be President in my own right."

CHAPTER FORTY-FOUR

It Takes So Little to Upset the Regular Action of the Heart

John Hay reported for duty at the White House the morning after the election and found Theodore still in the glow of victory. The president started in talking fast and didn't stop. He wanted to thank Hay personally, man to man, for putting himself on the line in the campaign. Hay was a singularly popular figure among the public, Roosevelt asserted, and chiefly because Americans trusted John Hay to preserve and protect the national dignity. The secretary of state graciously (and quietly) accepted the compliments from the president, until Roosevelt mentioned that a signal reason for the success at the polls was Hay's "willingness" to remain in office. Hay wondered for a second whether he should remind the president that he had not pledged any such willingness in public and that he was not at all certain he *would* stick around, but the president's private secretary entered the room with a new fistful of congratulatory letters and put an end to the discussion.

John Hay decided for the moment not to spend much time contemplating his future but simply to march one day at a time. He got up the next morning and double-timed through one of the busiest days he had ever witnessed in the State Department, which ended with the Russian ambassador, Count Cassini, in his private office worrying him—as he did almost weekly—about the United States' providing clandestine support to Japan in their war against Russia. The count demanded to know the meaning of Japanese prince Fushimi's upcoming visit.

By the time Hay dragged himself home that Thursday night, he was exhausted and jittery, and he had not yet entirely recovered from his recent attack of bronchitis. He was too tired to take any great satisfaction in notices such as the one in the *Spectator of London,* which called him "unquestionably one of the ablest, if not the ablest, of living diplomatists." He had little interest in answering the letters of congratulations that poured in, but he got some satisfaction in responding to a few, like the one from an old friend from the Lincoln days who was certain that the Republican victory put Hay next in line for the presidency in 1908. "Dear Mr. Solomons," Hay wrote. "The chances are very precarious of my being alive at that date, but if I am, I certainly shall not be a candidate for any office."

Theodore made the announcement the next afternoon, while chatting with a gaggle of reporters in his office. The newsmen were prodding Roosevelt about the makeup of the new cabinet. He had nothing really to say on that point, he explained, except perhaps—well—"You may state positively," the president offered, "that Mr. Hay will continue as Secretary of State up to the 4th of March, 1909."

Hay would not say it aloud, but he was angry at Theodore for making his announcement without the courtesy of first making a formal offer, and for refusing to heed Hay's warnings that he did not have much more work left in him. "I shall have to go along awhile longer," Hay lamented, "as it would be a scandal to contradict him."

HAY WAS AT a private meeting with John Morley, a British member of Parliament whom Roosevelt was then hosting at the White House, when the telegram came from Hay's sister back home in Warsaw, Illinois. His older brother, retired United States Army officer Leonard Hay, had just died at the old family homestead. Hay was trying to absorb this news just as Morley walked into his library, and he found himself fighting back growing swells of emotion. Hay could hear himself talking to the Right Honorable John Morley but was unsure what he was actually saying, and he felt relieved when the president came striding in a few minutes later to take hold of the conversation. Hay waited until after Morley had gone to explain his new tragedy to Roosevelt; he told the president he thought it best to go to Warsaw for the funeral, but he was so shaken he was unable to think straight. Theodore seemed to meet Hay's discomfort with his characteristic mien—*Get a grip on yourself, old man*—and Hay found himself incapable of articulating to the president the depth of the loss.

Hay worked fitfully the next day on a draft of the president's welcoming speech to Prince Fushimi, while an early blizzard roared off the water and into Lafayette Square. Clara Hay told her husband to drop his work for the week and get on a train to Warsaw to see his oldest brother buried, and Hay started making plans to do just that, when a new telegram from Illinois reported that the funeral would be the next day, which was too soon for Hay to get to the remote Mississippi River town. Hay's sister promised they would keep the body in a vault until John could get there for the interment.

The headlines in the newspapers were like daggers in Hay's person: SECRETARY OF STATE'S BROTHER DEAD . . . JOHN HAY'S BROTHER DIES. It shamed him to see Leonard Hay reduced to adjunct personhood. His brother had been his first and fiercest protector. As a boy, John had once dreamed that the two together were compelled to fight for their lives on the floor of the Coliseum in Rome, and John had stood helpless, watching as Leonard slayed a lion, and then felt himself being carried by his brother through a maze of tunnels that miraculously led to the Appian Way. Hay described this dream in a letter to the president a few days after his brother's death, trying to explain why he had been—and remained—so shaken by the loss. "I cannot talk about it—so I shall write you a word," Hay began his letter. "My brother was my first friend and my best. I owe him everything. . . . He was always my standard. He was not so quick at his books as I was, but far more sure. He taught me my Latin and Greek so that I made better recitations than he did, and got higher marks—which was a gross injustice. But he took more interest in my success than in his own. He made many sacrifices for me, which I, with the selfishness of a boy, accepted as a matter of course." There were scores of others who would recognize John Hay's gifts and propel him forward, but Leonard gave him the first push out of the valley of the Mississippi, where Leonard himself would remain. "He was my superior in every way but one—the gift of expression," Hay wrote to Theodore. "Now he has left us, and I never had a chance to get even with him for all he did for me when we were boys. My uncertain health, the weather, and other futilities have even kept me away from his funeral. I feel remorsefully unworthy of him."

CLARA HAY COULD see her husband heading for a crash, and she wanted him out of office or at least away from the pressures of Washington. Besides the ongoing bronchitis, her husband was suffering excruciating lumbar pain, vertigo, odd fluctuations in his heartbeat, and chest pain. Hay maintained that his chief malady was old age. "I feel a general flavor of mild decay," Hay told his friends, as if the flavor might somehow be soothing. Roosevelt encouraged Hay to forget his grief and his poor health by shouldering his pack and staying busy.

Hay kept up a steady, old-timey official gait; he was tidying up nearly a dozen separate arbitration treaties, which put into practical usage articles agreed upon at the multinational peace convention at The Hague a few years earlier. Hay had worked out bilateral treaties with France, Great Britain, and Germany compelling each side to submit to The Hague's Permanent Court of Arbitration disputes that did not rise to vital questions of independence, sovereignty, and national honor; and now it looked as if he was about to land Russia in the arbitration boat. The secretary of state had been assiduous about consulting the Senate throughout the negotiations, and the chairman of the Senate Foreign Relations Committee, Shelby Cullom, was saying he thought he could get the first of Hay's treaties through the Senate, no matter how loudly old Senator Morgan and a few others squawked.

The week before Christmas, Hay felt confident enough in his relations with the Senate to ask for a personal favor. "Dear Senator Spooner," he wrote to a key member of the Foreign Relations Committee and one of Theodore's strongest supporters in the upper chamber. "I suppose you will have in your hands the matter of the compliment recently paid me by the French Government, which requires the consent of Congress for me to accept it. . . . I enclose a copy of the letter which the French Embassy sent me on the 14th of last July. I have frequently been offered such distinctions, but have always declined them. The only reason for my making an exception in this case was that the President, whom I consulted in advance, thought that a compliment tendered in the words I have underlined could not be declined."

Hay was knocked back again in the last week of January by a new flare of bronchitis and vicious pains in his back and along his left side. He arose from his sickbed long enough to host a dinner for the members of the House Foreign Affairs Committee and the Senate Foreign Relations Committee and began to regret it as the hour approached ten o'clock and the nation's esteemed legislators were still at his house drinking his claret and babbling about congressional business. The only good news was that Cabot was feeling under the weather and left during the third course. Hay could feel his strength wane as the men began taking odds on ratification of the arbitration treaties. The vice president elect, Senator Charles W. Fairbanks, thought Morgan might be able to filibuster them unto death. John Spooner saw nothing but snags and shoals. By the time the night was done, Hay was convinced the treaties would not make it through in the current session. The evening's unhappy host was woozy with pain when he finally got upstairs to his bed that night, and he tossed and turned for a few uncomfortable hours. When he finally did go under, he dreamed that he had been condemned to be hanged as a deserter the next morning.

The next night, one of the senators voicing the loudest opposition to the treaties showed up at Hay's door. "He had mistaken the hour for the dinner, which was the night before," Hay reported of the spectacularly named Mississippian, Hernando DeSoto Money. "He sat with us and dined and remained till ten o'clock—with apparently not the slightest sense of embarrassment." Hay passed another fitful night abed and woke with a tender and raspy throat; his cough was worse than ever and the stitch in his left side had migrated into his shoulder.

Senator Henry Cabot Lodge stuck the first shiv in the secretary of state's back ten days later. He added an amendment effectively killing the recently negotiated commercial treaty with Canada. Cabot had decided a loud public show of protecting the fishermen in Gloucester, Massachusetts (where his son-in-law would have to run for reelection as congressman), was better politics for Cabot than was approving Hay's sweeping treaty of commercial reciprocity. "It seems to me as stupid a piece of bad manners as any country has ever been guilty of," Hay said privately.

Hay was busy negotiating a new treaty with Japan the next day when he got the news: the Senate had added to the arbitration treaties a blanket amendment that the president had warned would render the treaties worthless. Senator Spooner then attacked Secretary Hay for sophistry in preparing the text of the treaties to allow the executive to skirt the Senate ratification process. "The President appears to be bent on running foreign affairs himself, without consulting the Senate," said another senator. "Well, if he is looking for trouble of that kind he will find it."

Cabot, Spooner, and a few other senators blasted Hay for making the treaties public before submitting them to the Senate. Secretary of State Hay gave as good as he got. His next-day statement implicitly accused the Senate of cowardice for not simply voting the treaty down as a matter of principle but instead making "changes which are incompatible with the [treaties'] spirit and purpose" and leaving it for the executive to do the dirty work of a mercy killing.

Hay's best friends in the Senate answered, accusing him of something near dereliction of his duties for not being man enough to go to Capitol Hill to personally defend the treaties he had negotiated. The next slap at Hay was less benign. When Cullom attempted to report from committee to the Senate floor the bill authorizing Hay to accept the Grand Cross from the French government, Senator Spooner blocked it. This, Spooner lied, was the first he had ever heard of any such legislation.

IN EARLY MARCH, John Hay countersigned his own commission as secretary of state in Roosevelt's new second-term cabinet—over Clara Hay's objection. Clara had the better case, but all she could extract from her husband was a promise to take a six-week rest cure at the baths in the mountains of Germany that spring. Hay was already faltering as sailing day approached. He was still unable to shake his bronchitis, and any exertion left him faint or panting. His regular evening walks were harrowing endeavors, accompanied by constricting pains across his chest. He slept fitfully. He had no appetite. The White House staff had to help him climb the stairs to the president's office.

His last visitor at the State Department before the scheduled voyage was the

Russian ambassador, who exhausted him with complaints that the United States was still secretly aiding the Japanese. Count Cassini mewled gloomily about the many misfortunes Russia had suffered during its war with Japan, until Hay finally gathered the strength to stop him. "When will come the time of your diplomats?" Hay asked, and then he watched Cassini's shoulders sag. "We are condemned to fight," the count said. "We cannot honorably stop."

THE ADMINISTRATION MANAGED to keep Hay's poor health under wraps even as he set out for New York to begin his "vacation." John Hay and Theodore Roosevelt traveled up to the city on the same day, St. Patrick's Day, 1905, but separately. Hay went unnoticed in a quiet private railroad car and then shut himself into his bedroom in the city. The president took a special train north from Washington and arrived in New York in a hail of fanfare and publicity. He went directly to a town house in the East Seventies, where he gave away his niece Eleanor at her wedding to a distant cousin, Franklin Delano Roosevelt. Theodore left before the wedding dinner was complete, and Hay watched from his window as the presidential procession passed below, escorted by New York's famous Fighting Sixty-Ninth, on its way to Delmonico's, where Theodore was to be hosted by the Friendly Sons of St. Patrick. Roosevelt made an after-dinner speech to the Irishmen and then hied himself to the Hotel Astor to deliver a speech to the Sons of the American Revolution. By two o'clock in the morning, Theodore was sleeping peacefully in his private railcar as it hurtled through Delaware on its way back to the capital. Hay remained, though not particularly comfortably, in his bed.

John Hay had a leisurely breakfast the next morning but was hit with stabbing chest pain just before his carriage arrived to take him to the Thirteenth Street pier to board ship. Clara Hay and Henry Adams were traveling with Hay that day, and Clarence Hay, Henry White, and the Wadsworths were riding along to see them off. The docks were crawling with reporters when the party arrived, and the newsmen were watching as Hay faltered. The secretary of state could not make it up the three flights of stairs on his own power, nearly fainted twice, and finally had to resort to making the last short leg of the journey to the gangway in a wheelchair. As Henry White led Hay toward his stateroom, he whispered to his boss and friend, "We can't hold it any longer; they know now."

Once Hay was safely out of sight and in his berth, Mrs. Hay made a statement to the reporters. "He has been suffering from the grippe and has not fully recovered," she told them. "The climb up the stairs fatigued him. I hope not too much will be printed about it, as it is of little importance. . . . We hope that the trip will do him much good and result in his recovery, but we fear it will take much longer than he thinks before he is restored to his full health." Meanwhile reporters back in Washington were pounding at Hay's doctor's door, looking for answers. "Mr. Hay is suffering from exhaustion of the nerve centres, due to confinement and overwork," reported the *Sun,* which also recalled the secretary's reputation for extreme sensitivity and his tendency toward mental depression. "[The doctor] said this evening he fully believed that two months of rest and recreation would enable Mr. Hay to resume his official duties."

HAY WROTE FROM aboard ship to reassure his only remaining son that he would be OK. "I had my worst quarter of an hour on the dock at New York and have been gaining ever since," he told Clarence. "I have had my three meals daily and after the first week . . . I have walked the deck for a mile or two every day." On the ship's arrival in northern Italy, the United States consul in Genoa took one look at Hay and shipped him straight to a doctor, who diagnosed among other things nervous weakness and possibly anemia. He told Hay the chest pains were a result of "a sagging of the heart" and cautioned that he was not yet well enough to make the overland trip to Bad Nauheim and must take a fortnight's rest on the Riviera—under the doctor's care, of course. "He said," Hay reported, "my condition was one which was very common among public men."

When Hay arrived at Bad Nauheim ten days later (and already behind schedule), the spa's esteemed doctors Dr. Isidor Groedel and his son were unwilling to venture any definite prognosis before they had completed their exhaustive examinations, but they supposed Hay would need at least twenty baths, which meant five or more weeks at the spa. "At present I require absolute rest," Hay wrote after his second consultation with his doctors. "Must not walk up hill; must not talk while walking or walk after meals. [Dr. Groedel] is noncommittal as to my resignation. . . . Warned me especially against doing any work while here."

When the battery of blood tests and pulse and blood-pressure readings were complete, Groedel announced that Hay had an enlargement of the heart, which could be reversed. He laid out a strict diet, which was precisely the regimen Hay had already been observing. Hay stayed at Bad Nauheim for five weeks, not much cheered by his diet or by his fellow patients, one of whom insisted on regaling Hay with the grim details of his brother's death from enlargement of the heart. "There is very little youth and beauty to be seen here, the elderly and the ugly fill the shady streets and the alleys of the Park, with wan faces and crawling footsteps," Hay wrote to his daughter Alice. "But the main thing is the baths which are delightful; like being soused in a tub of warm apollinaris."

His chest pains diminished in the first few days and he found himself able to walk up a flight of stairs without feeling faint. The doctors presented him with rosy reports: "You seem better every day. We shall have excellent results." . . . "The enlargement of the heart is diminishing." . . . "The pulse much more regular." "You are better looking." Hay was not so able to throw pixie dust in his own eyes and was also alarmed at his reaction to word that the top United States diplomat in Germany intended to make a visit to Bad Nauheim. "The news annoyed me so that there was a sensible increase of the feeling of constriction as I went to my bath, and when young Groedel called he perceived that something was gone wrong by the status of my pulse," Hay admitted in his diary. "The discouraging thing about it is that it takes so little to upset the regular action of the heart, even after all the improvement of the last fortnight."

The correspondence from the State Department was spare and generally in the nature of ascertaining the boss's state of health or passing along well wishes. One cable came from the consul in Genoa, who had received a note from a mutual friend. "Here is what Sam Clemens writes me, under date of April 11: 'We are glad to know by the cable grams that Genoa treated Mr. Hay well, and that he is improving in the mild climate of Italy.' Then, in parentheses, and in [Clemens's] own handwriting—'It is a large 'we', there being eighty million of us.'"

The only visitors Hay allowed were old friends like Harry White and Frank Mason. "I had two priceless weeks . . . with poor dear Hay," Mason would report to Clemens not long after. "We were . . . in the suite of rooms just above the ones in which Mrs. Clemens and you and the girls lived during that happy summer away back about 1892 wasn't it? Well we talked and walked, told stories, and played that we were young again and I had a constant fight to keep away the great people who came to do him honor—for you know in Europe or rather international diplomacy Hay is looked up to as the Magnus Apollo."

THE DOCTORS PRONOUNCED Hay's heart in good health toward the end of his five-week stay, and when Hay asked what might then be the cause of the chest pain he felt on his walks, the doctor said it was only "neuralgia and would pass away." Toward the end of May, Hay sent the president news of his return date, though he made no promises that he would be ready to go back to work: "All this is very embarrassing," he wrote.

> If I were fit for work, I would gladly go back to my desk. If I were ready for the Knacker, I would at once get out of the way. But when all the doctors tell me I am going to get well, but that it will be a matter of some months yet, I feel that I ought not be a dead weight in the boat for an indefinite time. It would be easy for me to say "do as you please" and throw

> the job of deciding on you. But that would be a craven sort of thing, to add this other care to the many you bear. So that, if you do not want to make an appointment of an able bodied Secretary of State just now, we can let the matter rest till I see you next month, about the 16th or 17th, and perhaps by that time I shall be enough better, or worse, to give a decisive element to the problem.
>
> But of course I need not say that when you think a change would be, for any reason, advisable, I shall go. I don't say willingly, but as Browning says "go dispiritedly, glad to finish."

Theodore did not take the bait and refused to relieve Hay of his duties. Meanwhile word had got around that the American secretary of state was about to leave Bad Nauheim and then to pass briefly through Paris and London before sailing for home. The kaiser asked Hay to meet him in Berlin before he left Germany for good; the king of Belgium ("the rattlepated old lunatic," Hay called him) threatened to break into Hay's room at the baths; the Foreign Office in Paris wanted an audience with Hay, and so did the British foreign minister in London. And then the king of England, old Bertie, insisted that Hay could not go away from England without seeing him.

The doctors gave Hay very strict orders as he prepared to leave Bad Nauheim, which the patient recorded: "No cabbage, raisins, onions nor anything flatulent—no salmon, lobster, little red meat of any kind—no lively aerated water, no champagne. No sweets except the simplest form of pudding. No public speaking, not much animated conversation, especially after dinner or when walking. No fast walking, especially up hill. . . . He was especially severe as to the next two or three weeks. I was to see nobody, if possible, say nothing and see nothing amusing. He absolutely bars visits to the Foreign Offices in Paris & London."

"This opinion agrees so entirely with my own sensations, that I must be guided by it," Hay explained to the US Embassy in London, while asking them to send regrets to all invitations. "So I am to have no fun, and meet no personages, in Paris or London, or anywhere short of Washington. . . . I am very sorry, and very much ashamed to have to say this."

HIS SENSE OF shame got the better of him: Hay did see the king of Belgium when he showed up uninvited at Bad Nauheim. Hay had to sit and listen while Leopold II worried him toward a promise to prevent the Chinese government from buying up a Chinese railroad. Hay was not strong when he left Germany; he was gobbling an herb called valerian to tamp his anxieties and help him sleep. When he wasn't suffering actual chest pains, he simmered with "nervous malaise." Once Hay arrived for his brief visit to Paris, he spent much of his time in Henry Adams's sleek new Mercedes, making long, looping trips as far out as Versailles at "an incredible rate of speed." But when the French Foreign Office summoned him, Hay tossed out his doctor's orders and took the meeting.

Adams said his good-byes to his old friend in Paris and then reported to Lizzie Cameron: "His nerves are gone," Adams wrote. "He is in no better physical condition than when he sailed. . . . He had better go out, now that his excuse is good."

Three days in London promised as much business for Hay as it did fun or rest. He scheduled a long luncheon with Whitelaw Reid at his new residence, Dorchester House. Whitelaw had finally got his coveted ambassadorship to the Court of St. James's. "There is not much left of me," Hay wrote to Reid, "but I shall be glad and proud to see you, where I have long desired to see you, in a place you will not only fill but adorn."

Hay also took a long meeting with His Majesty's foreign minister, Lord Lansdowne, who wanted to talk through Far East policy and to ask about President Roosevelt's plans now that Japan and Russia were ready to accept his offer to personally handle their peace talks. Hay was at sea on that account: he had no idea what Theodore was up to. At the end of the hour-long meeting, Lansdowne reminded Hay of the king's ardent desire to meet once more with his old friend.

John Hay was unable to climb the stairs at Buckingham Palace, so the king met him in a private anteroom on the ground floor. The meeting was a confirmation that the work Hay had done in the previous seven years had not been for nothing. "[The king] began talking at once with great affability and fluency, laying great stress on the agreeable relations between our two countries," Hay would remember. "He was full of personal compliments to the President; exhibited a little feeling about the supposed efforts . . . to make trouble between us. . . . The King was very keen about having the English and American [naval] squadrons execute their maneuvers this summer in unison—'not against each other you understand, but together.'"

WHEN THE SS *Baltic* steamed out into the Atlantic for the voyage to New York, its most famous passenger was on edge. The trip had not had the effect Clara Hay had intended, and her husband's stubborn insistence on meeting the obligations of his office had cost him what little gain he had made. She hoped John would finally see the need to retire from office and save himself, but he had different ideas. Hay had already decided to make a brief visit to see the president in Washington when they arrived back in the States, just to make sure there was nothing urgent that needed his attention before he headed to the Fells for a full summer's rest. He would know in October, he figured, whether he was still fit for duty.

The third day at sea, Hay pulled out his diary and began sketching out a letter to Senator Shelby Cullom: "I rarely ask a favor personal to myself," Hay wrote,

> but I shall be greatly obliged to you if you will prevent any further consideration by the Senate of the Resolution you presented last winter permitting me to accept the distinction of Grand Cross of the Legion of Honor conferred upon me by the French Government. . . . It was felt by me and by those whom I consulted that it could not properly be declined; and that it was probable that no objection would be made in any quarter.
>
> In this I was mistaken. I was entirely unaware of the feeling existing towards me among some prominent members of my own party. But since it is evident that such a feeling exists, I beg that you will prevent the further consideration of your Resolution which failed of adoption last winter.

JOHN HAY HAD a vivid dream out at sea, on one of the last nights of his voyage home: He had gone to the White House to report for duty and found Abraham Lincoln in charge again. Hay was unsurprised in the dream to be in the presence of the Tycoon but felt awash in a deep and oppressive sadness. "[President Lincoln] was very kind and considerate, and sympathetic about my illness," was how Hay remembered the dream the next morning. "He said there was little work of importance on hand. He gave me two unimportant letters to answer. I was pleased that the slight order was within my power to obey."

CHAPTER FORTY-FIVE

I Didn't Wish to Be Useful to the World on Such Expensive Conditions

"Those were the days! —Those old ones," Sam Clemens wrote in declining an invitation to an upcoming reunion of his friends from 1860s California. "They will come no more. Youth will come no more. They were full to the brim with the wine of life; there have been no others like them. It chokes me up to think of them."

Clemens was up in the mountains of New Hampshire in June of 1905, anticipating the first anniversary of Livy's death, riding out awful dips of dark melancholy and swells of ungovernable rage. The sadness he accepted as the bill come due after thirty-five years of a life with Livy, and there was no harm in showing that to the world. But the bitterness he recognized as a perilous danger, and he was doing his best to keep it bottled up. His chief method in this was to just keep working. He had arrived at his rented summer cottage at the end of May and gone straight to his writing desk, working thirty-three of the first thirty-four days he was there. He churned out tens of thousands of words on two fanciful and unoffending little pieces of short fiction. At night after dinner, he would read the fruit of the day to Jean and to Isabel Lyon. These sessions were pleasant enough, but he found himself marking the absence of the prize members of his audience—Susy and Livy and even Clara, who remained in isolation at the sanatorium in Connecticut, trying to regain her mental equilibrium and her singing voice. Clemens was as encouraging as he could be at a distance.

"You have gotten back your sleep," he wrote to Clara on her birthday, June 8, 1905, in answer to her most recent missive. "It is great—there's nothing greater I reckon, among the blessings. . . . That your voice is stronger than it was, is most gratifying news. It means what the natural sleep does—that you are climbing handsomely health-ward. . . . Oh, lots and lots of love, dear little Black spider blatherskite. Father."

It made him lonesome to think of Clara by herself in Connecticut—when it didn't make him angry.

KATY LEARY WAS in her own room when she heard the racket from his office. Mr. Clemens must have thought he was alone. "Well! Damn this house! Goddamn this old place! Damn this climate! Damnedest room! Not a Goddamn thing here that anybody wants! Can't even find a single pin in the whole place!" Katy hadn't heard her boss talk this way since the day Livy died, when he vowed to swear off swearing for good. "You can never find a thing in this damned old place!" He was in the hall now, stalking, and growling. "Why, I had a new paper of pins only yesterday, and now some old idiot has come and *took all my pins away*!"

He saw Katy when he got to her doorway. "Katy! Are you here?"

"I've been here all the time, Mr. Clemens," she said.

"Well, I have been swearing," he admitted, embarrassed and apologetic. "There's no mistake about that, but this is the very *first* time I swore since I left Florence."

"To tell the truth, I was kind of amused listening to you," Katy told him. "I didn't mind it a bit. Bad language is the only thing that can take the deadness off *this* place. It would make *anybody* swear."

Katy found the pins and noted that Mr. Clemens, as he always did after such outbursts, "calmed down and was quiet as a lamb."

HE HAD TO *let it out* sometimes, when it felt as if he was choking on the bile that rose in his throat, but he was careful to confine his savaging to the inner circle, except for those times when he unleashed it on his publisher, who deserved it, after all. The hands at Harper & Brothers had made him—by a new and exclusive contract—the best-paid writer in the country, but they had also rewritten the rules on him a bit: they were no longer willing to take whatever matter "Mark Twain" desired to produce for publication. One of George Harvey's magazines had recently published "Twain's" screed against the murderous Czar Nicholas II of Russia, but editors had shied from "King Leopold's Soliloquy," an invented diatribe from the Belgian king, who was being charged publicly and accurately just then with genocide in the Congo. "They tell it all," Clemens's Leopold II whines, "how I am wiping a nation of friendless creatures out of existence by every form of murder, for my private pocket's sake, and how every shilling I get costs a rape, a mutilation or a life. But they never say, although they know it, that I have labored in the cause of religion at the same time and all the time, and have sent missionaries there (of a 'convenient stripe,' as they phrase it), to teach them the error of their ways and bring them to Him who is all mercy and love, and who is the sleepless guardian and friend of all who suffer. They tell only what is against me, they will not tell what is in my favor." When an editor at Harper & Brothers explained that the company was taking a pass on King Leopold, Clemens gave it away to be printed and sold by the Congo Reform Association.

The "War Prayer" was an even more risky attack, as Clemens seemed to be taking aim at his own country's methods of civilizing and reforming. He had tried the prayer on Jean one night when it was finished: "O Lord our God, help us to tear their soldiers to bloody shreds with our shells; help us to cover their smiling fields with the pale forms of their patriot dead; help us to drown the thunder of the guns with the wounded, writhing in pain; help us to lay waste their humble homes with a hurricane of fire; help us to wring the hearts of their unoffending widows with unavailing grief; help us to turn them out roofless with their little children to wander unfriended through wastes of their desolated land in rags & hunger & thirst." Jean was horrified and told her father he must put the piece where it belonged—in its pigeonhole and out of the sight of the reading public.

The editors at Harper & Brothers concurred. Clemens tried it a few days later on Dan Beard, who had illustrated his recent books: "For our sakes, who adore Thee, Lord, blast their hopes, blight their lives, protract their bitter pilgrimage, make heavy their steps, water their way with their tears, stain the white snow with the blood of their wounded feet!"

Beard was all for publishing it—somewhere, anywhere—and was ready to help, until Clemens stopped him. He was tired of fighting. "Only dead men can tell the truth in this world," he told Beard. "It can be published after I am dead."

SAM CLEMENS MIGHT sometimes wail at the timidity of Harper & Brothers, but he knew they were looking out for him. He would occasionally let fly about something he had read in the news, like the pogrom in Russia that left fifty thousand Jews dead, maimed, or displaced. "I wish somebody would assassinate the Russian [royal] Family," Clemens confided in one of his diatribes to Twichell. "So does every sane person in the world—but who has the grit to say so? Nobody."

He wouldn't say that in public, of course, and neither would he allow publication under his pen name of his private philosophy, which held that selfishness was at the heart of human nature. "Am I honest? I give my word of honor (private) I am not," he told Twichell. "For seven years I have suppressed a book which my conscience tells me I ought to publish. I hold it a duty to publish it. There are other difficult duties which I am equal to, but I am not equal to that one."

He had become mercenary at heart, but for all the best reasons; Clemens had worked too hard for too long—ever since he was thirteen years old!—and he had lost too much in his scrabble out of bankruptcy and certain disgrace to piss away his celebrated name—"Mark Twain"!—or to put in jeopardy the new pile of assets he had amassed. He had done it all for his wife and his daughters, hadn't he? Even if two of the four had not lived to benefit, Clara and Jean had. His only sole remaining duty was to them. Clara was thirty-one years old now and was still insistent on making her own name as a performer; she was as ambitious and headstrong and independent as her father, and he suspected none of these qualities was particularly fetching to suitors. Even if Clara did marry—and the talented Russian pianist Ossip Gabrilowitsch was a definite possibility—Jean was different. Her epilepsy made her unmarriageable, as far as Clemens could tell; her future depended entirely on him, and he meant to make her life after he was gone as full of ease and pleasure as he could.

Not that he wasn't tempted to let loose in print from his cottage perch in the hills of New Hampshire. President Roosevelt, for all his personal kindnesses to Clemens, made him crazy. Roosevelt's inane diatribes—and the almost daily evidence of what Poultney Bigelow liked to call the president's "refinement of cruelty and petty persecutions"—offered a big, chesty target for Clemens to work off some of his rage in public. But he refrained. In fact he didn't say much of anything from New Hampshire until the thirty-fifth day there, June 24, 1905, when Roosevelt started in on one of his garden-variety political lies, and Sam Clemens had to take a day off from his regular work just to purge. He wrote a long private letter to the poor Reverend Joe Twichell, his appointed "equilibrium restorer": "[Roosevelt] is all bluster, all pow-wow, all gas. He hasn't any real courage. . . . Even jelly McKinley was a man, compared with this kitten that masquerades in a lion's skin." And while he was at it, Clemens worked off a little extra of his stored spite on Roosevelt's recent diplomatic appointment. "Whitelaw Reid's father-in-law's money sent Ambassador to England! In the room of Choate, Hay, Phelps, Lowell & those others," he cried to Twichell. "Well, we sent all those fine giants to exhibit America's brains, perhaps it was time to send a dwarf to display cash."

CLEMENS WAS NOT pure rage and temper that summer; there was one man in the government he still regarded with fondness, the man who *should* be president, he said, "if we were a properly honest and grateful nation instead of an ungrateful one, a nation which has usually not been willing to have a chief magistrate of gold when it could get one of tin." The newspapers said this gold-plated icon of American officialdom was on his way to his own summer home in New Hampshire, not fifty miles away. Clemens was sorry his latest message had not caught up to John Hay. He had not liked the reports about Hay's state of health, so he had written him a little "buck up" note, but anonymously, because he did not want the secretary to feel obliged to answer it. "Dear & Honored Sir," it read.

> I never hear any one speak of you & your long role of illustrious services in other than terms of pride & praise—& out of the heart. I think I am right in believing you to be the only man in the civil service of the country the cleanness of whose motives is never questioned by any citizen, & whose acts proceed always upon a broad & high plane, never by accident or pressure of circumstance upon a narrow or low one. There are majorities that are proud of more than one of the nation's great servants, but I believe & I think I know, that you are the only one of whom the entire nation is proud. Proud & thankful.

SAM CLEMENS GOT the news with the rest of the world—dateline Newbury, New Hampshire, July 1: "John Hay, Secretary of State, died here to-day." The obituaries traced Hay's path over the previous two weeks. He had disembarked the SS *Baltic* in New York, made a brief visit at his daughter's country house on Long Island, reported to the president at the White House in Washington, and then to the State Department, where he had apparently resumed his official duties. Roosevelt had released Hay for the summer (Theodore thought he could handle the peace conference between Japan and Russia alone), so Secretary Hay had headed straight to the Fells in New Hampshire. He had arrived there on Saturday, June 24, suffered a frightening collapse the next day, but seemed to be rallying by week's end. The doctors and the family seemed sure of full recovery by the time Hay retired to his bed Friday night. He died a few hours later. "The last moments of the statesman were peaceful and the end came almost without a struggle," was a common report in the newspapers. This sounded like John Hay; he never *appeared* to struggle, whether he did or not.

The first telegram of the news had gone to the president. "My sense of deep personal loss, great though it is, is lost in my sense of the bereavement to the whole country in Mr. Hay's death," was the public statement Roosevelt released from Oyster Bay, where the president was so near to being able to enjoy his new trophy room paneled with beautifully burnished hardwoods imported tariff-free from the Philippines. "The American people have never had a greater Secretary of State than John Hay, and his loss is a National calamity."

Privately, Roosevelt was far less sentimental. John Hay was a lucky man, Theodore told their friends: he "fell in the harness, as I should suppose every man would wish to fall." Roosevelt was downright mean in a note to Secretary of War William Howard Taft: "For two years he has done little or nothing in the State Dept.," Roosevelt wrote. "What I didn't do myself wasn't done at all." John Hay's first boss and mentor in the foreign service, eighty-seven-year-old John Bigelow, was philosophical. "If this world's fame were still any object to [John Hay], his death probably was not premature," Bigelow wrote to a mutual friend. "There was no more glory in store for him as the mate of a ship [of] which Roosevelt was the Captain."

CLARA HAY PICKED up her husband's diary where he had left off. Her notes about John Hay's last week belied the newspaper accounts of a death "without struggle." A malignancy in Hay's prostate had made it almost impossible for him to pass urine. The doctors inserted an uncomfortable catheter, but he was still racked with what he described as "showers of pain" in his abdomen. While the physicians concentrated on his urinary issues and possible infection, the patient's chest pain continued without cease. Next came searing intestinal pains, and finally, after being in bed in the same position for almost a week, his entire body began to ache. "He did not complain to us," Clara wrote. "He did not like to make trouble."

Less than twelve hours before he died, Hay was signing official papers and dictating long letters back to the first assistant secretary of state. He would have kept at it longer, but Clara made him stop. "If you will promise me I will be better tomorrow," he grumbled to his wife, "I will wait."

The deathbed scene a few hours later was harrowing. When Clara arrived in his sickroom that night, she heard her husband groaning like an animal, and the doctors were frantically trying to inject him with nitroglycerin. Mrs. Hay was taken aback by the "look of horror on the nurse's face." Even in Clara Hay's genteel (and gentle) telling, her husband had suffered a demoralizing and painful final week of life—and kept working right to the end.

THE BIG DECISIONS fell to Clara Hay. Helen and Payne were in the middle of the Atlantic, heading to Europe to buy treasure to fill their glorious new Fifth Avenue mansion. There was no sense in postponing the funeral service for them. Clara decided to take her husband's body to Cleveland for burial immediately. He would lie in state at the chamber of commerce there and be buried in the Stone family plot. "As he told me once he did not care where I laid him and as our boy was there it seemed more like home," Clara would say.

The rain started early the second morning after John Hay's death and gathered force as the funeral party prepared to leave the Fells. Newspapers described the scene at the Hay house, where a wet horse-drawn wagon waited in somber stillness to receive the coffin. One of Hay's old Brown classmates, reading the description of that morning, was moved to pull out a volume of John Hay's poems and read "The Stirrup Cup," a verse of Hay's that he had always remembered.

> My short and happy day is done,
> The long and dreary night comes on;
> And at my door the Pale Horse stands,
> To carry me to unknown lands.
>
> His whinny shrill, his pawing hoof,
> Sound dreadful as a gathering storm;
> And I must leave this sheltering roof,
> And joys of life so soft and warm.

By the time the polished rosewood box carrying the secretary's body was loaded onto the wagon, covered with a rubber blanket, and lashed in place, the only road off the mountain had become a river of mud. "The body was attended only by an undertaker and Secretary Hay's coachman," reported Hay's old employer the *New York Tribune*.

> Both men walked, the coachmen leading the horse while the undertaker followed behind. Not a person was met along the lonely mountain road. The window shades of the few scattered farmhouses along the route were drawn. The rain fell in torrents as the funeral party proceeded along the muddy road.
>
> The trip to the Newbury station occupied nearly an hour. Almost all the residents of the little hamlet were assembled there awaiting the arrival of the funeral party, and when the wagon with the Secretary's body neared the station the crowd on the platform stood with heads bared.

Sam Clemens was one among the many famous men who released a public statement about John Hay. "My friendship with Mr. Hay & my admiration of him endured 38 years without impairment," it read. The reasons for this enduring admiration were not entirely obvious. In matters of politics and policy, and matters of race and class, and matters of mere personal style, there was an enormous gulf that separated the two men. But Clemens wasn't one to dwell on those differences or allow them to be the controlling factor in his estimation of John Hay. He still loved Hay for how they had been so alike, so long ago, when they were just two young men from remote and brutish Mississippi River towns, trying to cut their mark; he loved that Hay was still making that effort down to his final, painful end. That was courage, in Sam Clemens's book—the kind he respected in a man.

SAM CLEMENS SPOKE here and there about "patriotism" over the next few years. He even allowed a dangerous little phrase or two (the Philippines—a stain on our flag that can never be effaced) to sidle parenthetically into an interview or a speech. But that didn't happen often, and he kept his darker ideas on the subject to himself. "In the beginning of a change the patriot is a scarce man, & brave, & hated, & scorned," Clemens wrote in his notebook. "When his cause succeeds, the timid join him, for then it costs nothing to be a patriot. The soul & substance of what customarily ranks as patriotism is moral cowardice—and always has been. . . . We have thrown away the most valuable asset we had—the individual's right to oppose both flag & country when he (just *he,* by himself) believed them to be in the wrong. We have thrown it away."

Clemens had plenty of chances to prove wrong his own pitiable assertion. A week after John Hay's death, Secretary of War William Howard Taft stopped in San Francisco on his way to tour America's new Pacific holdings and took the time to explain the situation in the Philippines. "I am told there are quite a number of Filipinos who are in favor of absolute independence at once, and I am confronted with the repeated question, 'Shall we grant [the Filipinos] independence at once or are we right to show them that they cannot be made fit for independence at once?'" Taft said to the crowd at a banquet thrown him by the city's leading commercial organizations. And then he answered, "They are not yet ready for independence and if they talk of independence at the present time it is mere wind."

Clemens let it pass without remark, as he would similar episodes that followed. He began working again on his autobiographical dictations at the beginning of 1906, much of them to be embargoed until long after his death so that he could speak freely. But when news hit the papers in March that US soldiers had routed a group of "insurgent" Muslim natives on the island of Jolo, in the Philippine archipelago, the story grabbed his attention—and would not let go. The American army had reportedly wiped out a force of as many as six hundred

Moros who had taken up a defensive position inside a lava cone two thousand feet above sea level. Not a single one of these fighters survived the American attack. The Filipinos had been armed with their traditional knives and some old rifles, while the Americans had (with remarkable intrepidity, said the news dispatches) hauled their heavy artillery pieces up the crater wall to within range of the enemy encampment. On receiving news of American victory, President Roosevelt cabled a note to his old friend General Leonard Wood, the head military man in the region (a region that produced a very fine mahogany): "I congratulate you and the officers and men of your command upon the brilliant feat of arms wherein you and they so well upheld the honor of the American flag."

Second- and third-day newspaper reports started to suggest ugliness: a vast majority of the dead Moro "fighters" turned out to be women and children. Clemens was disgusted. His autobiographical dictations veered suddenly from his youth on the Mississippi to the American take-no-prisoners style of battle in the Philippines, which "had remained what it has been for eight years, in our army out there—the taste of Christian butchers." "With six hundred engaged on each side," he wrote, "we lost fifteen men killed outright, and we had thirty-two wounded—counting that nose and that elbow. The enemy numbered six hundred—including women and children—and we abolished them utterly, leaving not even a baby alive to cry for its dead mother. *This is incomparably the greatest victory that was ever achieved by the Christian soldiers of the United States*."

Clemens talked on and on, filling pages. "The next heading blazes with American and Christian glory like to the sun in the zenith: 'Death List is Now 900,'" he wrote, "I was never so enthusiastically proud of the flag till now!"

Clemens was still dictating matter on America's latest Benevolent Assimilation activities two days later. "The President's joy over the splendid achievement of his fragrant pet, General Wood, brings to mind an earlier Presidential ecstasy." He was still in this fury when Secretary Taft made public Leonard Wood's response to the charges of "wanton slaughter" in the recent battle. "I was present thruout practically entire action and inspected top of crater after action was finished," Wood had cabled to the War Department.

> Am convinced no man, woman or child was wantonly killed. Considerable number of women and children were killed in the fight—number unknown—for the reason that they were actually in the works when assaulted, and were unavoidably killed when hand-to-hand fighting took place in the narrow inclosed space. Moro women wore trousers and were dressed and armed like men, and charged with them. The children were in many cases used by the men as shields while charging troops. These incidents are much to be regretted, but it must be understood that the Moros,

> one and all, were fighting not only as enemies, but religious fanatics, believing Paradise to be their immediate reward if killed in action against Christians. They apparently desired that none be saved.

Wood's illogical assertions and flat-out lies settled affairs for Theodore Roosevelt. "This answer is, of course, entirely satisfactory," the president wrote in a message to Secretary of War Taft. "The officers and enlisted men under General Wood's command have performed a most gallant and soldierly feat in a way that confers added credit on the American army. They are entitled to the heartiest admiration and praise of all those of their fellow citizens who are glad to see the honor of the flag upheld by the courage of the men wearing the American uniform."

Clemens thought better of picking a fight—a fight he was unlikely to win. He tucked his Moro Crater Massacre manuscript into its pigeonhole, alongside a growing raft of material on Roosevelt.

> Mr. Roosevelt is the Tom Sawyer of the political world of the twentieth century; always showing off; always hunting for a chance to show off; in his frenzied imagination the Great Republic is a vast Barnum circus with him for a clown and the whole world for audience. . . . He represents what the American gentleman ought not to be, and does it as clearly, intelligibly, and exhaustively as he represents what the American gentleman *is*. We are by long odds the most ill-mannered nation, civilized or savage, that exists on the planet to-day, and our President stands for us like a colossal monument visible from all the ends of the earth. . . . Roosevelt is far and away the worst President we have ever had, and also the most admired and the most satisfactory.

There was one factor Clemens counted in Roosevelt's favor: he was only human, which was to say a helpless construct of a negligent Creator. "I say it seriously, not jestingly—that I am not laughing at Theodore, but only at the funny results of his make," Clemens once told Twichell. "I keep it clearly in mind—all the time—try to, anyway—that he had nothing to do with building any part of himself & is not in any way to blame for the resulting conduct."

HE DID NOT, of course, loose any of these considered judgments on the wider world, especially now that he was trying to get the president's backing on the one piece of politics in which Sam Clemens was truly *invested*: a new copyright law. The copyright protections for American authors had not changed for a generation; a writer could own his or her work for twenty-eight years and make petition for an additional fourteen. Only the author could renew, however; heirs and assignees lacked standing. Clemens, as a consequence, had already used an old trick of Walter Scott's—adding fresh material to old books in order to claim new copyright—but the minute Clemens died, he knew, the hourglass on his daughters' income would start running down. If the law remained unchanged, his earliest books would begin falling out of copyright and into the public domain in 1911.

Clemens had been lobbying for years for stronger copyright protection, and in December of 1906 he jumped at the invitation to testify in support of a bill that was finally beginning to move through Congress. America's best-known author put on a grand show in Washington, too; he showed up on Capitol Hill that cold winter day in the sort of effulgent summer-white suit he had first seen men wear in Hawaii, when it was still the Sandwich Islands and he was still a complete unknown. His talk was no less spectacularly odd than his dress, and no less deadly in earnest. "I like that bill," he told the Joint Committee on Patents, "and I like that extension from the present limit of copyright life of forty-two years to the author's life and fifty years after. I think that ought to satisfy any reasonable author, because it will take care of his children. Let the grandchildren take care of themselves. 'Sufficient unto the day.' That would satisfy me very well. That would take care of my daughters, and after that I am not particular."

His testimony ranged through property law and constitutional questions, and English common law, and a Clemens family history to make Clara cringe. "My copyrights produce to me annually a good deal more money than I have any use for. But those children of mine have use for that. . . . I like the fifty years' extension, because that benefits my two daughters, who are not as competent to earn a living as I am, because I have carefully raised them as young ladies, who don't know anything and can't do anything. So I hope Congress will extend to them that charity which they have failed to get from me."

CLARA CLEMENS WAS released from her hospital-jail and moved back to New York and into her father's lower Fifth Avenue town house, which they had furnished with the old family goods from the Hartford house. Clara wondered at her father; he had absorbed the hardest blows of his life, one after another, for the past ten years and was still "Youth." He was past seventy now and remained able to bound up their town house stairs two steps at a time. His shadow was longer than ever. When Clara made yet another concert "debut" in Connecticut at the end of 1906, her father devoured the stage lights. The next-day accounts were mainly a transcription of the talk "Mark Twain" gave after his daughter's recital. "I recall the occasion of my first appearance. San Francisco knew me then only as a reporter and I was to make my bow to San Francisco as a lecturer," was how newspapers from New York to Omaha to California quoted him, and they continued quoting him at length, while mentioning Clara only in passing.

Clara went without her famous father to make her British debut in the spring of 1908. "Well, I had him with me for two years in America, accompanying me, but I found he was so anxious to get on the platform and make a speech before I had finished singing, and the people seemed to want to hear him so much that I thought it safer to leave him behind," she told London reporters, who thought she must have inherited her sense of humor from her father. They were certain she was joking.

THEODORE ROOSEVELT SIGNED a new copyright act on his last day in office, March 4, 1909. The law was not all that Clemens had hoped for, but it gave him some measure of comfort. The twenty-eight-year term could now be extended an additional twenty-eight years, and Clara or Jean, as his heirs, held the right of renewal after he died. There was plenty of new copyrightable matter tucked away in his pigeonholes, including the dictations for his autobiography, which were pocked with the notation "Not to be used for fifty years."

Clemens meant to protect the value of "Mark Twain" to the end and against all comers, such as, for instance, the British novelist who had penned the randy little romance novel that introduced the aphrodisiac possibilities of a tiger-skin rug and a rose between clenched teeth. When Clemens privately praised the novel and its energetically adulterous main characters, Elinor Glyn all but demanded that "Mark Twain" boom her book in public because it would do such good for the poor benighted of the planet—as the truth always did. And it was his duty to tell the truth, Mrs. Glyn asserted, popular or not.

"She believed that when a man held a private unpleasant opinion of an educational sort which would get him hanged if he published it he ought to publish it anyway and was a coward if he didn't," Clemens wrote, ". . . but I said it would damn me before my time and I didn't wish to be useful to the world on such expensive conditions."

HENRY ROGERS DIED unexpectedly at his home in New York in May of 1909. On the morning Rogers suffered his massive fatal stroke, Clemens was on his way to the city from his new home in Connecticut to have lunch with his friend. Clemens got the news from Clara when he arrived at Grand Central around noon. His hands were shaking uncontrollably and tears welled in his eyes as reporters braced him outside the station. "I can't talk about it," was all Clemens had to offer. "I don't know what I shall do."

Almost all the obituaries noted the intense and unlikely friendship of "Mark Twain" and Henry Rogers. "Mr. Rogers took control of the writer's shattered resources and put him in a position of financial comfort," said one New York newspaper. None mentioned that Rogers was, on the day he died, in the middle of trying to untangle Clemens's most recent financial mishap.

Henry Rogers was a celebrated man, but an infamous one in some quarters—with a reputation as one of the great robber barons of the age. But what the hell did they know? Clemens bristled when people called Rogers's money "tainted," and he defended "Hell Hound" Rogers as he would defend a brother. "It's twice tainted," Clemens told one man. "'Tain't yours and 'tain't mine." The quality "which I most admired, and which was to me a constant reproach because I lacked it," Clemens would say, "was his unselfishness where a friend or a cause near his heart was concerned."

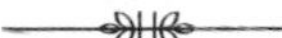

JEAN LEFT HIM next, and without warning. She had just come back to her father's home after more than two years in sanatoriums and hospitals. Clemens had built a big new house in Redding, Connecticut, on a property that was big enough for all the animals Jean wanted. Jean had been in Redding only seven months when Katy discovered her dead in her bathtub on the morning before Christmas, 1909. She had apparently suffered an epileptic seizure and drowned. Katy Leary alone took Jean's body to New York for the burial. Clara and Ossip had married by then and were living in Europe and unable to make it back in time. Sam Clemens refused to go. "I saw her mother buried," he told himself. "I said I would never endure that horror again; that I would never again look into the grave of any one dear to me. I have kept to that."

HE WAS CONVINCED his time was running out. He suspected he was suffering from congestive heart failure; he called it "tobacco heart." But he wasn't ready to give up, and he thought he might be able to make it through the winter if he got out of the frigid hills of Connecticut. So less than two weeks after Jean's death, he was boarding a ship in New York, ready to steam south into the Atlantic. Reporters at the pier wanted to know whether he was traveling with any family or friends. "This is my only companion and solace," he told them, waving his cigar. "It is about all I care for now, and I have been warned about making it too constant a companion. I detest the idea of shaking him though, for he and myself have been companions such a long time."

HE WAS NOT good for much in Bermuda and stuck close to the private residence where he was in hiding. "Yesterday I read *A Connecticut Yankee in King Arthur's Court* for the first time in more than 20 years," he recorded in his notebook. "I am prodigiously pleased with it—a most gratifying surprise."

Clemens had little interest in being social that winter, and he had *no* interest in being public. "I don't see anybody," he told a reporter who had tracked him to his sanctuary. "Nobody, nobody. I'm not, um, extravagantly well—I bark, bark, bark all the time. I can't talk to anybody." The reporter tried to stretch the visit by talking about the old books. She told him she loved *Huckleberry Finn* and *Tom Sawyer* "as my own soul."

"You ought to like 'em," he said. "I like 'em. Everybody likes 'em. They're very, very fine works of fiction. I guess I ought to know."

And then he told her, "You just recommend *them*. But don't recommend me to sightseers. I'm too old a bird to be caught. Besides, I'm going to charge an admission fee. It's a shilling a look." The effort of that little talk sent Sam Clemens into what the reporter described as a "terrible, racking cough that left him weak and gasping after each onslaught." When he got enough air, he carried on: "The price is going up—up—all—the time," he gasped. "Tomorrow it will be two shillings—the next day—three."

BY THE END of March, he was sure he was dying, and was anxious to be home. He summoned Clara to Connecticut and bought his return ticket. He was so weak the morning he left Bermuda that he had to be carried onto the boat; he boarded wearing a nightshirt and clinging to a pipe. He fought off death for another ten days, in the hopes of being able to see Clara one last time, fought it on the Atlantic and then up the seaboard and through New York City and all the way back to his own bed in Redding, Connecticut. He fought it until Clara and Ossip arrived from Europe two days later, and he was glad he had. The newlyweds brought big news: Clara was five months pregnant. The first grandchild of Sam and Livy Clemens was finally on the way.

Clara was with him when he died five days later, at a little after six o'clock in the evening, on April 21, 1910.

SAMUEL LANGHORNE CLEMENS had, by the time of his death, accomplished a great and heroic deed. His estate—sole surviving beneficiary, Clara Clemens Gabrilowitsch—included $70,000 in real property in Redding, $10,000 worth of home goods, $250,000 in stocks and bonds, his many (and still renewable) copyrights, and thousands of pages of pigeonholed literary material to be published at Clara's discretion. The total estimated value of the estate was $611,136.

Sam Clemens also left behind a sterling and beloved name—"Mark Twain"—whose future value could not be accurately foretold.

ACKNOWLEDGMENTS

THE FIRST SPARK of an idea for this book came while watching a friend of mine struggle with big issues of national and international import. I spent a lot of time on a separate editorial project with then Senator Joe Biden from 2005 through 2008, when he was the ranking member and then the chairman of the Senate Foreign Relations Committee. There were very few days in that time when Senator Biden wasn't trying to help make the outcome of the US wars in Afghanistan and Iraq a positive one. He was active, he was forceful, and most surprising to me at the time, he was optimistic to a fault, both in public and in private. But even this very capable public servant, with thirty years of experience in foreign affairs, in intelligence oversight, and in the general ways of Washington—even this man with an unwavering belief in the decency of US aims—had a hard time tracing a path to a happy ending.

What struck me at the time was that Senator Biden and every other important policymaker were carrying more than the burden of their own making—the hasty and unjustified bipartisan rush to war in Iraq. Biden and the rest were also dragging around the much more galumphing weight of history—history that stretched back past the advent of the United States as world sheriff in about 1947 and all the way to the country's popular and energetic overseas buccaneering in the Spanish-American War at the tail end of the nineteenth century. It made me want to explore the history and politics of that specific time.

None of the ideas or conclusions in this book can be attributed to Joe Biden. They are all mine. He is innocent of any such charges. I never talked with him about this project, because he has had more important things to do. But I will be forever grateful to him for taking me into his confidence and letting me near enough to see and understand the narrow band of choices American history has left to the men and women who are charged with shaping US foreign policy. I thank him for that, and I also thank former members of his staff, Ted Kaufman, Mark Gitenstein, Tony Blinken, and Puneet Talwar. They remind me that there are still plenty of men and women in government, on both sides of the aisle, trying to do the right thing.

This book, as all others I have been involved in, begins with Flip Brophy. Flip has been many things in my life: agent, cheerleader, therapist, life coach, financial savior, and most important, friend. Thank you again.

My editor at Algonquin, Chuck Adams, believed in this project and in me from the start and he continued to do so even when I gave him plenty cause to worry. Elisabeth Scharlatt, godmother to so many, thanks for letting me be one of the lucky beneficiaries of your special personal and professional aura. Rachel Careau was given the gargantuan task of copyediting this book. She did that, and so much more—with patience, endurance, and understanding. Thank you, Rachel. And thank you, Brunson Hoole, for assigning Rachel, and for keeping my train on the tracks.

I had many friends who let me bend their ears during the uncommonly long gestation period of this book. Thanks to David and Michaelyn Mitchell, Mark Gallogly and Lise Strickler, Curt and Paula Pesmen, Jim Kelly and Lisa Henrickson, Scott Yardley, and Sarah Masters. And a special shout-out to my pals Jane Leavy and John and Zoe Eisenberg, all of whom let me turn quiet rooms of their beach houses into temporary offices. And loudest of all to Michael Chin, who opened his San Francisco home to me for more than a month and supplied food, fun, and thoughtful conversation throughout. And thanks to the Spiegels of West Eighty-Third Street for providing the finest of daily shelter to me and mine. I thank my many colleagues in film and television who found ways to keep me employed when I needed to be: Rob Rapley, Jamila Wignot, and Sierra Pettengill in New York, as well as Mark Samels, Susan Bellows, Sarah Colt, and Randall MacLowry at *American Experience*. Thanks also to Bill Lacy and Scott Richardson at the Robert J. Dole Institute of Politics for occasionally gathering an audience on which I could surreptitiously test early lines from this book.

And then there is family. For nearly thirty years I have been blessed to share good laughter and better meatballs with my in-laws Rose Kukuc and Barbara and Robert Denninger. Thirty more would be good.

To my parents, Gary and Jean Zwonitzer, thanks for constructing the first supports beneath me, and for keeping them in good repair. My brothers Scot and Mike have inspired me with their toughness in the face of difficulty and jollied me with their sharp and cunning brands of humor. And thank you from afar to my other brother—my brother of choice, not of biology—Harland Abbott.

My son, Sam, and my daughter, Lila, received three separate educational degrees in the time it took me to finish this book. They also took jobs, signed leases, established good credit, gathered coteries of fine and respectable friends, traveled far and wide. It's not so much that they are extraordinarily accomplished, but that I am so slow. Thank you Sam and Lila, for not reminding me of this very often. And thank you most of all for being small forces for good and kindness in the world; this, to me, is what it truly means to be extraordinarily accomplished. You have done me more proud than any piece of work ever could.

Thanks finally to my wife, Gerri. Without you, Gerri, no book. Without you, nothing. And don't worry. It will get better.

A Note on Methods and Sources

I APPROACHED THE story of the last years of the lives of Sam Clemens and John Hay the way I was trained—as a reporter, allowing my subjects to be my guides. The things that occupied and interested them necessarily occupied and interested me. The letters, notebooks, and diaries of Clemens and Hay from 1895 to 1905 are the foundation of my understanding of them. These documents are happily accessible. The Mark Twain Papers and Project (in the Bancroft Library at the University of California, Berkeley) is the obvious starting point for Sam Clemens. This is as remarkable and active and welcoming a literary archive as exists on the planet. The Mark Twain Papers and Project is the repository of Sam Clemens's letters, notebooks, and manuscripts, and the editors and archivists there continue to produce work that deepens the understanding and appreciation of "Mark Twain." The editors' explanatory notes in the new three-volume *Autobiography of Mark Twain* alone are worth the price of admission and are a fabulous resource. I am particularly indebted to Victor Fischer and Michael B. Frank for the kindness they showed me while I was on site.

I made the attempt to read every letter Sam Clemens wrote and every notebook entry he made from 1895 to 1905 and much of what he produced from 1905 to 1910. My particular focus was on his correspondence with his closest confidants in this period: his friends Henry Rogers, Joseph Twichell, and William Dean Howells; his sister-in-law Susan Langdon Crane; his daughter Clara Clemens. Letters to his wife, Olivia Langdon Clemens, were fairly sparse in this time period as compared to earlier years, simply because Sam Clemens and his wife were not often apart. But what is there contains gold. Mrs. Clemens's correspondence with her daughters, Susy, Clara, and Jean, with her sister, Mrs. Crane; and with her friend Grace King was enormously helpful in filling in the story of the Clemens household and its mood at any given time.

The bulk of John Hay's correspondence (both personal and official) and his diaries from this time period are to be found among the John Hay Papers at the Library of Congress. The other important trove is the John Hay Papers at Brown University. As with Clemens, I tried to read all of Hay's personal correspondence and his key official correspondence from 1895 to 1905, as well as the diary Hay kept of the last couple of years of his life. Letters to and from Hay's close friends Henry Adams, Clarence King, and Whitelaw Reid; his brother-in-law Sam Mather; his coworkers Henry White and Alvey Adee; the British diplomat Cecil Spring Rice; and the British politicians Sir John Forbes Clark and Sir Robert Alfred Cunliffe were of particular help. So, too, was correspondence between Hay and the two presidents he served, William McKinley and Theodore Roosevelt, and the two secretaries of state he served while ambassador in London, John Sherman and William Day. Hay's letters to his daughter Helen Hay Whitney grew more interesting in the final years of his life. His letters to his wife, Clara Stone Hay, while rarely intimate, were both evocative and descriptive of his daily life when the two were apart, which appeared to be often in the last ten years of John Hay's busy public life.

All these archives contained correspondence between Sam Clemens and John Hay in the ten years from 1895 to 1905 and in the nearly thirty-year period of their friendship that preceded it.

IN PREPARING TO write each chapter, I first went back and reread the correspondence and the notebook and diary entries from the time period. Then I read the contemporaneous newspaper coverage, relevant official documents, transcripts of congressional investigations, and contemporaneous articles, memoirs, and letters produced by important characters in each chapter. The river of back-and-forth letters between Henry Cabot Lodge and Theodore Roosevelt, for instance, greatly informed the portrait of the two men in this book. Letters and writings of John Bigelow and his son Poultney Bigelow collected at the New York Public Library were a tool with which to reckon. John Bigelow was a mentor and boss to Hay when the younger man was beginning his diplomatic career. The two remained friends and correspondents to the end of Hay's life. John Bigelow was a keen observer of political events all his life and was also deeply interested in the Panama Canal and in the correct (as he saw it) kind of American expansion. John Bigelow's son Poultney became friends with Sam Clemens in the early 1890s and remained in touch. He was the only outsider allowed in the Clemens home with any regularity during the long, dark period in London after the death of Susy Clemens. Poultney covered a lot of ground himself. He was in Florida as the American expeditionary forces prepared to invade Cuba, and he reported from the Philippines also. Poultney Bigelow was also a childhood friend and lifelong acquaintance of Kaiser Wilhelm II, and his writings about the German emperor were full of insight and incident.

The Blount Report regarding the US-backed overthrow of the Hawaiian monarchy is a great resource for anybody who wants to understand this event. The dueling Morgan Report on the same subject has its own special value. The 1902 Senate investigation into the US occupation of the Philippines is a clear guide to official American thinking at the time. Filipino independence leaders like Emilio Aguinaldo and Felipe Agoncillo were not invited to testify at this hearing, but their contemporaneous writings and later memoirs give them voice. *Panama: The Creation, Destruction, and Resurrection* (1914), by Philippe Bunau-Varilla, is a compelling account of the shenanigans that made possible the Panama Canal, written by the man at the center of events.

Big and momentous events swirled around Sam Clemens and John Hay, but my aim was to keep a clear focus on these two men—on their trials, their triumphs, and their inextinguishable ambitions. William Roscoe Thayer's two-volume biography *The Life and Letters of John Hay* (1915), was an important secondary source, as was Tyler Dennett's *John Hay: From Poetry to Politics* (1934). John Taliaferro's new biography of Hay, which was published as I was lumbering to the finish of this manuscript, is a book to be commended. Hay deserved a new full-on biography and Taliaferro delivered one that should stand for another generation or two. On the Clemens side, the three-volume *Mark Twain: A Biography* (1912), by Albert Bigelow Paine, who was a Boswell to Clemens and the first editor of the Mark Twain Papers, is where all secondary sources begin. Whatever were his shortcomings, which generally grew from his desire to protect the reputation of Sam Clemens and the well-being of Clemens's only surviving daughter, Paine was an important friend and a confessor to Sam Clemens at the end of his long life. Paine saw with his own eyes, and tells plenty. There are scores of fine scholars and writers who have turned out excellent and insightful books and articles on the life and work of Sam Clemens. The bibliography includes the ones I found most helpful in understanding this small part of his story.

I also benefited from particular chapters of many more recent biographies of key figures in this story. I do want to say up front that Nell Irvin Painter's *The History of White People* was an enormous help in understanding the pseudo scholarly underpinnings of the misguided notions of racial hierarchy and Anglo-Saxon supremacy—misguided notions that infected so many happenings recounted in this book. Martha A. Sandweiss's book about Hay's dear friend Clarence King, *Passing Strange: A Gilded Age Tale of Love and Deception across the Color Line*, helped me to understand the painful personal costs of that sorry doctrine.

BIBLIOGRAPHY

Adams, Henry. *The Education of Henry Adams: An Autobiography*. Boston: Houghton Mifflin, 1918.

———. *Letters of Henry Adams (1892–1918)*. Edited by Worthington Chauncey Ford. Boston: Houghton Mifflin, 1938.

———. *The Letters of Henry Adams*. Vols. 4–6. Edited by J. C. Levenson et al. Cambridge: Harvard University Press, 1989.

Aguinaldo, Emilio. *True Version of the Philippine Revolution*. Tarlak: Philippine Islands, 1899.

Aguinaldo, Emilio, and Vicente Albano Pacis. *A Second Look at America*. New York: Robert Speller & Sons, 1957.

Barr, Robert. "Samuel L. Clemens, 'Mark Twain': A Character Sketch." *Idler* 13, no. 1 (February 1898): 23–29.

Beach, Edward L. *The United States Navy: A 200-Year History*. Boston: Houghton Mifflin, 1990.

Benfey, Christopher. *The Great Wave: Gilded Age Misfits, Japanese Eccentrics, and the Opening of Old Japan*. New York: Random House, 2003.

Bigelow, John. *Retrospections of an Active Life*. Vol. 4. New York: Doubleday, Page, 1913.

Bigelow, John, Papers. Manuscripts and Archives Division. New York Public Library.

Bigelow, Poultney. "In Camp at Tampa." *Harper's Weekly*, June 4, 1898, 550.

———. *Prussianism and Pacificism: The Two Wilhelms between the Revolutions of 1848 and 1918*. New York: G. P. Putnam's Sons, 1919.

———. *Seventy Summers*. 2 vols. New York: Longmans, Green, 1925.

Bigelow, Poultney, Papers. Manuscripts and Archives Division. the New York Public Library.

Bishop, Joseph Bucklin. "A Friendship with John Hay." *Century*, March 1906, 773–80.

———. *Notes and Anecdotes of Many Years*. New York: Charles Scribner's Sons, 1925.

———. *Theodore Roosevelt and His Time: Shown in His Own Letters*. Vol. 1. New York: Charles Scribner's Sons, 1920.

Bradley, James. *The Imperial Cruise: A Secret History of Empire and War*. New York: Little, Brown, 2009.

Brands, H. W. *TR: The Last Romantic*. New York: Basic Books, 1997.

Brown, Malcolm. *Reminiscences of a Pioneer Kauai Family with References and Anecdotes of Early Honolulu*. Honolulu: Thos. McVeagh, 1918.

Bunau-Varilla, Philippe. *Panama: The Creation, Destruction, and Resurrection*. New York: McBride, Nast, 1914.

Burton, Theodore E. *John Sherman*. Boston: Houghton, Mifflin, 1906.

Bush, Robert. *Grace King: A Southern Destiny.* Baton Rouge: Louisiana State University Press, 1983.

Carnegie, Andrew. "Distant Possessions—The Parting of the Ways." *North American Review* 167, no. 501 (August 1898): 239–48.

Carpenter, Teresa. *The Miss Stone Affair: America's First Modern Hostage Crisis.* New York: Simon & Schuster, 2003.

Cassini, Marguerite. *Never a Dull Moment.* New York: Harper & Brothers, 1956.

Chamberlin, Wilbur J. *Ordered to China: Letters of Wilbur J. Chamberlin, Written from China While Under Commission from the New York Sun during the Boxer Uprising of 1900.* New York: Frederick A. Stokes, 1903.

Churchill, Winston. *A Roving Commission: My Early Life.* New York: Charles Scribner's Sons, 1930.

Clay, Catrine. *King Kaiser Tsar: Three Royal Cousins Who Led the World to War.* New York: Walker, 2006.

Clemens, Clara. *My Father, Mark Twain.* New York: Harper & Brothers, 1931.

Cook's Tourists' Handbook for Egypt, the Nile, and the Desert. London: Thomas Cook & Son, 1897.

Cortissoz, Royal. *The Life of Whitelaw Reid.* 2 vols. New York: Charles Scribner's Sons, 1921.

Courtney, Steve. *Joseph Hopkins Twichell: The Life and Times of Mark Twain's Closest Friend.* Athens, University of Georgia Press, 2008.

Crosby, Travis L. *Joseph Chamberlain: A Most Radical Imperialist*. London: I. B. Tauris, 2011.

Cyriax, Edgar F. *The Elements of Kellgren's Manual Treatment.* New York: William Wood, 1904.

Dalton, Kathleen. *Theodore Roosevelt: A Strenuous Life.* New York: Alfred A. Knopf, 2002.

Darwin, John. *The Empire Project: The Rise and Fall of the British World-System, 1830–1970.* New York: Cambridge University Press, 2009.

Davis, Richard Harding. *Adventures and Letters of Richard Harding Davis*. Edited by Charles Belmont Davis. New York: Charles Scribner's Sons, 1917.

———. *The Cuban and Porto Rican Campaigns.* New York: Charles Scribner's Sons, 1898.

De Courcey, Anne. *The Viceroy's Daughters: The Lives of the Curzon Sisters.* New York: William Morrow, 2000.

Dennett, Tyler. *John Hay: From Poetry to Politics.* New York: Dodd, Mead, 1934.

Depew, Chauncey M. *My Memories of Eighty Years.* New York: Charles Scribner's Sons, 1922.

Dewey, George. *Autobiography of George Dewey: Admiral of the Navy.* New York: Charles Scribner's Sons, 1913.

Doty, Roxanne. *Imperial Encounters.* Minneapolis: University of Minnesota Press, 1996.

Dulles, Foster Rhea. "John Hay." In *An Uncertain Tradition: American Secretaries of State in the Twentieth Century,* edited by Norman A. Graebner. Westport, CT: Greenwood Press, 1980.

Emerson, Ralph Waldo. *English Traits.* Boston: Phillips, Sampson, 1856.

Fisher, Henry W. *Abroad with Mark Twain and Eugene Field: Tales They Told to a Fellow Correspondent*. New York: Nicholas L. Brown, 1922.

Foster, John W. *Diplomatic Memoirs*. 2 vols. Boston: Houghton Mifflin, 1909.

Freud, Sigmund. *Civilization and Its Discontents*. Edited and translated by James Strachey. New York: W. W. Norton, 1961.

Gilmour, David. *Curzon: Imperial Statesman*. New York: Farrar, Straus and Giroux, 2003.

Gilson, Willets. *Inside History of the White House: The Complete History of the Domestic and Official Life in Washington of the Nation's Presidents and Their Families*. New York: Christian Herald, 1908.

Grant, James. *Mr. Speaker: The Life and Times of Thomas B. Reed*. New York: Simon & Schuster, 2011.

Greene, F. V., et al. "Memoranda Concerning the Situation in the Philippines on August 30, 1898." Washington: Government Printing Office, 1899.

Hagner, Isabella. "Memoirs of Isabella Hagner, 1901–1905: Social Secretary to First Lady Edith Carow Roosevelt." *White House History*, no. 26.

Halstead, Murat. *The Story of the Philippines*. Chicago: Our Possessions, 1898.

Hay, Clara S., ed. *Letters of John Hay and Extracts from Diary*. 3 vols. Washington: printed but not published, 1908.

Hay, John. *Addresses of John Hay*. New York: Century, 1906.

———. *Castilian Days*. Boston: James R. Osgood, 1871.

———. *The Complete Poetical Works of John Hay, Including Many Poems Now First Collected with an Introduction by Clarence L. Hay*. Boston Houghton Mifflin, 1916.

Hay, John, Papers. John Hay Library, Brown University.

Hay, John, Papers. Library of Congress.

Hill, Hamlin. *Mark Twain: God's Fool*. New York: Harper & Row, 1973.

Howells, William Dean. *My Mark Twain: Reminiscences and Criticisms*. New York: Harper & Brothers, 1910.

Hullah, Annette. *Theodor Leschetizky*. New York: John Lane, 1906.

Hunt, Gaillard. *Department of State of the United States: Its History and Functions*. New Haven: Yale University Press, 1914.

James, Henry. *Richard Olney and His Public Service*. Boston: Houghton Mifflin, 1923.

Kaplan, Fred. *The Singular Mark Twain: A Biography*. New York: Doubleday, 2003.

King, Clarence. "The Education of the Future." *Forum* 13 (March 1892): 20–33.

———. [unsigned]. "Style and the Monument." *North American Review* 141, no. 348 (November 1885): 443–53.

King, Grace. *Memories of a Southern Woman of Letters*. New York: Macmillan, 1932.

Kohlsaat, H. H. *From McKinley to Harding: Personal Recollections of Our Presidents*. New York: Charles Scribner's Sons, 1923.

LaFeber, Walter. *The New Empire: An Interpretation of American Expansion, 1860–1898*. Ithaca: Cornell University Press, 1963.

Lambert, Angela. *Unquiet Souls: The Indian Summer of the British Aristocracy, 1880-1918*. London: Macmillan, 1984.

Larson, Thomas. "Our Samuel Clemens: Mark Twain in the Age of Personal Disclosure." *Southern Humanities Review* 38, no. 2 (spring 2004): 135–53.

Lazarovich-Hrebelianovich, Eleanor Hulda Calhoun. *Pleasures and Palaces*. New York: Century, 1915

Lears, Jackson. *Rebirth of a Nation: The Making of Modern America, 1877–1920*. New York: Harper Perennial, 2010.

Leary, Katy, and Mary Lawton. *A Lifetime with Mark Twain: The Memories of Katy Leary, for Thirty Years His Faithful and Devoted Servant.* New York: Harcourt, Brace, 1925.

Leech, Margaret. *In the Days of McKinley.* New York: Harper & Brothers, 1959.

Lodge, Henry Cabot. "England, Venezuela, and the Monroe Doctrine." *North American Review* 160, no. 463 (June 1895): 651–58.

———. "Our Blundering Foreign Policy." *Forum* 19 (March 1895): 8–17.

———. *Speeches and Addresses of Henry Cabot Lodge, 1884–1909.* Boston: Houghton Mifflin, 1909.

Long, John Davis. *America of Yesterday, as Reflected in the Journal of John Davis Long.* Edited Lawrence Shaw Mayo. Boston: Atlantic Monthly Press, 1923.

———. *The New American Navy*. 2 vols. New York: Outlook, 1903.

———. *Papers of John Davis Long, 1897–1904.* Edited by Gardner Weld Allen. [Boston] Massachusetts Historical Society, 1939.

Lowe, David Garrard. *Stanford White's New York.* New York: Doubleday, 1992.

Loving, Jerome. *Mark Twain: The Adventures of Samuel L. Clemens.* Berkeley: University of California Press, 2010.

Lynch, George. *The War of Civilisations: Being the Record of a "Foreign Devil's" Experiences with the Allies in China.* New York: Longmans, Green, 1901.

Lystra, Karen. *Dangerous Intimacy: The Untold Story of Mark Twain's Final Years.* Berkeley: University of California Press, 2004.

Marsh, Peter T. *Joseph Chamberlain: Entrepreneur in Politics.* New Haven: Yale University Press, 1994.

McCarthy, Justin. *British Political Portraits*. New York: Outlook, 1903.

McCullough, David. *Mornings on Horseback: The Story of an Extraordinary Family, a Vanished Way of Life, and the Unique Child Who Became Theodore Roosevelt*. New York: Simon Schuster, 1981.

McKinley, William. *Speeches and Addresses of William McKinley: From March 1, 1897 to May 30, 1900.* New York: Doubleday & McClure, 1900.

Miller, Stuart Creighton. *Benevolent Assimilation: The American Conquest of the Philippines, 1899–1903.* New Haven: Yale University Press, 1982.

Morgan, H. Wayne. *William McKinley and His America.* Rev. ed. Kent, OH: Kent State University Press, 2003.

Morgan, John Tyler. *Report from the Committee on Foreign Relations and Appendix in Relation to the Hawaiian Islands.* Washington: Government Printing Office, 1894.

Morison, Elting E., ed. *The Letters of Theodore Roosevelt,* Vol. 1. Cambridge, MA: Harvard University Press, 1951.

Morris, Edmund. *The Rise of Theodore Roosevelt*. New York: Random House, 2001.

———. *Theodore Rex.* New York: Random House, 2001.

Morris, Jan. *Pax Britannica: The Climax of an Empire*. New York: Harcourt Brace Jovanovich, 1968.

Morris, Roy, Jr. *Lighting Out for the Territory: How Samuel Clemens Headed West and Became Mark Twain.* New York: Simon & Schuster, 2010.

Nevins, Allan. *Henry White: Thirty Years of American Diplomacy.* New York: Harper & Brothers, 1930.

Newcomb, Ethel. *Leschetizky as I Knew Him.* New York: D. Appleton, 1921.

Olcott, Charles S. *The Life of William McKinley.* 2 vols. Boston: Houghton Mifflin, 1916.

O'Toole, Patricia. *The Five of Hearts: An Intimate Portrait of Henry Adams and His Friends, 1880–1918.* New York: Clarkson Potter, 1990.

Paine, Albert Bigelow. *Mark Twain, A Biography: The Personal and Literary Life of Samuel Langhorne Clemens.* 3 vols. New York: Harper & Brothers, 1912.

Painter, Nell Irvin. *The History of White People.* New York: W. W. Norton, 2010.

Parr, Henry Hallam. *Recollections and Correspondence, with a Short Account of His Two Sons, A. H. H. Parr and G. R. Parr.* Edited by Charles Fortescue-Brickdale. London: T. Fisher Unwin, 1917.

Pendel, Thomas F. *Thirty-Six Years in the White House.* Washington: Neale, 1902.

Philippine Review. Boston: Philippine Information Society, 1901–1902

Platt, Thomas Collier, and Louis J. Lang. *The Autobiography of Thomas Collier Platt.* New York: B. W. Dodge, 1910.

Pond, J. B. *Eccentricities of Genius: Memories of Famous Men and Women of the Platform and Stage.* New York: G. W. Dillingham, 1900.

Porter, Henry D. *William Scott Ament: Missionary of the American Board to China.* New York: Fleming H. Revell, 1911.

Powers, Ron. *Mark Twain: A Life.* New York: Simon & Schuster, 2005.

"The Problem of the Philippines: Speech of Hon. Henry M. Teller of Colorado, in the Senate of the United States, Tuesday, Wednesday, and Thursday, February 11, 12, and 13, 1902." Washington: Government Printing Office, 1902.

"Protest of Annexation by the Hawaiian Patriotic League and the Hawaiian Political Association, August 6, 1898." *Hawaiian Journal of Law & Politics* 1 (Summer 2004): 287–89.

Rasmussen, R. Kent. *Mark Twain A to Z: The Essential Reference to His Life and Writings.* New York: Oxford University Press, 1995.

Reid, Whitelaw. *Later Aspects of Our New Duties: An Address at Princeton University on Commemoration Day, October 21, 1899.* New York: Henry Hall, 1899.

———. *Making Peace with Spain: The Diary of Whitelaw Reid, September–December 1898.* Edited by H. Wayne Morgan. Austin: University of Texas Press, 1965.

———. *Rise to World Power: Selected Letters of Whitelaw Reid, 1895–1912.* Edited by David Contosta and Jessica R. Hawthorne. Philadelphia: American Philosophical Society, 1986.

———. *Some Consequences of the Last Treaty of Paris: Advances in International Law and Changes in National Policy.* London: John Lane, 1899.

Rhodes, James Ford. *The McKinley and Roosevelt Administrations.* New York: Macmillan, 1922.

Roberts, Andrew. *Salisbury: Victorian Titan.* London: Weidenfeld & Nicolson, 1999.

Robinson, Corinne Roosevelt. *My Brother Theodore Roosevelt.* New York: Charles Scribner's Sons, 1921.

Roosevelt, Theodore. "A Layman's Views on Specific Nomenclature." *Science*, April 30, 1897.

———. *Theodore Roosevelt: An Autobiography*. New York: Macmillan, 1913.

———. *The Winning of the West*. 4 vols. New York: G. P. Putnam's Sons, 1889–96.

Roosevelt, Theodore, and Henry Cabot Lodge. *Selections from the Correspondence of Theodore Roosevelt and Henry Cabot Lodge*. 2 vols. Edited by Henry Cabot Lodge. New York: Charles Scribner's Sons, 1925.

Ryder, C. Clifford. "Report upon the Epidemic of Cholera That Occurred in Honolulu during the Months of August and September, 1895." *Public Health Reports* 11, no. 8 (February 21, 1896): 166–68. Washington: Government Printing Office, 1896.

Sandweiss, Martha A. *Passing Strange: A Gilded Age Tale of Love and Deception across the Color Line*. New York: Penguin Press, 2009.

Scharnhorst, Gary. *Mark Twain: The Complete Interviews*. Tuscaloosa: University of Alabama Press, 2006.

Schriftgiesser, Karl. *The Gentleman from Massachusetts: Henry Cabot Lodge*. Boston: Little, Brown, 1944.

Shelden, Michael. *Mark Twain: Man in White: The Grand Adventure of His Final Years*. New York: Random House, 2010.

Silbey, David J. *A War of Frontier and Empire: The Philippine-American War, 1899–1902*. New York: Hill and Wang, 2007.

Simboli, Raffaele. "Mark Twain from an Italian Point of View." *Critic* 44 (June 1904): 518–24.

Smythe, Carlyle. "The Real Mark Twain." *Pall Mall Magazine* 16 (September 1898): 29–36.

Spring Rice, Cecil. *The Letters and Friendships of Sir Cecil Spring Rice*. 2 vols. Edited by Stephen Gwynn. Boston: Houghton Mifflin, 1929.

Stahr, Walter. *Seward: Lincoln's Indispensable Man*. New York: Simon & Schuster, 2012.

Stickney, Joseph L. *Admiral Dewey at Manila and the Complete Story of the Philippines*. Chicago: Imperial, 1899.

Stuart, Amanda Mackenzie. *Consuelo and Alva Vanderbilt: The Story of a Mother and Daughter in the Gilded Age*. New York: HarperCollins, 2005.

Taliaferro, John. *All the Great Prizes: The Life of John Hay, from Lincoln to Roosevelt*. New York: Simon & Schuster, 2013.

Tarbell, Ida. *All in the Day's Work: An Autobiography*. New York: Macmillan, 1939.

Thayer, William Roscoe. *The Life and Letters of John Hay*. 2 vols. Boston: Houghton Mifflin, 1915

Thomas, Evan. *The War Lovers: Roosevelt, Lodge, Hearst, and the Rush to Empire, 1898*. New York: Little, Brown, 2010.

Trask, David. *The War with Spain in 1898*. New York: Macmillan, 1981.

Traxel, David. *1898: The Tumultuous Year of Victory, Invention, Internal Strife, and Industrial Expansion That Saw the Birth of the American Century*. New York: Alfred A. Knopf, 1998.

Trombley, Laura Skandera. "'She Wanted to Kill': Jean Clemens and Postictal Psychosis." *American Literary Realism*, 37, no. 3 (Spring 2005): 225–37.

Twain, Mark. *Adventures of Huckleberry Finn.* New York: Charles L. Webster, 1885.

———. *The Autobiography of Mark Twain.* Edited by Charles Neider. New York: Harper Perennial Modern Classics, 2013.

———. *Autobiography of Mark Twain.* Vol. 1. Edited by Harriet Elinor Smith et al. Berkeley: University of California Press, 2010.

———. *Autobiography of Mark Twain.* Vol. 2. Edited by Benjamin Griffin and Harriet Elinor Smith et al. Berkeley: University of California Press, 2013.

———. *A Connecticut Yankee in King Arthur's Court.* New York: Charles L. Webster, 1889.

———. "The Czar's Soliloquy." *North American Review* 180, no. 580 (March 1905): 321–26.

———. "A Defence of General Funston." *North American Review* 174, no. 546 (May 1902): 613–24.

———. "Diplomatic Pay and Clothes." *Forum,* March 1899, 762–67.

———. "Extracts from Adam's Diary." *Harper's Monthly Magazine,* April 1901.

———. *Following the Equator: A Journey around the World.* Hartford: American, 1897.

———. *King Leopold's Soliloquy.* Boston: P. R. Warren, 1906.

———. *Mark Twain's Letters.* 2 vols. Arranged by Albert Bigelow Paine. New York: Harper & Brothers, 1917.

———. *Mark Twain's Speeches.* New York: Harper & Brothers, 1910.

———. "My Boyhood Dreams." *McClure's Magazine*, January 1900, 286–90.

———. "A Petition to the Queen of England." *Harper's New Monthly Magazine*, December 1887, 157–58.

———. *Roughing It.* Hartford: American, 1871.

———. "Stirring Times in Austria." *Harper's New Monthly Magazine*, March 1898, 530–40.

———. "To My Missionary Critics." *North American Review* 172, no. 533 (April 1901): 520–34.

———. "To the Person Sitting in Darkness." *North American Review* 172, no. 531 (February 1901) 161–76.

———. *What Is Man? And Other Philosophical Writings.* Edited by Paul Baender. Berkeley: University of California Press, 1973.

Twain, Mark, Papers. Bancroft Library. University of California, Berkeley.

United States Department of the Navy. *The War with Spain: Operations of the United States Navy on the Asiatic Station. Reports of Rear-Admiral George Dewey of the Battle of Manila Bay, May 1, 1898, and on the Investment and Fall of Manila, May 1 to August 13, 1898.* Washington: Government Printing Office, 1900.

United States Department of State. *Correspondence Concerning the Convention between the United States and Colombia for the Construction of an Inter-Oceanic Canal across the Isthmus of Panama.* Washington: Government Printing Office, 1903.

———. *Foreign Relations of the United States 1894: Affairs in Hawaii.* Washington: Government Printing Office, 1895.

———. *Papers Relating to the Foreign Relations of the United States.* Washington: Government Printing Office, 1895–1905.

United States House of Representatives. *The Story of Panama: Hearings on the Rainey Resolution before the Committee on Foreign Affairs of the House of Representatives.* Washington: Government Printing Office, 1913.

United States Senate. *Hearings before the Committee on the Philippines of the United States Senate.* Washington: Government Printing Office, 1902.

Wagenknecht, Edward. *The Seven Worlds of Theodore Roosevelt.* New York: Longmans, Green, 1958.

Watterson, Henry. *"Marse Henry": An Autobiography.* 2 vols. New York: George H. Doran, 1919.

White, Frank Marshall. "Mark Twain as a Newspaper Reporter." *Outlook*, December 24, 1910.

Widenor, William C. *Henry Cabot Lodge and the Search for an American Foreign Policy.* Berkeley: University of California Press, 1980.

Willis, Reesa. *Mark and Livy: The Love Story of Mark Twain and the Woman Who Almost Tamed Him.* New York: Atheneum, 1992.

Young, Kenneth Ray. *The General's General: The Life and Times of Arthur MacArthur.* Boulder, CO: Westview Press, 1989.

Zimmermann, Warren. *The First Great Triumph: How Five Americans Made Their Country a World Power.* New York: Farrar, Straus and Giroux, 2002.

INDEX

Note: Page numbers in italics refer to photographs.

Q

R